# SOC+

FOURTH EDITION

Robert Brym
University of Toronto

**NELSON**

# NELSON

**SOC+, Fourth Edition**
by Robert Brym

**Vice President, Product Solutions:**
Claudine O'Donnell

**Senior Publisher, Digital and Print Content:**
Leanna MacLean

**Marketing Manager:**
Claire Varley

**Content Manager:**
Toni Chahley

**Photo and Permissions Researcher:**
Julie Pratt

**Senior Production Project Manager:**
Jennifer Hare

**Copy Editor:**
June Trusty

**Proofreader:**
Linda Szostak

**Indexer:**
Belle Wong

**Design Director:**
Ken Phipps

**Post-secondary Project Manager:**
Pam Johnston

**Interior Design Revisions:**
Ken Cadinouche

**Cover Design:**
Courtney Hellam

**Cover Image:**
"With You Always" by Devan Shimoyama (2014). Courtesy of Samuel Freeman Gallery

**Compositor:**
MPS Limited

---

COPYRIGHT © 2020, 2018 by Nelson Education Ltd.

Printed and bound in Canada
1 2 3 4   21 20 19 18

For more information contact Nelson Education Ltd., 1120 Birchmount Road, Toronto, Ontario, M1K 5G4. Or you can visit our Internet site at nelson.com

Cognero and Full-Circle Assessment are registered trademarks of Madeira Station LLC.

ALL RIGHTS RESERVED. No part of this work covered by the copyright herein may be reproduced, transcribed, or used in any form or by any means—graphic, electronic, or mechanical, including photocopying, recording, taping, Web distribution, or information storage and retrieval systems—without the written permission of the publisher.

For permission to use material from this text or product, submit all requests online at cengage.com/permissions. Further questions about permissions can be emailed to permissionrequest@cengage.com

Every effort has been made to trace ownership of all copyrighted material and to secure permission from copyright holders. In the event of any question arising as to the use of any material, we will be pleased to make the necessary corrections in future printings.

**Library and Archives Canada Cataloguing in Publication Data**

Brym, Robert J., 1951-, author
    SOC+ / Robert Brym, University of Toronto. — Fourth edition.

Includes bibliographical references and index.
ISBN 978-0-17-686213-8 (softcover)

    1. Sociology.  2. Sociology—Canada.  I. Title.  II. Title: Sociology plus.

HM586.B792 2019        301
C2018-905884-6

ISBN-13: 978-0-17-686213-8
ISBN-10: 0-17-868213-7

# BRIEF CONTENTS

Preface xii

1. Introducing Sociology 2
2. Culture 32
3. Socialization 56
4. From Social Interaction to Social Organizations 77
5. Deviance and Crime 98
6. Social Stratification: Canadian and Global Perspectives 118
7. Race and Ethnicity 140
8. Sexualities and Genders 164
9. Families 188
10. Religion 211
11. Education 232
12. Health and Medicine 246
13. Mass Media and Mass Communication 266
14. Social Change: Technology, the Environment, and Social Movements 286
15. Sociology of Indigenous Peoples in Canada (online chapter)
    *by Jeffrey Denis*

References 309

Index 337

Chapters in Review CR-1

Appendix: Answers to Multiple-Choice Questions CR-50

# CONTENTS

**Preface** xii

## 1 Introducing Sociology 2

**My Road to Sociology** 3
**A Change of Mind** 3
**The Sociological Imagination** 4
Social Structures 4
**Origins of the Sociological Imagination** 6
The Scientific Revolution 6
The Democratic Revolution 6
The Industrial Revolution 8
**The Building Blocks of Sociology** 8
**Founders** 8
Émile Durkheim and Functionalism 8
Talcott Parsons and Robert Merton 9
Karl Marx and Conflict Theory 11
Max Weber 11
The Cultural Turn and Poststructuralism: Gramsci and Foucault 12
George Herbert Mead and Symbolic Interactionism 13
Harriet Martineau and Feminist Theory 14
Modern Feminism 15

**Sociological Theories and the Problem of Fashion** 15
Functionalist Theory 16
Conflict Theory 17
Symbolic Interactionist Theory 18
Feminism 19
**The Research Cycle** 22
Ethics in Sociological Research 23
**The Main Sociological Research Methods** 24
Experiments 24
Surveys 26
Field Research 27
Analysis of Existing Documents and Official Statistics 28
**Today's Challenges** 29
More Opportunity? 30
More Freedom? 30
Where Do You Fit In? 31

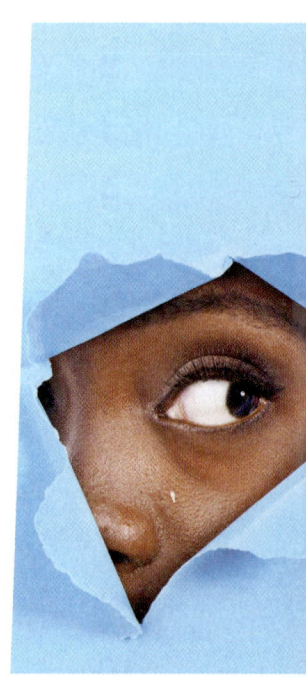

## 2 Culture 32

**Culture as Problem Solving** 33
**The Origins and Components of Culture** 34
Abstraction: Creating Symbols 34
Cooperation: Creating Norms and Values 35
Production: Creating Material Culture 35
Culture and Social Class 35
**Language** 36
The Sapir–Whorf Hypothesis 36
The Decline and Disappearance of Languages, Indigenous-Canadian and Other 37
**Culture and Ethnocentrism: A Functionalist Analysis** 39

**Culture as Freedom and Constraint** 40
Culture as Freedom 41
Multiculturalism 42
A Conflict Analysis of Culture: The Rights Revolution 44
From Diversity to Globalization 45
Postmodernism 46
Is Canada the First Postmodern Country? 48
**Culture as Constraint** 50
Rationalization 50
Consumerism 53
From Counterculture to Subculture 54

# 3 Socialization 56

## Social Isolation and Socialization 57
The Crystallization of Self-Identity 58

## The Symbolic-Interactionist Foundations of Childhood 59
The Looking-Glass Self 59
The "I" and the "Me" 60
Gender Differences 62
Civilization Differences 62

## Function, Conflict, Symbolic Interaction, and Gender: How Agents of Socialization Work 63
Family Functions 63
School Functions 64
School Conflicts 64
Symbolic Interactionism and the Self-Fulfilling Prophecy 64
Peer Groups 65
The Mass Media 66
The Mass Media and the Feminist Approach to Socialization 68
Resocialization and Total Institutions 68

## Socialization Across the Life Course 70
Adult Socialization and the Flexible Self 70
Self-Identity and the Internet 71

## Childhood, Adolescence, and Early Adulthood 72
The Emergence of Childhood and Adolescence 72

## Problems of Childhood, Adolescent, and Early Adult Socialization Today 73
Declining Adult Supervision and Guidance 73
Increasing Mass Media and Peer Group Influence 73
Declining Extracurricular Activities and Increasing Adult Responsibilities 73
The Vanishing Adolescent? 73
Millennials: The "Me" Generation? 74

# 4 From Social Interaction to Social Organizations 70

## Feminist Theory and Social Interaction 77

## Social Structure and Emotions 79
Emotional Labour 79

## Conflict Theories of Social Interaction 80
Competing for Attention 80
Interaction as Competition and Exchange 80

## Symbolic Interaction Theory and Social Interaction 81
Goffman's Dramaturgical Analysis 81
Verbal and Nonverbal Communication 82

## Networks, Groups, and Organizations 85
The Holocaust 85
How Social Groups Shape Our Actions 86

## Social Networks 89
The Value of Network Analysis 89

## Groups 92
Group Conformity 92
Primary and Secondary Groups 95

## Bureaucracy 95
Organizational Constraints and Freedom 97

# 5 Deviance and Crime 98

**The Social Definition of Deviance and Crime** 99
*The Difference between Deviance and Crime* 99

**Sanctions** 100
*Measuring Crime* 101
*Criminal Profiles* 102

**Explaining Deviance and Crime** 103
*Symbolic Interactionist Approaches to Deviance and Crime* 104
*Functionalist Explanations* 106
*Conflict Theories* 107
*Feminist Contributions* 109

**Punishment** 110
*The Medicalization of Deviance* 111
*The Prison* 112

**Moral Panic** 113
*Other Forms of Punishment: Two Extremes* 115

**Alternative Strategies** 115
*Rehabilitation* 115
*Decriminalization/Legalization* 116
*Diversion* 116

# 6 Social Stratification: Canadian and Global Perspectives 118

**Social Stratification: Shipwrecks and Inequality** 119

**Patterns of Social Inequality** 120
*Wealth* 120
*Income* 122
*Explanations of Income Inequality* 123
*Poverty* 125

**Is Stratification Inevitable? Three Theories** 127
*Marx's Conflict Theory* 127
*The Functionalist Theory of Davis and Moore* 130
*Weber's Compromise* 131

**Social Mobility** 133

**Politics and the Perception of Class Inequality** 135

**Global Inequality** 135
*Levels and Trends in Global Inequality* 135
*Modernization Theory: A Functionalist Approach* 136
*Dependency Theory: A Conflict Approach* 136
*Core, Periphery, and Semiperiphery* 138

# 7 Race and Ethnicity 140

**Defining Race and Intelligence** 141
*What Is Race?* 141
*Ethnicity, Culture, and Social Structure* 146
*Resources and Opportunities* 146

**Symbolic Interactionism and the Social Construction of Racial and Ethnic Identity** 147
*Labels and Identity* 147
*Choice vs. Imposition* 149

**Conflict Theories of Race and Ethnic Relations** 150
*Colonialism and Internal Colonialism* 150
*Canada's Indigenous Peoples* 150
*The Québécois* 153
*Black Canadians* 156
*Split Labour Markets and Asian Canadians* 158

**Some Advantages of Ethnicity** 160

**The Future of Race and Ethnicity in Canada** 161

# 8 Sexualities and Genders 164

**Sex, Intersex, Gender, Transgender** 165
*Sex and Intersex* 165
*Gender and Transgender* 166

**The Social Learning of Gender** 166
*Gender Theories* 166
*Essentialism* 166
*Functionalism and Essentialism* 167
*Social Constructionism and Symbolic Interactionism* 169
*Gender Socialization* 169
*The Mass Media and Body Image* 171
*Male–Female Interaction* 173

**Homosexuality** 173
*Sexual Orientation and Queer Theory* 175
*The Emergence of Homosexuality* 176

**Gender Inequality** 178
*The Earnings Gap* 178

**Male Aggression against Women** 180
*Sexual Assault* 180
*Explanations for Male Aggression against Women* 180
*Sexual Harassment* 182
*Gender Risk across 137 Countries* 183

**Toward 2089** 183
*Child Care* 184
*Equal Pay for Work of Equal Value* 185

**The Women's Movement** 185

# 9 Families 188

**Introduction** 189

**Is "The Family" in Decline?** 189

**Functionalism and the Nuclear Ideal** 191
*Functional Theory* 191
*Functions of the Nuclear Family* 192
*The Canadian Middle-Class Family in the 1950s* 192

**Power and Families** 196
*Love and Mate Selection* 196
*Marital Satisfaction* 197
*Divorce* 199
*Reproductive Choice* 200

*Housework and Child Care* 201
*Spousal Violence* 202

**Family Diversity** 202
*Heterosexual Cohabitation* 202
*Same-Sex Unions* 202
*Lone-Parent Families* 204
*Zero-Child Families* 204
*Mixed-Race Families: A Symbolic Interactionist Approach* 205

**Application of Major Sociological Theories** 205

**Family Policy** 206

# 10 Religion 210

**Religion** 211

**Classical Approaches in the Sociology of Religion** 212
*Durkheim's Functionalist Theory* 212
*Religion, Feminist Theory, and Conflict Theory* 213
*Weber and the Problem of Social Change: A Symbolic Interactionist Interpretation* 219

**The Rise, Decline, and Partial Revival of Religion** 221

*Secularization* 221
*Religious Revival and Religious Fundamentalism* 223
*The Revised Secularization Thesis* 224
*The Market Model* 226

**Religion in Canada** 227
*Church, Sect, and Cult* 227

**Religiosity** 229
*The Future of Religion* 230

# 11 Education 232

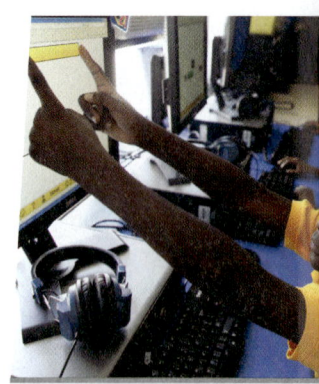

**The Rise of Mass Education** 233
*Uniform Socialization* 234
*Jobs and Earnings* 234
*Reasons for the Rise of Mass Education* 234

**Sociological Theories of Education** 235
*The Functions of Education* 235
*The Effect of Economic Inequality from the Conflict Perspective* 236

*Gender and Education: The Feminist Contribution* 240
*The Stereotype Threat: A Symbolic Interactionist View* 240

**The Corporatization of the University** 241

**Canadian Schools: Public Attitudes and International Comparison** 245

viii CONTENTS

# 12 Health and Medicine 246

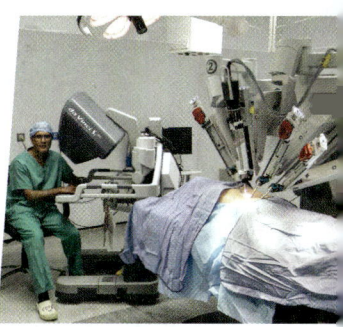

**The Black Death** 247

**Health and Inequality** 250
*Defining and Measuring Health* 250
*The Social Causes of Illness and Death* 250

**Class Inequality and Health Care** 253
*Intersectionality and Racial Inequalities in Health Care* 254
*Gender Inequalities in Health Care: The Feminist Contribution* 255

*Comparative Health Care from a Conflict Perspective* 256

**The Professionalization of Medicine** 258

**The Social Limits of Modern Medicine** 260
*Challenges to Traditional Medical Science* 261

# 13 Mass Media and Mass Communication 266

**The Significance of the Mass Media** 267
*Illusion Becomes Reality* 267
*What Are the Mass Media?* 268
*The Rise of the Mass Media* 268
*Causes of Media Growth* 270

**Theories of Media Effects** 271
*Functionalism* 271
*Conflict Theory* 273

*Interpretive Approaches* 275
*Feminist Approaches* 277

**Centralized Control and Resistance on the Internet** 280
*Access* 280
*Content* 281
*Online Piracy vs. Net Neutrality* 281
*The Rise of Social Media* 282

# 14 Social Change: Technology, the Environment, and Social Movements 286

**What Is Social Change?** 287

**Technology: Saviour or Frankenstein?** 287
*Technology and People Cause Social Change* 289
*How High Tech Became Big Tech* 290
*Global Warming* 291

**The Social Construction of Environmental Problems** 293
*The Social Distribution of Risk* 294

*Market vs. High-Tech Solutions to the Environmental Crisis* 296

**Social Movements** 297
*Breakdown Theory: A Functionalist Account* 298
*Solidarity Theory: A Conflict Approach* 299
*Framing Theory: The Contribution of Symbolic Interactionism* 300
*New Social Movements* 303

**Conclusion** 307

# 15 Sociology of Indigenous Peoples in Canada
## (online chapter) *by Jeffrey Denis*

*This chapter is available in the MindTap eBook*

**Introduction**

**Historical Development of Indigenous–Settler Relations**
Pre-Contact: Diverse and Independent Civilizations
Early Contact: Friends and Foes
Settler–Colonial Expansion: Land Dispossession and Coercive Assimilation
Confrontation, Healing, and Renewal

**Changing Images of Indigenous and Settler Peoples**
Indigenous Peoples Today

**Demographic and Social Characteristics**

**Social Inequalities**

**Explaining Inequality**
Biological and Cultural Deficit Theories
Sociological Theories: History, Culture, and Social Structure

**Diversity in Indigenous Communities**
Socioeconomic Diversity and Class Relations

**Gender Relations**
Male Violence against Indigenous Women
Indigenous Women's Leadership

**Public Awareness and Attitudes**

**Past, Present, and Future of Indigenous Resistance and Resurgence**

**Canada 150 and Beyond**

**Critical Thinking Questions**

**References**

# References 309
# Index 337
# Chapters in Review CR-1

**Chapter 1 in Review** *CR-1*
**Chapter 2 in Review** *CR-4*
**Chapter 3 in Review** *CR-7*
**Chapter 4 in Review** *CR-11*
**Chapter 5 in Review** *CR-14*
**Chapter 6 in Review** *CR-18*
**Chapter 7 in Review** *CR-22*
**Chapter 8 in Review** *CR-25*
**Chapter 9 in Review** *CR-28*

**Chapter 10 in Review** *CR-32*

**Chapter 11 in Review** *CR-36*

**Chapter 12 in Review** *CR-40*

**Chapter 13 in Review** *CR-44*

**Chapter 14 in Review** *CR-47*

**Appendix: Answers to Multiple-Choice Questions** *CR-50*

# PREFACE

## YOU NEED TO READ THIS PAGE. IT SUMMARIZES EVERYTHING IN THE BOOK. THE REST IS JUST COMMENTARY.

When I was a child growing up in New Brunswick in the 1950s, Lena White would come to our home from time to time and my mother would serve us lunch. Lena was Mi'kmaq. I was fond of her because she told good stories. During dessert, as we sipped tea with milk, Lena would spin tales about Glooskap, the Creator of the world. I liked Glooskap because he was mischievous, not just powerful. He regularly got into trouble and learned from his mistakes.

Here's a Glooskap story that I retell in Chapter 10, Religion: One day the wind was blowing so hard Glooskap couldn't paddle his canoe into the bay to hunt ducks. So he found the source of the wind: the flapping wings of the Wind Eagle. He then tricked the Wind Eagle into getting stuck in a crevice where he could flap no more. Now Glooskap could go hunting. However, the air soon grew so hot he found it difficult to breathe. The water became dirty and began to smell bad, and there was so much foam on it he found it hard to paddle. When he complained to his grandmother, she explained that the wind was needed to cool the air, wash the Earth, and move the waters to keep them clean. And so Glooskap freed the Wind Eagle, and the winds returned to the Earth. Glooskap decided it was better to wait for good weather and then go duck hunting rather than conquer the winds.

Like the tale of the Wind Eagle, many of the Glooskap stories Lena told me were about the need for harmony among humans and between humans and nature. You can imagine my surprise, therefore, when I got to school and learned about the European exploration of what some Indigenous groups called Turtle Island and the Europeans referred to as North America. My teachers taught me all about the glories of the *conquest* of nature—and of other people. I was taught that the Americas were unimaginably rich in resources. European rulers saw that by controlling this land they could increase their power and importance. Christians recognized new possibilities for spreading their religion. Explorers discerned fresh opportunities for rewarding adventures. Of course, I learned nothing about the violence visited on Indigenous peoples and on nature as the conquest of Turtle Island unfolded.

Stories of conquest and stories questioning the wisdom of conquest form the backbone of this book. Today, many people feel like the European explorers because we, too, have reached a new frontier. Our frontier is one of instant long-distance communication, globalized economies and cultures, and technological advances that often make the daily news seem like reports from a distant planet.

On the other hand, we understand that not all is hope and bright horizons. Our anticipation is mixed with dread. The global environment probably hasn't been in worse shape since the extinction of the dinosaurs. Wars and other acts of violence fill the daily news. Nations unexpectedly break up and reconstitute themselves in new and unanticipated forms. We celebrate the advances made by women and minorities only to find that some people oppose their progress, sometimes violently. Waves of migrants move between continents, often engendering animosity and conflict between previously separated peoples. New technologies make work more interesting and creative for some, offering unprecedented opportunities to become rich and famous—but they also make jobs more onerous and routine for others. The standard of living goes up for many people but stagnates or deteriorates for many more. Amid all this contradictory news, good and bad, uncertainty about the future prevails.

That's why I wrote this book. Its central theme is that we need to temper our headlong rush into the new frontier by listening carefully to Glooskap stories. They make more sense than ever.

I develop this theme by showing how sociology—the systematic study of human behaviour in a social context—can help us make sense of our lives, however uncertain they may appear to be. By revealing the opportunities and constraints we face, sociology can help teach us who we are and what we can become. Of course, we can't know what the future will bring. However, we can know the choices we confront and the likely consequences of our actions. From this point of view, sociology can help us create the best possible future. That has always been sociology's principal justification, and so it must be today.

My commentary on all of this begins in Chapter 1. However, instructors might want to finish the rest of this Preface before going there, since it outlines new features of the book and lets you know what to expect in this edition.

## Unique Features

*SOC+* introduces sociology by exploring how multiculturalism, globalization, the erosion of authority, international migration, technological development, and other social forces have destabilized identity and resulted in new patterns of social inequality.

The new edition engages students by drawing on examples from television, popular music, social media, and film. Many of the examples will likely be familiar to students—but not from a sociological perspective—so they will discover some eye-opening things about their everyday life in the following pages.

In particular, new **Sociology and the Media** boxed features explore television, social media, movies, and other media

phenomena that relate to the chapter topic. Covering everything from Donald Trump's assault on evidence-based research to implicitly racist TV ads and the limits of *The Book of Mormon*'s critique of religion, these features will engage and stimulate students to analyze media phenomena sociologically.

The fourth edition of *SOC+* has been thoroughly revised and updated. Notably, I've augmented the coverage of Indigenous Canadians throughout, including such topics as the ethics of research on First Nations people, the decline and disappearance of indigenous languages, indigenous rights and the rights revolution, Indigenous Canadians and critical race theory, and indigenous intermarriage. **Intersectionality** is a hot topic in sociology today, and I have given due weight to it here. In particular, I highlight intersectionality in discussions of violence against women, inequalities in health care, and occupational segregation. In addition, the topics of education and religion are now two separate chapters, giving increased attention to each of these vital areas.

The fourth edition of *SOC+* boasts a strong emphasis on the application of theory. Chapter 1 initiates this focus by analyzing fashion cycles as a running example of how each sociological perspective can open a different window on the social world. The theoretical emphasis continues in the new chapter pedagogy. Notably, I wrote new **Theories in Dispute** boxed features for nearly every chapter. They examine how different theories interpret timely issues in different ways. In some cases, I seek to reconcile the differences, in other cases to argue for the superiority of one theoretical approach over another, and in still others to call a draw and suggest the need for more research. This is not the kind of blind partisanship or bland "all theories are equal" approach that readers of many introductory sociology textbooks are all too familiar with. Rather, it is a simplified form of the kind of thing that most sociologists do in their everyday work. The issues explored in the new **Theories in Dispute** boxes include the impact of the Web on democracy, the interaction between genes and environment, the social and political context of extremist Islamic fundamentalism, and so on.

Continuing the focus on theoretical applications, I wrote new **Theories at a Glance** tables for nearly every chapter. The tables also appear in the **Chapter in Review** section for each chapter at the end of the book. They conveniently delineate how each chapter incorporates various theoretical perspectives. To help with retention, I included multiple-choice self-test questions at the end of each Chapter in Review. Combined, these features will serve as a study guide that students will truly find useful.

## Ancillaries

A full range of high-quality ancillaries has been prepared to help instructors and students get the most out of *SOC+*, Fourth Edition.

## Supplements for Instructors

### About the Nelson Education Teaching Advantage (NETA)

The **Nelson Education Teaching Advantage (NETA)** program delivers research-based instructor resources that promote student engagement and higher-order thinking to enable the success of Canadian students and educators. To ensure the high quality of these materials, all Nelson ancillaries have been professionally copyedited.

Be sure to visit Nelson Education's **Inspired Instruction** website at **nelson.com/inspired/** to find out more about NETA. Don't miss the testimonials of instructors who have used NETA supplements and seen student engagement increase!

### Instructor Resources

All NETA and other key instructor ancillaries are provided in the Instructor Resources at **nelson.com/instructor**, giving instructors the ultimate tool for customizing lectures and presentations.

**NETA Test Bank:** This resource was written by Lauren Barr at Western University. It includes over 1500 multiple-choice questions written according to NETA guidelines for effective construction and development of higher-order questions. The Test Bank was copyedited by a NETA-trained editor. Also included are true/false, short answer, and essay questions. Test Bank files are provided in Word format for easy editing and in PDF format for convenient printing, whatever your system.

The NETA Test Bank is available in a new, cloud-based platform. **Testing Powered by Cognero®** is a secure online testing system that allows you to author, edit, and manage test bank content from any place you have Internet access. No special installations or downloads are needed, and the desktop-inspired interface, with its drop-down menus and familiar, intuitive tools, allows you to create and manage tests with ease. You can create multiple test versions in an instant and import or export content into other systems. Tests can be delivered from your learning management system, your classroom, or wherever you want.

**NETA PowerPoint:** Microsoft® PowerPoint® lecture slides for every chapter have been created by Christopher Helland of Dalhousie University. There is an average of 40 slides per chapter, many featuring key figures, tables, and photographs from *SOC+*. NETA principles of clear design and engaging content have been incorporated throughout, making it simple for instructors to customize the deck for their courses.

**Image Library:** This resource consists of digital copies of figures, short tables, and photographs used in the book. Instructors may use these jpegs to customize the NETA PowerPoint or create their own PowerPoint presentations.

**NETA Instructor's Manual:** This resource was written by Amanda Zavitz-Gocan at Fanshawe College. It is organized according to the textbook chapters and addresses key educational concerns, such as typical stumbling blocks student face and how to address them.

**MindTap:** MindTap for *SOC+* is a personalized teaching experience with relevant assignments that guide students to analyze, apply, and elevate thinking, allowing you to measure skills and promote better outcomes with ease. A fully online learning solution, MindTap combines all student learning tools—readings, multimedia, activities, and assessments—into a single Learning Path that guides the student through your curriculum. You may personalize the experience by customizing the presentation of these learning tools to your students, even seamlessly introducing your own content directly into the Learning Path.

## Student Ancillaries

Stay organized and efficient with **MindTap**—a single destination with all the course material and study aids you need to succeed. Built-in apps leverage social media and the latest learning technology. For example:

- ReadSpeaker will read the text to you.
- Flashcards are pre-populated to provide you with a jump start for review—or you can create your own.
- You can highlight text and make notes in your MindTap Reader. Your notes will flow into Evernote, the electronic notebook app that you can access anywhere when it's time to study for the exam.
- Self-quizzing allows you to assess your understanding.

Visit **NelsonBrain.com** to start using **MindTap**. Enter the Online Access Code from the card included with your text. If a code card is *not* provided, you can purchase instant access at NelsonBrain.com.

# ACKNOWLEDGMENTS

Anyone who has gone sailing knows that when you embark on a long voyage, you need more than a compass. Among other things, you need a helm operator blessed with a strong sense of direction and an intimate knowledge of likely dangers. You need crew members who know all the ropes and can use them to keep things intact and in their proper place. And you need sturdy hands to raise and lower the sails. On the voyage to complete this book, the crew demonstrated all these skills. I am especially grateful to my publisher, **Leanna MacLean**, who saw this book's promise from the outset, understood clearly the direction I had to take to develop its potential, and on several occasions steered me clear of threatening shoals. I am also deeply indebted to the following crew members:

**Toni Chahley**, developmental editor

**Jennifer Hare**, production project manager

**Claire Varley**, marketing manager

**June Trusty**, copy editor

**Linda Szostak**, proofreader

**Julie Pratt**, permissions coordinator and photo researcher

**Tim Melnyk**, research assistant

Finally, I thank the following reviewers for their guidance, which helped shape this new edition:

**Lauren Barr**, Western University

**Timothy Epp**, Redeemer University College

**Merle Fuller**, Lethbridge College

**Cindy Gervais**, Fleming College

**Antoine Goulem**, Seneca College

**Maureen Murphy-Fricker**, Conestoga College

**John Patterson**, Canadore College

**Geraint Osborne**, University of Alberta

**Alexander Shvarts**, Humber College

*Robert Brym*

# Introducing Sociology

# 1

## LEARNING OBJECTIVES:

In this chapter, you will learn to

- **LO1** Define sociology.
- **LO2** Identify the social relations that surround you, permeate you, and influence your behaviour.
- **LO3** Describe how the Scientific, Democratic, and Industrial Revolutions gave rise to the sociological imagination.
- **LO4** Appreciate that values, theory, and research form the building blocks of the sociological enterprise.
- **LO5** Summarize the four main schools of sociological theory.
- **LO6** Distinguish the four main methods of collecting sociological data.
- **LO7** Explain how sociology can help us deal with major challenges that face society today.

# MY ROAD TO SOCIOLOGY

"When I started university at the age of 18," says Robert Brym, "I was bewildered by the variety of courses I could choose from. Having now taught sociology for decades and met thousands of undergraduates, I am quite sure most students today feel as I did then.

"One source of confusion for me was uncertainty about why I was in university in the first place. Like you, I knew higher education could improve my chance of finding good work. But, like most students, I also had a sense that higher education is supposed to provide something more than just the training necessary to start a career that is interesting and pays well. Several high school teachers and a guidance counsellor had told me that university was also supposed to 'broaden my horizons' and teach me to 'think critically.' I wasn't sure what they meant, but they made it sound interesting enough to encourage me to know more. In my first year, I decided to take mainly 'practical' courses that might prepare me for a law degree (economics, political science, and psychology). However, I also enrolled in a couple of other courses to indulge my 'intellectual' side (philosophy, drama). One thing I knew for sure: I didn't want to study sociology.

"Sociology, I came to believe, was thin soup with uncertain ingredients. When I asked a few second- and third-year students in my dorm what sociology is, I received different answers. They variously defined sociology as the science of social inequality, the study of how to create the ideal society, the analysis of how and why people assume different roles in their lives, and a method for figuring out why people don't always do what they are supposed to do. I found all this confusing and decided to forgo sociology for what seemed to be tastier courses."

## **LO1** A CHANGE OF MIND

"Despite the opinion I'd formed, I found myself taking no fewer than four sociology courses a year after starting university. That revolution in my life was partly due to the influence of an extraordinary professor I happened to meet just before I began my second year. He set me thinking in an altogether new way about what I could and should do with my life. He exploded some of my deepest beliefs. He started me thinking sociologically.

> **sociology** The systematic study of human behaviour in social context.
>
> **social structures** Stable patterns of social relations.
>
> **sociological imagination** The quality of mind that enables one to see the connection between personal troubles and social structures.

"Specifically, he first encouraged me to think about the dilemma of all thinking people. Life is finite. If we want to make the most of it, we must figure out how best to live. That is no easy task. It requires study, reflection, and the selection of values and goals. Ideally, he said, higher education is supposed to supply students with just that opportunity. Finally, I was beginning to understand what I could expect from university apart from job training.

"The professor also convinced me that sociology in particular could open up a new and superior way of comprehending my world. Specifically, he said, it could clarify my place in society, how I might best manoeuver through it, and perhaps even how I might contribute to improving it, however modestly. Before beginning my study of sociology, I had always taken for granted that things happen in the world—and to me—because physical and emotional forces cause them. Famine, I thought, is caused by drought, economic success by hard work, marriage by love, suicide by bottomless depression, rape by depraved lust. But now this professor repeatedly threw evidence in my face that contradicted my easy formulas. If drought causes famine, why have so many famines occurred in perfectly normal weather conditions or involved some groups hoarding or destroying food so others would starve? If hard work causes prosperity, why are so many hard workers poor? If love causes marriage, why does violence against women and children occur in so many families? And so the questions multiplied.

"As if it were not enough that the professor's sociological evidence upset many of my assumptions about the way the world worked, he also challenged me to understand sociology's unique way of explaining social life. He defined **sociology** as the systematic study of human behaviour in social context. He explained that social causes are distinct from physical and emotional causes. Understanding social causes can help clarify otherwise inexplicable features of famine, marriage, and so on. In public school, my teachers taught me that people are free to do what they want with their lives. However, my new professor taught me that the organization of the social world opens some opportunities and closes others, thus limiting our freedom and helping to make us what we are. By examining the operation of these powerful social forces, he said, sociology can help us to know ourselves, our capabilities, and limitations. I was hooked. And so, of course, I hope you will be, too."

When I sat down to plan this book, I figured I stood the best chance of hooking you if I drew lots of examples from aspects of social life that you enjoy and know well, such as contemporary music, fashion, sports, the Web, social networking, and other aspects of popular culture. Chances are that popular culture envelopes you and makes you feel as comfortable as your favourite pair of pants. Our aim is to show you that underlying the taken-for-granted fabric of your life are patterns of social relations that powerfully influence your tastes, your hopes, your actions, and your future—even though you may be only dimly aware of them now.

# LO² THE SOCIOLOGICAL IMAGINATION

## SOCIAL STRUCTURES

You have known for a long time that you live in a society. Until now, you may not have fully appreciated that society also lives in you. Patterns of social relations affect your innermost thoughts and feelings, influence your actions, and help shape who you are Sociologists call stable patterns of social relations **social structures**.

Nearly 60 years ago, the great American sociologist C. Wright Mills (1916–62) wrote that the sociologist's main task is to identify and explain the connections between people's personal troubles, the changing social structures in which they are embedded, and ways they can contribute to improving their lives and the state of the world. He called the ability to see these connections the **sociological imagination**. Mills wrote:

> [People] do not usually define the troubles they endure in terms of historical change.... Seldom aware of the intricate connection between the patterns of their own lives and the course of world history, ordinary [people] do not usually know what this connection means for the kind of [people] they are becoming and for the kind of history-making in which they might take part.... What they need...is a quality of mind that will help them to [see]...what is going on in the world and...what may be happening within themselves. It is this quality...that...may be called the sociological imagination. —C. Wright Mills (1959: 3–4)

To gain a better sense of what Mills meant by the sociological imagination, consider a story that has been repeated, with variations, many times. A 50-year-old woman loses a good job on the assembly line of a southern Ontario car plant when production moves to

Mexico. After half a year of collecting Employment Insurance, she manages to land a job at the checkout counter of a local Walmart. She earns less than half of her previous salary. She had hoped to help her son pay tuition when he started college, but can no longer afford that because her income is now barely enough to pay for food, rent, and utilities. Her son is a good student but he now has to delay his plan to go to college for at least a couple years while he earns tuition money. The woman blames herself for not being able to land a better job. She becomes depressed. To cope, she starts smoking and drinking more—and taking high-interest payday loans to feed her habits. The son's resentment and anger toward his mother grow, so they argue a lot. Family life, once happy, becomes miserable.

Will the woman develop a chronic illness because of the stress, the smoking, and the drinking? Will the son get caught stealing clothes he can't afford? Will he ever make it to college? Or will they apply the sociological imagination to their situation and come to realize that their personal troubles are the result of powerful social forces that they can help to control?

Here is what the sociological imagination could teach them: Since the 1970s, many large North American corporations have been moving manufacturing industries to low-wage countries like Mexico and China so that they can pay workers less and earn bigger profits. Millions of North Americans have seen their steady, relatively high-paying jobs vanish. Their quality of life has gone downhill. Yet some countries have been able to withstand the challenge of the deindustrialization that is taking place in many rich countries. For instance, in Denmark, the government gives people who lose jobs relatively generous unemployment benefits for a couple of years, organizes programs that retrain them for skilled jobs that are in high demand, and requires that they complete such a program. Denmark therefore suffers nothing like the growing unemployment and poverty that grips parts of southern Ontario, let alone the United States, where government programs are even less generous and economic inequality is higher.

## The Four Levels of Social Structure

An important step in broadening your sociological awareness involves recognizing that four levels of social structure surround and permeate us. Think of these structures as concentric circles radiating out from you (Figure 1.1):

1. **Microstructures** are patterns of intimate social relations formed during face-to-face interaction. Families and friendship cliques are examples of microstructures.
2. **Mesostructures** are patterns of social relations in organizations that involve people who are often not intimately acquainted and who often do not interact face to face. Social organizations such as colleges and government bureaucracies are examples of mesostructures.
3. **Macrostructures** are overarching patterns of social relations that lie above and beyond mesostructures. One such macrostructure is **patriarchy**, the system of power relations and customary practices that help to ensure male dominance in economic, political, and other spheres of life.
4. **Global structures** are the fourth level of society that surrounds and permeates us. Economic relations among countries and patterns of worldwide travel and communication are examples of global structures.

> **microstructures** Patterns of social relations formed during face-to-face interaction.
>
> **mesostructures** Patterns of social relations in organizations that involve people who are often not intimately acquainted and who often do not interact face to face.
>
> **macrostructures** Overarching patterns of social relations that lie outside and above one's circle of intimates and acquaintances.
>
> **patriarchy** A system of power relations and customary practices that help to ensure male dominance in economic, political, and other spheres of life.
>
> **global structures** Patterns of social relations that lie outside and above the national level.

**FIGURE 1.1 The Four Levels of Social Structure**

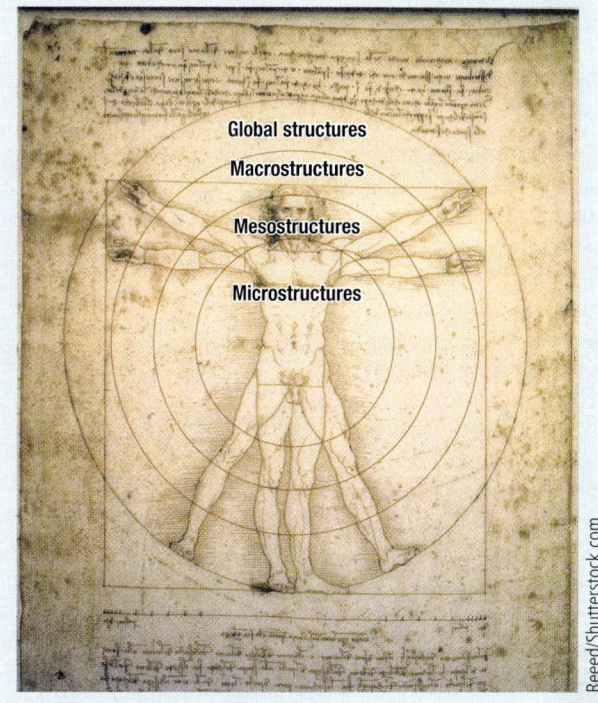

Source: Vitruvian Man by Leonardo Da Vinci.

Personal problems are connected to social structures at the micro, meso, macro, and global levels. Whether the personal problem involves finding a job, keeping a marriage intact, or acting justly to end world poverty, considering the influence of social structures on us broadens our understanding of the problems we face and suggests appropriate courses of action.

# LO³ ORIGINS OF THE SOCIOLOGICAL IMAGINATION

The sociological imagination is only a couple of hundred years old. Although in ancient and medieval times some philosophers wrote about society, their thinking was not sociological. They believed that God and nature controlled society. These philosophers spent much of their time sketching blueprints for the ideal society and urging people to follow those blueprints. They relied on speculation rather than evidence to reach conclusions about how society worked. The sociological imagination was born when three revolutions pushed people to think about society in an entirely new way—the Scientific, Democratic, and Industrial Revolutions.

**Scientific Revolution** This revolution in thinking began in Europe about 1550. It promoted the view that conclusions about the workings of the world should be based on solid evidence, not just speculation.

**theory** Speculation about the way observed facts are related.

**Democratic Revolution** This political upheaval began about 1770, as citizens of France and the United States started demanding an increased say in the way they were governed. By eventually achieving popular control of government, they demonstrated that societies do not have to be ruled by kings and queens who claim their authority is ordained by God. Instead, society can be organized and run by ordinary people. This idea prepared the ground for the notion that a science of society aimed at improving human welfare is possible.

## THE SCIENTIFIC REVOLUTION

The **Scientific Revolution** began about 1550. It encouraged the view that sound conclusions about the workings of the world must be based on evidence, not speculation. Many people link the Scientific Revolution to specific ideas, such as Copernicus's theory that Earth revolves around the Sun. (A **theory** is a speculation about the way observed facts are related.) However, science is less a collection of ideas than a method of inquiry. For instance, in 1609, Galileo pointed his newly invented telescope at the heavens, made some careful observations, and showed that his observations fit Copernicus's theory. This is the core of the scientific method: using evidence to make a case for a particular point of view. By the mid-1600s, some philosophers were calling for a science of society. When sociology emerged as a distinct discipline in the nineteenth century, commitment to the scientific method was one firm pillar of the sociological imagination. It remains so today, although some people are trying to undermine it (see the Sociology and the Media boxed feature, Donald Trump's Assault on Evidence).

## THE DEMOCRATIC REVOLUTION

The **Democratic Revolution** began about 1770, as citizens of France and the United States started demanding an increased say in the way they were governed. Before the Democratic Revolution, most people thought that God ordained kings and queens to rule. The American Revolution (1775–83) and the French Revolution (1789–99) helped to undermine that idea. These democratic upheavals showed that society could quickly experience massive change. They proved that ordinary people could replace unsatisfactory rulers and assume control themselves. The implications for social thought were profound. By demonstrating that human intervention could change the social order for the better, the Democratic Revolution prepared the ground for the idea that a science of society could play a big role in overcoming social problems and improving human welfare. Much of the justification for sociology as a science arose out of the democratic revolutions that shook Europe and North America.

*Liberty Leading the People*. Eugene Delacroix, 1830. The democratic forces unleashed by the French Revolution suggested that people are responsible for organizing society and that human intervention can therefore solve social problems. As such, democracy was a foundation stone of sociology.

# SOCIOLOGY AND THE MEDIA

## Donald Trump's Assault on Evidence

Donald Trump noisily opposes racial and sexual diversity, abortion, and scientific evidence that threatens his many prejudices. It was therefore only mildly shocking when, on December 14, 2017, White House officials informed analysts at the government-funded Centers for Disease Control and Prevention in Atlanta that certain words, including "diversity," "transgender," "fetus," and "science-based," were now prohibited in their reports (Sun and Eilperin, 2017). Apparently, this move is part of an attempt to suppress research on a wide range of pressing social issues.

The great intuition that launched the Scientific Revolution nearly 500 years ago was that humans do not know the answers to their most important questions (Harari, 2014: 251). In contrast, Donald Trump and many of his supporters think they've got all the answers. That is why Trump has cut science funding and why some top scientists are leaving the United States for more hospitable climates, including France and Canada (Flores, 2017; Semeniuk, 2018; Silcoff, 2018; Vidal, 2017).

Trump's bias extends to what he calls "fake news," that is, any broadcast or printed item that challenges his prejudices, regardless of how firmly the report is based on evidence from reliable sources, including high-quality research in the natural and social sciences. For example, on especially cold days, Trump likes to ridicule press reports about climate change and global warming—reports that are backed by a mountain of research and a strong scientific consensus. He has ordered the deletion or alteration of scientific information on government websites, reduced public access to scientific data, made it more difficult for government scientists to speak publicly about their work, and weakened science-based pollution standards without scientific justification. In his first year as president, Trump broadcast hundreds of tweets attacking evidence-based media stories that ran counter to his prejudices—while making countless demonstrably false or misleading statements in public (Coll, 2017).

Canadians have been less victimized by anti-evidence politicians than Americans have (Adams, 2017: 43–45). Moreover, Canadians respect traditional news reports and the evidence on which they are based much more than Americans do: nearly 70 percent of Canadians trust traditional news sources, compared to

The 45th president of the United States of America

just over 30 percent of Americans (Russell, 2016). Still, the media crisis to the south reminds us that we need to resist those who question the validity of news reports backed by solid evidence.

Many people take the mass media for granted or consider it only a form of entertainment. However, Trump's resistance to evidence-based policy illustrates that the media can be a rich source of sociological insight. Accordingly, in each chapter of this book, I explore an aspect of the media to help you see that even taken-for-granted aspects of everyday life have deeper meaning if you apply the sociological imagination to understanding them.

### Critical Thinking Questions

- Could a Canadian government resemble the Trump government in its approach to science?
- People trust news outlets when they read reports backed by evidence from reliable sources that are verified by subsequent events. How can you discover which news sources are reputable and trustworthy?

**Industrial Revolution** This rapid growth of mechanized industry began in Britain in the 1780s. The application of science and technology to industrial processes, the creation of factories, massive migration from countryside to city, and the formation of an industrial working class transformed society and caused a host of social problems that attracted the attention of social thinkers.

**values** Ideas about what is right and wrong, good and bad, desirable and undesirable, beautiful and ugly.

**research** The systematic observation of facts for the purpose of showing that a theory is false. When research fails to show that a theory is false, investigators are obliged to conclude that the theory is valid—but only until further notice, that is, unless and until someone shows it is false.

**social solidarity** A property of social groups that increases with the degree to which a group's members share beliefs and values, and the frequency and intensity with which they interact.

**rate** The number of times an event happens in a given period per 100 000 members of the population.

# THE INDUSTRIAL REVOLUTION

The **Industrial Revolution** began about 1780. It created a host of new and serious social problems that attracted the attention of social thinkers. As a result of the growth of mechanized industry, masses of people moved from countryside to city, worked agonizingly long hours in crowded and dangerous mines and factories, lost faith in their religions, confronted faceless bureaucracies, and reacted to the filth and poverty of their existence by means of strikes, crime, revolutions, and wars. Scholars had never seen a sociological laboratory like this. The Scientific Revolution suggested that a science of society was possible. The Democratic Revolution suggested that people can intervene to improve society. The Industrial Revolution now presented social thinkers with a host of pressing social problems crying out for solution. They responded by giving birth to the sociological imagination.

## LO4 THE BUILDING BLOCKS OF SOCIOLOGY

All of the natural and social sciences, including sociology, rest on three building blocks: theories, research, and values.

As noted earlier, a *theory* is a conjecture about the way observable facts are related. A theory may take many forms—a casual hunch ("He keeps staring at me because he thinks I'm handsome"), a mathematical formula ($E = mc^2$), and so on. However, regardless of form, and irrespective of whether they concern the relationship between attractiveness and sexual interest or between energy, mass, and speed, all theories venture ideas about how observable facts are related.

**Research** is the systematic observation of facts for the purpose of showing that a theory is false. When research fails to show that a theory is false, investigators are obliged to conclude that the theory is valid—but only until further notice, that is, unless and until someone shows it is false.

When people formulate theories, their values inevitably influence them. **Values** are ideas about what is right and wrong, good and bad, desirable and undesirable, beautiful and ugly. For instance, Albert Einstein's values, perhaps even his religious outlook, led him to believe that the universe is orderly and predictable, and that the scientist's job is to discover the underlying physical laws that make it so. That is why in 1927 he objected to Werner Heisenberg's theory that trying to measure both the speed and position of subatomic particles at the same time must yield unpredictable results. Einstein refused to accept that unpredictability is inevitable, famously stating that "God does not play dice." In his view, laws governing the speed and position of subatomic particles *must* exist. As far as we know, he was wrong, but that's what his values led him to think (Hawking, 2018). Sometimes values lead to the formulation of valid theories, sometimes not.

Émile Durkheim, Karl Marx, and Max Weber (pronounced VAY-ber) stood close to the origins of three of the main theoretical traditions in sociology: functionalism, conflict theory, and symbolic interactionism. A fourth theoretical approach, feminism, has arisen in recent decades to correct deficiencies in the three long-established traditions. It will become clear as you read this book that many more theories exist in addition to these four. However, because these four traditions have been especially influential in the development of sociology, I present a thumbnail sketch of each of them next.

## LO5 FOUNDERS
### ÉMILE DURKHEIM AND FUNCTIONALISM

Émile Durkheim (1858–1917) is generally considered to be the first modern sociologist. He argued that human behaviour is influenced by "social facts" or the social relations in which people are embedded. He illustrated his argument in a famous study of suicide (Durkheim, 1951 [1897]).

Many scholars of the day believed that psychological disorders cause suicide, but Durkheim's analysis of European government statistics and hospital records demonstrated no correlation between rates of psychological disorder and suicide rates in different categories of the population. Instead, he found that suicide rates varied with different degrees of **social solidarity** in different population categories. (A **rate** is the number of times an event happens in a given period per 100 000 members of the population.)

tightly knit. Elderly people were more prone than young and middle-aged people were to take their own lives when faced with misfortune because they were most likely to live alone, to have lost a spouse, and to lack a job and a wide network of friends (see Figure 1.3).

Durkheim's argument is an early example of functionalist theory. Functionalist theory focuses on how human behaviour is governed by social structures that are based mainly on shared values and that contribute to social stability.

## TALCOTT PARSONS AND ROBERT MERTON

By the 1930s, functionalism was popular in North America and it remained so until the 1960s. Talcott Parsons (1902–79) was its leading proponent. He argued that society is well integrated and in equilibrium when the family successfully raises new generations, the military successfully defends society against external threats, schools are able to teach students the skills and values they need to function as productive adults, and religions create a shared moral code among people (Parsons, 1951).

Émile Durkheim (1858–1917) was the first professor of sociology in France and is considered to be the first modern sociologist. In *The Rules of Sociological Method* (1938 [1895]) and *Suicide* (1951 [1897]), he argued that human behaviour is shaped by "social facts," or the social context in which people are embedded. In Durkheim's view, social facts define the constraints and opportunities within which people must act. Durkheim was also keenly interested in the conditions that promote social order in "primitive" and modern societies, and he explored this problem in depth in such works as *The Division of Labor in Society* (1997 [1893]) and *The Elementary Forms of the Religious Life* (1976 [1915/1912]).

According to Durkheim, the greater the degree to which a group's members share beliefs and values, and the more frequently and intensely they interact, the more social solidarity exists in the group. In turn, the higher the level of social solidarity, the more firmly anchored individuals are to the social world and the less likely they are to commit suicide if adversity strikes. In other words, Durkheim found that groups with a high degree of social solidarity had lower suicide rates than groups with a low degree of solidarity—at least up to a point (see Figure 1.2). For instance, married people were half as likely as unmarried people were to commit suicide because marriage typically created social ties and a kind of moral cement that bound the individuals to society. Women were less likely to commit suicide than men were because women were generally more involved in the intimate social relations of family life. Jews were less likely to commit suicide than Christians were because centuries of persecution had turned them into a group that was more defensive and

S. D. Clark (1910–2003) received his PhD from the University of Toronto. He became the first chair of the Department of Sociology at that institution. Born in Lloydminster, Alberta, he became known for his studies of Canadian social development as a process of disorganization and reorganization on a series of economic frontiers (Clark, 1968). The influence of functionalism on his work is apparent in his emphasis on the way society re-establishes equilibrium after experiencing disruptions caused by economic change.

## FIGURE 1.2 Durkheim's Theory of Suicide

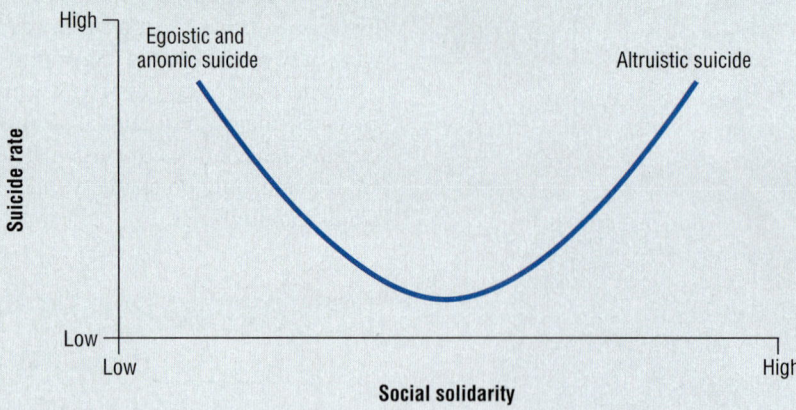

Durkheim's theory of suicide states that the suicide rate declines and then rises as social solidarity increases. Suicide in low-solidarity settings may be egoistic or anomic. **Egoistic suicide** results from the poor integration of people into society because of weak social ties to others. Someone who is unemployed and unmarried is thus more likely to commit suicide than is someone who is employed and married. **Anomic suicide** occurs when vague norms govern behaviour. The rate of anomic suicide is likely to be high among people living in a society that lacks a widely shared code of morality. Durkheim called suicides that occur in high-solidarity settings *altruistic*. **Altruistic suicide** occurs when norms tightly govern behaviour. Soldiers who knowingly give up their lives to protect comrades commit altruistic suicide out of a deep sense of patriotism and comradeship.

Source: From BRYM/ROBERTS/STROHSCHEIN/LIE. *Sociology: Your Compass for a New World,* 6E. © 2019 Nelson Education Ltd. Reproduced by permission. www.cengage.com/permissions

## FIGURE 1.3 Suicide by Age and Sex, Canada, 2015

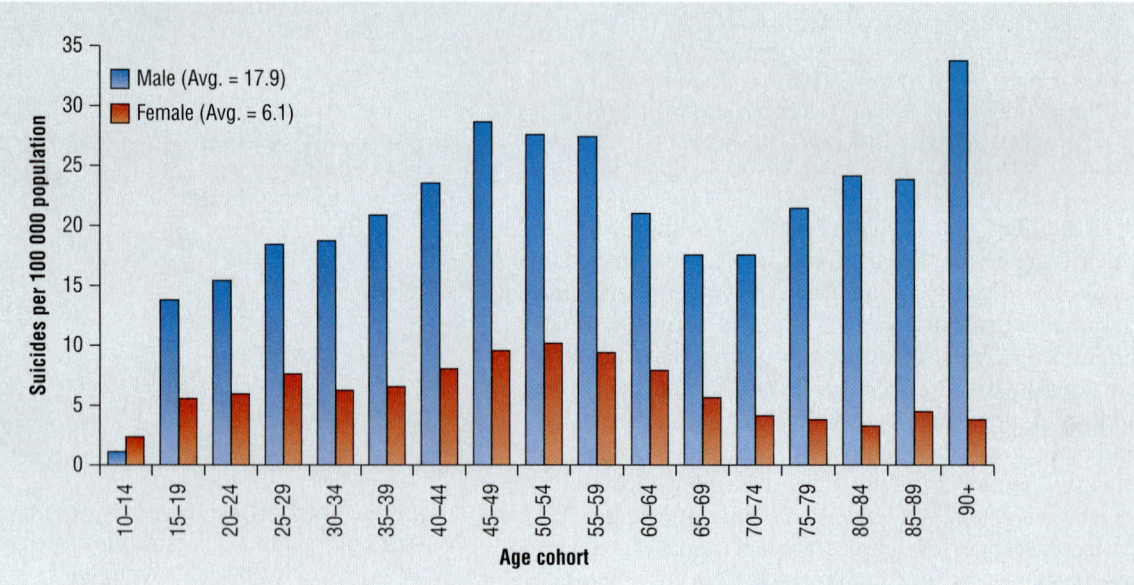

The most recent data on suicide by age and sex in Canada suggest the need to revise Durkheim's theory in some respects. While men are about three times more likely than women to take their own lives, as was the case in Durkheim's France, the suicide rate among teenagers, young adults, and middle-aged people is much higher. Moreover, the suicide rate declines for women over the age of 54, contrary to Durkheim's findings. Be a sociological theorist: Outline your own explanation for these differences between late nineteenth-century France and early twenty-first-century Canada.

Source: Statistics Canada. 2018. CANSIM Table 1020561. https://www150.statcan.gc.ca/t1/tbl1/en/tv.action?pid=1310039401 (retrieved 27 June 2018).

However, Robert Merton (1910–2003), the other leading functionalist of the day, criticized Parsons for exaggerating the degree to which members of society share common values and social institutions contribute to social harmony. Merton proposed that social structures may have different consequences for different groups, and some of those consequences may be disruptive or have **dysfunctions** (Merton, 1968 [1949]). Moreover, said Merton, although some functions are **manifest functions** (intended and easily observed), others are **latent functions** (unintended and less obvious). For instance, a manifest function of schools is to transmit skills from one generation to the next. A latent function of schools is to encourage the development of a separate youth culture that often conflicts with parents' values (Coleman, 1961; Hersch, 1998).

## KARL MARX AND CONFLICT THEORY

Karl Marx (1818–83) observed the destitution and discontent produced by the Industrial Revolution and proposed a very different argument about the way societies develop (Marx, 1904 [1859]; Marx and Engels, 1972 [1848]). He focused on the study of **social classes**, the positions people occupy in a hierarchy that is shaped by the source or amount of their income and wealth. (Marx emphasized *source* of income as the determinant of a person's class position; others have emphasized *amount* of income.) **Class conflict,** the struggle between classes to resist and overcome the opposition of other classes, lies at the centre of Marx's ideas. In his writings lie the seeds of conflict theory, which highlights the tensions underlying existing social structures and the capacity of those tensions to burst into the open and cause social change.

Specifically, Marx argued that owners of industry are eager to improve the way work is organized and to adopt new tools, machines, and production methods because these innovations allow them to produce more efficiently, earn higher profits, and drive inefficient competitors out of business. However, the drive for profits also causes capitalists to concentrate workers in larger and larger establishments, keep wages as low as possible, and invest as little as possible in improving working conditions. Consequently, wrote Marx, a large and growing class of poor workers comes to oppose a small and shrinking class of wealthy owners.

Marx believed that workers would ultimately become aware of belonging to the same exploited class. He called this awareness **class consciousness**. He believed that working-class consciousness would encourage the growth of trade unions and labour parties. According to Marx, these organizations would eventually seek to put an end to private ownership of property, replacing it with a communist society, defined as a system in which there is no private property and everyone shares property and wealth according to their needs.

## MAX WEBER

Although some of Marx's ideas have been usefully adapted to the study of contemporary society, his predictions about the inevitable collapse of capitalism were soon questioned.

Karl Marx (1818–83) was a revolutionary thinker whose ideas affected not just the growth of sociology but also the course of world history. He held that major sociohistorical changes are the result of conflict between society's main social classes. In his major work, *Capital* (1967 [1867–94]), Marx argued that capitalism would produce such misery and collective power among workers that they would eventually take control of government and create a classless society in which production would be based on human need rather than profit.

Alfredo Dagli Orti/REX/Shutterstock

> **egoistic suicide** The type of suicide that results from a lack of integration of the individual into society because of weak social ties to others.
>
> **anomic suicide** The type of suicide that occurs when norms governing behaviour are vaguely defined.
>
> **altruistic suicide** The type of suicide that occurs when norms govern behaviour so tightly that individual actions are often in the group interest.
>
> **dysfunctions** Effects of social structures that create social instability.
>
> **manifest functions** Visible and intended effects of social structures.
>
> **latent functions** Less visible and unintended effects of social structures.
>
> **social classes** Positions people occupy in a hierarchy that is shaped by the source or amount of their income and wealth.
>
> **class conflict** The struggle between classes to resist and overcome the opposition of other classes.
>
> **class consciousness** Awareness of being a member of a social class.

Other social thinkers pointed out that Marx did not understand how investing in technology would make it possible for workers to toil fewer hours under less oppressive conditions. Nor did he foresee that higher wages, better working conditions, and welfare-state benefits would pacify manual workers. Still, although Weber and others called into question the particulars of Marx's ideas, we can identify the general principles of conflict theory in Marx's writings—an emphasis on macro-level structures, the centrality of inequality in understanding social life, and the role of conflict in causing social change.

## THE CULTURAL TURN AND POSTSTRUCTURALISM: GRAMSCI AND FOUCAULT

In the 1960s and 1970s, conflict theory took what has been called a "cultural turn." Increasingly, conflict theorists directed their attention to the ways in which language, music, literature, fashion, movies, advertising, and other elements of culture express domination by the powerful and resistance by others.

The origins of a cultural approach to the study of social conflict are found in essays written in the early twentieth century by Italian Marxist Antonio Gramsci (pronounced GRAM-shee). In Gramsci's view, ruling classes establish their dominance partly by controlling jobs, using force, and the like. However, they also exercise power in softer ways. In particular, they fund the development, transmission, and learning of ideas that seem to embody the values of everyone but are actually biased in favour of ruling-class dominance. Gramsci wrote that **cultural hegemony** exists if these values become so deeply entrenched that the great majority of people accept them as common sense (Gramsci, 1957; 1971). Subordinate classes can resist cultural hegemony, Gramsci wrote, but only if they develop ideas and institutions that express and support their own cultural preferences. Later writers extended Gramsci's argument to include dominant, taken-for-granted ideas about race, ethnicity, sexuality, and so on.

The notion that culture is the site of ongoing conflict between dominant and subordinate classes and other groups was further developed in France from the 1950s to the 1980s by Michel Foucault (pronounced Foo-CŌ). Foucault made his case by studying new forms of regulation that accompany capitalist industrialization. He showed that, as the goal of maximizing economic productivity grows in importance, criminals, the physically infirm, the mentally ill, and ordinary students and workers are subjected to new structures of control in prisons, hospitals, mental institutions, workplaces, schools, and universities. According to Foucault, modern institutions sometimes use violence to regulate behaviour but they more often rely on new technologies and the *internalization* of control

Max Weber (1864–1920), Germany's greatest sociologist, profoundly influenced the development of the discipline worldwide. Engaged in a lifelong "debate with Marx's ghost," Weber held that economic circumstances alone do not explain the rise of capitalism. As he showed in *The Protestant Ethic and the Spirit of Capitalism* (1958 [1904–05]), independent developments in the religious realm had unintended beneficial consequences for capitalist development in some parts of Europe. He also argued that capitalism would not necessarily give way to socialism. Instead, he regarded the growth of bureaucracy and the overall "rationalization" of life as the defining characteristics of the modern age. These themes were developed in *Economy and Society* (1968 [1914]).

Max Weber (1864–1920), a German sociologist who wrote his major works two or three decades after Marx died, was among the first to criticize Marx's argument (Weber, 1946). Weber observed the rapid growth of the service sector of the economy, with its many nonmanual workers and professionals. He argued that many members of these occupational groups stabilize society because they enjoy higher status and income than do manual workers employed in the manufacturing sector. In addition, Weber showed that class conflict is not the only driving force of history. In his view, politics and religion are also important sources of historical change.

**cultural hegemony** Involves the control of a culture by dominant classes and other groups to the point where their values are universally accepted as common sense.

12 CHAPTER 1 Introducing Sociology

mechanisms. For example, modern institutions are physically, technologically, and socially designed so authorities can easily observe the behaviour of inmates, patients, workers, and students. Authorities may not always watch their "clientele," but knowing that they *may* be under the watchful eye of authorities, inmates and others usually act as if they *are* being observed. Before capitalist industrialization, control took place almost exclusively through force, but now more subtle and effective mechanisms of regulation are employed. (Michel Foucault, 1973, 1977, and 1988)

Power, Foucault held, is exercised in every social interaction, but every social interaction is also subject to resistance by subordinates. Thus, the exercise of power is unstable. Dominant groups and individuals must continuously renew power relations to maintain control, but sometimes they fail, giving subordinates the opportunity to assert their interests.

Foucault was part of a movement in French social thought known as **poststructuralism.** Earlier social thinkers had argued that social relations and cultures form structures, or stable determinants of the way people think and act. These "structuralists" typically categorized elements of social relations and of culture as binary opposites: male versus female, civilized versus uncivilized people, black versus white races, and so on (Derrida, 2004: 41). In contrast, poststructuralists, Foucault among them, denied the stability of social relations and of cultures, their capacity always to shape how people think and act, and the tidy categorization of social and cultural elements as binary opposites. According to the poststructuralists, the social world is a more fluid and complex place, and people are more often the agents of their own destiny than earlier social theorists ever imagined.

To better understand these ideas, consider that many of us casually use the term "the opposite sex" in everyday speech without giving it much thought. Yet embedded in this term is a faulty set of assumptions based on a distribution of power that favours some categories of people at the expense of others. As noted in the body of this chapter and as developed in Chapter 8, Sexualities and Genders, it is factually incorrect to assume that men and women are opposites in their sexual identities, preferences, and behaviours. It is more accurate to say that men and women are arrayed along one scale with respect to their sexual identities, a second scale with respect to their sexual preferences, and a third scale with respect to their sexual behaviours, and their positions on these scales can change in different circumstances.

When we think that men remain clustered on one extreme of a single scale and women on the other—when we think of women and men as fixed "opposites"—we oversimplify the complexity of real flesh-and-blood people. We also ignore that many women and men are not so neatly pigeonholed. Those who are not neatly categorized are simply defined out of existence by our casual use of language and the underlying fact that some people have more power than others to name things.

## GEORGE HERBERT MEAD AND SYMBOLIC INTERACTIONISM

We noted earlier that Weber criticized Marx's interpretation of the development of capitalism. Among other things, Weber argued that early capitalist development was not caused by favourable economic circumstances alone. In addition, he said, certain *religious* beliefs encouraged robust capitalist growth. In particular, sixteenth- and seventeenth-century Protestants believed that their religious doubts could be reduced and a state of grace assured if they worked diligently and lived modestly. Weber called this belief the **Protestant ethic.** He believed it had an unintended effect: people who held to the Protestant ethic saved and invested more money than others did. Consequently, capitalism developed most vigorously where the Protestant ethic took hold. He concluded that capitalism did not develop simply as a result of the operation of economic forces, as Marx argued. Instead, it depended partly on the religious *meaning* that individuals attached to their work (Weber, 1958 [1904–05]). In much of his research, Weber emphasized the need to understand people's motives and the meanings they attach to things to gain a clear sense of the significance of their actions.

At the University of Chicago, George Herbert Mead (1863–1931) thought along the same lines as Weber. He was the driving force behind the early study of how the individual's sense of self is formed in the course of interaction with other people (Mead, 1934). As such, he was a founder of the school of thought that came to be known as symbolic interactionism, which examines how various aspects of social life, including fashion, convey meaning and thereby assist or impede communication (Blumer, 1969).

Mead understood that human communication involves seeing yourself from other people's points of view. For example, let's say you're standing outside talking to two classmates. One winks at you. How do you know what the wink means, that is, what your classmate wants to communicate?

**poststructuralism** A school of thought that originated in mid-twentieth-century France, it denied the stability of social relations and of cultures, their capacity to always shape how people think and act, and the tidy categorization of social and cultural elements as binary opposites.

**Protestant ethic** The sixteenth- and seventeenth-century belief that religious doubts can be reduced and a state of grace assured if people work diligently and lived modestly. According to Weber, the Protestant ethic had the unintended effect of increasing savings and investment, thus stimulating capitalist growth.

Conflict theory became especially popular in North America in the 1960s and 1970s, a period that was rocked by major labour unrest, peace demonstrations on university campuses, the rise of the Black Power movement and the Quebec separatist movement, and the emergence of contemporary feminism. Strikes, demonstrations, and riots were almost daily occurrences in the 1960s and 1970s, and it seemed evident to many sociologists of that generation that conflict among classes, nations, races, and generations was the very essence of social life. For example, John Porter (1921–79) was Canada's premier sociologist in the 1960s and 1970s. Born in Vancouver, he received his PhD from the London School of Economics. He spent his academic career at Carleton University in Ottawa, where he served as chair of the Department of Sociology and Anthropology, Dean of Arts and Science, and Academic Vice-president. His major work, *The Vertical Mosaic* (1965), is a study of class and power in Canada. Firmly rooted in conflict theory, it influenced a generation of Canadian sociologists in their studies of social inequality, elite groups, French–English relations, and Canadian–American relations.

Erving Goffman (1922–82) was born in Mannville, Alberta. He studied sociology and anthropology at the University of Toronto. He completed his PhD at the University of Chicago and pursued his academic career at the University of California, Berkeley, and the University of Pennsylvania. Goffman developed an international reputation for his "dramaturgical" approach to symbolic interactionism, which views social life much like the enactment of a play, with defined roles and props, and front stage and backstage performances.

If the wink occurs while you are trying to pull a trick on the third classmate, it might signify that the winker knows what you're up to. If the winker has hinted earlier that she might be interested in going out on a date with you, the wink might signify that her interest has grown. If the wind is blowing, it might mean that some dust got in her eye. According to Mead, you must figure out the meaning of the wink by using your imagination to understand the social context of your interaction, take the winker's point of view for a moment and see yourself as she sees you. Only to the degree that you see yourself from her point of view—only to the extent that you succeed in "taking the role of the other,"

as Mead put it—will you be able to understand accurately what she means by winking at you.

All human communication depends on being able to take the role of the other, wrote Mead. And it is only by taking the role of the other and seeing ourselves as others see us hundreds of times every day that we can develop a sense of who we are. Mead concluded that our sense of self is not present from birth. It emerges only gradually as we interact with others and use symbols such as words and gestures to communicate with them.

With its emphasis on the construction of meaning during social interaction, Mead's work gave birth to symbolic interactionism, a theoretical tradition that continues to be a major force in sociology today.

## HARRIET MARTINEAU AND FEMINIST THEORY

Few women figured prominently in the early history of sociology. The demands placed on them by the nineteenth-century family and the lack of opportunity in the larger society prevented most of them from attaining a higher education and making major contributions to the discipline. Women who made their mark on sociology in its early years tended to have unusual biographies. Some of them introduced gender issues that were ignored by Marx, Durkheim, Weber, Mead, and other early sociologists.

Appreciation for the sociological contribution of these pioneering women has grown in recent years because concern regarding gender issues has come to form a substantial part of the modern sociological enterprise.

For example, Harriet Martineau (1802–76) is often called the first woman sociologist. Born in England to a prosperous family, she never married. She supported herself comfortably from her journalistic writings. Martineau wrote one of the first books on research methods and undertook critical studies of slavery, factory laws, and gender inequality. She was a leading advocate of voting rights and higher education for women and of gender equality in the family. As such, Martineau was one of the first feminists (Martineau, 1985).

## MODERN FEMINISM

Despite its early stirrings, feminist thinking had little impact on sociology until the mid-1960s, when the rise of the modern women's movement drew attention to the many remaining inequalities between women and men. Because of feminist theory's major influence on sociology, it can fairly be regarded as sociology's fourth major theoretical tradition. Modern feminism has several variants (see Chapter 8, Sexualities and Genders). However, the various strands of feminist theory have in common a focus on patriarchy (the male domination of women), the conviction that gender inequality is a consequence of structures of power and social conventions rather than biological necessity, and a readiness to examine the operation of patriarchy in micro- and macro-settings.

To show how much farther we can see by using theory as our guide, I now illustrate how the four traditions outlined above improve our understanding of an aspect of social life familiar to everyone: the world of fashion.

Margrit Eichler (1942–) was born in Berlin, Germany. She received her PhD at Duke University in the United States before beginning her academic career in Canada. She served as chair of the Department of Sociology at the Ontario Institute for Studies in Education (University of Toronto) and was the first director of the Institute for Women's Studies and Gender Studies at the University of Toronto. Eichler is internationally known for her work on feminist methodology (Eichler, 1987). Her work on family policy in Canada has influenced students, professional sociologists, and policy-makers for decades (Eichler, 1988).

## SOCIOLOGICAL THEORIES AND THE PROBLEM OF FASHION

In the late 1990s, one of the main fashion trends among white, middle-class girls between the ages of 11 and 14 was the Britney Spears look: bare midriff, highlighted hair, wide belt, glitter purse, and big wedge shoes or Skechers Energy sneakers. However, in 2002, a new pop star, Avril Lavigne, was rising in the pop charts. Nominated for a 2003 Grammy Award in the "Best New Artist" category, the 17-year-old skater punk from the small town of Napanee in eastern Ontario affected a shaggy, unkempt look. She sported worn-out T-shirts, plaid shirts, baggy pants, undershirts, ties, backpacks, chain wallets, and, for shoes, Converse Chuck Taylors. As Avril Lavigne's popularity soared, some young girls switched their style from glam to neo-grunge (Tkacik, 2002).

That switch is just one example of the fashion shifts that occur periodically and with increasing frequency in popular culture. A rock idol or movie star helped by a carefully planned marketing campaign captures the imagination of some people, who start dressing in the style of the star—until another star catches their fancy and influences yet another style change. Market research shows that musicians are more influential than any other type of celebrity on young people's fashion choices. More than 7 out of 10 women and 6 out of 10 men turn to musicians for style inspiration. Based on such findings, Nordstrom has gone so far as to create detailed instructional YouTube videos to teach young consumers how to emulate the fashion styles of Vince Staples, Cassey Veggies, Hailee Steinfeld, Olivia Holt, Bahari, Vic Mensa, and so on (search "style mix designed by Nordstrom"). Ironically, despite such carefully planned corporate strategies, young consumers say they are highly influenced by musicians because of their authenticity, that is, the belief that musicians alone control their style to express who they really are (Vevo, 2017).

Why then do fashion shifts take place? Sociologists explain fashion cycles in four ways: functionalist, conflict,

Britney Spears

Avril Lavigne

symbolic interactionist, and feminist. Each explanation derives from a major theoretical tradition in sociology.

## FUNCTIONALIST THEORY

One way of interpreting fashion shifts (or any other social phenomenon) is through a functionalist lens. In general, **functionalist theory** rests on three ideas:

1. *Social structure*. Human behaviour is governed by stable patterns of social relations, or social structures.
2. *Social function*. The most important thing we can know about social structures is how they operate or function to maintain social stability (or fail to do so).
3. *Values*. Social structures are based mainly on shared values.

Let's see how these ideas apply to the analysis of fashion cycles (Davis, 1992).

Functionalists note that exclusive fashion houses in Paris, Milan, New York, and London show new styles every season. Some of the new styles catch on among the rich clientele of big-name designers. Wealthy people value ways of distinguishing themselves from the non-wealthy, and the main appeal of wearing expensive, new fashions is that it provides a means of achieving such distinction. Thus, the fashion industry is a social structure that performs an important social function. By allowing people of different rank to distinguish themselves from one another, it helps to promote social stability insofar as it reinforces the ordered layering of society. If fashion didn't perform this function, we wouldn't have fashion cycles.

> **functionalist theory** Holds that (1) human behaviour is governed by stable patterns of social relations, or social structures; (2) the most important thing we can know about social structures is how they maintain social stability or fail to do so; and (3) social structures are based mainly on shared values.

Functionalists note that the ebb and flow of fashion sped up in the twentieth century thanks to technological advances in clothes manufacturing. Inexpensive knock-offs could now quickly reach markets accessible to nearly everyone. Consequently, new styles needed to be introduced more often so fashion could continue to perform its function of helping to preserve the system of social stratification.

Functionalism offers a pretty accurate account of the way fashion trends worked until the 1960s, but after that fashion became more democratic. Paris, Milan, New York, and London are still important fashion centres, but new fashion trends are increasingly initiated by lower classes, minority racial and ethnic groups, and people who spurn "high" fashion altogether. Today, big-name designers are more likely to be influenced by the inner-city styles of hip-hop rather than vice versa. New fashions no longer trickle down from the upper classes and a few high-fashion centres. People in the upper classes are nearly as likely to adopt fashions trends that can originate just about anywhere in the social order. Thus, although functionalist theory helps us make sense of fashion cycles in the first half of the twentieth century, it doesn't provide a satisfactory explanation of fashion cycles since then.

## CONFLICT THEORY

Recognizing the declining validity of functionalism as an explanation for fashion cycles since the mid-twentieth century, some sociologists turned to conflict theory. Like functionalism, **conflict theory** rests on three ideas:

1. *Social structure*. Human behaviour is governed by social structures.
2. *Inequality*. Social structures are characterized by inequalities of wealth and power.
3. *Conflict and change*. Members of privileged and subordinate groups engage in a continuous struggle to increase their advantages, one at the expense of the other. Consequently, social structures are unstable; sometimes they rupture, leading to social change or even social transformation.

**conflict theory** Holds that (1) human behaviour is governed by social structures; (2) social structures are characterized by inequalities of wealth and power; and (3) members of privileged and subordinate groups engage in a continuous struggle to increase their advantages, one at the expense of the other, so social structures sometimes rupture and are transformed.

In short, conflict theory highlights the tensions underlying existing social arrangements and the capacity of those tensions to burst and cause social change.

From the point of view of a conflict theorist, fashion cycles are a means by which owners and other big players in the clothing, advertising, and entertainment industries make big profits. They introduce new styles frequently because they make more money when they encourage people to buy new clothes often. Doing so has the added advantage of keeping consumers distracted from the many social, economic, and political problems that might otherwise cause them to express dissatisfaction with the existing social order and even rebel against it. Conflict theorists therefore believe that fashion helps to maintain a precarious system of inequality between ordinary consumers and big players in fashion-related industries—an equilibrium that can be disrupted by the underlying tensions between them.

Women's jeans were first manufactured in 1934. Since then, denim styles have gone through many fashion cycles, some of which are illustrated here. Would you wear bell-bottom jeans? Why or why not?

## FIGURE 1.4 Quick! New Wardrobe Required!

How the fashion colour palette changed from spring 2017 to spring 2018.

Source: Images used with the permission of Pantone LLC. PANTONE® and other Pantone trademarks are the property of, and are used with the written permission of, Pantone LLC. PANTONE Color identification is solely for artistic purposes and not intended to be used for specification. © Pantone LLC, 2017. All rights reserved.

**symbolic interactionist theory** Holds that (1) human behaviour is governed by the meanings people attach to other people and to things in their social environment; (2) other people and things become meaningful in the course of interpersonal communication; and (3) people create their social circumstances and do not merely react to them.

Conflict theorists have a point. Fashion *is* a big and profitable business. Owners *do* introduce new styles frequently to make more money. For example, they have created the Color Marketing Group (known to insiders as the "Color Mafia"), a committee that meets regularly to help change the palette of colour preferences for consumer products. According to one committee member, the Color Mafia makes sure that "the mass media,…fashion magazines and catalogs, home shopping shows, and big clothing chains all present the same options" each season (Mundell, 1993; see Figure 1.4)

Yet the Color Mafia and other influential elements of the fashion industry are not all-powerful. In fact, some fashion trends initiated by industry owners flop. Thus, when the fashion industry proclaimed 1970 "the year of the midi-skirt," all hell broke loose. Mini-skirted women organized protest marches against skirts hanging six inches below the knee. Men publicly objected that the midi interfered with their ogling. One author wrote in an influential magazine that the fashion industry had so much invested in the midi that "no amount of protest will stem the tide of the longer skirt" (quoted in Chrisman-Campbell, 2014). He was wrong. The midi-skirt was a huge failure. Fashion flops like this illustrate what conflict theorists mean when they say that all social relations are unstable, with subordinates sometimes subverting the best-laid plans of the wealthy and the powerful. Fashion decisions are made partly by consumers.

This insight raises an interesting question. If fashion decisions are made partly by consumers, why do they make certain choices rather than others? Unfortunately, both functionalist and conflict theory are silent on this question. For answers, we must turn to a third theoretical tradition in sociology—symbolic interactionist theory.

## SYMBOLIC INTERACTIONIST THEORY

The three core ideas of **symbolic interactionist theory** are as follows:

1. *Meaning*. Human behaviour is governed by the meanings people attach to other people and to things in their social environment.

Women demonstrate against the midi-skirt in 1970.

18  CHAPTER 1  Introducing Sociology

2. *Interpersonal communication.* Other people and things become meaningful in the course of interpersonal communication.
3. *Human agency.* People help to create their social circumstances and do not merely react to them. While functionalists and conflict theorists emphasize the degree to which people's behaviour is influenced by whether they are rich or poor, male or female, black or white, and so on, symbolic interactionists emphasize human creativity—how people routinely interpret their circumstances in novel ways, change their minds, make choices, and alter their circumstances.

From a symbolic interactionist point of view, clothes are symbols that communicate meaning. (A **symbol** is a meaningful representation of something.) Clothes announce to the world who their wearers are. They thus help to establish the kind of interaction that takes place among people.

Specifically, the fashion industry feeds on the fact that a person's identity or sense of self is always a work in progress. True, we develop a self-conception as we mature. We come to think of ourselves as members of one or more families, occupations, communities, classes, ethnic and racial groups, and countries. We develop patterns of behaviour and belief associated with each of these social categories. However, social categories change over time and so do we as we move within and through those categories and as we age. Consequently, our identities are in flux. When our identities change, clothes help us express our shifting identities. They convey whether we are rich, sexually available, athletic, conservative, and much more, thus telling others how we want them to see us and the kinds of people with whom we want to associate.

At some point, you may become less conservative, less sexually available, and so on. Your clothing style is likely to change accordingly. (Of course, the messages people try to send through their style of clothing may be misinterpreted.) The fashion industry invests much effort trying to discern which new styles might capture current needs for self-expression among various categories of the population. Fashion cycles result from this effort and from clothing's ability to grease the wheels of symbolic interaction.

## FEMINISM

**Gender**—one's personal sense of being masculine or feminine, conventionally defined—is a central part of everyone's identity. Because clothes are one of the most important means of expressing gender, feminist theorists have done a lot of interesting work on fashion.

Sociological feminism's three key ideas may be summarized as follows:

1. *Patriarchy.* The system of male domination of women—patriarchy—is the most important social structure affecting a person's opportunities in life.
2. *Power and social convention.* Male domination and female subordination are determined not by biological necessity but by structures of power and social convention. From this point of view, women are subordinate to men only because men enjoy more legal, economic, political, and cultural rights.
3. *Micro- and macro-level.* While functionalism and conflict theorists tend to focus on macrostructures, and symbolic interactionist theorists tend to focus on microstructures, feminist theorists are inclined to examine the operation of patriarchy in both macro- and micro-level settings.

> **symbol** A meaningful representation of something.
>
> **gender** One's personal sense of being masculine or feminine, conventionally defined.

How have feminist ideas been applied to the analysis of fashion? Here we must distinguish two generations of thought. In the 1970s, feminist sociologists tended to view fashion as a feature of male domination. After all, they noted, fashion is mainly a female preoccupation. It takes a lot of time and money to choose, buy, and clean clothes. Fashionable clothing is often impractical and uncomfortable, sometimes even unhealthy (prolonged wearing of four-inch heels are murder on women's feet). They concluded that, in a sense, fashion imprisons women. Moreover, they

Lady Gaga at a MuchMusic Video Awards show

**sexuality** One's capacity for sexual feelings.

continued, fashion's focus on youth, slenderness, and eroticism diminishes women by turning them into sexual objects.

If feminists from the 1970s could have time-travelled to 2010 and viewed Lady Gaga and Beyoncé's "Telephone" music video, they likely would have been aghast. When Lady Gaga gets strip-searched at the start of the music video and then enters the prison exercise yard clad in little more than chains, they would have thought she was glorifying rape and the strict control of women. After Lady Gaga and Beyoncé escape prison and fasten vanity plates on their car identifying it as a "Pussy Wagon," our imaginary feminists from the 1970s would have said that the singers are reducing women to sexual objects for the pleasure of men.

In recent years, a new generation of feminist sociologists have offered a diametrically opposed interpretation of women's fashion. They see it as a vehicle of female empowerment insofar as it allows women to use their **sexuality**—their capacity for sexual feelings—to assert their interests. To remain with our example, they view Lady Gaga as a continuation of the girl-power movement that first emerged in 1996 with the release of the Spice Girls' hit single, "Wannabe." They note that, in "Telephone," Lady Gaga and Beyoncé go so far as to poison the men who treat them as sexual objects, and that at a MuchMusic Video Awards show, Lady Gaga's bra shot flames, suggesting that she is not just hot but also powerful and independent. As Lady Gaga once said, "Some women choose to follow men, and some women choose to follow their dreams. If you're wondering which way to go, remember that your career will never wake up and tell you it doesn't love you anymore" (Spines, 2010: 54; see also Bauer, 2010; Powers, 2009).

In sum, functionalism helps us understand how fashion cycles operated until the 1960s to reinforce inequality. Conflict theory helps us see the tensions underlying the apparently stable social arrangements of the fashion industry. Symbolic interactionism explains how fashion assists communication and the drawing of boundaries between different population categories. Feminism explores the ambiguities of gender identity that underlie fashion. Although each type of sociological explanation clarifies a different aspect of fashion, all four allow us to probe beneath a taken-for-granted part of our world and learn something new and surprising about it. Thus, one promise of the four main types of sociology's main theories, summarized in Theories at a Glance, Sociology's Main Theories, is that when you see the next hit music video by Rihanna or Drake, you will think differently and more deeply about the social world and how you manoeuver through it.

A caution is necessary at this point. To a degree, the four theories to which you've been introduced focus on different aspects of social life (see the "Main foci" column

## THEORIES AT A GLANCE

### Sociology's Main Theories

| Theory | Main Level(s) of Analysis | Main Foci | Main Question |
|---|---|---|---|
| Functionalism | Macro | Social structure; social function; values | How do social structures and the values underlying them contribute to social stability? |
| Conflict theory | Macro | Social structure; inequality; social conflict and change | How does the structure of inequality between privileged groups seeking to maintain their advantages and subordinate groups seeking to increase theirs lead to conflict and often to social change? |
| Symbolic interactionism | Micro | Meaning; interpersonal communication; human agency | How do people communicate to make their social settings meaningful, thus helping to create their social circumstances? |
| Feminism | Macro and micro | Patriarchy; power and social convention | How do social conventions maintain male dominance and female subordination, and how do these conventions get overturned? |

of the Theories at a Glance box). If a sociologist happens to be interested in more than one aspect, she may borrow ideas from more than one tradition. Insofar as the four theories have different foci, they are complementary.

However, sometimes theories are not complementary; they may make different conjectures about the relationship between the same facts. Figure 1.5 illustrates this circumstance. The non-overlapping parts of the circles in Figure 1.5 suggest that theories *complement* each other when they explain how facts are related in *different* aspects of social life. We saw this in our analysis of fashion. The overlapping parts of the circles in Figure 1.5 illustrate that theories *compete* against each other when they offer *contradictory* explanations of how facts are related in the *same* aspects of social life.

It is especially when theories compete to explain the same things that research is most useful. Research can influence theoretical development by providing grounds for *rejecting* or *modifying* one or more theories or *synthesizing* two or more theories. Because research designed to test theories is a large part of what sociologists do, I devote a box in each chapter to showing how research can influence knowledge by giving us grounds for rejecting, modifying, or synthesizing theories. In the boxed feature, Theories in Dispute, The Problem of Sexuality, I begin with an example of rejection.

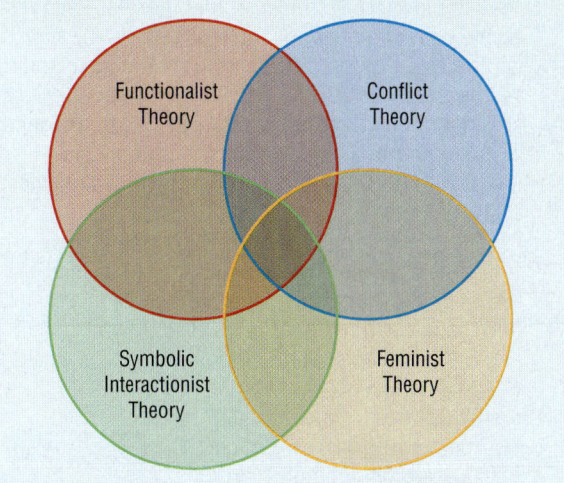

FIGURE 1.5 Competing and Complementary Theories

Sociological theories *complement* each other when they explain how facts are related in *different* areas of social life (non-overlapping parts of the circles). Sociological theories *compete* when they offer *contradictory* explanations of how facts are related in the *same* areas of social life (overlapping parts of the circles).

# THEORIES IN DISPUTE

## The Problem of Sexuality

Functionalists argue that most people value families in which wives and husbands play different roles, with husbands working in the paid labour force and wives focused on raising children and managing the household without pay. Supposedly, this division labour exists because parents think that educating their daughters to be nurturing and sensitive, and their sons to be rational, self-assured, and competitive, will prepare them for adulthood. In the functionalist view, teaching girls and boys to act in such conventional ways helps to maintain social order, while homosexuality and lesbianism are socially disruptive phenomena that are sensibly scorned (Parsons, 1942).

Underlying the functionalist perspective is the idea that nearly all males think of themselves as masculine, conventionally defined, and want to have sexual relations with females, while nearly all females think of themselves as feminine, conventionally defined, and want to have sexual relations with males. Said differently, functionalists claim that biological sex, sociological gender, and social-psychological sexuality are binary (standing in an either/or relationship) and perfectly aligned.

French sociological theorists challenged these ideas beginning in the 1970s. They called themselves *poststructuralists* because they claimed that social structures and cultural standards are not as rigid or structured as functionalists held, nor are they binary. For example, biological sex, sociological gender, and social-psychological sexuality vary along continua: people can be more or less male or female biologically, they can feel more or less masculine or feminine (conventionally defined), and they can be more or less attracted to members of their sex heterosexual. Some people choose to alter the sex, gender, and sexuality that have been assigned to them by physicians, parents, and teachers (Foucault, 1990 [1978]; see Chapter 8, Sexualities and Genders).

Research helped to resolve the dispute between functionalist and poststructuralist theories. Here, I summarize just one such effort. It focuses on sexuality (Vrangalova and Savin-Williams, 2012). Researchers asked 1784 people (half of them men, half women) to define their sexuality as heterosexual, mostly heterosexual, bisexual, mostly gay/lesbian, gay/lesbian, questioning/uncertain, or other. They then asked these people to situate themselves along two dimensions: degree of sexual attraction to men and women, and number of men and women with whom they had had a genital sexual experience. The results for five categories of women are arrayed in Figure 1.6.

Note that for all five sexual orientations, women are on average simultaneously attracted to same-sex and other-sex partners, albeit to varying degrees. For example, women who define themselves as heterosexual (signified by green squares) scored 4.9 out of 5 on other-sex attraction and 1.5 out of 5 on same-sex attraction. It also shows that, for all five sexual orientations, women have had on average more than one male and at least one female sexual partner. For example, heterosexual women had on average 10.2 other-sex partners and 1.7 same-sex partners. The pattern for men differs only in detail.

In short, this research convincingly shows that one aspect of the functionalist theory is invalid. It is simply incorrect to think that most people's sexual feelings and behaviour are binary.

### Critical Thinking Questions

- Some people refuse to believe that sex, gender, and sexuality are not binary. What sociological factors might explain their refusal?
- A small percentage of babies are born with ambiguous genitalia, in which case parents and doctors commonly opt for early "corrective" surgery. What are the pros and cons of this decision?

**FIGURE 1.6** Same/Other Sexual Attraction and Number of Same/Other Sex Partners for Women of Five Sexual Orientations

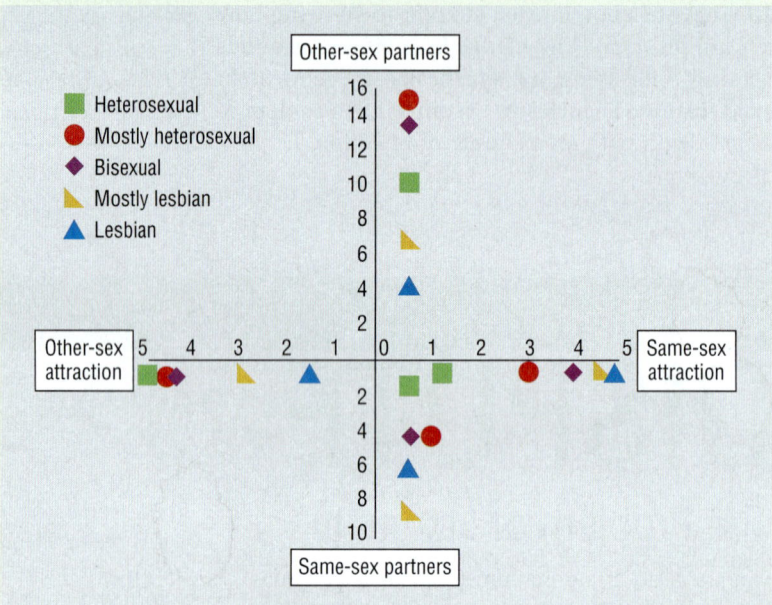

Note: To avoid crowding, the graph does not include the small number of subjects who identified themselves as questioning/uncertain or other.
Source: Robert Brym, compiled from Zhana Vrangalova and Ritch C. Savin-Williams. 2012. "Mostly Heterosexual and Mostly Gay/Lesbian: Evidence for New Sexual Orientation Identities." *Archives of Sexual Behavior* 41: 85–101.

# THE RESEARCH CYCLE

Since, importantly, conducting research allows us to invalidate theories, it's worth devoting some time to understanding what research entails.

Sociological research is a cyclical process that involves six steps (see Figure 1.5). The first step is *formulating a research question*. A research question must be stated so that it can be answered by systematically collecting and analyzing sociological data. Not all questions must be stated in this way. For instance, we don't need data of any sort to answer the question "Does God exist? We need faith or lack of faith. In contrast, any question purporting to be in the least scientific can be answered only with

## FIGURE 1.7 The Research Cycle

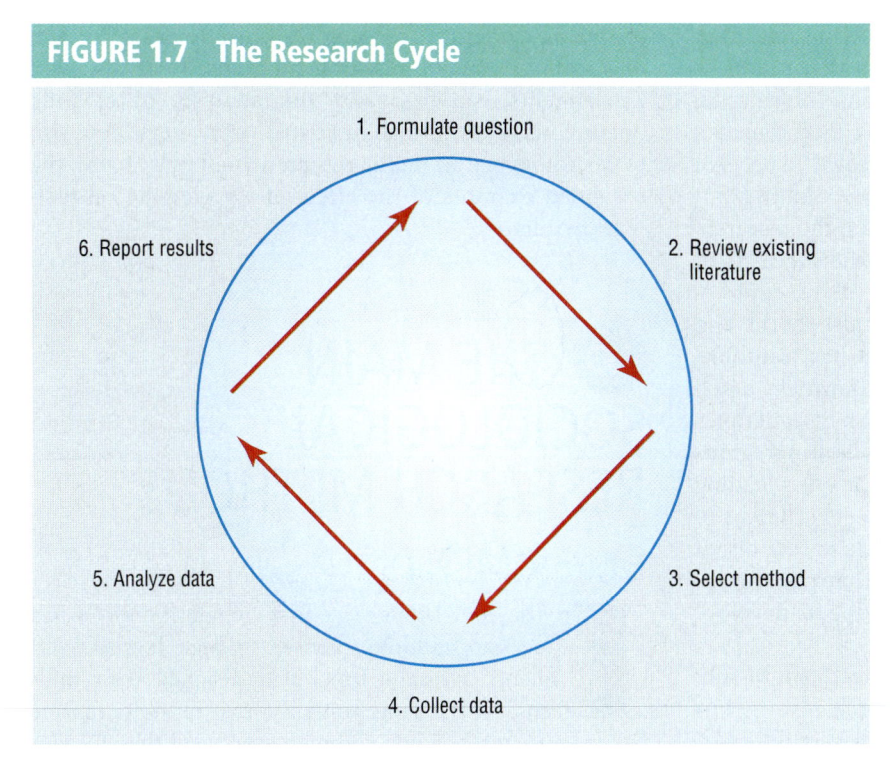

1. Formulate question
2. Review existing literature
3. Select method
4. Collect data
5. Analyze data
6. Report results

Source: From Brym/Lie. *Sociology*, 1E. © 2009 Nelson Education Ltd. Reproduced by permission. www.cengage.com/permissions

observable data in hand. Sociological research can answer a question like "Why are some people more religious than others?" or "Why is there less economic inequality in Sweden than in Canada, and less in Canada than in the United States?" Answers to such questions require evidence, not faith.

The second step in the research process involves *reviewing the existing research literature*. Chances are, a researcher won't be the first person to formulate a particular sociological question. She must elaborate her research question in light of what other sociologists have already debated and discovered. Why? Because reading the relevant sociological literature stimulates the researcher's sociological imagination, allows her to refine her initial questions, and prevents duplication of effort.

*Selecting a research method* is the third step in the research cycle. As we will see in detail later in this chapter, each data collection method has its own strengths and weaknesses. Each method is therefore best suited to studying a different kind of problem. When choosing a method, researchers must keep these strengths and weaknesses in mind.

The fourth step in the research cycle involves *collecting data* by observing subjects, interviewing them, reading documents produced by or about them, and so on. Many researchers think this is the most exciting stage of the research cycle because it brings them face to face with the puzzling sociological reality that so fascinates them.

Other researchers find the fifth step in the research cycle—*analyzing the data*—the most exciting. That is because, during data analysis, they can learn things that nobody knew before. At this stage, data confirm some of the researcher's expectations and confound others, requiring her to think creatively about familiar issues, reconsider the relevant theoretical and research literature, and abandon pet ideas. That is why Figure 1.7 is an oversimplification. In fact, data analysis often results in the researcher reformulating her initial research question, reviewing additional literature, and reanalyzing her data before moving on to step six.

Research is not useful to the sociological community, the subjects of the research, or the wider society if researchers do not complete the sixth step—publishing the results in a report, a scientific journal, or a book. Publication serves another important function, too: it allows other sociologists to scrutinize and criticize the research. On that basis, errors can be corrected and new and more sophisticated research questions can be formulated for the next round of research. Science is a social activity governed by rules defined and enforced by the scientific community. These rules include ethical considerations.

## ETHICS IN SOCIOLOGICAL RESEARCH

Researchers recognize that they must respect their subjects' rights throughout the research cycle. This means, first, that researchers must do their subjects no harm. This is the right to *safety*. Second, research subjects must have the right to decide whether their attitudes and behaviours may be revealed to the public and, if so, in what way. This is the right to *privacy*. Third, researchers cannot use data in a way that allows them to be traced to a particular subject. This is the subject's right to *confidentiality*. Fourth, subjects must be told how the information they supply will be used. They must also be allowed to judge the degree of personal risk involved in answering questions so they can decide whether they may be studied and, if so, in what way. This is the right to *informed consent*.

All of the ethical principles just listed refer to the protection of the rights of individual subjects, not to the protection of community rights. Supplementing individual protections, Canada's First Nations have recently asserted their collective right to control the data that is collected about them and the research that produces the data in the first place (First Nations Information Governance Centre, 2018). This means that Canada's First Nations claim the authority to control all aspects of research yielding data on First Nations, including planning, reviewing, approving, and managing the research, and owning, accessing, and possessing the products of the research.

Such control is intended to minimize harm and maximize benefits to a community that has traditionally not been consulted by outside authorities, much of whose research has not benefited and has sometimes harmed First Nations people. To cite just one egregious example, from 1948 to 1953, some of Canada's leading nutritionists were funded by the federal government to deprive Indigenous students in residential schools of basic nutrients for extended periods so they could measure the effect of malnutrition on childhood development (Mosby, 2013).

Ethical issues arise not only in the treatment of subjects but also in the treatment of research results. For example, plagiarism is a concern in academic life, especially among students who write research papers and submit them to professors for evaluation. One study found that 38 percent of university students admitted to committing "cut and paste" plagiarism when writing essays (Edmundson, 2003), while another found that 51 percent of high school students admitted to cheating on an exam (Josephson Institute, 2012). And it's probably not news to you that you can easily buy ready-made essays.

Increased plagiarism is a consequence of the availability of the Web and the common view that everything on it is public and therefore does not have to be cited. That view is wrong. In fact, we must identify, credit, and reference the author when we make any use of another person's written work, whether it is published, unpublished, or available electronically (American Sociological Association, 1999: 16). Making such ethical standards better known can help remedy the problem of plagiarism.

So can better policing. Powerful Web-based applications are now available that help college and university instructors determine whether essays are plagiarized in whole or in part (for example, see www.turnitin.com). Perhaps the most effective remedy, however, is for instructors to ensure that what they teach really matters to their students. If they do, students won't be as inclined to plagiarize because they will regard essay writing as a process of personal discovery. You can't cut and paste or buy enlightenment (Edmundson, 2003).

Bearing in mind this thumbnail sketch of the research cycle, I devote the rest of this chapter to exploring its fourth and fifth steps—gathering and analyzing evidence. In doing so, I briefly describe each of sociology's major research methods: field research, experiments, surveys, and the analysis of existing documents and official statistics. To introduce you to sociology's four main research methods, I use the extended example of the effect of TV viewing on real-world violence.

## LO6 THE MAIN SOCIOLOGICAL RESEARCH METHODS

### EXPERIMENTS

In the mid-1960s, the first generation of North American children exposed to high levels of TV violence virtually from birth reached their mid-teens. At the same time, the rate of violent crime began to increase. Some commentators said that TV violence made violence in the real world seem normal and acceptable. As a result, they concluded, North American teenagers in the 1960s and subsequent decades were more likely than pre-1960s teens to commit violent acts. The increasing prevalence of violence in movies, and later in video games and popular music, seemed to add weight to their conclusion.

Social scientists soon started investigating the connection between media and real-world violence using

Aggressive behaviour among children is common, from siblings fighting to bullying in the schoolyard. Since the inception of home TV, social scientists have sought to find strong research designs capable of examining the causal effects, if any, of viewing violence on television.

experimental methods. An **experiment** is a carefully controlled artificial situation that allows researchers to isolate presumed causes and measure their effects precisely (Campbell and Stanley, 1963).

Experiments use a procedure called **randomization** to create two similar groups. Randomization involves assigning individuals to the groups by chance processes. For example, researchers may ask 50 children to draw a number from 1 to 50 from a covered box. The researchers assign children who draw odd numbers to one group and those who draw even numbers to the other group. By assigning subjects to the two groups using a chance process and repeating the experiment many times, researchers ensure that each group has the same proportion of boys and girls, members of different races, children highly motivated to participate in the study, and so on.

After randomly assigning subjects to the two groups, the researchers put the groups in separate rooms and give them toys to play with. They observe the children through one-way mirrors, rating each child in terms of the aggressiveness of his or her play. Precise scoring criteria will have been decided beforehand (for example, hitting a toy = 1; hitting another child = 5). This is the child's initial score on the dependent variable, aggressive behaviour. The **dependent variable** is the presumed effect in any cause-and-effect relationship.

Then the researchers introduce the supposed (or hypothesized) cause to one group—now called the **experimental group**. For example, they may show children in the experimental group an hour-long TV program in which many violent acts occur. They do not show the program to children in the other group, now called the **control group**. In this case, the violent TV show is the "independent variable." The **independent variable** is the presumed cause in any cause-and-effect relationship.

Immediately after the children see the TV show, the researchers again observe the children in both groups at play. Each child's play is given a second aggressiveness score. By comparing the aggressiveness scores of the two groups before and after only one of the groups has been exposed to the presumed cause, an experiment can determine whether the presumed cause (watching violent TV) has the predicted effect (increasing violent behaviour; see Table 1.1).

Experiments have the advantage of allowing researchers to isolate the single cause of theoretical interest and measure its effect with high **reliability**, that is, consistently from one experiment to the next. Yet many sociologists argue that experiments are highly artificial situations. They believe that removing people from their natural social settings lowers the **validity** of experimental results, that is, the degree to which they measure what they are actually supposed to measure.

Why do experiments on the effects of media violence lack validity? First, in the real world, violent behaviour usually means attempting to harm another person physically. Shouting or kicking a toy is not the same thing. In fact, acting out in this way may enable children to relieve frustrations in a fantasy world, lowering their chance of acting violently in the real world. Second, aggressive behaviour is not controlled in the laboratory setting as it is in the real world. If a boy watching a violent TV show stands up and delivers a karate kick to his brother, a parent or other caregiver is likely to take action to prevent a recurrence. In the lab, lack of disciplinary control may facilitate unrealistically high levels of aggression (Felson, 1996).

An **association** between two variables exists if the value of one variable changes with the value of the other. For example, if the percentage of people who approve of a man punching another man is *higher* among those who watch three or more hours of TV a day than it is among those who watch less than three hours of TV a day, a *positive*

> **experiment** A carefully controlled artificial situation that allows researchers to isolate hypothesized causes and precisely measure their effects.
>
> **randomization** A process that, in an experiment, assigns individuals to groups by chance processes.
>
> **dependent variable** The presumed effect in a cause-and-effect relationship.
>
> **experimental group** The group that is exposed to the independent variable in an experiment.
>
> **control group** The group that is not exposed to the independent variable in an experiment.
>
> **independent variable** The presumed cause in a cause-and-effect relationship.
>
> **reliability** The degree to which a measurement procedure yields consistent results.
>
> **validity** The degree to which a measure actually measures what it is intended to measure.
>
> **association** The relationship between two variables if the value of one variable changes with the value of another.

**TABLE 1.1  Steps in a Simple Experiment**

|  | Time 1 | Time 2 | Time 3 | Time 4 |
|---|---|---|---|---|
| Control group | Randomize assignment of subjects to group. | Measure dependent variable. | Do not introduce independent variable. | Measure dependent variable again. |
| Experimental group | Randomize assignment of subjects to group. | Measure dependent variable. | Introduce independent variable. | Measure dependent variable again. |

**survey** A data collection method in which people are asked questions about their knowledge, attitudes, or behaviour, either in a face-to-face or telephone interview or by completion of a questionnaire.

**sample** The part of the population of interest that is selected for analysis.

**population** The entire group about which the researcher wants to generalize.

**closed-ended questions** Survey questions that provide respondents with a list of permitted answers. Each answer is given a numerical code so that the data can later be easily input into a computer for statistical analysis.

**open-ended questions** Survey questions that allow respondents to answer in their own words.

association exists between the two variables. If the percentage of people who approve of a man punching another man is *lower* among those who watch three or more hours of TV a day, a *negative* association exists between the two variables. The greater the percentage difference between frequent and infrequent TV viewers, the stronger the association. Table 1.2 shows results from a survey on this subject. Sixty-nine percent of respondents who watched TV zero to two hours a day approved of punching, compared with 65 percent of respondents who watched TV three hours or more. Is this a positive or a negative association?

## SURVEYS

Surveys are the most widely used sociological research method, and they also have been used to measure the effects of media violence on behaviour. Overall, the results of surveys show a weaker relationship between exposure to violent mass media and violent behaviour than do experiments, and some surveys show no relationship at all between these two variables (Anderson and Bushman, 2002; Huesmann et al., 2003; Johnson et al., 2002; see Table 1.2).

In a **survey**, people are asked questions about their knowledge, attitudes, or behaviour. All survey researchers aim to study part of a group—a **sample**—to learn about the whole group of interest—the **population**. To reliably generalize about the population based on findings from a sample, researchers must be sure that the characteristics of the people in the sample match those of the population. To draw a sample from which one can safely generalize, researchers must choose respondents at random, and an individual's chance of being chosen must be known and greater than zero.

When sociologists conduct a survey, they may mail a form containing questions to respondents. Respondents then mail the completed questionnaire back to the researcher. Alternatively, sociologists may conduct face-to-face interviews in which questions are presented to the respondent by the interviewer during a meeting. Sociologists may also conduct surveys by means of telephone interviews or online.

Questionnaires may contain two types of questions. A **closed-ended question** provides the respondent with a list of permitted answers. Each answer is given a numerical code so the data can later be easily input into a computer for statistical analysis. Often, the numerical results of surveys are arranged in tables like Table 1.2. An **open-ended question** allows respondents to answer in their own words. Open-ended questions are particularly useful

| TABLE 1.2 | Watching TV and Approval of Punching Violence (percentage) |||| 
|---|---|---|---|
| Approved of punching | TV Viewing: 0–2 Hours/Day (% viewers who approved) | TV Viewing: 3+ Hours/Day (% viewers who approved) | TV Viewing: Total (% viewers who approved) |
| Yes | 69 | 65 | 67 |
| No | 31 | 35 | 33 |
| Total | 100 | 100 | 100 |
| Number of interviews | 5188 | 5022 | 10 210 |

Source: National Opinion Research Center. 2006. *General Social Survey, 1972–2004*. Chicago: University of Chicago.

To interpret this or any other table, you must first pay attention to what adds up to 100 percent. Generally, the columns of a table, representing the independent variable, add up to 100 percent. Thus, Table 1.2 table says that 69 percent *of people who watched TV 0–2 hours a day* approved of a man punching an adult male. It does *not* say that 69 percent of all people who approved of a man punching an adult male watched TV 0–2 hours a day. We know this because the categories of the "TV viewing" variable equals 100 percent.

To test your understanding, calculate the actual number of respondents represented by the following percentages in the table: 69%, 65%, 31%, and 35%. Answers are given in the box below.

> Answers
> 69% = (69/100) × 5188 = 3580 respondents; 65% = (65/100) × 5022 = 3264 respondents; 31% = (31/100) × 5188 = 1608 respondents; 35% = (35/100) × 5022 = 1758 respondents

Researchers collect information through surveys by asking people in a representative sample an identical set of questions. People interviewed on a downtown street corner do not constitute a representative sample of Canadian adults, because the sample might not include people who live outside the urban core, it underestimates the number of older people and people with disabilities, it does not take into account regional diversity, and so on.

field research is a **qualitative method** (it analyzes observational or speech data in narrative form); see Figure 1.8.

When they go into the field, researchers come prepared with strategies to ensure that their observations are accurate. One such strategy is **detached observation**, which involves classifying and counting the behaviour of interest according to a predetermined scheme. Although useful for some purposes, two main problems confound direct observation. First, the presence of the researcher may cause **reactivity**—the observed people may conceal certain things or act artificially to impress the researcher. Second, the meaning of the

> **field research** The systematic observation of people in their natural settings.
>
> **quantitative method** A research method that analyzes numerical data statistically.
>
> **qualitative method** A research method that analyzes observational or speech data in narrative form.
>
> **detached observation** A type of field research that involves classifying and counting the behaviour of interest according to a predetermined scheme.
>
> **reactivity** The tendency of people who are being observed by a researcher to react to the presence of the researcher by concealing certain things or acting artificially to impress the researcher.

when researchers don't have enough knowledge to create a meaningful and complete list of possible answers.

While surveys often have high reliability, researchers must take special measures to ensure that survey questions elicit valid responses. In particular, they must guard against four dangers:

1. Excluding certain categories of the population from the sample
2. Refusal of some people to participate in the survey
3. Unwillingness of some respondents to answer questions frankly
4. Asking confusing, leading, or inflammatory questions or questions referring to several unimportant or noncurrent events

Much of the art and science of survey research involves overcoming these threats to validity (Babbie and Roberts, 2018). Surveys tend to show a weaker relationship than do experiments between exposure to violent mass media and violent behaviour. That may be because survey researchers have developed more valid measures of violent behaviour than experimenters have.

## FIELD RESEARCH

The method that comes closest to people's natural social settings is **field research**. Field research involves systematically observing people wherever they associate. While experimental and survey research are **quantitative methods** (they analyze numerical data statistically),

### FIGURE 1.8  Qualitative and Quantitative Research

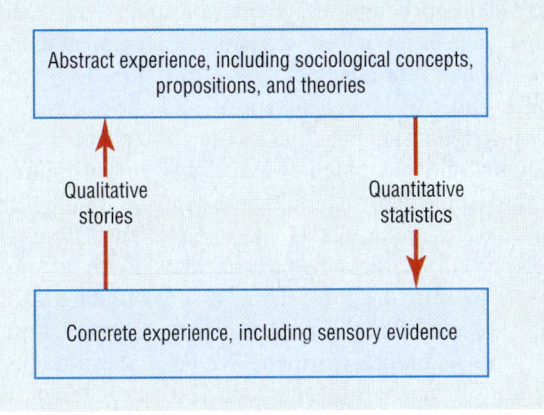

Sociology research is conducted in two ways. *Qualitative* research works from the bottom up: it starts from observations of human interaction and uses these observations to build general statements about how social life operates. *Quantitative* research works from the top down: it begins from general ideas about how social life operates and tests the validity of these ideas by turning observations of social life into numbers that can be analyzed statistically.

Source: From BRYM/ROBERTS/STROHSCHEIN/LIE. *Sociology: Your Compass for a New World*, 6E. © 2019 Nelson Education Ltd. Reproduced by permission. www.cengage.com/permissions

**participant observation** A type of field research that involves carefully observing people's face-to-face interaction and participating in their lives over a long period, thus achieving a deep and sympathetic understanding of what motivates them.

**analysis of existing documents and official statistics** A nonreactive research method that involves the use of diaries, newspapers, published historical works, and statistics produced by government agencies, all of which are created by people other than the researcher for purposes other than sociological research.

observed behaviour may remain obscure to the researcher. A wink may be an involuntary muscle contraction caused by a speck of dust, a signal that the winker is joking, a sign of affection, an indication of a secret being kept, or a sexual come-on. We can't know what a wink means just by observing it.

To avoid reactivity and understand the meaning of behaviour, we must be able to see it in its social context and from the point of view of the people we are observing. To do that, researchers must immerse themselves in their subjects' world by learning their language and their culture in depth. When sociologists observe a social setting systematically *and* take part in the activities of the people they are studying, they engage in **participant observation** research (Lofland and Lofland, 2006 [1971]).

Participant observation research helps us better understand how media violence may influence youth violence. Sociologists have spent time in schools where shooting rampages have taken place. They have lived in the neighbourhoods where shooting rampages occurred. They have interviewed students, teachers, neighbours, and shooters' family members. And they have studied police and psychological reports and the shooters' own writings (Harding, Fox, and Mehta, 2002; Sullivan, 2002). Sociologists have concluded that only a small number of young people who are weakly connected to family, school, community, and peers are at risk of translating media violence into violent behaviour. Lack of social support allows them to magnify their personal problems, and if guns are available, they are prone to using violent media messages as models for their own behaviour. In contrast, for the great majority of young people, violence in the mass media is just a source of entertainment and a fantasy outlet for emotional issues (Anderson, 2003).

Like other research methods, participant observation has strengths and weaknesses. On the plus side, it allows researchers to develop a deep and sympathetic understanding of the way people see the world. It is especially useful in the "exploratory" stage of research, when investigators have only a vague sense of what they are looking for and little sense of what they will discover. On the minus side, because participant observation research usually involves just one researcher in one social setting, it is difficult to know if other researchers would measure things in the same way (this is the problem of reliability), and it is difficult to know how broadly findings may be generalized to other settings.

## ANALYSIS OF EXISTING DOCUMENTS AND OFFICIAL STATISTICS

The fourth important sociological research method involves **analysis of existing documents and official statistics** that are created by people other than the researcher for purposes other than sociological research.

The three types of existing documents that sociologists have mined most deeply are diaries, newspapers, and published historical works. Census data, police crime reports, and records of key life events are perhaps the most frequently used sources of official statistics. For example, Statistics Canada is a federal government agency. Among many other official statistics, it publishes the results of a twice-a-decade compulsory census that asks all adult Canadians about their household composition, employment, income, ethnic background, language use, housing, and so on. It also publishes an annual *Uniform Crime Reporting Survey* that lists the number of police-reported crimes in Canada, classifying them by the location and type of crime, the age and sex of offenders and victims, and other variables.

Census and crime data put the limited effect of media violence on violent behaviour into perspective. For example, researchers have discovered big differences in violent behaviour when they compare the United States and Canada. The homicide rate (the number of murders per 100 000 people) has historically been about four times higher in the United States. Yet TV programming, movies, and video games are highly similar in the two countries, so exposure to media violence can't account for the difference. Researchers instead attribute the difference in homicide rates to the higher level of economic and racial inequality and the wider availability of handguns in the United States (Government of Canada, 2002; Lenton, 1989; National Rifle Association, 2005; Sternheimer, 2014).

Existing documents and official statistics have several advantages over other types of data. They can save researchers time and money because they are usually available at no cost in libraries or on the Web. Official statistics usually cover entire populations and are collected using rigorous and uniform methods, yielding highly reliable data. Existing documents and official statistics are especially useful for historical analysis. Finally, because the analysis of existing documents and official statistics does not require live subjects, reactivity is not a problem. The researchers' presence does not influence the subjects' behaviour.

Existing documents and official statistics also share one big disadvantage: They are not created with researchers' needs in mind. In a sense, researchers using existing documents and official statistics start at step 5 of the research cycle (refer back to Figure 1.5) and then work within the limitations imposed by available data, including biases that reflect the interests of the individuals and organizations that created the data.

The preceding discussion should give you a pretty good idea of the basic methodological issues that confront any sociological research project. You should also know the strengths and weaknesses of some of the most widely used data collection techniques (see Table 1.3). In the remainder of this chapter, I outline what you can expect to learn from the rest of this book.

## LO7 TODAY'S CHALLENGES

Earlier I wrote that the Industrial Revolution caused masses of people to move from countryside to city, work agonizingly long hours in crowded and dangerous mines and factories, lose faith in their religions, confront faceless bureaucracies, and react to the filth and poverty of their existence by means of strikes, crime, revolutions, and wars. Most of the founders of sociology developed their ideas to better understand the causes and consequences of the Industrial Revolution. It was the great sociological puzzle of their time. This fact raises two interesting questions: What are the great sociological puzzles of *our* time? How are today's sociologists responding to the challenges presented by the

Homelessness is an increasing focus of public policy, but public support may not be adequate if the homeless are not counted properly in the census. Statistics Canada started including a count of the homeless in the 2001 census. However, because the count is based on information about the use of shelters and soup kitchens, combined with an attempt at street counts, these numbers are only rough estimates.

### TABLE 1.3 Strengths and Weaknesses of the Four Main Sociological Research Methods

| Method | Strengths | Weaknesses |
| --- | --- | --- |
| Experiment | High reliability; excellent for establishing cause-and-effect relationships | Low validity for many sociological problems because of the unnaturalness of the experimental setting |
| Survey | Good reliability; useful for establishing cause-and-effect relationships | Validity problems exist unless researchers make strong efforts to deal with them |
| Participant observation | Allows researchers to develop a deep and sympathetic understanding of the way people see the world; especially useful in exploratory research | Low reliability and generalizability |
| Analysis of existing documents and official statistics | Often inexpensive and easy to obtain; provides good coverage; useful for historical analysis; nonreactive | Often contains biases reflecting the interests of the data creators rather than the interests of the researcher |

Source: From BRYM/LIE. *Sociology*, 1E. © 2009 Nelson Education Ltd. Reproduced by permission. www.cengage.com/permissions.

> **Postindustrial Revolution** The technology-driven shift from manufacturing to service industries and the consequences of that shift for virtually all human activities.
>
> **globalization** The process by which formerly separate individuals, groups, institutions, economies, states, and cultures are becoming tied together and people are becoming increasingly aware of their growing interdependence.

social settings in which *we* live? The rest of this book answers these questions in depth.

It would be wrong to suggest that just a few key issues animate the research of tens of thousands of sociologists around the world. Hundreds of debates enliven sociology today. Some focus on small issues relevant to particular fields and geographical areas, others on big issues that seek to characterize the entire historical era for humanity as a whole. It seems to me that the greatest sociological puzzles of our time are the causes and consequences of the Postindustrial Revolution and globalization.

The **Postindustrial Revolution** is the technology-driven shift from employment in factories to employment in offices, and the consequences of that shift for nearly all human activity. As a result of the Postindustrial Revolution, around 80 percent of Canadian workers now provide services, while just 20 percent produce things (Statistics Canada, 2017). Women have been drawn into the system of higher education and the paid labour force in large numbers. Types of family structures have multiplied. Computers, the Internet, and social media have helped to change the way we work, study, entertain ourselves, and interact with one another.

**Globalization** is the process by which formerly separated individuals, groups, institutions, economies, states, and cultures are becoming tied together and people are becoming increasingly aware of their growing interdependence (Giddens, 1990: 64; Guillén, 2001; Harari, 2014). Especially in recent decades, rapid increases in the volume of international trade, travel, and communication have broken down the isolation and independence of most countries and people. Also contributing to globalization is the growth of many institutions that bind corporations, companies, and cultures together. These processes have caused people to depend more than ever on people in other countries for products, services, ideas, and even a sense of identity.

## MORE OPPORTUNITY?

Some sociologists think that globalization and postindustrialism will enhance the quality of life. They say it will generate more equality of opportunity, that is, better chances for *all* people to get an education, influence government policy, and find creative, interesting, challenging, and rewarding jobs. However, as you read this book, it will become clear that, although great strides have been made in providing economic and educational opportunities for women, limiting discrimination, and spreading democracy, all of these seemingly happy stories have a dark underside.

For example, it turns out that the number of routine jobs with low pay and few benefits is growing faster than the number of creative, high-paying jobs. Inequality between the wealthiest and poorest people has grown substantially in recent decades. An enormous opportunity gulf still separates women from men. Racism and discrimination are still very much a part of our world and are intensifying in some places. Our health care system is in trouble just as our population is aging rapidly and most in need of health care. Disasters sometimes follow technological advances. Just think of the giant oil spill in the Gulf of Mexico in 2010, the catastrophic nuclear reactor meltdown in Japan in 2011, and the Fort McMurray, Alberta, wildfire of 2016–17 that destroyed an area larger than Prince Edward Island and that scientists linked to global warming caused by the burning of fossil fuels (De Souza, 2016).

Meanwhile, many of the countries that claim to be new democracies are only superficially democratic, while others have regressed to non-democratic status. Canadians and citizens of many other postindustrial societies are increasingly cynical about the ability of their political systems to respond to their needs and are looking for alternative forms of political expression. The absolute number of desperately poor people in the world continues to grow, as does the gap between rich and poor nations. Many people attribute the world's most serious problems to globalization. They have formed organizations and movements—some of them violent—to oppose it. In short, equality of opportunity is an undeniably attractive ideal, but it is unclear whether it is the inevitable outcome of a globalized, postindustrial society.

## MORE FREEDOM?

We may say much the same about the ideal of freedom. In an earlier era, most people retained their religious, ethnic, racial, and sexual identities for a lifetime, even if they were not particularly comfortable with them. They often remained in social relationships that made them unhappy. One of the major themes of this book is that many people are now freer to construct their identities and form social relationships in ways that suit them. To a greater degree than ever before, it is possible to *choose* who you want to live with, who you want to marry (or whether you want to marry at all), how many children to have (if any), who you want to associate with, and how you want to engage with them. The postindustrial and global era frees people from traditional constraints by encouraging virtually instant global communication, international migration, greater acceptance of sexual diversity and a variety of family forms, the growth of ethnically and racially diverse cities, and so on.

Again, however, we must face the less rosy aspects of postindustrialism and globalization. In the following chapters, we show how increased freedom is experienced only within certain limits and how social diversity is limited by a strong push to conformity in some spheres of life. For instance, we can choose a far wider variety of consumer products than ever before, but consumerism itself increasingly seems a compulsory way of life. Moreover, it is a way of life that threatens the natural environment. Large, impersonal bureaucracies and standardized products and services dehumanize both staff and customers. The tastes and the profit motive of vast media conglomerates govern most of our diverse cultural consumption and arguably threaten the survival of distinctive national cultures. Powerful interests are trying to shore up the traditional nuclear family even though it does not suit many people. As these examples show, the push for uniformity counters the trend toward growing social diversity.

In short, postindustrialism and globalization may make us freer in some ways, but they also place new constraints on us.

## WHERE DO YOU FIT IN?

Our overview of themes in this book drives home the fact that we live in an era "suspended between extraordinary opportunity... and global catastrophe" (Giddens, 1987: 166). A whole range of issues, just some of which I have listed, continue to stare us in the face and profoundly affect the quality of our everyday lives.

Giving in to despair and apathy is one possible response to these complex issues, but it is not a response that humans often favour. If it were our nature to give up hope, we would still be sitting around half-naked in the mud outside a cave. People are more inclined to look for ways of improving their lives and this period of human history is full of opportunities to do so. We have, for example, advanced to the point at which for the first time we have the means to feed and educate everyone in the world. Similarly, it now seems possible to erode some of the inequalities that have always been the major source of human conflict.

Sociology offers useful advice on how to achieve these goals—for sociology is more than just an intellectual exercise. It is also an applied science with practical, everyday uses. Sociologists teach at all levels, from high school to graduate school. They conduct research for local, provincial/territorial, and federal governments; colleges and universities; corporations; the criminal justice system; public opinion firms; management consulting firms; trade unions; social service agencies; international nongovernmental organizations; and private research and testing firms. They are often involved in the formulation of public policy, the creation of laws and regulations by organizations and governments. This is because sociologists are trained not just to see what is, but to see what is possible (see Careers in Sociology on the MindTap website).

So please consider this book an invitation to explore your society's—and your own—possibilities. I don't provide easy answers. However, I am sure that if you try to grapple with the questions I raise, you will find that sociology can help you figure out where you fit into society and how you can make society fit you.

## READY TO STUDY?

### IN THE BOOK YOU CAN:

- Refer to the Chapter in Review section at the back of the book to have a summary of the chapter and key terms handy.
- Test your knowledge of chapter contents by answering the multiple-choice questions in the Chapter in Review section. Answers are in the appendix at the end of the book.

### ONLINE YOU CAN:

- Stay organized and efficient with MindTap—a single destination with all the course material and study aids you need to succeed.
- Flashcards are pre-populated to provide you with a jump start for review—or you can create your own.
- You can highlight text and make notes in your MindTap Reader.
- Prepare for tests with quizzes.

GO TO NELSON.COM/STUDENT TO PURCHASE THESE DIGITAL RESOURCES.

# 2
# Culture

Emanuele Cremaschi/Getty Images News

# LO¹ CULTURE AS PROBLEM SOLVING

Sidney Crosby won't sign a team jersey until he plays a regular season hockey game in it. DeMar DeRozan kisses the back of each hand at the start of each basketball game. Such superstitions among athletes are common. In fact, back in the 1970s, one study found that 137 intercollegiate athletes at the University of Western Ontario practised 6.6 superstitions each on average (Gregory and Petrie, 1975). Superstitions are widespread because they perform a useful social function. Research shows that, in general, superstitions help athletes reduce anxiety and improve self-confidence and performance (Damisch, Stoberock, and Mussweiler, 2010).

Athletes like Sidney Crosby, shown here, often develop superstitions to help them manage stress. If such superstitions are socially transmitted and shared, they become part of culture.

## LEARNING OBJECTIVES:

In this chapter, you will learn to

- **LO¹** Define culture and its main components.
- **LO²** Explain how culture helps humans adapt and thrive in their environments.
- **LO³** Recognize the centrality of language in all cultures.
- **LO⁴** Appreciate that assessing other cultures from the standpoint of your own culture impairs sociological understanding.
- **LO⁵** Distinguish ways in which culture makes people freer as it becomes more diverse, multicultural, and globalized.
- **LO⁶** Identify ways in which culture places limits on people's freedom.

**culture** The socially transmitted practices, languages, symbols, beliefs, values, ideologies, and material objects that people create to deal with real-life problems.

**society** A number of people who interact, usually in a defined territory, and share a culture.

**abstraction** The human capacity to create general ideas or ways of thinking that are not linked to particular instances.

**symbols** Things that carry particular meanings, including the components of language, mathematical notations, and signs. Symbols allow us to classify experience and generalize from it.

It is not just athletes who invent routines to help them stop worrying and focus on the job at hand. Soldiers going off to battle, university students about to write final exams, and other people in high-stress situations behave similarly. Some wear a lucky piece of jewellery or item of clothing. Others say special words or a quick prayer. Still others cross themselves.

And then there are people who engage in more elaborate rituals. For example, sociologists at the University of Manitoba interviewed 300 university students about their superstitious practices before final exams. One student felt she would do well only if she ate a sausage and two eggs sunny-side-up on the morning of each exam. The sausage had to be arranged vertically on the left side of her plate and the eggs placed to the right of the sausage so they formed the "100" percent she was aiming for (Albas and Albas, 1989). The ritual may have had a more direct influence on her cholesterol level than on her grade. Indirectly, however, it may have had the desired effect—to the degree it helped to relieve her anxiety and relax her, she may have done better in exams.

All elements of **culture**—the socially transmitted ideas, practices, and material objects that people create to deal with real-life problems—begin in the way that superstitions do: People confront a need and invent a solution. The Winnipeg student ate those eggs and sausage to help her deal with the real-life problem of anxiety. Similarly, tools help people solve the problem of how to plant crops and build houses. Religion helps people give meaning to life and come to terms with death. Tools and religion are elements of culture because they help people solve real-life problems.

Note, however, that religion, technology, and other elements of culture differ from the superstitions of athletes and undergraduates in one important respect: Superstitions are often unique to the individuals who create them. In contrast, religion and technology are widely shared. They are passed from one generation to the next. How does cultural sharing take place? Through human interaction, communication, and learning. A **society** involves people interacting socially and sharing culture, usually in a defined geographical area. Culture, then, is the sum of the *socially transmitted* ideas, practices, and material objects that enable people to adapt to, and thrive in, their environments.

# LO² THE ORIGINS AND COMPONENTS OF CULTURE

You can appreciate the importance of culture for human survival by considering the predicament of early humans about 100 000 years ago. They lived in harsh natural environments. They had poor physical endowments, being slower runners and weaker fighters than many other animals. Yet, despite these disadvantages, they survived. More than that, they prospered and came to dominate nature. Domination was possible largely because humans were the smartest creatures around. Their sophisticated brains enabled them to create cultural survival kits of enormous complexity and flexibility. These cultural survival kits contained three main tools: the capacity to engage in abstraction, cooperation, and production. Each tool was a uniquely human talent, and each gave rise to a different element of culture.

## ABSTRACTION: CREATING SYMBOLS

Human culture exists only because we can think abstractly. **Abstraction** is the capacity to create **symbols** or general ideas that carry particular meanings. Languages and mathematical notations are sets of symbols. They allow us to classify experience and generalize from it. For instance, we recognize that we can sit on many objects but that only some of those objects have four legs, a back, and space for one person. We distinguish the latter from other objects by giving them a name: "chairs." By the time a baby reaches the end of her first year, she has heard that word repeatedly and understands that it refers to a certain class of objects. True, a few chimpanzees have been taught to make some signs with their hands. In this way, they have learned some words and how to string together a few simple phrases. However, even these extraordinarily intelligent animals cannot learn any rules of grammar, teach other chimps what they know, or advance much beyond the vocabulary of a human toddler. Abstraction at anything beyond the most rudimentary level is a uniquely human capacity. The ability to abstract enables humans to learn and transmit knowledge in a way no other animal can.

# COOPERATION: CREATING NORMS AND VALUES

The ability to cooperate is a second factor that enables human culture to exist. **Cooperation** involves creating a complex social life by establishing **norms** or generally accepted ways of doing things, and values or ideas about what is right and wrong, good and bad, desirable and undesirable, beautiful and ugly. For example, family members cooperate to raise children. In the process, they develop and apply norms and values about which child-rearing practices are appropriate and desirable.

Different times and places give rise to different norms and values. In our society, non-Indigenous parents might ground children for swearing, but in pioneer days, non-Indigenous parents would typically "beat the devil out of them." In contrast, Indigenous parents rarely physically disciplined their children. They preferred teasing and public embarrassment as a means of social control, and they tended to get uncles and aunts to enforce discipline so as not to alienate their children (Muir and Bohr, 2014). "Never in anger" was the first rule of child discipline among the Inuit (Briggs, 1970). As these examples suggest, by analyzing how people cooperate and produce norms and values, we can learn much about what distinguishes one culture from another.

## Three Types of Norms: Folkways, Mores, and Taboos

If a man walks down a busy street wearing nothing on the top half of his body, he is violating a **folkway**. If he walks down the street wearing nothing on the bottom half of his body, he is violating a **more** (the Latin word for "custom," pronounced MORE-ay). Folkways are norms that specify social *preferences*. Mores are norms that specify social *requirements*. People are usually punished when they violate norms but the punishment is usually minor if the norm is a folkway. Some onlookers will raise their eyebrows at the shirtless man. Others will shake their head in disapproval. In contrast, the punishment for walking down the street without pants is bound to be moderately harsh. Someone is bound to call the police, probably sooner than later (Sumner, 1940 [1907]). The strongest and most central norm is a **taboo**. When someone violates a taboo, it causes revulsion in the community and punishment is severe. Incest is one of the most widespread taboos.

# PRODUCTION: CREATING MATERIAL CULTURE

Finally, culture relies on the human capacity to engage in **production**; we can make and use tools and techniques that improve our ability to take what we want from nature. Sociologists call such tools and techniques **material culture**. All animals take from nature to subsist, and an ape may sometimes use a rock to break another object or use a stick to keep its balance in a fast-flowing stream. However, only humans are sufficiently intelligent and dexterous to *make* tools and use them to produce everything from food to computers. Understood in this sense, production is a uniquely human activity.

Table 2.1 illustrates each of the basic human capacities and their cultural offshoots in the field of medicine. As in all fields of human endeavour, abstraction, operation, and production give rise to specific kinds of ideas, norms, and elements of material culture.

# CULTURE AND SOCIAL CLASS

A society's core cultural elements are widely shared. However, culture is not homogeneous across all sectors of society. Significant variation in culture is evident in different classes, ethnic and racial groups, genders, and regions. To illustrate this point, think about the

---

**cooperation** The human capacity to create a complex social life by sharing resources and working together.

**norms** Generally accepted ways of doing things.

**folkway** The least important type of norm—a norm that evokes the least severe punishment when violated.

**more** A core norm that most people believe is essential for the survival of their group or their society.

**taboo** The strongest type of norm. When someone violates a taboo, it causes revulsion in the community, and punishment is severe.

**production** The human capacity to make and use tools. It improves our ability to take what we want from nature.

**material culture** The tools and techniques that enable people to accomplish tasks.

---

By cooperating, people are able to accomplish things that no one person could possibly do alone.

> **high culture** Culture consumed mainly by upper classes.
>
> **popular culture (or mass culture)** Culture consumed by all classes.
>
> **dominant culture** Helps rich and powerful categories of people exercise control over others.
>
> **subordinate culture** Contests dominant culture to varying degrees.
>
> **language** A system of symbols strung together to communicate thought.

relationship between culture and social class.

Sociologists distinguish **high culture** from **popular culture** or **mass culture**. High culture includes opera, ballet, classical music, fine art, and literature. Popular or mass culture includes movies, TV shows, and rock, hip hop, and country music. Popular or mass culture is consumed by many people in all social classes. In contrast, as French sociologist Pierre Bourdieu (1986) emphasized, the consumption of high culture tends to be restricted to upper classes. That is because appreciating the fine points of high culture requires a certain type of education or training that takes considerable time and money to attain. This fact makes high culture more accessible to people in upper classes and less accessible to people in lower classes.

Sociologists who study the political effects of culture often distinguish **dominant culture** from **subordinate culture**. Dominant culture helps rich and powerful categories of people exercise control over others. Subordinate culture contests dominant culture to varying degrees.

Take the widely held notion that anyone can become rich if he or she works hard and makes smart choices. That belief is part of our dominant culture insofar as it is widely shared and justifies the wealth that rich people enjoy by making it seem as if rich people became wealthy just by virtue of their cleverness and diligence. It ignores the economic and other advantages that many rich people inherit from their parents. It also plays down the fact that many people who are not rich would like to make the right choices but lack the means to do so. Some people who want to attend medical school just can't afford it. The belief that hard work and smart choices alone determine success helps to justify the transmission of valued resources from rich and powerful adults to their children while obscuring the difficulties that others may face in their effort to move up the socioeconomic hierarchy.

To the degree that members of lower classes agree that hard work and good choices alone make people rich, they accept a core idea of dominant culture. However, many members of lower classes are skeptical about this belief because they work hard but experience social constraints that prevent them and their offspring from becoming rich: diseases and accidents related to the kinds of jobs they do, insufficient money to help their children attend college, university, and professional school, and so on. (For survey evidence supporting this claim, see the Politics and the Perception of Class Inequality section in Chapter 6, Social Stratification: Canadian and Global Perspectives.) Such skepticism is part of their subordinate culture, and in certain circumstances it may boil over into outright rebellion against upper class ideas and institutions. I analyze the circumstances that encourage such rebellion in Chapter 14, Social Change: Technology, the Environment, and Social Movements.

Even the idea that there is a "proper" way to speak English is part of the dominant culture. After all, well-to-do people are more likely to speak "proper" English than others are. And even if they don't, they can most easily afford to send their children to elite schools where they can learn the right accent, a rich vocabulary, and authoritative grammatical structures. Meeting "the right sort of people" depends in part on learning how to talk to them. In this sense, proper English is a cultural tool that allows people to join useful social networks and exclude the less fortunate from them.

# LO³ LANGUAGE

## THE SAPIR–WHORF HYPOTHESIS

Language is in fact one of the most important parts of any culture. A **language** is a system of symbols strung together to communicate thought. Equipped with language, we can

### TABLE 2.1 The Building Blocks of Culture

| The Human Capacity for… | Abstraction | Cooperation | Production |
| --- | --- | --- | --- |
| Gives rise to these elements of culture | ideas | norms and values | material culture |
| In medicine, for example, | *theories* are developed about how a certain drug might cure a disease | *experiments* are conducted to test whether the drug works as expected | *treatments* are developed on the basis of the experimental results |

Source: Adapted from Robert Bierstedt, 1963, *The Social Order: An Introduction to Sociology*, New York: McGraw-Hill.

share understandings, pass experience and knowledge from one generation to the next, and make plans for the future. In short, language allows culture to develop. Consequently, sociologists commonly think of language as a cultural invention that distinguishes humans from other animals.

In the 1930s, Edward Sapir and Benjamin Lee Whorf proposed an influential argument about the connections among experience, thought, and language. It is now known as the **Sapir–Whorf hypothesis** (Whorf, 1956). It holds that we experience important things in our environment and form concepts about those things (Path 1 to 2 in Figure 2.1). Then, we develop language to express our concepts (Path 2 to 3). Finally, language itself influences how we see the world (Path 3 to 1).

For example, different types of camels are important in the environment of nomadic Arabs, and different types of snow are important in the lives of the Inuit in Canada's Far North and Alaska, and the Sami people in northern Finland, Norway, Russia, and Sweden (Path 1 to 2). Consequently, nomadic Arabs have developed many words for different types of camels and the Inuit and the Sami have developed many terms for different types of snow (Path 2 to 3). Distinctions that these people see may elude us because types of camels and snow are less important in our environment (Krupnik and Müller-Wille, 2010; Neil, 2014). On the other hand, terms that are familiar to every Canadian hockey fan—poke-check, slot, five-hole, tic-tac-toe—are unlikely to have equivalents in, say, Japanese, and in the absence of this vocabulary, the fine points of the game are likely to be less apparent.

In turn, language obliges people to think in certain ways (Path 3 to 1). If you are walking in a park, you will know whether a certain tree is in front of you, behind you, to the left, or to the right. When asked where the tree is, you will use such directions to describe its position. We think "egocentrically," locating objects relative to ourselves. However, egocentric directions have no meaning for speakers of Tzeltal in southern Mexico or of Guugu Yimithirr in Queensland, Australia. They lack concepts and words for "left," "right," and so on. They think geographically, and will say that the tree is to the "north," "south," "east," or "west." Trained from infancy to attend to geographic direction, Tzeltal speakers are obliged to think in those terms. If a tree to the north is located behind them and they are asked where the tree is, they will point to themselves, as if they don't exist. Reportedly, a Tzeltal speaker can be blindfolded, put in a dark room, and spun around 20 times until he's dizzy yet still point without hesitation to the north, south, east, and west (Boroditsky, 2010; Deutscher, 2010).

Taking an example closer to home, income and power inequality between women and men encourages some men to use terms like *fox, babe, bitch, ho,* and *doll* to refer to women. The use of such words in itself influences men to think of women simply as sexual objects. Feminist theorists argue that thinking about women in this way sustains a **rape culture** on college and university campuses and in society as a whole. In a rape culture, sexual harassment, slut-shaming, the trivialization of rape, victim-blaming, and sexual assault are widespread and, for large sections of the population, these actions seem normal. As some members of the Me Too movement emphasize, if men are ever going to think of women as equals, actual gender inequality will have to be reduced—and the language some men use to refer to women will also have to change.

> **Sapir–Whorf hypothesis** Holds that we experience certain things in our environment and form concepts about those things. We then develop language to express our concepts. Finally, language itself influences how we see the world.
>
> **rape culture** A culture in which sexual harassment, slut-shaming, the trivialization of rape, victim-blaming, and sexual assault are widespread and, for large sections of the population, these actions seem normal.

### FIGURE 2.1 The Sapir–Whorf Hypothesis

Triangle diagram with vertices: Experience (1, top), Conceptualization (Thought) (2, bottom right), Verbalization (Language) (3, bottom left). Arrows flow 1 → 2 → 3 → 1.

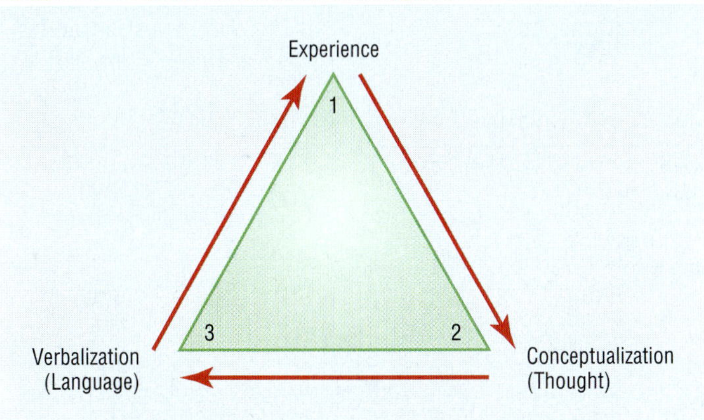

Source: From BRYM/ROBERTS/STROHSCHEIN/LIE. *Sociology: Your Compass for a New World*, 6E. © 2019 Nelson Education Ltd. Reproduced by permission. www.cengage.com/permissions.

## THE DECLINE AND DISAPPEARANCE OF LANGUAGES, INDIGENOUS-CANADIAN AND OTHER

Someone once defined language as a dialect supported by an army and a navy (Weinreich, 1945: 13). This definition makes a lot of sense if we consider changes in language use worldwide. For centuries, Great Britain, the United States, France, Portugal, and Spain gained economic, political, and cultural influence over much of the world by employing military violence, supporting sympathetic local governments, helping to create new educational systems, fostering the spread of the mass media, and encouraging the use of their national languages. The rise of English (and, to a lesser degree, French, Portuguese, and Spanish) has meant the elimination or endangerment of thousands of languages around the world spoken by the tribes of Papua New Guinea; the native peoples of the Americas; the national and tribal minorities of Asia, Africa, and Oceania; and marginalized European peoples, such as the Irish and the Basques. More than half the people in the world speak just 23 languages but there are 7099 living languages in the world. Some 34.8 percent of the world's languages are endangered, with the rate of extinction now being about 600 languages per century (Simons and Fennig, 2017). *All* of Canada's Indigenous languages fall into the "endangered" category.

How did Canada's more than 70 Indigenous languages become endangered? To make way for European colonists' farms, industries, railroads, and towns, the government segregated most Indigenous people on "reserves," often by force. However, Sir John A. Macdonald, our first prime minister, saw the reserve system as a problem when it came to educating children. As he wrote in 1879:

> When...the child lives with its parents, who are savages, and though he may learn to read and write, his habits and...mode of thought are Indian. He is simply a savage who can read and write. It has been strongly impressed upon myself... that Indian children should be withdrawn as much as possible from the parental influence, and the only way to do that would be to put them in central training industrial schools where they will acquire the habits and modes of thought of white men (quoted in Joseph, 2016).

Here we have the core idea for what became Canada's residential school system, a network of government-funded, church-run schools that over the course of their existence housed and trained some 150 000 Indigenous children. The residential schools aimed to help the children "escape" their cultures, facilitating their assimilation into white, European-Canadian culture. After being removed from their families, they were placed in an alien environment where malnourishment and abuse—emotional, physical, and sexual—were widespread. Some 4 percent of the children died while in the "care" of residential school staff members. Any hint of Indigenous culture was strictly forbidden. Use of Indigenous languages was punished (Brym, 2018a: 125–46).

The effect on Indigenous language use was telling. As late as the 1951 census, fully 87.4 percent of Indigenous Canadians said they could still speak an Indigenous language. By 1996, the figure had plummeted to 29.3 percent. In that year, the last residential school was shut down, but by then the capacity to sustain Indigenous languages had been so massively eroded that the figure continued to fall. In 2016, just 15.5 percent of Canada's 1.67 million Indigenous people claimed they could carry on a conversation in an indigenous language. Today, most of Canada's Indigenous languages are spoken by fewer than 1000 people (Burnaby and Beaujot, 1987: 36; Statistics Canada, 2017t; Table 2.2). True, some young people are now learning an Indigenous language as a second language, but not enough to stem the decline.

Much of the culture of a people—its prayers, humour, conversational styles, technical vocabulary, myths, and way of thinking—is expressed through language. Therefore, the loss of language amounts to the disappearance of traditions, and in some cases, even identity, and their replacement by the traditions and identity of a colonial power. These days, television, movies, and the Web play a leading role in speeding the loss (Woodbury, 2003).

**TABLE 2.2 Speakers of Indigenous Languages in Canada, 2016**

| Language Group | Speakers | Geographical Concentration of Speakers |
| --- | --- | --- |
| Algonquian (Cree, etc.) | 175 825 | Manitoba, Quebec, Ontario, Alberta, Saskatchewan |
| Inuit (Inuktitut, etc.) | 42 065 | Nunavut, Quebec |
| Athabaskan (Dene, etc.) | 23 455 | Saskatchewan, Northwest Territories, British Columbia |
| Salish (Shuswap, etc.) | 5 620 | British Columbia |
| Siouan (Stoney, etc.) | 5 400 | Alberta, Manitoba |
| Iroquoian (Mohawk, etc.) | 2 715 | Ontario, Quebec |
| Other | 6 180 | British Columbia |
| Total | 260 550 | |

Source: Statistics Canada. 2017. "The Aboriginal languages of First Nations people, Métis and Inuit." http://www12.statcan.gc.ca/census-recensement/2016/as-sa/98-200-x/2016022/98-200-x2016022-eng.cfm (retrieved 9 January 2017).

# LO 4 CULTURE AND ETHNOCENTRISM: A FUNCTIONALIST ANALYSIS

Despite its central importance in human life, culture is often invisible. That is, people tend to take their own culture for granted. It usually seems so sensible and natural that they rarely think about it. In contrast, people are sometimes startled when confronted by cultures other than their own. The ideas, norms, values, and techniques of other cultures may seem odd, irrational, and even inferior.

Judging another culture exclusively by the standards of our own is known as **ethnocentrism.** Ethnocentrism impairs sociological analysis. This fact can be illustrated by Marvin Harris's (1974) functionalist analysis of a practice that seems bizarre to many Westerners: cow worship among Hindus in India.

Many Hindus refuse to slaughter cattle and eat beef because, for them, the cow is a religious symbol of life. In India, some pin-up calendars portray the heads of beautiful women with the bodies of fat white cows, milk jetting out of each teat. Cows are permitted to wander the streets, defecate on the sidewalks, and stop to chew their cud in busy intersections or on railroad tracks, forcing traffic to a complete halt. In Chennai, police stations maintain fields where stray cows that have fallen ill can graze and be nursed back to health. The government even runs old-age homes for cows, where dry and decrepit cattle are kept free of charge. All of this special care seems mysterious to most Westerners, for it takes place amid poverty and hunger that could presumably be alleviated if only people would slaughter "useless" cattle for food instead of squandering scarce resources to feed and protect these animals.

According to Harris (1974: 3–32), however, ethnocentrism misleads many Western observers. Cow worship, it turns out, is an economically rational practice, especially in rural areas. For one thing, most Indian peasants can't afford tractors, so cows are needed to give birth to oxen, which are in high demand for plowing. For another, the cows produce hundreds of millions of kilograms of recoverable manure, half of which is used as fertilizer and the other half as a cooking fuel. With oil, coal, and wood in short supply, and with the peasants unable to afford chemical fertilizers, cow dung is, well, a godsend.

What is more, cows in India don't cost much to maintain because they eat mostly food that is not fit for human consumption. And they represent an important source of protein as well as a livelihood for members of low-ranking castes, who have the right to eat beef and dispose of the bodies of dead cattle. (A **caste** is a hereditary class authorized by religion.) These "untouchables" form the workforce of India's large leather craft industry. The protection of cows by means of cow worship is thus a sensible and efficient economic practice. It seems irrational only when judged by the standards of Western agribusiness.

Harris's (1974) analysis of cow worship in India is interesting for two reasons. The first lesson is about ethnocentrism: If you refrain from judging other societies by the standards of your own, you will have taken an important first step toward developing a sociological understanding of culture.

The second lesson is that functionalist theory can illuminate otherwise mysterious social practices. You will recall from Chapter 1 the functionalist claim that social structures have consequences that make social order possible. Some of those consequences are manifest functions that are intended and easily observed, while others are latent functions that are unintended and less obvious

> **ethnocentrism** The tendency to judge other cultures exclusively by the standards of your own.
>
> **caste** Hereditary class authorized by religion.

Many Westerners find the Indian practice of cow worship bizarre, but it performs several useful economic functions and is, in that sense, rational. By viewing cow worship exclusively as an outsider (or, for that matter, exclusively as an insider), we fail to see its rational core.

(Merton, 1968 [1949]). Harris discovered that cow worship performs a range of latent functions, showing how a particular social practice has unintended consequences that make social order possible.

## LO5 CULTURE AS FREEDOM AND CONSTRAINT

Some sociologists emphasize the way in which culture acts as an independent variable *causing* the establishment of certain patterns of social relations. Other sociologists emphasize the way in which culture acts a dependent variable. From the latter viewpoint, culture is an *effect* of certain patterns of social relations.

Harris's analysis of cow worship in India illustrates the second case. In Harris's view, social relations in India—in particular, social relations that result in a relatively low level of economic development—are such that the protection of cows becomes an economic necessity. The social necessity presumably gives rise to an aspect of Hinduism: the belief among individuals that cows are holy. Some conflict theorists take a similar view about the relationship between social relations and cultural consequences.

Symbolic interactionists take the opposing view. For them, people are not empty vessels into which society pours a defined assortment of beliefs, symbols, and values. Rather, elements of culture result from human creativity and choice; we are at liberty to give meaning to the people and things in our environment. Culture is the outcome of our choices, and culture shapes and constrains our social relations. Some poststructuralists hold a similar view about the relationship between human creativity as the source of culture and of structured social relations.

In the remainder of this chapter, I probe these two faces of culture—culture as freedom and culture as constraint (see the Theories in Dispute boxed feature, The Problem of Caste).

## THEORIES IN DISPUTE

### The Problem of Caste

The "two faces of culture" metaphor is a convenient way of reconciling opposing views. One view is that culture is a source of freedom insofar as it allows people to create social structures. In this sense, culture is a cause or an independent variable. The opposing view is that culture is an effect of social structure—a dependent variable that constrains human behaviour. However, on reflection, the metaphor may seem like a cop-out; it's difficult to see how something and its opposite can both be true. To see how it is possible to reconcile these apparently conflicting arguments, let's consider competing analyses of the Indian caste system.

The caste system divided Indian society into groups and subgroups arranged in a rigid hierarchy authorized by religion. Being born into a particular caste meant that you had to work in the distinctive occupations reserved for that caste and engage in a range of rituals and social practices that kept you socially segregated within it.

In an influential study, French anthropologist/sociologist Louis Dumont sought to demonstrate that Hinduism gave rise to the system of inequality known as the caste system (Dumont, 1980 [1966]). For instance, Hinduism promoted the idea of reincarnation, claiming that any attempt to improve one's social position would ensure rebirth in a lower position. Accordingly, an observant Hindu would not dare seek to advance himself for fear of being reborn as, say, a dung beetle. Hinduism thus created and perpetuated India's system of inequality.

York University sociologist Hira Singh challenged Dumont's theory (Singh, 2014). He showed that each caste had a different relationship to land. Caste position was highest among those who owned the most land, lower for those who owned less land, still lower for those who leased land, and lowest for those who neither owned nor leased land but had to work it. In his judgment, the caste system was caused not by Hinduism but by a social structure, namely the system of land ownership in India. Hinduism was merely a set of ideas that justified the caste system.

The caste system may well have been linked to patterns of land ownership, as Singh argues, but it is difficult to understand how it could have been initiated and maintained without the existence of widespread and deeply held beliefs that made it seem necessary. After all, in the absence of such beliefs, lower castes would have been free to rebel

### FIGURE 2.2 Reconciling the Two Faces of Culture

Culture as an independent variable (Dumont)

Hinduism → Caste system

Culture as a dependent variable (Singh)

Patterns of land ownership → Caste system

Reconciliation

Patterns of land ownership → Caste system ← Hinduism
Patterns of land ownership → Hinduism

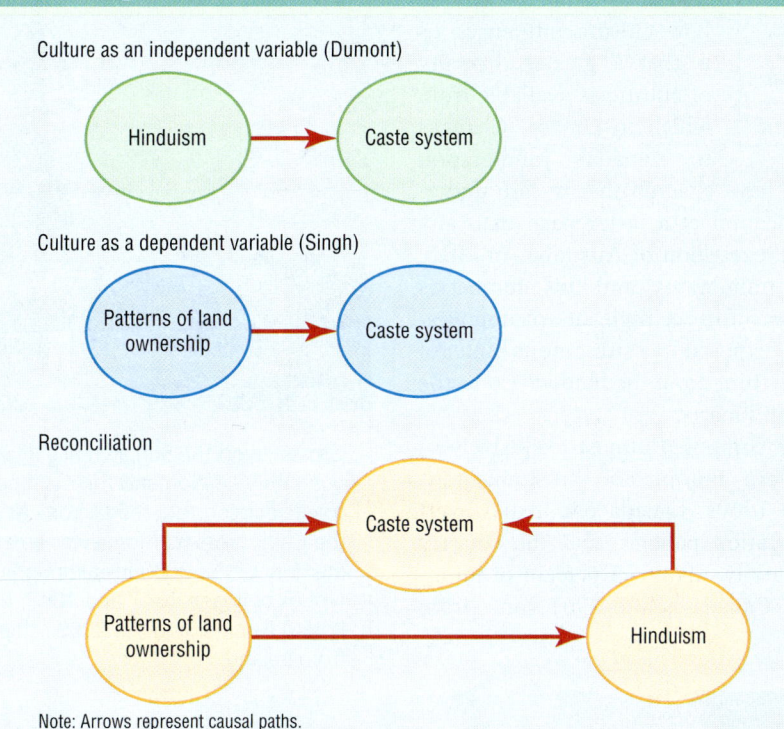

Note: Arrows represent causal paths.

Source: Robert Brym

against India's hereditary system of stark inequality. As Dumont contends, Hinduism provided those beliefs, in particular, belief in reincarnation and the need to remain in the social position into which one is born. Apparently, culture *can* be both an independent and a dependent variable, as Figure 2.2 illustrates.

### Critical Thinking Questions
- To which theoretical traditions are Dumont's and Singh's ideas the closest?
- How are Max Weber's ideas about early Protestantism similar to Dumont's ideas about Hinduism? How are they different? Consult the Appendix of Chapter 1, Introducing Sociology, for hints.

## CULTURE AS FREEDOM

This is a nice room tonight. When I look out, I see all kinds of different people. I see Black, White, Asian, everybody hangin' out, havin' a good time.... This type of thing is not going to be able to happen about 300 years from now. You realize that?... You realize there's not going to be any more White people? There's not going to be any more Black people? Everyone's going to be beige.... It's true, the whole world's mixing. There's nothing you can do about it. Eventually, we're all going to become some hybrid mix of Chinese and Indian. It's inevitable. They're the two largest populations in the world. So you can run from us now. But sooner or later, we're going to hump you.... But I'm thinkin' if we're all going to mix anyway, let's start mixing people now that would never normally mix just to see what we'll get. You know, hook up a Jamaican with an Italian. They could have little Pastafarians. I'm Indian. I could hook up with a Jewish girl and we could have little Hinjews. A woman from the Philippines, a guy from Holland—little Hollapinos. A guy from Cuba, a woman from Iceland—little Ice-cubes. A French and a Greek—Freaks. A German and a Newfie—little Goofies. It's gonna happen. We might as well help it along.

—Russell Peters (2009)

**multiculturalism** A federal government policy that promotes and funds the maintenance of culturally diverse communities, thus strengthening the trend toward cultural diversification.

Part of the reason we are increasingly able to choose how culture influences us is that a greater diversity of culture is available from which to choose. Changes to Canada's immigration policy since the 1960s have ensured that we are undergoing cultural diversification at a faster pace than any other country, with the exception of Australia. In 2016, we admitted 296 346 immigrants, and this number is expected to grow in the future. A high rate of immigration ensures that we are exposed to a sumptuous buffet of cultural options in everything from the food we eat to the people we date, court, and marry.

Canada used to be composed almost exclusively of Christians from northern Europe and an Indigenous minority. Then, in the 1960s, Canada eliminated overt racism from its immigration policies, and the country began to diversify culturally. About 95 percent of immigrants who arrived in Canada before 1961 came from

Grosse Île on the St. Lawrence River was Quebec's quarantine station and the main point of entry for immigrants coming to Canada from 1832 to 1937. In 1909, the Celtic cross memorial was erected to honour the memory of the 3000 Irish immigrants who perished from typhus between 1847 and 1848, during the Great Irish Potato Famine, and the 2000 others who died in transit from Ireland.

Europe and the United States. Between 2011 and 2016, about 87 percent of immigrants came from places *outside* Europe and the United States (Statistics Canada, 2017j; Figure 2.3). Because of the inflow of immigrants from such places as the Philippines, India, China, and Pakistan, more than 22 percent of the population is now composed of members of visible minority groups. About three-quarters of visible-minority Canadians reside in Toronto, Vancouver, and Montreal, with most of the rest residing in Edmonton, Calgary, and Winnipeg.

## MULTICULTURALISM

In the 1970s, the Canadian government adopted a policy of **multiculturalism**, making Canada the world's first officially multicultural society. Multicultural policy promotes and funds the maintenance of culturally diverse communities, thus strengthening the trend toward cultural diversification (Fleras and Elliott, 2002). The multiculturalist principle is enshrined in the Canadian Charter of Rights and Freedoms, which forms the first part of the 1982 Constitution Act. With the passage of the 1988 Canadian Multiculturalism Act, the government confirmed its commitment to recognizing all Canadians as "full and equal participants in Canadian society."

Russell Peters

## FIGURE 2.3  Immigration Population in Canada

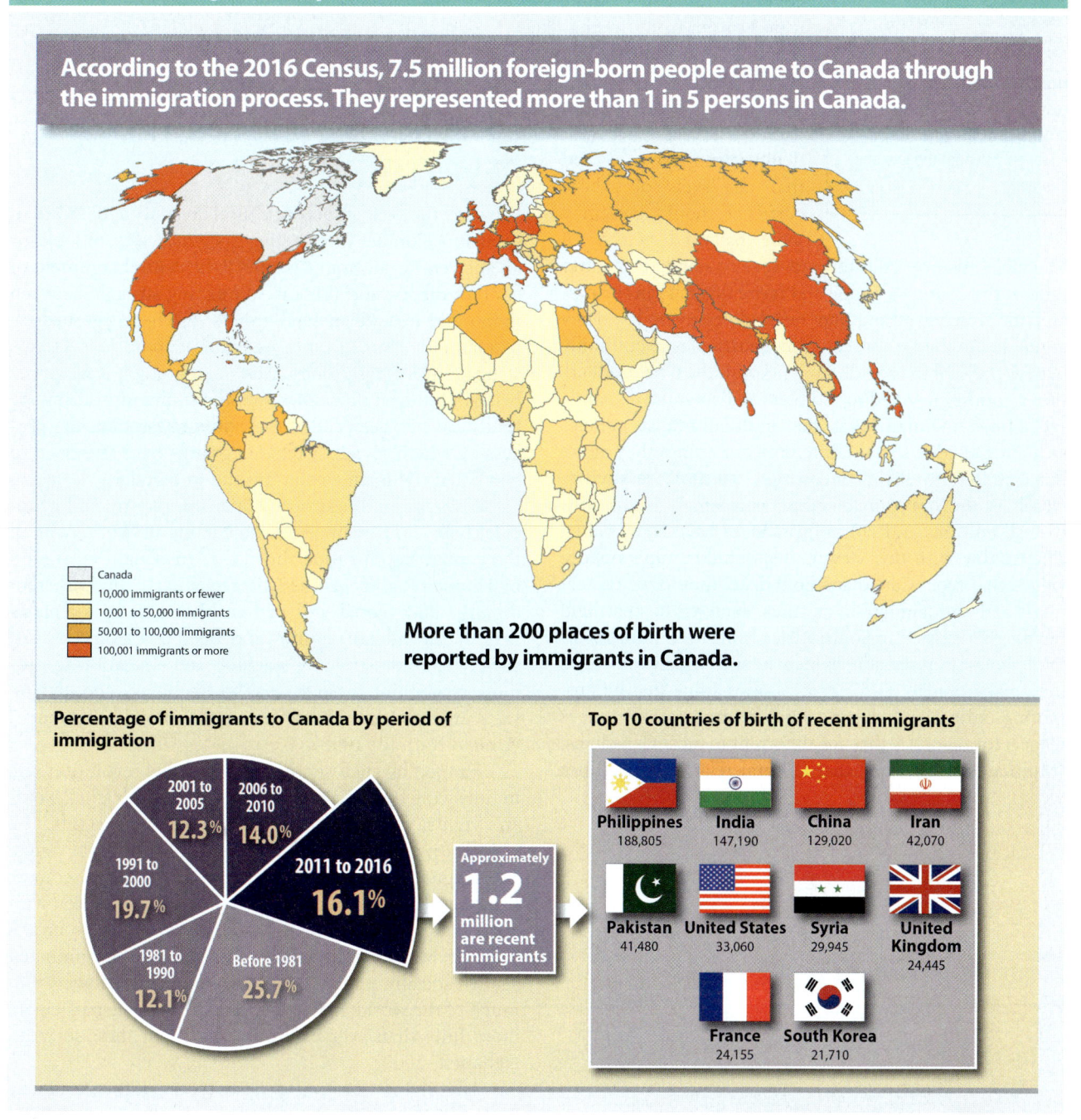

According to the 2016 Census, 7.5 million foreign-born people came to Canada through the immigration process. They represented more than 1 in 5 persons in Canada.

Legend:
- Canada
- 10,000 immigrants or fewer
- 10,001 to 50,000 immigrants
- 50,001 to 100,000 immigrants
- 100,001 immigrants or more

More than 200 places of birth were reported by immigrants in Canada.

**Percentage of immigrants to Canada by period of immigration**

- 2001 to 2005: 12.3%
- 2006 to 2010: 14.0%
- 2011 to 2016: 16.1%
- 1991 to 2000: 19.7%
- 1981 to 1990: 12.1%
- Before 1981: 25.7%

Approximately 1.2 million are recent immigrants

**Top 10 countries of birth of recent immigrants**

- Philippines 188,805
- India 147,190
- China 129,020
- Iran 42,070
- Pakistan 41,480
- United States 33,060
- Syria 29,945
- United Kingdom 24,445
- France 24,155
- South Korea 21,710

Source: Statistics Canada. 2017j. "Immigrant population in Canada." https://www150.statcan.gc.ca/n1/pub/11-627-m/11-627-m2017028-eng.htm (retrieved 10 January 2018).

Some of the effects of multiculturalism are evident in Canada's schools ("Canada," 2018). Although each province and territory holds jurisdiction over education, it was common until recent decades for schools across Canada to stress the common elements of our culture, history, and society. Students learned the historical importance of the "charter groups"—the English and the French—in Canadian history. School curricula typically neglected the contributions of non-white, non-French, and non-English people to Canada's literary, artistic, and scientific development. Moreover, students learned little about the less savoury aspects of Canadian history, including Canada's racist immigration policies that sought to preserve Canada's "English stock" by restricting or denying entry to certain groups, including Chinese, black people, and Jews (see Chapter 7,

> **cultural relativism** The belief that all cultures have equal value.
>
> **rights revolution** The process by which socially excluded groups have struggled to win equal rights under the law and in practice.

Race and Ethnicity). In general, history books were written from the perspective of the victors, not the vanquished.

For the past several decades, advocates of multiculturalism have argued that all levels of school curricula should present a more balanced picture of Canadian history, culture, and society—one that better reflects the country's ethnic and racial diversity in the past and its growing ethnic and racial diversity today. They argue that to the extent that school curricula are culturally biased, they fail to provide students with the type of education a country devoted to multiculturalism must demand.

Critics maintain that our multiculturalist policies weaken Canada's social fabric. For one thing, they argue that multiculturalism encourages **cultural relativism**, which is the opposite of ethnocentrism. It is the idea that all cultures and cultural practices have equal value. The trouble with this view is that some cultures oppose values that most Canadians hold dear. Should we respect racist and antidemocratic cultures, such as the apartheid regime that existed in South Africa from 1948 until 1992? Or female circumcision, which is still widely practised in Somalia, Sudan, and Egypt? Critics argue that by promoting cultural relativism, multiculturalism encourages respect for practices that are abhorrent to most Canadians. (Multiculturalists reply that cultural relativism need not be taken to an extreme. *Moderate* cultural relativism encourages tolerance and should be promoted.)

## A CONFLICT ANALYSIS OF CULTURE: THE RIGHTS REVOLUTION

What are the social roots of cultural diversity and multiculturalism? Conflict theory suggests where we can look for an answer. Recall from Chapter 1 the central argument of conflict theory: social life is an ongoing struggle between more- and less-advantaged groups. Privileged groups try to maintain their advantages, while subordinate groups struggle to increase theirs. And sure enough, if we probe beneath cultural diversification and multiculturalism, we find what has been called the **rights revolution**, the process by which socially excluded groups have struggled to win equal rights under the law and in practice.

After the outburst of nationalism, racism, and genocidal behaviour among the combatants in World War II, the United Nations proclaimed the Universal Declaration of Human Rights in 1948. It recognized the "inherent dignity" and "equal and inalienable rights of all members of the human family" and held that every part of society should "strive by teaching and education to promote respect for these rights and freedoms" and "secure their universal and effective recognition and observance" (United Nations, 1998).

Fanned by such sentiment, the rights revolution was in full swing by the 1960s. Today, Indigenous rights, women's rights, minority rights, gay and lesbian rights, the rights of people with special needs, constitutional rights, and language rights are all part of our political discourse. Because of the rights revolution, democracy has been widened and deepened. The rights revolution is by no means finished. Many categories of people are still discriminated against socially, politically, and economically. However, in much of the world, a widening circle of people participate more fully than ever before in the life of their societies (Ignatieff, 2000).

The rights revolution raises some difficult issues. For example, some members of groups that have suffered extraordinarily high levels of discrimination historically, such as Indigenous Canadians, Chinese Canadians, and others, have demanded reparation in the form of money, symbolic gestures, land, and political autonomy (see Chapter 7, Race and Ethnicity). Much controversy surrounds the extent to which today's citizens are obligated to compensate past injustices.

Such problems notwithstanding, the rights revolution is here to stay and it affects our culture profoundly. Specifically, the rights revolution fragments Canadian culture by (1) legitimizing the grievances of groups that were formerly excluded from full social participation, and

The Canadian Charter of Rights and Freedoms forms the first part of the 1982 Constitution Act. Section 27 states: "This Charter shall be interpreted in a manner consistent with the preservation and enhancement of the multicultural heritage of Canadians."

(2) renewing Canadians' pride in their identity and heritage. Our history books, our literature, our music, our use of languages, and our very sense of what it means to be Canadian have diversified culturally. White, male, heterosexual property owners of northern European origin are still disproportionately influential in Canada, but our culture is no longer dominated by them in the way that it was just 50 or 60 years ago.

## FROM DIVERSITY TO GLOBALIZATION

The cultural diversification we witness today is not evident in preliterate or tribal societies. In such societies, cultural beliefs and practices are virtually the same for all group members. For example, many tribal societies organize **rites of passage**. These cultural ceremonies mark the transition from one stage of life to another (e.g., from childhood to adulthood) or from life to death (e.g., funerals). Some involve elaborate procedures, such as body painting and carefully orchestrated chants and movements. They are conducted in public, and no variation from prescribed practice is allowed. Culture is homogeneous (Durkheim, 1976 [1915/1912]).

In contrast, pre-industrial western Europe and North America were rocked by artistic, religious, scientific, and political forces that fragmented culture. The Renaissance, the Protestant Reformation, the Scientific Revolution, the French and American Revolutions—between the fourteenth and eighteenth centuries, all of these movements involved people questioning old ways of seeing and doing things. Science placed skepticism about established authority at the very heart of its method. Political revolution proved nothing was ordained about who should rule and how they should do so. Religious dissent ensured that the Catholic Church would no longer be the supreme interpreter of God's will in the eyes of all Christians. Authority and truth became divided as never before.

Cultural fragmentation picked up steam during industrialization, as the variety of occupational roles grew and new political and intellectual movements crystallized. Its pace is quickening again today as a result of globalization. Globalization, as defined in Chapter 1, is the process by which formerly separate individuals, groups, institutions, economies, states, and cultures are becoming tied together and people are becoming increasingly aware of their growing interdependence.

Globalization has many roots. International trade and investment are expanding. Members of different

> **rites of passage** Cultural ceremonies that mark the transition from one stage of life to another (e.g., baptisms, confirmations, weddings) or from life to death (e.g., funerals).

Canada continues to diversify culturally.

> **postmodernism** Culture characterized by an eclectic mix of cultural elements from different times and places, the erosion of authority, and the decline of consensus around core values.

ethnic and racial groups are migrating and coming into sustained contact with one another. A growing number of people from these diverse groups date, court, and marry across religious, ethnic, and racial lines. Influential "transnational" organizations have been created, such as the International Monetary Fund, the European Union, Greenpeace, Amnesty International, and *Médecins sans frontières*. Inexpensive international travel and communication make contacts between people from diverse cultures routine. The mass media make Ryan Gosling and *13 Reasons Why* as well-known in Warsaw as in Winnipeg, while hip-hop is as popular in Senegal as it is in Saskatoon. Globalization, in short, eliminates political, economic, and cultural isolation, bringing people together in what Canadian communications guru Marshall McLuhan (1964) called a "global village." Because of globalization, people are less obliged to accept the culture into which they are born and freer to combine elements of culture from a wide variety of historical periods and geographical settings.

The Coca-Cola Company was one of the first American companies to go global.

## POSTMODERNISM

Some sociologists think that so much cultural fragmentation and reconfiguration has taken place in the last few decades that a new term is needed to characterize the culture of our times: **postmodernism**.

Scholars often characterize the last half of the nineteenth century and the first half of the twentieth century as the era of modernity. During this hundred-year period, belief in the inevitability of progress, respect for authority, and consensus around core values characterized much of Western culture. In contrast, postmodern culture involves an eclectic mix of elements from different times and places, the erosion of authority, and the decline of consensus around core values. Let us consider each of these aspects of postmodernism in turn.

### Blending Cultures

A mixing of diverse elements from different times and places is the first aspect of postmodernism. In the postmodern era, it is easier to create individualized belief systems and practices by blending facets of different cultures and historical periods. Take religion. Although 73 percent of Canadians still say they believe in God or a higher power and 69 percent continue to identify as Christians, increasing numbers now identify themselves as adherents of non-Christian religions (7 percent) or as having no religious affiliation (24 percent) (Bibby, 2017: 66, 223; Chapter 10, Religion). In addition, Canadians are increasingly showing a willingness to combine conventional religious beliefs with a wide assortment of supernatural beliefs and practices, including astrology, tarot, New Age mysticism, psychic phenomena, and communication with the dead (Bibby, 1987: 233; 2001: 195; 2017: 174).

Simply put, we have many more ways to express our spirituality than we used to. A person can easily construct a personalized religion by drawing on different religions, much like consumers shopping in a mall. Meanwhile, churches, mosques, synagogues, and other religious institutions have diversified their offerings to appeal to the spiritual, leisure, and social needs of religious consumers and retain their loyalties in the competitive market for congregants and parishioners (Finke and Stark, 1992).

### Erosion of Authority

The erosion of authority is the second aspect of postmodernism. Half a century ago, Canadians were likely to defer to authority in the family, schools, politics, and medicine. Today, we are more likely to challenge authority and hold parents, teachers, politicians, and doctors in lower regard. In the 1950s, for example, Robert Young played the firm, wise, and

A hallmark of postmodernism is the combining of cultural elements from different times and places. In 2007, an addition to the Royal Ontario Museum known as the Michael Lee-Chin Crystal, was opened in Toronto. In the eyes of some, it is a postmodern marvel. In the eyes of others, it is a postmodern nightmare.

46 CHAPTER 2 Culture

**FIGURE 2.4  Belief in God or a Higher Power by Age Cohort, Canada, 1985 and 2015**

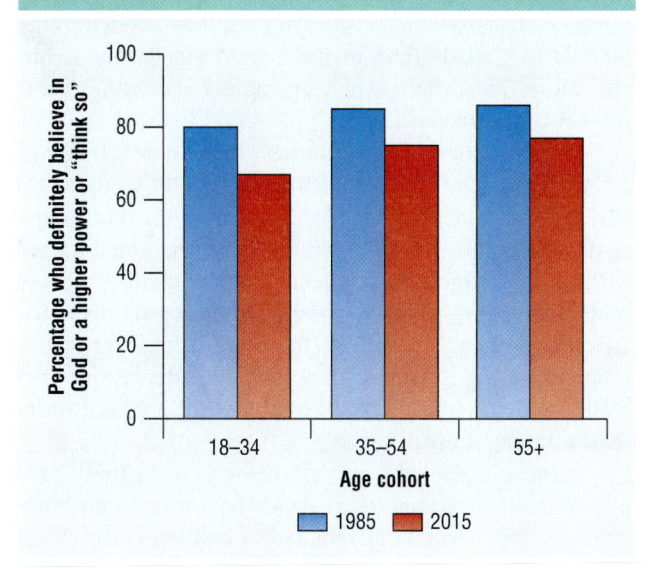

Sources: Reginald Bibby, 1985. *Project Canada National Survey Series*; Reginald Bibby and Angus Reid, 2015. Angus Reid Institute Religion Survey.

**FIGURE 2.5  Voter Turnout in Canadian Federal Elections, 1958–2015**

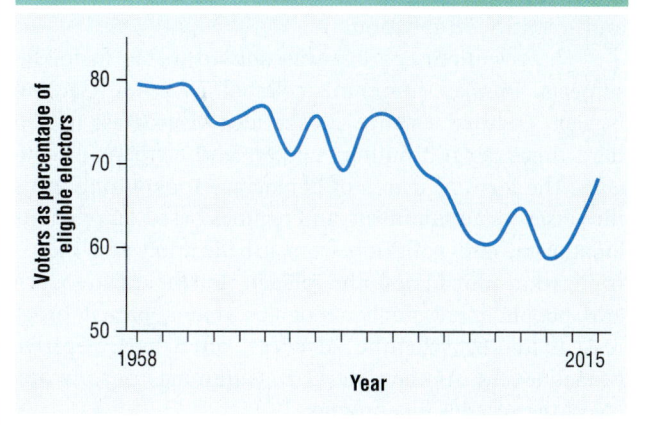

Sources: Elections Canada. 2012. "Voter Turnout at Federal Elections and Referendums." http://www.elections.ca; 2016. "Retrospective Report on the 42nd General Election of October 19, 2015." http://www.elections.ca/content.aspx?section=res&dir=rec/eval/pes2015/ege&document=p1&lang=e#a4 (retrieved 10 January 2016).

always-present father in the TV hit *Father Knows Best*. In the 2010s, the typical TV father is more like Homer Simpson or Phil Dunphy in *Modern Family*: a fool. Another illustration of the erosion of authority concerns belief in God or a higher power. Surveys stretching over the past three decades show not only that the percentage of Canadians saying they are inclined to believe in God or a higher power has declined but that the decline is largest in the youngest age cohort (Figure 2.4). Finally, consider that voting and other forms of conventional politics are less popular than they used to be—an indication, one could argue, of a decline in political authority (Figure 2.5).

## Instability of Core Values

The decline of consensus around core values is the third aspect of postmodernism. Half a century ago, most people's values remained stable during their adult lives and many values were widely accepted. Today, value shifts are more rapid and consensus has broken down on many issues. For example, in the middle of the twentieth century, most adults remained loyal to one political party from one election to the next. However, specific issues and personalities have increasingly eclipsed party loyalty as the driving forces of Canadian politics (Johnston, 2012). Today, people are more likely to vote for different political parties in succeeding elections than they were in 1950.

The decline of consensus can also be illustrated by considering the fate of "big historical projects." For most of the past 200 years, consensus throughout the world was built around big historical projects. Various political and social movements convinced people they could take history into their own hands and create a glorious future just by signing up. German Nazism was a big historical project. Its followers expected the Reich to enjoy 1000 years of power. Communism was an even bigger big historical project, mobilizing hundreds of millions of people for a future that promised to end inequality and injustice for all time. However, the biggest and most successful big historical project was

The father figure of postmodernism?

not so much a social movement as a powerful idea—the belief that progress is inevitable and that life will always improve, mainly because of the spread of democracy and scientific innovation.

The twentieth century was unkind to big historical projects. Russian communism lasted 74 years. German Nazism endured a mere 12. The idea of progress fell on hard times, as 100 million soldiers and civilians died in wars; the forward march of democracy took wrong turns into fascism, communism, and regimes based on religious fanaticism; and pollution from urbanization and industrialization threatened the planet. In the postmodern era, people increasingly recognize that apparent progress, including scientific advances, often have negative consequences. As the poet E. E. Cummings once wrote, "Nothing recedes like progress."

## IS CANADA THE FIRST POSTMODERN COUNTRY?

Until the mid-1960s, the image of Canadians among most sociologists was that of a stodgy people: peaceful, conservative, respectful of authority, and therefore unlike our American cousins.

According to conventional wisdom, the United States was born in open rebellion against the British motherland. Its western frontier was lawless. Vast opportunities for striking it rich bred a spirit of individualism. Consequently, American culture became an anti-authoritarian culture.

Canada developed differently in this conventional view. It became an independent country not through a revolutionary upheaval but in a more gradual, evolutionary manner. The North-West Mounted Police and two hierarchical churches (Roman Catholic and Anglican) first imposed themselves on Indigenous peoples in order to establish an administrative arm that opened up the land to European settlement (Miller, 2018 [1989]). This imposition laid the foundation for a more or less orderly society before the era of mass settlement, rather than permitting the emergence of a "Wild West." Beginning with the Hudson's Bay Company, large corporations quickly came to dominate the Canadian economy, hampering individualism and the entrepreneurial spirit. Consequently, Canadian culture became a culture of deference to authority. That, at least, was the common view until the 1960s (Lipset, 1963).

Although the contrast between deferential Canadian culture and anti-authoritarian American culture had validity 50 or 60 years ago, it is inaccurate today (Adams, 1997: 62–95). As we have seen, the questioning of authority spread throughout the Western world beginning in the 1960s. Nowhere, however, did it spread as quickly and thoroughly as in Canada. Canadians used to express more confidence in big business than Americans did, but surveys now show the opposite. Canadians used to be more religious than Americans were, but that is no longer the case. Fewer Canadians (in percentage terms) say they believe in God and fewer attend weekly religious services. Confidence in government has eroded more quickly in Canada than in the United States. Americans are more patriotic than Canadians, according more respect to the state.

Finally, Americans are more likely than Canadians are to regard the traditional nuclear family as the ideal family form and to think of deviations from tradition—same-sex couples, single-parent families, cohabitation without marriage—as the source of a whole range of social problems. Thus, whether sociologists examine attitudes toward the family, the state, the government, religion, or big business, they now find that Americans are more deferential to traditional institutional authority than Canadians are.

Because Canadians are less deferential to traditional institutional authority than Americans are, some commentators say that Canadians lack a distinct culture. For example, American patriotism sparks awareness of great national accomplishments in art, war, sports, science, and, indeed, all fields of human endeavour. Anthems, rituals, myths, and festivities celebrate these accomplishments and give Americans a keen sense of who they are and how they differ from non-Americans. Not surprisingly, therefore, a larger percentage of Americans than of Canadians think of themselves in unhyphenated terms—as "Americans" plain and simple rather than, say, Italian-Americans. In Canada, a larger percentage of the population thinks of itself in hyphenated terms; compared with the Americans, our identity is qualified, even tentative.

Does this mean that Canadians lack a distinct national culture? Hardly. It means that although American culture is characterized by a relatively high degree of deference to dominant institutions, Canadian culture is characterized by a relatively high degree of tolerance and respect for diversity. We are more likely than Americans are to favour gender equality, accept gay and lesbian relationships, and encourage bilingualism and multiculturalism. Characteristically, a large international survey by a condom manufacturer found that Americans have sex more often than Canadians do, but Canadians are more likely to say that the pleasure of their partner is very important. As public opinion pollster Michael Adams wrote, "Twenty-five years of public-opinion polling in Canada has taught me a seemingly paradoxical truth: Canadians feel *strongly* about their *weak* attachments to Canada, its political institutions and their fellow citizens. In other words, they feel strongly about the right to live in a society that allows its citizens to be detached from ideology and critical of organizations, and not to feel obliged to be jingoistic or sentimentally patriotic. Canadians *lack* of nationalism is, in many ways, a distinguishing feature of the country" (Adams, 1997: 171).

# THEORIES AT A GLANCE

## Culture

| Theory | Main Question | Application |
|---|---|---|
| Functionalism | How do social structures and the values underlying them contribute to social stability? | Cow worship is a practice that seems bizarre to many Westerners but it makes sense if one considers its useful functions. As Harris noted, most Indian peasants can't afford tractors, so cows are needed to give birth to oxen, which are in high demand for plowing. Moreover, cows produce hundreds of millions of kilograms of recoverable manure, half of which is used as fertilizer and the other half as a cooking fuel—and all of which is useful in a society with oil, coal, wood, and chemical fertilizers too expensive for many peasants to afford. Cows in India don't cost much to maintain because they eat mostly food that is not fit for human consumption. And they represent an important source of protein as well as a livelihood for members of low-ranking castes, who have the right to eat beef and dispose of the bodies of dead cattle. These "untouchables" form the workforce of India's large leather craft industry. The protection of cows by means of cow worship is thus a functional practice.<br><br>Manifest functions are intended and easily observed, while latent functions are unintended and less obvious. Harris discovered that cow worship performs a range of latent functions, showing how a particular social practice has unintended consequences that make social order possible. |
| Symbolic interactionism | How do people communicate to make their social settings meaningful, thus helping to create their social circumstances? | Functionalists and conflict theorists view culture as an effect of patterns of social relations. Symbolic interactionists view culture as a result of human creativity and choice. From the latter viewpoint, freedom to choose one's culture has been enhanced over the past half-century by the ethnic and religious diversification of Canadian society, the development of Canada's policy of multiculturalism, the efforts of groups formerly excluded from full participation in Canadian economic and political life to assert their rights, and globalization. Some analysts regard the freedom to choose one's culture as having advanced to the point where it is necessary to characterize our culture as postmodern—a culture that blends elements from various times and places, erodes authority, and renders core values unstable. |
| Conflict theory | How does the structure of inequality between privileged groups seeking to maintain their advantages and subordinate groups seeking to increase theirs lead to conflict and often to social change? | Conflict theorists argue that if we probe beneath cultural diversification and multiculturalism, we find the rights revolution, the process by which socially excluded groups have struggled to win equal rights under the law and in practice. Today, Indigenous rights, women's rights, minority rights, gay and lesbian rights, the rights of people with special needs, constitutional rights, and language rights are all part of our political discourse. Because of the rights revolution, democracy has been widened and deepened. Many categories of people are still discriminated against socially, politically, and economically. However, in much of the world, a widening circle of people participate more fully than ever before in the life of their societies because they have engaged in conflict with privileged groups. |
| Feminism | How do social conventions maintain male dominance and female subordination, and how can these conventions be overturned? | Income and power inequality between women and men encourages some men to use terms like fox, babe, bitch, ho, and doll to refer to women. The use of such words in itself influences men to think of women as sexual objects. Feminist theorists argue that thinking about women in this way sustains a rape culture in which sexual harassment, slut-shaming, the trivialization of rape, victim-blaming, and sexual assault are widespread and, for large sections of the population, these actions seem normal. As some feminists emphasize, if men are ever going to think of women as equals, actual gender inequality will have to be reduced—and male language conventions used to refer to women will also have to change. |

**rationalization** The application of the most efficient means to achieve given goals and the unintended, negative consequences of doing so.

In short, Canadian culture *is* distinctive, and its chief distinction may be that it qualifies us as the first thoroughly postmodern society.

## LO6 CULTURE AS CONSTRAINT

We noted earlier that culture has two faces. One we labelled *freedom*, the other *constraint*. Diversity, globalization, and postmodernism are all aspects of the new freedoms that culture allows us today. We now turn to an examination of two contemporary aspects of culture that act as constraining forces on our lives: rationalization and consumerism.

### RATIONALIZATION

At the turn of the twentieth century, the great German sociologist Max Weber coined the term **rationalization** to describe the application of the most efficient means to achieve given goals and the unintended, negative consequences of doing so. He claimed that rationalization was creeping into all spheres of life (Figure 2.6). In Weber's view, rationalization is one of the most constraining aspects of contemporary culture (Weber, 1958 [1904–05]): 181).

The constraining effects of rationalization are evident, for example, even in something as basic as the way we measure and use time. People did not always let the clock determine the pace of daily life. The first mechanical clocks were installed in public squares in Germany seven centuries ago to signal the beginning of the workday, the timing of meals, and quitting time. Workers were accustomed to enjoying a flexible and vague work schedule regulated only approximately by the seasons and the rising and setting of the Sun. The strict regime imposed by the work clocks made their lives harder. They staged uprisings to silence the clocks, but to no avail. City officials sided with employers and imposed fines for ignoring the work clocks (Thompson, 1967).

Today, few people rebel against the work clock. This is especially true of urban North American couples who are employed full-time in the paid labour force and have young children. For them, life often seems an endless round of waking up at 6:30 a.m.; getting everyone washed and dressed; preparing the kids' lunches; getting the kids out the door in time for the school bus or the car pool; driving to work through rush-hour traffic; facing the speed-up at work resulting from the recent downsizing; driving back home through rush-hour traffic; preparing dinner; taking the kids to their soccer game; returning home to clean up the dishes and help with homework; getting the kids washed, their teeth brushed, and then into bed; and (if they have not brought some office work home) grabbing an hour of TV before collapsing, exhausted, for 6½ hours' sleep before the story repeats itself (Statistics Canada, 2011).

Life tends to be less hectic for residents of small towns, unmarried people, couples without young children, retirees, and the unemployed. But the lives of others are typically so packed with activities that they must carefully regulate time and parcel out each moment so they can tick off one item after another from an ever-growing list of tasks that need to be completed on time. After 700 years of conditioning, allowing clocks to precisely regulate our activities seems the most natural thing in the world, although there is of course nothing natural about it.

The regulation of time ensures efficiency. It maximizes how much work you get done in a day. It enables trains to run on schedule, university classes to begin punctually, and business meetings to start on time. However, many people complain that life has become too hectic to enjoy. A popular restaurant in Japan has even installed a punch-clock for its customers. The restaurant offers all you can eat for 35 yen per minute. As a result, "the diners rush in, punch the clock, load their trays from the buffet table, and concentrate intensely on efficient chewing and swallowing, trying not to waste time talking to

**FIGURE 2.6 The Rationalization of Chinese Script**

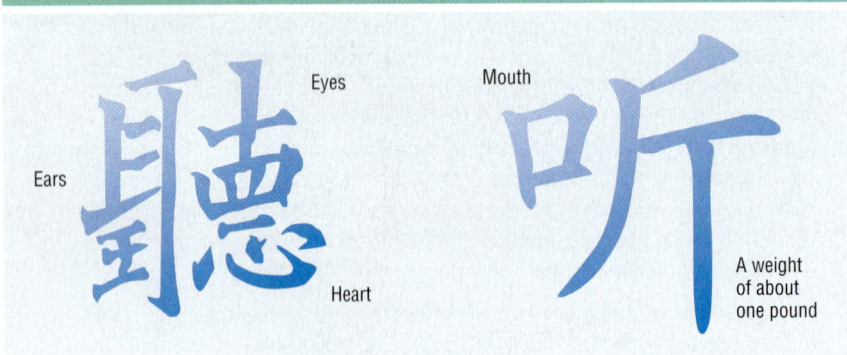

聽 — Ears, Eyes, Heart
听 — Mouth, A weight of about one pound

Shown here are the Chinese characters for "listening" (t'ing) in traditional Chinese script (left) and simplified, modern script (right). Each character is composed of several word-symbols. In traditional script, listening is depicted as a process involving the eyes, the ears, and the heart. It implies that listening demands the utmost empathy and involves the whole person. In contrast, modern script depicts listening as something that involves merely one person speaking and the other "weighing" speech. Modern Chinese script has been rationalized. Has empathy been lost in the process?

their companions before rushing back to punch out" (Gleick, 2000: 244). Some upscale restaurants in New York and Los Angeles have gotten in on the act. An increasingly large number of business clients are so pressed for time, they pack in two half-hour lunches with successive guests. The restaurants oblige, making the resetting of tables "resemble the pit-stop activity at the Indianapolis 500" (Gleick, 2000: 155). As these examples illustrate, a *rational* means (the use of the work clock) has been applied to a *given goal* (maximizing work) but has led to an *irrational end* (a too-hectic life). For another example with which you are only too familiar, see Sociology and the Media, Smartphones, Social Media, and the Two Faces of Culture.

## SOCIOLOGY AND THE MEDIA

### Smartphones, Social Media, and the Two Faces of Culture

The data are in, and they show that most Canadians find digital technology liberating. Some 77 percent of Canadians over the age of 17 report that digital technology helps them communicate with others, 66 percent claim it saves them time, and 52 percent say it helps them make more informed decisions. For Canadians under the age of 45, the corresponding percentages are significantly higher (Figure 2.7).

Wireless communication has a downside too, as has been evident for some time (see the *Punch* cartoon). For example, smartphones and social media shrink attention spans. Research sponsored by Microsoft Canada shows that the average attention span of adults fell by a third from 2000 to 2013. Among younger Canadians, attention spans are shrinking the most (Microsoft Canada, 2015: 6–7).

And what happens when you don't have your smartphone with you? One social psychologist wanted to find out. He asked university undergraduates to give him their smartphones. He then had each of them

*(Continued)*

## FIGURE 2.7  The Internet and Digital Technology

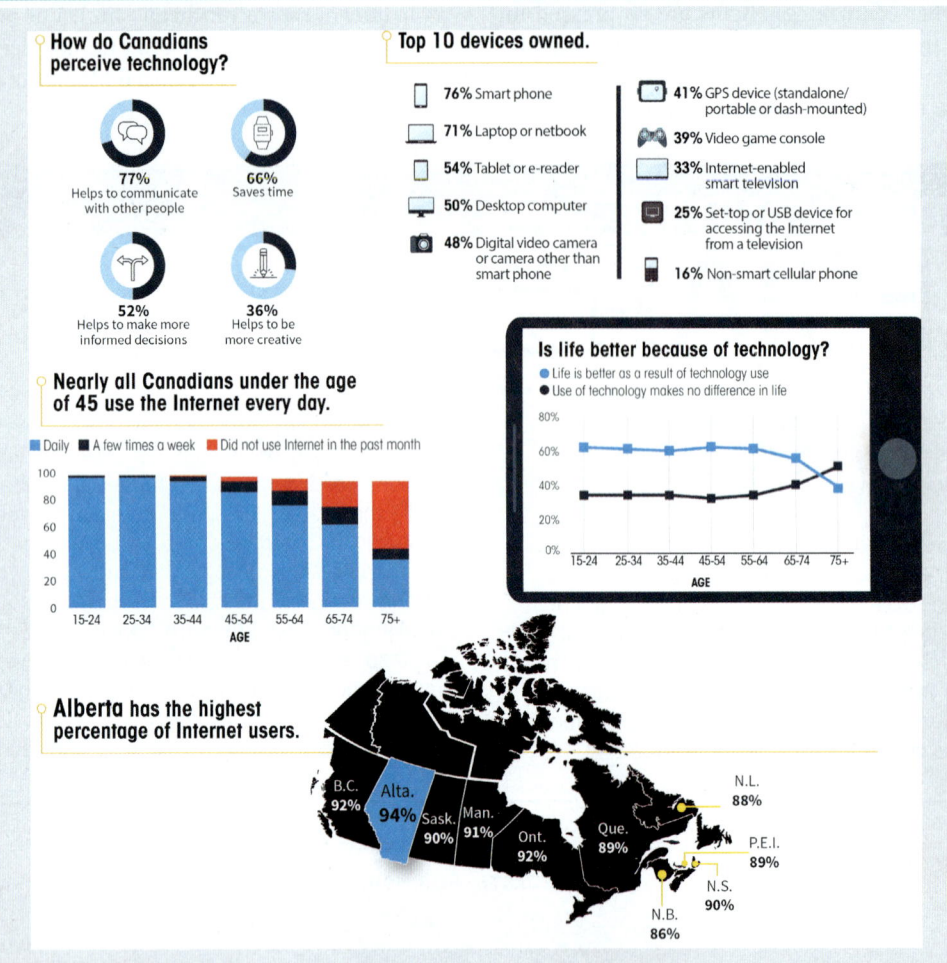

**How do Canadians perceive technology?**
- 77% Helps to communicate with other people
- 66% Saves time
- 52% Helps to make more informed decisions
- 36% Helps to be more creative

**Top 10 devices owned.**
- 76% Smart phone
- 71% Laptop or netbook
- 54% Tablet or e-reader
- 50% Desktop computer
- 48% Digital video camera or camera other than smart phone
- 41% GPS device (standalone/portable or dash-mounted)
- 39% Video game console
- 33% Internet-enabled smart television
- 25% Set-top or USB device for accessing the Internet from a television
- 16% Non-smart cellular phone

**Nearly all Canadians under the age of 45 use the Internet every day.**

**Is life better because of technology?**

**Alberta has the highest percentage of Internet users.**
- B.C. 92%
- Alta. 94%
- Sask. 90%
- Man. 91%
- Ont. 92%
- Que. 89%
- N.L. 88%
- P.E.I. 89%
- N.S. 90%
- N.B. 86%

Source: Statistics Canada. 2018. "The Internet and digital technology." https://www.statcan.gc.ca/pub/11-627-m/index-eng.htm (retrieved 10 January 2018).

---

spend 15 minutes alone in a lab. During that time they could do only one of two things: sit quietly and think or push a button that gave them a mild electric shock. Twenty-five percent of the women and 67 percent of the men were so bored sitting quietly and thinking that they chose to shock themselves for entertainment (Wilson et al., 2014). Desperate circumstances call for desperate measures.

Sean Parker, co-founder of Napster (the first Internet file-sharing program) and the first president of Facebook, says he knows why attention spans are shrinking. According to Parker, social media platforms are designed so users constantly expect to receive a reward such as a "like" or gain new knowledge such as the latest gossip about Kim Kardashian. Receiving such a reward releases a spurt of dopamine in the brain. Dopamine is a neurotransmitter widely believed to be associated with addiction. Research support the view that social media platforms are built to get people addicted to them so audiences will grow and audience members will remain logged on, thus allowing platform owners to earn more ad revenue (Smith, 2018).

One study found that British smartphone users say they look at their phones 75 times a day—but under observation the figure turned out to be more like 150 times a day, which works out to once every 6.4 waking minutes. A series of American studies found that the number of times Americans touched their smartphone screens grew from 8 billion in 2015 to 12 billion in 2017. The average number of minutes per day people spend on social media increased by 50 percent from 2012 to 2017. Most Canadians believe that smartphones and social media liberate us, and in some sense they do—but it turns out they also constrain us by becoming a compulsion (Andrew-Gee, 2018; Deloitte, 2017).

The effects of such constraint include neglect of loved ones, decreased capacity to focus, and increased risk of anxiety and depression among children and adolescents (Andrew-Gee, 2018). Here I have space to discuss just the first effect, and only briefly.

Nobody likes to be ignored, so you've likely been annoyed when someone you are trying to talk to starts texting on her smartphone, sometimes for minutes at a time. For babies and children, the consequences of such distraction are more serious than mere annoyance. Women are increasing their smartphone use while breastfeeding, breaking eye contact with their babies. That is unfortunate because research shows that eye contact between breastfeeding mothers and babies aids communication, learning, and emotional bonding.

Research also shows that many children between the ages of 4 and 18 are developing a deep sense of frustration and loss because their parents often get pulled away from them by their cellphones (Steiner-Adair and Barker, 2013). Of course, nobody wants babies and children to be deprived of necessary emotional support, which is necessary for healthy development. However, the constraints imposed by smartphones and social media are apparently often strong enough to override our thoughtful preferences.

"Cuffberry" by David Murray

### Critical Thinking Questions
- In what ways has your smartphone made you freer?
- In what ways has your smartphone constrained you?

## CONSUMERISM

In a famous study, Max Weber argued that early Protestants believed they could reduce their religious doubts and attain a state of grace if they worked diligently and lived modestly. They believed that "the care for external goods should lie on one's shoulders only 'like a light cloak, which can be thrown aside at any moment.'" However, Weber continued, "fate decreed that the cloak should become an iron cage" (Weber, 1958 [1904-05]: 181). Weber's "iron cage" remark points to a second constraining aspect of culture, already evident in the early twentieth century: consumerism. **Consumerism** is the tendency to define ourselves in terms of the goods and services we purchase.

The rationalization process, when applied to the production of goods and services, enables us to produce more efficiently, to have more of just about everything than previous generations did. However, it is consumerism that ensures that most of the goods we produce will be bought. We have lots of choices, of course. We can select from dozens of styles of running shoes, cars, toothpaste, and all the rest. We can also choose to buy items that help define us as members of a particular **subculture**, adherents of a set of distinctive values, norms, and practices within a larger culture. But, individual tastes aside, most of us have one thing in common: we tend to be good consumers. We are motivated by advertising, which is based on the accurate insight that people will tend to be regarded as cultural outcasts if they fail to conform to stylish trends. By creating those trends, advertisers push us to buy, even if doing so requires that we work more and incur large debts. That is why the "shop-till-you-drop" lifestyle of many North Americans prompted French sociologist Jean Baudrillard to remark pointedly that even what is best in North America is compulsory (Baudrillard, 1988 [1986]).

> **consumerism** The tendency to define ourselves in terms of the goods and services we purchase.
>
> **subculture** A set of distinctive values, norms, and practices within a larger culture.

Recent advances in artificial intelligence promise to boost consumerism to new heights. Amazon claims that by 2020 it will automatically be delivering products to people *before they know they want them* (Pittis, 2018). This is not just a simple matter of figuring out the rate at which your household uses toilet paper and delivering two dozen rolls of your favourite brand before you run out. Knowing Lin's pattern of behaviour on the Web—opinionated posts, product selections, news and musical preferences, and so on—Amazon will know that Lin adores Ariana Grande, that Grande is performing in Lin's city on May 24, that Lin has a boyfriend, and that his birthday is coming up that very week. Based on this information, Amazon will decide to email Lin two concert tickets for the quality of seats she has bought in the past. Returns will be free but Lin's credit card will automatically be charged if she uses the tickets. "What a good idea," Lin may very well say when she reads the email, "and how convenient that Amazon did nearly all the thinking for me!"

"And to all a good night." It's 1:30 a.m. on December 26 in Ottawa. The temperature is −9°C. Canadians dutifully line up for a Boxing Day sale that begins in five hours. Similar scenes occur across Canada, including Saskatoon and Winnipeg, where the temperature drops to −30°C.

## FROM COUNTERCULTURE TO SUBCULTURE

In concluding our discussion of culture as a constraining force, we note that consumerism is remarkably effective at taming countercultures. **Countercultures** are subversive subcultures. They oppose dominant values and seek to replace them. The hippies of the 1960s formed a counterculture and so do environmentalists today.

Countercultures rarely pose a serious threat to social stability. Most often, the system of social control, of rewards and punishments, keeps countercultures at bay. In our society, consumerism acts as a social control mechanism that normally prevents countercultures from disrupting the social order. It does that by transforming deviations from mainstream culture into means of making money and by enticing rebels to become entrepreneurs (Frank and Weiland, 1997). The development of hip-hop helps to illustrate the point (Brym, 2018e: 13–31).

Hip-hop originated in the American inner city in the 1970s. At the time, manufacturing industries were leaving for suburban or foreign locales, where land values were lower and labour was less expensive. Unemployment among black youth rose to more than 40 percent. At the same time, many middle-class black people left the inner city for the suburbs. Their migration robbed the remaining young people of successful role models. It also eroded the taxing capacity of municipal governments, leading to a decline in public services. Meanwhile, the American public elected conservative governments at the state and federal levels. They cut school and welfare budgets, thus deepening the destitution of ghetto life (Piven and Cloward, 1977: 264–361, 1993; Wilson, 1987).

With few legitimate prospects for advancement, poor black American youth in the inner city turned increasingly to crime and, in particular, to the drug trade. In the late 1970s, cocaine was expensive and demand for the drug was flat. Consequently, in the early 1980s, Colombia's Medellin drug cartel introduced a less expensive form of cocaine called "crack." Crack was inexpensive, it offered a quick and intense high, and it was highly addictive. It offered many people a temporary escape from hopelessness and soon became wildly popular in the inner city. Turf wars spread as gangs tried to outgun each other for control of the local traffic. The sale and use of crack became so widespread it corroded much of what was left of the inner city black American community (Davis, 1990).

The shocking conditions described above gave rise to a shocking musical form: hip-hop. Stridently at odds with the values and tastes of both white people and middle-class black Americans, hip-hop described and glorified the mean streets of the inner city while holding the police, the mass media, and other pillars of society in contempt. Furthermore, hip-hop tried to offend middle-class sensibilities, black and white, by using highly offensive language.

In 1988, more than a decade after its first stirrings, hip-hop reached its political high point with the release of the album *It Takes a Nation of Millions to Hold Us Back* by Chuck D and Public Enemy. In "Don't Believe the Hype," Chuck D accused the mass media of maliciously distributing lies. In "Black Steel in the Hour of Chaos," he charged the FBI and the CIA with assassinating the two great leaders of the black American community in the 1960s, Martin Luther King and Malcolm X. In "Party for Your Right to Fight," he blamed the federal government for organizing the fall of the Black Panthers, the radical black nationalist party of the 1960s. Here, it seemed, was an angry expression of subcultural revolt that could not be tamed.

However, the seduction of big money did much to mute the political force of hip-hop. As early as 1982, with the release of Grandmaster Flash and the Furious Five's "The Message," hip-hop began to win acclaim from mainstream rock music critics. With the success of Run-DMC and Public Enemy in the late 1980s, it became clear there was a big audience for hip-hop. Significantly, much of that audience was composed of white youths. As one music critic wrote, they "relished… the subversive 'otherness' that the music and its purveyors represented" (Neal, 1999: 144). Sensing the opportunity for profit, major media corporations, such as Time/Warner, Sony, CBS/Columbia, and BMG Entertainment, signed distribution deals with the small independent recording labels that had formerly been the exclusive distributors of hip-hop CDs. In 1988, *Yo! MTV Raps* debuted on MTV. The program brought hip-hop to middle America.

Most hip-hop recording artists proved they were eager to forgo political relevancy for commerce. For instance, WU-Tang Clan started a line of clothing called WU-Wear,

**countercultures** Subversive subcultures that oppose dominant values and seek to replace them.

and, with the help of major hip-hop recording artists, companies as diverse as Tommy Hilfiger, Timberland, Starter, and Versace began marketing clothing influenced by ghetto styles. Independent labels such as Phat Farm and Fubu also prospered. Puff Daddy reminded his audience in his 1999 CD, *Forever:* "nigga get money, that's simply the plan." According to *Forbes* magazine, he became one of the country's 40 richest men under 40. By 2005, having renamed himself Diddy, he had his own line of popular clothing.

The members of Run-DMC once said that they "don't want nobody's name on my behind" but those days were long past by the early 1990s. Hip-hop was no longer just a musical form but a commodity with spinoffs. Rebellion had been turned into mass consumption. Hip-hop's radicalism had given way to the lures of commerce. A counterculture had become a subculture.

Radical political currents in hip-hop still exist. For example, in 2012, Macklemore and Ryan Lewis's first hit, "Same Love," criticized homophobia in hip-hop and promoted gay rights. Their single, "Thrift Shop," which topped the *Billboard* "Hot 100" for six weeks and won a Grammy award for best rap song in 2014, is a critique of mindless consumerism. Kendrick Lamar's 2015 single, "Alright," became a rallying cry for the Black Lives Matter movement, which protests the disproportionate police violence visited on black people. Lamar won a coveted Pulitzer Prize for his work in 2018, but in terms of popularity, he is a minor current in the North American hip-hop universe. A list of the 100 wealthiest hip-hop artists ranks him 92nd. Macklemore ranks 66th ("Top 100 Richest Rappers & Hip-Hop Artists," 2018).

Radical currents seem to be more common outside North America. In Senegal, the playing of hip-hop highly critical of the government is widely believed to have helped topple the ruling party in the 2000 election. In France, North African youth living in impoverished and segregated slums use hip-hop to express their political discontent,

Kendrick Lamar

and some analysts say the genre helped mobilize youth for antigovernment rioting in 2005 (Akwagyiram, 2009). *Rais Lebled* [Mr. President], a song by Tunisian rapper El Général, became the anthem of young people participating in the democratic uprisings in Tunisia, Egypt, and elsewhere in the Arab world in 2011: "Mr. President, your people are dying/People are eating rubbish/Look at what is happening/Miseries everywhere, Mr. President/I talk with no fear/Although I know I will get only trouble/I see injustice everywhere" (Ghosh, 2011).

In North America, however, hip-hop has become for the most part an apolitical commodity that increasingly appeals to a racially heterogeneous, middle-class audience. As one of hip-hop's leading analysts and academic sympathizers writes, "the discourse of ghetto reality or 'hood authenticity' remains largely devoid of political insight or progressive intent" (Forman, 2001: 121). The fate of hip-hop is testimony to the capacity of consumerism to change countercultures into mere subcultures, thus constraining dissent and rebellion.

## READY TO STUDY?

### IN THE BOOK YOU CAN:

- Refer to the Chapter in Review section at the back of the book to have a summary of the chapter and key terms handy.
- Test your knowledge of chapter contents by answering the multiple-choice questions in the Chapter in Review section. Answers are in the appendix at the end of the book.

### ONLINE YOU CAN:

- Stay organized and efficient with MindTap—a single destination with all the course material and study aids you need to succeed.
- Flashcards are pre-populated to provide you with a jump start for review—or you can create your own.
- You can highlight text and make notes in your MindTap Reader.
- Prepare for tests with quizzes.

GO TO NELSON.COM/STUDENT TO PURCHASE THESE DIGITAL RESOURCES.

# 3 Socialization

## LEARNING OBJECTIVES:

In this chapter, you will learn to

- **LO¹** Recognize that human abilities remain undeveloped unless social interaction unleashes them.
- **LO²** Explain how one's sense of self emerges and changes as one interacts socially with others.
- **LO³** Compare change over the past century in the socializing influence of the family, schools, peer groups, and the mass media.
- **LO⁴** Appreciate that people's identities change faster, more often, and more completely than they did just a couple of decades ago.
- **LO⁵** List the factors transforming the character of childhood, adolescence, and early adulthood today.
- **LO⁶** Identify how the socialization patterns of Canadian youth have changed over the past half-century due to declining adult supervision

and guidance, increasing mass media and peer group influence, and increasing assumption of substantial adult responsibilities to the neglect of extracurricular activities.

## LO¹ SOCIAL ISOLATION AND SOCIALIZATION

One day in 1800, a 10- or 11-year-old boy walked out of the woods in southern France. He was filthy, naked, and unable to speak, and he had not been toilet trained. After being taken by the police to a local orphanage, he repeatedly tried to escape and refused to wear clothes. No parent ever claimed him. He became known as "the wild boy of Aveyron." A thorough medical examination found no major abnormalities of either a physical or a mental nature. Why, then, did the boy seem more animal than human? Because, until he walked out of the woods, he had been raised in isolation from other humans (Shattuck, 1980).

Similar horrifying reports lead to the same conclusion. Occasionally, a child is found locked in an attic or a cellar, where he or she saw another person for only short periods each day to receive food. Like the wild boy of Aveyron, such children rarely develop normally. Typically, they remain uninterested in games. They cannot form intimate social relationships with other people. They develop only the most basic language skills.

Some of these children may suffer from congenitally low intelligence. The amount and type of social contact they had before they were discovered is unknown. Some may have been abused, so their condition may not be due to social isolation alone. However, these examples do at least suggest that the ability to learn culture and become human is only a potential. To be actualized, **socialization** must unleash this potential. Socialization is the process by which people learn their culture. They do so by (1) entering into and disengaging from a succession of roles and (2) becoming aware of themselves as they interact with others. A **role** is the behaviour expected of a person occupying a particular position in society.

> **socialization** The process by which people learn their culture. They do so by (1) entering into and disengaging from a succession of roles and (2) becoming aware of themselves as they interact with others.
>
> **role** A set of behaviours expected of a person occupying a particular position in society.

Convincing evidence of the importance of socialization in unleashing human potential comes from a study conducted by René Spitz (1945, 1962). Spitz compared children who were being raised in an orphanage with children who were being raised in a nursing home attached to a women's prison. Both institutions were hygienic and provided good food and medical care. However, the children's mothers cared for the babies in the nursing home, whereas only six nurses cared for the 45 babies in the orphanage. The orphans therefore had much less contact with other people. Moreover, from their cribs, the nursing home infants could see a slice of society. They saw other babies playing and receiving care. They saw mothers, doctors, and nurses talking, cleaning, serving food, and providing medical treatment. In contrast, the caregivers in the orphanage would hang sheets from the cribs to prevent the infants from seeing the activities of the institution. Depriving the infants of social stimuli for most of the day apparently made them less demanding.

Social deprivation had other effects too. Because of the different patterns of child care just described, by the age of 9 to 12 months, the orphans were more susceptible to infections and had a higher death rate than the babies in the nursing home. By the time they were two to three years old, all of the children from the nursing home were walking and talking, compared with fewer than 8 percent of the orphans. Normal children begin to play with their own genitals by the end of their first year. Spitz found that the orphans began this sort of play only in their fourth year. He took this as a sign that they might have an impaired sexual life when they reached maturity. This outcome has been observed in rhesus monkeys raised in isolation. Spitz's natural experiment thus amounts to quite compelling evidence for the importance of childhood socialization in making us fully human. Without childhood socialization, most of our human potential remains undeveloped.

## THE CRYSTALLIZATION OF SELF-IDENTITY

The formation of a sense of self continues in adolescence (a particularly turbulent period of self-development) and, indeed, throughout life. To paint a picture of the socialization process in its entirety, I first review the main theories of how a sense of self develops during early childhood. I then discuss the operation and relative influence of society's main socializing institutions or agents of socialization: families, schools, peer groups, and the mass media. In these settings, we learn, among other things, how to control our impulses, think of ourselves as members of different groups, value certain ideals, and perform various roles. You will see that these agents do not always work hand in hand to produce happy, well-adjusted adults. They often give mixed messages, teaching children and adolescents different and even contradictory lessons. You will also see that although recent developments give us more freedom to decide who we are, this often makes socialization more disorienting than it used to be.

Next, I examine how decreasing supervision and guidance by adult family members, increasing assumption of adult responsibilities by youths, and declining participation in extracurricular activities are changing the nature of childhood and adolescence today. Some analysts even say that childhood and adolescence are vanishing before our eyes. Finally, I examine conflicting interpretations of the so-called Millennial generation, born between the early 1980s and early 2000s. These analyses lead to the conclusion that the development of self-identity is often a difficult and stressful process—and is becoming more so.

The contours of the self are formed during childhood. I therefore begin by discussing the most important social-scientific theories of how the self originates in the first years of life.

> In the 1960s, researchers Harry and Margaret Harlow placed baby rhesus monkeys in various conditions of isolation to study the animals' reactions. Among other things, they discovered that baby monkeys raised with an artificial mother made of wire mesh, a wooden head, and the nipple of a feeding tube for a breast were later unable to interact normally with other monkeys. However, when the artificial mother was covered with soft terry cloth, the infant monkeys clung to it for comfort and later exhibited less emotional distress. Infant monkeys preferred the cloth mother even when it had less milk than the wire mother. The Harlows concluded that emotional development requires affectionate cradling (Suomi and Leroy, 1982).

# LO² THE SYMBOLIC-INTERACTIONIST FOUNDATIONS OF CHILDHOOD

## THE LOOKING-GLASS SELF

Socialization begins soon after birth. Infants cry out, driven by elemental needs, and are gratified by food, a clean diaper, comfort, and affection. Because their needs are typically satisfied immediately, they do not at first seem able to distinguish themselves from their main caregivers, usually their mothers. However, they soon begin developing a self-image or sense of **self**—a set of ideas and attitudes about who they are as independent beings. How does this happen? And why does the baby's sense of self continue to change as the baby ages and eventually dies an old man?

> **self** A set of ideas and attitudes about who one is as an independent being.

For millennia, the common view of socialization likened people to acorns, in the sense that both acorns and people have growth potential and develop in stages set by their inherent characteristics. A crude biological version of that view persists to this day (see Theories in Dispute, Sociology, Biology, and the Interaction between Genes and Environment). It holds that our biological

## THEORIES IN DISPUTE

### Sociology, Biology, and the Interaction between Genes and Environment

Many sociologists are inclined to reject the notion that biology plays more than a potentiating or limiting role in human development. They readily admit that people are biologically programmed to grow arms. They also acknowledge that people can flap their arms as vigorously as they like but still won't be able to fly on their own. However, many sociologists are reluctant to entertain the idea that specific patterns of behaviour derive from people's biological makeup. Instead, sociologists focus on socialization—the way families, schools, peer groups, and the mass media influence how we think of ourselves and how we act.

The trouble is there are not many biologists who think as narrowly as some sociologists imagine. For example, few scholars in the life sciences contend that a one-to-one relationship exists between specific genes and certain patterns of behaviour, with particular genes making some people aggressive, for instance. Instead, modern biology recognizes that there is a strong interaction between genes and environment, with environmental factors (including sociological forces) able to modify genes, and genes able to modify the effect of social forces on behaviour. That is why a variant of the MAOA gene does not by itself lead to an antisocial psychiatric disorder in young adulthood—but people with that gene variant who were badly mistreated before the age of five are significantly more likely to develop the disorder (Caspi et al., 2002). Here then is a fruitful field for collaboration between biologists and sociologists, an area of inquiry that many sociologists have ignored because they haven't been sufficiently open to appreciating the gene–society interaction (Shanahan, Bauldry, and Freeman, 2010).

Studies of gene–society interactions face big challenges, ranging from the fact that behaviours may be influenced by entire networks of genes acting in concert to the fact that people can't be used for experimental genetic-sociological research. We know that some genes can be turned on and off, and change the rate at which they make proteins, because of change in a person's stress level, social status, and connectedness to other people. That may be enough to convince more sociologists that no inherent conflict exists between biological and sociological theories of human development, and that much room exists for cross-disciplinary learning.

#### Critical Thinking Questions

- Can you draw causal diagrams showing the relationship between genes and society according to (a) the crude biological theory, (b) the crude sociological theory, and (c) the gene–society interaction theory?
- Why can't people be used for experimental genetic-sociological research?

**looking-glass self** Cooley's term for the way our sense of self depends largely on how we see ourselves evaluated by others.

**I** According to Mead, the subjective and impulsive aspect of the self that is present from birth.

**me** According to Mead, the objective component of the self that emerges as people communicate symbolically and learn to take the role of the other.

**significant others** The people who play important roles in the early socialization experiences of children.

makeup ensures that babies suckle, toddlers walk, adolescents have sex, adults start forgetting things, and elderly people pass away. Presumably, our sense of who we are changes in lockstep with these and other biologically determined milestones.

In contrast, the symbolic interactionist model of socialization thinks of people as the imaginative, two-legged creatures that you and I deal with every day. From the symbolic interactionist point of view, socialization is a creative process that takes place in human groups. To be sure, inherent biological (and psychological) traits set broad potentials and limits to what people can become. The broader society and culture define the general outlines of people's beliefs, symbols, values, and roles. However, as symbolic interactionists emphasize, people are continually socialized in face-to-face settings where they interact with others. In those settings they imaginatively interpret, accept, and sometimes reject the opportunities and demands of socialization in ways that suit them.

At the beginning of the twentieth century, American sociologist Charles Horton Cooley set symbolic interactionist thinking into motion. He proposed that our sense of self depends largely on how we see ourselves evaluated by others; our self is, he insisted, a **looking-glass self** (Cooley, 1902: 152).

Cooley observed that when we interact with others, they react to us with words and gestures. This allows us to imagine how we appear to them. We then judge how others evaluate us. Finally, from these judgments we develop a self-concept or a set of feelings and ideas about who we are. Said differently, our feelings about who we are depend largely on how we see ourselves judged by others. Just as we see our physical body reflected in a mirror, so we see our social selves reflected in people's reactions to us. Thus, when teachers evaluate students negatively, students may develop a negative self-image that causes them to do poorly in school. Research suggests that poor performance may have as much to do with teachers' negative evaluations as with students' innate abilities (Weinstein, Gregory, and Strambler, 2004; Chapter 11, Education). Here, succinctly put, are the hallmarks of symbolic interactionism—the idea that in the course of face-to-face communication, people engage in a creative process of attaching meaning to things.

# THE "I" AND THE "ME"

George Herbert Mead (1934) took up and developed Cooley's idea of the looking-glass self. Mead noted that a subjective and impulsive aspect of the self is present from birth. Mead called it the **"I."** He also recognized that a storehouse of culturally approved standards emerges as part of the self during social interaction. Mead called this objective social component of the self the "**me**." He drew attention to the unique human capacity to "take the role of the other" as the source of the me.

Mead understood that human communication involves seeing yourself from other people's points of view. If you're eating lunch with a friend, you need to interpret whether her sudden grimace means her food tastes awful, you said something offensive, or something else entirely. Of course, you can ask. But you often find the answer to such questions by using your imagination to take the other person's point of view for a moment and see yourself as she sees you. In other words, you see yourself objectively as a me to interpret your friend's communicative act. All human communication depends on being able to take the role of the other, wrote Mead. Thus, one's sense of self emerges from people using symbols, such as words and gestures, to communicate. It follows that the me is not present from birth. It emerges only gradually during social interaction (see Sociology and the Media, I, Me, and *Revenge Body*).

## Stages of Development

Mead saw the self as developing in four stages of role-taking:

1. At first, children learn to use language and other symbols by imitating important people in their lives, such as their mother and father. Mead called such people **significant others.** This stage lasts until the age of about two.

2. Second, until they reach the age of about six, children pretend to be other people. That is, they use their imaginations to role-play in games, such as "house," "school," and "doctor."

3. Third, around the time they reach the age of seven, children learn to play complex games that require them to take the role of several other people simultaneously. In baseball, for example, the infielders have to be aware of the expectations of everyone in the infield. A shortstop may catch a line drive. If she wants to make a double play, she must almost instantly be aware that a runner is trying to reach

# SOCIOLOGY AND THE MEDIA

## I, Me, and *Revenge Body*

It began with *Extreme Makeover* in 2002. In a typical episode, a team comprising a plastic surgeon, a personal trainer, a hairdresser, and a wardrobe consultant refashioned a woman's exterior. The cameras recorded the woman's doubts and suffering, but also her resilience and determination. In the end, when she saw the finished product, her self-esteem skyrocketed and her family and friends became ecstatic over her Cinderella transformation.

As of 2018, Wikipedia listed 80 English-language "makeover" and "lifestyle change" reality TV shows that offered fast solutions to problems of housing, career, intimate relations, wardrobe, and so on. Local variants of many of these shows were available for Canadian audiences. The latest was Khloe Kardashian's *Revenge Body*. The show featured young women who had been dumped by their husbands. After spending countless hours at the gym, dieting rigorously, allowing talented hairdressers and makeup artists to beautify them, scoring a gorgeous new wardrobe, and posting umpteen selfies on Facebook, they finally got what they wanted: a body so alluring that exes who saw the photos broke down crying and wanted desperately to rekindle the romance.

Of course, almost everyone wants to be attractive and have a good job, a long-lasting intimate relationship with another adult, and material comforts. However, makeover reality TV shows like *Revenge Body* teach viewers that all we need to be happy is the achievement of commercially manufactured ideas of what constitutes the perfect body, face, career, partner, house, and wardrobe. Said differently, their common message is that the surest path to self-awareness and self-fulfillment involves accepting images generated by others as ideals. To be happy, all you have to do is please other people, including the lout who dumped you because he was unable to appreciate your intelligence, compassion, and good humour.

Mead would say that makeover reality TV shows make it seem as if all worthwhile self-development comes from the "me"—the objectification supplied, in this case, largely by marketing experts—not from thoughtful exploration of the creative "I." The tough questions posed by ancient Greek philosophy—Who am I? What do I need to make me happy?—have no relevance in this context. Arguably, shows like *Revenge Body* turn answers to these difficult questions into instant and, for most people, unrealistic solutions focusing on the commercial images others provide. They teach us little about how to know ourselves and thus how to live happily.

*Revenge Body*, Khloe Kardashian's reality TV show, is based on the idea that happiness comes from having the perfect body, face, house, partner, career, and so on—as defined by advertisers. Do realistic alternatives to this vision exist or does the show make a valid point?

### Critical Thinking Questions
- At what point(s) in the life cycle—childhood, adolescence, early adulthood, mature adulthood, retirement—are people most influenced by commercially generated ideals?
- Why do you think such influence is strongest at a particular point (or particular points) in the life cycle?

**generalized other** According to Mead, a person's image of cultural standards and how they apply to him or her.

second base and that the person playing second base expects her to throw there. If she hesitates, she probably cannot execute the double play.

4. Once a child can think in this complex way, he or she can begin the fourth stage in the development of the self, which involves taking the role of what Mead called the **generalized other**. Years of experience may teach an individual that other people, employing the cultural standards of their society, usually regard him or her as funny or temperamental or intelligent. A person's image of these cultural standards and how they are applied to him or her is what Mead meant by the generalized other.

Since Mead, psychologists interested in the problem of childhood socialization have analyzed how the style, complexity, and abstractness of thinking (cognitive skills) develop in distinct stages from infancy to the late teenage years (Piaget and Inhelder, 1969). Others have analyzed how the ability to think morally develops in stages (Kohlberg, 1981). However, from a sociological point of view, it is important to emphasize that the development of cognitive and moral skills is more than just the unfolding of a person's innate characteristics. As you will now see, the structure of a person's society and his or her position in it also influences socialization because they influence the kinds of people with whom one is most likely to interact.

## GENDER DIFFERENCES

One of the best-known examples of how social position affects socialization comes from the research of Carol Gilligan. Gilligan showed that sociological factors help explain differences in the sense of self that boys and girls usually develop. That is because parents and teachers tend to pass on different cultural standards to each gender. Such adult authorities usually define the ideal woman as eager to please and therefore not assertive. Most girls learn this lesson as they mature. The fact that girls usually encounter more male and fewer female teachers and other authority figures as they grow up reinforces the lesson. Consequently, much research shows that girls tend to develop lower self-esteem than boys do, although it seems doubtful that teenage girls in general experience the decline in self-esteem that Gilligan detected in her early work (Kling et al., 1999). Gilligan's most influential work dates from the 1990s (Brown and Gilligan, 1992). To a degree, gender socialization has changed since then. However, as you will learn later in this chapter, change has been more modest than you might first think.

## CIVILIZATION DIFFERENCES

In a like manner, sociological factors help explain the development of different style of thinking in different civilizations (Cole, 1995; Vygotsky, 1987). Consider, for example, the contrast between ancient China and ancient Greece.

In part because of complex irrigation needs, the rice agriculture of ancient southern China required substantial cooperation among neighbours. It had to be centrally organized in an elaborate hierarchy within a large state. Harmony and social order were therefore central to ancient Chinese life. Ancient Chinese thinking, in turn, tended to stress the importance of mutual social obligation and consensus rather than debate. Ancient Chinese philosophy focused on the way in which whole systems, not analytical categories, cause processes and events.

In contrast, the hills and seashores of ancient Greece were suited to small-scale herding and fishing. As a result, ancient Greece was less socially complex than ancient China was. It was more politically decentralized. It gave its citizens more personal freedom. As a result, philosophies tended to be analytical, which means, among other things, that processes and events were viewed as the result of discrete causes rather than whole systems. Markedly different civilizations grew up on these different cognitive foundations. Ways of thinking depended less on people's innate characteristics than on the structure of society (Nisbett et al., 2001).

Clearly, society plays a major role in shaping the way we think and the way we think of ourselves (refer back to the Sociology and the Media feature in this chapter). The early symbolic interactionists discovered the fundamental social process by which the self develops, and later researchers emphasized the gender, civilizational, and other social bases of diverse socialization patterns.

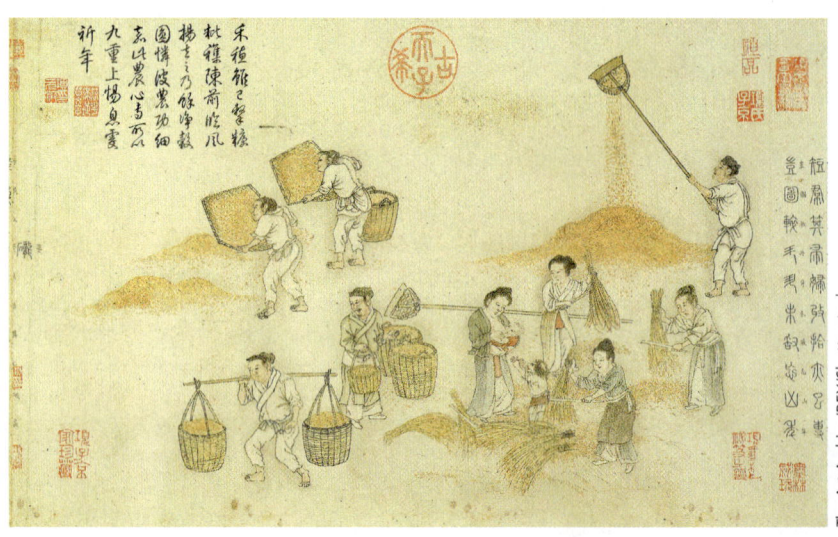

## LO³ FUNCTION, CONFLICT, SYMBOLIC INTERACTION, AND GENDER: HOW AGENTS OF SOCIALIZATION WORK

Early work on childhood socialization leaves two key questions unanswered. First, does socialization help to maintain social order or does it give rise to conflict that has the potential to change society? Second, if society socializes people, how much freedom do individuals have to choose, modify, or even reject these influences? Functionalists, conflict theorists, symbolic interactionists, and feminists answer these key questions differently:

- Functionalists emphasize how socialization helps to maintain orderly social relations. They also play down the freedom of choice that individuals enjoy in the socialization process.
- Conflict and feminist theorists typically stress the discord based on class, gender, and other divisions that is inherent in socialization and that sometimes causes social change.
- Symbolic interactionists highlight the creativity of individuals in attaching meaning to their social surroundings. They focus on the many ways in which we often step outside of, and modify, the values and roles that authorities try to teach us.

Whether it maintains order or engenders conflict, shapes us or allows us to shape it, the socialization process operates through a variety of social institutions, including families, schools, peer groups, and, in modern times, the mass media. Let us now consider how these various "agents of socialization" work. As we do so, please take careful note of the functionalist, conflict, symbolic-interactionist, and feminist interpretations embedded in our discussion.

### FAMILY FUNCTIONS

Few sociologists would disagree with the functionalist claim that the family is the most important agent of **primary socialization**, the process of mastering the basic skills required to operate in society during childhood. After all, the family is well suited to providing the kind of careful, intimate attention required for primary socialization. It is a small group, its members are in frequent face-to-face contact, and most parents love their children and are therefore highly motivated to care for them. These characteristics make most families ideal for teaching small children everything from language to their place in the world.

Note, however, that the socialization function of the family was more pronounced a century ago, partly because adult family members were more readily available for child care and supervision than they are today. As industry grew across Canada, families left farming for city work in factories and offices. Many women had to work outside the home for a wage to maintain an adequate standard of living for their families. Fathers spent less time working with children on the family farm. Fathers partly compensated by spending somewhat more time caring for their children. However, because divorce rates have increased and many fathers have less contact with their children after divorce, children probably see less of their fathers on average now than they did a century ago.

In some countries, such as Sweden and France, the creation of state-funded child-care facilities compensated for these developments by helping teach, supervise, and discipline children (see Chapter 9, Families). In Canada, however, child care—and therefore childhood socialization—became a big social problem, leading in some cases to child neglect and abuse. Families are still the most important agent of primary socialization, but they are less important than they once were, and they sometimes function poorly.

> **primary socialization** The process of acquiring the basic skills needed to function in society during childhood. Primary socialization usually takes place in the family.

CHAPTER 3 Socialization  63

The family is still an important agent of socialization, although its importance has declined since the nineteenth century.

## SCHOOL FUNCTIONS

For children over the age of five, the child-care problem was resolved partly by the growth of the public school system, which became increasingly responsible for **secondary socialization**, or socialization outside the family after childhood. In addition, industry needed better-trained and better-educated employees. Therefore, by the early twentieth century, every province had passed laws prescribing the ages between which a child had to attend school. Today, about 87 percent of Canadians between the ages of 25 and 64 have completed high school, 64 percent have postsecondary qualifications, and 26 percent have a university degree (Statistics Canada, 2016d). This makes Canadians among the most highly educated people in the world.

## SCHOOL CONFLICTS

Instructing students in academic and vocational subjects is the school's manifest function. One of its latent functions is to teach what sociologists call the **hidden curriculum**. The hidden curriculum instructs students in what will be expected of them in the larger society once they graduate—it teaches them to be conventionally "good citizens." Most parents approve. According to one survey conducted in several highly industrialized countries, the capacity of schools to socialize students is more important to the public than all academic subjects except math (Galper, 1998).

**secondary socialization** Socialization outside the family after childhood.

**hidden curriculum** Teaches students what will be expected of them as conventionally good citizens once they leave school.

**Thomas theorem** "Situations we define as real become real in their consequences."

**self-fulfilling prophecy** An expectation that helps bring about what it predicts.

What is the content of the hidden curriculum? In the family, children tend to be evaluated on the basis of personal and emotional criteria. As students, however, they are led to believe that they are evaluated solely on the basis of their performance on impersonal, standardized tests. They are told that similar criteria will be used to evaluate them in the work world. The lesson is, of course, only partly true. As you will see in Chapter 7 (Race and Ethnicity), Chapter 8 (Sexualities and Genders), and Chapter 11 (Education), it is not just performance but also class, gender, sexual orientation, and racial criteria that help to determine success in school and in the work world. But the accuracy of the lesson is not the issue here. The important point is that the hidden curriculum does its job if it convinces students that they are judged on the basis of performance alone. Similarly, a successful hidden curriculum teaches students punctuality, respect for authority, the importance of competition in leading to excellent performance, and other conformist behaviours and beliefs that are expected of good citizens, conventionally defined.

The idea of the hidden curriculum was first proposed by conflict theorists, who, you will recall, see an ongoing struggle between privileged and disadvantaged groups whenever they probe beneath the surface of social life (Willis, 1984). Their research on socialization in schools highlights the way many students—especially those from working-class and racial-minority families—struggle against the hidden curriculum.

Conflict theorists acknowledge that schools teach many working-class and racial-minority students to act like conventional good citizens. However, they also note that a disproportionately large number of such students reject the hidden curriculum because their experience and that of their friends, peers, and family members make them skeptical about the ability of school to open good job opportunities for them. As a result, they rebel against the authority of the school. Expected to be polite and studious, they openly violate rules and neglect their work. Consequently, they do poorly in school and eventually enter the work world near the bottom of the socioeconomic hierarchy. Paradoxically, the rebellion of some working-class and racial-minority students against the hidden curriculum typically helps to sustain the overall structure of society, with all of its privileges and disadvantages.

## SYMBOLIC INTERACTIONISM AND THE SELF-FULFILLING PROPHECY

Early in the twentieth century, symbolic interactionists proposed the **Thomas theorem**, which holds that "situations we define as real become real in their consequences" (Thomas, 1966 [1931]: 301). They also developed the closely related idea of the **self-fulfilling prophecy**, an expectation that helps to cause what it predicts. Our analysis of the hidden curriculum suggests that the expectations of working-class and racial-minority students often act as self-fulfilling prophecies. Expecting to achieve little if they play by the rules, they reject the rules and so achieve little.

The self-fulfilling prophecy does not operate only among students. Teachers, too, develop expectations that help to cause what they predict. In one famous study, two researchers informed the teachers in a primary school that they were going to administer a special test to the pupils to predict intellectual "blooming." In fact, the test was just a standard IQ test. After the test, they told teachers which students they could expect to become high achievers and which students they could expect to become low achievers. In fact, the researchers assigned pupils to the two groups at random. At the end of the year, the researchers repeated the IQ test. They found that the students singled out as high achievers scored significantly higher than those singled out as low achievers. Because the only difference between the two groups of students was that teachers expected one group to do well and the other to do poorly, the researchers concluded that teachers' expectations alone influenced students' performance (Rosenthal and Jacobson, 1968).

In a more recent Canadian study, 21 teachers were asked to review fictitious student records of 24 Grade 7 students and decide what kind of class each should attend in Grade 8: supplemental (remedial), regular, or rapid advance. The records included information on the student's grades, background, and academic history from Grades 4 to 7. Eight students were identified as Indigenous, eight as English-as-a-second-language (ESL) students, and eight as neither. In each of these three categories, students were matched in terms of achievement. For example, two students in each category were identified as low achievers, four as middle achievers, and two as high achievers.

One teacher paid attention only to students' grades. Consequently, she placed two Indigenous students, two ESL students, and two other students in the remedial class. She displayed no bias. However, eight other teachers placed at least one student in the remedial class. In seven of the eight cases, the student was Indigenous or ESL, indicating how biased expectations can restrict students' learning opportunities (Riley and Ungerleider, 2012: 330).

The clear implication of this research is that if a teacher believes that poor or minority-group children are likely to do poorly in school, chances are they will. That is because students who are members of groups that are widely expected to perform poorly are channelled into low-performance classes and/or internalize low social expectations. They may feel anxious about their performance, and anxiety lowers their performance level. After half a century of research and growing awareness of the effects of the self-fulfilling prophecy in education, it continues to operate among Indigenous Canadian and other racial-minority students (López, 2017).

## PEER GROUPS

Like schools, **peer groups** are agents of socialization whose importance grew in the twentieth century. Peer groups consist of individuals who are not necessarily friends but who are about the same age and of similar status. (**Status** refers to a recognized social position an individual can occupy.) Peer groups help children and adolescents to separate from their families and develop independent sources of identity. They particularly influence such lifestyle issues as appearance, social activities, and dating. In fact, from middle childhood through adolescence, the peer group is often the dominant socializing agent.

As you probably have learned from your own experience, conflict often exists between the values promoted by parents and those promoted by the adolescent peer group. Issues such as tobacco, drug, and alcohol use; hair and dress styles; political views; musical taste; and curfew times are likely to become points of conflict between the generations. About 4 percent of Canadians between the ages of 12 and 17 smoke cigarettes daily or occasionally and have five or more drinks per occasion at least 12 times a year (Statistics Canada, 2017b; Figure 3.1).

Adolescent peer groups are controlled by youth, and through them, young people begin to develop their

> **peer groups** A person's peer group comprises people who are about the same age and of similar status as that person. The peer group acts as an agent of socialization.
>
> **status** A recognized social position that an individual can occupy.

**FIGURE 3.1 Smoking, Heavy Drinking, and Perceived Life Stress, Canadians, 12–17 Years Old**

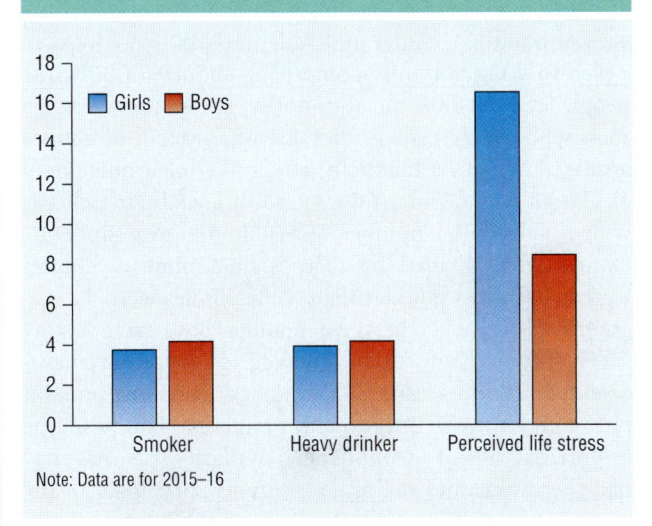

Note: Data are for 2015–16

Source: Statistics Canada. 2017b. Canadian health characteristics, two-year period estimates, by age group and sex, Canada, provinces, territories and health regions. http://www5.statcan.gc.ca/cansim/a47 (retrieved 17 January 2017).

**gender roles** The behaviours associated with widely shared expectations about how males and females are supposed to act.

own identities. They do this by rejecting some parental values, experimenting with new elements of culture, and engaging in various forms of rebellious behaviour. Such rejection is typically a group phenomenon, not just a matter of individual choice. Thus, one Canadian survey found that 12- and 13-year-old Canadians who identified themselves as belonging to a group that did "risky" things were up to seven times more likely than others were to report smoking, disorderly conduct, skipping school at least once, and attaching low importance to marks. They were also much more likely to report at least three instances of stealing and fighting. Of 12- and 13-year-olds who smoked, 84 percent reported having three or more friends who also smoked, while only 26 percent of their nonsmoking counterparts claimed that three or more of their friends smoked. Although parents' smoking behaviour—especially that of mothers—was linked to a youth's decision to smoke, the influence of peers was far greater (Statistics Canada, 1999).

I don't want to overstate the significance of adolescent–parent conflict. For one thing, the conflict is usually temporary. Once adolescents mature, the family usually exerts a more enduring influence on many important issues. Research shows that, on average, families have more influence than peer groups do over the educational aspirations and the political, social, and religious preferences of adolescents and university students (Bibby, 2001: 55).

A second reason one shouldn't exaggerate the extent of adolescent–parent discord is that peer groups are not just sources of conflict. They also help integrate young people into the larger society. A study of preadolescent children in a small North American city illustrates the point well. Over eight years, two sociologists conducted in-depth interviews at schools with children between the ages of 8 and 11 (Adler and Adler, 1998). They lived in a well-to-do community comprising about 80 000 white people and 10 000 racial-minority group members. In each school they visited, they found a system of cliques arranged in a strict hierarchy, much like the arrangement of classes and racial groups in adult society. In schools with a substantial number of visible-minority students, cliques were divided by race. Visible-minority cliques were usually less popular than white cliques were.

In all schools, the most popular boys were highly successful in competitive and aggressive achievement-oriented activities, especially athletics. The most popular girls came from well-to-do and permissive families. One important basis of the students' popularity was that they had the means and the opportunity to participate in the most interesting social activities, ranging from skiing to late-night parties. Physical attractiveness was also an important basis of girls' popularity.

Elementary school peer groups thus prepared these youngsters for the class and racial inequalities of the adult world and the gender-specific criteria that would often be used to evaluate them as adults, such as competitiveness in the case of boys and attractiveness in the case of girls. (For more on gender socialization, see the discussion of the mass media in the next section and in Chapter 8, Sexualities and Genders.) What we learn from this research is that peer groups function not only to help adolescents form an independent identity by separating them from their families, but also to teach them how to adapt to the ways of the larger society.

## THE MASS MEDIA

Like the school and the peer group, the mass media became increasingly important socializing agents in the twentieth and twenty-first centuries. In fact, we spend more hours per week interacting with the mass media than we do sleeping, working, or going to school. On average, Canadians use the Internet, TV, radio and newspapers 82.5 hours per week. Assuming adults sleep on average 7 hours per day, usage of these media amounts to 69 percent of waking time, with Internet usage alone accounting for nearly 31 percent of waking time (Young, 2016: 5, 8).

The mass media constitute such an influential socializing agent today that I devote Chapter 13 (Mass Media and Mass Communication) to the subject. Here, I accomplish two tasks to introduce you to the topic. First, I describe the reach of television and the Internet, the two mass media that consume most of our time. Second, I illustrate the impact of the mass media by discussing how they help to teach people **gender roles** or the behaviours associated with widely shared expectations about how males and females are supposed to act.

The mass media include television, the Internet, radio, movies, videos, CDs, newspapers, magazines, and books. Television reaches more Canadians than any other mass medium does—98 percent of adults. Watching more hours of television is associated with having relatively few years of formal education and being more than 49 years old, among other factors (Television Bureau of Canada, 2015: 172, 174, 178).

In terms of reach, the Internet is catching up fast. In fact, in Figure 3.2, it is literally off the chart. The Internet has not yet achieved the reach of television because many elderly Canadians do not use it, but on average Canadians spend more time using the Internet than any other mass medium. (In contrast, the reach and usage of radio and newspapers are declining over time; see Figure 3.2.)

Worldwide, the number of Internet users jumped from a mere 40 million in 1996 to 3.9 billion in 2017, nearly 52 percent of the world's population of all ages (Internet World Stats, 2012; 2017). The most startling gains in

## FIGURE 3.2 Media Usage, Canada, 2001 and 2016: Reach by Time

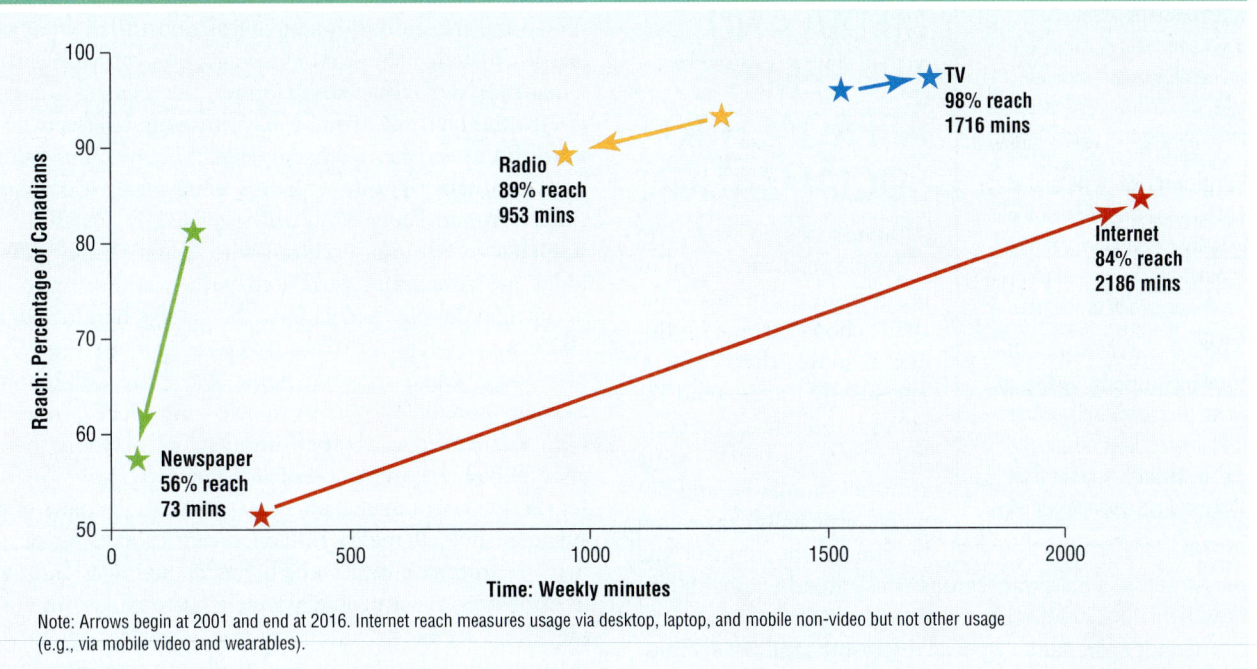

- Newspaper: 56% reach, 73 mins
- Radio: 89% reach, 953 mins
- TV: 98% reach, 1716 mins
- Internet: 84% reach, 2186 mins

Note: Arrows begin at 2001 and end at 2016. Internet reach measures usage via desktop, laptop, and mobile non-video but not other usage (e.g., via mobile video and wearables).

Source: IAB Canada, "CMUST 2016 Executive Summary," Rob Young, December 2016. https://iabcanada.com/research/cmust/ (retrieved 13 January 2018). Reproduced by permission.

Internet use occur particularly among young people and those with more years of formal education. For example, Canadians between the ages of 18 and 24 spend about three times more time on the Internet than do Canadians over the age of 49. Much of this time is spent using Netflix and social media, including Facebook, Twitter, Instagram, Snapchat, and so on. Seventy-five percent of Canadians between the ages of 18 and 34 have a Facebook profile, and 60 percent of them visit Facebook more than once a day (Forum Research Inc., 2015; Figure 3.3).

## FIGURE 3.3 Penetration of Leading Social Networks in Canada

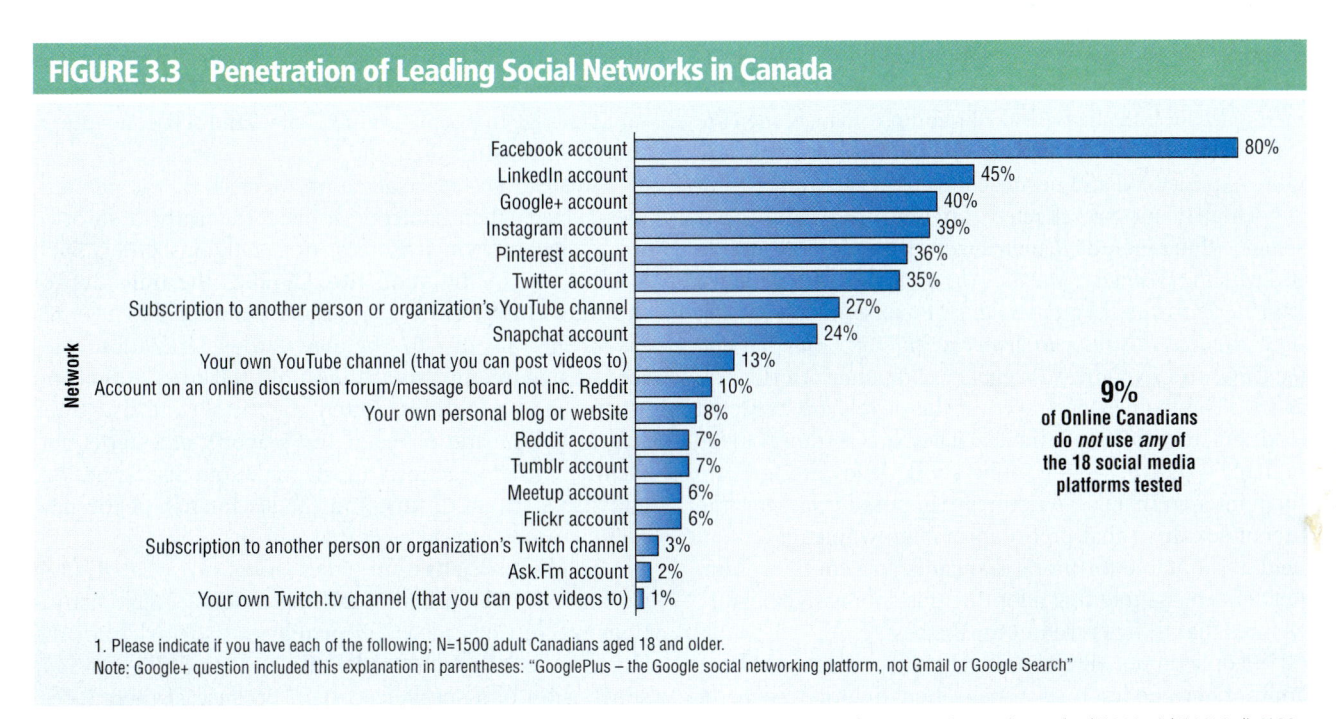

| Network | % |
|---|---|
| Facebook account | 80% |
| LinkedIn account | 45% |
| Google+ account | 40% |
| Instagram account | 39% |
| Pinterest account | 36% |
| Twitter account | 35% |
| Subscription to another person or organization's YouTube channel | 27% |
| Snapchat account | 24% |
| Your own YouTube channel (that you can post videos to) | 13% |
| Account on an online discussion forum/message board not inc. Reddit | 10% |
| Your own personal blog or website | 8% |
| Reddit account | 7% |
| Tumblr account | 7% |
| Meetup account | 6% |
| Flickr account | 6% |
| Subscription to another person or organization's Twitch channel | 3% |
| Ask.Fm account | 2% |
| Your own Twitch.tv channel (that you can post videos to) | 1% |

**9%** of Online Canadians do *not* use *any* of the 18 social media platforms tested

1. Please indicate if you have each of the following; N=1500 adult Canadians aged 18 and older.
Note: Google+ question included this explanation in parentheses: "GooglePlus – the Google social networking platform, not Gmail or Google Search"

Source: Forum Research Inc. 2015. "Instagram tops in user satisfaction." Retrieved July 6, 2015 (http://poll.forumresearch.com/data/Federal%20Social%20Media%20News%20Release%20%282015%2001%2006%29%

**resocialization** What occurs when powerful socializing agents deliberately cause rapid change in a person's values, roles, and self-conception, sometimes against that person's will.

**initiation rite** A ritual that signifies the transition of the individual from one group to another and helps to ensure his or her loyalty to the new group.

**total institutions** Settings in which people are isolated from the larger society and under the strict control and constant supervision of a specialized staff.

# THE MASS MEDIA AND THE FEMINIST APPROACH TO SOCIALIZATION

Although people are free to choose socialization influences from the mass media, they choose some influences more than others. Specifically, they tend to choose influences that are more pervasive, fit existing cultural standards, and are made especially appealing by those who control the mass media. This point can be illustrated by considering how feminist sociologists analyze gender roles.

Gender roles are of special interest to feminist sociologists, who claim that people are not born knowing how to express masculinity and femininity in conventional ways. Instead, say feminist sociologists, people *learn* gender roles, in part through the mass media.

The learning of gender roles through the mass media begins when small children see that only a kiss from Prince Charming will save Snow White from eternal sleep. This is an early lesson about who can expect to be passive and who potent. The lesson continues in magazines, romance novels, television, advertisements, music, and the Internet. For example, a central theme in Harlequin romance novels (the world's top sellers in this genre) is the transformation of women's bodies into objects for men's pleasure. In the typical Harlequin romance, men are expected to be the sexual aggressors. They are typically more experienced and promiscuous than the women.

These themes are reflected in a listing of Harlequin bestsellers, which include *Reunited with Her Surgeon Prince; In Bed with the Wrangler; Mending the Doctor's Heart; Reunited with Her Parisian Surgeon; Soldier's Promise; Greek Tycoon; Inexperienced Mistress; To Tempt a Stallion; Seduction and the CEO;* and *Executive's Pregnancy Ultimatum* (Harlequin, 2018). The women portrayed in the novels are expected to desire love before intimacy. They are assumed to be sexually passive, giving only subtle cues to indicate their interest in male overtures. Supposedly lacking the urgent sex drive that preoccupies men, women are often held accountable for moral standards and contraception. Readers are assured that adopting this submissive posture ensures that things turn out for the best.

People do not always passively accept messages about appropriate gender roles. They often interpret them in unique ways and sometimes resist them. For the most part, however, they try to develop skills that will help them perform gender roles in a conventional way. Of course, conventions change. What children learn about femininity and masculinity today is less sexist than what they learned just a generation or two ago. (As you will learn in Chapter 8, Sexualities and Gender, this change is largely due to the fact that women have become relatively more powerful in the past 50 or 60 years and have increasingly asserted their right to equality with men.) Comparing *Cinderella* and *Snow White* with *Tangled*, for example, we immediately see that children who watch Disney movies today are sometimes presented with more assertive and heroic female role models than the passive heroines of the 1930s and 1940s. Yet we must not exaggerate the degree of change. *Cinderella* and *Snow White* are still popular movies. Moreover, for every *Tangled* and *Frozen*, there is a *Little Mermaid*, a movie that simply modernizes old themes about female passivity and male conquest.

As the learning of gender roles through the mass media suggests, not all media influences are created equal. We may be free to choose which media messages influence us. However, most people are inclined to choose the messages that are most widespread, most closely aligned with existing cultural standards, and made most enticing by the mass media. As feminist sociologists remind us, in the case of gender roles, these messages support conventional expectations about how males and females are supposed to act.

# RESOCIALIZATION AND TOTAL INSTITUTIONS

In concluding our discussion of socialization agents, I must underline the importance of resocialization in the lifelong process of social learning. **Resocialization** takes place when powerful socializing agents deliberately cause rapid change in people's values, roles, and self-conception, sometimes against their will.

You can see resocialization at work in the ceremonies staged when someone joins a fraternity, a sorority, the Canadian Armed Forces, or a religious order. Such a ceremony, or **initiation rite**, signifies the transition of the individual from one group to another and ensures his or her loyalty to the new group. Initiation rites require new recruits to abandon old self-perceptions and assume new identities. Often the rites comprise three stages: (1) separation from the person's old status and identity (ritual rejection); (2) degradation, disorientation, and stress (ritual death); and (3) acceptance of the new group culture and status (ritual rebirth).

Much resocialization takes place in what Erving Goffman (1961) called **total institutions**. Total institutions are settings in which people are isolated from the larger society and under the strict control and constant supervision of a specialized staff. Because of their "pressure cooker" atmosphere, resocialization in total institutions is often rapid and thorough, even in the absence

## THEORIES AT A GLANCE
### Socialization

| Theory | Main Question | Application |
|---|---|---|
| Functionalism | How do social structures and the values underlying them contribute to social stability? | Families and schools contribute to social order because they are the main agents of primary and secondary socialization, respectively. |
| Conflict theory | How does the structure of inequality between privileged groups seeking to maintain their advantages and subordinate groups seeking to increase theirs lead to conflict and often to social change? | The experience of many minority-group and working-class students teaches them that even if they adhere to the hidden curriculum, it is unlikely they will become highly successful. Therefore, they often rebel against school authority—which helps to ensure they will not become highly successful. |
| Symbolic interactionism | How do people communicate to make their social settings meaningful, thus helping to create their social circumstances? | The expectations of students and teachers influence the learning opportunities and performance of students. The operation of self-fulfilling prophecies helps to ensure that, on average, working-class and minority-group students will have inferior learning opportunities and achieve lower grades than other students do. |
| Feminism | How do social conventions maintain male dominance and female subordination, and how do these conventions get overturned? | Media messages typically support conventional expectations about how males and females are supposed to behave. However, women's increasing power over the past 50 or 60 years has led them to assert their right to equality with men, and to a degree this change is reflected in the mass media. |

of initiation rites. Asylums, prisons, drug and alcohol rehabilitation centres, and armies are examples of total institutions. Typically, drug or alcohol rehabilitation takes three to six months in a highly structured, drug-free setting in a remote location. Basic training in the Canadian Forces takes three-and-a-half months at the Canadian Forces Leadership and Recruit School in Saint-Jean-sur-Richelieu, about 50 km outside Montreal.

A new engineering student at the University of Toronto is dyed purple as part of an initiation rite.

A famous failed experiment illustrates the immense resocializing capacity of total institutions (Haney, Banks, and Zimbardo, 1973; Zimbardo, 1972). In the early 1970s, a group of researchers at Stanford University created their own mock prison. They paid about two dozen male volunteers to act as guards and inmates. The volunteers were mature, emotionally stable, intelligent, university students from middle-class American and Canadian homes. None had a criminal record.

By the flip of a coin, half of the volunteers were designated prisoners and the other half guards. The guards made up their own rules for maintaining law and order in the mock prison. The prisoners were picked up by city police officers in a squad car, searched, handcuffed, fingerprinted, booked at the police station, and taken blindfolded to the mock prison. At the mock prison, each prisoner was stripped, deloused, put into a uniform, given a number, and placed in a cell with two other inmates.

To better understand what it means to be a prisoner or a prison guard, the researchers wanted to observe and record social interaction in the mock prison for two weeks. However, they were forced to end the experiment abruptly after only six days because what they witnessed frightened them. In less than a week, the prisoners and prison guards could no longer tell the difference between the roles they were playing and their "real" selves. Much of the

**anticipatory socialization**
Learning the norms and behaviours of the roles to which one aspires.

socialization these young men had undergone over a period of about 20 years was quickly suspended.

About a third of the guards began to treat the prisoners like despicable animals, taking pleasure in cruelty. Even the guards who were regarded by the prisoners as tough but fair stopped short of interfering in the tyrannical and arbitrary use of power by the most sadistic guards.

All of the prisoners became servile and dehumanized, thinking only about survival, escape, and their growing hatred of the guards. Had they been thinking as university students, they could have walked out of the experiment at any time. Some of the prisoners did, in fact, beg for parole. However, by the fifth day of the experiment they were so programmed to think of themselves as prisoners that they returned docilely to their cells when their request for parole was denied.

The Stanford prison experiment suggests that your sense of self and the roles you play are not as fixed as you may think. Radically alter your social setting and, like the university students in the experiment, your self-concept and patterned behaviour are also likely to change. Such change is most evident among people undergoing resocialization in total institutions. However, the sociological eye is able to observe the flexibility of the self in all social settings—a task made easier by the fact that the self has become more flexible over time. We now turn to an examination of the growing flexibility of the self.

## LO⁴ SOCIALIZATION ACROSS THE LIFE COURSE

### ADULT SOCIALIZATION AND THE FLEXIBLE SELF

The development of the self is a lifelong process. When young adults enter a profession or get married, they must learn new occupational and family roles. Retirement and old age present an entirely new set of challenges. Giving up a job, seeing children leave home and start their own families, losing a spouse and close friends are all changes later in life that require people to think of themselves in new ways and to redefine who they are.

Many new roles are predictable. To help us learn them, we often engage in **anticipatory socialization**, which involves beginning to take on the norms and behaviours of the roles to which we aspire. (Think of 12-year-old fans of *Pretty Little Liars* learning from the show what it might mean to be a young adult.) Other new roles are unpredictable. You might unexpectedly fall in love and marry someone from a different ethnic, racial, or religious group. You might experience a sudden and difficult transition from peace to war. If so, you will have to learn new roles and adopt new cultural values or at least modify old ones. Even in adulthood, the self remains flexible.

Today, people's identities change faster, more often, and more completely than they did just a few decades ago. One important factor contributing to the growing flexibility of the self is globalization. As we saw in Chapter 2, Culture, people are now less obliged to accept the culture into which they are born. Because of globalization, they are freer to combine elements of culture from a wide variety of historical periods and geographical settings.

A second factor increasing our freedom to design ourselves is our growing ability to fashion new bodies from old. People have always

American Private Lynndie England became infamous when photographs were made public showing her and other American soldiers abusing Iraqi prisoners in obvious contravention of international law. "She's never been in trouble. She's not the person that the photographs point her out to be," said her childhood friend Destiny Gloin (quoted in "Woman Soldier," 2004). Ms. Gloin was undoubtedly right. Private England at Abu Ghraib prison was not the Lynndie England from high school. As in the Stanford prison experiment, she was transformed by a structure of power and a culture of intimidation that made the prisoners seem subhuman.

defined themselves partly in terms of their bodies; your self-conception is influenced by whether you're a man or a woman, tall or short, healthy or ill, conventionally attractive or plain. However, our bodies used to be fixed by nature. People could do nothing to change the fact that they were born with certain features and grew older at a certain rate. Now, however, you can change your body, and therefore your self-conception, radically and virtually at will—if, that is, you can afford it. Bodybuilding, aerobic exercise, and weight reduction regimens are more popular than ever. Plastic surgery allows people to buy new breasts, noses, lips, eyelids, and hair—and to remove unwanted fat, skin, and hair from various parts of their bodies.

In 2016, more than 1.7 million North Americans underwent cosmetic surgery, over five times more than in 1992. In order of popularity, the most common procedures were breast augmentation, liposuction, nose reshaping, eyelid surgery, and face lift. In addition, some 15.4 million North Americans underwent collagen, Botox, and other "minimally invasive" procedures in 2015, about 220 times more than in 1992 (American Society of Plastic Surgeons, 2017: 5).

Other body-altering procedures include sex-change operations and organ transplants. In North America alone, more than 125 000 people need a lifesaving organ transplant at any given time. Brisk, illegal international trade in human hearts, lungs, kidneys, livers, and eyes enables well-to-do people (mainly in Canada, the United States, the United Kingdom, Australia, and Saudi Arabia) to enhance and extend their lives at the expense of poor people (mainly in China, India, Brazil, the Philippines, and South Africa; Scutti, 2013).

As these examples illustrate, many new opportunities for changing one's body and therefore one's self-conception have been introduced in recent decades.

**virtual communities** An association of people, scattered across the city or around the world, who communicate via computer about a subject of common interest.

## SELF-IDENTITY AND THE INTERNET

Further complicating the process of identity formation today is the growth of the Internet. In the 1980s and early 1990s, most observers believed that social interaction by means of computer would involve only the exchange of information between individuals. They were wrong. Computer-assisted social interaction profoundly affects how people think of themselves as they form social networks and **virtual communities**—associations of people, scattered across town or across the planet, who communicate via the Internet about subjects of common interest (Brym and Lenton, 2001; Haythornthwaite and Wellman, 2002).

Because social networks and virtual communities allow people to conceal their identities, they are free to assume new identities and discover parts of themselves they were formerly unaware of. Shy people can become bold, normally assertive people can become voyeurs, old people can become young, straight people can become gay, and women can become men (see Chapter 13, Mass Media and Mass Communication). Experience on the Internet reinforces the point that the self has become increasingly flexible in recent decades, and people are freer than ever to shape their selves as they choose.

However, as you'll now see, this freedom comes at a cost, particularly for young people. To appreciate the cost, we first consider what childhood and adolescence looked like a few centuries ago.

# LO5 CHILDHOOD, ADOLESCENCE, AND EARLY ADULTHOOD

In preindustrial societies, children were considered to be small adults. From a young age, they were expected to conform as much as possible to the norms of the adult world. That was largely because children were put to work as soon as they could contribute to the welfare of their families. Often, this contribution meant doing chores by the age of 5 and working full-time by the age of 10 or 12. Marriage, and thus the achievement of full adulthood, was common by the age of 15 or 16.

Beginning around 1600 in Europe and North America, the idea of childhood as a distinct stage of life emerged.

Child labour during the Industrial Revolution

The feeling grew among well-to-do Europeans and North Americans that boys should be allowed to play games and receive an education that would allow them to develop the emotional, physical, and intellectual skills they would need as adults. Until the nineteenth century, girls continued to be treated as "little women" (the title of Louisa May Alcott's famous 1868–69 novel). Most working-class children didn't enjoy much of a childhood until the twentieth century. Only in the last century did the idea of childhood as a distinct and prolonged stage of life become universal in the West (Ariès, 1962 [1960]).

## THE EMERGENCE OF CHILDHOOD AND ADOLESCENCE

The idea of childhood emerged when and where it did because of social necessity and social possibility. Prolonged childhood was *necessary* in societies that required better-educated adults to do increasingly complex work, because childhood gave young people a chance to prepare for adult life. Prolonged childhood was *possible* in societies where improved hygiene and nutrition allowed most people to live more than 35 years, the average lifespan in Europe in the early seventeenth century. In other words, before the late seventeenth century, most people did not live long enough to permit the luxury of childhood. Moreover, there was no social need for a period of extended training and development before the comparatively simple demands of adulthood were thrust on young people.

In general, wealthier and more complex societies whose populations enjoy a long average life expectancy stretch out the pre-adult period of life. For example, we saw that in Europe in the seventeenth century, most people reached mature adulthood by the age of about 16. In contrast, in such countries as Canada today, most people are considered to reach mature adulthood only around the age of 30, by which time they have completed their formal education, possibly married, and "settled down." Once teenagers were relieved of adult responsibilities, a new term had to be coined to describe the teenage years: *adolescence*. Subsequently, the term *young adulthood* entered popular usage as an increasingly large number of people in their late teens, 20s, and early 30s delayed marriage to attend university.

Although terms such as *adolescence* and *young adulthood* describing the stages of life were firmly entrenched in North America by the middle of the twentieth century, some of the categories of the population they were meant to describe began to change dramatically. Somewhat excitedly, some analysts began to write about the "disappearance" of childhood and adolescence (Friedenberg, 1959; Postman, 1982).

Although undoubtedly overstating their case, these social scientists did identify some of the social forces responsible for the changing character of childhood and adolescence in recent decades. We examine these social forces in the concluding section of this chapter.

# LO6 PROBLEMS OF CHILDHOOD, ADOLESCENT, AND EARLY ADULT SOCIALIZATION TODAY

The socialization patterns of Canadian youth have changed considerably over the past half-century. The change is largely due to declining adult supervision and guidance, increasing mass media and peer group influence, and increasing assumption of substantial adult responsibilities to the neglect of extracurricular activities. Let us consider each of these developments in turn.

## DECLINING ADULT SUPERVISION AND GUIDANCE

In Canada, adults in the paid labour force living with a spouse or a child spend about 20 percent less time in activities with family members during a typical workday than they did in 1986. The main reason? They spend more time at work (Turcotte, 2007). Because adults have less time to spend with their children than they used to, young people are increasingly left alone to socialize themselves and build their own community.

This community sometimes revolves around high-risk behaviour. As noted earlier, about 4 percent of Canadians between the ages of 12 and 17 smoke and about the same percentage engage in binge drinking. It is not coincidental that the peak hours for juvenile crime are between 3 p.m. and 6 p.m. on weekdays—that is, after school and before most parents return home from work (Hersch, 1998: 362; Statistics Canada, 2017b). These research findings suggest that many of the teenage behaviours commonly regarded as problematic result from declining adult guidance and supervision.

## INCREASING MASS MEDIA AND PEER GROUP INFLUENCE

Declining adult supervision and guidance also leave North American youth more susceptible to the influence of the mass media and peer groups. In an earlier era, family, school, church, and community usually taught young people more or less consistent beliefs and values. Now, however, the mass media and peer groups often pull young people in different directions from the school and the family, leaving them uncertain about what constitutes appropriate behaviour and making the job of growing up more stressful than it used to be (refer back to Figure 3.1).

## DECLINING EXTRACURRICULAR ACTIVITIES AND INCREASING ADULT RESPONSIBILITIES

Extracurricular activities are important for adolescent personality development. These activities provide opportunities for students to develop concrete skills and thereby make sense of the world and their place in it. In schools today, academic subjects are too often presented as disconnected bits of knowledge that lack relevance to the student's life. Drama, music, and athletics programs are often better at giving students a framework within which they can develop a strong sense of self, because they are concrete activities with clearly defined rules. By training and playing hard on a hockey team, mastering an instrument, or acting in plays, students can learn something about their physical, emotional, and social capabilities and limitations, about what they are made of, and about what they can and cannot do. These are just the sorts of activities adolescents require for healthy self-development (Brym, 2006).

If you're like most young Canadians today, you spend fewer hours per week on extracurricular activities associated with school than your parents did when they went to school. Many young Canadians are simply too busy with homework, household chores, child-care responsibilities, and part-time jobs to enjoy the benefits of school activities outside the classroom. Canadian teens average more than seven hours of paid and unpaid labour per day, spending nearly 50 hours a week on school work, homework, paid work, and housework—a 50-hour workweek. About half of Canadian teenagers work at jobs averaging 15 hours a week. Canadian teens work more than teens do in the United States, the United Kingdom, France, Australia, and other rich countries (Bibby, 2001: 35; Siad, 2007).

## THE VANISHING ADOLESCENT?

Some analysts wonder whether the assumption of adult responsibilities, the lack of extracurricular activities, declining adult supervision and guidance, and increasing mass media and peer group influence are causing childhood and adolescence to disappear. As early as 1959, one sociologist spoke of "the vanishing adolescent" in North American society (Friedenberg, 1959). Four decades later, another commentator remarked, "I think that we who were small in the early sixties were perhaps the last generation who actually had a childhood, in the…sense of…a space distinct in roles and customs from the world of adults, oriented around children's own needs and culture rather than around the needs and culture of adults" (Wolf, 1997: 13). Childhood and adolescence became universal categories of social thought and experience in the twentieth century. Under the impact of the social forces discussed above, however, the experience and meaning of childhood and adolescence now seem to be changing radically.

Half of McDonald's employees are under the age of 18.

## MILLENNIALS: THE "ME" GENERATION?

Notwithstanding the changes just enumerated, many commentators characterize North Americans born between the early 1980s and the early 2000s—so-called "Millennials"—as spoiled brats. Now the largest living generation, more numerous than even their baby boomer parents born between the mid-1940s and the mid-1960s, Millennials are the first generation to have come of age during the twenty-first century. They grew up with smartphones, laptops, social media, and ATMs. Presumably, they are you.

In the popular press and more than a few articles and books by learned academics, you are called a member of the entitled "Me" generation. Ostensibly, you think only about yourself because you were poorly socialized. Your parents gave you too much freedom to do what you wanted, your teachers gave you a participation award for placing ninth in track and field competitions, and now you feel that the world owes you a living. You are (as a cover of *Time* magazine put it a few years ago), "lazy, entitled narcissists who still live with their parents" (Stein, 2013). Go to Google images and type in "Millennials" to see what you look like in the popular imagination.

The reality is of course different (Cairns, 2017). Spoiled kids from well-to-do families are not a new phenomenon; after all, *The Great Gatsby* was published in 1925. Far from all children from well-to-do families are spoiled. And in any case most Millennials are not from well-to-do families. They are not characters straight out of Lena Dunham's *Girls*.

True, between 2001 and 2016, the share of young Canadian adults between the ages of 20 and 34 who were married or living common-law fell from 49 percent to 42 percent. About 35 percent of young adults now live with a parent—a figure that has been increasing since 2001 (Statistics Canada, 2017s). However, the reasons for this residential pattern are largely economic. Despite strenuous efforts, many Millennials can't find good jobs. Many still have to pay off large student loans. According to a 2017 survey, 67 percent of Canadian college and university graduates under the age of 40 said they were in debt when they graduated. Some 62 percent of them still had an average of $16,816 remaining on their student

Millennials in the popular imagination

loans at the time of the survey. On average, they expected it would take another five years to pay off their debt (Ipsos, 2017). Moreover, many Millennials are priced out of the housing market because rents and real estate prices are so high. That's why, among Canadian cities, Toronto, with its housing costs out of sight, leads the pack; more than 47 percent of young adults in Toronto live with their parents, 12 percent above the national average.

If Millennials want more, who can blame them? Their parents wanted a house, a good job, and a family of their own. The difference is that they had the good fortune to be born during the post-World War II economic boom, so the great majority of them could afford to achieve their dreams. Their children face unimagined economic difficulties. Blaming them for their own misfortune is the very opposite of exercising the sociological imagination.

## READY TO STUDY?

### IN THE BOOK YOU CAN:

- Refer to the Chapter in Review section at the back of the book to have a summary of the chapter and key terms handy.
- Test your knowledge of chapter contents by answering the multiple-choice questions in the Chapter in Review section. Answers are in the appendix at the end of the book.

### ONLINE YOU CAN:

- Stay organized and efficient with MindTap—a single destination with all the course material and study aids you need to succeed.
- Flashcards are pre-populated to provide you with a jump start for review—or you can create your own.
- You can highlight text and make notes in your MindTap Reader.
- Prepare for tests with quizzes.

**GO TO NELSON.COM/STUDENT TO PURCHASE THESE DIGITAL RESOURCES.**

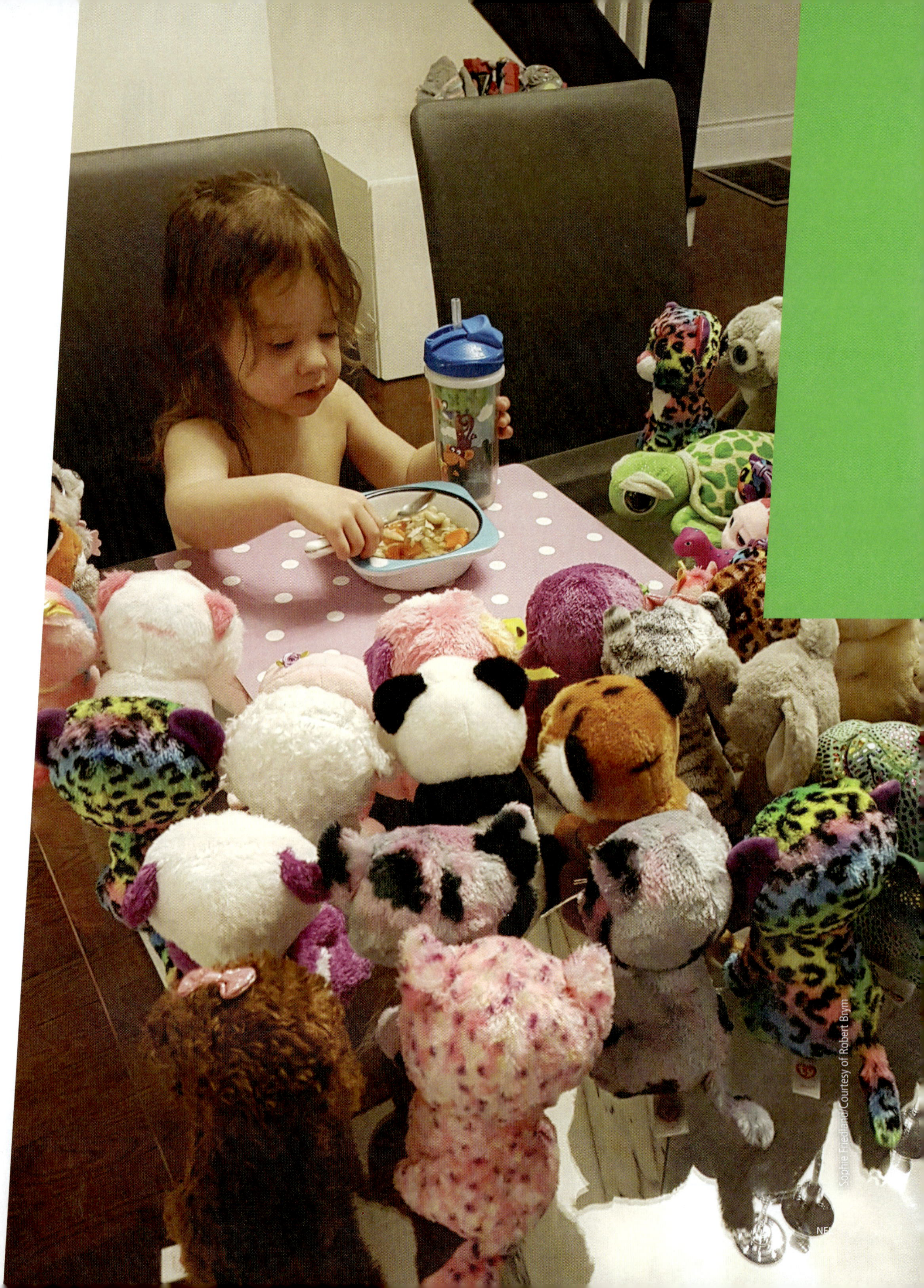

Sophie Friedland/Courtesy of Robert Brym

# 4
# From Social Interaction to Social Organizations

## LEARNING OBJECTIVES:

In this chapter, you will learn to

- **LO1** Define *social interaction* as people communicating face to face, acting and reacting in relation to one another.
- **LO2** Identify how various aspects of social structure influence the texture of emotional life.
- **LO3** Recognize that in social interaction, nonverbal communication is extremely important.
- **LO4** See how emotional and material resources flow through patterns of social relations called *social networks*.
- **LO5** Explain how social groups bind people together, impose conformity on them, and separate them from non-group members.
- **LO6** Appreciate that bureaucracies can often be made more efficient by adopting more democratic structures with fewer levels of authority.

## LO1 FEMINIST THEORY AND SOCIAL INTERACTION

A researcher and his assistants once eavesdropped on 1200 conversations of people laughing in public places, such as shopping malls (Provine, 2000). When they heard someone laughing, they recorded who laughed (the speaker, the listener, or both) and the gender of the speaker and the listener. To simplify things, they eavesdropped only on two-person groups.

They found that women laugh more than men do in everyday conversations. The biggest discrepancy in laughing occurred when the speaker was a woman and the listener was a man. In such cases, women laughed more than twice as often as men did. However, even when a man spoke and a woman listened, the woman was more likely to laugh than the man was.

Research also shows that men are more likely than women are to engage in long monologues and interrupt when others are talking (Tannen, 1994a, 1994b). They are also less likely to ask for help or directions because doing so would imply a reduction in their authority. Much male–female conflict results from these differences. A stereotypical case is the lost male driver and the helpful female passenger. The female passenger, seeing that the male driver is lost, suggests that they stop and ask for directions. The male driver does not want to ask for directions because he thinks that would make him look incompetent. If both parties remain firm in their positions, an argument is bound to result.

**Social interaction** involves communication among people acting and reacting to one another. Feminist sociologists are especially sensitive to gender differences in social interactions like those just described. They see that gender often structures interaction patterns.

Consider laughter. If we define *status* as a recognized social position, it is generally true that people with higher status (in this case, men) get more laughs, whereas people with lower status (in this case, women) laugh more. That is perhaps why class clowns are nearly always boys. Laughter in everyday life, it turns out, is not as

> **social interaction** Involves people communicating face to face or via computer, acting and reacting in relation to other people. It is structured around norms, roles, and statuses.

**role conflict** Occurs when two or more statuses held at the same time place contradictory role demands on a person.

**role strain** Occurs when incompatible role demands are placed on a person in a single status.

### FIGURE 4.1 Role Set and Status Set

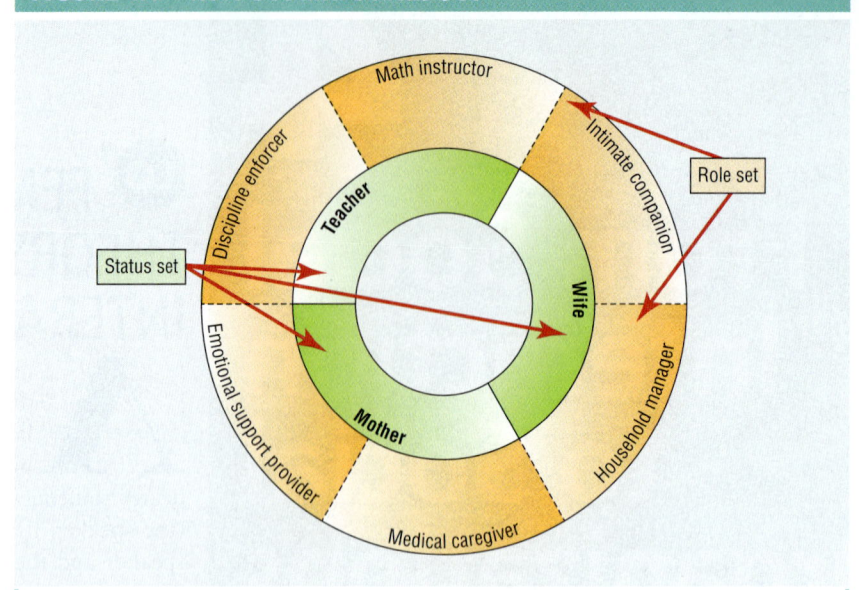

People can occupy several statuses at the same time, such as mother, wife, and teacher, as shown in this figure. When considered together, these statuses form a status set. Similarly, role sets are made up of all the roles (expected behaviours) for each status. For example, the expected behaviours associated with the status of wife include being an intimate companion and assuming certain responsibilities as a manager of the household. In this figure, dashed lines are used to separate roles, while solid lines are used to separate statuses.

Source: From BRYM/ROBERTS/STROHSCHEIN/LIE. *Sociology: Your Compass for a New World*, 6E. © 2019 Nelson Education Ltd. Reproduced by permission. www.cengage.com/permissions.

spontaneous as you may think. It is often a signal of who has higher or lower status. Social structure influences who laughs more.

Social statuses are just one of the three building blocks that structure all social interactions. The others are roles and norms. A *role* is a set of expected behaviours. Whereas people *occupy* a status, they *perform* a role (see Figures 4.1 and 4.2). Students may learn to expect that when things get dull, the class clown will brighten their day. The class clown will rise to the occasion, knowing that his classmates expect him to do so. A *norm* is a generally accepted way of doing things.

### FIGURE 4.2 Role Conflict and Role Strain

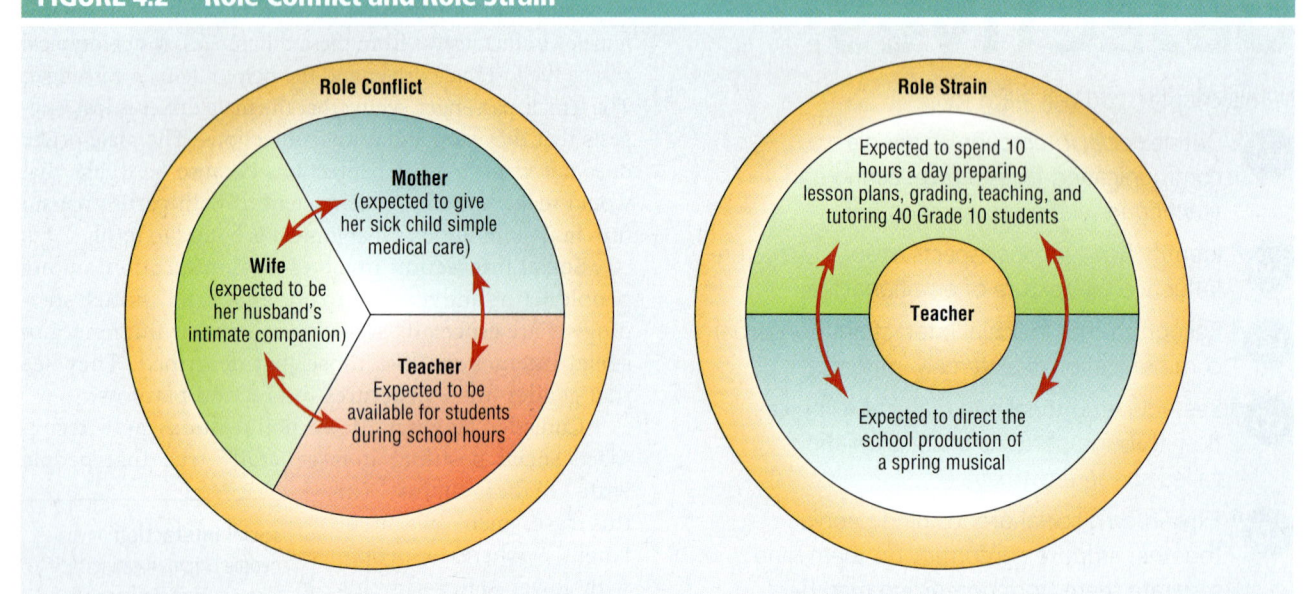

When a person holds two or more statuses with different role demands, the result is **role conflict**. How might a woman occupying the three statuses shown on the left experience role conflict? When a person holds a single status with incompatible role demands, the result is **role strain**.

Source: From BRYM/ROBERTS/STROHSCHEIN/LIE. *Sociology: Your Compass for a New World*, 6E. © 2019 Nelson Education Ltd. Reproduced by permission. www.cengage.com/permissions.

Classroom norms are imposed by instructors, who routinely punish class clowns for distracting their classmates from the task at hand.

## LO² SOCIAL STRUCTURE AND EMOTIONS

Just as statuses, roles, and norms structure laughter, they influence other emotions, although their influence is often not apparent. In fact, most people think that emotions are a lot like the common cold. In both cases, an external disturbance causes a reaction that people presumably experience involuntarily. The external disturbance could be exposure to a virus that causes us to catch a cold or a grizzly bear attack that causes us to experience fear. In either case, we can't control our body's patterned response. Emotions, like colds, just happen to us.

Feminists were among the first sociologists to note the flaw in the view that emotional responses are typically involuntary. Seeing how often women, as status subordinates, must *control* their emotions, they generalized the idea. Emotions don't just happen to us, they argued. We manage them. If a grizzly bear attacks you in the woods, you can run as fast as possible or calm yourself, lie down, play dead, and silently pray for the best. You are more likely to survive the grizzly bear attack if you control your emotions and follow the second strategy. You will also temper your fear with a new emotion: hope (see Figure 4.3).

When people manage their emotions, they usually follow certain cultural "scripts," like the culturally transmitted knowledge that lying down and playing dead gives you a better chance of surviving a grizzly bear attack. We usually know the culturally designated emotional response to a particular external stimulus and we try to respond appropriately. If people don't succeed in achieving the culturally appropriate emotional response, they are likely to feel guilt, disappointment, or (as in the case of the bear attack) something much worse.

Sociologist Arlie Russell Hochschild is a leading figure in the study of **emotion management**. In fact, she coined the term. She argues that emotion management involves people obeying "feeling rules" and responding appropriately to the situations in which they find themselves (Hochschild, 1979, 1983). So, for example, people talk about the "right" to feel angry and they acknowledge that they "should" have mourned a relative's death more deeply. We have conventional expectations not only about what we should feel but also about how much we should feel, how long we should feel it, and with whom we should share those feelings. For example, we are expected to mourn the end of a love relationship. Shedding tears would be regarded as a completely natural reaction among Canadians today, but if you shot yourself—as was the fad among some European Romantics in the early nineteenth century—then you would be regarded as deranged. If you went on a date with someone new half an hour after breaking up with your long-time girlfriend or boyfriend, then most people would regard you as callous. Norms and rules govern our emotional life.

> **emotion management** The act of obeying "feeling rules" and responding appropriately to situations.
>
> **emotional labour** Emotion management that many people do as part of their job and for which they are paid.

### EMOTIONAL LABOUR

Hochschild distinguishes emotion management (which everyone does in everyday life) from **emotional labour** (which many people do as part of their job and for which they are paid). We've all seen teachers deal with students who routinely hand in assignments late, pass notes, chatter during class, talk back, and act as class clowns. Those teachers do emotional labour. Sales clerks, nurses, and flight attendants must also be experts in emotional labour. They

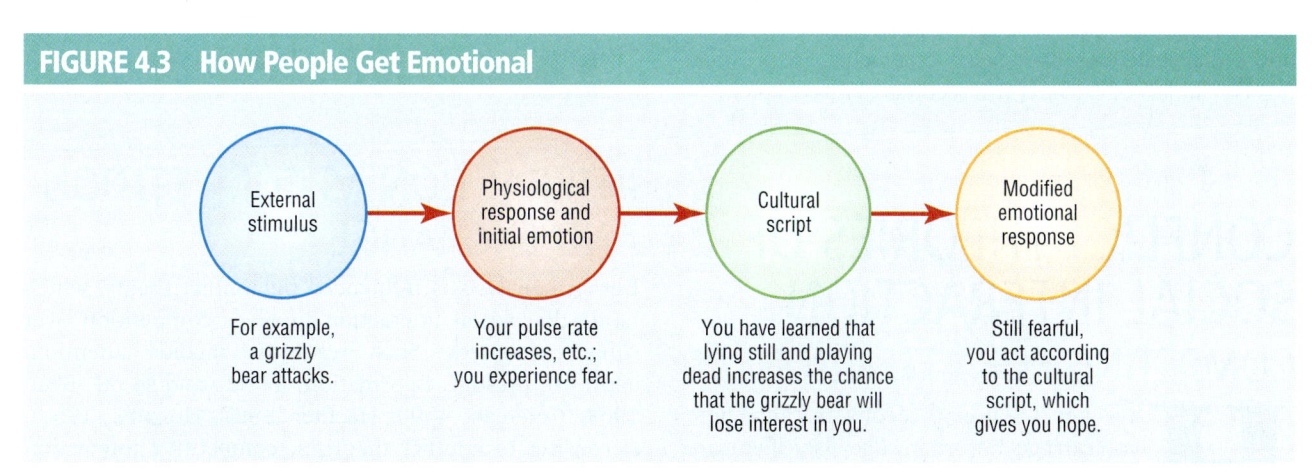

**FIGURE 4.3  How People Get Emotional**

External stimulus → Physiological response and initial emotion → Cultural script → Modified emotional response

- For example, a grizzly bear attacks.
- Your pulse rate increases, etc.; you experience fear.
- You have learned that lying still and playing dead increases the chance that the grizzly bear will lose interest in you.
- Still fearful, you act according to the cultural script, which gives you hope.

Source: From BRYM/ROBERTS/STROHSCHEIN/LIE. *Sociology: Your Compass for a New World*, 6E. © 2019 Nelson Education Ltd. Reproduced by permission. www.cengage.com/permissions.

spend a considerable part of their workday dealing with other people's misbehaviour, anger, rudeness, and unreasonable demands. They also do promotional and public relations work on behalf of the organizations that employ them. ("We hope you enjoyed your flight on Air Canada and that we can serve you again the next time you travel.") In all of these tasks, they carefully manage their own emotions while trying to keep their clientele happy and orderly.

Hochschild estimates that in North America nearly half of the jobs that women do and one-fifth of the jobs that men do involve substantial amounts of emotional labour. More women than men do emotional labour because they are typically better socialized to undertake caring and nurturing roles.

Note, too, that as the focus of the economy shifts from the production of goods to the production of services, the market for emotional labour grows. More and more people are selected, trained, and paid for their skill in emotional labour. Consequently, business organizations increasingly govern the expression of feelings at work, which becomes less spontaneous and authentic over time. This process affects women more than it does men because women do more emotional labour than men do.

These observations fly in the face of common sense. We typically think of our interactions as outcomes of our emotional states. We interact differently with people depending on whether they love us, make us angry, or make us laugh. We usually think our emotions are evoked involuntarily and result in uncontrollable action. However, emotions are not as unique, involuntary, and uncontrollable as people often believe. Underlying the turbulence of emotional life is a measure of order and predictability governed by sociological principles.

Just as building blocks need cement to hold them together, so norms, roles, and statuses require a sort of "social cement" to prevent them from falling apart and to turn them into a durable social structure. What is the nature of the cement that holds the building blocks of social life together? Asked differently, exactly how is social interaction maintained? This is the most fundamental sociological question we can ask, because it is really a question about how social structures, and society as a whole, are possible. It is the subject of the next two sections of this chapter.

# CONFLICT THEORIES OF SOCIAL INTERACTION
## COMPETING FOR ATTENTION

Have you ever been in a conversation where you can't get a word in edgewise? If you are like most people, this situation is bound to happen from time to time. The longer a one-sided conversation persists, the more neglected you feel. You may make increasingly less subtle attempts to turn the conversation your way. But if you fail, you may decide to end the interaction altogether. If this experience repeats itself—if the person you're talking to consistently monopolizes conversations—you're likely to want to avoid getting into conversations with him or her in the future. Maintaining interaction (and maintaining a relationship) requires that both parties' need for attention is met.

Most people don't consistently try to monopolize conversations. If they did, there wouldn't be much talk in the world. In fact, taking turns is one of the basic norms that govern conversations; people literally take turns talking to make conversation possible. Nonetheless, a remarkably large part of all conversations involves a subtle competition for attention. Consider the following snippet of dinner conversation:

> John: "I'm feeling really starved."
> Mary: "Oh, I just ate."
> John: "Well, I'm feeling really starved."
> Mary: "When was the last time you ate?"

Sociologist Charles Derber recorded this conversation (Derber, 1979: 24). John starts by saying how hungry he is. The attention is on him. Mary implies that she's not hungry; the attention shifts to her. John insists he's hungry, shifting attention back to him. Mary finally allows the conversation to focus on John by asking him when he last ate. John thus "wins" the competition for attention.

Derber recorded 1500 conversations in family homes, workplaces, restaurants, classrooms, dormitories, and therapy groups. He concluded that North Americans usually try to turn conversations toward themselves. They usually do so in ways that go unnoticed. Nonetheless, says Derber, the typical conversation is a covert competition for attention. Derber is careful to point out that conversations are not winner-take-all competitions. Unless both people in a two-person conversation receive some attention, the interaction is likely to cease. Therefore, conversation typically involves the exchange of attention.

## INTERACTION AS COMPETITION AND EXCHANGE

Derber's analysis is influenced by conflict theory, which holds that social interaction involves competition over valued resources. Such resources include attention, approval, prestige, information, money, and so on (Blau, 1964; Coleman, 1990; Hechter, 1987; Homans, 1961). According to conflict theorists, competitive interaction involves people seeking to gain the most—socially, emotionally, and economically—while paying the least.

From this point of view, the chance of a relationship enduring increases if it provides the interacting parties with payoffs. Ultimately, then, payoffs make social order possible. On the other hand, unequal payoffs mean trouble. The greater the inequality of payoffs to interacting parties, the greater the chance that conflict will erupt and lead to a breakdown in the interaction. Thus, conflict never lies far below the surface of competitive social interactions marked by substantial inequality (Bourdieu, 1977 [1972]; Collins, 1982).

# SYMBOLIC INTERACTION THEORY AND SOCIAL INTERACTION

Is social interaction *always* a competitive and conflict-prone struggle over valued resources, as conflict theorists suggest? A moment's reflection suggests otherwise. People frequently act in ways they consider fair or just, even if that does not maximize their personal gain (Gamson, Fireman, and Rytina, 1982). Some people even engage in altruistic or heroic acts from which they gain nothing and risk much. The plain fact is that social life is richer than conflict theorists would have us believe. Selfishness and conflict are not the only bases of social interaction.

When people behave fairly or altruistically, they are interacting with others based on *norms* they have learned. These norms say they should act justly and help people in need, even if it costs a lot to do so. How then do people learn norms (as well as roles and statuses)? The first step involves what George Herbert Mead called "taking the role of the other," that is, seeing yourself from the point of view of the people with whom you interact (see Chapter 3, Socialization). According to Mead, we interpret other people's words and nonverbal signals to understand how they see us, and we adjust our behaviour to fit their expectations about how we ought to behave. During such symbolic interaction, we learn norms and adopt roles and statuses (Mead, 1934).

Such social learning is different from studying a user manual or a textbook. It involves constantly negotiating and modifying the norms, roles, and statuses that we meet as we interact with others, shaping them to suit our preferences. People learn norms, roles, and statuses actively and creatively, not passively and mechanically (Berger and Luckmann, 1966; Blumer, 1969; Strauss, 1993). Let's explore this theme by considering the ingenious ways in which people manage the impressions they give to others during social interaction.

# GOFFMAN'S DRAMATURGICAL ANALYSIS

One of the most popular variants of symbolic interactionism is **dramaturgical analysis**. As first developed by Erving Goffman (1959), dramaturgical analysis takes literally Shakespeare's line from *As You Like It*: "All the world's a stage, and all the men and women merely players."

From Goffman's point of view, people constantly engage in role-playing. This fact is most evident when we are "front stage" in public settings. Just as being front stage in a play requires the use of props, gestures, and memorized lines, so does acting in a public space. A server in a restaurant, for example, must dress in a uniform, smile, and recite fixed lines ("How are you? My name is Sam and I'm your server today. May I get you a drink before you order your meal?"). When the server goes "backstage," he or she can relax from the front-stage performance and discuss it with co-workers ("Those kids at table six are driving me nuts!"). Thus, we often distinguish between our public roles and our "true" selves.

Note, however, that even backstage we engage in role-playing and impression management; it's just that we are less likely to be aware of it. For instance, in the kitchen, a server may try to present herself in the best possible light to impress another server so that she can eventually ask him out for a date. Thus, the implication of dramaturgical analysis is that there is no single self, just the ensemble of roles we play in various social contexts. Servers in restaurants play many roles off the job. They play on basketball teams, sing in church choirs, and hang out with friends at shopping malls. Each role is governed by norms about what kind of clothes to wear, what kind of conversation to engage in, and so on. Everyone plays on many front stages in everyday life.

They do not always do so enthusiastically. If a role is stressful, people may engage in role distancing. **Role distancing** involves giving the impression of just "going through the motions" but lacking serious commitment to a role. Thus, when people think a role they are playing is embarrassing or beneath them, they typically want to give their peers the impression that the role is not their "true" self. "My parents force me to sing in the church choir"; "I'm working at McDonald's just to earn a few extra dollars, but I'm going back to college next semester"; "This old car I'm driving is just a loaner." These are the kinds of rationalizations individuals offer when distancing themselves from a role.

> **dramaturgical analysis** Views social interaction as a sort of play in which people present themselves so that they appear in the best possible light.
>
> **role distancing** Involves giving the impression that we are just going through the motions and that we lack serious commitment to a role.

Onstage, people typically try to place themselves in the best possible light; they engage in "impression management." For example, a study of McMaster University medical school in Hamilton, Ontario, found that when students enter medical school, they quickly adopt a new vocabulary and wear a white lab coat to set themselves apart from patients. They try to model their behaviour after the doctors who have authority over them. When dealing with patients, they may hide their ignorance under medical jargon to maintain their authority. They may ask questions they know the answer to so that they can impress their teachers. According to one third-year student: "The best way of impressing [advisers] with your competence is asking questions you know the answer to. Because if they ever put it back on you, 'Well what do *you* think?' then you can tell them what you think and you'd give a very intelligent answer because you knew it. You didn't ask it to find out information. You ask it to impress people." Medical students don't take a course in how to act like a doctor, but they learn their new role in the course of impression management (Haas and Shaffir, 1987).

We'll now discuss briefly the way people use words and nonverbal signals to communicate in face-to-face interaction. Having a conversation is actually a wonder of intricate complexity. As you will see, even today's most advanced supercomputer cannot conduct a natural-sounding conversation with a person.

## LO³ VERBAL AND NONVERBAL COMMUNICATION

In the 1950s, an article appeared in a British newspaper trumpeting the invention of an electronic translating device at the University of London. According to the article, "As fast as [a user] could type the words in, say, French, the equivalent in Hungarian or Russian would issue forth on the tape" (quoted in Silberman, 2000: 225). The report was an exaggeration, to put it mildly. It soon became a standing joke that if you asked a computer to translate "The spirit is willing, but the flesh is weak" (Matthew 26:41) into Russian, the output would read, "The vodka is good, but the steak is lousy." Today, we are closer to high-quality machine translation than we were in the 1950s. However, a practical universal translator exists only on *Star Trek*.

## The Social Context of Language

Why can people translate better than computers can? Because computer programs find it difficult to make sense of the *social and cultural context* in which language is used. The same words can mean different things in different settings, so computers, lacking contextual cues, routinely botch translations. That is why machine translation works best when applications are restricted to a single social context—say, weather forecasting or oil exploration. In such cases, specialized vocabularies and meanings specific to the context of interest are built into the program. Ambiguity is reduced and computers can "understand" the meaning of words well enough to translate them with reasonable accuracy. Similarly, humans must be able to reduce ambiguity and make sense of words to become good translators. They do so by learning the nuances of meaning in different cultural and social contexts over an extended time. *Nonverbal* cues assist them in that task.

## Facial Expressions, Gestures, and Body Language

Social interaction typically involves a complex mix of verbal and nonverbal messages. The face alone is capable of more than 1000 distinct expressions, reflecting the whole range of human emotion. Arm movements, hand gestures, posture, and other aspects of body language send many more messages to a person's audience.

A caution is necessary here. Based on weak research conducted in the 1960s and early 1970s, many advertisers, motivational speakers, and popular psychology articles baldly assert even today that 93 percent of communication is nonverbal (Dean, 2007; Mehrabian, 1972). This is a gross exaggeration, as a study conducted in Vancouver a few years ago showed (Small et al., 2015). Researchers recorded eight hours of everyday interactions of staff and residents in two homes for the elderly. In one facility, all of the residents

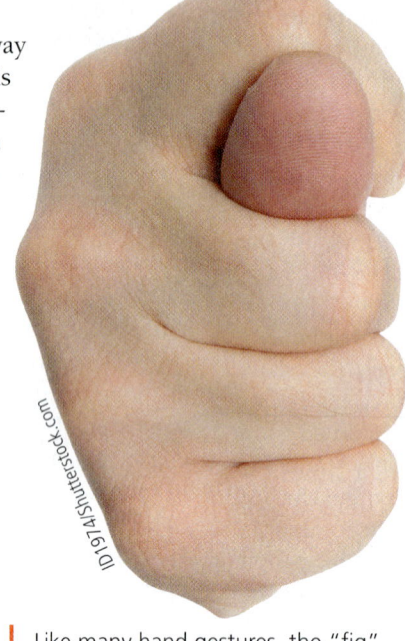

---

Like many hand gestures, the "fig" means different things in different times and places. You probably know it as a sign that adults make when they play with children and pretend "I've got your nose." But in ancient Rome, the fig was meant to convey good luck; in India it represents a threat; and in Russia, Turkey, and South Korea it means "Screw you." It signifies the letter "t" in the American Sign Language alphabet, but it had to be modified in the International Sign Language alphabet to avoid giving offence.

were of Chinese origin. Only 29 percent of them spoke some English, while just 26 percent of the staff spoke some Chinese. In the second facility, the residents spoke Punjabi, Italian, Dutch, English, Polish, Tagalog, or Hindi as a first language. About 69 percent of them spoke at least some English. The staff spoke either English or Tagalog. Because of the linguistic diversity of these facilities—typical of big-city Canada—much communication was reduced to smiling, pointing, and a variety of other gestures and facial expressions. At best, all that could be communicated in most cases were the simplest of messages: "eat," "nice job," "my foot hurts," and the like. Relying mainly on nonverbal signals severely impaired communication.

But make no mistake, nonverbal messages do matter, often a lot. To cite just one example, a few years ago researchers set up an experiment in which first- and second-year undergraduates at the University of New Brunswick viewed recordings of Liberal Party candidates giving campaign talks (Everitt, Best, and Gaudet, 2016). When female candidates used assertive, expressive, or choppy hand movements, students' evaluations of the candidates dropped significantly. When male candidates used the same hand movements, students' evaluations of the candidates rose significantly. Female candidates were more likely to receive support if they remained calm and contained, while male candidates were more likely to receive support if their nonverbal behaviour was assertive. The young Canadian students' culturally defined expectations about the appropriate nonverbal behaviour of women versus men strongly influenced their evaluations of the candidates.

Despite the wide variety of facial expressions in the human repertoire, most researchers believe that the facial expressions of six emotions are similar across cultures. These six emotions are happiness, sadness, anger, disgust, fear, and surprise (Ekman, 1978). However, since the late 1990s, some researchers have questioned whether a universally recognized set of facial expressions reflects basic human emotions. Among other things, critics have argued that "facial expressions are not the readout of emotions but displays that serve social motives and are mostly determined by the presence of an audience" (Fernandez-Dols et al., 1997: 163). From this point of view, a smile will reflect pleasure if it serves a person's interest to present a smiling face to his or her audience. Conversely, a person may be motivated to conceal anxiety by smiling or to conceal pleasure by suppressing a smile.

At times, different cultural expectations can lead to colossal misunderstanding. Until recently, it was considered rude among educated Japanese to say "no." Disagreement was instead conveyed by discreetly changing the subject and smiling politely. Consequently, it was common for visiting North Americans to think that their Japanese hosts were saying "yes" because of the politeness, the smile, and the absence of a "no" when in fact they were saying "no."

Similarly, no gesture or body posture means the same thing in all societies and all cultures. In our society, people point with an outstretched hand and an extended finger. However, people raised in other cultures tip their head or use their chin or eyes to point out something. We nod our heads "yes" and shake "no," but others nod "no" and shake "yes."

Finally, note that people in all societies communicate by manipulating the space that separates them from others (Hall, 1959, 1966). Sociologists commonly distinguish four zones that surround us. The size of these zones varies from one society to the next. In North America, an intimate zone extends about 0.5 metres from the body. It is restricted to people with whom we want sustained, intimate physical contact. A personal zone extends from about 0.5 metres to 1.5 metres away. It is reserved for friends and acquaintances. We tolerate only a little physical intimacy from such people. The social zone is situated in the area roughly 1.5 metres to 3.5 metres away from us. Apart from a handshake, no physical contact is permitted from people we restrict to that zone. The public zone starts around 3.5 metres from our bodies. It is used to distinguish a performer or a speaker from an audience.

## Status Cues

Aside from facial expressions, gestures, and body language, nonverbal communication takes place by means of **status cues**, or visual indicators of other people's social position. Goffman (1959) observed that when individuals come into contact, they typically try to acquire information that will help them define the situation and make interaction easier. That goal is accomplished in part by attending to status cues.

Although status cues can be useful in helping people define the situation and thus greasing the wheels of social interaction, they also pose a danger: status cues can quickly degenerate into **stereotypes**, or rigid views of how members of various groups act, regardless of whether individual group members really behave that way. Stereotypes create social barriers that impair interaction or prevent it altogether.

For instance, every year in Toronto, police officers stop, question, and document hundreds of thousands of people on foot, on bicycles, and in cars. They write down each person's name, phone number, date of birth, address, height, weight, race, and the names of that person's associates. This procedure is commonly called "carding." Reasons for carding include "general investigation," "loitering,"

> **status cues** Visual indicators of a person's social position.
>
> **stereotypes** Rigid views of how members of various groups act, regardless of whether individual group members really behave that way.

Among other things, body language communicates the degree to which people conform to gender roles, or widely shared expectations about how males and females are supposed to act. In these illustrations, which postures suggest power and aggressiveness? Which suggest compliance? Which are "appropriate" to the person's gender? Recently, efforts have been made to change traditional, gender-appropriate postures. For example, some women have promoted an end to "manspreading" on subways and urged women to "lean in" more aggressively during formal meetings. Do you witness such change in your everyday life?

## FIGURE 4.4  Likelihood of Black People Being Stopped for Carding by Toronto Police in 72 Police Districts

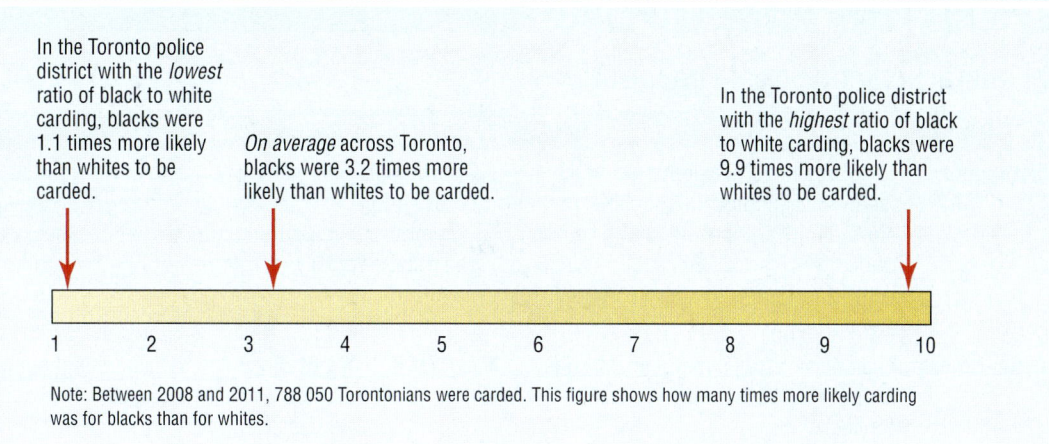

In the Toronto police district with the *lowest* ratio of black to white carding, blacks were 1.1 times more likely than whites to be carded.

*On average* across Toronto, blacks were 3.2 times more likely than whites to be carded.

In the Toronto police district with the *highest* ratio of black to white carding, blacks were 9.9 times more likely than whites to be carded.

Note: Between 2008 and 2011, 788 050 Torontonians were carded. This figure shows how many times more likely carding was for blacks than for whites.

Between 2008 and 2011, 788 050 Torontonians were carded. This figure shows how many times more likely carding was for black people than for white people. For example, on average, black people were 3.2 times more likely to be carded than white people were.

Source: *Toronto Star*. 2015. "Known to police." http://www.thestar.com/news/gta/knowntopolice.html (retrieved 22 July 2015).

---

"suspicious activity," "related to a radio call," or "as a result of a traffic stop." In the great majority of cases, no charge or arrest results. Less than a fifth of the people who are carded have had a criminal record in the preceding decade.

In Toronto's 72 police districts, black people are on average 3.2 times more likely than white people to be carded, although they represent just 8.4 percent of the city's population (City of Toronto, 2015; *Toronto Star*, 2015; see Figure 4.4). The people *least* likely to be stopped while driving are older, highly educated Asian females. The people *most* likely to be stopped while driving are young, highly educated black males (Wortley, Brownfield, and Hagan, 1996). Presumably, young black men who are highly educated drive relatively expensive cars because they earn relatively high incomes, so they are regarded with particular suspicion by the police! In this case, a social cue has become a stereotype that guides police policy. Many black people, the great majority of whom never commit an illegal act, view this police practice as harassment. Racial stereotyping therefore helps perpetuate the sometimes poor relations between the black community and law enforcement officials.

As our discussion shows, face-to-face interaction may at first glance appear to be straightforward and unproblematic. Most of the time, it is. However, underlying the surface of human communication is a wide range of cultural assumptions, unconscious understandings, and nonverbal cues that make interaction possible. You will now see that social structures also underlie social interaction, but before turning to that lesson you might want to review some of what you have just learned (see Theories at a Glance, Social Interaction and Social Organizations).

# NETWORKS, GROUPS, AND ORGANIZATIONS

## THE HOLOCAUST

In 1941, the large stone and glass train station was one of the proudest structures in Smolensk, a city of about 100 000 people on Russia's western border. Always bustling, it was especially busy on the morning of June 28. Besides the usual passengers and well-wishers, hundreds of Soviet Red Army soldiers were nervously talking, smoking, writing hurried letters to their loved ones, and sleeping fitfully on the station floor while waiting for their train. Nazi troops had invaded the nearby city of Minsk in Belarus a couple of days before. The Soviet soldiers were being positioned to defend Russia against the inevitable German onslaught.

My father, then in his 20s, had been standing in line for nearly two hours to buy food when he noticed flares arching over the station. Within seconds, Stuka bombers, the pride of the German air force, swept down, releasing their bombs just before pulling out of their dive. Inside the station, shards of glass, blocks of stone, and mounds of earth fell indiscriminately on sleeping soldiers and nursing mothers alike. Everyone panicked. People trampled over one another to get out. In minutes, the train station was rubble.

Nearly two years earlier, my father had managed to escape Poland when the Nazis invaded his hometown near Warsaw. Now he was on the run again. By the time the Nazis occupied Smolensk a few weeks after their dive

## THEORIES AT A GLANCE

### Social Interaction and Social Organizations

| Theory | Main Question | Application |
|---|---|---|
| Conflict theory | How does the structure of inequality between privileged groups seeking to maintain their advantages and subordinate groups seeking to increase theirs lead to conflict and often to social change? | A large part of everyday conversation involves a subtle competition for attention. In fact, much social interaction is a competitive struggle in which people seek to gain the most—socially, emotionally, and economically—while paying the least. |
| Symbolic interactionism | How do people communicate to make their social settings meaningful, thus helping to create their social circumstances? | People frequently act in ways they consider fair or just, even if it does not maximize their personal gain. Some people even act altruistically. Thus, selfishness and conflict are not the only bases of social interaction.<br><br>When people behave fairly or altruistically, they are interacting with others based on norms they have learned. These norms say they should act justly and help people in need, even if it costs a lot to do so. |
| Feminism | How do social conventions maintain male dominance and female subordination, and how do these conventions get overturned? | Women laugh more than men do in everyday conversations. Men are more likely than women are to engage in long monologues and interrupt when others are talking. They are also less likely to ask for help or directions because doing so would imply a reduction in their authority. These research findings suggest that social interaction is structured by the relative power of women and men. |

bombers destroyed its train station, my father was deep in the Russian interior, serving in a workers' battalion attached to the Soviet Red Army.

My father was one of 300 000 Polish Jews who fled eastward into Russia before the Nazi genocide machine could reach them. The remaining 3 million Polish Jews were killed in various ways. Some died in battle. Many more, like my father's mother and younger siblings, were rounded up like diseased cattle and shot. However, most of Poland's Jews wound up in the concentration camps. Those deemed unfit were shipped to the gas chambers. Those declared able to work were turned into slaves until they could work no more. Then they, too, met their fate. A mere 9 percent of Poland's 3.3 million Jews survived World War II. The Nazi regime was responsible for the death of about 6 million Jews in Europe.

One question that always perplexed my father about the war was this: How was it possible for many thousands of ordinary Germans—products of what he regarded as the most advanced civilization on earth—to systematically murder millions of defenceless and innocent Jews, Romani ("Gypsies"), gays and lesbians, and people with mental disabilities in the death camps? To answer this question adequately, one must use sociological concepts.

## HOW SOCIAL GROUPS SHAPE OUR ACTIONS

The conventional, nonsociological answer to the question of how ordinary Germans could commit the crime of the twentieth century is that many Nazis were evil, sadistic, or deluded enough to think that Jews and other undesirables threatened the existence of the German people. Therefore, in the Nazi mind, the innocents had to be killed. This answer is given in the Oscar-winning movie *Schindler's List* and many other accounts. While this answer is accurate for a certain proportion of the German population (Goldhagen, 1996), it is not the whole story. Sociologists emphasize three additional factors:

1. *Norms of solidarity demand conformity.* When we form relationships with friends, lovers, spouses, teammates, and comrades-in-arms, we develop shared ideas, or *norms of solidarity*, about how we should behave toward them to sustain the relationships. Because these relationships are emotionally important to us, we sometimes pay more attention to norms of solidarity than to the morality of our actions. For example, a study of the Nazis who roamed the Polish countryside to shoot and kill Jews and other "enemies" of Nazi Germany found

that the soldiers often did not hate the people they systematically slaughtered, but they had few qualms about their actions (Browning, 1992). They simply developed deep loyalty to one another. They felt they had to get their assigned job done or face letting down their comrades. Thus, they committed atrocities partly because they just wanted to maintain group morale, solidarity, and loyalty. They committed evil deeds not because they were extraordinarily bad but because they were quite ordinary—ordinary in the sense that they acted to sustain their friendship ties and to serve their group, just like most people would.

The case of the Nazi regime may seem extreme, but other instances of going along with criminal behaviour uncover a similar dynamic at work. Why do people rarely report crimes committed by corporations? Employees may worry about being reprimanded or fired if they become whistle-blowers, but they also worry about letting down their co-workers. Why do gang members engage in criminal acts? They may seek financial gain, but they also regard crime as a way of maintaining a close social bond with the other gang members.

A study of Polish Christians who helped save Jews during World War II helps clarify why some people violate group norms (Tec, 1986). The heroism of these Polish Christians was not correlated with their educational attainment, political orientation, religious background, or even attitudes toward Jews. In fact, some Polish Christians who helped save Jews were quite anti-Semitic. Instead, these Christian heroes were for one reason or another estranged or cut off from mainstream norms. Because they were poorly socialized into the norms of their society, they were freer not to conform and instead to act in ways they believed were right. We could tell a roughly similar story about corporate whistle-blowers or people who turn in members of their gang. They are disloyal from an insider's point of view but heroic from an outsider's point of view, often because they have been poorly socialized into the group's norms.

2. *Structures of authority tend to render people obedient.* Most people find it difficult to disobey authorities because they fear ridicule, ostracism, and punishment. This was demonstrated in a famous experiment conducted by social psychologist Stanley Milgram (1974). (As its name implies, social psychology straddles the border between sociology and psychology.)

Milgram informed his subjects that they were taking part in a study on punishment and learning. He brought each subject to a room where a man was strapped to a chair. An electrode was attached to the man's wrist. The subject sat in front of a console. It contained 30 switches with labels ranging from "15 volts" to "450 volts" in 15-volt increments. Labels ranging from "Slight Shock" to "Danger: Severe Shock" were pasted below the switches. The experimental subjects were told to administer a 15-volt shock for the man's first wrong answer and then increase the voltage each time he made an error.

> **bureaucracy** A large, impersonal organization composed of many clearly defined positions arranged in a hierarchy.

The man strapped in the chair was, in fact, an actor. He did not actually receive a shock. As the experimental subject apparently increased the current, however, the actor began to writhe, shouting for mercy and begging to be released. If the experimental subjects grew reluctant to administer more current, Milgram assured them the man strapped in the chair would be fine and insisted that the success of the experiment depended on the subject's obedience. The subjects were, however, free to abort the experiment at any time.

Some 71 percent of experimental subjects administered shocks of 285 volts or more, even though the switches at that level were labelled "Intense Shock," "Extreme Intensity Shock," and "Danger: Severe Shock" and despite the fact that the actor appeared to be in great distress at this level of current (see Figure 4.5).

Milgram's experiment suggests that when people are introduced to a structure of authority, they are inclined to obey those in power. This is the case even if the authority structure is new and artificial, even if the people are free to walk away from it with no penalty, and even if they think that by remaining in its grip they are inflicting terrible pain on another human being. In this context, the actions and inactions of German citizens in World War II become more understandable if no more forgivable.

In recent years, Milgram's research has been carefully reviewed and found wanting in some respects (see the Theories in Dispute boxed feature, Obedience to Authority: Ethics and Validity). Nonetheless, the experiment still holds important lessons for the study of obedience.

3. *Bureaucracies are highly effective structures of authority.* The Nazi genocide machine was also effective because it was bureaucratically organized. As Max Weber (1964 [1947]) defined the term, a **bureaucracy** is a large, impersonal organization comprising many clearly defined positions arranged in a hierarchy. A bureaucracy has a permanent, salaried staff of qualified experts and written goals, rules, and procedures. Staff members typically try

**FIGURE 4.5  Obedience to Authority Increases with Separation from the Negative Effects of a Person's Actions**

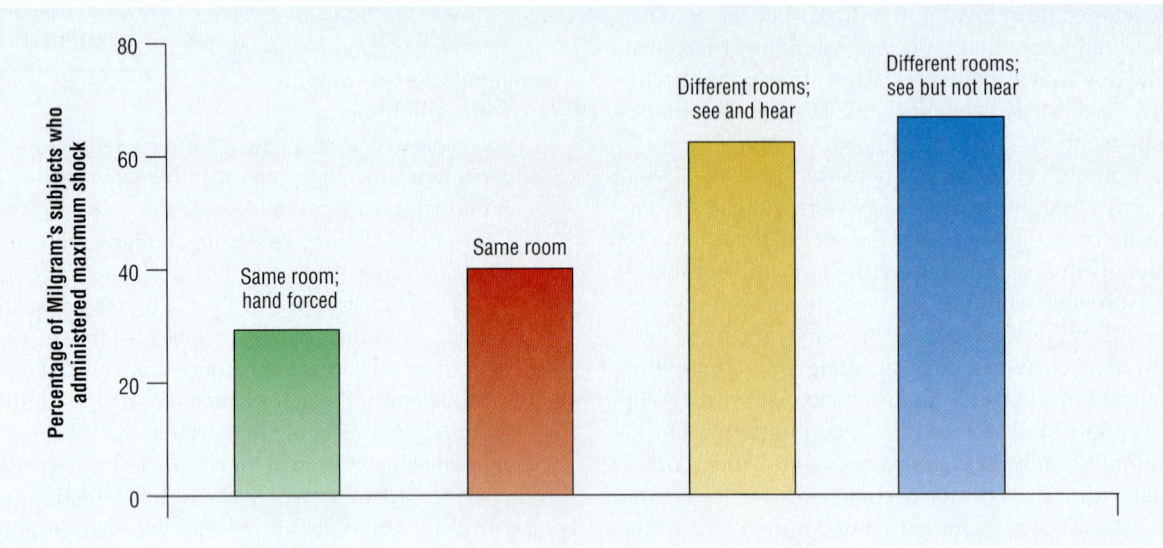

[Bar chart showing Percentage of Milgram's subjects who administered maximum shock:
- Same room; hand forced: ~30%
- Same room: ~40%
- Different rooms; see and hear: ~63%
- Different rooms; see but not hear: ~68%]

Milgram's experiment supports the view that separating people from the negative effects of their actions increases the likelihood of compliance.

Source: Adapted from "Closeness of the Victim" from *Obedience to Authority,* Chapter 4. Stanley Milgram. Copyright © 1994 by Stanley Milgram.

## THEORIES IN DISPUTE

### Obedience to Authority: Ethics and Validity

Australian social psychologist Gina Perry (2013) spent four years scouring Milgram's personal archive at Yale University and interviewing every living person who participated in his experiments back in the 1960s and early 1970s. Perry discovered ethical lapses in Milgram's research, including his failure to screen out emotionally vulnerable subjects. She found that the deeper he got into the experiments, the more he pushed subjects to obey: one woman was urged 26 times to give high-voltage shocks before she finally complied and was categorized as "obedient." Perry exposed the fact that Milgram selectively suppressed some data so the experiments' findings would more strongly support his central claim. Finally, she questioned whether Milgram's experiments mirrored what one would find in the real world.

Milgram's ethical and methodological breaches are undeniable. However, experiments can and should be replicated to see if initial results are reliable. If initial experiments fail to adhere to high ethical and methodological standards, replications should improve on them. And, in fact, more than 20 ethically and methodologically superior variants of the Milgram experiment have been conducted since the 1970s. In most cases they support Milgram's core finding (see, for example, Burger, 2009). Thus, while social psychologists continue to debate Milgram's theory of obedience, my reading of the literature leads me to conclude that it still has validity, even in real-world settings (Browning, 1992).

### Critical Thinking Questions

- What do ongoing debates about the Milgram experiments tell us about how useful experiments are as tests of sociological theory?
- Should one be permitted to use data from research that is marred by ethical breaches or should such data be embargoed?

to find ways to run their organization more efficiently. *Efficiency* means achieving the bureaucracy's goals at the least cost.

The goal of the Nazi genocide machine was to kill Jews and other undesirables. To achieve that goal with maximum efficiency, the job was broken into many small tasks. Most officials performed only one function, such as checking train schedules, organizing entertainment for camp guards, maintaining supplies of Zyklon B gas, and removing ashes from the crematoria. The full horror of what was happening eluded many officials or at least could be conveniently ignored as they concentrated on their jobs, most of them far removed from the gas chambers and death camps in occupied Poland.

Many factors account for variations in Jewish victimization rates across Europe during World War II. One factor was bureaucratic organization. Not coincidentally, the proportion of Jews killed was highest not in the Nazi-controlled countries where the hatred of Jews was most intense (for example, Romania), but in countries where the Nazi bureaucracy was best organized (for example, Holland (Bauman, 1989; Sofsky, 1997 [1993]).

In short, the sociological reply to the question posed by my father is that it was not just blind hatred but also the nature of groups and bureaucracies that made it possible for the Nazis to kill innocent people so ruthlessly.

## LO⁴ SOCIAL NETWORKS

Suppose someone asked you to deliver a letter to a complete stranger on the other side of the country by using only acquaintances to pass the letter along. You give the letter to an acquaintance, who gives the letter to one of his or her acquaintances, and so on. Research shows that, on average, it would take no more than about six acquaintances to get the letter to the stranger. This fact suggests that in a fundamental sociological sense, we live in a small world. Just a few social ties separate us from everyone else.

Our world is small because we are enmeshed in overlapping sets of social relations, or social networks. Although any particular individual may know a small number of people, his or her family members, friends, co-workers, and others know many more people who extend far beyond that individual's personal network. So, for example, I am likely to be a complete stranger to you. Yet your professor may know me, or someone who knows someone who knows me. Probably no more than two links separate me from you. Put differently, although our personal networks are small, they lead quickly to much larger networks. We live in a small world because our social networks connect us to the larger world.

> **social network** A bounded set of units that are linked by the exchange of material or emotional resources.

Sociologists define a **social network** as a bounded set of units (individuals, organizations, countries, and so on) linked by the exchange of material or emotional resources, everything from money to friendship. The patterns of exchange determine the boundaries of the network. Network members exchange resources more frequently with each other than with non-members. Individuals in a network think of themselves as network members. Social networks may be formal (i.e., defined in writing) or informal (i.e., defined only in practice). The people you know personally form the boundaries of your personal network. However, each of your network members is linked to people in other social networks. This is what connects you to people you have never met, creating a "small world" that extends far beyond your personal network.

## THE VALUE OF NETWORK ANALYSIS

The study of social networks is not restricted to ties among individuals (Wasserman and Faust, 1994; Wellman and Berkowitz, 1997 [1988]). The units of analysis (or *nodes*) in a network can be individuals, groups, organizations, and even countries. Thus, social network analysts have examined everything from intimate relationships between lovers to diplomatic relationships among nations.

Unlike organizations, most networks lack names and offices. There is a Boy Scouts of Canada but no Asian Trading Bloc. In a sense, networks lie beneath the more visible collectivities of social life, but that makes them no less real or important. Some analysts claim that we can gain only a partial sense of why certain things happen in the social world by focusing on highly visible collectivities. From their point of view, the whole story requires probing below the surface and examining the network level. The study of social networks clarifies a wide range of social phenomena, including how people find jobs, form communities, and find marriage partners (see the Sociology and the Media feature, *The Big Sick*).

### Finding a Job

Many people learn about important events, ideas, and opportunities from their social networks. Friends and acquaintances often introduce you to everything from

# SOCIOLOGY AND THE MEDIA

## The Big Sick

This really happened. Actor Kumail Nanjiani fell deeply in love with his girlfriend, writer Emily V. Gordon, *after* they broke up and *during* the time she was in a coma. She revived, and they got married three months later. Then Judd Apatow made a charming comedy out of the story.

The drama in *The Big Sick* hinges on the fact that Kumail and Emily come from different groups. She is a white American. He is from a traditional Pakistani family. Kumail and Emily broke up because Kumail's family strenuously objected to his dating a woman who was not of Pakistani origin. They wanted to arrange a marriage for him, as is the tradition. The breakup occurred because Kumail couldn't take the pressure and Emily couldn't take the slight.

It all worked out in the end to the everlasting joy of the young couple, but this is a sweet story with a bitter pill that many young people from immigrant families must swallow. Amman and abba (or baba and mama or ina and ama or ima and aba or eomma and appa—the phenomenon is common to all ethnicities and races) typically want their offspring to marry within the group. You know why: it's hard for the immigrant generation in a country like Canada to imagine that their family will witness the weakening and eventual disappearance of the culture in which they were raised and which they cherish.

Kumail and Emily share a laugh in *The Big Sick*.

You also know why the immigrant generation's children (first-generation Canadians) and especially grandchildren (second-generation Canadians) are often tempted to marry outside the group. Their first language is French or English. They attend Canadian schools, feel comfortable with Canadian culture, and befriend Canadians from the entire range of ethnic and racial groups. Consequently, many of them find it perfectly natural to date and eventually establish a long-term intimate relationship with a person from outside their group. See Figure 4.6 for the percentage of second-generation Canadians from various racial and ethnic groups who are married or living common-law and have formed a union with someone from outside their group.

What you may not know is why one person is likely to marry within the group while another is less likely to do so. Sociological research suggests that three sets of factors influence whether you're in or out (Kalmijn, 1998: 398–404):

1. *Resources.* Most people want a mate who has similar values, tastes, and knowledge. These resources are more likely to be aligned with those of the cultural mainstream for minority group members who are more culturally assimilated. One would therefore expect to find more intermarriage among culturally assimilated minority group members. In addition, most people want to maximize the financial assets and status they gain from marriage. Minority group members with more financial assets and higher status are likely to be more appealing to those in the cultural mainstream. Therefore, one would expect a higher rate of intermarriage among minority group members with relatively high status and good financial prospects.

2. *Third parties.* Because marriage between people from different groups may threaten the cohesion of one or both groups, third parties often intervene to prevent marriages outside the group. Families, neighbourhoods, communities, and religious institutions raise young people to identify with the group they belong to and think of themselves as different from members of other groups. They also apply sanctions to young people who threaten to marry outside the group; Kumail Nanjiani's mother refused to talk to him when she found

## FIGURE 4.6  Mixed Unions among Second-Generation Canadians (percentage)

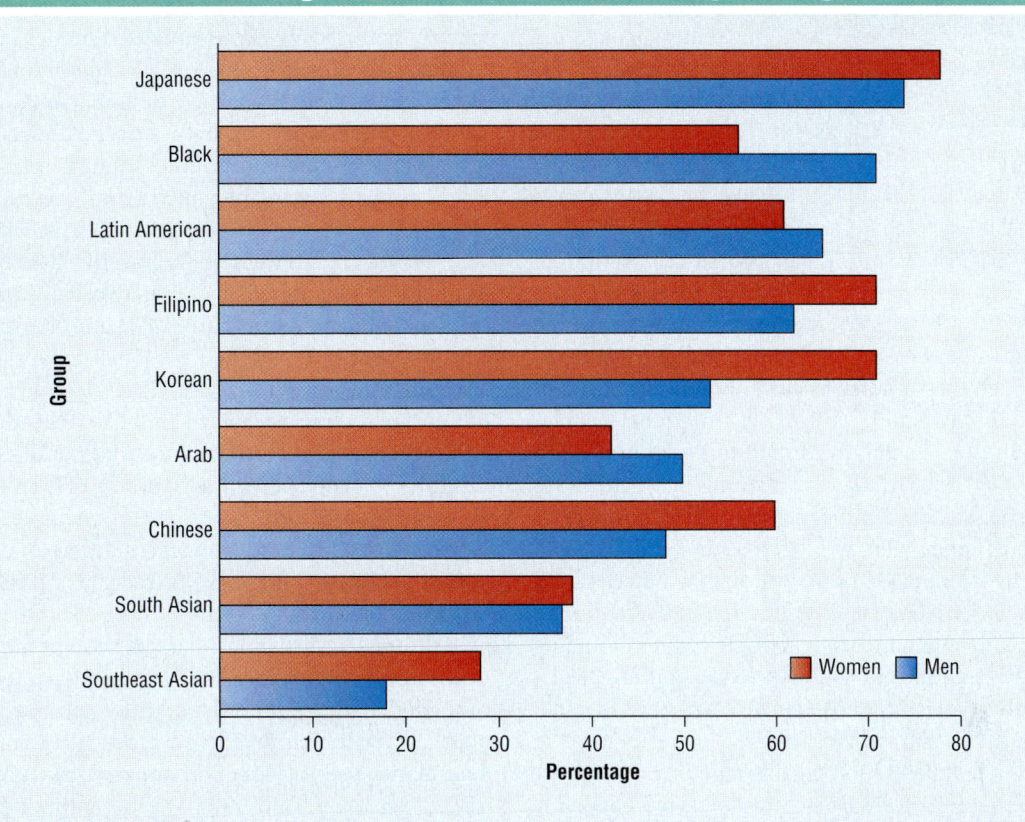

[Bar chart showing mixed union percentages by group and gender (Women in orange, Men in blue):
- Japanese: Women ~78, Men ~75
- Black: Women ~56, Men ~71
- Latin American: Women ~62, Men ~65
- Filipino: Women ~71, Men ~62
- Korean: Women ~71, Men ~54
- Arab: Women ~42, Men ~50
- Chinese: Women ~60, Men ~48
- South Asian: Women ~38, Men ~36
- Southeast Asian: Women ~28, Men ~18]

Source: From Richard Alba (2017). "Immigration and Mainstream Expansion in Canada and the United States," pp. 11–27 in Robert Brym, ed., *Immigration and the Future of Canadian Society*. Proceedings of the Second S. D. Clark Symposium on the Future of Canadian Society (Oakville ON: Rock's Mills Press). Reproduced by permission.

out about his relationship with Emily Gordon. Members of ethnic and racial groups that are less assimilated and more highly organized are more likely to play this third-party role, so their offspring are less likely to out-marry than are the offspring of members of other ethnic and racial groups.

3. *Demography.* The chance of marrying inside one's group increases with the group's size and geographical concentration. If you are a member of a small group or a group that is dispersed geographically, there may simply be too few prospects in your immediate social setting from which to choose. In that case, you stand a greater chance of choosing a mate from outside your group. In addition, the ratio of men to women in a group influences the degree to which members of each sex marry inside or outside the group. For instance, war or imprisonment may eliminate many male group members as potential marriage partners. This may encourage female group members to marry outside the group. Finally, because in a country like Canada people usually meet potential spouses in school, at work, in bars, and in clubs, the degree to which these settings are socially segregated influences mate selection. You are more likely to marry outside your group if socially heterogeneous meeting places are available and you frequent them.

## Critical Thinking Questions

- The groups in Figure 4.6 are ranked from those with the highest average rate of out-marriage at the top to those with the lowest average rate of out-marriage at the bottom. How do groups at the top differ from those at the bottom in ways that might explain differences in the average rate of out-marriage?
- Among the second-generation Canadians in Figure 4.6, women are more likely to out-marry than are men in six cases (Japanese, Filipino, Korean, Chinese, South Asian, and Southeast Asian). Men are more likely to out-marry than women in three cases (black, Latin American, and Arab). What might account for this difference?

> **social group** A group composed of one or more networks of people who identify with one another and adhere to defined norms, roles, and statuses.
>
> **social category** A group composed of people who share similar status but do not identify with one another.

an interesting university course or a great restaurant to a satisfying occupation or a future spouse. Social networks aren't the only source of information, but they are highly significant.

Consider how people find jobs. Do you look in the "Help Wanted" section of your local newspaper, scan the Internet, or walk around certain areas of town looking for "Employee Wanted" signs? Although these strategies are common, people often learn about employment opportunities from other people.

What kind of people? According to sociologist Mark Granovetter (1973), you may have strong or weak ties to another person. You have strong ties to people who are close to you, such as family members and friends. You have weak ties to mere acquaintances, such as people you meet at parties and friends of friends. In his research, Granovetter found that weak ties are more important than strong ties in finding a job, which is contrary to common sense. You might reasonably assume that a mere acquaintance wouldn't do much to help you find a job, whereas a close friend or relative would make a lot more effort in this regard. However, by focusing on the flow of information in personal networks, Granovetter found something different. Mere acquaintances are more likely to provide useful information about employment opportunities than friends or family members because people who are close to you typically share overlapping networks. Therefore, the information they can provide about job opportunities is often redundant.

In contrast, mere acquaintances are likely to be connected to *diverse* networks. They can therefore provide information about many different job openings and make introductions to many different potential employers. Moreover, because people typically have more weak ties than strong ties, the sum of weak ties holds more information about job opportunities than does the sum of strong ties. These features of personal networks allowed Granovetter to conclude that the "strength of weak ties" lies in their diversity and abundance.

## Urban Networks

We rely on social networks for a lot more than job information. Consider everyday life in the big city. We often think of big cities as cold and alienating places where few people know one another. In this view, urban acquaintanceships tend to be few and functionally specific; we know someone fleetingly as a bank teller or a server in a restaurant but not as a whole person. Even dating can involve a series of brief encounters. In contrast, people often think of small towns as friendly, comfortable places where everyone knows everyone else (and everyone else's business). Indeed, some of the founders of sociology emphasized just this distinction. Notably, German sociologist Ferdinand Tönnies (1988 [1887]) contrasted *community* with *society*. According to Tönnies, a community is marked by intimate and emotionally intense social ties, whereas a society is marked by impersonal relationships held together largely by self-interest. A big city is a prime example of a society in Tönnies's judgment.

Tönnies's view prevailed until network analysts started studying big-city life in the 1970s. Where Tönnies saw only sparse, functionally specific ties, network analysts found elaborate social networks, some functionally specific and some not. For example, Barry Wellman and his colleagues studied personal networks in Toronto (Wellman, Carrington, and Hall, 1997 [1988]). They found that each Torontonian had an average of about 400 social ties, including immediate and extended kin, neighbours, friends, and co-workers. These ties provided everything from emotional aid (for example, visits after a personal tragedy) and financial support (small loans) to minor services (fixing a lawn mower) and information of the kind Granovetter studied.

Strong, enduring ties that last a long time are typically restricted to immediate family members, a few close relatives and friends, and a close co-worker or two. Beyond that, however, people rely on a wide array of ties for different purposes at different times. Downtown residents sitting on their front stoops on a summer evening, sipping beverages, and chatting with neighbours as the kids play road hockey may be less common than they were 50 years ago. However, the automobile, public transportation, the telephone, and the Internet help people stay in close touch with a wide range of contacts for a variety of purposes (Haythornwaite and Wellman, 2002). Far from living in an impersonal and alienating world, the lives of today's city dwellers are network-rich.

## LO⁵ GROUPS

A **social group** consists of one or more social networks, the members of which identify with one another, routinely interact, and adhere to defined norms, roles, and statuses. In contrast, social categories consist of people who share similar status but do not routinely interact or identify with one another. Coffee drinkers form a **social category**. Members of a family, sports team, or college form groups. Groups exert enormous influence on us.

## GROUP CONFORMITY

*Mean Girls* tells the story of 17-year-old Cady Heron (played by Lindsay Lohan) who, after being homeschooled in Africa by her archaeologist parents, is

Cady Heron (Lindsay Lohan) learns about group boundaries in *Mean Girls*.

plunked down into a suburban high school when the family moves back to the United States. The ways of the school bewilder her, so a friend prepares "Cady's Map to North Shore High School." It shows the layout of the cafeteria, with tables neatly labelled "Varsity Jocks," "J. V. Jocks," "Plastics," "Preps," "Fat Girls," "Thin Girls," "Black Hotties," "Asian Nerds," "Cool Asians," "Cheerleaders," "Burnouts," and so on.

If you drew a map of your high school cafeteria—even your college or university cafeteria—the labels might be different, but chances are they would represent cliques that are just as segregated as North Shore High was. Everywhere, group members tend to dress and act alike, use the same slang, like and dislike the same kind of music, and demand loyalty, especially in the face of external threat. All groups demand conformity and, to varying degrees, they get it, although, of course, group loyalties may change with changing social circumstances.

## The Asch Experiment

A famous experiment conducted by social psychologist Solomon Asch shows how group pressure creates conformity (Asch, 1955). Asch gathered seven men, one of whom was the experimental subject. The other six were Asch's confederates. Asch showed the seven men a card with a line drawn on it. He then showed them a second card with three lines of varying lengths drawn on it (see Figure 4.7).

How are disconnected individuals turned into cohesive teams through social interaction and the sharing of symbols?

CHAPTER 4 From Social Interaction to Social Organizations

**FIGURE 4.7** The Asch Experiment

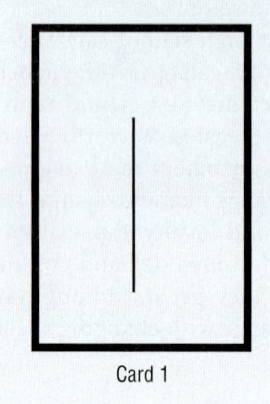

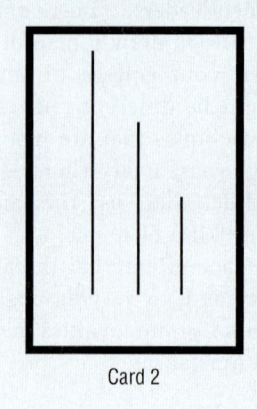

Card 1    Card 2

One by one, he asked the confederates to judge which line on card 2 was the same length as the line on card 1. The answer was obvious. One line on card 2 was shorter than the line on card 1. One line was longer. One was exactly the same length. Yet, as instructed by Asch, all six confederates said that either the shorter or the longer line was the same length as the line on card 1. When it came time for the experimental subject to make his judgment, he typically overruled his own perception and agreed with the majority. Only 25 percent of Asch's experimental subjects consistently gave the right answer. Asch thus demonstrated how easily group pressure can overturn individual conviction and result in conformity.

## Groupthink and Bystander Apathy

The power of groups to ensure conformity is often a valuable asset. Sports teams couldn't excel without the willingness of players to undergo personal sacrifice for the good of the group, nor could armies function. In fact, as sociologists have demonstrated and as high-ranking military officers have observed, group cohesion—not patriotism or bravery—is the main factor motivating soldiers to engage in combat (Marshall, 1947: 160–61; Stouffer et al., 1949). As one soldier says in the movie *Black Hawk Down*: "When I go home people will ask me: 'Hey, Hoot, why do you do it, man? What, you some kinda war junkie?' You know what I'll say? I won't say a goddamn word. Why? They won't understand. They won't understand why we do it. They won't understand that it's about the men next to you. And that's it. That's all it is."

**groupthink** Group pressure to conform despite individual misgivings.

**bystander apathy** Occurs when people observe someone in an emergency but do not offer help because they feel no responsibility for the incident and justify their inaction by the fact that others are not responding to it.

However, being a "good team player" can have a downside, because group consensus can sometimes be misguided or dangerous. Dissent might save the group from making mistakes, but the pressure to conform despite individual misgivings—sometimes called **groupthink** (Janis, 1972)—can lead to disaster. For instance, groupthink was at work in high-level meetings preceding the space shuttle *Columbia* disaster in 2003. Transcripts of those meetings at the National Aeronautics and Space Administration (NASA) show that the official who ran shuttle management meetings, a non-engineer, believed from the outset that foam insulation debris could not damage the spacecraft. She dismissed the issue and cut off discussion when an engineer expressed his concerns. The others present quickly fell into line with the person running the meeting (Wald and Schwartz, 2003). A few days later, damage caused by foam insulation debris caused *Columbia* to break apart on re-entry into Earth's atmosphere. Seven astronauts died.

The concept of **bystander apathy** is related to the idea of groupthink. Bystander apathy occurs when people observe someone in an emergency but do not offer help. One case that attracted worldwide attention in 2011 involved a two-year-old toddler in Foshan, China, who was seriously injured when she wandered into the path of a van. Surveillance footage showed that the driver did not stop. A second truck then drove over the child. Again, the driver did not stop. More than a dozen people turned a blind eye when they walked by the critically injured child. Finally, a trash collector pulled her off the road and managed to track down her mother. The child later died in hospital (to see the YouTube video of this incident, use the search term "tragic accident at Foshan").

Studies of bystander apathy suggest that, in general, as the number of bystanders increases, the likelihood of any one bystander helping a person in distress decreases because the greater the number of bystanders, the less responsibility any one individual feels. This behaviour shows that people usually take their cues for action from others and again demonstrates the power of groups over individuals.

## Group Boundaries: Competition and Self-Esteem

The boundaries separating groups often seem unchangeable and even natural. They are not. In general, groups construct boundaries to assert their dominance, increase their self-esteem, or compete for scarce resources, such as jobs (Barth, 1969; Levine and Campbell, 1972; Tajfel, 1981). Sometimes this involves redrawing group boundaries. A survivor of the Nazi occupation of Amsterdam recalls the following in her memoir:

> During the occupation, there had been just two kinds of Dutch people: those who collaborated [with the Nazis] and those who resisted. Political

and religious and class differences had been forgotten. It was simply we Dutch against our German oppressor. After the liberation, the unity quickly disappeared and people again divided into groups and factions that were at odds with each other. Everyone returned to his old ways, his old class, to his own political group (Gies with Gold, 1987: 244).

The *Robbers Cave Study* is a classic experiment that illustrates the conditions leading to the crystallization of group boundaries (Sherif et al., 1988 [1961]). Researchers took two groups of 11-year-old boys to a summer camp at Robbers Cave State Park in Oklahoma. The boys were strangers to one another, and the two groups were kept apart for about a week. They swam, camped, and hiked. Each group chose a name for itself, and the boys printed their group's name on their caps and T-shirts. Then the two groups met. A series of athletic competitions was set up between them. Soon, each group became highly antagonistic toward the other. Each group came to hold the other in low esteem. The boys ransacked cabins, started food fights, and stole various items from members of the other group. Thus, under competitive conditions, the boys quickly drew sharp group boundaries.

The investigators next stopped the athletic competitions and created several apparent emergencies whose solution required cooperation between the two groups. One such emergency involved a leak in the pipe supplying water to the camp. The researchers assigned the boys to teams comprising members of *both* groups. Their job was to inspect the pipe and fix the leak. After engaging in several such cooperative ventures, the boys started playing together without fighting. Once cooperation replaced competition and the groups ceased to hold each other in low esteem, group boundaries melted away as quickly as they had formed. Significantly, the two groups were of equal status—the boys were all white, middle-class, and 11 years old—and their contact involved face-to-face interaction in a setting where norms established by the investigators promoted a reduction of group prejudice. Social scientists today recognize that such conditions must be in place before group boundaries fade (Sternberg, 1998: 512).

## Reference Groups

So far, we have focused almost exclusively on face-to-face interaction in groups. However, people also interact with other group members in their imagination. Take reference groups, for example. A **reference group** is composed of people against whom an individual evaluates his or her situation or conduct. Put differently, members of a reference group function as "role models." Reference groups may influence us even though they represent a largely imaginary ideal. For instance, the advertising industry promotes certain body ideals that many people try to emulate, although we know that hardly anyone looks like a runway model or a Barbie doll.

## PRIMARY AND SECONDARY GROUPS

Many kinds of social groups exist. However, sociologists make a basic distinction between primary and secondary groups. In a **primary group**, norms, roles, and statuses are agreed on but are not put into writing. Social interaction creates strong emotional ties, extends over a long period, and involves a wide range of activities. It results in group members knowing one another well. The family is the most important primary group.

A **secondary group** is larger and more impersonal than a primary group is. Compared with primary groups, social interaction in secondary groups creates weaker emotional ties. It extends over a shorter period and involves a narrow range of activities. It results in most group members having at most a passing acquaintance with one another. Your sociology class is an example of a secondary group.

Many secondary groups are **formal organizations**, or secondary groups designed to achieve explicit objectives. In complex societies like ours, the most common and influential formal organizations are bureaucracies. We now turn to an examination of these often frustrating but necessary organizational forms.

> **reference group** A group of people against whom an individual evaluates his or her situation or conduct.
>
> **primary group** A social group in which norms, roles, and statuses are agreed on but are not put into writing. Social interaction leads to strong emotional ties. It extends over a long period and involves a wide range of activities. It results in group members knowing one another well.
>
> **secondary group** A social group that is larger and more impersonal than a primary group. Compared with primary groups, social interaction in secondary groups creates weaker emotional ties. It extends over a shorter period and involves a narrow range of activities. It results in most group members having at most a passing acquaintance with one another.
>
> **formal organizations** Secondary groups designed to achieve specific and explicit objectives.

## LO6 BUREAUCRACY

Earlier, we noted that Weber regarded bureaucracies as the most efficient type of secondary group. This runs against the grain of common knowledge. In everyday speech, when someone says "bureaucracy," people commonly think of bored clerks sitting in small cubicles spinning out endless trails of red tape that create needless waste and frustrate the goals of clients. The idea that bureaucracies are efficient may seem odd.

How can we square the reality of bureaucratic inefficiencies—even tragedies—with Weber's view that bureaucracies are the most efficient type of secondary group? The answer is twofold. First, we must recognize that when Weber wrote about the efficiency of bureaucracy, he was comparing it with older organizational forms. These had operated on the basis of either traditional practice ("We do it this way because we've always done it this way") or the charisma of their leaders ("We do it this way because our chief inspires us to do it this way"). Compared with such "traditional" and "charismatic" organizations, bureaucracies are generally more efficient.

Second, we must recognize that Weber thought bureaucracies could operate efficiently only in the ideal case. He wrote extensively about some of bureaucracy's less admirable aspects in the real world. In other words, he understood that reality is often messier than the ideal case. In reality, bureaucracies vary in efficiency. Therefore, rather than proclaiming bureaucracy efficient or inefficient, we need to find out what makes bureaucracies work well or poorly.

One factor underlying bureaucratic inefficiency is size. The larger the bureaucracy, the more difficult it is for functionaries to communicate. Moreover, bigger bureaucracies make it easier for rivalries and coalitions to form.

A second factor underlying bureaucratic inefficiency is social structure. Figure 4.8 shows a typical bureaucratic structure: a hierarchy. The bureaucracy has a head, below which are three divisions, below which are six departments. As you move up the hierarchy, the power of the staff increases. Note also the red lines of communication that join the various bureaucratic units. Departments report only to their divisions. Divisions report only to the head.

Usually, the more levels in a bureaucratic structure, the more difficult communication becomes because people have to communicate indirectly, through department and division heads, rather than directly with one another. Information may be lost, blocked, reinterpreted, or distorted as it moves up the hierarchy, or an excess of information may cause top levels to become engulfed in a paperwork blizzard that prevents them from clearly seeing the needs of the organization and its clients. Bureaucratic heads may have only a vague and imprecise idea of what is happening "on the ground" (Wilensky, 1967).

Consider also what happens when the lines of communication directly joining departments or divisions are weak or nonexistent. As the lines joining units in Figure 4.8 suggest, Department A1 may have information that could help Department B1 do its job better, but A1 may have to communicate that information indirectly through the division level. At the division level, the information may be lost, blocked, reinterpreted, or distorted. Thus, just as people who have authority may lack information, people who have information may lack the authority to act on it directly (Crozier, 1964).

In the business world, large bureaucratic organizations are sometimes unable to compete against smaller, innovative firms, particularly in industries that are changing quickly. This situation occurs partly because innovative firms tend to have more democratic organizational structures with fewer levels of authority, such as the network illustrated in Figure 4.9. Note that the network structure has fewer levels than the traditional bureaucratic structure in Figure 4.8. Moreover, in the network structure, lines of communication link all units. In the traditional bureaucratic structure, information flows only upward.

Much evidence suggests that bureaucracies with fewer levels of authority, decentralized decision making, and multiple lines of communication produce more satisfied workers, happier clients, and bigger profits. Some of this evidence comes from Sweden and Japan. Beginning in the early 1970s, such corporations as Volvo and Toyota were at the forefront of bureaucratic innovation. They began eliminating middle-management positions. They allowed worker participation in a variety of tasks related to their main functions. They delegated authority

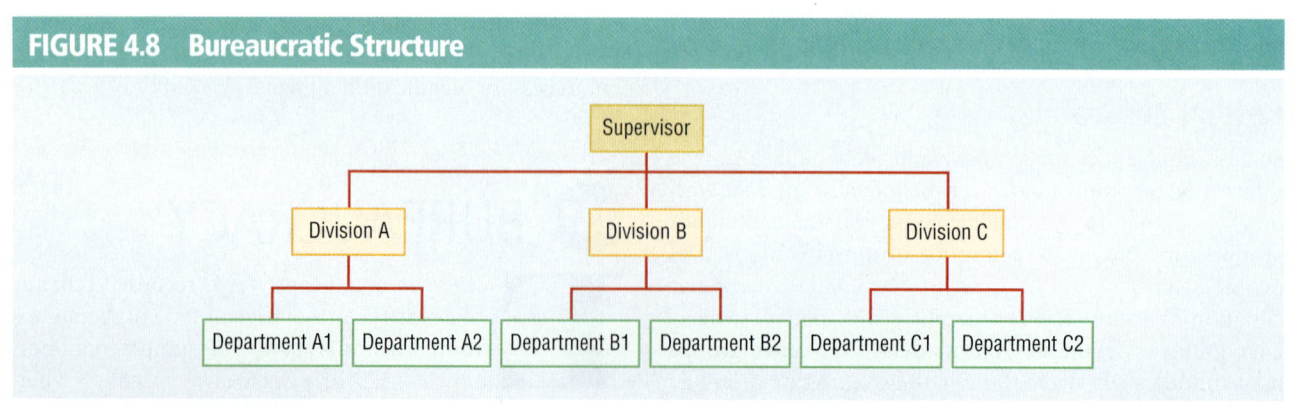

**FIGURE 4.8 Bureaucratic Structure**

Source: From BRYM/ROBERTS/STROHSCHEIN/LIE. *Sociology: Your Compass for a New World*, 6E. © 2019 Nelson Education Ltd. Reproduced by permission. www.cengage.com/permissions.

### FIGURE 4.9 Network Structure

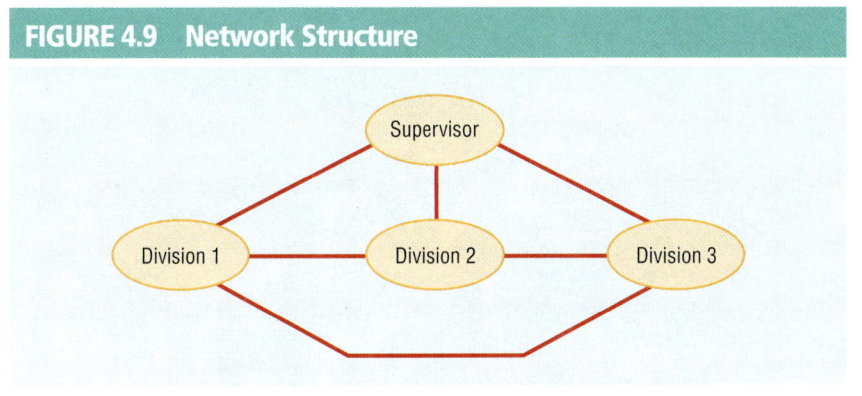

Source: From BRYM/ROBERTS/STROHSCHEIN/LIE. *Sociology: Your Compass for a New World*, 6E. © 2019 Nelson Education Ltd. Reproduced by permission. www.cengage.com/permissions.

to autonomous teams of a dozen or so workers that were allowed to make many decisions themselves. They formed "quality circles" of workers to monitor and correct defects in products and services. As a result, product quality, worker morale, and profitability improved. Today, these ideas have spread well beyond the Swedish and Japanese automobile industries and are evident in many large North American companies, both in the manufacturing and the service sectors.

## ORGANIZATIONAL CONSTRAINTS AND FREEDOM

In the second half of this chapter, I emphasized the capacity of networks, groups, and bureaucracies to constrain human behaviour. As you saw, such social collectivities can even encourage dangerously high levels of conformity, compel people to act against their better judgment, and dominate people in a vise of organizational rigidities.

I stressed the constraining aspect of social collectivities because I wanted to counter the commonsense view that motives alone determine the way people act. In conclusion, however, we should remember that people are often free to exercise two options other than bowing to the will of their social collectivities. One option is to struggle against the constraints imposed on them.

Knowledge, including sociological knowledge, can help in this regard. Recall the Milgram experiment in which subjects administered what they thought were painful shocks to people just because the experimenters told them to. In one replication of the experiment years later, many of the subjects refused to go along with the demands of the experimenters. Some invoked the example of the Nazis to justify their refusal to comply. Others mentioned Milgram's original experiment. Their knowledge, some of it perhaps gained in sociology courses, enabled them to resist unreasonable demands (Gamson, Fireman, and Rytina, 1982).

The second option is to leave the oppressive collectivity. Sometimes people even leave and then form a new social collectivity—a lobby, a union, a political party, a social movement. People are always free to form new social collectivities that can counteract old ones. Embedded in social relations, we can use them for good or evil.

## READY TO STUDY?

### IN THE BOOK, YOU CAN:

- Refer to the Chapter in Review section at the back of the book to have a summary of the chapter and key terms handy.
- Test your knowledge of chapter contents by answering the multiple-choice questions in the Chapter in Review section. Answers are in the appendix at the end of the book.

### ONLINE YOU CAN:

- Stay organized and efficient with MindTap—a single destination with all the course material and study aids you need to succeed.
- Flashcards are pre-populated to provide you with a jump start for review—or you can create your own.
- You can highlight text and make notes in your MindTap Reader.
- Prepare for tests with quizzes.

GO TO NELSON.COM/STUDENT TO PURCHASE THESE DIGITAL RESOURCES.

# 5
# Deviance and Crime

# LO¹ THE SOCIAL DEFINITION OF DEVIANCE AND CRIME

If you happen to come across members of the Tukano tribe in northern Brazil, don't be surprised if they greet you with a cheery "Have you bathed today?" You would probably find the question insulting, but think how you would feel if the Yanomamö people in Brazil's central highlands greeted you. An anthropologist reports that when he first encountered the Yanomamö, they rubbed mucus and tobacco juice into their palms, then inspected him by running their filthy hands over his body (Chagnon, 1992). He must have been relieved to return to urban Brazil and be greeted with a simple kiss on the cheek.

Rules for greeting people vary widely from one country to the next and among different cultural groups within one country. That is why a marketing company created an animated website showing business travellers how to greet their hosts in the 15 countries where the firm does business ("Business of Touch," 2006). After all, violating local norms can cause great offence and result in the loss of a contract, a fact that one visitor to South Korea found out too late. He beckoned his host with an index finger, after which the host grew quiet. He discovered after he lost the deal that Koreans beckon only cats and dogs with an index finger. If you want to beckon someone politely in South Korea, you should do so with all four fingers facing down, much like Canadians wave goodbye.

Because norms vary widely, deviance is relative. What some people consider normal, others consider deviant, and vice versa. No act is deviant in and of itself. People commit deviant acts only when they break a norm and cause others to react negatively. From a sociological point of view, *everyone* is a deviant in one social context or another.

## THE DIFFERENCE BETWEEN DEVIANCE AND CRIME

**Deviance** involves breaking a norm and evoking a negative reaction from others. Societies establish some norms as laws. **Crime** is

**deviance** Departure from a norm that evokes a negative reaction from others.

**crime** Deviance that is against the law.

## LEARNING OBJECTIVES:

In this chapter, you will learn to

- LO¹ See how people define deviance and crime differently in different times and places.
- LO² Interpret differences in crime rates over time and between different population categories.
- LO³ Apply a variety of sociological theories to the analysis of various aspects of deviant and criminal behaviour.
- LO⁴ Learn how forms of punishment have changed historically.
- LO⁵ Explain how fear of crime is subject to manipulation by political and commercial groups that benefit from it.
- LO⁶ Identify workable alternatives to tough prison regimes.

**law** A norm stipulated and enforced by government bodies.

**formal punishment** Penalization by the judicial system for breaking a law.

**informal punishment** A mild sanction that is imposed during face-to-face interaction rather than by the judicial system.

**stigmatization** Process of negatively evaluating people because of a marker that distinguishes them from others.

deviance that breaks a **law**, which is a norm stipulated and enforced by government bodies.

Just as deviance is relative, so is crime. Consider that a list of famous people who have been labelled criminals would include Socrates, Jesus, Louis Riel, Mahatma Ghandi, Martin Luther King, Jr., and Nelson Mandela. For many people today, these historical figures are heroes. In contrast, those who planned and participated in the extermination of Jews, Romani ("Gypsies"), leftists, and gays and lesbians in Nazi Germany were acting in a way that was defined as law-abiding at the time in Germany. You would probably consider the actions taken by the Nazis in Germany, rather than the actions of Jesus or Martin Luther King, Jr., to be criminal. That is because norms and laws have changed dramatically. Today, anyone who advocates or promotes genocide commits a crime under Canadian law. We conclude that what is considered a crime in some times and places is considered perfectly normal in other times and places.

## SANCTIONS

Many otherwise deviant acts go unnoticed or are considered too trivial to warrant negative *sanctions*, or actions indicating disapproval. People who are observed committing more serious acts of deviance are typically punished, either informally or formally.

**Formal punishment** results from people breaking laws. For example, criminals are usually formally punished by having to serve time in prison, pay a fine, or perform community service. **Informal punishment** is mild. It may involve raised eyebrows, a harsh stare, an ironic smile, gossip, ostracism, "shaming," or **stigmatization** (Braithwaite, 1989). When people are stigmatized, they are negatively evaluated because of visible characteristics that distinguish them from others (Goffman, 1963). For example, a study of newspaper portrayals of prostitutes in Victoria, British Columbia, shows that, in the 1980s, prostitutes were stigmatized as fallen women who spread disease and crime in public places and were themselves to blame for their moral failings. In the 1990s and 2000s, the stigmatization of prostitutes changed, as prostitutes were increasingly characterized as victims of ruthless pimps,

violent clients, and the global sex trade. The content of the stigma changed, but in both periods, negative and sensationalistic evaluations largely prevented serious discussion of how prostitution could be regulated to decrease risk to sex workers and their clients (Hallgrimsdottir, Phillips, and Benoit, 2006).

Types of deviance and crime vary in terms of the *severity of the social response*, which ranges from mild disapproval to capital punishment (Hagan, 1994). They vary also in terms of the *perceived harmfulness* of the deviant or criminal act. Note that actual harmfulness is not the only issue here—*perceived* harmfulness is involved too. Coca-Cola got its name because, in the early part of the last century, it contained a derivative of cocaine. Now cocaine is an illegal drug because people's perceptions of its harmfulness changed.

Finally, deviance and crime vary in terms of the *degree of public agreement* about whether an act should be considered deviant. Even the social definition of murder varies over time and across cultures and societies. For example, at the beginning of the twentieth century, Inuit communities sometimes deliberately allowed newborns to freeze to death. This was not considered to be a punishable offence if community members agreed that investing scarce resources in keeping the newborn alive could endanger everyone's well-being. Similarly, whether we classify the death of a miner as accidental or a case of manslaughter depends on the kind of worker safety legislation in existence. Some societies have more stringent worker safety rules than others, and deaths considered accidental in some societies are classified as criminal offences in others. So we see that, even when it comes to serious crimes, social definitions are variable.

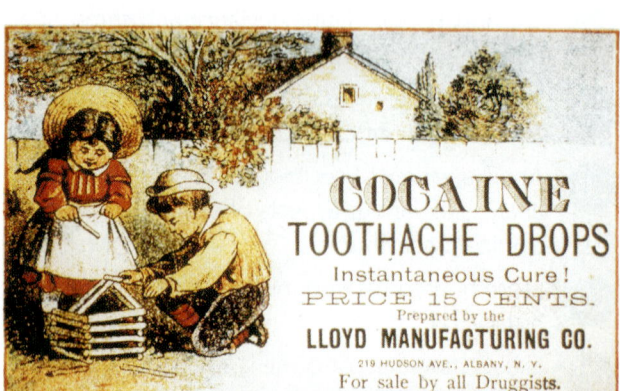

One of the determinants of the seriousness of a deviant act is its perceived harmfulness. Perceptions vary historically, however. For instance, until the early part of the twentieth century, cocaine was considered a medicine. It was an ingredient in cold formulas and toothache drops, and in these forms it was commonly given to children.

# LO² MEASURING CRIME

Some crimes are more common than others are, and rates of crime vary over place and time and across different social groups. I now describe some of these variations and then I'll review the main sociological explanations of crime and deviance.

First, a word about crime statistics. Information on crime collected by the police is the main source of crime statistics. Since 1962, the Canadian Centre for Justice Statistics (CCJS), in co-operation with the policing community, has collected police-reported crime statistics through the Uniform Crime Reporting (UCR) Survey. UCR data reflect reported crime that has been substantiated by police. Information collected by the survey includes the number of criminal incidents, the clearance status of those incidents, and persons-charged information. The UCR survey produces a continuous historical record of crime and traffic statistics reported by every police agency in Canada.

These statistics have two main shortcomings. First, much crime is not reported to the police. This is particularly true of so-called **victimless crimes**, which involve violations of the law in which no victim steps forward and is identified. Communicating for the purposes of prostitution, illegal gambling, and the use of illegal drugs are all victimless crimes. In addition, many common or "Level 1" assaults go unreported because the assailant is a friend or relative of the victim. Many victims of sexual assault are also reluctant to report the crime because they are afraid they will be humiliated or not believed and stigmatized by making the crime public.

The second main shortcoming of official crime statistics is that authorities and the wider public decide which criminal acts to report and which to ignore. If, for instance, the authorities decide to crack down on drugs, more drug-related crimes will be counted, not because more drug-related crimes are committed, but because more drug criminals are apprehended. Changes in legislation, which either create new offences or amend existing offences, also influence the number of recorded offences. Recognizing these difficulties, students of crime often supplement official crime statistics with other sources of information.

**Self-report surveys** are especially useful. In such surveys, respondents are asked to report their involvement in criminal activities, either as perpetrators or as victims. Self-report data compensate for many of the problems associated with official statistics. In general, self-report surveys report approximately the same rate of serious crime as official statistics do, but find two to three times the rate of less-serious crimes.

Self-report surveys tell us that a majority of Canadians have engaged in some type of criminal activity and that about a quarter of the population in any given year believes that they have been the victim of crime. These large proportions remind us that committing an act in violation of the law does not automatically result in being officially labelled a criminal. The process of criminal labelling can be likened to a funnel, wide at one end and narrow at the other. To be officially identified as a criminal, an individual's law-violating behaviour must first be observed and felt to justify action. The behaviour must be reported to the police who, in turn, must respond to the incident, decide that it warrants further investigation, file a report, and make an arrest. Next, the accused person must appear at a preliminary hearing (an arraignment) and a trial. If the person does not plead guilty, the possibility always exists that he or she will not be convicted because guilt has not been proven "beyond a reasonable doubt."

> **victimless crimes** Violations of the law in which no victim has stepped forward and been identified.
>
> **self-report surveys** Surveys in which respondents are asked to report their involvement in criminal activities, either as perpetrators or as victims.
>
> **victimization surveys** Surveys in which people are asked whether they have been victims of crime.

In **victimization surveys**, people are asked whether they have been victims of various crimes within a certain period. Although these types of surveys date back to the mid-1960s in the United States, no national victimization survey was conducted in Canada until 1988. As of this writing, the latest such survey was conducted in 2014. It examined householders' experience with crime, including the impact of victimization and perceptions of personal safety (Perreault, 2015). It found that Canadians reported just 31 percent of victimization incidents to the police, with property crimes more likely to be reported than were crimes against persons. In part, this tendency reflects the requirement by insurance companies that individuals seeking compensation for property stolen or damaged as the result of a criminal act must file a police report. With the exception of vandalism, all major categories of victimization were down since 1999. Although victimization surveys provide detailed information about crime victims, they provide less reliable data about offenders.

Bearing these caveats in mind, what does the official record show? Most Canadians would be understandably alarmed to hear that, in 2016, nearly 1.9 million Criminal Code incidents (excluding traffic incidents) were reported to police agencies (Keighley, 2017). They might assume that each of these incidents mirrored the violent, dramatic, and lurid offences that daily media reports bring to our attention (Statistics Canada, 2018h). But that is not the case. In 2016, nearly 86 percent of Criminal Code incidents involved no violence at all

**FIGURE 5.1** Police-Reported Crime Rates, Canada, 1962–2016 (rate per 100 000 population)

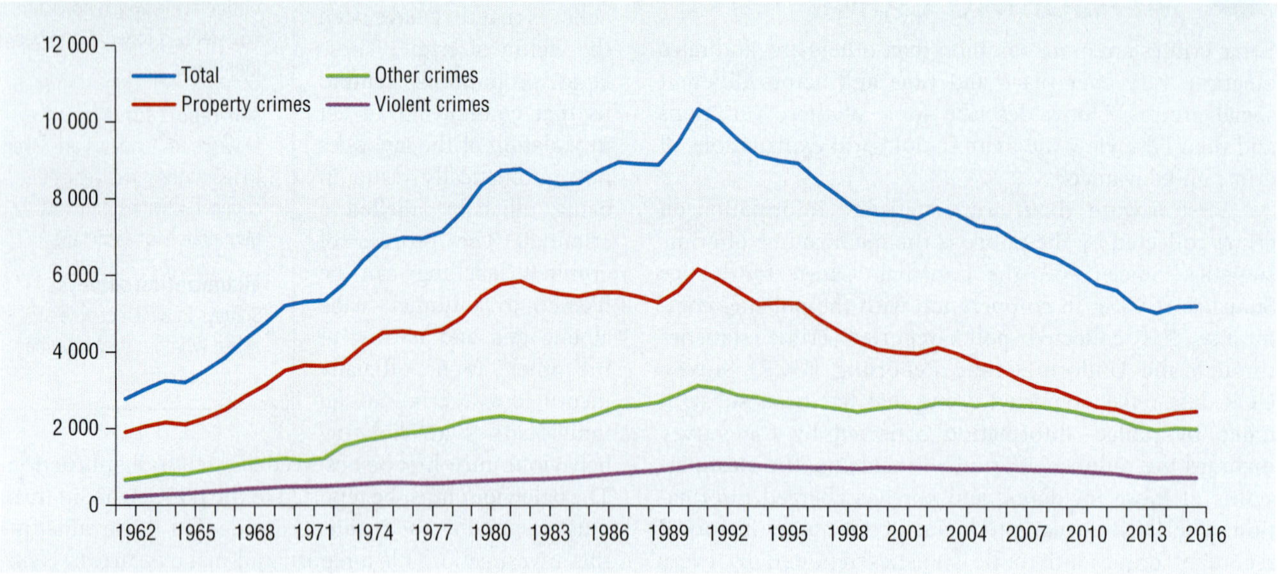

Source: Kathryn Keighley, 2017. "Police-reported crime statistics in Canada, 2016." http://www.statcan.gc.ca/pub/85-002-x/2017001/article/54842-eng.htm (retrieved 21 January 2018).

(see Figure 5.1). True, the 2016 Canadian crime rate was more than twice as high as it was in 1962. However, the long crime wave that began its upswing in the early 1960s peaked in 1992 (when it was about four times the 1962 level) and then fell steadily. In 2013, the crime rate was at its lowest level since 1969, and in 2016 it stood at about the same level as the 1970 rate. How can we explain the decline?

First, a growing number of well-trained troops are fighting crime. Today, there are about 69 000 police officers in Canada (Greenland and Alam, 2017). Recent declines in Canada's crime rate may reflect the introduction of community policing initiatives, enforcement efforts that target specific types of crime, the refinement of case management methods, improvements in the field of forensics, and crime prevention efforts.

Second, the people most prone to street crime are young men, but Canada is aging and the percentage of young people in the population has declined in recent decades.

Third, the unemployment rate has followed a downward trend since 1992 (it stood at 12.1 percent in November 1992 and 5.7 percent in December 2017). Economic conditions have favoured a decrease in crime because the factor most strongly correlated with the crime rate is the male unemployment rate.

Finally, and more controversially, some researchers argue that declining crime rates may be linked to the legalization of abortion (Donahue and Levitt, 2001). They observe that the crime rate started to decline 19 years after abortion was legalized, suggesting that the decline occurred because, with the legalization of abortion, proportionately fewer unwanted children were in the population. They argue that unwanted children are more prone to criminal behaviour than wanted children are because they tend to receive less parental supervision and guidance.

Some people believe that putting more people in prison and imposing tougher penalties on criminals also lower crime rates. For reasons discussed later, I disagree.

# CRIMINAL PROFILES

## Age and Gender

Men account for more than three-quarters of Canadian criminal court cases. However, with almost every passing year, women compose a slightly higher percentage of arrests (Mahony, 2013). This change is partly due to the fact that, in the course of socialization, traditional social controls and definitions of femininity are less often being imposed on women (see Chapter 8, Sexualities and Genders).

Most crime is committed by people who have not reached middle age. The 15- to 24-year-old age cohort is the most prone to criminal behaviour, with 18-year-olds having the highest crime rate. The percentage of 15- to 24-year-olds who are charged with a *violent* crime is about twice as high as the percentage of 15- to 24-year-olds in the population. For *property* crimes, the percentage is about three times higher (Brennan, 2013; Savoie, 2002: 3).

## Race

Analysis of official statistics reveals that race is also a factor in who is arrested. Although Indigenous peoples represent about 4 percent of Canada's population, they account for nearly a quarter of the federal inmate population—31 percent in the case of women (Bellrichard, 2018). The overrepresentation of Indigenous peoples in Canada's prisons is particularly marked in the Prairie provinces and the northern territories, where they form a relatively large part of the population. For example, in Saskatchewan Penitentiary, nearly two-thirds of inmates are Indigenous (Office of the Correctional Investigator, 2013).

There are five reasons for the overrepresentation of Indigenous peoples in Canada's prisons (Hartnagel, 2000). First, a disproportionately large number of Indigenous people are poor. Although the great majority of poor people are law-abiding, poverty and its handicaps are associated with elevated crime rates. Second, the Indigenous population is younger than the rest of the population and, as we have seen, young people are most crime-prone. Third, Indigenous people tend to commit so-called **street crimes**—breaking and entering, robbery, assault, and the like—that are more detectable than **white-collar crimes** such as embezzlement, fraud, copyright infringement, false advertising, and so on. Fourth, the police, the courts, and other institutions may discriminate against Indigenous peoples. As a result, Indigenous peoples may be more likely to be apprehended, prosecuted, and convicted. Fifth, contact with Western settlers and Western culture disrupted social life in Indigenous communities (see Chapter 7, Race and Ethnicity). The disruption led to a weakening of social control over community members. Some people think that certain "races" are *inherently* more law-abiding than others, but they are able to hold such an opinion only by ignoring the powerful *social* forces that cause so many Indigenous peoples to be incarcerated in Canada (Roberts and Gabor, 1990).

Most of the factors listed above also account for the above-average incarceration rate among black Canadians. Occupying a relatively low class position, engaging mainly in street crime as opposed to white-collar crime, and facing a discriminatory criminal justice system, black people are more likely than are white people to be motivated to commit criminal acts, to be detected and apprehended, and to be prosecuted, convicted, and jailed.

The claim that the criminal justice system engages in discriminatory practices based on race may be difficult for some Canadians to accept, but research suggests that the claim is credible. For instance, a Toronto survey on who gets stopped for police checks found that older and better-educated white people and Asians with no criminal record are significantly less likely to be stopped for police searches than are younger and less well-educated white people and Asians with a criminal record. In contrast, age, education, and lack of a criminal record do not insulate black people from searches. In fact, better-educated and well-to-do black people are *more* likely to be stopped and searched by police than are less well-educated and poorer black people. These findings suggest that Toronto police keep a closer eye on black people than they do on white people and Asians, and are particularly suspicious of black people with an education and money (Wortley and Tanner, 2008).

> **street crimes** Crimes including arson, break and enter, assault, and other illegal acts are disproportionately committed by people from lower classes.
>
> **white-collar crimes** Illegal acts committed by respectable, high-status people in the course of work.

## LO3 EXPLAINING DEVIANCE AND CRIME

When Segun Akinsanya was two years old, his parents moved the family from Nigeria to Canada. Segun's father earned a chemistry degree from the University of Waterloo and, after graduation, ran a water filtration business in rural Quebec, while Segun's mother pursued a nursing degree. Segun won math awards and played chess. His father wanted him to become a doctor.

When he was eight years old, Segun's mother died in a car accident. Segun started acting out in school, getting detention, and being sent to the principal's office. When some older boys on the school bus called him a nigger, he got into his first of what would become near weekly fist fights.

Segun's father started seeing a woman who lived in Toronto, so the family moved to that city's Scarborough district when Segun was 12 years old. One day on his way to play basketball, some boys from his class asked Segun if he wanted to hang out. Eager to make friends, he agreed. They promptly punched and kicked him until he was lying on the ground, crying. He didn't realize it then, but he had just been initiated into a crew. Within a few months, he was handing off brown paper bags full of drugs to customers outside convenience stores.

Segun's father was still running his business in Quebec and travelling a lot, leaving Segun unsupervised. By the age of 14, feeling that he had no one in his life, Segun was one of the estimated 6000 kids in Toronto's street gangs. Years later, Segun acknowledged that street gangs "gave me a sense of power and belonging that I couldn't find anywhere else" (Akinsanya, 2016). His popularity and influence grew as he became more deeply involved in a life of violent crime. In 2006, after slicing a drug dealer's aorta with a knife, he was apprehended and charged with second-degree murder. A plea bargain resulted in a sentence of manslaughter with a five-year sentence.

In prison, Segun became deeply depressed. He started meeting with a priest to talk about his past mistakes and

Segun Akinsanya

attending an anger management class. He became an amateur sociologist, conducting written surveys to find out what led his fellow inmates to a life of crime. He wrote a 60-page curriculum for a program to help marginalized youth; he wanted to start such a program when he got out of jail.

When he was released, he started implementing his plan. He began working with several programs designed to help marginalized youth, received grants to expand his work, landed his first paying job with the Youth Justice Education Program, and worked toward his BA in human geography (a sister discipline of sociology) at the University of Toronto. It is a path that, unfortunately, far too few people in Segun's position have chosen or been able to execute.

Segun's story prompts one to ask: What makes engaging in crime an attractive prospect for so many people? In general, why do deviance and crime occur at all? Sociologists rely on symbolic interactionism, functionalism, conflict theories, and feminist theories for explanations.

## SYMBOLIC INTERACTIONIST APPROACHES TO DEVIANCE AND CRIME

People may learn deviant and criminal behaviour when they interact with others. Identifying the social circumstances that promote the learning of deviant and criminal roles is a traditional focus of symbolic interactionists.

### Learning Deviance

The idea that becoming a habitual deviant or criminal is a learning process that occurs in a social context was firmly established by Howard S. Becker's classic study of marijuana users (Becker, 1963: 41–58). In the 1940s, Becker financed his PhD studies by playing piano in Chicago jazz bands. He used the opportunity to carefully observe 50 of his musician colleagues, informally interview them in depth, and write up detailed field notes after performances.

Becker found that jazz musicians had to pass through a three-stage learning process before becoming regular marijuana users. Failure to pass a stage meant failure to learn the deviant role and become a regular user. These are the three stages:

1. *Learning to smoke the drug in a way that produces real effects.* First-time marijuana smokers do not ordinarily get high. To do so, they must learn how to smoke the drug in a way that ensures a sufficient dosage to produce intoxicating effects (taking deep drags and holding their breath for a long time). This process takes practice, and some first-time users give up, typically claiming that marijuana has no effect on them and that people who claim otherwise are just fooling themselves. Others are more strongly encouraged by their peers to keep trying. If they persist, they are ready to advance to stage two.

2. *Learning to recognize the effects and connect them with drug use.* Those who learn the proper smoking technique may not recognize that they are high or they may not connect the symptoms of being high with smoking the drug. They may get hungry, laugh uncontrollably, play the same song for hours on end, and yet still fail to realize that these are symptoms of intoxication. If so, they will stop using the drug. Becker found, however, that his musician associates typically asked experienced users how they knew whether they were high. Experienced users identified the symptoms of marijuana use and helped novices make the connection between what they were experiencing and smoking the drug. Once they made that connection, novices were ready to advance to stage three.

3. *Learning to enjoy the perceived sensations.* Smoking marijuana is not inherently pleasurable. Some users experience a frightening loss of self-control (paranoia). Others feel dizzy, uncomfortably thirsty, itchy, forgetful, or dangerously impaired in their ability to judge time and distance. If these negative sensations persist, marijuana use will cease. However, Becker found that experienced users typically helped novices redefine negative sensations as pleasurable. They taught novices to laugh at their impaired judgment, take pleasure in quenching their deep thirst, and find deeper meaning in familiar music. If and only if novices learned to define the effects of smoking as pleasurable did they become habitual marijuana smokers.

Learning *any* deviant or criminal role requires a social context in which experienced deviants or criminals teach novices the tricks of the trade. It follows that more exposure to experienced deviants and criminals increases the chance that an individual will come to value a deviant or criminal lifestyle and consider it normal (Sutherland, 1939, 1949). Moreover, the type of deviant or criminal who predominates in one's social environment has a bearing on the type of deviant or criminal that a novice will become.

For example, depending on the availability of different types of deviants and criminals in their neighbourhoods, delinquent youths will turn to different types of crime. In some areas, delinquent youths are recruited by organized crime, such as the Mafia. In areas that lack organized crime networks, delinquent youths are more likely to create gangs. Thus, the relative availability of different types of deviants and criminals influences the type of deviant or criminal role a delinquent youth learns (Cloward and Ohlin, 1960).

## Labelling

One night in Regina, after a night of heavy drinking, two 20-year-old university students, Alex Ternowetsky and Steven Kummerfield, both white and middle class, picked up Pamela George, an Indigenous single mother who occasionally worked as a prostitute. They drove the woman outside the city limits, forced her to perform oral sex without pay, and then beat her to death.

Ternowetsky and Kummerfield were charged with first-degree murder. However, Justice Ted Malone of the Saskatchewan Court of Queen's Bench instructed the jurors to consider mitigating circumstances: the two men had been drinking, and George was "indeed a prostitute." Therefore, the jury found the two men guilty of the lesser charge of manslaughter. Members of the victim's family were appalled, Indigenous leaders outraged. Tone Cote of the Yorkton Tribal Council said the sentence would send the message that "it's all right for little white boys to go out on the streets, get drunk and use that for an excuse to start hunting down our people." As if to prove his point, Ternowetsky and Kummerfield were set free just five years after their conviction ("19 years ago," 2015; "Full parole," 2000)

**labelling theory** Holds that deviance results not so much from the actions of the deviant as from the response of others, who label the rule breaker a deviant.

**Labelling theory**, a variant of symbolic interactionism, holds that deviance results not just from the actions of the deviant but also from the responses of others. From this point of view, terms like *deviant* or *criminal* are not applied automatically when a person engages in rule-violating behaviour; others must define some actions as deviant and other actions as normal. Moreover, authorities typically exercise considerable discretion in how seriously they treat a deviant act, as the example of Ternowetsky and Kummerfield suggests. Note too that some people, such as Pamela George, who are the victims of such acts, may find themselves labelled as deviant by authorities (and the public) because they are members of a stigmatized group (Matsueda, 1988, 1992) (see the Sociology and the Media boxed feature, *Highway of Tears* and the Problem of Intersectionality).

## SOCIOLOGY AND THE MEDIA

### *Highway of Tears* and the Problem of Intersectionality

Highway 16 is northern British Columbia's east–west corridor, stretching from Prince Rupert on the Pacific coast to Alberta's Jasper National Park. Because the region has a poorly developed public transportation system and many people who are too poor to own their own vehicles, hitchhiking is common along the highway.

In June 2017, a transit service covering just over half of the British Columbia portion of Highway 16 started operating on alternating days. That was too late for the more than 40 women who were murdered or disappeared near the highway between 1969 and 2011. Only one of the murders has been solved to date. Most of the victims were Indigenous.

*Highway of Tears* (available on Netflix) won the best documentary award at the Malibu Film Festival and the Vancouver International Women in Film Festival. It details the horrible events that have taken place near Highway 16 and investigates their causes. As the movie progresses, it becomes clear that we are dealing here with a case of what sociologists call *intersectionality*—the way in which gender and/or race, class, and sexuality combine to produce unique outcomes with respect to health, education, income, and other aspects of life (Crenshaw, 2016).

Consider homicide as an outcome. In Canada between 1991 and 2012, 705 Indigenous women and 3284 non-Indigenous women were victims of homicide. The homicide rate was 2.3 for every 100 000 non-Indigenous women and 14.1 for every

*(Continued)*

CHAPTER 5 Deviance and Crime

100 000 Indigenous women. Being a non-Indigenous woman in Canada was associated with a certain risk of becoming a homicide victim, but the risk was 6.3 times higher for Indigenous women (Royal Canadian Mounted Police, 2015; Statistics Canada, 2013a). This is clear evidence of intersectionality insofar as the female/Indigenous and female/non-Indigenous categories had widely different homicide rates. More evidence of intersectionality exists. For example, Indigenous women represent about 5 percent of Canada's female population but 60 percent of the country's missing women and girls.

While a large percentage of female homicides are committed by relatives and friends of the victims, Indigenous women are significantly more likely than are non-Indigenous women to be murdered by a stranger. Some 84 percent of all female homicide cases in Canada are solved but the comparable rate for Indigenous female homicide cases is about 50 percent (Native Women's Association of Canada, 2015; Royal Canadian Mounted Police, 2015).

*Highway of Tears* traces the roots of this case of intersectionality to the way people of white European origin have dealt with Indigenous peoples since settler times. Because settlers wanted choice land for farming, mining, and, later, railways and hydro-electric power plants, they forced Indigenous peoples out of their settlements and onto reserves that often lacked adequate access to food and clean water, and typically provided few jobs. (According to *Highway of Tears*, in some communities in northern British Columbia, up to 92 percent of Indigenous peoples are unemployed.) By thus destroying the Indigenous way of life, settlers created a substantially impoverished population largely dependent on the state.

In addition, the government, aided by the Catholic Church and various Protestant denominations, removed scores of thousands of Indigenous children from their families and placed them in residential schools, forcing them to give up their culture and their language, abusing many of them physically, sexually, and mentally, and preventing them from learning basic parenting skills. A deeply ingrained racist attitude toward Indigenous peoples oozed from this swamp. In this context, and especially in the four Western provinces, where Indigenous peoples form 8.6 percent of the population (three times the percentage for the rest of Canada), some people have gone so far as to treat Indigenous women like things to be violated, then discarded (Statistics Canada, 2017a). *Highway of Tears* movingly tells their stories.

### Critical Thinking Questions

- A national inquiry into murdered and missing Indigenous women and girls was proposed during the tenure of the 2006–2015 Conservative government. Prime Minister Harper's response to the proposal was that disproportionate Indigenous female homicide is not a sociological phenomenon but just a matter of bad people committing murder. What evidence in this boxed feature suggests that Harper was wrong?
- In later chapters you will learn about disparities in Indigenous/non-Indigenous educational attainment, health, and income. What do you anticipate discovering about the causes of these disparities?

## FUNCTIONALIST EXPLANATIONS

If symbolic interactionists focus on the learning and labelling of deviant and criminal roles, functionalists direct their attention to the social dysfunctions that lead to deviant and criminal behaviour.

### Émile Durkheim

Functionalist thinking on deviance and crime originated with Durkheim (1938 [1895]), who made the controversial claim that deviance and crime are beneficial for society. For one thing, he wrote, when someone breaks a rule, it provides others with a chance to condemn and punish the transgression, remind them of their common values, clarify the moral boundaries of the group to which they belong, and thus reinforce social solidarity. For another, Durkheim claimed, deviance and crime help societies adapt to social change. Martin Luther King, Jr., was arrested in Alabama in February 1965 for taking part in a demonstration supporting the idea that black people should be allowed to vote, but later that year the passage of the Voting Rights Acts made it a crime to *prevent* black people from voting in the United States. King's crime (and similar crimes by other civil rights activists) brought about positive social change, demonstrating the validity of Durkheim's point about the potentially positive functions of some types of deviance and crime.

### Robert Merton

Robert Merton (1938) further developed Durkheim's theory by emphasizing the *dysfunctions* of deviance and crime. Merton argued that cultures often teach people to value material success. Just as often, however, societies do not provide enough legitimate opportunities for everyone to succeed. In Merton's view, such a discrepancy between cultural ideals and structural realities is dysfunctional, producing what he called **strain**.

Most people who experience strain will nonetheless force themselves to adhere to social norms, Merton wrote. He called this option "conformity." The rest adapt by engaging in one of four types of action. Rejecting the society's goals and its institutionalized means of achieving them, they may drop out of conventional society ("retreatism").

> **strain** The result of a culture teaching people to value material success, but society failing to provide enough legitimate opportunities for everyone to succeed.

**FIGURE 5.2  Merton's Strain Theory of Deviance**

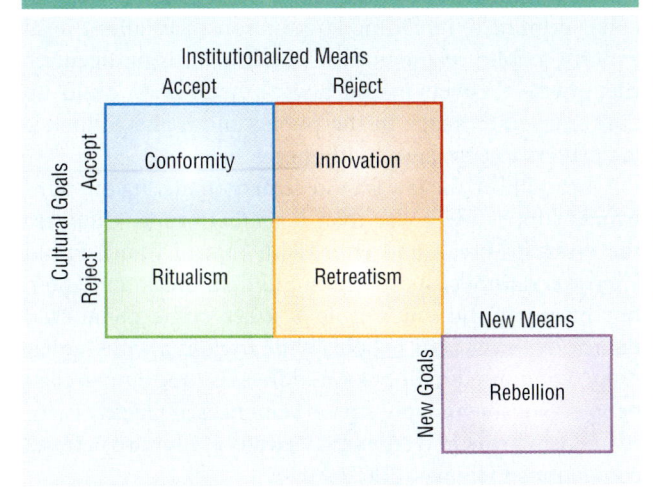

Sources: From BRYM/ROBERTS/STROHSCHEIN/LIE. *Sociology: Your Compass for a New World*, 6E. © 2019 Nelson Education Ltd. Reproduced by permission. www.cengage.com/permissions; adapted from Robert K. Merton, 1938, "Social Structure and Anomie." *American Sociological Review* 3: 672–82.

Rejecting the goals of conventional society but continuing to follow them, they may engage in "ritualism." Accepting cultural goals and creating novel means of achieving them results in "innovation." Although some innovators are business geniuses like Henry Ford and Steve Jobs, some are criminals. Finally, rejecting cultural goals and finding new means of achieving new goals involves "rebellion"—the hippies of the 1960s represent this last form of adaptation to strain (see Figure 5.2).

## Criminal Subcultures

Not only individuals adapt to the strain caused by social dysfunction—some social groups adapt by forming criminal gangs. Gang members feel that the legitimate world has rejected them—and they have a point. Although black people and Indigenous peoples constitute less than 7 percent of the country's population, 25 percent of Canadian youth gang members are black and 21 percent are Indigenous (Public Safety Canada, 2012). Little wonder. Black people and Indigenous peoples are the two groups that experience the highest levels of discrimination in Canadian society. A disproportionately large number of young men from these groups reject the legitimate world and turn to crime, in the process developing distinct norms and values—a criminal subculture (Cohen, 1955; Wortley and Tanner, 2008).

An important part of any gang subculture consists of the justifications its members spin for their criminal activities. These justifications make illegal activities appear morally acceptable and normal, at least to the gang members. Typically, criminals deny personal responsibility for their actions ("It wasn't my fault!") or deny the wrongfulness of the act ("I was just borrowing it."). They condemn those who pass judgment on them ("The cops are bigger crooks than anyone!"). They claim their victims get what they deserve ("She had it coming to her."). And they appeal to higher loyalties, particularly to friends and family ("I had to do it because he dissed my gang."). Such rationalizations enable criminals to clear their consciences and get on with the job (Sykes and Matza, 1957).

Although deviants may depart from mainstream culture in many ways, they are strict conformists when it comes to the norms of their own subculture. They tend to share the same beliefs, dress alike, eat similar food, and adopt the same mannerisms and speech patterns. Although most members of the larger society consider gang subcultures deviant, gang members strongly discourage deviance *within* the subculture, which is governed by strict rules of obedience and hierarchy.

## Functionalism and the Relationship between Crime and Class

One of the main problems with functionalist accounts is that they exaggerate the connection between crime and class. Many self-report surveys find, at most, a weak tendency for criminals to come disproportionately from lower classes. Some self-report surveys report no such tendency at all, especially among young people and for less serious types of crime (Weis, 1987). A stronger correlation exists between *serious street crimes* and class. Armed robbery and assault, for instance, are more common among people from lower classes. A stronger correlation also exists between *white-collar* crime and class. Middle-class and upper-class people are most likely to commit fraud and embezzlement, for example. Thus, generalizations about the relationship between class and crime must be qualified by taking into account the severity and type of crime (Braithwaite, 1981).

Note also that official statistics usually exaggerate class differences because they are more accurate barometers of street crime than suite (white-collar) crime. More police surveillance occurs in lower-class neighbourhoods than in upper-class boardrooms, and widely cited police statistics do not record some white-collar crimes because they are handled by agencies other than the police. As we will now see, conflict theories help to overcome functionalism's inadequate explanation of the relationship between crime and class.

# CONFLICT THEORIES

Conflict theorists maintain that rich and powerful members of society impose deviant and criminal labels on others, particularly those who challenge the existing social order. Meanwhile, the rich and powerful are usually able to use their money and influence to escape punishment for their own misdeeds.

Steven Spitzer (1980) summarizes this school of thought. He notes that capitalist societies are based on private ownership of property. Moreover, their smooth functioning depends on the availability of productive labour and respect for authority. When thieves steal, they challenge

**control theory** Holds that the rewards of deviance and crime are ample. Therefore, nearly everyone would engage in deviance and crime if they could get away with it. The degree to which people are prevented from violating norms and laws accounts for variations in the levels of deviance and crime.

private property. Theft is therefore a crime. When so-called bag ladies and drug addicts drop out of conventional society, they are defined as deviant because their refusal to engage in productive labour undermines a pillar of capitalism. When young, politically volatile students demonstrate and militant trade unionists strike, they, too, represent a threat to the social order. Authorities may therefore define them as deviant.

Of course, Spitzer notes, the rich and powerful engage in deviant and criminal acts too. However, they are less likely to be reported, convicted, and prosecuted for criminal acts than other people are (Blumberg, 1989; Clinard and Yeager, 1980; Hagan, 1989; Sherrill, 1997; Snider, 1999; Sutherland, 1949). *Reporting* is less frequent because much white-collar crime takes place in private and is therefore difficult to detect. For instance, corporations may collude to fix prices and divide markets—both crimes—but executives may make such decisions in boardrooms, private clubs, and homes that are not generally subject to police surveillance. *Conviction* and *prosecution* are less frequent partly because wealthy white-collar criminals, including corporations, can afford legal experts, public relations firms, and advertising agencies that advise their clients on how to bend laws, build up their corporate image in the public mind, and influence lawmakers to pass laws "without teeth."

In addition, the law is more lenient in meting out punishment for white-collar than for street crime. Compare the crime of break and enter with that of fraud. Fraud almost certainly costs society more than break and enter, but breaking and entering is a street crime committed mainly by lower-class people, while fraud is a white-collar crime committed mainly by middle-class and upper-class people. Not surprisingly, prison sentences are nearly twice as likely in break and enter convictions as they are in fraud convictions (Thomas, 2002: 9).

## Social Control

Conflict theorists argue that the rich and powerful exercise disproportionate control over the criminal justice system and are therefore able to engage in deviance and crime with relative impunity. One variant of conflict theory, **control theory**, generalizes this argument. According to control theorists, nearly everyone would like to have the fun, pleasure, excitement, and profit that deviance and crime promise. Moreover, they say, if we could get away with it, most of us would commit deviant and criminal acts to acquire more of those rewards. For control theorists, the reason most of us do not engage in deviance and crime is that we are prevented from doing so. In contrast, deviants and criminals break norms and laws because social controls imposed by various authorities are too weak to ensure conformity.

Travis Hirschi developed the control theory of crime (Gottfredson and Hirschi, 1990; Hirschi, 1969). He argued that adolescents are more prone to deviance and crime than adults are because they are incompletely socialized and therefore lack self-control. Adults and adolescents may both experience the impulse to break norms and laws, but adolescents are less likely to control that impulse. Hirschi went on to show that the adolescents who are most prone to delinquency are likely to lack four types of social control. They tend to have few social *attachments* to parents, teachers, and other respectable role models; few legitimate *opportunities* for education and a good job; few *involvements* in conventional institutions; and weak *beliefs* in traditional values and morality. Because of the lack of control stemming from these sources, these adolescents are relatively free to act on their deviant impulses. For similar reasons, boys are more likely to engage in juvenile delinquency than girls are, and people who experience job and marital instability are more likely than others are to engage in crime (Hagan, Simpson, and Gillis, 1987; Peters, 1994; Sampson and Laub, 1993). Tighter social control by authorities in all spheres of life decreases the frequency of deviant and criminal acts.

Canadian millionaire Conrad Black was convicted in 2007 of fraud and obstruction of justice. Sentenced to six and a half years in prison, he was released on bail after serving two and a half years, partly because some charges were dropped.

# FEMINIST CONTRIBUTIONS

Although conflict theory shows how the distribution of power in society influences the definition, detection, and prosecution of deviance and criminality, it neglects the consequences of something you will learn about in detail in Chapter 8, Sexualities and Genders: On average, women are less powerful than men are in all social institutions. Feminist sociologists hold that gender-based power differences influence the framing of laws and therefore the definition and detection of crime and the prosecution of criminals.

To support their claim, feminists note that, until recently, many types of crime against women were largely ignored in Canada and most other parts of the world. This was true even when the crime involved non-consensual sexual intercourse, an act that was defined under Canadian criminal law as *rape* before 1983 and is now considered a form of *sexual assault*. Admittedly, the authorities sometimes severely punished rapes involving strangers. However, so-called date and acquaintance rape were rarely prosecuted, while Canadian law viewed marital rape as a contradiction in terms, as if it were logically impossible for a woman to be raped by her husband. Law professors, judges, police officers, rapists, and even victims did not think date rape was "real rape" (Estrich, 1987). Similarly, judges, lawyers, and social scientists rarely discussed physical violence against women and sexual harassment until the 1970s. Governments did not collect data on the topic, and few social scientists showed any interest in it. Relative powerlessness allowed many women to be victimized, while the violence against them often went unnoticed by the larger society and their assailants went free.

It follows from the feminist argument that a shift in the distribution of power between women and men would alter this state of affairs. And in fact, that is precisely what happened after about 1970. A series of changes to Canadian criminal law since 1970 have emphasized that non-consensual sexual acts are sexual assaults. The new laws have helped raise people's awareness of date, acquaintance, and marital rape. Sexual assault is more often prosecuted now than it used to be. The same is true for other types of violence against women and for sexual harassment. These changes occurred because women's position in the economy, the family, and other social institutions has improved since 1970. Women now have more autonomy in the family, earn more, and enjoy more political influence. They also created a movement for women's rights that heightened concern about crimes disproportionately affecting them (MacKinnon, 1979). Social definitions of crimes against women changed as women became more powerful in Canadian society.

In the 1970s, some feminists expected that growing gender equality would also change the historical tendency for women to be far less crime-prone than men are. They reasoned that control over the activities of girls and women would weaken, thus allowing them to behave more like men. Widely publicized cases of violent crime by teenage girls add weight to such claims, and official data, while not dramatic, also support them. As Figure 5.3 shows, the

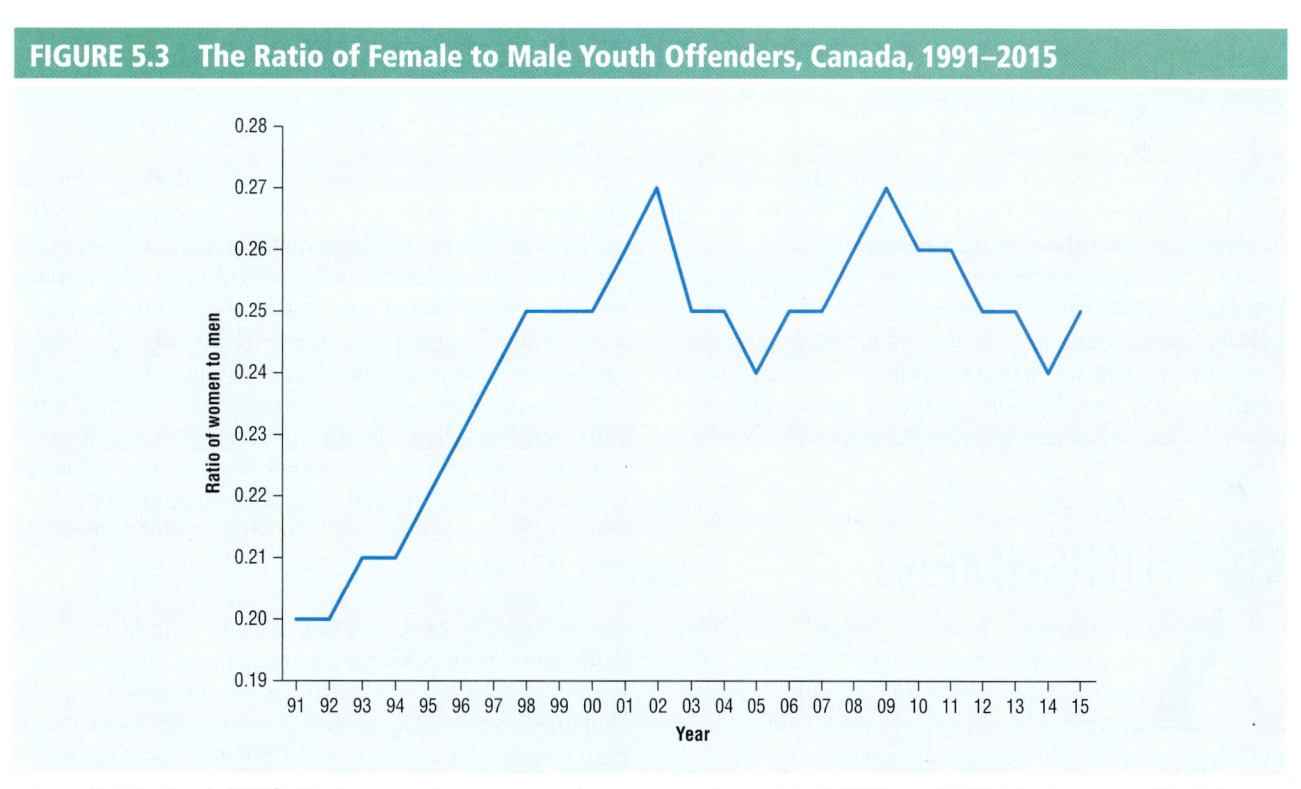

**FIGURE 5.3   The Ratio of Female to Male Youth Offenders, Canada, 1991–2015**

Source: Statistics Canada (2018f). "Youth courts, guilty cases by type of sentence, annually (number)." CANSIM Table 2520067. Retrieved January 22, 2018 (https://www150.statcan.gc.ca/t1/tbl1/en/tv.action?pid=3510004101).

## THEORIES AT A GLANCE

### Deviance and Crime

| Theory | Main Question | Application |
|---|---|---|
| Symbolic interactionism | How do people communicate to make their social settings meaningful, thus helping to create their social circumstances? | Deviant and criminal roles must be learned in the course of social interaction if they are to become habitual activities. Moreover, deviance results not just from the actions of the deviant but also from the responses of others, who define some actions as deviant and other actions as normal. |
| Functionalism | How do social structures and the values underlying them contribute to social stability? | Deviance and crime have positive functions for society insofar as they provide opportunities to clarify societal values, define moral boundaries, increase social solidarity, and allow useful social change. They also have dysfunctions. In particular, if societies do not provide enough legitimate opportunities for everyone to succeed, strain results, one reaction to which is to find alternative and illegitimate means of achieving one's goals. |
| Conflict theory | How does the structure of inequality between privileged groups seeking to maintain their advantages and subordinate groups seeking to increase theirs lead to conflict and often to social change? | The rich and powerful are most likely to impose deviant and criminal labels on others, particularly those who challenge the existing social order. The rich and powerful are also often able to use their money and influence to escape punishment for their own misdeeds. Most people do not engage in deviance and crime because they are prevented from doing so by authorities. Deviants and criminals break norms and laws because social controls imposed by various authorities are too weak to ensure their conformity. |
| Feminist theory | How do social conventions maintain male dominance and female subordination, and how do these conventions get overturned? | Changes over time in the distribution of power between women and men influence the degree to which crimes against women are identified and prosecuted, and the degree to which women become criminals. |

ratio of female to male youths convicted of crime rose from 0.20 to 0.25 between 1991 and 1999, and then fluctuated between 0.24 and 0.27 between 1999 and 2015.

In sum, many theories contribute to understanding the social causes of deviance and crime (see Theories at a Glance, Deviance and Crime). Each focuses on a different aspect of the phenomena, so familiarity with all of them allows us to develop a fully rounded appreciation of the complex processes surrounding the sociology of deviance and crime.

## LO4 PUNISHMENT

All societies seek to ensure that their members obey norms and laws. All societies impose sanctions on rule breakers. However, the *degree* of social control varies over time and place. *Forms* of punishment also vary.

In many respects people are freer today than ever. We elect leaders, choose consumer products, change religions, and so on. In other respects, however, social control has intensified over time. Much of the regimentation of modern life is tied to the growth of capitalism and the state. Factories require strict labour regimes, with workers arriving and leaving at fixed times and, while there, performing fixed tasks at a fixed pace. Institutions regulated by the state's armies, police forces, public schools, health care systems, and other bureaucracies also demand strict work regimes, curricula, and procedures. These institutions existed on a much smaller scale in pre-industrial times or did not exist at all. Today, they penetrate our lives and sustain strong norms of belief and conduct (Foucault, 1977 [1975]).

Electronic technology makes it possible for authorities to exercise more effective social control than ever. With millions of cameras mounted in public places and workplaces, some sociologists say we now live in a "surveillance society" (Lyon and Zureik, 1996). Spy cameras enable observers to see deviance and crime that would otherwise go undetected and to take quick action to apprehend rule breakers. Moreover, when people are aware of the presence of surveillance cameras, they tend to alter their behaviour. For example, attentive shoplifters migrate to stores that lack electronic surveillance. On factory floors and in offices, workers display more conformity to management-imposed work norms when they're aware of surveillance cameras. On campuses, surveillance cameras inhibit at least some students from engaging in organized protests (Boal, 1998).

Among the most important recent developments in social control are the "medicalization of deviance" and the widespread use of prisons. Let us examine these reactions to deviance and crime in turn.

## THE MEDICALIZATION OF DEVIANCE

Increasingly, we deal with deviance by medicalizing it. The **medicalization of deviance** refers to the fact that "medical definitions of deviant behaviour are becoming more prevalent in...societies like our own" (Conrad and Schneider, 1992: 28–29). In an earlier era, much deviant behaviour was labelled as evil. Deviants tended to be chastised, punished, and otherwise socially controlled by members of the clergy, neighbours, family members, and the criminal justice system. Today, however, a person prone to drinking sprees is more likely to be declared an alcoholic and treated in a detoxification centre. A person predisposed to violent rages is more likely to be medicated. A person inclined to overeating is more likely to seek therapy and, in extreme cases, surgery. A heroin addict is more likely to seek the help of a methadone program. As these examples illustrate, what used to be regarded as willful deviance is now often regarded as involuntary deviance. Increasingly, what used to be defined as evil is defined as "sickness." As our definitions of deviance change, deviance is increasingly coming under the sway of the medical and psychiatric establishments.

### The Spread of Mental Disorders

Some mental disorders have obvious organic causes, such as chemical imbalances in the brain. Researchers can often identify these problems precisely, treat them with drugs or other therapies, and conduct experiments to verify their existence and establish the effectiveness of one treatment or another. Little debate takes place over whether such ailments should be listed in the psychiatrist's "bible," the *Diagnostic and Statistical Manual of Mental Disorders* (DSM-5).

The organic basis for other ailments is unclear. In such cases, social values and political conflict can determine whether they are listed in the DSM-5. For instance, in the 1970s and 1980s, North American psychiatrists fiercely debated whether neurosis, posttraumatic stress disorder (PTSD), homosexuality, and self-defeating personality disorder were real mental disorders. In the end, homosexuality was dropped from an earlier version of the DSM-5, largely in response to the efforts of liberal-minded psychiatrists, as was self-defeating personality disorder, thanks to the efforts of feminists.

> **medicalization of deviance**
> The process of applying medical definitions to deviant behaviour, a practice that is becoming more prevalent.

Neurosis was retained at the insistence of Freudians. PTSD was added to an earlier version of the DSM-5 after a strenuous lobbying campaign by Vietnam War veterans and their supporters (Scott, 1990). These cases illustrate that the medicalization of deviance is in part a social and political process.

In the mid-nineteenth century there was just one officially recognized mental disorder: idiocy/insanity. The current edition of the DSM-5, published in 2013, lists 294. As the number of mental disorders has grown, so has the proportion of North Americans presumably affected by them. In the mid-nineteenth century, few people were defined as suffering from mental disorders, but one respected survey conducted in the early 1990s found that 48 percent of people will suffer from a mental disorder—very broadly defined, of course—during their lifetime (Blazer et al.,1994; Shorter, 1997: 294).

The number and scope of mental disorders have grown partly because North Americans are now experiencing more stress than ever before, mainly because of the increased demands of work and a growing time crunch. At the same time, traditional institutions for dealing with mental health problems are less able to cope with them. The weakening authority of religious institutions and the weakening grip of the family over the individual leave the treatment of mental health problems more open to the medical and psychiatric establishments.

The cultural context also stimulates inflation in the number and scope of mental disorders. North Americans are inclined to turn their problems into medical and psychological issues, sometimes without inquiring deeply into the disadvantages of doing so. For example, in 1980, the term "attention deficit disorder" (ADD) was coined to label hyperactive and inattentive schoolchildren, mainly boys. By the mid-1990s, doctors were writing more than 6 million prescriptions a year for Ritalin, an amphetamine-like compound that controls ADD.

Evidence shows that some children diagnosed with ADD have certain problems with their brain chemistry. Yet the diagnosis of ADD is typically conducted clinically, that is, by interviewing and observing children to see if they exhibit signs of serious inattention, hyperactivity, and impulsivity. This means that many children diagnosed with ADD may have no organic disorder at all. Some cases of ADD may be due to the school system failing to capture children's imagination. Some may involve children acting out because they are deprived of attention at home. Some may involve plain, old-fashioned youthful enthusiasm.

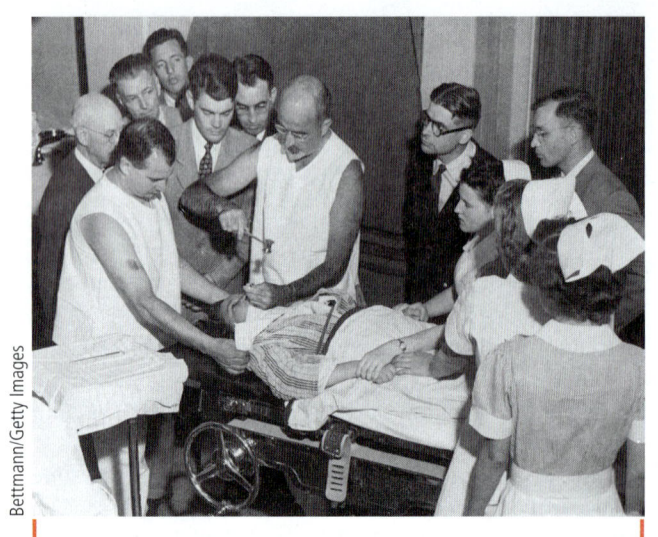

In the 1930s, lobotomies began to be performed to deal with some deviants and criminals. Here, Dr. Walter Freeman performs a lobotomy in the 1930s using an instrument like an ice pick, which he invented for the procedure.

In pre-industrial societies, criminals who committed serious crimes were put to death, often in ways that seem cruel by today's standards. One method involved hanging them upside down, bound and alive, so that starving dogs could rip them apart.

(Doctors at Dalhousie University Medical School in Halifax made a plausible case that Winnie the Pooh suffered from ADD; see Shea et al., 2000.) However, once hyperactivity and inattentiveness in school are defined as a medical and psychiatric condition, officials routinely prescribe drugs to control the problem and tend to ignore possible social causes.

Finally, we have witnessed inflation in the number and scope of mental disorders because various professional organizations have an interest in it. Consider PTSD. There is no doubt that PTSD is a real condition and that many veterans suffer from it. However, once the disorder was officially recognized in the 1970s, some therapists trivialized the term. By the mid-1990s some therapists were talking about PTSD "in children exposed to movies like *Batman*" (Shorter, 1997: 290). Some psychiatric social workers, psychologists, and psychiatrists may magnify the incidence of such mental disorders because doing so increases their stature and their patient load. Others may do so simply because the condition becomes trendy. Whatever the motive, overdiagnosis is the result.

# THE PRISON

## Origins

As societies industrialized, imprisonment became one of the most important forms of punishment for criminal behaviour (Garland, 1990; Morris and Rothman, 1995). In pre-industrial societies, criminals were publicly humiliated, tortured, or put to death, depending on the severity of their transgressions. In the industrial era, depriving criminals of their freedom by putting them into prison seemed more civilized (Durkheim, 1973 [1899–1900]).

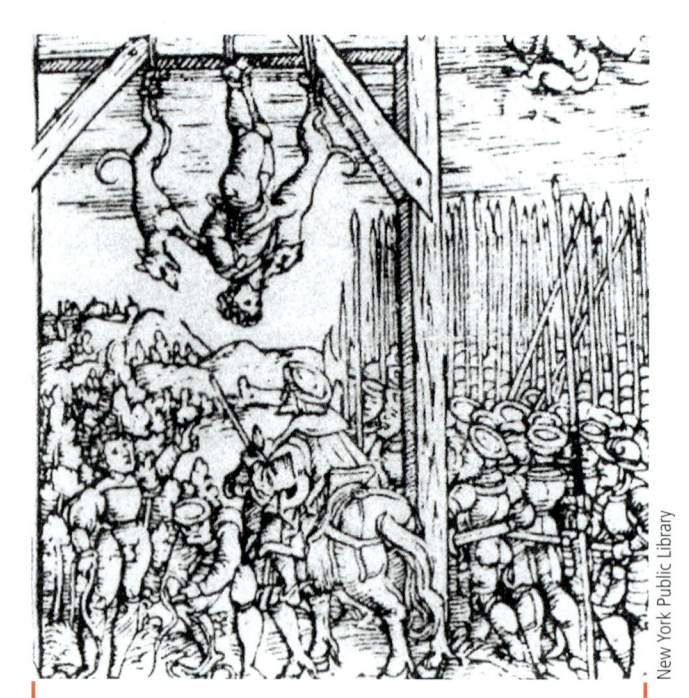

## Goals of Incarceration

Some people still take a benign view of prisons, even seeing them as opportunities for *rehabilitation*. They believe that prisoners, while serving time, can be taught to become productive citizens on release. In Canada, this idea predominated from the 1950s to the early 1970s, when many prisons sought to reform criminals by offering them psychological counselling, drug therapy, skills training, education, and other programs that would help at least the less-violent offenders reintegrate into society.

Today, however, many Canadians scoff at the idea that prisons should aim to rehabilitate criminals. Instead, they demand more incarceration of offenders for longer terms and see little reason to improve prison conditions. Some see prison as a means of *deterrence*. In this view, people will be less inclined to commit crimes if they know they are likely to be caught and serve long and unpleasant prison terms. Others think of prisons as institutions of *revenge*. They believe that depriving criminals of their freedom and forcing them to live in poor conditions is fair retribution for their illegal acts. Still others regard prisons as institutions of *incapacitation*. From this viewpoint, the chief function of the prison is to keep criminals out of society as long as possible to ensure they can do no more harm.

There are about 10.6 million prisoners in the world, nearly half of them in the United States, Russia, China, and Brazil. As Figure 5.4 shows, some 114 of every

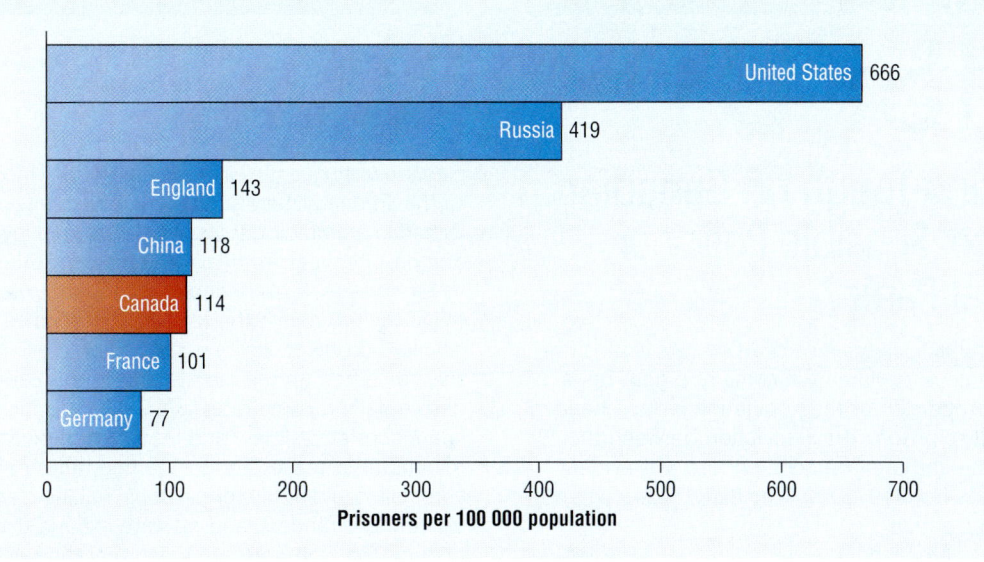

## FIGURE 5.4  Rate of Imprisonment, Selected Countries

| Country | Prisoners per 100 000 population |
|---|---|
| United States | 666 |
| Russia | 419 |
| England | 143 |
| China | 118 |
| Canada | 114 |
| France | 101 |
| Germany | 77 |

Source: World Prison Brief, Institute for Criminal Policy Research. 2017. "Highest to Lowest—Prison Population Rate." http://www.prisonstudies.org/highest-to-lowest/prison-population-total (retrieved 22 January 2018).

100 000 Canadians are in prison, which makes Canada's incarceration rate higher than that of some European countries, such as France and Germany, but below the world average. The United States ranks second in the world with 666 inmates per 100 000 people (first place goes to the tiny African island nation of Seychelles). Some 4.4 percent of the world's population lives in the United States—and 20.2 percent of the world's prisoners (International Centre for Prison Studies, 2017).

The size of the U.S. prison population has more than quadrupled since 1980, yet little evidence supports the view that throwing more people into jail lowers the crime rate in the United States or anywhere else for that matter. In fact, many sociologists have shown that prison often has the opposite effect, turning small-time crooks into hardened criminals (Ore and Birgden, 2003). Why then has the U.S. prison population grown so quickly?

## LO 5 MORAL PANIC

Some analysts say that the United States has been gripped by **moral panic**, or widespread fear that crime poses a grave threat to society's well-being. Partly in response to lurid news stories and TV dramas that direct attention to the most notorious and atypical crimes, many members of the public incorrectly conclude that most crime is violent and predatory and that the current crime rate endangers just about everyone, even though it has been falling since the early 1990s (Goode and Ben-Yehuda, 1994).

Powerful interests benefit from moral panics that result in higher incarceration rates. In particular:

**moral panic** Widespread fear that occurs when many people fervently believe that some form of deviance or crime poses a profound threat to society's well-being.

1. The mass media benefit from moral panic because it allows them to earn hefty profits. They publicize every major crime because crime draws big audiences, and big audiences mean more revenue from advertisers. Fictional crime programs draw tens of millions of additional viewers to their TVs.

2. The crime prevention and punishment industry benefits from moral panic for much the same reason. Prison construction and maintenance firms, firearms manufacturers, and home security companies are big businesses that flourish in a climate of moral panic.

3. The criminal justice system is a huge bureaucracy with many employees. They benefit from moral panic because increased spending on crime prevention, control, and punishment secures their jobs and expands their turf.

4. Most important, moral panic is useful politically insofar as it can help candidates get elected. Many politicians have found it expedient to instill fear of crime in the public, criticize opponents for being "soft on crime," and promise voters that endorsing a "get-tough" policy will bring them more security. Such arguments have formed the basis of entire political careers, as Canadians learned just a few years ago (see Theories in Dispute, Getting Tough on Canadian Crime: Sensible Policy or Moral Panic?).

# THEORIES IN DISPUTE

## Getting Tough on Canadian Crime: Sensible Policy or Moral Panic?

In general, a society's incarceration rate is sensitive to its crime rate. When the crime rate goes up, a higher proportion of the population is apprehended and sent to prison. The association between the crime rate and the incarceration rate was evident in Canada from 1978 until the early 2000s, as Figure 5.5 shows.

Then something unexpected happened. After 2004, the incarceration rate went up while the crime rate *fell*. A moral panic gripped many Canadians.

The Conservative party was a major force driving the moral panic from the years leading up to its 2006 election victory until 2014, a year before it lost power to the Trudeau Liberals. Over the objections of most Canadian criminologists, sociologists, and lawyers, and despite pleas from law enforcement officials as far away as Texas, where "get-tough" measures failed to curb crime, the former Conservative government (2006 to 2015) passed a crime bill in 2012 that ratcheted up the moral panic in this country despite falling crime rates. Bill C-10 introduced new criminal offences, new and increased mandatory minimum sentences, longer waiting times before criminals could apply for pardons, harsher sentencing for young offenders, and plans to expand the prison system. The Conservatives were operating on the theory that getting tough on crime would contain the crime rate. But on the evidence, it made little sense to imprison a higher proportion of Canadians when crime rates were falling. The theory did,

**FIGURE 5.5** Adult Incarceration Rate and Crime Rate, Canada, 1978–2015

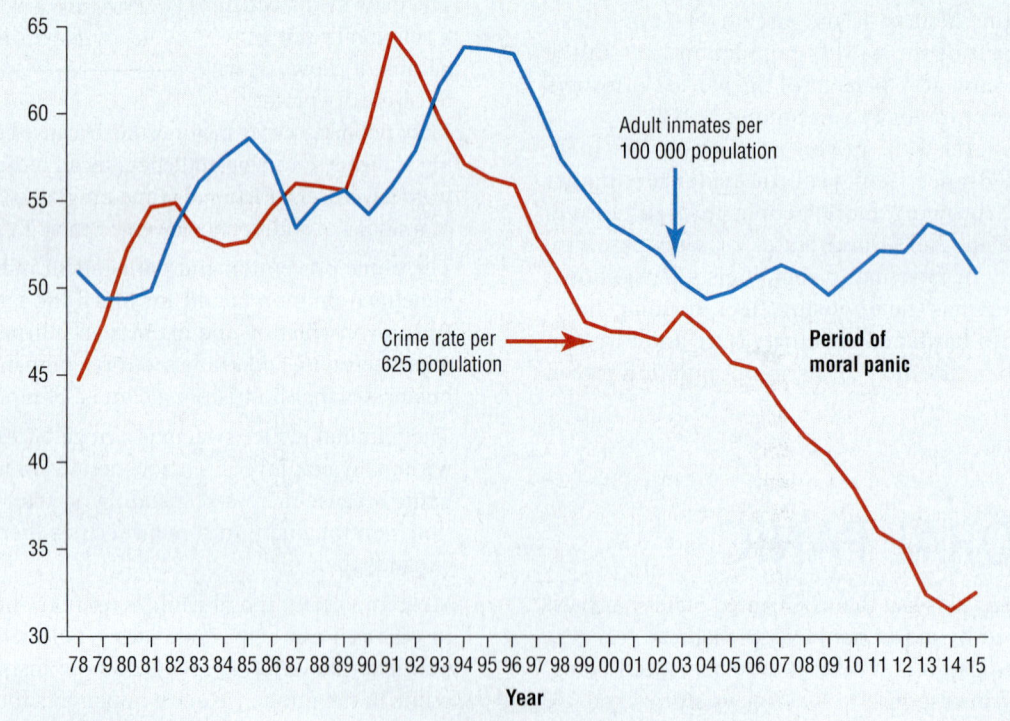

Note: To be able to place the incarceration rate and the crime rate on the same scale, the crime rate has been calculated per 625 population rather than the standard 100 000 population.

Sources: Statistics Canada. 2018a. "Adult correctional services, average counts of offenders in federal programs, annually." CANSIM Table 2510006; Kathryn Keighley, 2017. "Police-reported crime statistics in Canada, 2016."

Former Conservative Prime Minister Stephen Harper and former Minister of Public Safety Vic Toews championed efforts to get tough on crime by engineering a moral panic.

however, make for effective politics. Convincing some Canadians that they were experiencing a dangerous crime wave when in fact they were not helped some political candidates get elected and join the government.

### Critical Thinking Questions
- In the absence of a moral panic, what is the relationship between the crime rate and the incarceration rate?
- In the event of moral panic, how does the relationship between the crime rate and the incarceration rate change?

## OTHER FORMS OF PUNISHMENT: TWO EXTREMES

Imprisonment is not the only form of punishment for criminal acts. In concluding this chapter, we consider two of the most hotly debated issues concerning other forms of punishment: (1) Should Canada reintroduce the death penalty for the most violent criminals? (2) Should we more often use strategies other than imprisonment for non-violent criminals?

### Capital Punishment

Between 1859 and 1962, 710 Canadians were hanged by the state. Capital punishment has not been employed in Canada since 1962 and was formally abolished in 1976, but most Canadians favour its re-introduction. Approximately 6 in 10 Canadians favour punishing homicide with the death penalty, about the same proportion as Americans (Brennan, 2012; Jones, 2014).

Although the death penalty ranks high as a form of revenge, it is questionable whether it is much of a deterrent. First, murder is often committed in a rage, when the perpetrator is not thinking entirely rationally and is unlikely to consider the costs and consequences of his or her actions coolly. Second, the United States has capital punishment, but its homicide rate is much higher than that of Canada and western European countries that do not practise capital punishment (Mooney et al., 2001: 131).

We must also note that capital punishment is hardly a matter of blind justice. Research conducted in the United States reveals that, other things being equal, killers of white people are more likely to receive death sentences than are killers of black people, especially if the murderer is black (Culver, 1992). Social class is also a factor. A study conducted in Texas found that people represented by court-appointed lawyers were 28 percent more likely to be convicted than those who could afford to hire their own lawyers and, once convicted, 44 percent more likely to be sentenced to death (Vago and Nelson, 2003: 205). It is doubtful that we can view the death penalty as a justly administered punishment.

Sometimes people favour capital punishment because they think it saves money. They argue that killing someone costs less than keeping the person alive in prison for the rest of his or her life. However, the experience of the United States suggests otherwise. In that country, where an exhaustive system of judicial review is required before anyone is executed, trials of capital cases cost more than $2.6 million each on average—enough to keep a person in prison in Canada for almost 40 years (Costanzo, 1997).

Finally, in assessing capital punishment, it is important to remember that mistakes are common. Nearly 40 percent of death sentences in the United States since 1977 have been overturned because of new evidence or mistrial (Haines, 1996). In Canada, the wrongful convictions of Donald Marshall, Guy Paul Morin, David Milgaard, and many others for murders they did not commit should be sufficient to remind us that the wheels of justice do not always turn smoothly.

## LO6 ALTERNATIVE STRATEGIES

### REHABILITATION

In recent years, sociologists and criminologists have promoted three main ways to reform our prison regime. First, they have argued that we should reconsider rehabilitation. Advocates of rehabilitation

**recidivism rate** The percentage of imprisoned people who commit another crime, usually within two years after release from prison.

**restorative justice** Focuses not on punishment but on rehabilitating offenders through reconciliation with victims and the larger community.

suggest that the **recidivism rate**—the percentage of convicted offenders who commit another crime, usually within two years of release from prison—can be reduced by means of education and job training, individual and group therapy, substance abuse counselling, behaviour modification, and simply treating prisoners with dignity.

Although some people think that such a system would do nothing to lower the recidivism rate and promote the reintegration of criminals into society, the Scandinavian experience suggests otherwise. It is based on the idea that the more closely a prison resembles the outside world, the easier it will be to train less violent prisoners to function well outside the prison. Thus, Danish prisoners with sentences shorter than five years live in prisons without walls, barbed wire fences, and gun towers. They wear their own clothes, shop inside the prison, cook their own meals, attend classes, work 37 hours a week, and are allowed a private family visit every week—unless they are married and have a child under the age of three, in which case the entire family can live in the prison with them. (Larson, 2013; Reiter, Sexton, and Sumner, 2016)

And the result? Denmark's recidivism rate for offenders of all types two years after release is about 29 percent, compared to 41 percent in Canada's less rehabilitative system (Fazel and Wolf, 2015). These figures suggest that, at least for less violent offenders, a get-tough approach to imprisonment is less effective than a rehabilitative approach.

## DECRIMINALIZATION/ LEGALIZATION

A second proposed reform to our prison regime involves the decriminalization or legalization of certain actions. (Decriminalization allows for fines or other non-prison penalties; legalization does not.)

The production, distribution, and possession of cannabis became a crime in Canada in 1923. Criminalization restricted supply and encouraged the growth of organized crime to meet demand. It contributed to violence in society and put many Canadians in prison, even for the possession of small quantities of cannabis for personal use. However, in the twenty-first century, it became obvious to most politicians, employees of the criminal justice system, social scientists, and members of the public that legalization would be less harmful to society than the existing state of affairs. Reformers were convinced that legalization would put criminals out of business, shrink the size of the prison population, create legitimate business and employment opportunities for Canadians, and provide a new source of tax revenue for governments. Consequently, the use of cannabis was legalized for medical purposes in 2013 and for recreational purposes in 2018 (Rough, 2017; Statistics Canada, 2018b).

Portugal decriminalized (but did not legalize) the use or possession of *all* drugs in 2001, viewing addiction to heroin and other hard drugs as a medical issue rather than a criminal problem. The Portuguese government's goal is harm reduction, not punishment. Accordingly, it funds countrywide needle exchange programs; centres for the detoxification and treatment of addicts, including the replacement of heroin with methadone; and training, employment, and housing opportunities that allow former addicts to become reintegrated into society. Since 2001, Portugal has witnessed a decline in drug use among adolescents and adults; drug-related prosecutions; HIV infections among drug users; and drug-related deaths—all indicators that decriminalization has worked as planned (European Monitoring Centre for Drugs and Drug Addiction, 2011).

## DIVERSION

The third reform to tough prison regimes that has been proposed in recent years involves reducing the number of incarcerated offenders by diverting them from the court and prison systems.

Diversion procedures handle tens of thousands of youth cases every year. For example, the Victim Offender Reconciliation Program allows victims and offenders to meet under controlled conditions. To be considered candidates for the program, offenders must first acknowledge that they are guilty of the act they have been accused of committing. Victims have the opportunity to explain to the victim the full impact of the criminal act. Offenders must then seek reconciliation with the victim by, say, apologizing and agreeing to financial compensation. Most cases referred for diversion involve a minor offence, such as theft under $5000. Offenders selected for the program generally complete the provisions of the agreements they make (Tufts, 2000).

Similarly, the Supreme Court of Canada has urged judges to "take into account the primary importance of restorative justice principles within Indigenous conceptions of sentencing," especially for less-serious offences (Hendrick and Farmer, 2002: 11). **Restorative justice** addresses the harm caused by crime, holds the offender responsible, and gives the parties affected the chance to articulate their needs. It thus supports "healing, reintegration, the prevention of future harm, and reparation, if possible" (Federal-Provincial-Territorial Working Group on Restorative Justice Subcommittee on Public and Justice Sector Education, 2009). The restorative justice model views crime as behaviour that violates people and relationships rather than just the state and its laws. Although the behaviour of the offender is condemned, the essential value of the individual is affirmed and the offender reassured that, through conformity, the stigma associated with a crime can be removed.

A summary of 25 years of research on the subject allowed analysts to compare the effectiveness of restorative and nonrestorative justice programs in terms of victim satisfaction, offender satisfaction, restitution compliance, and reduction in recidivism (Latimer, Dowden, and Muise, 2007). In brief, the researchers found that participating in a restorative justice program resulted in higher victim satisfaction ratings, higher restitution compliance, and lower recidivism rates than participating in a nonrestorative justice program did. Analysis of the comparative effectiveness of restorative justice programs on offender satisfaction was inconclusive.

All of these reforms serve to remind us, yet again, that crime and deviance are social constructs.

## READY TO STUDY?

### IN THE BOOK YOU CAN:

- ❏ Refer to the Chapter in Review section at the back of the book to have a summary of the chapter and key terms handy.
- ❏ Test your knowledge of chapter contents by answering the multiple-choice questions in the Chapter in Review section. Answers are in the appendix at the end of the book.

### ONLINE YOU CAN:

- ❏ Stay organized and efficient with MindTap—a single destination with all the course material and study aids you need to succeed.
- ❏ Flashcards are pre-populated to provide you with a jump start for review—or you can create your own.
- ❏ You can highlight text and make notes in your MindTap Reader.
- ❏ Prepare for tests with quizzes.

**GO TO NELSON.COM/STUDENT TO PURCHASE THESE DIGITAL RESOURCES.**

# 6

# Social Stratification: Canadian and Global Perspectives

# SOCIAL STRATIFICATION: SHIPWRECKS AND INEQUALITY

Writers and filmmakers sometimes tell stories about shipwrecks and their survivors to make a point about social inequality. They use the shipwreck as a literary device that allows them to sweep away all traces of privilege and social convention. What remains are human beings stripped to their essentials, guinea pigs in an imaginary laboratory for the study of wealth and poverty, power and powerlessness, esteem and disrespect.

The tradition began with Daniel Defoe's *Robinson Crusoe*, first published in 1719. Defoe tells the story of an Englishman marooned on a desert island. His strong will, hard work, and inventiveness turn the poor island into a thriving colony. Defoe was one of the first writers to portray capitalism favourably. He believed that people get rich if they possess the virtues of good businesspeople—and stay poor if they don't.

The 1974 Italian movie *Swept Away* tells almost exactly the opposite story. In the movie, a beautiful woman, one of the idle rich, boards her yacht for a cruise in the Mediterranean. She is condescending and abrupt in her interactions with the hardworking deckhands. They do their jobs but seethe with resentment. Then comes the storm. The yacht is shipwrecked. Only the beautiful woman and one handsome deckhand remain alive, marooned on a desert island. Now equals—both have only each other—the two survivors soon have passionate sex and fall in love.

All is well until the day of their rescue. As soon as they return to the mainland, the woman resumes her haughty ways. She turns her back on the deckhand, who is reduced again to the role of a common labourer. Thus, the movie sends the audience three harsh messages. First, it is possible to be rich without working hard, because a person can inherit wealth. Second, people can work hard without becoming rich. Third, something about the structure of society causes inequality, because inequality disappears only on the desert island, where there is no society as we know it.

*Titanic* is a more recent movie on the shipwreck-and-inequality theme. At one level, the movie shows that class differences are important. For example, in first class, living conditions are luxurious, whereas in third class, they are cramped. In fact, on the *Titanic*, class differences spell the difference between life and death. After the *Titanic*

## LEARNING OBJECTIVES:

In this chapter, you will learn to

- **LO1** Describe how wealth and income inequality in Canada have changed in recent decades.
- **LO2** List the factors underlying income inequality.
- **LO3** Appreciate the social origins of poverty.
- **LO4** Understand why different sociologists argue that high levels of inequality are necessary, will inevitably disappear, or vary under identifiable conditions.
- **LO5** Recognize how people move up and down the structure of inequality.
- **LO6** Analyze change in the magnitude of inequality on a world scale.
- **LO7** Contrast competing explanations for the persistence of global inequality.

**social stratification** The way society is organized in layers or strata.

**power** Defined by Weber as the ability to achieve one's goals, even against the resistance of others.

strikes the iceberg off the coast of Newfoundland and Labrador, the ship's crew prevents second- and third-class passengers from entering the few available lifeboats. They give priority to rescuing first-class passengers. Consequently, 75 percent of third-class passengers perished, compared with 39 percent of first-class passengers (Table 6.1).

As the tragedy of the *Titanic* unfolds, however, another, contradictory theme emerges. Under some circumstances, we learn, class differences can be insignificant. In the movie, the sinking of the *Titanic* is the backdrop to a fictional love story about a wealthy young woman in first class and a working-class youth in the decks below. The sinking of the *Titanic* and the collapse of its elaborate class structure give the young lovers an opportunity to cross class lines and profess their devotion to each other. At one level, then, the movie *Titanic* is an optimistic tale that holds out hope for a society in which class differences matter little.

*Robinson Crusoe, Swept Away,* and *Titanic* raise many of the issues I address in this chapter. What are the sources of social inequality? Do determination, industry, and ingenuity shape the distribution of advantages and disadvantages in society, as the tale of *Robinson Crusoe* portrays? Or is *Swept Away* more accurate? Do certain patterns of social relations underlie and shape that distribution? Is *Titanic's* first message of social class differences still valid? Does social inequality still have big consequences for the way we live? What about *Titanic's* second message? Can people overcome or reduce inequality in society? If so, how?

To answer these questions, I first sketch patterns of social stratification in Canada and globally. I then critically review major theories of **social stratification,** the way society is organized in layers or strata. Finally, I analyze the movement of individuals up and down the stratification system over time and their perceptions of the stratification system.

# LO¹ PATTERNS OF SOCIAL INEQUALITY

## WEALTH

Most adults' wealth (or net worth) includes a dwelling (minus the mortgage), a car (minus the loan), some appliances and furniture (minus the credit card balance), and some savings. Owning a nice house and a good car and having a substantial sum of money invested securely enhances your sense of well-being. You know you have a cushion to fall back on in difficult times, and you know you don't have to worry about paying for your children's postsecondary education or how you will make ends meet during retirement.

Wealth is also **power**, which Weber defined as the ability to achieve one's goals, even against the resistance of others (Weber, 1964 [1947]: 152). For example, wealth can buy political influence. Campaign contributions to political parties and donations to favourite political causes increase the chance that policies you favour will become law.

Wealth even improves your health. If you can afford to engage in leisure pursuits, turn off stress, consume high-quality food, and employ superior medical services, you are likely to live a healthier and longer life than someone who lacks these advantages.

In 2018, the 100 wealthiest Canadians enjoyed a net worth between $1.01 billion and $41.14 billion (Canada's Richest People, 2018). These sums are so large they are hard to imagine. You can begin to grasp them by considering that if you spent $1000 a day, it would take you nearly three years to spend $1 million. How long would it take you to spend $1 billion? If you spent $1000 a day, you couldn't spend the entire sum in a lifetime. It would take nearly 3000 years to spend $1 billion at the rate of $1000 a day—and that assumes you don't invest part to earn still more money.

Another way of putting the wealth gap into perspective is to note that the two wealthiest in Canada

### TABLE 6.1   Survivors of the 1912 *Titanic* Disaster by Class (percentage)

|  | First Class | Second Class | Third Class | Crew |
|---|---|---|---|---|
| Children | 100 | 100 | 34.2 | n.a. |
| Women | 97.2 | 86.0 | 46.1 | n.a. |
| Men | 32.6 | 8.3 | 16.2 | 21.7 |
| Total | 62.5 | 41.4 | 25.2 | 21.7 |

Source: Adapted from Charles Anesi. 1997. "The Titanic Casualty Figures." Based on British Parliamentary Papers, Shipping Casualties (Loss of the Steamship "Titanic"), 1912, cmd. 6352, Report of a Formal Investigation into the circumstances attending the foundering on the 15th April, 1912, of the British Steamship "Titanic," of Liverpool, after striking ice in or near Latitude 41° 46′ N., Longitude 50° 14′ W., North Atlantic Ocean, whereby loss of life ensued. (London: His Majesty's Stationery Office, 1912). http://www.anesi.com/titanic.htm (retrieved 11 March 2010).

(the Thomson family and Galen Weston, Sr.) have the same amount of wealth as the 11 million Canadians at the bottom of the wealth ladder, who comprise 31 percent of the Canadian population (Thompson, 2017) But perhaps oil baron John Paul Getty, named the world's richest man by the *Guinness World Book of Records* in 1966, said it best when a *Playboy* reporter interviewed him:

> *Playboy*: It's been reported that you are the first man in history with a fortune in excess of a billion dollars.
>
> Getty: I have no idea. But if you can count your money, you're not a billionaire.

See Sociology and the Media, *All the Money in the World*.

Official statistics give us insight into how net worth (assets minus debt) changed between 1999 and 2016. The median net worth of Canadian families rose from $144 500 in 1999 to $295 100 in 2016—an increase of 104 percent, taking inflation into account. (The median separates the bottom and top halves of a category so, for example, in 2016, half of Canadians owned assets worth more than $295 100 and half owned assets worth less.) Much of this increase was due to the soaring value of real estate in some cities, notably Toronto, Hamilton, Vancouver, and Victoria.

Figure 6.1 divides Canadian families and unattached individuals into the poorest fifth (or "quintile"), the second-poorest fifth, the middle fifth, the second-richest fifth, and the richest fifth. Over the period in question, the biggest winner by far was the top quintile. The median net worth of the wealthiest fifth of Canadians rose from $2.8 million in 1999 to $6.9 million in 2016. In stark contrast, the net worth of the poorest fifth of Canadians increased by a mere $3000 between 1999 and 2016, but even so their debt exceeded the value of their assets by $1400 at the end of this period.

Finally, note that in 2016 the top quintile owned more than two-thirds of all wealth in the country, the second quintile owned just over a fifth, the middle quintile less than a tenth, and the second poorest quintile less than one-fortieth. The bottom quintile had no wealth at all.

## SOCIOLOGY AND THE MEDIA

### All the Money in the World

John Paul Getty inherited a sizable sum from his multi-millionaire father, who made his fortune in the oil fields of Oklahoma. However, the bulk of his wealth resulted from a 1949 deal he made with Ibn Saud, the first King of Saudi Arabia. In exchange for a 60-year concession to a barren tract of land near the Kuwaiti border, Getty paid Ibn Saud $9.5 million. Four years later, he struck oil, and by 1953 he was pumping 16 million barrels a year.

*All the Money in the World* is a jaw-dropping Ridley Scott film about the 1973 Rome kidnapping of John Paul Getty's 16-year-old grandson by a Calabrian-organized crime group. It features Michelle Williams as the grandson's mother, Canadian acting legend Christopher Plummer as Getty (nominated for an Oscar for his performance), and Mark Wahlberg as Getty's adviser. Why jaw-dropping? Because the kidnappers demanded $17 million in ransom but the notoriously miserly Getty figured he could claim only $2.2 million as a tax deduction, so he refused to pay a penny more, even though he professed to love his grandson and even after the kidnappers sent him his grandson's ear and threatened to send additional body parts until he paid up. The kidnappers would go no lower than $3 million. Getty finally gave his son a loan of $800 000 to pay the balance—at 4 percent interest (Weber, 2011).

I imagine pretty well everyone left the theatre asking themselves how anyone calling himself a human being act could act so despicably, haggling over the life of a cherished grandchild. But I doubt the audience reaction had much influence on their general attitudes toward the rich. Research shows that most middle-class people actually tend to favour the rich over the middle class, at least implicitly (Horwitz and Diovidio, 2017). In an 18-country survey, Canadians ranked second to Australians in thinking that the rich deserve their wealth (Americans placed third) (Globescan, 2012).

That may help explain why so many people are fascinated with the lives of rich people, devouring TV shows like *Trust*, *Succession*, *Dynasty*, *Billions*, *Empire*, *Downton Abbey*, *Gossip Girl*, *Odd Mom Out*, and the many iterations of *The Real Housewives* franchise. A high level of inequality has negative consequences for society, weakening democracy by allowing the rich to exercise disproportionate political influence and preventing the poor from receiving adequate health care, for example. However, for many people, the fascination and implicit approval remain strong.

### Critical Thinking Question

- Why do most middle-class people implicitly favour the rich and think the rich deserve their wealth?

## FIGURE 6.1 Median Net Worth of Families and Unattached Individuals, by Quintile, Canada, 1999–2016 (in 2016 dollars)

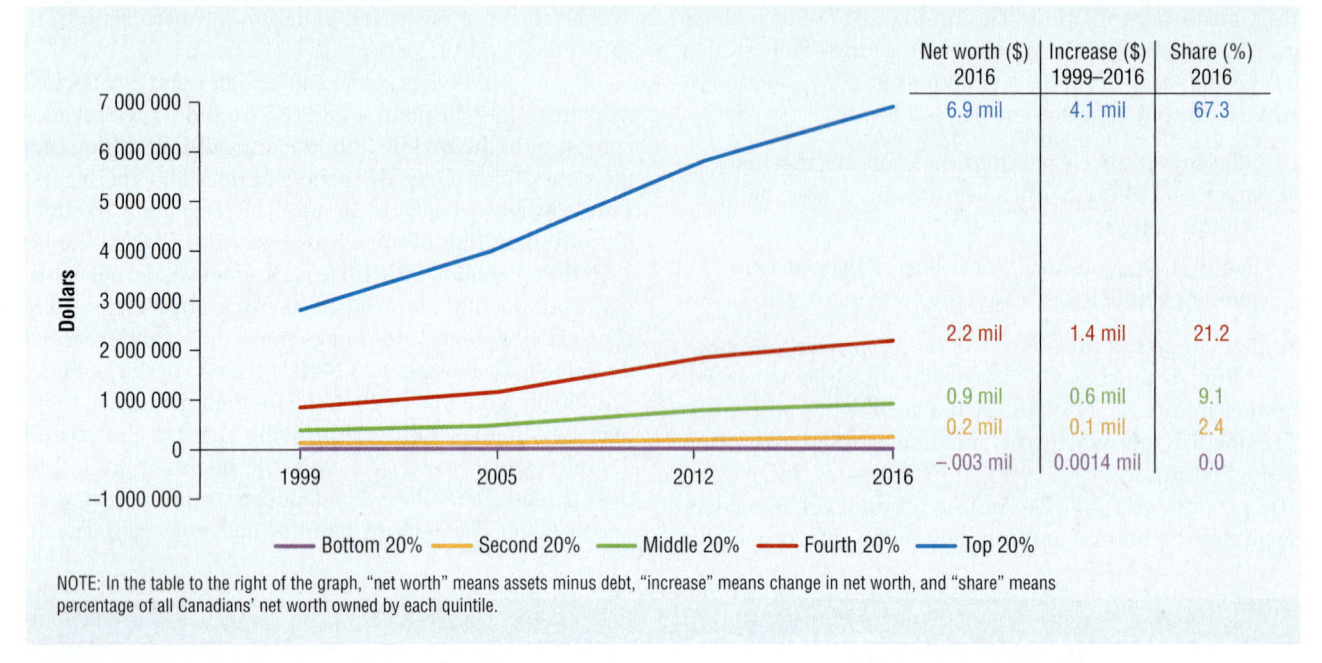

|  | Net worth ($) 2016 | Increase ($) 1999–2016 | Share (%) 2016 |
|---|---|---|---|
| Top 20% | 6.9 mil | 4.1 mil | 67.3 |
| Fourth 20% | 2.2 mil | 1.4 mil | 21.2 |
| Middle 20% | 0.9 mil | 0.6 mil | 9.1 |
| Second 20% | 0.2 mil | 0.1 mil | 2.4 |
| Bottom 20% | −.003 mil | 0.0014 mil | 0.0 |

NOTE: In the table to the right of the graph, "net worth" means assets minus debt, "increase" means change in net worth, and "share" means percentage of all Canadians' net worth owned by each quintile.

Source: Adapted from Statistics Canada (2017q). "Survey of Financial Security (SFS), assets and debts by net worth quintile, Canada, provinces and selected census metropolitan areas (CMAs)." CANSIM 205-0004 (https://www150.statcan.gc.ca/t1/tbl1/en/tv.action?pid=1110004901) (retrieved 27 January 2018)

A popular song during the Great Depression (1929–39) claimed that "the rich get richer and the poor get poorer." Figure 6.1 shows that the song is half-right as a description of changing net worth in dollars in recent years. In Canada, the rich are getting a lot richer while the poor remain pretty much in place, owning less than nothing.

## INCOME

Income is the amount of money earned in a given period. Today, the average Canadian family earns about 21 times more than the average Canadian family did in 1950, but that is less impressive than it sounds. More than half the gain is due to inflation. After all, a soft drink that once cost a dime now costs a dollar. Moreover, the average number of earners per family increased as more women entered the paid labour force. As a result, more people are now generating the income of the average family than was the case in 1950. Even so, Canadian families earn considerably more now than they did 60 years ago, partly because they are more productive. That is, the average worker is more skilled and is using more sophisticated technology to produce more goods and services per hour of work.

How has the distribution of income changed over time? Is income inequality growing or shrinking? To answer these questions, Figure 6.2 divides Canadian families and unattached individuals into quintiles, but this time by annual income, not wealth. It shows the percentage of all income earned in Canada in a year by quintile. A completely unequal distribution would exist if the top quintile earned 100 percent of the country's

## FIGURE 6.2 Share of Annual After-Tax Income, Canadian Families and Unattached Individuals, by Quintile, 1976 and 2011 (percentage)

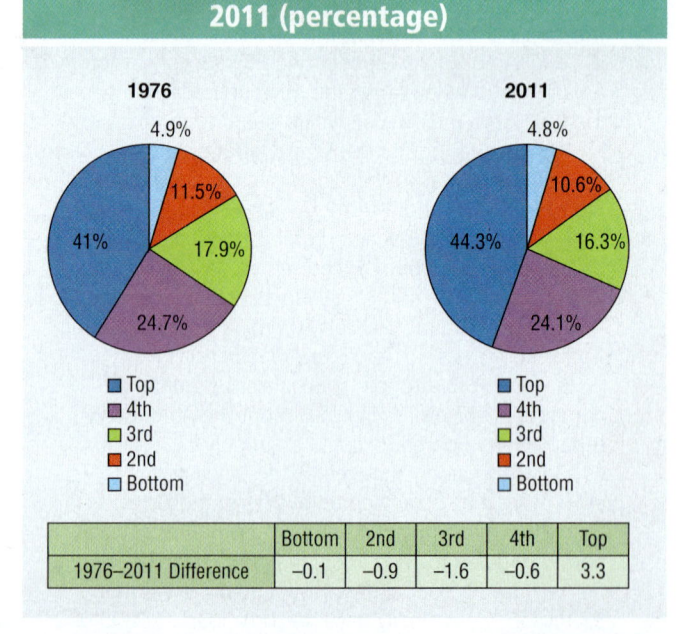

**1976**
- Top: 41%
- 4th: 24.7%
- 3rd: 17.9%
- 2nd: 11.5%
- Bottom: 4.9%

**2011**
- Top: 44.3%
- 4th: 24.1%
- 3rd: 16.3%
- 2nd: 10.6%
- Bottom: 4.8%

|  | Bottom | 2nd | 3rd | 4th | Top |
|---|---|---|---|---|---|
| 1976–2011 Difference | −0.1 | −0.9 | −1.6 | −0.6 | 3.3 |

Source: Statistics Canada. 2015e. "Market, total and after-tax income, by economic family type and income quintiles, 2011 constant dollars, annually." CANSIM Table 202–0701. (https://www150.statcan.gc.ca/t1/tbl1/en/tv.action?pid=1110017301) (retrieved 27 July 2015).

income. A completely equal distribution would exist if each quintile earned 20 percent of the country's income.

Figure 6.2 shows that in 2011, the bottom quintile of families and unattached individuals earned just 4.8 percent of all income, while the top quintile earned 44.3 percent. This means that the richest 20 percent of families earned $4.43 of every $10 earned in Canada. Moreover, the distribution of income has become more unequal since 1976. All quintiles earned a smaller share of total national income in 2011 than in 1976—except for the top quintile, which earned 3.3 percent more. This pattern mirrors the trend in most rich countries: income gaps have been widening. Specifically, looking at the year-by-year trend from 1976 to 2015, we see that income inequality increased in Canada from the early 1990s to the early 2000s and then levelled off (Figure 6.3).

The income data just reported represent the money that Canadian households earn after paying income tax and receiving government benefits. Canada has a welfare state. The government collects taxes and redistributes them in the form of social assistance payments, Employment Insurance payments, child tax credits, GST credits, and so on. The richest fifth of Canadians lose about a fifth of their income to income tax, while the poorest fifth of Canadians see their incomes increase by nearly two-thirds as a result of government transfer payments. If Canadians relied only on the market to distribute income, inequality would be much greater.

Differences in income inequality are evident within Canada too. Income inequality is lowest in Prince Edward Island and New Brunswick and highest in Ontario and Alberta. However, the biggest geographical differences are between Toronto, Montreal, Vancouver, and Calgary, on the one hand, and the rest of the country, on the other. Canada's four largest cities, with 38 percent of the country's population, have witnessed the country's biggest increases in income inequality in recent decades. Between 1982 and 2014, the increase in household income inequality was fully four times larger in Calgary than in the rest of the country (Fong, 2017: 5, 11-12)

## LO 2 EXPLANATIONS OF INCOME INEQUALITY

What explains the distribution of income? Why are some people rich and others poor? You know that some individuals earn high salaries because of their natural talent. Sidney Crosby (hockey), Andrew Wiggins (basketball), Ryan Gosling (acting), and Drake (rap music) are Canadians

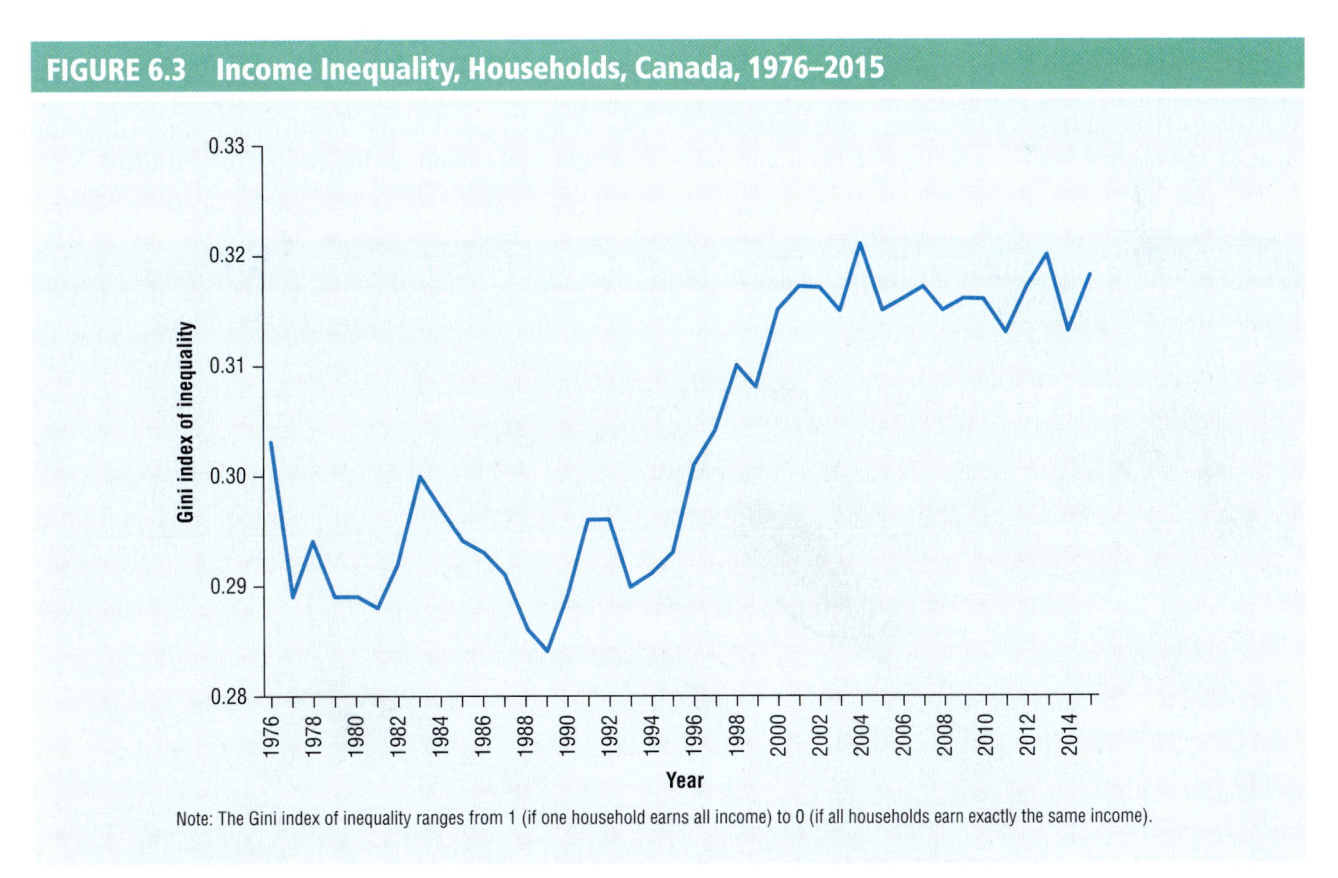

### FIGURE 6.3  Income Inequality, Households, Canada, 1976–2015

Note: The Gini index of inequality ranges from 1 (if one household earns all income) to 0 (if all households earn exactly the same income).

Source: Based on data from OECD (2018), Income inequality (indicator). https://data.oecd.org/inequality/income-inequality.htm/doi: 10.1787/459aa7f1-en. (retrieved 27 January 2018).

> **economic capital** Economic capital is ownership of land, real estate, industrial plants and equipment, and stocks and bonds.
>
> **human capital** Investment in education and training.
>
> **social capital** The social networks to which people are connected and that give them varying degrees of access to others who are well-positioned.

whose success on the world stage has provided them with substantial earnings. The principal reason for their excellence is a natural endowment in athletics, music, and so on. A genetic gift sets them apart. At the other end of the economic spectrum, some people suffer the genetic misfortune of Down syndrome or schizophrenia—conditions that usually prevent them from earning big salaries. However, people at both ends of the spectrum are exceptions. Sociologists believe that for the vast majority of people, genes play only a minor role in determining income.

Even for people with a natural talent in the performing arts or athletics, effort is essential. Practice and years of dedication to the basics of a profession are common to all who enjoy success. Effort is also significant for many Canadians who spend long hours at work—whether amassing billable hours in a law practice, doing endless chores in a small business, or working overtime at a construction site. However, although diligence and perseverance might be necessary conditions for rewards, they are not sufficient. Effort alone does not result in high income.

The most important determinant of income for most people is capital in its various forms. **Economic capital** is ownership of land, real estate, industrial plants and equipment, and stocks and bonds. Capital generates income and can be inherited, so being born into a rich family almost automatically ensures one of a substantial income.

A second form of capital is **human capital**, or investment in education and training. Just as productivity increases by upgrading manufacturing plants and introducing new technology, productivity gains can result from investment in the skills and abilities of people. Jobs requiring advanced skills are increasingly numerous in Canada, and the importance of education remains one of the most important determinants of occupation and income (Statistics Canada, 2003a: 9). As the Canadian occupational structure moves farther away from its traditional resource-based foundation to a more mature, knowledge-driven economy, the importance of education will continue to grow (see Table 6.2).

Much evidence supports a human capital interpretation of the link between schooling and incomes. However, it is not a complete explanation for why people earn what they earn. For example, in the legal profession, almost everyone makes the same human capital investment; every lawyer acquires a law degree. Yet economic rewards vary even for people with the same experience and type of legal practice. Notably, female lawyers earn less on average than male lawyers do, even if they are matched in terms of experience and type of practice (Kay and Hagan, 1998).

Part of the reason that people with the same amount of human capital may receive different economic rewards is that they possess different amounts of social capital. **Social capital** refers to people's networks or connections. Individuals are more likely to succeed if they have strong bonds of trust, cooperation, mutual respect, and obligation with well-positioned individuals or families. Knowing the right people, and having strong links to them, helps

### TABLE 6.2 Average Hourly Wage by Broad Occupational Group, 2016

| Occupational Group | Average Annual Earnings |
| --- | --- |
| Management | 40.25 |
| Natural and applied sciences | 33.45 |
| Education, law, and social, community, and government services | 33.20 |
| Health | 31.80 |
| Art, culture, recreation, and sport | 27.35 |
| Business, finance, and administration | 26.00 |
| Trades, transport, and equipment operators | 25.85 |
| Natural resources, agriculture, and related production | 22.15 |
| Manufacturing and utilities | 21.90 |
| Sales and service | 18.85 |

Source: Statistics Canada. 2017c. "Chart 1: Average full-time hourly wage by broad occupational group, 2016." CANSIM Table 285-0050. http://www.statcan.gc.ca/daily-quotidien/170615/cg-a001-eng.htm (retrieved 28 January 2018).

in finding opportunities and taking advantage of them (Coleman, 1988).

A related version of this argument is captured in the notion of cultural capital (Bourdieu and Passeron, 1990). **Cultural capital** comprises the set of social skills people have: their ability to impress others, to use tasteful language and images effectively to influence and persuade people. Although the notion of social capital stresses networks and connections with others, the idea of cultural capital emphasizes impression management skills and ability to influence others. In different ways, both concepts emphasize being part of the right "social club."

What the concepts of social and cultural capital also have in common is the idea that families higher in the social hierarchy enjoy more capital of all types. Connections and culture help you find a good job. The hiring of new recruits, then, depends on the talent, effort, and skills that people bring to the interview, but it also depends on the connections and culture that people have. Indeed, culture and connections often influence who gets an interview.

In sum, natural talent, effort, and capital (economic, human, social, and cultural) all influence how much people earn.

## LO3 POVERTY

### Defining Poverty

At the bottom of the income distribution are the homeless. In recent decades, the number of people with no fixed address has increased considerably. Nobody knows exactly how many Canadians are homeless, but in cities across the country, people sleep under bridges, in back alleys, behind dumpsters, and in thickets in public parks. They do so night after night, month after month.

Homelessness is a manifestation of **poverty**. Exactly how many Canadians are poor is a matter of debate. Poverty lacks an agreed-on definition. A first disagreement occurs around whether poverty should be defined in absolute or relative terms. An absolute definition of poverty focuses on essentials, suggesting that poor families have inadequate resources to acquire the necessities of life (food, clothing, and shelter). Agreement on "essentials" depends on values and judgments (Sarlo, 2001). What is essential varies from time to time, place to place, and group to group. Many of our ancestors lived without indoor plumbing, and some Canadians still do, but most people would define indoor plumbing as essential. A family could survive on a steady diet of cod and potatoes, but most would define such a family as poor.

A relative poverty line also has certain drawbacks. Two issues are central: relative to what, and how relative? Whether poverty ought to be defined narrowly in terms of economic measures (e.g., income) or more broadly with respect to community standards (e.g., safety of working conditions, environmental quality, type of housing) illustrates this second area of disagreement. Most definitions tend to be narrow, focusing primarily on income. But even if a relative poverty line is defined narrowly, how relative ought it to be? One-third of average income? One-half? Some other fraction?

Yet another disagreement plagues any definition. Should poverty be defined on the basis of income or consumption? Because "bare essentials" is a core idea in any definition of poverty, it makes good sense to think about, and measure, poverty as the cost of purchasing bare essentials. Deprivation occurs when a family cannot acquire the essentials, not necessarily when income is too low. Income and consumption are correlated, of course, but wealthy people can live off their savings, even with low income.

In one sense, the definition of poverty means little to a homeless person sleeping on a hot air vent. The immediate experience of poverty by families in remote coastal communities, single parents in the urban core, and marginal Prairie farmers is unaffected by whether poverty is defined absolutely or relatively, narrowly or broadly, by income or by consumption. However, the definition of poverty is consequential for these people because social policies are enacted, or not enacted, based on levels and trends in poverty. Definitions matter.

> **cultural capital** The widely shared, high-status cultural signals (attitudes, preferences, formal knowledge, behaviours, goals, and credentials) used for social and cultural inclusion and exclusion.
>
> **poverty** Lacks an agreed-on definition. Analysts disagree whether poverty should be defined in absolute or relative terms and whether it should be based on income or consumption. Canada does not have an official poverty line. Statistics Canada reports a low-income measure (half the median household income, adjusted for family size), below which people are considered to be in the low-income category.

Answers to the question of why some people are poor vary from individual-level to structural explanations.

CHAPTER 6 Social Stratification: Canadian and Global Perspectives

Politics can reshape the distribution of income and the system of inequality by changing laws governing people's right to own property. Politicians can also alter patterns of inequality by entitling people to various welfare benefits and by redistributing income through tax policies. When politicians de-emphasize poverty, legislative efforts to maintain or expand welfare benefits and redistribute income are less likely. A definition of poverty showing fewer poor Canadians implies little need for government action. Conversely, for politicians and political parties supporting the poor, a definition of poverty showing a growing proportion of poor people is beneficial to their cause.

Poverty definitions are also important for political reasons. A democratic society depends on the full participation of all citizens—everyone has the right to vote, anyone can run for political office, and everyone's voice should influence political choices. The proportion of Canadians who are poor is a measure of how well democracy is working. Can someone without a permanent home or someone in a family with bare cupboards participate fully in national affairs?

Statistics Canada does not attempt to estimate the number of Canadians who are poor. Instead, it calculates several low-income measures. One is the LIM-AT (low-income measure, after tax). It is a relative, income-based measure that defines low income as half the national median household income, adjusted for family size. In 2015, 14.2 percent of Canadians in households (4.8 million people) were in the low-income category by this definition. In 1989, Parliament vowed to put an end to child poverty by 2000, but in 2015, 17 percent of Canadians under the age of 18 were still in the low-income category (Statistics Canada, 2017h).

## Myths about Poverty

The language people use to speak of the poor is often revealing. For example, referring to someone as "poor but honest" or "poor but virtuous" suggests that the speaker views such combinations as unlikely and feel it necessary to single out those who possess both characteristics as exceptions to the rule. Popular mythology also depicts the poor— especially those who receive public assistance ("on welfare")—as lazy, irresponsible, and lacking in motivation, abilities, and moral values. These images are potent and contribute to stereotypes of the "deserving" and the "undeserving" poor (for example, war veterans and children versus "welfare bums" and those "looking for a handout"). However, research conducted in the past few decades shows that many stereotypes about the poor are myths:

- *Myth 1: People are poor because they don't want to work.* The myth that poor people don't want to work ignores that many poor people can't work because of poor health or a disability or because they must take care of their young children due to inadequate public child-care provisions in Canada. Moreover, it ignores that many poor people work full-time, and many more work part-time. Still, having a job is no guarantee of escaping poverty because the minimum wage set by provincial and territorial governments is so low. In 2015, the minimum wage varied from $10.20 (in Alberta and Saskatchewan) to $12.50 (in the Northwest Territories), with an unweighted provincial and territorial average of $10.69. Working 50 weeks at 40 hours a week for $10.69 an hour would earn a person $21 380 a year—$753 below LIM-AT. That's why many Canadians have been pushing provincial governments to raise the minimum wage. On January 1, 2018, Alberta's minimum wage was $13.60 an hour; Ontario's minimum wage was $14. At the beginning of 2018, the unweighted provincial and territorial average minimum wage was just $11.02 an hour, a gain of a paltry 33 cents in three years.
- *Myth 2: Most poor people are immigrants.* Actually, only recent immigrants experience poverty rates significantly higher than the Canadian-born, and recent immigrants are only a small fraction of all Canadian immigrants. Moreover, once they are established, immigrants have lower poverty rates than do people born in Canada (National Council of Welfare, 2004).
- *Myth 3: Most poor people are trapped in poverty.* In fact, 80 percent of people with low income in a given year escape poverty in less than a year; and another 12 percent escape within two years (Statistics Canada, 2010a). I conclude that most people try to move out of difficult financial circumstances and most succeed, at least for a time.

## Explaining Poverty

General explanations for the existence of poverty range from individual-level to structural explanations. Individual-level explanations focus on the characteristics of people who are poor, asking how they differ from people who are not poor. This type of explanation focuses on causes that lie within the person. Someone is poor, according to this logic, because of a personal attribute, such as low intelligence or a behavioural abnormality.

Some evidence suggests that individual attributes do explain a small amount of poverty. For example, people with disabilities have a higher risk of living in poverty than do others. Not all people with disabilities live in poverty, however, and the vast majority of people living in poverty do not have a disability. As this example illustrates, most poverty is not a consequence of people's characteristics.

A related explanation focuses on people's acquired attitudes: low self-esteem, lack of motivation to achieve, and an inability to delay gratification. Based on this logic, poverty persists because poor families employ inadequate child-rearing practices that create bad attitudes. A related version of this argument identifies a "culture of poverty," a way of thinking and acting supposedly shared by poor families. A culture of poverty is said to reinforce and perpetuate itself through poor upbringing and ill-formed personalities.

Two objections undermine this type of social-psychological explanation. First, descriptions of poverty stressing a culture of depression, lack of hope, and fatalism may be accurate, but these states of mind are typically *effects* of poverty, not its causes. Second, many people who are poor do work, are religious, don't smoke or drink, and so on. Therefore, evidence that supports explanations founded on these personal deficits is often lacking.

Another type of explanation has greater currency in sociology. It stresses the organization of the economy as the principal cause of poverty. Capitalist economies feature periods of low unemployment and high profits followed by high unemployment and low profits. During recessions, many people lose their jobs and fall into poverty. Moreover, as we have seen, people with minimum-wage jobs don't earn enough to escape poverty. From this point of view, the lack of good jobs, especially during recessions, is the major cause of poverty.

Other analysts stress social policy as a factor affecting poverty levels. For example, as noted above, if you received the minimum hourly wage while working full-time year-round, you would still be poor, especially if you had children to support. In this sense, minimum-wage legislation is a social policy that creates a group of working poor.

However, the social world is not that simple. If minimum wages were to rise too much or too quickly or during an economic downturn, so too might the level of unemployment; some employers might not be able to afford a sudden big jump in wages. Debate over these issues continues, but the point is that our social policies affect people's well-being, and understanding the consequences of policies is critical.

The tax system illustrates another way that social policies affect poverty. A *progressive* tax system is one in which income is taxed at a higher rate the more one earns. For example, in a progressive tax system, a person with $50 000 a year of taxable income may pay 25 percent of that amount in income tax while a person with $100 000 a year of taxable income may pay 40 percent of that amount in income tax. In Canada, although income tax is progressive, the overall tax system is approximately neutral. That is, most Canadian families pay about the same percentage of their total income in tax. That is because four factors undermine the "Robin Hood" effect of progressive income tax:

1. Taxes other than income tax, such as the HST, fuel tax, and property tax, are regressive; the tax rate is the same for everyone who pays these taxes, regardless of their income.
2. Higher income earners are able to shelter part of their income from taxation by investing extra cash in registered education savings plans (RESPs) and registered retirement savings plans (RRSPs).
3. Higher income earners tend to own investments that generate dividends and profits, which are taxed at a lower rate than are wages and salaries.
4. The very rich can hire tax lawyers and accountants to channel money to overseas "tax havens" such as Panama and avoid taxation altogether. Canada loses between $6 and $7.8 billion in tax revenue annually due to such tax evasion (Oved, 2016).

These four mechanisms help to keep one out of seven Canadians below the low-income line.

Finally, other sociologists stress ways of thinking, or ideological perspectives, as explanations for poverty. Negative images of various groups lead to an undervaluing of the ways of life of Indigenous peoples, recent immigrants, and members of visible minority groups. Discrimination follows from undervaluation. Discrimination causes poverty because it leads to less success in finding jobs and, when jobs are found, to more unsteady and low-paying work.

Is poverty inevitable? Perhaps, but the extent of poverty can be substantially reduced. Many western European governments have established job-training and child-care programs that allow more poor people to take jobs with livable wages and benefits. Consequently, poverty rates in these countries are lower than in Canada (see Theories in Dispute, The Feminization of Poverty?). In the five Scandinavian countries combined (Denmark, Finland, Iceland, Norway, and Sweden), the poverty rate is half that of Canada's (Statista, 2018c).

The observation that it is possible to reduce the extent of poverty raises a more general issue: Is inequality inevitable? That question has concerned sociologists since the mid-nineteenth century. We next review some classical answers to shed light on our prospects today.

# LO4 IS STRATIFICATION INEVITABLE? THREE THEORIES

## MARX'S CONFLICT THEORY

Karl Marx was the founder of conflict theory in sociology. It is ironic, therefore, that social stratification and the accompanying conflict between classes were *not* inevitable in Marx's view (Marx, 1904 [1859]; Marx and Engels, 1972 [1848]). He believed that capitalist growth would eventually produce a society without classes and therefore without class conflict.

# THEORIES IN DISPUTE

## The Feminization of Poverty?

In the 1970s, North American feminist sociologists claimed to have identified a considerable and growing gap between women and men in the extent of poverty. Specifically, they meant that (1) women were more likely to be low-income earners than men were, and (2) the low-income gap between women and men was growing (Duffy and Mandell, 2014: 116–20). These observations came to be known as the *feminization of poverty* thesis.

The data suggest that while (1) is correct, (2) is not. As Figure 6.4 indicates, in 1976, the low-income gap between women and men was 3.1 percent. It reached a high point of 3.6 percent in 1980. Since then, however, the low-income gap has fallen pretty consistently. By 2015, the low-income rate among Canadian women was just 1 percent higher than the comparable rate among Canadian men. These figures contradict the view that the low-income gap between women and men is large and growing.

Nonetheless, the gap between women and men living in poverty is real, and it is especially large among people in one-parent families and among the elderly (although there have been improvements over time even among these categories of the population).

**FIGURE 6.4  Male–Female Gap in Low Income, Canada, 1976–2015**

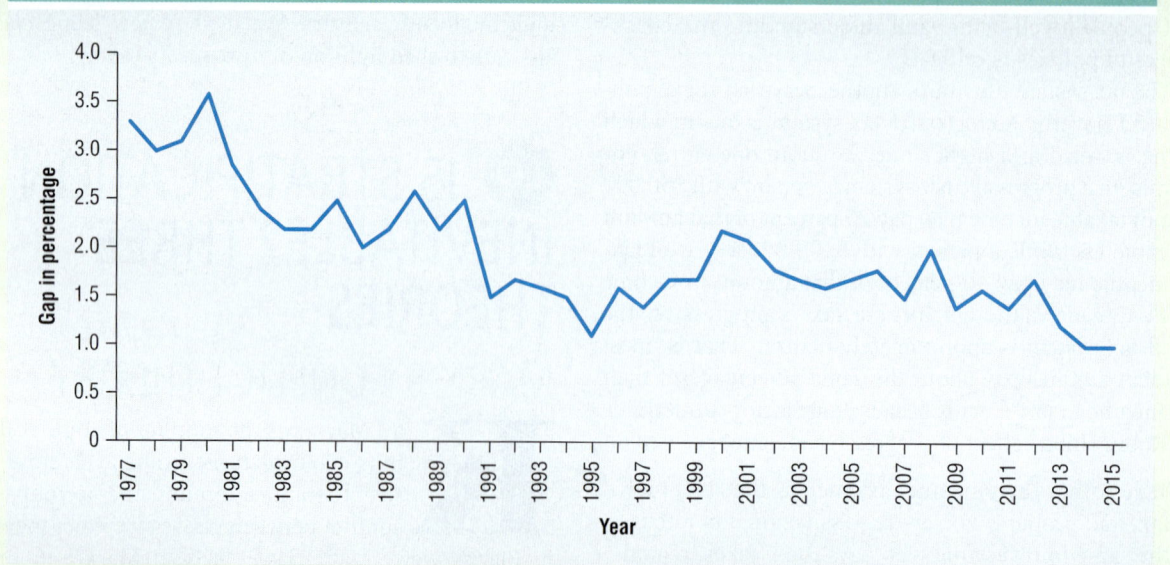

Source: Statistics Canada. 2017l. "Low income statistics by age, sex and economic family type, Canada, provinces and selected census metropolitan areas (CMAs), annually." CAMSIM Table 2060041. http://www.statcan.gc.ca/daily-quotidien/140225/dq140225b-eng.htm (retrieved 27 January 2018)

The female–male poverty gap is largely a function of women's position in the labour market compared to that of men. Women typically spend fewer years working in the paid labour force than men do because they assume the bulk of domestic and child-rearing responsibilities in most families. This means that they usually accumulate smaller pensions and more modest savings than men do. When they are working in the paid labour force, women typically earn less than men do, again minimizing their savings and pensions. Moreover, relatively low wages for women means that the advantage of working for a wage as compared to collecting social assistance payments is smaller for women than for men. Women are therefore more likely than men are to collect social assistance payments and sink into poverty. Finally, women live an average of five years longer than men do, so their financial resources have more time to deplete.

## Critical Thinking Questions

- One reason the Scandinavian countries have a relatively low poverty rate is that they have found a way to get most low-income single mothers (who would otherwise be their children's sole caregivers) into the paid labour force. How do you think they have accomplished this feat?
- Apart from the suggestions you've made answering question 1, how could the male–female gap in low income be eliminated?

In Marx's sense of the term, **class** is determined by a person's "relationship to the means of production" or the source of that person's income. The source of income is profit if the person owns a factory or a mine. It is a wage if he or she must work as a labourer in a factory or a mine. Accordingly, Marx argued that capitalist societies have two main classes: the ownership class (or **bourgeoisie**, to use his term) and the working class (or what Marx termed the **proletariat**), distinguished from each other by whether they own productive property (factories, mines, and so on).

According to Marx, during the Industrial Revolution that began in Great Britain in the late eighteenth century, industrial owners were eager to adopt new tools, machines, and production methods so they could produce goods more efficiently and earn higher profits. Such innovations had unforeseen consequences. First, some owners were driven out of business by more efficient competitors. They were forced to become members of the working class. Together with former peasants pouring into the cities from the countryside to take factory jobs, this circumstance caused the working class to grow. Second, the drive for profits motivated owners to concentrate workers in increasingly larger factories, keep wages as low as possible, and invest as little as possible in improving working conditions. Thus, as the bourgeoisie grew richer and smaller, the proletariat grew larger and more impoverished.

Marx also believed that capitalism would experience increasingly severe economic crises of "overproduction" or "underconsumption" because the impoverished proletariat would be unable to afford to buy all that industry could produce. During such crises, businesses would go bankrupt, unemployment would spread, and workers would become more aware of the severity of their exploitation. Their growing sense of "class consciousness" would encourage the growth of unions and workers' political parties which, according to Marx, would eventually try to create a new "communist" society in which there would be no private wealth. Instead, under communism, everyone would share wealth, said Marx, contributing to the welfare of society according to their ability and taking according to their need.

## Critical Evaluation of Marx's Conflict Theory

For five reasons, things did not work out the way Marx had predicted. First, industrial societies did not polarize into two opposed classes engaged in bitter conflict. Instead, a large and heterogeneous middle class of white-collar workers emerged. Some of them were nonmanual employees. Others were professionals. Many of them enjoyed higher income and status than manual workers did. With a bigger stake in capitalism than propertyless manual workers had, nonmanual employees and professionals generally acted as a stabilizing force in society.

Second, although Marx correctly argued that investment in technology makes it possible for capitalists to earn high profits, he did not expect investment in technology also to make it possible for workers to earn higher wages and toil fewer hours under less oppressive conditions. Yet that is just what happened.

**class** According to Marx, a grouping that is determined by a person's relationship to the means of production or the source of that person's income. In Weber's usage, class position is determined by a person's "market situation," including the possession of goods, opportunities for income, level of education, and level of technical skill.

**bourgeoisie** Owners of the means of production, including factories, tools, and land, according to Marx. They do not do any physical labour. Their income derives from profits.

**proletariat** The term Marx gave to the working class. Members of the proletariat perform physical labour but do not own means of production. They are thus in a position to earn wages.

> **functional theory of stratification** Argues that (1) some jobs are more important than others, (2) people must make sacrifices to train for important jobs, and (3) inequality is required to motivate people to undergo these sacrifices.

Third, many workers supported political parties that promoted improved state benefits, including employment insurance and health care, and they went on strike to demand higher wages from their employers. Their efforts won them improved living standards, which in turn tended to pacify them.

Fourth, communism took root not where industry was most highly developed, as Marx predicted, but in semi-industrialized countries, such as Russia in 1917 and China in 1949. Moreover, instead of evolving into classless and democratic societies, new forms of privilege and authoritarianism emerged under communism. According to a Russian quip from the 1970s, "Under capitalism, one class exploits the other, but under communism it's the other way around." Many workers consequently became disillusioned with the promises of communism.

Fifth, businesspeople developed new ways to avert economic crises and prolong the life of capitalism by stimulating demand. To encourage people to buy more things, they began advertising on a massive scale, which created new "needs." To give people the means to buy new things they could not otherwise afford, businesspeople created easy credit. And to ensure that people frequently replaced the new things they bought, they started designing things to break down. Light bulbs with short 1000-hour lifespans, nylon stockings that developed runs after being worn just a few times, and inkjet printers containing a chip that made them die after printing a set number of pages were among the abundant fruits of such "planned obsolescence."

# THE FUNCTIONALIST THEORY OF DAVIS AND MOORE

In the mid-twentieth century, American sociologists Kingsley Davis and Wilbert Moore proposed a **functional theory of stratification** that, in contrast to Marx's theory, asserts the *inevitability* of social stratification (Davis and Moore, 1945). Davis and Moore observed that jobs differ in importance. A judge's work, for example, contributes more to society than does the work of a janitor. This presents a problem: How can people be motivated to undergo the long training they need to serve as judges, physicians, engineers, and so on? Higher education is expensive. You earn little if any money while studying. Clearly, an incentive is needed to motivate the most talented people to train for the most important jobs. The incentives, said Davis and Moore, are money and prestige. More precisely, social stratification is necessary (or functional) because the prospect of high rewards motivates people to undergo the sacrifices needed to get a higher education. Without substantial inequality, Davis and Moore concluded, the most talented people would have no incentive to become judges, physicians, and so on.

## Critical Evaluation of Functionalism

Although the functional theory of stratification may at first seem plausible, we can quickly uncover one of its chief flaws by imagining a society with just two classes of people—physicians and farmers. The farmers grow food. The physicians tend the ill. Then, one day, a rare and deadly virus strikes. The virus has the odd property of attacking only physicians. Within weeks, there are no more doctors in our imaginary society. As a result, the farmers are much worse off. Cures for their ailments are no longer available. Soon the average farmer lives fewer years than his or her predecessors. The society is less well off, although it manages to survive.

Now imagine the reverse. Again, we have a society comprising only physicians and farmers. Again, a rare and lethal virus strikes. This time, however, the virus has the odd property of attacking only farmers. Within weeks, the physicians' stores of food are depleted. After a few more weeks, the physicians start dying of starvation. The physicians who try to become farmers catch the new virus and expire. Within months, the society has been wiped out. Who, then, does the more important work, physicians or farmers? Our thought experiment suggests that farmers do, for without them, society cannot exist.

From a historical point of view, we can say that *none* of the jobs regarded by Davis and Moore as important would exist without the physical labour done by people in so-called less important jobs. To sustain the witch doctor in a tribal society, hunters and gatherers had to produce enough for their own subsistence plus a surplus to feed, clothe, and house the witch doctor. To sustain the royal court in an agrarian society, peasants had to produce enough for their own subsistence plus a surplus to support the royal family. By using taxes, tithes, and force, government and religious authorities have taken surpluses from ordinary working people for thousands of years. Among other things, these surpluses were used to establish the first institutions of higher learning in the thirteenth century. Out of these, modern universities and colleges developed.

The question of which occupations are most important is thus not clear-cut. To be sure, physicians earn a lot more money than farmers today, and they also enjoy more prestige. But it is not because their work is more important in any objective sense of the word.

Sociologists have noted other problems with the functional theory of stratification (Tumin, 1953). First, it stresses how inequality helps society discover talent but it ignores the pool of talent lying undiscovered because of inequality. Bright and energetic adolescents may be forced

generation. Like *Robinson Crusoe*, the functional theory correctly emphasizes that talent and hard work often result in abundant material rewards. However, it is also the case that inheritance allows parents to transfer wealth to children, regardless of the children's talent. By one count, more than one-quarter of Canada's billionaires inherited a substantial part of their fortunes, most came from solidly middle-class and upper-middle-class families, and only one of them rose from rags to riches (Forbes.com, 2010).

> **status groups** Groups that differ from one another in terms of the prestige or social honour they enjoy and in terms of their style of life.

## WEBER'S COMPROMISE

Like the functionalists, Max Weber argued that the emergence of a classless society is highly unlikely. Like Marx, however, Weber recognized that under some circumstances people can act to lower the level of inequality in society.

Writing in the early twentieth century, Weber held that a person's class position is determined by his or her "market situation," including the possession of goods, opportunities for income, level of education, and level of technical skill. Accordingly, in Weber's view, four main classes exist in capitalist societies: large property owners, small property owners, propertyless but relatively highly educated and well-paid employees, and propertyless manual workers (Weber, 1946: 180–95).

Weber also recognized that two types of groups other than classes—status groups and parties—have a bearing on the way a society is stratified. **Status groups** differ from one another in the prestige or social honour they enjoy and in their lifestyle. Celebrities form an especially high-ranking status group in North America. Some enjoy prestige because they are rich or talented. Others enjoy prestige just because they attract a lot of attention. Consider Kim Kardashian. She first drew the attention of the mass media by hanging out with Paris Hilton. She received wider notice after the leak of a sex tape with her former boyfriend. She has no extraordinary talents and her family was not especially rich, although their reality TV show improved their economic

Are farmers or physicians more important to society?

to drop out of high school to help support themselves and their families. Capable and industrious high school graduates may be forced to forgo a postsecondary education because they can't afford it. Inequality may encourage the discovery of talent but only among those who can afford to take advantage of the opportunities available to them. For the rest, inequality prevents talent from being discovered.

Second, the functional theory of stratification fails to examine how advantages are passed from generation to

Roy Thomson, Canada's wealthiest man in 1976

Ken Thomson, Roy's son, Canada's wealthiest man in 1996

David Thomson, Roy's grandson, Canada's wealthiest man in 2016

CHAPTER 6 Social Stratification: Canadian and Global Perspectives 131

**parties** In Weber's usage, organizations that seek to impose their will on others.

**social mobility** Movement up or down the stratification system.

status a lot. Nor did power catapult her into a high-status rank. She became well-known largely because of her "well-knownness" (Boorstin, 1992: 57). As such, she illustrates how social honour alone can bestow rank on individuals.

In Weber's usage, **parties** are not just political groups but, more generally, organizations that seek to impose their will on others through the exercise of power (Weber, 1946: 152). Control over parties, especially large bureaucratic organizations, does not depend just on wealth. A person can head a military, scientific, political, or other bureaucracy without being rich, just as a person can be rich and still have to endure low prestige.

Weber argued that to draw an accurate picture of a society's stratification system, we must analyze classes, status groups, and parties as somewhat independent bases of social inequality. Each basis of stratification influences the others. For example, one political party may want to tax the rich and distribute benefits to the poor, thus increasing opportunities for upward mobility. Another political party may want to cut taxes to the rich and decrease benefits to the poor, thus decreasing opportunities for upward mobility.

The class system will be affected in different ways depending on which party comes to power. From this point of view, nothing is inevitable about the level of social stratification in society. We are neither headed inexorably toward classlessness nor are we bound to endure high levels of inequality. Instead, the level of social stratification depends on the complex interplay of class, status, and party, and their effect on **social mobility**, or movement up and down the stratification system. We devote the next section to exploring these themes.

*Kim Kardashian is famous for being famous.*

## THEORIES AT A GLANCE

### Stratification

| Theory | Outline |
|---|---|
| Marx's conflict theory | In capitalist societies, the two main classes are the bourgeoisie (who own but do not work productive property) and the proletariat (who work but do not own productive property). During the Industrial Revolution, industrial owners were eager to become more productive so they could earn higher profits. Less efficient owners were driven out of business and forced to join the working class, where they were joined by former peasants pouring into the cities looking for factory jobs. The drive for profits motivated owners to concentrate workers in increasingly larger factories, keep wages as low as possible, and invest as little as possible in improving working conditions. Thus, as the bourgeoisie grew richer and smaller, the proletariat grew larger and more impoverished. Marx also believed that the impoverished proletariat would be unable to afford to buy all that industry could produce, creating economic crises, during which businesses would go bankrupt, unemployment would spread, and workers would become more aware of the severity of their exploitation. Their growing sense of "class consciousness" would encourage the growth of unions and workers' political parties that would eventually try to create a new, classless society in which there would be no private wealth. |

| Theory | Outline |
|---|---|
| Davis and Moore's functionalist theory | Davis and Moore observed that some jobs are more important than others, and important jobs require considerable education. Incentives are needed to motivate the most talented people to train for the most important jobs. The incentives, said Davis and Moore, are money and prestige. Thus, social stratification is necessary (or functional) because the prospect of high rewards motivates people to undergo the sacrifices needed to get a higher education. Without substantial inequality, Davis and Moore concluded, the most talented people would have no incentive to become judges, physicians, and so on. |
| Weber's compromise | Weber argued that the emergence of a classless society is highly unlikely but under some circumstances people can act to lower the level of inequality in society. He also held that a person's class position is determined by his or her possession of goods, opportunities for income, level of education, and level of technical skill. Four main classes based on these factors exist in capitalist societies: large property owners, small property owners, propertyless but relatively highly educated and well-paid employees, and propertyless manual workers.<br><br>Weber also recognized that two types of groups other than classes—status groups and parties—have a bearing on the way a society is stratified. Status groups differ from one another in the prestige or social honour they enjoy and in their lifestyle. Parties are organizations that seek to impose their will on others through the exercise of power. Just as a person can be rich and have low prestige, so control over parties does not depend just on wealth. Weber argued that to draw an accurate picture of a society's stratification system, we must analyze classes, status groups, and parties as somewhat independent bases of social inequality. |

## LO 5 SOCIAL MOBILITY

Mordecai Richler's *The Apprenticeship of Duddy Kravitz* (1959) is one of the classics of modern Canadian literature. Made into a 1974 film starring Richard Dreyfuss as Duddy, it is the story of a poor 18-year-old Jewish Montrealer in the mid-1940s who is desperately seeking to establish himself in the world. To that end, he waits on tables, smuggles drugs, drives a taxi, produces wedding and bar mitzvah films, and rents out pinball machines. He is an obnoxious charmer with relentless drive, a young man so fixed on making it that he is even willing to sacrifice his girlfriend and his only friend and co-worker to achieve his goals. We cannot help but admire Duddy for his relentless ambition, even while we are shocked by his unprincipled guile.

Part of what makes *The Apprenticeship of Duddy Kravitz* universally appealing is that it could be a story about anyone. It is not just some immigrants and their children who may start out as pushy little people engaged in shady practices and unethical behaviour. As Richler reminds us repeatedly, many of the wealthiest establishment families in Canada and elsewhere started out in just this way. Duddy, then, is a universal symbol of "upward mobility"—and the compromises with ethical standards that people sometimes make to achieve it.

Much of our discussion to this point has focused on how we describe inequality and how we explain its persistence. Here I take up a different, although related, set of questions. To what extent are we trapped in a disadvantaged social position or assured of maintaining an advantaged position?

At birth, do all people have the same freedom to gain wealth and fame? Are the opportunities we enjoy—our "life chances" as Weber called them—equally accessible to everyone?

Sociologists use the term *social mobility* to refer to the dynamics of the system of inequality and, in particular, to movement up and down the stratification system over time. If we think about inequality as either a hierarchy of more or less privileged positions or a set of higher and lower social classes, an important question is how much opportunity people have to change positions. Typically, change has been measured by using one of two benchmarks: your first full-time job and the position of your parents in the hierarchy. Comparing your first job with your current job is an examination of occupational or **intragenerational mobility**. Comparing the occupations of parents with their children's current occupation is an examination of the inheritance of social position or **intergenerational mobility**.

Whichever benchmark is used, social mobility analysts are interested in the openness or fluidity of society. Open or fluid societies have greater equality of access to all positions in the hierarchy of inequality, both the low and the high. Regardless of your social origins, in more open societies you are more likely to rise or fall to a position that reflects your capabilities. In contrast, in closed or rigid societies, your social origins have major consequences for where you are located in the hierarchy of inequality. In such societies, poverty

> **intragenerational mobility**
> Social mobility that occurs within a single generation.
>
> **intergenerational mobility**
> Social mobility that occurs between generations.

**ascription-based stratification system** A system in which your family's station in life determines your own fortunes

**achievement-based stratification system** A system in which your own talents determine your lot in life

begets poverty, wealth begets wealth. In feudal Europe or in the Indian caste system, your birth determines your fate—you are a peasant or a lord, a Brahmin or a Dalit, based on the position of the family to which you are born.

In modern times, societies have become more open. The circumstances of your birth do not completely determine your fate. Think about the changes in Canadian society over the past century. A mainly agrarian, resource-based economy has transformed into a modern, advanced postindustrial nation. We have experienced substantial growth in well-paying occupations in finance, marketing, management, and the professions. To what extent have people from all walks of life, from all economic backgrounds, been able to benefit from this transformation?

In the 1950s and 1960s, proponents of the functional theory of stratification and human capital theory imagined that equality of opportunity would predominate.

Parents' socioeconomic status strongly influences children's educational attainment.

They argued that as more and more skilled jobs are created in the new economy, the best and the brightest must rise to the top to take those jobs and perform them diligently. We would then move from an **ascription-based stratification system** to an **achievement-based stratification system**. In a system of inequality based on ascription, your family's station in life determines your own fortunes. In a system based on achievement, your own talents determine your lot in life. If you achieve good grades in school, your chance of acquiring a professional or managerial job rises.

Other sociologists cautioned that this scenario of high individual social mobility might not follow from the transformation of the economy. They emphasized how advantaged families have long attempted to ensure that their offspring will inherit their advantages (Collins, 1979).

On the world stage, Blossfeld and Shavit (1993) demonstrated that in 11 of 13 advanced industrial countries, little evidence supports the view that greater equality of opportunity exists in societies with expanding education systems (Sweden and the Netherlands are the two exceptions). In most countries, the openness of the system of inequality did not increase over the last half of the twentieth century. Richard Wanner tested these ideas using Canadian data. He asked whether the growth of education—more high schools, colleges, and universities—benefited people from all social backgrounds equally (Wanner, 1999).

If in earlier decades the chances of children from poorer families going to university were small, then these chances should have increased in more recent decades if ascription were weakening. As measures of socioeconomic background, Wanner (1999) used mother's and father's education and father's occupation. He tested his central question by using detailed information from a sample of 31 500 Canadians. Wanner found that class-based ascription still operates strongly. Despite the fact that more Canadians are acquiring more years of schooling and more degrees than ever, the long arm of family socioeconomic background continues to exert a strong hold on educational attainment. The link between family advantage and children's educational achievement has not weakened (see Chapter 11, Education).

Explanations for how and why this occurs remain a matter of controversy (Davies, 1999). One explanation focuses on the way the school system has become increasingly differentiated. New high school programs have proliferated. These include storefront schools for at-risk students in poorer neighbourhoods, language-immersion streams, private schools, and enriched learning tracks. These different types of schools tend to enroll students from different socioeconomic backgrounds. Students from lower socioeconomic backgrounds tend to take various routes through high school vocational programs and college diploma programs. Students from higher socioeconomic backgrounds typically continue on to university. That is how it is possible for Canadians to acquire more years of schooling and more degrees while the link between family background and educational achievement persists.

Finally, note that young people are especially likely to experience limited upward mobility if they enter the job market during a recession, a period of declining economic activity (Harvey and Kalwa, 1983). During a recession, unemployment increases, making it harder to find a job. Young people who do find a job must often take work below the level for which they are trained. When the economic downturn ends and employment picks up, employers are inclined to hire not the young people who have been unemployed or underemployed for a few years, but a still more junior cohort of young people, who tend to be better trained and willing to work for lower wages. Thus, young people who enter the job market during a recession are likely to experience relatively low upward mobility over their entire careers. The Great Recession of 2008–09 created a cohort of job market entrants, many of them with university and college degrees, who now realize that they may never achieve the economic successes of their parents' generation (Smith, 2012).

## POLITICS AND THE PERCEPTION OF CLASS INEQUALITY

Unfortunately, we have to go back more than two decades to find a study of how Canadians perceive their stratification system (Pammett, 1997). The study is based on a survey of more than 22 000 respondents in 18 countries, including Canada. Among other questions, respondents were asked if large differences in income are necessary for national prosperity. Canadians were among the most likely to disagree with that view. They also tended to think that deep class divisions are not necessary for national prosperity.

So why then do Canadians think inequality continues to exist? One of the survey questions asked respondents how strongly they agree or disagree with the view that "inequality continues because it benefits the rich and powerful." Most Canadians agreed with that statement. Only about a quarter of them disagreed with it in any way. Another question asked respondents how strongly they agree or disagree with the view that "inequality continues because ordinary people don't join together to get rid of it." Again, most Canadians agreed, with less than a third disagreeing in any way.

Despite widespread awareness of inequality and considerable dissatisfaction with it, most Canadians are opposed to the government playing an active role in reducing inequality. Most do not want governments to provide citizens with a basic income. They tend to oppose government job-creation programs. They even resist the idea that governments should reduce income differences through taxation. Most Canadians remain individualistic and self-reliant. On the whole, they persist in the belief that opportunities for mobility are abundant and that it is up to the individual to make something of those opportunities by means of talent and effort.

Significantly, however, all of the attitudes summarized above vary by class position. For example, discontent with the level of inequality in Canadian society is stronger at the bottom of the stratification system than at the top. The belief that Canadian society is full of opportunities for upward mobility is stronger at the top of the class hierarchy than at the bottom. We find considerably less opposition to the idea that government should reduce inequality as we move down the stratification system. This permits us to conclude that, if Canadians allow inequality to persist, it is because the balance of attitudes—and of the power that supports those attitudes—favours continuity over change.

## LO6 GLOBAL INEQUALITY

### LEVELS AND TRENDS IN GLOBAL INEQUALITY

Despite the existence of considerable social stratification in Canada, we live in one of the 20 or so richest countries in the world—an elite club that also includes the United States, Japan, Australia, Germany, France, the United Kingdom, and a dozen or so other western European countries. In contrast, the world's poor countries cover much of Africa and parts of South America and Asia. Inequality between rich and poor countries is staggering. In Manhattan, pet owners can treat their cats to US$100-a-plate birthday parties. In Cairo (Egypt) and Manila (the Philippines), garbage dumps are home to entire families who sustain themselves by picking through the refuse.

The average income of citizens in the highly industrialized countries far outstrips that of citizens in the developing societies. According to the 2016 census, the median annual income of Canadian households was $70 336—18 times the world average. Half of Canadians are in the richest 4 percent of the world's population ("How Rich Am I?" 2018). About 800 million people in the world (more than 11 percent of the global population) are malnourished, while the citizens of the 20 or so rich, highly industrialized countries spend more on pet food than it would take to provide basic education or water and sanitation or basic health and nutrition for everyone in the world (World Hunger Education Service, 2015; Table 6.3).

Has global inequality increased or decreased over time? Since 1975, the annual income gap between the 20 or so richest countries and the rest of the world has grown enormously. The share of world income going to the top

> **modernization theory**
> Holds that global inequality results from various dysfunctional characteristics of poor societies: lack of investment capital, Western-style business techniques, stable Western-style governments, and a Western mentality.
>
> **dependency theory** Holds that global inequality is the result of patterns of domination and submission between rich and poor countries. From this point of view, rich countries have impoverished poor countries in order to enrich themselves.

10 percent of individuals increased, and the share of world income going to the bottom 20 percent of individuals fell. Since 1980, the world's richest 0.1 percent increased their wealth by the same amount as the poorest half of the world's population (Milanovic, 2018). True, the number of people in the world living on $1 a day or less peaked in 1950 and then started to decline gradually. Still, nearly half of the world's population lives on $2 a day or less (Milanovic, 2005; Figure 6.5).

Statistics never speak for themselves. We need theories to explain them. Let us now outline and critically assess the two main theories that seek to explain the origins and persistence of global inequality.

> A half-hour's drive from the centre of Manila, the capital of the Philippines, an estimated 70 000 Filipinos live off a 22-hectare mountain of rotting garbage 45 metres high. It is infested with flies, rats, dogs, and disease. On a lucky day, residents can earn up to $5 retrieving scraps of metal and other valuables. On a rainy day, the mountain of garbage is especially treacherous. In July 2000, an avalanche buried 300 people alive. People who live on the mountain of garbage call it "The Promised Land."

## LO7 MODERNIZATION THEORY: A FUNCTIONALIST APPROACH

Two main sociological theories claim to explain global inequality. The first, **modernization theory**, is a variant of functionalism. According to modernization theory, global inequality results from various dysfunctional characteristics of poor societies. Specifically, modernization theorists say the citizens of poor societies lack sufficient *capital* to invest in Western-style agriculture and industry. They lack rational Western-style *business techniques* of marketing, accounting, sales, and finance. As a result, their productivity and profitability remain low. They lack stable Western-style *governments* that could provide a secure framework for investment. Finally, they lack a Western *mentality*: values that stress the need for savings, investment, innovation, education, high achievement, and self-control in having children (Inkeles and Smith, 1976; Rostow, 1960).

It follows that people living in rich countries can best help their poor cousins by transferring Western culture and capital to them and eliminating the dysfunctions. Only then will the poor countries be able to cap population growth, stimulate democracy, and invigorate agricultural and industrial production. Government-to-government foreign aid can accomplish some of this. Much work also needs to be done to encourage Western businesses to invest directly in poor countries and to increase trade between rich and poor countries.

## DEPENDENCY THEORY: A CONFLICT APPROACH

Proponents of **dependency theory**, a variant of conflict theory, have been quick to point out the chief flaw in modernization theory (Baran, 1957; Cardoso and Faletto, 1979; Wallerstein, 1974–89). For more than 500 years, the most powerful countries in the world have deliberately impoverished the less powerful countries. Focusing on internal characteristics blames the victim rather than the perpetrator of the crime. It follows that an adequate theory of global inequality should not focus on the internal characteristics of poor countries. Instead, it should follow the principles of conflict theory and focus on patterns of domination and submission—specifically, in this case, on the relationship between rich and poor countries. That is just what dependency theory does.

According to dependency theorists, less global inequality existed in 1500 and even in 1750 than today. However, beginning around 1500, the armed forces of the world's most powerful countries subdued and then annexed or colonized most of the rest of the world. The Industrial Revolution began around 1780. It enabled the western European countries, Russia, Japan, and the United States to

## TABLE 6.3 Global Priorities (in US$ billions)

| | |
|---|---|
| Additional annual cost, basic education for everyone in the world[1] | $6.3 |
| Additional annual cost, water and sanitation for everyone in the world[1] | 12.4 |
| Annual dog and cat food sales, United States[2] | 18.6 |
| Additional, annual cost, reproductive health care for all women in the world[1] | 18.6 |
| Additional annual cost, basic health and nutrition for everyone in the world[1] | 20.1 |
| Annual global perfume sales[3] | 27.5 |
| Annual TV advertising, United States[3] | 60.0 |
| Annual global revenue, strip clubs[3] | 75.0 |
| Annual global revenue, cocaine sales[4] | 88.0 |
| Annual beer sales, United States[3] | 96.0 |
| Annual global arms sales[5] | $1700.0 |

[1] U.S. Bureau of Labor Statistics. "CPI Inflation Calculator." http://data.bls.gov/cgi-bin/cpicalc.pl?cost1=1&year1=1998&year2=2011 (retrieved 28 December 2012); Negative Population Growth. "Total Midyear World Population, 1950–2050." http://www.npg.org/facts/world_pop_year.htm (retrieved 28 December 2012); United Nations. *World Development Report 1998* (New York: Oxford University Press): 37. United Nations data for 1998 are adjusted for world population increase, 1998–2011, and the U.S. consumer price index, 1998–2011.

[2] Pet Food Institute. 2012. "U.S. Pet Food Sales." http://www.petfoodinstitute.org/Index.cfm?Page=USPetFoodSales (retrieved 28 December 2012).

[3] Statistic Brain. 2012. http://www.statisticbrain.com/ (retrieved 28 December 2012).

[4] United Nations. 2012. "The global cocaine market." http://www.unodc.org/documents/wdr/WDR_2010/1.3_The_globa_cocaine_market.pdf (retrieved 28 December 2012).

[5] Global Issues. "World Military Expenditures." 2012. http://www.globalissues.org/article/75/world-military-spending#WorldMilitarySpending (retrieved 28 December 2012).

## FIGURE 6.5 World Poverty

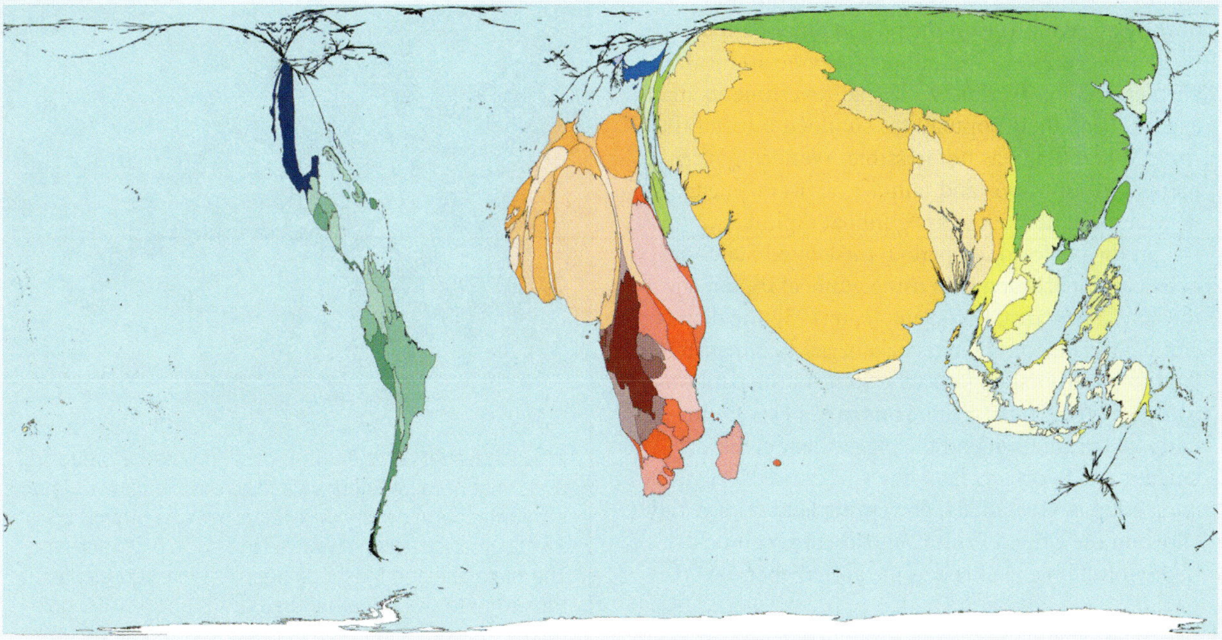

Note: The size of each country is proportional to the percentage of people in that country living on US$2 a day or less in purchasing power.
Source: University of Sheffield. 2006. "Absolute Poverty." http://www.worldmapper.org/posters/worldmapper_map180_ver5.pdf (retrieved 11 March 2010). ©Copyright 2006 SASI Group (University of Sheffield) and Mark Newman (University of Michigan).

**core countries** Capitalist countries that are the world's major sources of capital and technology (the United States, Japan, and Germany)

**peripheral countries** The world's major sources of raw materials and cheap labour (the former colonies)

**semiperipheral countries** Former colonies that are making considerable headway in their attempt to become prosperous

amass enormous wealth that they used to extend their global reach. They forced their colonies to become a source of raw materials, cheap labour, investment opportunities, and markets for the conquering nations. The colonizers thereby prevented industrialization and locked the colonies into poverty.

In the decades following World War II, nearly all of the colonies in the world became politically independent. However, dependency theorists say that exploitation by direct political control was soon replaced by new means of achieving the same end: substantial foreign investment, support for authoritarian governments, and mounting debt.

1. *Substantial foreign investment.* Multinational corporations invested in the poor countries to siphon off wealth in the form of raw materials and profits. True, they created some low-paying jobs in the process, but they created many more high-paying jobs in the rich countries where the raw materials were used to produce manufactured goods. They also sold part of the manufactured goods back to the poor unindustrialized countries for additional profit.

2. *Support for authoritarian governments.* According to dependency theorists, multinational corporations and rich countries continued their exploitation of the poor countries in the postcolonial period by giving economic and military support to local authoritarian governments. These governments managed to keep their populations subdued most of the time. When that was not possible, Western governments sent in troops and military advisers, engaging in what became known as "gunboat diplomacy."

In the postcolonial period, the United States has been particularly active in using gunboat diplomacy in Central America. For example, in 1952 the democratic government of Guatemala began to redistribute land to impoverished peasants. Some of the land was owned by the United Fruit Company, a U.S. multinational corporation and the biggest landowner in Guatemala. Two years later, the CIA backed a right-wing coup in Guatemala, preventing land reform and allowing the United Fruit Company to continue its highly profitable business as usual (LaFeber, 1993).

3. *Mounting debt.* The governments of the poor countries struggled to create transportation infrastructures (airports, roads, harbours, and so on), build their education systems, and deliver safe water and at least the most basic health care to their people. To accomplish these tasks, they had to borrow money from Western banks and governments. Some rulers also squandered money on luxuries. As a result, debt—and the interest payments that inevitably accompany debt—grew every year. Crushing interest payments leave governments of poor countries with too little money for development tasks. Foreign aid helps, but not much. Foreign aid to the world's developing countries is only one-seventh the amount that the developing countries pay to Western banks in loan interest (United Nations, 2004: 201).

# CORE, PERIPHERY, AND SEMIPERIPHERY

Although dependency theory provides a more realistic account of the sources of global inequality than modernization theory does, it leaves a big question unanswered: How have some countries managed to escape poverty and start rapid economic development? After all, the world does not consist of just **core countries** that are major sources of capital and technology (the United States, Japan, and Germany) and **peripheral countries** that are major sources of raw materials and cheap labour (the former colonies). In addition, a middle tier of **semiperipheral countries**

In 1893, leaders of the British mission pose before taking over what became Rhodesia and is now Zimbabwe. To raise a volunteer army, every British trooper was offered about 23 square kilometres of native land and 20 gold claims. The Matabele and Mashona peoples were subdued in a three-month war. Nine hundred farms and 10 000 gold claims were granted to the troopers and about 100 000 cattle were stolen, leaving the native survivors without a livelihood. Forced labour was subsequently introduced by the British so that the natives could pay a £2 a year tax.

consists of former colonies that are making considerable headway in their attempts to become prosperous (South Korea, Taiwan, and Israel, for example; Wallerstein, 1974–89). Comparing poor peripheral countries with the more successful semiperipheral countries allows us to identify the circumstances that have helped some poor countries overcome the worst effects of colonialism. The semiperipheral countries differ from the peripheral countries in four main ways, which I outline next (Kennedy, 1993: 193–227; Lie, 1998).

## Type of Colonialism

Around the turn of the twentieth century, Taiwan and Korea became colonies of Japan. They remained so until 1945. However, in contrast to the European colonizers of Africa, Latin America, and other parts of Asia, the Japanese built up the economies of their colonies. They established transportation networks and communication systems. They built steel, chemical, and hydro-electric power plants. After Japanese colonialism ended, Taiwan and South Korea were thus at an advantage compared with the former colonies of, say, Britain and France. South Korea and Taiwan could use the Japanese-built infrastructure and Japanese-trained personnel as springboards to development.

## Geopolitical Position

Although the United States was the leading economic and military power in the world by the end of World War II, it began to feel its supremacy threatened in the late 1940s by the Soviet Union and China. Fearing that South Korea and Taiwan might fall to the communists, the United States poured unprecedented aid into both countries in the 1960s. It also gave the countries large, low-interest loans and opened its domestic market to Taiwanese and South Korean products. Because the United States saw Israel as a crucially important ally in the Middle East, Israel also received special economic and military assistance. Other countries with less strategic importance to the United States received less help in their drive to industrialize.

## State Policy

A third factor that accounts for the relative success of some countries in their efforts to industrialize and become prosperous concerns state policies. As a legacy of colonialism, the Taiwanese and South Korean states were developed on the Japanese model. They kept workers' wages low, restricted trade union growth, and maintained quasi-military discipline in factories. Moreover, by placing high taxes on consumer goods, limiting the import of foreign goods, and preventing their citizens from investing abroad, they encouraged their citizens to put much of their money in the bank. This situation created a large pool of capital for industrial expansion. The South Korean and Taiwanese states also gave subsidies, training grants, and tariff protection to export-based industries from the 1960s onward. (Tariffs are taxes on foreign goods.) These policies did much to stimulate industrial growth. Finally, the Taiwanese and South Korean states invested heavily in basic education, health care, roads, and other public goods. A healthy and well-educated labour force, combined with good transportation and communication systems, laid solid foundations for economic growth.

## Social Structure

Taiwan and South Korea are socially cohesive countries, which makes it easy for them to generate consensus around development policies. It also allows them to get their citizens to work hard, save a lot of money, and devote their energies to scientific education.

Social solidarity in Taiwan and South Korea is based partly on the sweeping land reform they conducted in the late 1940s and early 1950s. By redistributing land to small farmers, both countries eliminated the class of large landowners, who opposed industrialization. Land redistribution got rid of a major potential source of social conflict. In contrast, many countries in Latin America and Africa have not undergone land reform. The United States often intervened militarily in Latin America to prevent land reform because U.S. companies profited handsomely from the large plantations they owned (LaFeber, 1993).

Another factor underlying social solidarity in Taiwan and South Korea is that neither country suffered from internal conflicts like those that wrack Africa south of the Sahara desert. British, French, and other western European colonizers often drew the borders of African countries to keep antagonistic tribes in the same jurisdiction and often sought to stir up tribal conflict. Keeping tribal tensions alive made it possible to play one tribe against another, which made it easier for imperial powers to dominate. This policy led to much social and political conflict in postcolonial Africa. Today, the region suffers from frequent civil wars, coups, and uprisings. It is the most conflict-ridden area of the world. The high level of internal conflict acts as a barrier to economic development.

In sum, postcolonial countries that enjoy a solid industrial infrastructure, strategic geopolitical importance, strong states with strong development policies, and socially cohesive populations are in the best position to join the ranks of the rich countries in the coming decades. Countries that have some of these characteristics are likely to experience economic growth and an increase in the well-being of their populations. Such countries include China, India, Chile, Thailand, Indonesia, Mexico, Turkey, Russia, and Brazil. We conclude that, as is the case for social stratification within highly developed countries like Canada, the existing level of global inequality is not inevitable and can under some circumstances change for the better. I take up this theme again in the book's final chapter, Chapter 14, Social Change: Technology, the Environment, and Social Movements.

Courtesy of Teresa Peterson

# 7
# Race and Ethnicity

## LEARNING OBJECTIVES:

In this chapter, you will learn to

**LO¹** Recognize that race and ethnicity are socially constructed variables rather than biological or cultural constants.

**LO²** Analyze why racial and ethnic labels and identities change over time and place.

**LO³** Appreciate that conquest and domination are among the most important forces leading to the crystallization of distinct ethnic and racial identities.

**LO⁴** Describe the ways in which identifying with a racial or ethnic group can be economically, politically, and emotionally advantageous.

**LO⁵** Understand that Canada is among the world's most tolerant countries and home to persistent racial inequality.

# LO¹ DEFINING RACE AND INTELLIGENCE

## WHAT IS RACE?

### Race and Intelligence

In the 1920s, Peter Sandiford, a professor in the Department of Education at the University of Toronto, administered some IQ tests and concluded that Canada must adopt a policy of selective immigration to ensure that "misfits" and "defectives" are kept out of the country. He encouraged the immigration of Britons, Germans, and Danes, and discouraged the immigration of Poles, Italians, Greeks, and Asians. The latter groups scored low on his IQ tests, and he believed that their apparent intellectual inferiority was rooted in their biological makeup (McLaren, 1990). Around the same time in the United States, Jewish immigrants were scoring lower than non-Jews on IQ tests. Influential people used these results as an argument against Jewish immigration. In modern times, black immigrants have, on average, scored below European Americans on IQ tests. Some people say this justifies slashing budgets for schools where many black people live. Why invest good money in schooling, such people ask, if low IQ scores are rooted in biology and therefore fixed?

People who argue against the immigration of certain groups and better education for black people ignore two facts. First, IQ scores are remarkably flexible. Sandiford's low-IQ Asians are among the stars of the Canadian system of higher education today. As Jews experienced upward mobility and could afford better education, their IQ scores rose to above-average levels. Enriched educational facilities routinely boost the IQ scores and achievements of poor black children (Campbell and Ramey, 1994; Gould, 1996). We are obliged to conclude that the social setting in which a person is raised and educated has a big impact on IQ. The average IQ of members of racial and ethnic groups has nothing to do with biology (Nisbett, 2011).

### Race and Sports

Nonetheless, the view persists that races differ biologically (see the boxed feature Sociology and the Media, Racist TV Ads). For instance, we commonly hear that, for biological reasons, black people are better at sports than white people are. Is there any evidence to support that belief? At first glance, the evidence might seem strong. Roughly two-thirds of NFL and NBA players are black. Black men of West African descent hold the 200 fastest 100-metre-dash times, all under 10 seconds. North and East Africans regularly win 40 percent of the top international distance-running honours yet represent only a fraction of 1 percent of the world's population (Entine, 2000; Lapchick, 2017),

## SOCIOLOGY AND THE MEDIA

### Racist TV Ads

You've probably seen TV ads for genetic testing companies like 23 and Me and Ancestry (if not, you might want to visit www.iSpot.tv to search for the ads by company name). One ad begins with a woman who used to think she was Hispanic but now marks "other" on a form asking about race or ethnicity because DNA testing revealed she's "really" 33 percent Indigenous and just 31 percent Iberian (Spanish or Portuguese).

Such ads share with many racist ideologies the view that our essential racial or ethnic makeup is inscribed in our biology, not our social conditions. DNA testing companies may deny that each group's supposedly inborn characteristics and abilities can be arranged in a hierarchy of superiority and inferiority. However, the very idea that each racial or ethnic group is distinct by nature is itself racist. It's also based on bad science.

Let's deal with the bad science part first. To identify the unique genetic characteristics of racial and ethnic groups, companies first create "reference samples" of group members to which they can later compare individuals who pay to be tested. So, for example, they might send agents to northern Nigeria to find some people who claim to be Hausa and pay them for saliva samples. DNA testing reveals that members of the sample have a certain proportion of various genetic characteristics. Those proportions became the standard by which the company later judges the likelihood that paying customers are of Hausa origin.

Members of the sample are selected as a matter of convenience, not in such a way as to be representative of all Hausa. Nor are they "pure" Hausa. Africa boasts the greatest human genetic diversity of any continent. It has witnessed much internal migration and intermarriage over tens of thousands of years. There are about 400 officially recognized ethnic groups in Nigeria alone, and no ethnic group is confined to a single geographical area. It is therefore likely that some of the ancestors of the Hausa reference sample had children with, say, Yorubas or Igbos—or with Portuguese, English or Dutch traders, who started arriving in the fifteenth century.

Some members of the reference sample who are in fact Yorubas or Igbos might have said they are Hausa just to earn a fee for their saliva. Thus, when a paying customer is told that she is 51 percent Hausa, all it means is that there is a certain similarity between her and the non-representative, racially and ethnically heterogeneous sample the company assembled. It does not mean that she is predominantly Hausa. It is in fact highly unlikely that a homogeneous, representative sample of Hausa could ever be created. The problem is magnified when companies create reference samples of such hugely genetically diverse categories as "West African."

The racist character of such DNA testing resides in the fact that it reinforces the assumption that ethnic and racial groups are distinct by nature, that we are really what our DNA says we are racially and ethnically. To illustrate the danger of such thinking, consider how this assumption plays out in modern medicine. Researchers have discovered that black residents of North America are more prone than white residents are to certain types of cancer. Much of the medical community considers this finding important because it can lead to the production of medicines designed to maximize benefits for black patients. What the medical profession commonly ignores is that black people are much more likely than white people are to work in and live near industries and toxic waste dumps that emit pollutants that cause genetic mutations leading to cancer (Brym, 2018d). The workers in one factory producing a carcinogenic herbicide were found to have a prostate cancer rate 8.4 times above normal. Eighty percent of the workers were black. Was it the workers' genetic mutations that were fundamentally responsible for

On its website, 23 and Me shows the genetic profile of one Jamie King, colour coded by the racial and ethnic markers in each of his chromosomes (23 and Me, 2018). It shows that Jamie is 41.0 percent southern European, 34.4 percent Native American, and 0.3 percent northwestern European. If Jamie was brought up to think he is of Scottish origin, should he now give up the Highland Fling for flamenco? If he fancies a wee dram, should we attribute that to his upbringing or the discredited theory that Indigenous peoples are genetically susceptible to alcoholism (Ehlers, 2007; Szalavitz, 2015)?

Sources: 23 and Me. 2018. "See sample report." https://www.23andme.com/en-ca/dna-reports-list (retrieved 1 February 2018); Cindy L. Ehlers. 2007. "Variations in ADH and ALDH in Southwest California Indians." *Alcohol Research Current Reviews* 30(1): 14–17; Maia Szalavitz. 2015. "No, Native Americans aren't genetically more susceptible to alcoholism." *The Verge* 2 October. https://www.theverge.com/2015/10/2/9428659/firewater-racist-myth-alcoholism-native-americans (retrieved 3 February 2018).

the cancer or the working and living conditions of the disproportionate number of black people? Any industry that feeds into the idea that differences between racial and ethnic groups are genetic rather than social is racist insofar as it obscures the roots of racial and ethnic inequality under the cover of "science" (Duster, 2015: 6).

### Critical Thinking Question

- Draw diagrams for the cause-and-effect arguments in this boxed feature and in the Chapter 3 boxed feature, Theories in Dispute: Sociology, Biology, and the Interaction between Genes and Environment. Are the arguments compatible or contradictory?

Although these facts are undeniable, the argument for the genetic basis of black athletic superiority begins to falter once we consider two additional points. First, nobody has ever identified genes linked to general athletic superiority. Second, black athletes do not perform unusually well in many sports, such as swimming, hockey, cycling, tennis, gymnastics, soccer, and equestrian events. The idea that black people are in general superior athletes is simply untrue.

Sociologists have identified certain social conditions that lead to high levels of participation in sports. These operate on all groups of people, whatever their race. Specifically, people who face widespread prejudice and discrimination often enter professional sports in disproportionately large numbers for lack of other ways to improve their social and economic standing. For such people, other avenues of upward mobility tend to be blocked. (**Prejudice** is an attitude that judges a person on his or her group's real or

**prejudice** An attitude that judges a person on his or her group's real or imagined characteristics.

**discrimination** Unfair treatment of people because of their group membership.

imagined characteristics. **Discrimination** is unfair treatment of people because of their group membership.) For example, it was not until the 1950s that prejudice and discrimination against North American Jews began to decline appreciably. Until then, Jews played a prominent role in some professional sports, such as boxing, baseball, and basketball. When the New York Knicks played their first game on November 1, 1946, beating the Toronto Huskies 68–66, the starting lineup for New York consisted of Ossie Schechtman, Stan Stutz, Jake Weber, Ralph Kaplowitz, and Leo "Ace" Gottlieb—an all-Jewish squad ("Do You Know...?" n.d.). Similarly, Koreans in Japan today are subject to considerable prejudice and discrimination. They often pursue careers in professional sports. In contrast, Koreans in Canada face less prejudice and discrimination. Few become professional athletes.

The idea that black people are genetically superior to white people in athletic ability is the complement of the idea that they are genetically inferior to white people in intellectual ability. Both ideas have the effect of reinforcing black–white inequality. For although there are just a few thousand professional athletes in North America, there are millions of pharmacists, graphics designers, lawyers, systems analysts, police officers, nurses, and people in other interesting occupations that offer steady employment and good pay. By promoting outstanding athletes such as Andrew Wiggins as role models for youth, the idea of "natural" black athletic superiority and intellectual inferiority in effect asks black youth to bet on a high-risk proposition—that they will make it in professional sports. At the same time, it deflects attention from a much safer bet—that they can achieve upward mobility through academic excellence.

## Racial Mixing

Another problem undermines the argument that genes determine the behaviour of racial groups: it is impossible to neatly distinguish races based on genetic differences. A high level of genetic mixing has taken place. In Canada in the eighteenth and nineteenth centuries, French settlers and Indigenous peoples merged to form the Métis. In the United States in the same period, it was

Who is the safer role model—Andrew Wiggins, Canadian star forward of the Minnesota Timberwolves, or Dr. Anderson Ruffin Abbott, who became the first Canadian-born black doctor in 1861 and rose to the position of surgeon-in-chief at the Toronto General Hospital?

common for white male slave owners to rape black female slaves, who then gave birth to children of mixed race. We know from the census that racial intermarriage has been increasing in Canada since at least 1871 (for recent data, please refer back to Chapter 4, Figure 4.6, Mixed Unions among Second-Generation Canadians). The differences among black, white, Asian, and so forth are often anything but clear-cut.

Most experts on the subject believe we all belong to one human race, which originated in Africa (Cavalli-Sforza, Menozzi, and Piazza, 1994). They argue that subsequent migration, geographical separation, and inbreeding led to the formation of more or less distinct races. However, particularly in modern times, humanity has experienced so much intermixing that race as a biological category has lost nearly all meaning. Should we therefore drop the term *race* from the vocabulary of science?

## A Sociological Definition of Race

Sociologists say "no." We do so because *perceptions* of race continue to affect the lives of most people profoundly. Everything from your wealth to your health is influenced by whether others see you as black, white, brown, or something else. Race as a sociological concept is thus a valuable analytical tool as long as people who use the term remember that it refers to socially significant physical differences such as skin colour rather than to biological differences that shape behaviour patterns. Said differently, perceptions of racial difference are socially constructed and often arbitrary. How arbitrary? The Irish and the Jews were once regarded as black by some people, and today many northern Italians still think of southern Italians from Sicily and Calabria as black (Gilman, 1991; Ignatiev, 1995; Roediger, 1991).

Finally, then, we can define **race** as a social construct used to distinguish people in terms of one or more physical markers. However, this definition raises an interesting question. If race is merely a social construct and not a useful biological term, why do we commonly use perceptions of physical difference to distinguish groups of people in the first place? Why, in other words, does race matter?

Most sociologists believe that race matters because it allows social inequality to be created and perpetuated. The English who colonized Ireland, the Americans who went to Africa looking for slaves, and the Germans who used the Jews as a scapegoat to explain their deep economic and political troubles after World War I, all created systems of racial domination. (A **scapegoat** is a disadvantaged person or category of people that others blame for their own problems.)

Once colonialism, slavery, and concentration camps were established, behavioural differences developed between subordinates and their masters. For example, North American slaves and Jewish concentration camp inmates, with little motivating them to work hard except the ultimate threat of the master's whip, tended to do only the minimum work necessary to survive. Their masters noticed this and characterized their subordinates as inherently slow and unreliable workers (Collins, 1982: 66–69). In this way, racial stereotypes are born. The stereotypes then embed themselves in popular lore, journalism, literature, and political debate, reinforcing racial inequalities (see Figure 7.1). So we can see that race matters to the degree that it helps create and maintain systems of social inequality.

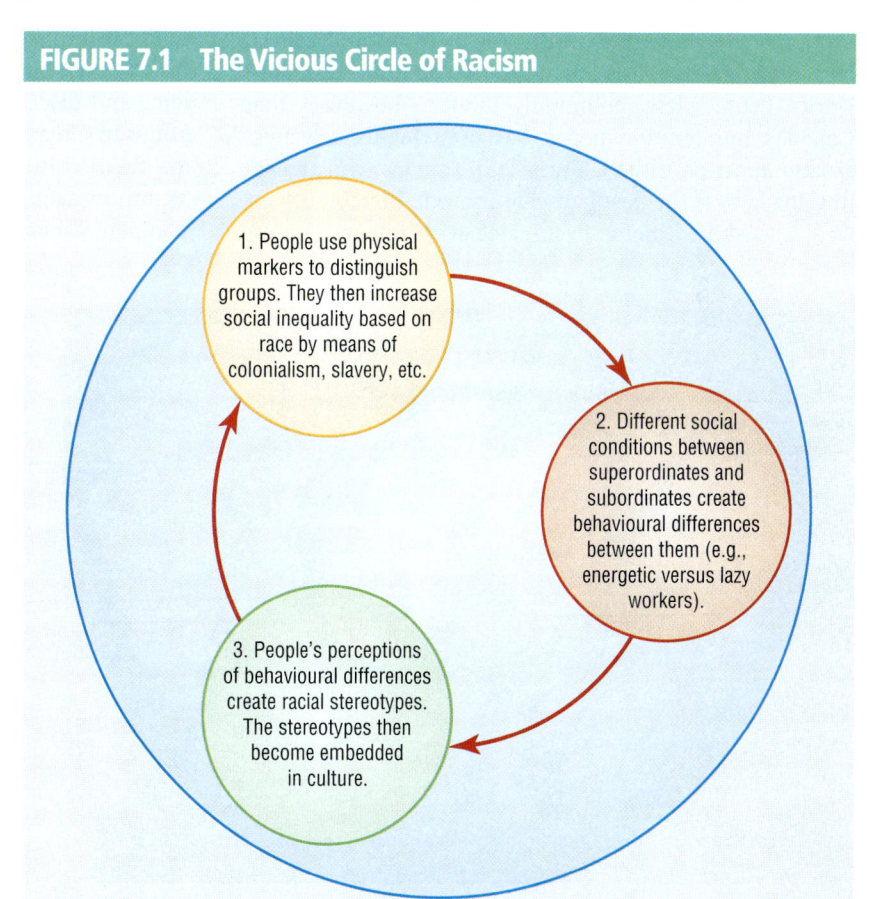

**race** A social construct used to distinguish people in terms of one or more physical markers, usually with profound effects on their lives.

**scapegoat** A disadvantaged person or category of people whom others blame for their own problems.

### FIGURE 7.1 The Vicious Circle of Racism

1. People use physical markers to distinguish groups. They then increase social inequality based on race by means of colonialism, slavery, etc.

2. Different social conditions between superordinates and subordinates create behavioural differences between them (e.g., energetic versus lazy workers).

3. People's perceptions of behavioural differences create racial stereotypes. The stereotypes then become embedded in culture.

Source: From BRYM/ROBERTS/STROHSCHEIN/LIE. *Sociology: Your Compass for a New World*, 6E. © 2019 Nelson Education Ltd. Reproduced by permission. www.cengage.com/permissions.

# ETHNICITY, CULTURE, AND SOCIAL STRUCTURE

**ethnic group** Comprises people whose perceived cultural markers are deemed socially significant. Ethnic groups differ from one another in terms of language, religion, customs, values, ancestors, and the like.

Race is to biology as ethnicity is to culture. A *race* is a socially defined category of people whose perceived *physical* markers are socially significant. An **ethnic group** comprises people whose perceived *cultural* markers are socially significant. Ethnic groups differ from one another in terms of language, religion, customs, values, ancestors, and the like. However, just as physical distinctions do not *cause* differences in the behaviour of various races, so cultural distinctions are often not by themselves the major source of differences in the behaviour of various ethnic groups. In other words, ethnic values and other elements of ethnic culture have less of an effect on the way people behave than we commonly believe. That is because *social-structural* differences frequently underlie cultural differences.

An example will help drive home the point. People often praise Chinese and Korean Canadians and other economically successful groups for their cultural values, including an emphasis on education, family, and hard work. People less commonly notice, however, that Canada's immigration policy has been highly selective. For the most part, the Chinese and Koreans who arrived in Canada over the past half-century were literate, urbanized, and skilled. Some even came with financial assets (Li, 1995; Wong and Ng, 1998). They certainly confronted prejudice and discrimination, but far less than that reserved for the descendants of slaves or members of Canada's Indigenous peoples.

These social-structural conditions facilitated Chinese and Korean success. They gave members of these groups a firm basis on which to build and maintain a culture emphasizing education, family, and other middle-class virtues. In contrast, descendants of slaves and members of Canada's Indigenous peoples were typically illiterate and unskilled a century ago and they experienced more prejudice and discrimination than did other ethnic or racial groups in Canada. These social-structural disadvantages—not their culture—made them less economically successful on average than Koreans and Chinese have been (compare Table 7.1).

**TABLE 7.1 Percentage Low-Income by Selected Groups and Immigration Status, Canada**

|  | White | Black | Chinese | Arab |
|---|---|---|---|---|
| Immigrants | 13.6 | 28.5 | 25.1 | 36.7 |
| Non-immigrants | 11.7 | 30.8 | 17.9 | 34.7 |

Notes: This table shows the percentage of people over the age of 15 below the low-income cutoff in each group. For an explanation of how low income is measured, see Chapter 6. The percentages are probably low because of problems with the data source (Brym, 2014) but no evidence suggests that underestimates are higher in one group than in another.

Source: Statistics Canada. 2015h. *National Household Survey* (NHS) PUMF, 2011: individuals file. https://www150.statcan.gc.ca/n1/en/catalogue/99M0001X2011001 (retrieved 2 August 2015).

## RESOURCES AND OPPORTUNITIES

What matters most in determining the economic success of an ethnic or racial group are the *resources* that people possess (notably literacy, education, urbanity, and financial assets) and the *economic opportunities* open to them. To appreciate the latter point, compare Canada in the mid-twentieth century with Canada today.

In the 1950s, Canada was a society sharply stratified along ethnic and racial lines. The people with the most power and privilege were of British origin. WASPs (white Anglo-Saxon Protestants) controlled almost all of the big corporations in the country and dominated politics. Immigrants who arrived later enjoyed less power and privilege. Even among them, big economic differences were evident,

Literate, urbanized, skilled immigrants with financial assets tend to be more upwardly mobile than other immigrants are.

with European immigrants enjoying higher status than immigrants of Asian ancestry, for example.

John Porter, one of the founders of modern Canadian sociology, called mid-twentieth-century Canada a **vertical mosaic**, a highly ethnically and racially stratified society. He thought that the retention of ethnic and racial culture was a big problem in Canada because it hampered the upward mobility of immigrants. In his view, the Canadian value system encouraged the retention of ethnic culture, making Canada a low-mobility society (Porter, 1965, 1979: 91).

By the 1970s, however, many Canadian sociologists, including Porter himself, had to reject or at least qualify the view that ethnic and racial culture determines economic success or failure. Events upset their earlier assumptions. The Canadian economy grew quickly in the decades after World War II. Many members of ethnic and racial-minority groups were economically successful despite ethnic and racial prejudice and discrimination. Economic differences among ethnic groups and among most racial groups diminished. Among the wealthiest Canadians and among politicians at all levels of government, ethnic and racial diversity increased. Such diversity became even more evident among professional groups.

The term **visible minority** is a government designation unique to Canada. It refers to non-Indigenous people who are "non-Caucasian in race or non-white in colour," including South Asian, Chinese, black, Filipino, Latin American, Arab, southeast Asian, West Asian, Korean, and Japanese Canadians (Statistics Canada, 2016e). For the most part, visible-minority status has little bearing on educational, occupational, and income attainment in Canada, especially among the Canadian-born (Boyd, 2017; Lautard and Guppy, 2014). There are exceptions. For example, black men born in Canada continue to face discrimination that significantly impedes their upward mobility, as do Indigenous Canadians. However, for the great majority of Canadians in the decades after World War II, ethnic and racial culture mattered less than the structure of mobility opportunities in determining a person's economic success.

From the 1990s to the 2010s, recent immigrants who were members of some visible-minority groups were significantly less successful economically than we would expect given their educational and other resources (refer back to Table 7.1). However, their cultural values had little to do with that. Canada experienced an unusually high rate of unemployment in the 1990s, hovering around 10 percent until late in the decade. That situation made it more difficult than in previous decades for recently arrived visible-minority immigrants to succeed economically. In addition, although many minority immigrants are selected to come to Canada because they are highly educated, their credentials are often not recognized by employers here. The mechanisms for receiving accreditation for foreign credentials are poorly developed in this country and need to be improved (Reitz, 2011).

Finally, labour force and housing discrimination are ongoing problems for visible-minority Canadians. Numerous studies conducted in Toronto, Montreal, and Vancouver document that job and housing applications are less likely to result in interviews if the applicant has a name that does not sound like that of a white person or if the applicant speaks on the phone with a non-Canadian accent (Hogan and Berry, 2011; Oreopoulos and Dechief, 2011). The relative lack of success of recent visible-minority immigrants thus reinforces our point. In addition to the resources a person possesses, it is the structure of opportunities for economic advancement that determines income and occupational and educational attainment. Ethnic or racial culture by itself plays at most a minor role (Boyd, 2017).

> **vertical mosaic** A highly ethnically and racially stratified society.
>
> **visible minority** A government designation unique to Canada; refers to non-Indigenous people who are "non-Caucasian in race or non-white in colour," including South Asian, Chinese, black, Filipino, Latin American, Arab, southeast Asian, West Asian, Korean, and Japanese Canadians

In sum, we see that racial and ethnic inequality are more deeply rooted in social structure than in biology and culture. The biological and cultural aspects of race and ethnicity are secondary to their sociological character when it comes to explaining inequality. The interesting question from a sociological point of view is why social definitions of race and ethnicity change. We now consider that issue.

# LO2 SYMBOLIC INTERACTIONISM AND THE SOCIAL CONSTRUCTION OF RACIAL AND ETHNIC IDENTITY

## LABELS AND IDENTITY

To varying degrees, racial and ethnic identities are fluid. Social contexts, and in particular the nature of a person's relations with members of other racial and ethnic groups, shape and continuously reshape a person's racial and ethnic identity and the manner in which he or she expresses it. Enduring change often occurs when one attends school in a new country or marries someone from a different racial group. Fleeting change can take place over the

**First Nations** Consist of status Indians and non-status Indians.

**Status Indians** Indigenous people who live throughout Canada and are registered as Indians under the Indian Act, most of whom belong to a band that signed a treaty with the Crown.

**Non-status Indians** Indigenous people who live throughout Canada and were once Status Indians but lost that status.

**Métis** Canadians of Indigenous and European (usually French) origin who reside mainly in the western provinces and Ontario.

**Inuit** Indigenous Canadians who reside in the country's northern regions.

course of a day as a person moves from homogeneous to heterogeneous racial and ethnic settings and back again. Change your social context and your racial and ethnic self-conception and expression eventually change too.

Consider Italian Canadians. Around 1900, Italian immigrants thought of themselves as people who came from a particular town or perhaps a particular province, such as Sicily or Calabria. They did not usually think of themselves as Italians. Italy became a unified country only in 1861. A few decades years later, many Italian citizens still did not identify with their new Italian nationality. In both Canada and the United States, however, government officials and other residents identified the newcomers as Italians. The designation at first seemed odd to many of the new immigrants. However, over time it stuck. Immigrants from Italy started thinking of themselves as Italian Canadians because others defined them that way. A new ethnic identity was born (Yancey, Ericksen, and Leon, 1979).

As symbolic interactionists emphasize, the development of racial and ethnic labels and ethnic and racial identities is typically a process of negotiation. For example, members of a group may have a racial or an ethnic identity, but outsiders may impose a new label on them. Group members may then reject, accept, or modify the label. The negotiation between outsiders and insiders eventually results in the crystallization of a new, more or less stable ethnic identity. If the social context changes again, the negotiation process begins anew.

One such case involves the labelling of the Indigenous peoples by European settlers. When Christopher Columbus landed in North America in 1492, he assumed he had reached India. He called the Indigenous peoples "Indians" and the misnomer stuck—not only among European settlers but to some degree also among many Indigenous peoples themselves. Indigenous peoples still identified themselves in tribal terms—as Mi'kmaq or Mohawk or Haida—but they typically thought of themselves collectively and *in opposition to European settlers* as Indians. A new identity was thus grafted onto tribal identities because Indigenous peoples confronted a group that had the power to impose a name on them.

Since the 1960s, Indigenous North Americans have begun to vigorously assert themselves culturally and politically, asserting pride in their languages, art, and customs and making legal claims to the lands that were taken from them.

In time, however, an increasingly large number of Indigenous people began to reject the term "Indian." White settlers and their governments took land from the Indigenous peoples, forced them onto reserves, and thus caused their resentment, anger, and solidarity to grow. Especially since the 1960s, Indigenous North Americans have begun to fight back culturally and politically, asserting pride in their languages, art, and customs and making legal claims to the lands that were taken from them.

One aspect of their resistance involved questioning use of the term *Indian* (and *Eskimo*). Today, many Indigenous Canadians prefer to use their tribal names as a re-assertion of pride in their heritage. Many non-Indigenous North Americans accept these names out of respect for Indigenous North Americans and in recognition of their neglected rights.

The government distinguishes three main groups of Indigenous Canadians for administrative purposes: First Nations, Métis, and Inuit. **First Nations** consist of **Status Indians** (Indigenous people who live throughout Canada and are registered as Indians under the Indian Act, most of whom belong to a band that signed a treaty with the Crown; and **non-status Indians** (people who were once Status Indians but lost that status). **Métis** are Canadians of Indigenous and European (usually French) origin who reside mainly in the western provinces and Ontario. **Inuit** are Indigenous Canadians who reside in the country's northern regions (Figure 7.2).

In short, new and more or less stable ethnic identities have been negotiated as the power struggle between Indigenous peoples and more recent settlers continues. As the social context changed, the negotiation of ethnic identities proceeded apace.

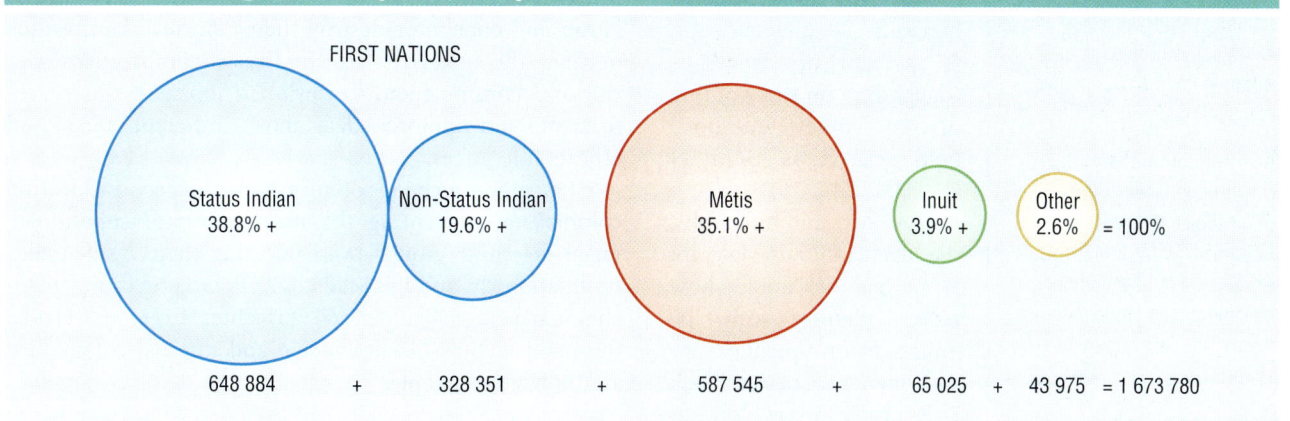

## FIGURE 7.2 Indigenous Population by Self-Identification, Canada

**FIRST NATIONS**

Status Indian 38.8% + Non-Status Indian 19.6% + Métis 35.1% + Inuit 3.9% + Other 2.6% = 100%

648 884 + 328 351 + 587 545 + 65 025 + 43 975 = 1 673 780

Note: Except for the "Other" category, all people represented in this chart reported a single Indigenous identity in the 2011 National Household Survey. The "Other" category includes people who reported multiple Indigenous identities or declared Indigenous identities not included elsewhere.

Source: Statistics Canada. 2017a. "Aboriginal identity population by both sexes, total - age, 2016 counts, Canada, provinces and territories, 2016 Census—25% Sample data." http://www12.statcan.gc.ca/census-recensement/2016/dp-pd/hlt-fst/abo-aut/Table.cfm?Lang=Eng&S=99&O=A&RPP=25 (retrieved 2 February 2018).

## CHOICE VS. IMPOSITION

The idea that race and ethnicity are socially constructed does not mean that everyone can always choose their racial or ethnic identity freely. Wide variations exist over time, between societies, and within societies in the degree to which people can exercise such freedom.

The Canadians with the most freedom to choose their ethnic identity are white people whose ancestors arrived in Canada more than two generations ago. For example, identifying as an Irish Canadian no longer has the negative implications it did in, say, 1900. Then, the English Protestant majority typically regarded working-class Irish Catholics as often drunk, inherently lazy, and born superstitious. Strong anti-Irish sentiment often erupted in conflict and meant that the Irish found it difficult to escape their ethnic identity even if they wanted to. Since then, however, Irish Canadians have followed the path taken by many other white European groups: They have achieved upward mobility and blended with the majority.

As a result, Irish Canadians no longer find their identity imposed on them. Instead, they can choose whether to march in a St. Patrick's Day parade, enjoy the remarkable contributions of Irish authors to English-language literature and drama, and take pride in the athleticism and artistry of Riverdance. For them, ethnicity is largely a symbolic matter, as it is for the other white European groups that have undergone similar social processes. Herbert Gans defines **symbolic ethnicity** as "a nostalgic allegiance to the culture of the immigrant generation, or that of the old country; a love for and a pride in a tradition that can be felt without having to be incorporated in everyday behaviour" (Gans, 1991: 436).

In contrast, most black Canadians lack the freedom to enjoy symbolic ethnicity. They may well take pride in their cultural heritage. However, their identity as black people is not optional because a considerable number of non-blacks are racists and impose black identity on them daily. **Racism** is the belief that a visible characteristic of a group, such as skin colour, indicates group inferiority and justifies discrimination. **Institutional racism** is bias that is inherent in social institutions and is often not noticed

> **symbolic ethnicity** A nostalgic allegiance to the culture of the immigrant generation or that of the old country that is not usually incorporated into everyday behaviour.
>
> **racism** The belief that a visible characteristic of a group, such as skin colour, indicates group inferiority and justifies discrimination.
>
> **institutional racism** Bias that is inherent in social institutions and is often not noticed by members of the majority group.

A St. Patrick's Day parade in Toronto

**colonialism** Involves people from one country invading and taking political, cultural, and economic control over people in another country.

**internal colonialism** Involves one race or ethnic group subjugating another in the same country. It prevents assimilation by segregating the subordinate group in terms of jobs, housing, and social contacts.

**assimilation** The process by which a minority group blends into the majority population and eventually disappears as a distinct people in the larger society.

**expulsion** The forcible removal of a population from a territory claimed by another population.

**genocide** The intentional extermination of an entire population defined as a race or a people.

by members of the majority group. Surveys show that between 30 percent and 55 percent of Canadians (depending on the wording of the survey question) hold racist views (Henry et al., 2001: 147–51).

In his autobiography, the black militant Malcolm X poignantly noted how racial identity can be imposed on people. He described one of his black PhD professors as "one of these ultra-proper-talking Negroes" who spoke and acted snobbishly. "Do you know what white racists call black PhDs?" asked Malcolm X. "He said something like, 'I believe that I happen not to be aware of that….' And I laid the word down on him, loud: 'Nigger!'" (X, 1965: 284). Malcolm X's point is that it doesn't matter to a racist whether a black person is a professor or a panhandler, a genius or a fool, a saint or a criminal. Where racism is common, racial identities are compulsory and therefore at the forefront of a person's self-identity.

As the contrast between Irish Canadians and black Canadians suggests, then, relations among racial and ethnic groups can take different forms. We next examine how various forms of inequality promote conflict between racial and ethnic groups and thus help to sustain racial and ethnic distinctiveness.

# LO3 CONFLICT THEORIES OF RACE AND ETHNIC RELATIONS

## COLONIALISM AND INTERNAL COLONIALISM

Conflict theorists argue that one of the most important mechanisms that has promoted inequality and conflict between racial and ethnic groups is colonialism. **Colonialism** involves people from one country invading another. In the process, the invaders gain control over the native population and change or destroy their culture. The invaders develop the belief that the natives are inherently inferior and confine them to unskilled jobs. All this serves to create and reinforce ideas about "inherent" racial and ethnic differences.

Once entrenched, colonizers may engage in **internal colonialism**, preventing the **assimilation** of subordinate racial or ethnic groups by segregating them residentially, occupationally, and in social contacts ranging from friendship to marriage (Blauner, 1972; Hechter, 1974). In Canada, the main victims of colonialism and internal colonialism are Indigenous peoples, the Québécois, and black people.

## CANADA'S INDIGENOUS PEOPLES

The words that best describe the treatment of Canada's Indigenous peoples by European immigrants are expulsion and genocide. **Expulsion** is the forcible removal of a population from a territory claimed by another population. **Genocide** is the intentional extermination of an entire population defined as a race or a people.

Both concepts are dramatically illustrated by the plight of the Beothuk, the First Nations inhabitants of what is today Newfoundland and Labrador. The Beothuk were Algonkian-speaking hunter–gatherers. In the sixteenth century, Europeans used Newfoundland and Labrador as a fishing port, returning to Europe each year after the fishing season. In the seventeenth century, year-round European settlement began. This caused a revolution in the life of the Beothuk because the Europeans viewed them as a nuisance. They offered incentives to Mi'kmaq Indians from Nova Scotia to kill off the Beothuk. The Beothuk population declined and gradually withdrew from European contact.

As European settlement grew in the eighteenth century, the Beothuk were pushed into the interior. There they competed for scarce resources with fur traders. Eventually the Beothuk were reduced to a small refugee population living off the meagre resources of the Newfoundland and Labrador interior. The expulsion of the Beothuk from their traditional territories because of European colonization led to their eventual extinction. Today, all that remains of the Beothuk aside from their tragic history and a few artifacts is a statue outside the Newfoundland and Labrador provincial legislature in St. John's.

The story of the Beothuk is an extreme case. However, *all* First Nations had broadly similar experiences. In the eighteenth and especially the nineteenth centuries, as the European settlers' fur trade gave way to the construction of railroads, the harvesting of agricultural products and timber, and the mining of minerals, oil, and gas, First Nations people were shunted aside so the Canadian economy could grow. Contact with Europeans exposed them to infectious diseases against which they had little resistance. Relocation on reserves cut off their access to food and clean water. The historical record shows that many European settlers understood that their actions would likely lead to the extinction of the First Nations population, and their expectations were nearly borne out. Between the time of first contact in the sixteenth century and the early 1920s, the Indigenous population of Canada plummeted by 75 percent, about the same as the percentage of European Jews killed by the Nazis during World War II and the percentage of Armenians killed by the Turks in the Ottoman Empire during World War I—the two great genocides of the twentieth century (Brym, 2018b).

European settlers sought to "assimilate" the First Nations. The 1876 Indian Act underlined the importance of transforming a hunting–gathering people into an agricultural labour force (Menzies, 1999). Sir John A. Macdonald, Canada's first prime minister, spoke of the need "to do away with the tribal system and assimilate the Indian people in all respects with the inhabitants of the Dominion, as speedily as they are fit to change" (quoted in Montgomery, 1965: 13).

First Nations people understood the settlers' actions as an attempt to obliterate their heritage. No other conclusion seems warranted when one considers the collaboration between government and various churches in establishing Canada's 130 "residential schools." The government and the churches removed First Nations children from their families and forced them to study in boarding schools. There, they were prevented from speaking their languages and practising their religions, and were compelled to adopt the dominant, white European culture.

Physical abuse was common in the residential schools. About a fifth of First Nations Canadians now living on reserves attended residential schools in their youth, and about 70 percent of them experienced physical abuse while enrolled (Reading and Wien, 2009: 22). Four percent of the 150 000 children who attended residential schools died while they were in the schools' "care." Between 1942 and 1952, some were deprived of basic nutrients as part of a government-funded experiment (Mosby, 2013).

According to 12 000 pages of testimony collected by the Ontario Provincial Police between 1992 and 1998 and only recently made public, the nuns who ran St. Anne's residential school near James Bay in northeastern Ontario

The Canadian policy of assimilation. In its annual report of 1904, the Department of Indian Affairs published these photographs of Thomas Moore of the Regina Industrial School, "before and after tuition."

administered discipline in especially gruesome ways, tying children to their beds, placing them in straitjackets, and strapping them into the special chair the school had built to deliver electric shocks. Some children were force-fed spoiled fish and rancid horsemeat that made them vomit. Then they were forced to eat the vomit (Barrera, 2018).

Sexual abuse of children attending residential schools was also widespread. One survivor of St. Anne's recalled that, while having her first period, a nun started rubbing her breasts and stomach, then moved down between her legs. When the girl resisted, the nun explained that "the devil's inside you" and they had to get the devil out. She then forced the girl into a straitjacket and continued the sexual assault. The nun was never charged (Barrera, 2018).

Adding insult to cruelty, early historical writing about Canada depicted the First Nations as evil personified. Typically, *The History of the Dominion of Canada*, a book widely used in Canadian schools at the turn of the twentieth century, devoted just five pages to First Nations people. The book describes them as "cruel," "rude," "false," "crafty," "savages," and "ferocious villains" who plotted against the Europeans with "fiendish ingenuity" (Clement, 1897: 12 and 13). Canadian schoolbooks continued to portray members of the First Nations in pretty much this way until the mid-twentieth century.

Throughout North America, the confrontation with European culture undermined the way of life of the First Nations. Because of internal colonialism and, in particular, expulsion from their traditional lands and genocidal actions on the part of European settlers, Canada's First Nations were prevented from practising their traditional ways and from assimilating into the larger society. Most of them languished on reserves and, more recently, in urban slums. There they experience extraordinarily high rates of unemployment, poverty, ill health, and violence (see Table 7.2).

It is a credit to Canada's First Nations that they have made significant progress in recent decades despite the many obstacles just listed. In 1950, only about 200 businesses were owned or operated by members of First Nations in Canada. Today, the figure is more than 30 000. British Columbia's first Indigenous lawyer was called to the bar in 1962. Today, there are about 200 Indigenous lawyers in the province. Nearly half of Indigenous Canadians between the ages of 25 and 64 have a postsecondary qualification, and more than 13 percent of Indigenous women between the ages of 25 and 44 have a university degree.

While these figures are still significantly below the comparable figures for non-Indigenous people, they have skyrocketed since 2001, especially for women; while there were just a few hundred Indigenous Canadians in university in the 1970s, today there are about 30 000, two-thirds of them women. Moreover, while non-Indigenous Canadians and Indigenous men have seen their participation rate in the paid labour market decline since the 2008-09 recession, Indigenous women have seen their participation rate increase.

Employment growth has been especially robust in high-paying, knowledge-based sectors including finance, education, and professional services. Successful Indigenous Canadians can now be found in all walks of life—among musicians (Susan Aglukark, Tanya Tagaq, A Tribe Called Red), jurists/senators (Senator Murray Sinclair of Manitoba, first Indigenous judge appointed in Manitoba), athletes (Carey Price, star goalie of the Montreal Canadiens), writers (Joseph Boyden, Thomas King), filmmakers (Alanis Obomsawin), politicians (Leona Aglukkaq, Shelly Glover), and so on (Denis, 2016; Griner, 2013; Law Society of British Columbia, 2015; Mendelson, 2006; Statistics Canada, 2013g; TD Economics, 2015).

Especially since the 1960s, Canada's First Nations have taken legal action against the Canadian government

### TABLE 7.2 Relative Well-Being of Indigenous People in Canada

| Measure of Well-Being | Indigenous Peoples in Canada |
| --- | --- |
| Unemployment rate vs. the national rate | 2.1 times |
| Median income vs. the national average | 60 percent |
| Incarceration rate vs. the national rate | 10 times |
| Homicide rate vs. the national rate | 6.1 times |
| Infant mortality rate vs. the national rate | 2.3 times |
| Life expectancy vs. the national average | 91 percent |
| Dropout rate vs. the national average* | 2.7 times |

*20- to 24-year-olds without a high school diploma, and not in school.

Source: From Scott Gilmore, "Out of sight, out of mind." http://www.macleans.ca/news/canada/out-of-sight-out-of-mind-2/ (retrieved 2 August, 2015). Originally published in *Maclean's*™ magazine on Feb. 2, 2015. Used with permission of Rogers Media Inc. All rights reserved.

Carey Price, star goalie of the Montreal Canadiens. His mother is former chief of the Ulkatcho First Nation in British Columbia. She has earned a Juris Doctor of Law degree and now has a business in her home community.

to have treaty rights recognized and have periodically demonstrated in protest against the conditions of their existence (Miller, 2018 [1989]: 273–95). These actions have resulted in court cases finding in favour of Indigenous land claims and have done much to raise awareness of, and sympathy toward, the plight of Indigenous Canadians among the non-Indigenous population of Canada. The formal apology of the Harper government on behalf of all Canadians for the residential schools (2008), the formation of the Truth and Reconciliation Commission to document the stories of survivors of the residential schools system (2008), and Prime Minister Trudeau's pursuit of a papal apology for the residential schools (2017) are evidence of a new tone in relations between Indigenous and non-Indigenous Canadians. (In 2018, the Pope announced that he would not apologize.)

The most recent episode of Indigenous protest, the Idle No More movement, erupted in late 2012 after the federal government, eager to see new oil and gas pipelines built from Alberta to the British Columbia coast, weakened the consultation and approval process for construction along Canada's waterways. Pipeline construction increases the risk of serious environmental damage, and some of the affected territory is on Indigenous reserves. First Nations demonstrations against the new legislation began in Saskatchewan, and protesters later began blocking rail lines in British Columbia, Ontario, and Quebec. The chief of a reserve in northern Ontario claiming to be part of the Idle No More movement went on a hunger strike to force a meeting with the governor-general and publicize the plight of her people. The latest wave of Indigenous protest raises once again the question of whether and in what form non-Indigenous Canadians should take responsibility for past and current injustices. (See Theories in Dispute, From the Contact Hypothesis to Critical Race Theory.)

## THE QUÉBÉCOIS

In Canada, colonialism and internal colonialism involved not just expulsion but also **conquest**, the forcible capture of land and the economic and political domination of its inhabitants. For example, as part of their centuries-long struggle to control North America, the English conquered New France and its 60 000 Canadien settlers in 1759. They thereby

**conquest** The forcible capture of land and the economic and political domination of its inhabitants.

# THEORIES IN DISPUTE

## From the Contact Hypothesis to Critical Race Theory

McMaster university sociologist Jeff Denis spent 18 months living in Fort Frances, a mill and mining town of about 8000 residents in northwestern Ontario, two hours' drive from the Manitoba border. During his stay, he interviewed and systematically observed the interactions of white and Indigenous residents, the latter comprising about one-quarter of the population. His goal was to test the well-established *contact hypothesis*. The contact hypothesis holds that racial and ethnic prejudice will be reduced to the degree that majority and minority group members will engage in friendly, informal, personal interaction (Denis, 2015; Pettigrew and Tropp 2006).

Denis observed a high level of such interaction and even intermarriage between white and Indigenous people in the Fort Frances region. In line with the contact hypothesis, he expected to discover little or no prejudice among white people who were in close contact with Indigenous people. He found nothing of the sort.

One type of prejudice is *victim blaming*, which involves holding the targets of wrongful action responsible for harm that befalls them. Accordingly, Denis asked white people in Fort Frances to think about the main reasons why Indigenous people are more likely than non-Indigenous people to be poor. Half of his respondents, and half of his respondents with close Indigenous friends, placed all of the blame on Indigenous people themselves. About one-quarter of his respondents, and one-quarter of his respondents with close Indigenous friends, placed half the blame on Indigenous people themselves.

Most whites also rejected policies designed to improve Indigenous living conditions and resented people who fought for Indigenous rights. Although many of them were perfectly friendly and even on intimate terms with Indigenous people, they claimed that the subordinate position of Indigenous people in the social order was appropriate given their behaviour, and that improvements in their social standing should come about only through their own efforts.

Denis's finding leaves an intriguing question unanswered. How is it possible for members of a majority group to like and even love individual members of a minority group—to claim that they are "colour-blind"—yet still believe that the minority group as a whole deserves to rest at the bottom of Canada's social hierarchy? To answer this question, we must turn to critical race theory.

*Critical race theory* insists that racial and ethnical prejudice and discrimination are embedded in institutionalized ideologies and practices, not necessarily in the conscious actions of individuals (Weiner, 2012). From this point of view, it is possible in principle that (1) *nobody* in a society is prejudiced against individual members of a minority group, while (2) legal, educational, health, and other institutions operate in such a manner as to discriminate against the minority group, and (3) many members of the majority justify the existing social hierarchy. The assumptions of genetic testing for race and ethnicity, discussed earlier in this chapter in the boxed feature Sociology and the Media, Racist TV Ads, constitute an example of institutionalized racism in science. Here are a few other examples in other institutions:

- High self-esteem is critically important to learning. A school system that teaches only the contributions of white people to human culture boosts the self-esteem of white students while failing to nurture the self-esteem of Indigenous students, thus placing them at a learning disadvantage.
- Saskatchewan farmer Gerald Stanley, a white man, was charged with second degree murder in the case of Colten Boushie, an Indigenous man. In 2018, a jury found Stanley not guilty. In murder trials, the guilt or innocence of the accused is supposed to be decided by a jury that reflects community norms. More than a fifth of the population of Battleford, the town where the trial took place, is Indigenous—but the jury was all-white, an especially big problem because anti-Indigenous prejudice is stronger in rural and small-town Saskatchewan than anywhere else in Canada. Why was the jury all-white? Because, during jury selection, the lawyers were allowed to reject a certain number of potential jurors without giving a reason for doing so. This practice is known as "peremptory challenge." Stanley's lawyer acted completely within the law by rejecting all potential jurors who were Indigenous. The exercise of peremptory challenge had racist implications in and of itself, just like other aspects of the Canadian legal system do (Butt, 2018).
- Health professionals recognize that the tendency of Indigenous Canadians to consume too much sugar, salt, and fat, and not enough lean protein, vegetables, and complex carbohydrates is extremely bad for their health. However, if you live in remote areas of the country, healthy food is too expensive to buy. A kilo of apples costs about $8.80 in the Northwest Territories versus $3.40 in Toronto. The term *food insecurity* refers

to inadequate access to food because of financial constraints. The most food-insecure jurisdiction in Canada by far is Nunavut at 46.8 percent of households; 60 percent of Nunavut's children live in food-insecure households (PROOF, 2018). From this perspective, Canada's food distribution system is an agent of institutionalized racism.

In general, if the social and historical conditions of disadvantaged clients, students, and patients are not taken into account in the operation of courts, schools, and hospitals, these institutions will operate to perpetuate disadvantages. It will even be possible to blame victims for their own misfortune, while being colour-blind with respect to one's treatment of individuals.

## Critical Thinking Questions

- You are a critical race theorist. Explain the rise of the Quebec separatist movement.
- Which is the more sociological argument, the contact hypothesis or critical race theory?

created a system of ethnic stratification that remained in place for more than 200 years and became a major source of political conflict (McRoberts, 1988).

The British recognized that any attempt to impose their language, religion, laws, and institutions on the former French colony could result in unacceptably high levels of resistance and conflict. Therefore, they tried to accommodate farmers and the Catholic clergy by reinforcing their rights and privileges. The British believed this would win the allegiance of these two Canadien groups, who would in turn help to build loyalty to Britain among the population as a whole. In contrast, the British undermined the rights and privileges of Canadien merchants engaged mainly in the fur trade. They took over virtually all large-scale commerce. In this manner, big business became a British domain while agriculture, religion, and politics remained the province of the French. This pattern of ethnic stratification remained intact for two centuries.

By 1950, most farmers had been transformed into urban industrial workers. Some Québécois had become physicians, lawyers, and members of the "new middle class" of administrators, technicians, scientists, and intellectuals. However, the upper reaches of the stratification system remained overwhelmingly populated by people of British origin. Social separation reinforced economic segregation. The French and the British tended to speak different languages, live in different towns and neighbourhoods, interact occasionally, befriend one another infrequently, and intermarry rarely. The novel that became emblematic of the social relations between French and English in Quebec is appropriately entitled *Two Solitudes* (MacLennan, 1945).

Apart from its rigid system of ethnic stratification, Quebec in the middle of the twentieth century was remarkable because of its undeveloped government services. Health, education, and welfare institutions were largely controlled by the Catholic Church. Intervention of the government in economic matters was almost unknown. Because of this political backwardness, members of Quebec's new middle class, together with blue-collar workers, began campaigning to modernize the provincial political system in the late 1940s. They pressed for more liberal labour laws that would recognize the right of all workers to form unions and to strike. They wanted state control over education and a new curriculum that stressed the natural and social sciences rather than the classical languages and catechism. They desired a government that would supply a wide range of social services to the population. They demanded that the state provide better infrastructure for economic development and assist francophone entrepreneurs in expanding their businesses. The partial realization of these aims in the 1960s came to be known as the Quiet Revolution.

However, the modernization of the Quebec state failed to resolve four issues:

1. *The potential demographic decline of the Québécois.* By 1981, Québécois women were giving birth to fewer children on average than women in any other province. In fact, they were having fewer than the 2.1 children women must bear on average to ensure that the size of the population does not decline (Romaniuc,

René Levesque (1922–87), the founder of the Parti Québécois and the twenty-third premier of Quebec

**slavery** The ownership and control of people.

1984: 14–18). Noticing this trend in the 1970s, many Québécois felt their very existence was endangered.

2. *The assimilation of immigrants into English culture.* Fears of demographic decline were reinforced by the preference of most new immigrants to have their children educated in English-language schools. Together with the falling birth rate, this development threatened to diminish the size—and therefore, potentially, the power—of Quebec's francophone population.

3. *Persistent ethnic stratification.* The Quiet Revolution helped create many thousands of jobs for highly educated francophones—but almost exclusively in the government bureaucracy, the educational system, and new Crown corporations, such as Hydro-Québec. It became apparent in the 1970s that management positions in the private sector remained the preserve of English-origin Canadians.

4. *The continued use of English as the language of private industry.* English remained the language of choice in the private sector because the largest and technologically most advanced businesses were controlled by English Canadians and Americans. This situation was felt particularly keenly when the expansion of the state sector, and therefore the upward mobility of the francophone new middle class, slowed in the 1970s.

Because of the issues just listed, many Québécois came to believe that the survival and prosperity of their community required active state intervention in non-francophone institutions. For example, many Québécois came to believe that most shares of banks, trust companies, and insurance firms should be held in Quebec and that these financial institutions should be obliged to reinvest their profits in the province. They argued that the state should increase its role as economic planner and initiator of development and should forbid foreign ownership of cultural enterprises. Finally, the Québécois increasingly demanded compulsory French-language education for the children of most immigrants, obligatory use of French among private-sector managers, and French-only signs in public places.

Most Québécois regarded these proposals as the only means by which their community could survive and attain equality with other groups. Moreover, because the Quebec state did not have the legal authority to enact some of the proposed changes, they felt that the province ought to negotiate broader constitutional powers with the federal government. A large minority of Québécois went a step further. They became separatists, convinced that Quebec ought to become a politically sovereign nation, albeit a nation economically associated with Canada.

The pro-independence Parti Québécois won the provincial election in 1976. In 1980, it held a referendum to see whether Quebecers favoured "sovereignty association." Nearly 60 percent voted "no." A second referendum was held in 1995. This time, the forces opposed to sovereignty association won by the narrowest of margins—about 1 percent. The sovereignty question then subsided, and the Parti Québécois lost provincial elections in 2003, 2007, and 2008. It promised yet another referendum but failed to deliver when it regained power from 2012–14. Over the last few decades, Quebec has won increasing powers from the federal government. The educational and economic standing of its population has improved considerably. That is why Canada's future is now less uncertain than it was when the social, political, and economic inequalities caused by the conquest were more evident.

## BLACK CANADIANS

We have seen that colonialism and internal colonialism, whether accomplished by expulsion or conquest, create big barriers to assimilation that can endure for centuries. A third form of colonial action—slavery—creates similar barriers. **Slavery** is the ownership and control of people.

By about 1800, 24 million Africans had been captured and placed on slave ships headed to North, Central, and South America. Because of violence, disease, and shipwreck, fewer than half survived the passage. Black slaves were bought and sold in Canada until at least the 1820s. Only in 1833, when the British government banned slavery throughout the British Empire, did the practice become illegal in all of what is now Canada. Slavery was abolished in the United States 30 years later.

It is true that the extent of slavery in Canada paled in comparison with its widespread use in the United States,

> TO BE SOLD,
>
> A BLACK WOMAN, named PEGGY, aged about forty years; and a Black boy her son, named JUPITER, aged about fifteen years, both of them the property of the Subscriber.
>
> The Woman is a tolerable Cook and washer woman and perfectly understands making Soap and Candles.
>
> The Boy is tall and strong of his age, and has been employed in Country business, but brought up principally as a House Servant—They are each of them Servants for life. The Price for the Woman is one hundred and fifty Dollars—for the Boy two hundred Dollars, payable in three years with Interest from the day of Sale and to be properly secured by Bond &c.— But one fourth less will be taken in ready Money.
>
> PETER RUSSELL.
>
> York, Feb. 10th 1806.

*Upper Canada Gazette, February 10, 1806*

Many distinguished people were slave owners, including Peter Russell, who held positions in the executive and legislative councils and became administrator of Upper Canada.

where tobacco and cotton production depended entirely on the work of dirt-cheap black labour. It is also true that for decades Canada served as the terminus of the "underground railway," a network that smuggled escaped slaves out of the United States to freedom in Canada. As Martin Luther King, leader of the American civil rights movement in the 1950s and 1960s, said in Toronto in 1967:

> Deep in our history of struggle for freedom Canada was the North Star. The Negro slave knew that far to the north a land existed where a fugitive slave, if he survived the horrors of the journey, could find freedom. The legendary underground railroad started in the south and ended in Canada. Our spirituals, now so widely admired around the world, were often codes. We sang of "heaven" that awaited us, and the slave masters listened in innocence, not realizing that we were not speaking of the hereafter. Heaven was the word for Canada and the Negro sang of the hope that his escape on the underground railroad would carry him there. One of our spirituals, "Follow the Drinking Gourd," in its disguised lyrics contained directions for escape. The gourd was the big dipper, and the North Star to which its handle pointed gave the celestial map that directed the flight to the Canadian border.
>
> —Martin Luther King*

What King neglected to mention is that after the American Civil War (1861–65), the Canadian government reversed its practice of allowing black settlement. Government policy required the rejection of most immigration applications by black people. The policy reflected a deeply felt prejudice on the part of the Canadian population that persisted throughout the twentieth century (Sissing, 1996). Moreover, social relations between black Canadians and the white European majority were anything but intimate and based on equality. Until the mid-twentieth century, blacks tended to do unskilled labour and be residentially and socially segregated—for example, in the Halifax community of Africville, established around 1850 by runaway American slaves (Clairmont and Magill, 1999).

Canadian immigration policy was liberalized in the 1960s. Racial and ethnic restrictions were removed. Immigrants were now admitted on the basis of their potential economic contribution to Canada, their close family ties with Canadians, or their refugee status (see Table 7.3). As a result, Canada became a much more racially and ethnically diverse society. Today, about three-quarters of Canadian immigrants are members of visible-minority groups, most of them from Africa, Asia, and

Jacob Lawrence's *The Great Migration* series of paintings illustrates the mass exodus of black Americans from the south to the north in search of a better life. Many former slaves came to Canada by the "underground railway," a network of blacks and whites who opposed slavery. The former slaves settled mainly in southern Ontario after Lieutenant Governor John Graves Simcoe signed the Upper Canadian Act Against Slavery in 1793.

### TABLE 7.3 Immigrants by Category, Canada, 2015

| Category | Number | Percentage |
| --- | --- | --- |
| Family class | 65 490 | 24.1 |
| Economic | 170 384 | 62.7 |
| Refugee and other humanitarian | 35 922 | 13.2 |
| Other | 49 | 0 |
| Total | 271 845 | 100.0 |

Source: *Annual Report to Parliament on Immigration*. 2016. https://www.canada.ca/en/immigration-refugees-citizenship/corporate/publications-manuals/annual-report-parliament-immigration-2016.html#abintro (retrieved 31 January 2018).

---

* Martin Luther King. 1967. Conscience for Change. Toronto: CBC Learning Systems. Reprinted by arrangement with The Heirs to the Estate of Martin Luther King Jr., c/o Writers House as agent for the proprietor New York, NY. Copyright: © 1967 Dr. Martin Luther King, Jr. © renewed 1995 Coretta Scott King.

> **split labour market** Exists where low-wage workers of one race and high-wage workers of another race compete for the same jobs. In that situation, high-wage workers are likely to resent the presence of low-wage competitors. Conflict is bound to result, and racist attitudes develop or become reinforced.

South and Central America. Among them, according to the 2016 census, are nearly 1.2 million blacks. They form Canada's third-largest visible minority (after Chinese and East Indians), representing 3.5 percent of the population and more than one-fifth of the visible-minority population.

With the influx of new immigrants in recent decades, the social standing of Canada's black community has improved significantly. Many new immigrants had completed postsecondary education before their arrival. Others attended colleges and universities in Canada. Nonetheless, black Canadians still tend to interact little with white Canadians of European descent, especially in their intimate relations, and they still tend to live in different neighbourhoods. The likelihood that black men find employment in highly skilled occupations is still lower than the likelihood of white men attaining such employment, even if we compare groups that are identical in terms of years of education, field of study, and a range of demographic factors (Boyd, 2017). Like the aftermath of expulsion and genocide, the aftermath of slavery—prejudice, discrimination, disadvantage, and segregation—continues to act as a barrier to the incorporation of black Canadians as equal partners in Canadian society.

## SPLIT LABOUR MARKETS AND ASIAN CANADIANS

We have seen how the theory of colonialism and internal colonialism explains the persistence of inequality and segregation among racial and ethnic groups. A second theory that focuses on the social-structural barriers to assimilation is the theory of the **split labour market**, first proposed by sociologist Edna Bonacich (1972). Bonacich's theory explains why racial identities are reinforced by certain labour market conditions. In brief, she argues that where low-wage workers of one race and high-wage workers of another race compete for the same jobs, high-wage workers are likely to resent the presence of low-wage competitors and conflict is bound to result. Consequently, racist attitudes develop or are reinforced.

Resentment certainly crystallized during the early years of Asian immigration in Canada. Chinese, then Japanese, and later Sikhs were allowed into Canada from about the 1850s to the early 1920s for one reason: to provide scarce services and cheap labour in the booming West. Chinese-owned restaurants, grocery stores, laundries, and import businesses dotted the West, especially British Columbia, by the early twentieth century (Li, 1998; Whitaker, 1987).

Numerically more important were the Asian labourers who worked in lumbering, mining, and railway construction. For example, 15 000 Chinese men were allowed into Canada to complete construction of the final and most difficult section of the Canadian Pacific Railway (CPR), which involved blasting tunnels and laying rail along dangerous Rocky Mountain passes. The Chinese were paid half the wages of white workers. It is said that they "worked like horses" and "dropped like flies" because of exposure, disease, malnutrition, and explosions. Three Chinese workers died for every kilometre of track laid.

Asian immigration in general was widely viewed as a threat to cherished British values and institutions, an evil to be endured only as long as absolutely necessary. Therefore, once the CPR was completed in 1885, the Chinese were no longer welcome in British Columbia. A prohibitively expensive "head tax" equal to two months' wages was placed on each Chinese immigrant. The tax was increased tenfold in 1903. In 1923, Chinese immigration

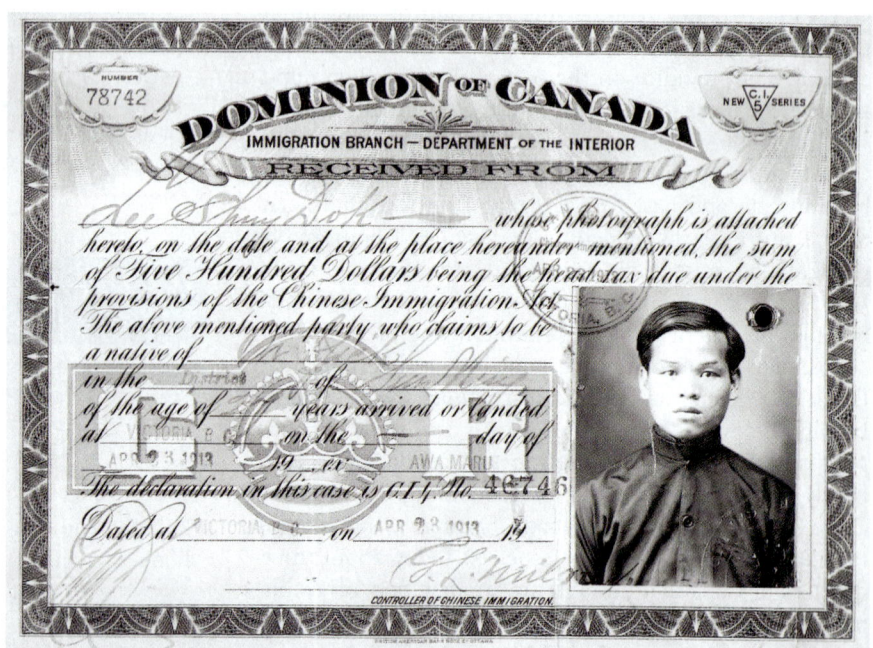

> **Head Tax Certificate:** In an example of legislated racism, immigrants from China were required by law to pay a "head tax" to enter Canada between 1885 and 1923. The tax began at $50 and rose as high as $500.

was banned altogether. During the Great Depression, more than 28 000 Chinese were deported because of high unemployment. Asian immigration did not resume on a large scale until the 1960s, when racial criteria were finally removed from Canadian immigration regulations.

Underlying European-Canadian animosity against Asian immigration was a split labour market. The fact that Asian immigrants were willing to work for much lower wages than European Canadians fuelled deep resentment among European Canadians, especially when the labour market was flooded with too many job seekers. European Canadians formed "exclusion leagues" to pressure the government to restrict Asian immigration, and on occasion they even staged anti-Asian riots, notably in Vancouver in 1907. Such actions solidified racial identities among both the rioters and the victims of the riots and made assimilation extremely difficult.

In sum, the theory of split labour markets, like the theory of internal colonialism, emphasizes the social-structural roots of race and ethnicity. The groups that have had most trouble assimilating into the British values and institutions that dominate Canadian society are those that were subjected to genocidal actions, expulsion from their native lands, conquest, slavery, and split labour markets. These circumstances have left a legacy of racism that has created social-structural impediments to assimilation, such as forced segregation in low-status jobs and low-income neighbourhoods.

## THEORIES AT A GLANCE
### Race and Ethnicity

| Theory | Main Question | Application |
|---|---|---|
| Conflict theory | How does the structure of inequality between privileged groups seeking to maintain their advantages and subordinate groups seeking to increase theirs lead to conflict and often to social change? | **Colonialism** involves people from one country invading another and engaging in **conquest**, the forcible capture of land, and the economic and political domination of its inhabitants. In the process of gaining control over the native population, the colonizers change or destroy the Indigenous culture, develop the belief that the natives are inherently inferior, and confine them to unskilled jobs.<br><br>**Genocide** (the intentional extermination of an entire population defined as a race or a people) and expulsion (the forcible removal of a population from a territory claimed by another population) often accompany colonialism. Once entrenched, colonizers may engage in internal colonialism, preventing the assimilation of subordinate racial or ethnic groups by segregating them residentially, occupationally, and in social contacts ranging from friendship to marriage.<br><br>**Slavery** (the ownership and control of people) has also been a consequence of colonialism in certain times and places. Colonialism can also give rise to **split labour markets**, where low-wage workers of one race and high-wage workers of another race compete for the same jobs. In that situation, high-wage workers are likely to resent the presence of low-wage competitors. Conflict is bound to result and racist attitudes to develop or become reinforced. |
| Symbolic interactionism | How do people communicate to make their social settings meaningful, thus helping to create their social circumstances? | Racial and ethnic identity and the labels that people attach to different racial and ethnic groups are social constructs that emerge from, and are transformed by, social relations between previously separated peoples. Racial differences are not the inevitable outcome of physical or biological differences. Ethnic differences are based more on social-structural than cultural differences.<br><br>High levels of **pluralism** (the retention of racial and ethnic culture combined with equal access to basic social resources) and **assimilation** (the process by which a minority group blends into the majority population and eventually disappears as a distinct people in the larger society) are associated with low levels of **prejudice** (an attitude that judges a person on his or her group's real or imagined characteristics), **discrimination** (unfair treatment of people because of their group membership), and institutionalized racism (embeddedness of prejudice and discrimination in established ideologies and practices, not in the conscious actions of individuals). |

# LO4 SOME ADVANTAGES OF ETHNICITY

Conflict theories emphasize how social forces outside a racial or an ethnic group create inequality and bind group members together, preventing their assimilation into the dominant values and institutions of society. They focus on the disadvantages of race and ethnicity. Moreover, they deal only with the most disadvantaged minorities. The theories have less to say about the internal conditions that promote group cohesion and in particular about the value of group membership. They do not help us understand why some European Canadians of Greek or German or Irish origin continue to participate in the life of their ethnic communities, even if their families have been in the country for more than two or three generations.

High levels of immigration renew racial and ethnic communities by providing them with new members who are familiar with ancestral languages and customs. Part of the reason that ethnic communities remain vibrant in Canada is that immigration continues at a rapid pace; only Australia and Israel have a larger percentage of immigrants than Canada does. However, as we have seen, little of Canada's current immigration is composed of white Europeans. Immigration levels do not explain the persistence of ethnic identity among members of some white ethnic groups of European origin.

Among white European groups, three main factors enhance the value of continued ethnic group membership:

1. *Ethnic group membership can have economic advantages.* The economic advantages of ethnicity are most apparent for immigrants, who often lack extensive social contacts and fluency in English or French. They commonly rely on members of their ethnic group to help them find jobs and housing. In this way, immigrant communities become tightly knit. However, some economic advantages extend into the third generation and beyond. For example, community solidarity is an important resource for "ethnic entrepreneurs," businesspeople who operate largely within their ethnic community. They draw on their community for customers, suppliers, employees, and credit, and they may be linked economically to the homeland as importers and exporters. They often pass on their businesses to their children, who in turn can pass the businesses on to the next generation. In this way, strong economic incentives encourage some people to remain ethnic group members, even beyond the immigrant generation (Kariv et al., 2009).

2. *Ethnic group membership can be politically useful.* Consider, for instance, the way some Canadians reacted to the rise of separatism in Quebec in the 1960s. To bridge the growing divide between francophone Quebec and the rest of the country, the federal government under Pierre Trudeau's Liberals had promoted a policy of bilingualism. French and English were made official languages. The policy meant that federal government services would be made available in both languages and instruction in French would be encouraged in English schools.

   Members of some ethnic groups, such as people of Ukrainian origin in western Canada, felt neglected by this turn of events. They saw no reason for the French to be accorded special status and wanted a share of the resources available for promoting ethnic languages and cultures. As a result, the Trudeau government proclaimed a new policy of multiculturalism in 1971. Federal funds became available for the promotion of Ukrainian and all other ethnic cultures in Canada. This episode bolstered western support for the Liberal Party and softened western opposition to bilingualism. Moreover, it helped to stimulate ethnic culture and ethnic identification throughout the country. We thus see that ethnicity can be a political tool for achieving increased access to resources.

3. *Ethnic group membership tends to persist because of the emotional support it provides.* Like economic benefits, the emotional advantages of ethnicity are most apparent in immigrant communities. Speaking the ethnic language and sharing other elements of one's native culture are valuable sources of comfort in an alien environment. However, even beyond the second generation, ethnic group membership can perform significant emotional functions. For example, some ethnic groups have experienced unusually high levels of prejudice and discrimination involving expulsion or genocide. For people who belong to such groups, the resulting trauma is so severe it can be transmitted

Many immigrants to Canada were processed at Pier 21, located in Halifax, Nova Scotia. It opened its doors in 1928. As the era of ocean travel was coming to an end, the Immigration Service left Pier 21 in March 1971.

for several generations. In such cases, ethnic group membership offers security in a world still seen as hostile long after the threat of territorial loss or annihilation has disappeared (Bar-On, 1999).

Ethnic group membership also offers emotional support beyond the second generation by providing a sense of rootedness. Especially in a highly mobile, urbanized, technological, and bureaucratic society such as ours, ties to an ethnic community can be an important source of stability and security (Isajiw, 1978).

Note also that retaining ethnic ties beyond the second generation has never been easier. Immigration used to involve cutting all or most ties to a country of origin because of the high cost of travel and long-distance telephone calls. Lack of communication encouraged assimilation in people's newly adopted countries. Today, however, ties to the ancestral communities are often maintained in ways that sustain ethnic culture. Many people can afford to visit relatives abroad or bring relatives to Canada for visits. Many more use telephone, Skype, WhatsApp, texting and e-mail to keep in touch. People receive radio and TV broadcasts in their mother tongue, act as conduits for foreign investment, and send money to relatives abroad. This sort of intimate and ongoing connection with the motherland is typical of most recent immigrant communities in North America. Thanks to inexpensive international travel and communication, some ethnic groups have become **transnational communities**, the boundaries of which extend between or among countries.

In sum, ethnicity remains a vibrant force in Canadian society for a variety of reasons. Even some white Canadians whose families settled in this country more than two generations ago have reason to identify with their ethnic group. Bearing this in mind, what is the likely future of race and ethnic relations in Canada? I conclude by offering some tentative answers to that question.

**transnational communities** Communities whose boundaries extend between or among countries.

## LO5 THE FUTURE OF RACE AND ETHNICITY IN CANADA

The world comprises more than 200 countries and more than 5000 ethnic and racial groups. As a result, no country is ethnically and racially homogeneous and in many countries, including Canada, the largest ethnic group forms less than half of the population. True, Canada's British roots remain important. Our parliamentary democracy is based on the British model. The Queen's representative, the governor general, is our head of state. We still celebrate Queen Victoria's birthday (May 24).

English is the country's predominant language, with 56 percent of Canadians over the age of 14 claiming it as their mother tongue in the 2016 census. Our French patrimony is also strong, especially of course in Quebec. Nationwide, nearly 21 percent of Canadians claim French as their mother tongue (Statistics Canada, 2017f.) Nonetheless, Canada is one of the most racially and ethnically heterogeneous societies, and it will become still more diverse in coming decades (see Table 7.4 and Table 7.5).

### TABLE 7.4 Canada's 25 Largest Ethnic Groups, 2016

| | | | | | |
|---|---|---|---|---|---|
| Canadian | 11 135 965 | East Indian | 1 374 710 | Portuguese | 482 610 |
| English | 6 320 085 | Ukrainian | 1 359 655 | Welsh | 474 805 |
| Scottish | 4 799 010 | Dutch | 1 111 655 | Norwegian | 463 275 |
| French | 4 670 595 | Polish | 1 106 585 | Spanish | 396 460 |
| Irish | 4 627 000 | Filipino | 837 130 | American | 377 410 |
| German | 3 322 405 | Other British Isles | 644 695 | Swedish | 349 640 |
| Chinese | 1 769 195 | Russian | 622 445 | Hungarian | 348 085 |
| Italian | 1 587 970 | Métis | 600 000 | Jamaican | 309 485 |
| First Nations | 1 525 565 | | | | |

Notes:
1. Respondents were allowed to select more than one ethnic identity, so the number of responses, shown here is larger than the number of people in each category.
2. A change in question wording excluded more than half of Canada's roughly 390 000 Jews from being counted as Jews in the 2016 census. Statistics Canada is working to correct the problem in the 2021 census. See Brym (2017); Della Pergola (2016).

Source: Statistics Canada (2017f). "Ethnic Origin, both sexes, age (total), Canada, 2016 Census – 25% Sample data." http://www12.statcan.gc.ca/census-recensement/2016/dp-pd/hlt-fst/imm/Table.cfm?Lang=E&T=31&Geo=01&SO=4D (retrieved 31 January 2018).

### TABLE 7.5  Population by Visible-Minority Group, Canada, 2016 and 2031 (projected)

| Group | 2016 Thousands | % | 2031 Thousands | % |
|---|---|---|---|---|
| South Asian | 1 925 | 5.6 | 3 640 | 8.7 |
| Chinese | 1 577 | 4.6 | 2 714 | 6.4 |
| Black | 1 199 | 3.5 | 1 809 | 4.3 |
| Filipino | 780 | 2.3 | 1 020 | 2.4 |
| Arab | 523 | 1.5 | 930 | 2.2 |
| Latin American | 447 | 1.3 | 733 | 1.7 |
| Southeast Asian | 313 | 0.9 | 449 | 1.1 |
| West Asian | 264 | 0.8 | 523 | 1.2 |
| Korean | 189 | 0.5 | 407 | 1.0 |
| Japanese | 93 | 0.3 | 142 | 0.3 |
| Multiple visible minorities | 232 | 0.7 | n.a. | n.a. |
| Other visible minorities | 132 | 0.4 | 489 | 1.2 |
| Subtotal | 7 675 | 22.3 | 12 855 | 30.6 |
| Rest of population | 26 786 | 77.7 | 29 222 | 69.4 |
| Total | 34 461 | 100.0 | 42 078 | 100.0 |

Notes:
1. "n.a." = not available.
2. For 2031, "Multiple visible minorities" are included in the "Other visible minorities" category.

Sources: Statistics Canada, 2010c. "Projections of the Diversity of the Canadian Population, 2006 to 2031," 91-551-XIE 2010001, 2006 to 2031. Released March 9, 2010; 2017r. "Visible minority (visible minority), both sexes, age (total), Canada, provinces and territories, 2016 Census–25% Sample data." http://www12.statcan.gc.ca/census-recensement/2016/dp-pd/hlt-fst/imm/Table.cfm?Lang=E&T=41&Geo=00&SP=1&vismin=2&age=1&sex=1 (retrieved 31 January 2018).

As racial and ethnic diversity has increased, Canadian ethnic and race relations have changed. Two hundred years ago, Canada was a society based on genocide, expulsion, conquest, slavery, and segregation. Today, we are a society based on segregation, **pluralism**, and assimilation—pluralism being understood as the retention of racial and ethnic culture combined with equal access to basic social resources. On a scale of tolerance, Canada has come a long way in the past 200 years (see Figure 7.3).

Canada is a tolerant land compared with other countries, too. A survey of 44 countries found that only Canada boasts a majority of the population with a positive view of immigrants—and a strong majority at that (77 percent) (Pew Research Center, 2002). Each year between 2010 and 2017, a representative sample of nearly 60 000 people worldwide were asked to rank countries in terms of how welcoming they are. Canada ranked first in five of the eight years and second in the other three years (Reputation Institute, 2018).

Growing tolerance certainly does not imply the absence of ethnic and racial discrimination and stratification. Although Canada is becoming less ethnically and racially stratified from one census to the next, serious problems remain (Lautard and Guppy, 2014). For one thing, Indigenous Canadians are making insufficiently rapid progress in their efforts to raise their educational and economic standing. Most of them remain clustered near the bottom of Canada's socioeconomic hierarchy. For another, the upward mobility of immigrants, three-quarters of whom are members of visible-minority groups, has slowed since the early 1990s. Therefore, if present trends continue, Canada's mosaic will continue to be stratified, mainly along racial lines. Unless dramatic changes occur, a few groups will continue to enjoy less wealth, income, education, good housing, health care, and other social rewards than other Canadians do.

**pluralism** The retention of racial and ethnic culture combined with equal access to basic social resources.

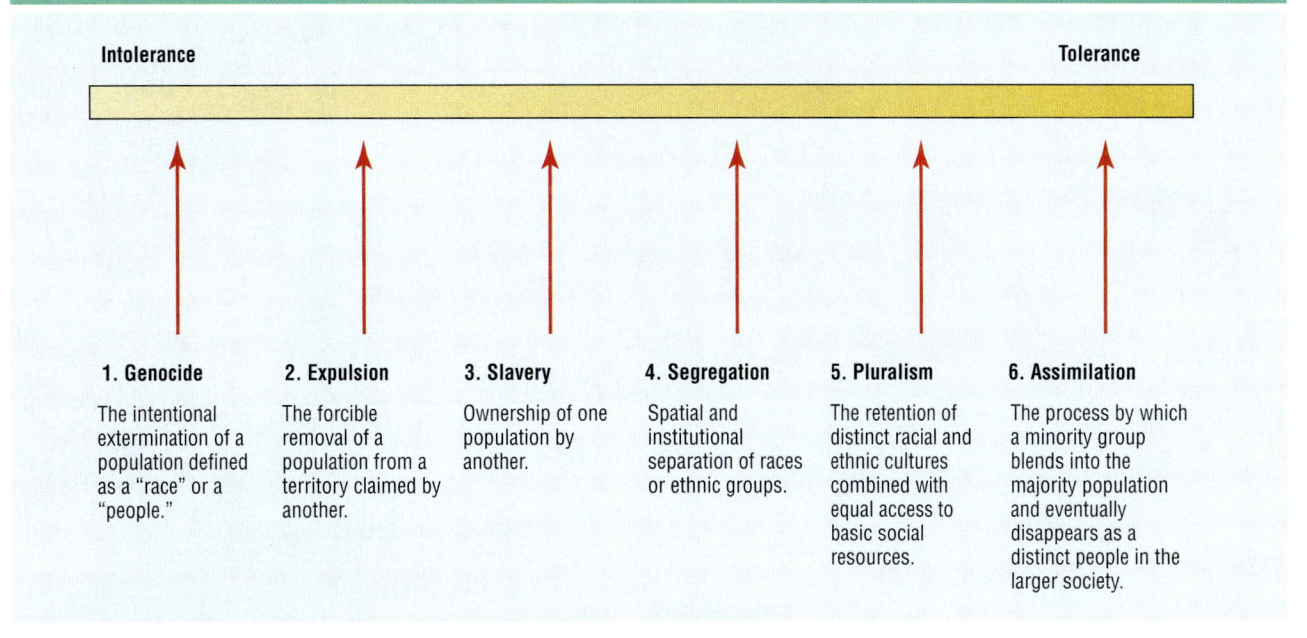

## FIGURE 7.3  Six Degrees of Separation: Types of Ethnic and Racial Group Relations

Intolerance ⟶ Tolerance

**1. Genocide** — The intentional extermination of a population defined as a "race" or a "people."

**2. Expulsion** — The forcible removal of a population from a territory claimed by another.

**3. Slavery** — Ownership of one population by another.

**4. Segregation** — Spatial and institutional separation of races or ethnic groups.

**5. Pluralism** — The retention of distinct racial and ethnic cultures combined with equal access to basic social resources.

**6. Assimilation** — The process by which a minority group blends into the majority population and eventually disappears as a distinct people in the larger society.

Source: From KORNBLUM. *Sociology in a Changing World*, 4E. © 1997 South-Western, a part of Cengage Learning, Inc. Reproduced by permission. www.cengage.com/permissions.

## READY TO STUDY?

### IN THE BOOK YOU CAN:

- Refer to the Chapter in Review section at the back of the book to have a summary of the chapter and key terms handy.
- Test your knowledge of chapter contents by answering the multiple-choice questions in the Chapter in Review section. Answers are in the appendix at the end of the book.

### ONLINE YOU CAN:

- Stay organized and efficient with MindTap—a single destination with all the course material and study aids you need to succeed.
- Flashcards are pre-populated to provide you with a jump start for review—or you can create your own.
- You can highlight text and make notes in your MindTap Reader.
- Prepare for tests with quizzes.

GO TO NELSON.COM/STUDENT TO PURCHASE THESE DIGITAL RESOURCES.

# 8
# Sexualities and Genders

## LEARNING OBJECTIVES:

In this chapter, you will learn to

**LO 1** Distinguish biologically determined sex from socially constructed gender.

**LO 2** Apply major sociological theories to the analysis of gender.

**LO 3** Appreciate that gender is shaped largely by the way parents raise children, teachers interact with pupils, and the mass media portray ideal body images.

**LO 4** Identify the social forces pushing people toward heterosexuality.

**LO 5** Recognize that the social distinction between men and women serves as an important basis of inequality in the workplace.

**LO 6** Explain how male aggression against women is rooted in gender inequality.

**LO 7** Outline social policies that could lower the level of inequality between women and men.

# LO 1 SEX, INTERSEX, GENDER, TRANSGENDER

## SEX AND INTERSEX

At the 1976 Montreal Olympics, Bruce Jenner set a new world record in the decathlon, vaulting to fame as the world's greatest athlete. His picture appeared on a cereal box, and in the following decades he acted in a series of TV shows and became a successful race car driver. He got married for the third time in 1991, to Kris Kardashian. Beginning in 2007, they appeared in the reality TV show, *Keeping Up with the Kardashians*.

Jenner and Kardashian legally divorced in March 2015. A month later, Jenner announced in a TV interview that, since he was a teenager, he had been upset with the sex and gender he had been assigned at birth. He said that, in the 1980s, he had cross-dressed and taken hormone replacement therapy, stopping only when he became involved with Kris Kardashian. He also said that her inability to deal with the issue that lay at the core of his identity contributed to the dissolution of their marriage. Jenner now says he thinks of himself as a woman, which is why he changed his first name to Caitlyn. She says she has never been attracted to men, but she underwent sex reassignment surgery in 2017. She considers herself asexual (Bissinger, 2015; Lee, 2015; Sawyer, 2015).

Caitlyn Jenner's story raises a host of issues concerning sexualities and genders, the subject of this chapter. What is the difference between sex and gender? How are sex and gender related? Are there just two sexes and genders? What makes a person more or less male or female? How do members of society deal with sexual diversity? These are among the questions we will touch on here.

I begin by noting that **sex** depends fundamentally on one's genetic makeup. The overwhelming majority of people are born with 23 pairs of chromosomes, one pair of which determines their sex. If a person's sex chromosome is of the XX variety, she will be a woman. If a person's sex chromosome is of the

> **sex** One's sex depends on one's genetic makeup—specifically, on whether one's sex chromosome is XX (female), XY (male) or X, XXY, XXYY, and so on; the latter sex chromosomes often result in a person who does not fit into conventional male or female sex categories.

CHAPTER 8 Sexualities and Genders

**intersex** Intersex people do not fit into conventional male or female sex categories. Often, intersex people do not have a sex chromosome that is XX or XY and their genitals, reproductive system, and secondary sexual characteristics (such as breasts and body hair) are not distinctly male or female in the conventional sense of the terms.

**gender** One's sense of being male or female and playing masculine or feminine roles in ways defined as appropriate by your culture and society.

**gender identity** A person's identification with, or sense of belonging to, a particular sex—biologically, psychologically, and socially.

**transgender** People who are uncomfortable with the gender assigned to them at birth or who do not fit neatly into conventional male or female gender categories.

**essentialism** A school of thought that views gender differences as a reflection of biological differences between women and men.

**social constructionism** A school of thought that views gender differences as a reflection of the different social positions occupied by women and men.

---

XY variety, he will be a man. However, other sex chromosome types occur naturally: X, XXY, XXYY, and so on. Such combinations often result in people who are **intersex**, that is, they do not fit the conventional male or female sex categories. Their genitals, reproductive system, and secondary sexual characteristics such as breasts and body hair may not be distinctly male or female in the conventional sense of the terms. It is estimated that 1.7 percent of people lie somewhere between male and female as conventionally understood (Fausto-Sterling, 2000; Hird, 2005).

## GENDER AND TRANSGENDER

Being male or female involves not just biological characteristics but also certain "masculine" and "feminine" feelings, attitudes, and behaviours. Accordingly, sociologists distinguish biological sex from sociological **gender**. One's gender comprises the feelings, attitudes, and behaviours typically associated with being male or female. **Gender identity** is your identification with, or sense of belonging to, a particular sex—psychologically, socially, and usually biologically. When you behave according to widely shared expectations about how males or females are supposed to act, you adopt a *gender role*.

Before her sex reassignment surgery, Caitlyn Jenner was not intersex. She was a man sexually. However, her gender identity did not correspond with her sex. She was (and remains) a woman in terms of gender identity. People like Jenner who are uncomfortable with the gender assigned to them at birth or who do not fit neatly into conventional male or female gender categories are considered **transgender**. There are no survey-based estimates of the percentage of Canadians who identify as transgender, but the best estimate from the United States is 0.3 percent (Gates, 2011).

Neither biologists nor social scientists have yet developed convincing explanations for why sex and gender identity may not correspond (Lips, 2014: 18). However, we do know that, unlike sex, gender is not determined solely by biology, a subject to which we now turn.

# THE SOCIAL LEARNING OF GENDER

## LO² GENDER THEORIES

Most arguments about the origins of gender differences in human behaviour adopt one of two perspectives. Some analysts see gender differences as a reflection of naturally evolved tendencies, and they argue that society must reinforce those tendencies if it is to function smoothly. Sociologists call this perspective **essentialism** because it views gender as part of the nature or "essence" of one's biological and social makeup (Weeks, 1986). Functionalists typically view gender in essentialist terms.

Other analysts see gender differences mainly as a reflection of the different social positions occupied by women and men. Sociologists call this perspective **social constructionism** because it views gender as "constructed" by people's interaction with social structure and culture. Conflict, feminist, and symbolic interactionist theories focus on various aspects of the social construction of gender.

## ESSENTIALISM

Sociobiologists and evolutionary psychologists have proposed a popular essentialist theory. They argue that humans instinctively try to ensure that their genes are passed on to future generations. However, they say, men and women develop different strategies for achieving that goal. A woman has a bigger investment than a man does in ensuring the survival of her offspring because she produces only a small number of eggs during her reproductive life. At most, she can give birth to about 20 children. It is therefore in a woman's best interest to maintain primary responsibility for her genetic children and to seek out the single mate who can best help support and protect them. In contrast, men can produce as many as a billion sperm per ejaculation and this feat can be replicated daily (Saxton, 1990: 94–95). To maximize their chance of passing on their genes to future generations, men must have many sexual partners.

Many sociobiologists and evolutionary psychologists claim that male sexual jealousy leading to violence is part of a "reproductive strategy."

According to sociobiologists and evolutionary psychologists, as men compete with other men for sexual access to many women, competitiveness and aggression emerge (DeSteno and Salovey, 2001). Women, says one evolutionary psychologist, are greedy for money, while men want casual sex with women, treat women's bodies as their property, and react violently to women who incite male sexual jealousy. These are supposedly "universal features of our evolved selves" that contribute to the survival of the human species (Buss, 2000). Thus, from the point of view of sociobiology and evolutionary psychology, gender differences in behaviour are based on biological differences between women and men.

## FUNCTIONALISM AND ESSENTIALISM

Functionalists reinforce the essentialist viewpoint when they claim that traditional gender roles help to integrate society (Parsons, 1942; Popenoe, 1988). In the family, they note, women traditionally specialize in raising children and managing the household. Men traditionally work in the paid labour force. Each generation learns to perform these complementary roles by means of gender role socialization. For boys, the essence of masculinity is a series of "instrumental" traits such as rationality, self-assuredness, and competitiveness. For girls, the essence of femininity is a series of "expressive" traits, such as nurturance and sensitivity to others.

Boys and girls first learn their respective gender traits in the family as they see their parents going about their daily routines. The larger society also promotes gender role conformity. It instills in men the fear that they won't be attractive to women if they are too feminine, and it instills in women the fear that they won't be attractive to men if they are too masculine. In the functionalist view, then, learning the essential features of femininity and masculinity integrates society and allows it to function properly.

Conflict and feminist theorists disagree sharply with the essentialist account (see the boxed feature, Theories in Dispute, A Critique of Essentialism from the Conflict and Feminist Perspectives).

### Conflict Theory

Conflict theorists dating back to Marx's collaborator, Friedrich Engels, locate the root of male domination in class inequality (Engels, 1970 [1884]). According to Engels, men gained substantial power over women when preliterate societies were first able to produce more than their members needed for their own subsistence. At that point, some men gained control over the economic surplus. They soon devised two means of ensuring that their offspring would inherit the surplus. First, they imposed the rule that only men could own property. Second, by means of socialization and force, they ensured that women remained sexually faithful to their husbands. As industrial capitalism developed, Engels wrote, male domination increased because industrial capitalism made men still wealthier and more powerful while it relegated women to subordinate domestic roles.

### Feminist Theory

Feminist theorists doubt that male domination is so closely linked to the development of industrial capitalism. For one thing, they note that gender inequality is greater in agrarian than in industrial capitalist societies. For another, male domination is evident in societies that call themselves socialist or communist. These observations lead many feminists to conclude that male domination is rooted less in industrial capitalism than in the patriarchal authority relations, family structures, and patterns of socialization and culture that exist in most societies (Lapidus, 1978: 7).

Despite this disagreement, conflict and feminist theorists concur that behavioural differences between women and men result less from any essential differences between them than from men being in a position to advance their interests over the interests of women. From the conflict and feminist viewpoints, functionalism, sociobiology, and evolutionary psychology can themselves be seen as examples of the exercise of male power, that is, as rationalizations for male domination and sexual aggression.

# THEORIES IN DISPUTE

## A Critique of Essentialism from the Conflict and Feminist Perspectives

Conflict and feminist theorists have lodged four main criticisms against essentialism. First, essentialists ignore the historical and cultural variability of gender and sexuality. Wide variations exist in what constitutes masculinity and femininity. Moreover, the level of gender inequality and the rate of male violence against women, both of which appear universal to the essentialists, vary widely too, as discussed at length later in this chapter. Where women and men are treated equally, criteria for mate selection become more similar, gender differences in math and science scores disappear, and young women and men "hook up" with equal frequency (Ayalon and Livneh, 2013; Goldman and Penner, 2016; Smiler, 2011; 2013). Such variation deflates the idea that there are essential and universal behavioural differences between women and men.

Second, conflict and feminist theorists point out that essentialism tends to generalize from the average, ignoring variations within gender groups. On average, women and men do differ in some respects. For example, one of the best-documented gender differences is that men are on average more verbally and physically aggressive than women are. However, when sociobiologists and evolutionary psychologists say men are inherently more aggressive than women are, they make it seem as if this is true of all men and all women. As Figure 8.1 shows, however, it is not. When trained researchers measure verbal or physical aggressiveness, scores vary widely within gender groups. Aggressiveness is distributed so that considerable overlap exists between women and men. Many women are more aggressive than the average man and many men are less aggressive than the average woman.

A third criticism of essentialism made by conflict and feminist theorists is that no direct evidence directly supports the essentialists' major claims. For instance, sociobiologists and evolutionary psychologists have not identified any of the genes that, they claim, cause male jealousy, female nurturance, and the unequal division of labour between men and women, and so forth.

Finally, the essentialist explanations for gender differences ignore the role of power. Essentialists assume that existing behaviour patterns help ensure the survival of the species and the smooth functioning of society. However, as conflict and feminist theorists argue, this assumption overlooks the fact that men are usually in a position of greater power and authority than women are. This fact accounts well for many gender differences, as you will now learn.

### Critical Thinking Question

- Some people think that male–female differences in average testosterone levels account for differences in many male–female behaviours, ranging from aggressiveness to occupational choice. Others think that gender socialization influences testosterone levels. What do you think?

**FIGURE 8.1** The Distribution of Aggressiveness among Men and Women

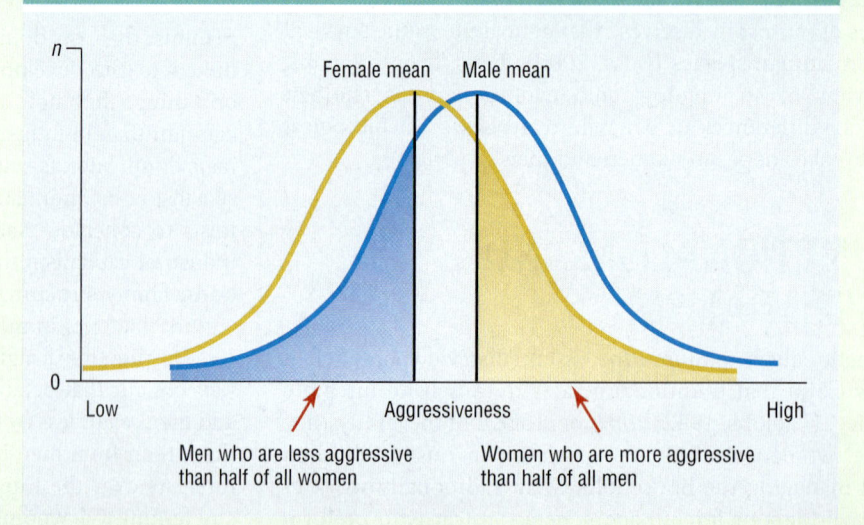

Men who are less aggressive than half of all women

Women who are more aggressive than half of all men

# SOCIAL CONSTRUCTIONISM AND SYMBOLIC INTERACTIONISM

As we have seen, essentialism is the view that masculinity and femininity are inherent and universal traits of men and women, whether because of biological or social necessity or some combination of the two. In contrast, social constructionism is the view that *apparently* natural or innate features of life, such as gender, are actually sustained by *social* processes that vary historically and culturally. As such, conflict and feminist theories can be regarded as types of social constructionism. So can symbolic interactionism.

Symbolic interactionists, you will recall, focus on the way people attach meaning to things in the course of their everyday communication. One of the things to which people attach meaning is what it means to be a man or a woman. We illustrate the symbolic interactionist approach by first considering how boys and girls learn masculine and feminine roles in the family and at school. We then show how gender roles are maintained in the course of everyday social interaction and through advertising in the mass media.

## LO3 GENDER SOCIALIZATION

Barbie dolls have been around since 1959. Based on the creation of a German cartoonist, Barbie is the first modern doll modelled after an adult. (Lili, the German original, became a life-sized pornographic doll.) Some industry experts predicted mothers would never buy their little girls a doll with breasts. Were *they* wrong. Mattel now sells about 10 million Barbies and 20 million accompanying outfits annually. According to Mattel, the average American girl between the ages of 3 and 11 owns 10 Barbie dolls; the average British or Italian girl owns 7, and the average French or German girl owns 5. The Barbie trademark is worth US$2 billion, making it the most valuable toy brand in the world ("Life in plastic," 2002).

In one study, researchers asked young adolescent girls their opinions about Barbie. One girl responded: "She is the perfect person when you are little that everyone wants to be like" (quoted in Kuther and McDonald, 2004: 48). One ideal that Barbie stimulates among many girls concerns body image. Barbie is a scale model of a woman with an hourglass figure. Researchers who compared Barbie's gravity-defying body with the actual proportions of several representative groups of adult women concluded that the probability of this body shape was less than 1 in 100 000 (Norton et al., 1996). (Ken's body shape is far more realistic at 1 in 50.) Experimental studies demonstrate that young girls who play with Barbie are more likely than girls who play with dolls that have ordinary proportions to view their own bodies negatively and think that ultra-thin bodies are ideal (Jellinek, Myers, and Kellet, 2016; Slater and Tiggemann, 2016.

A comparable story, with competition and aggression as its theme, could be told about how boys' toys, such as GI Joe and Transformers, teach stereotypical male roles. True, a movement to market more gender-neutral toys arose in the 1960s and 1970s; there is now even a Presidential Barbie. However, a strong tendency remains to market toys based on gender. Typically, in the 1990s, Mattel produced a pink, flowered Barbie computer for girls with fewer educational programs than its blue Hot Wheels computer for boys. And researchers who measured change in the neck, arm, forearm, waist, thigh, and calf circumferences of five popular male "action figures" from 1980 to 2005 found significant increases in all their measurements, except for the waist (Baghurst et al., 2006).

Yet toys are only part of the story of gender socialization and hardly its first or final chapter. Research conducted in the early 1970s showed that from birth, infant boys and girls who are matched in length, weight, and general health are treated differently by parents—fathers in particular. Girls tend to be identified as delicate, weak, beautiful, and cute; boys as strong, alert, and well-coordinated. One experiment found that when viewing a videotape of a nine-month-old infant, subjects tended to label its startled reaction to a stimulus as "anger" if the child had earlier been identified by the experimenters as a boy, and as "fear" if it had earlier been identified as a girl, *regardless of the infant's actual sex*. More recent research shows that although parents' gender-stereotyped perceptions of newborns have declined, especially among fathers, they have not disappeared (Gauvain et al., 2002).

Parents, and especially fathers, are more likely to encourage their sons to engage in boisterous and competitive play and discourage their daughters from doing likewise. In general, parents tend to encourage girls to engage in cooperative, role-playing games (Fagot, Rodgers, and Leinbach, 2000; Parke, 2001, 2002). These different play patterns lead to the heightened development of verbal and emotional skills among girls and to more concern with winning and the establishment of hierarchy among boys. Boys are more likely than girls are to be praised for assertiveness. Girls are more likely than boys are to be rewarded for compliance. Given this early socialization, it seems perfectly "natural" that boys' toys stress aggression, competition, spatial manipulation, and outdoor activities, while girls' toys stress nurturing, physical attractiveness, and indoor activities.

Only someone who has spent very little time in the company of children would think they are passive objects of socialization. They are not. Parents, teachers, and other authority figures typically try to impose their ideas of appropriate gender behaviour on children, but children creatively interpret, negotiate, resist, and self-impose these ideas all the time. Gender, we might say, is something that is done, not just given (Messner, 2000; West and Zimmerman, 1987). This is nowhere more evident than in the way children play.

## Gender Segregation and Interaction

In a classic study, sociologist Barrie Thorne (1993) observed a Grade 4 and Grade 5 classroom in which the teacher periodically asked the children to choose their own desks. With the exception of one girl, they always segregated *themselves* by gender. Similarly, when children played chasing games in the schoolyard, groups often *spontaneously* crystallized along gender lines. The teacher often reaffirmed such gender boundaries by pitting the boys against the girls in spelling and math contests. These contests were marked by cross-gender antagonism and expression of within-gender solidarity.

However, Thorne also observed many cases of boys and girls playing together. She also noticed considerable "boundary crossing." Boundary crossing involves boys playing stereotypically girls' games and girls playing stereotypically boys' games. The most common form of boundary crossing involved girls who were skilled at sports that were central to the boys' world, such as soccer, baseball, and basketball. Boys and girls also interacted easily and without strong gender identities coming to the fore in activities requiring cooperation, such as a group project. Mixed-gender interaction was also more common in less public and crowded settings; boys and girls were more likely to play together and in a relaxed way in the relative privacy of their neighbourhoods. In contrast, in the schoolyard, where they were under the scrutiny of their peers, gender segregation and antagonism were more evident.

Thorne's research makes two important contributions to our understanding of gender socialization. First, children are actively engaged in the process of constructing gender roles. They are not just passive recipients of adult demands. Second, while schoolchildren tend to segregate themselves by gender, boundaries between boys and girls are sometimes fluid and sometimes rigid, depending on social circumstances. In other words, the content of children's gendered activities is by no means fixed.

This is not to suggest that adults have no gender demands and expectations. They do, and their demands and expectations contribute importantly to gender socialization. For instance, many schoolteachers and guidance counsellors still expect boys to do better in science and math and girls to achieve higher marks in English. Parents often reinforce these stereotypes in their evaluation of different activities.

In single-sex schools, girls experience faster cognitive development; higher occupational aspirations and attainment; greater self-esteem and self-confidence; and more teacher attention, respect, and encouragement in the classroom. They also develop more egalitarian attitudes toward the role of women in society. Why? Because such schools place more emphasis on academic excellence and less on physical attractiveness and heterosexual popularity. They provide more successful same-sex role models, and they eliminate sex bias in teacher–student and student–student interaction because there are no boys around (Hesse-Biber and Carter, 2000: 99–100).

Adolescents must usually start choosing courses in school by the age of 14 or 15. By then, their **gender ideologies** are well formed. Gender ideologies are sets of interrelated ideas about what constitutes appropriate masculine and feminine roles and behaviour. One aspect of gender ideology becomes especially important around Grades 9 and 10: adolescents' ideas about whether, as adults, they will focus mainly on the home or on paid work outside the home or on a combination of the two. Adolescents usually make course choices with gender ideologies in mind. Boys are strongly inclined to consider only their careers in making course choices. Most girls are inclined to consider both home responsibilities and careers, although a minority considers only home responsibilities and another minority considers only careers. Consequently, boys tend to choose career-oriented courses, particularly in math and science, more often than girls do.

In college and university, the pattern is accentuated. Because they expect to devote a large part of their lives to child-rearing and housework, the course choices of young women typically lead to less demanding, lower-paying jobs (Hochschild with Machung, 1989: 15–18). Although women have made big inroads in such fields as law and medicine in recent decades, the top fields of study for university and college graduates still indicate the continuing impact of gender ideologies on Canadian men and women (Table 8.1). I examine the wage gap between women and men in the second half of this chapter.

## THE MASS MEDIA AND BODY IMAGE

The social construction of gender does not stop at the school steps. Outside school, children, adolescents, and adults continue to negotiate gender roles as they interact with the mass media.

If you systematically observe the roles played by women and men on TV programs and in ads one evening, you will probably discover a pattern noted by sociologists since the 1970s. Women will more frequently be seen cleaning house, taking care of children, modelling clothes, and acting as objects of male desire. Men will more frequently be seen in aggressive, action-oriented, and authoritative roles. The effect of these messages on viewers is to reinforce the normality of traditional gender roles.

**TABLE 8.1 Percentage of Women Who Graduated from Canadian Universities and Colleges, by Field of Study, 2015**

| Field of Study | % Women |
| --- | --- |
| Architecture, engineering, & related technologies | 18 |
| Mathematics, computer, & information sciences | 28 |
| Personal, protective, & transportation services | 45 |
| Agriculture, natural resources, & conservation | 52 |
| Physical & life sciences & technologies | 56 |
| Personal improvement & leisure | 57 |
| Business, management, & public administration | 57 |
| Humanities | 62 |
| Visual & performing arts & communications technologies | 62 |
| Social & behavioural sciences & law | 71 |
| Education | 77 |
| Health & related fields | 78 |

Source: Statistics Canada. 2017n. "Postsecondary graduates by institution type, sex and field of study (both sexes)." http://www.statcan.gc.ca/tables-tableaux/sum-som/l01/cst01/educ70a-eng.htm (retrieved 4 February 2018).

Survey data show that body dissatisfaction is widespread, and the mass media play an important role in generating body discomfort in both adults and adolescents (see the Sociology and the Media boxed feature, The Body Mass Index of *Playboy* Playmates of the Month). One study asked 391 students (average age: 13) about their favourite TV characters. On average, they strongly favoured thin characters, and the more they liked thin characters, the more dissatisfaction they expressed about their own body. Girls were more dissatisfied with their body weight than boys were, and were more likely than boys to have dieted. Another study of 259 women between the ages of 18 and 29 discovered that greater engagement with photo activities on Facebook and celebrity images and health and

**gender ideology** A set of ideas about what constitutes appropriate masculine and feminine roles and behaviour.

# SOCIOLOGY AND THE MEDIA

## The Body Mass Index of *Playboy* Playmates of the Month

Assume that *Playboy* "Playmate of the Month" centrefolds represent the North American ideal body type for women. From information in the magazine, it is possible to calculate the body mass index (BMI) of 689 centrefolds from December 1953 to May 2016 (see Figure 8.2). (The BMI is equal to body mass in kilograms divided by the square of body height in metres.) The BMI of *Playboy* centrefolds declined about 5 percent from 1953 to 2016. According to the accepted standard, a BMI of less than 18.5 indicates an underweight woman. By this benchmark, the average *Playboy* centrefold has been underweight since about 2000. A BMI greater than 25.0 is the accepted standard for an overweight woman. From 1978–79 to 2004, the average BMI for Canadian women rose about 6 percent, from 25.2 to 26.7.

### Critical Thinking Questions

- What are the cross-time trends in the body weight of Canadian women versus *Playboy* playmates of the month?
- What consequences, if any, might the two trends have?

**FIGURE 8.2** Body Mass Index (BMI) of 689 *Playboy* Centrefolds, December 1953–May 2016

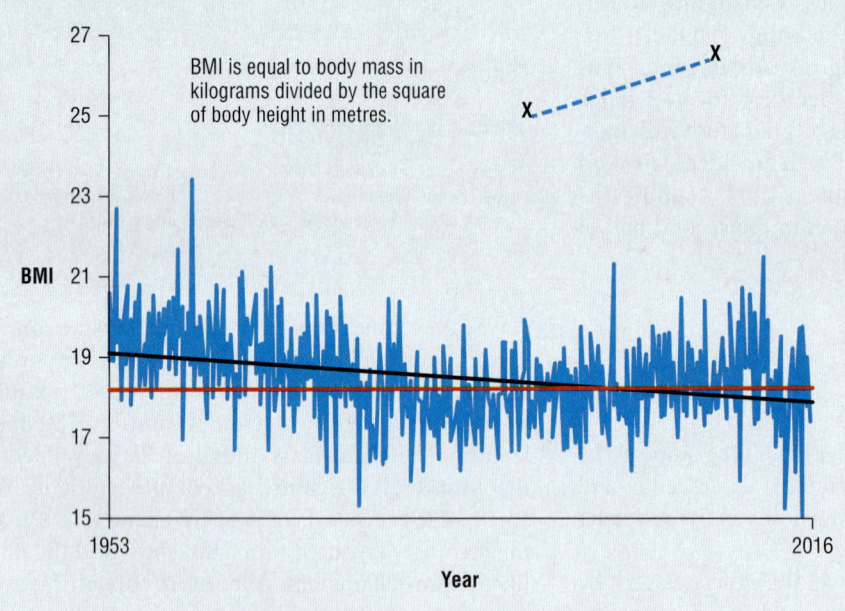

The average BMI of Canadian women (represented by the dotted line) was 25.2 in 1978–79 and 26.7 in 2004—a rise of 6 percent. A BMI of 25.0 is considered overweight.

The red line represents a BMI of 18.5. A BMI of less than 18.5 is considered underweight. The average *Playboy* centrefold has been underweight since about 2000.

The black line is the trend line. The average BMI of *Playboy* centrefolds fell about 6 percent from 1953 to 2016.

Sources: Michael Tjepkema, n.d., "Measured Obesity: Adult Obesity in Canada: Measured Height and Weight"; Statistics Canada, *Nutrition: Findings from the Canadian Community Health Survey*, Issue No. 1; Wikipedia. 2018. "List of *Playboy* Playmates of the Month." https://en.wikipedia.org/wiki/List_of_Playboy_Playmates_of_the_Month (retrieved 4 February 2018).

fitness accounts on Instagram were associated with an increased drive for thinness and more surveillance of one's own body (Cohen, Newton-John, and Slater, 2017; Eyal and Te'eni-Harari, 2013).

Most Canadians have dieted, and women are far more likely than men are to attempt losing weight, even if they fall within the range of healthy weights. Some are willing to live dangerously; many smokers say they smoke to

Hailey Baldwin was #1 on *Maxim* magazine's "Hot 100" list for 2017. What made her "hot"?

control their weight. Between 0.3 percent and 1 percent of women between the ages of 15 and 24 suffer from anorexia nervosa (characterized by weight loss, excessive exercise, food aversion, distorted body image, and an intense and irrational fear of body fat and weight gain) and bulimia (characterized by cycles of binge eating and purging through self-induced vomiting or the use of laxatives, purgatives, or diuretics) (Hoek, 2007).

Men, too, are influenced by male body ideals as portrayed in the mass media. Research shows that exposure to lean, muscular images of men increases male anxiety and the desire to become leaner and more muscular (Taylor and Fortaleza, 2016). That is undoubtedly why an increasing number of men are developing anorexia and bulimia as well as "reverse anorexia," characterized by obsessive bodybuilding and the consumption of steroids (Strother et al., 2012).

## MALE–FEMALE INTERACTION

The gender roles children learn in their families, at school, and through the mass media form the basis of their social interaction as adults. For instance, by playing team sports, boys tend to learn that social interaction is most often about competition, conflict, self-sufficiency, and hierarchical relationships (leaders versus the led). They understand the importance of taking centre stage and boasting about their talents. Because many of the most popular video games for boys exclude female characters, use women as sex objects, or involve violence against women, they reinforce some of the most unsavoury lessons of traditional gender socialization. To cite just one example, in *Grand Theft Auto*, a player can have sex with a prostitute, beat her up, and steal his money back. On the other hand, by playing with dolls and baking sets, girls tend to learn that social interaction is most often about maintaining cordial relationships, avoiding conflict, and resolving differences of opinion through negotiation. They understand the importance of giving advice and not promoting themselves or being bossy.

> **glass ceiling** A social barrier that makes it difficult for women to rise to the top level of management.

Gender-specific interaction styles have serious implications for who is heard and who gets credit at work. For instance, Deborah Tannen's research discovered the typical case of the female office manager who doesn't want to seem bossy or arrogant. Eager to preserve consensus among her co-workers, she spends much time soliciting their opinions before making an important decision. However, her boss perceives her approach as indecisive and incompetent. He wants to recruit leaders for upper-management positions, so he overlooks the woman and selects an assertive man for a senior job that just opened up (Tannen, 1994a: 132).

The contrasting interaction style between male and female managers can lead to women not getting credit for competent performance. That is why they sometimes complain about a **glass ceiling**, a social barrier that makes it difficult for them to rise to the top level of management. As we will see soon, factors other than interaction styles—such as outright discrimination and women's generally greater commitment to family responsibilities—also restrict women's upward mobility. But gender differences in interaction styles also play a role in constraining women's career progress.

## LO⁴ HOMOSEXUALITY

The preceding discussion identifies powerful social forces that push us to define ourselves as conventionally masculine or feminine in behaviour and appearance. For most people, gender socialization by the family, the school, and the mass media is compelling and sustained by daily interactions. A minority of people, however, resist conventional gender

# THEORIES AT A GLANCE

## Genders and Sexualities

| Theory | Main Question | Application |
|---|---|---|
| Functionalism | How do social structures and the values underlying them contribute to social stability? | Functionalists reinforce the essentialist viewpoint that gender roles are inherent when they claim that traditional gender roles help to integrate society. From this point of view, in the family, women traditionally specialize in raising children and managing the household. Men traditionally work in the paid labour force. Each generation learns to perform these complementary roles by means of gender role socialization in the family.<br><br>According to functionalists, the larger society also promotes gender role conformity. It instills in men the fear that they won't be attractive to women if they are too feminine, and it instills in women the fear that they won't be attractive to men if they are too masculine. In the functionalist view, then, learning the essential features of femininity and masculinity as conventionally understood integrates society and allows it to function properly. |
| Conflict theory | How does the structure of inequality between privileged groups seeking to maintain their advantages and subordinate groups seeking to increase theirs lead to conflict and often to social change? | Conflict theorists dating back to Engels locate the root of male domination in class inequality. According to Engels, men gained substantial power over women when preliterate societies were first able to produce more than their members needed for their own subsistence. At that point, some men gained control over the economic surplus. They soon devised two means of ensuring that their offspring would inherit the surplus. First, they imposed the rule that only men could own property. Second, by means of socialization and force, they ensured that women remained sexually faithful to their husbands.<br><br>As industrial capitalism developed, Engels wrote, male domination increased because industrial capitalism made men still wealthier and more powerful, while it relegated women to subordinate domestic roles. |
| Symbolic interactionism | How do people communicate to make their social settings meaningful, thus helping to create their social circumstances? | One of the things to which people attach meaning is what it means to be male or female. Boys and girls first learn masculine and feminine roles in their interactions in the family and at school, and these lessons are reinforced by the mass media. |
| Feminism | How do social conventions maintain male dominance and female subordination, and how do these conventions get overturned? | Feminist theorists doubt that male domination is closely linked to the development of industrial capitalism. They note that gender inequality is greater in agrarian than in industrial capitalist societies. Moreover, male domination is evident in societies that call themselves socialist or communist. These observations lead many feminists to conclude that male domination is rooted less in industrial capitalism than in the patriarchal authority relations, family structures, and patterns of socialization and culture that exist in most societies.<br><br>Despite this disagreement, conflict and feminist theorists concur that behavioural differences between women and men result less from any essential differences between them than from men being in a position to advance their interests over the interests of women. |

roles. **Heterosexuals** are people who desire sexual partners of the opposite sex, **homosexuals** are people who prefer sexual partners of the same sex, and **bisexuals** are people who enjoy sexual partners of either sex. People usually call homosexual men *gays* and homosexual women *lesbians*.

Because of widespread animosity toward homosexuals, some people who engage or want to engage in same-sex acts do not identify themselves as gay, lesbian, or bisexual (Flowers and Buston, 2001; Herdt, 2001). However, sexuality has two dimensions apart from identity: desire and behaviour. Identity, desire, and behaviour are not perfectly correlated. For instance, one can express homosexual desire or have same-sex sexual partners without identifying as a homosexual (Michael et al., 1994: 174–79).

One survey of North American college students showed that homosexual experiences and desires are far more frequent than is homosexual identification. Men were 3.5 times more likely to say they had homosexual experiences and desires than they were to identify as gay. Women were 5.6 times more likely to say they had same-sex sexual experiences or desires than to identify as lesbians (Figure 8.3).

What might account for the male–female difference? One possibility is that many heterosexual men find sex between women exciting, so a considerable number of young women engage in sexual acts with other women for the benefit of men—a growing phenomenon according to analysts who have observed the party, bar, and club scenes in recent years (Rupp and Taylor, 2010).

## SEXUAL ORIENTATION AND QUEER THEORY

Research not only confirms that sexuality is multidimensional but also calls into question whether the conventional characterization of people as heterosexual, bisexual, or gay/lesbian adequately captures the range of sexual orientations in human populations. **Sexual orientation** refers to a person's preference(s) with respect to sexual partners.

You were introduced to research concerning variability in sexuality in Chapter 1 in the Theories in Dispute feature, The Problem of Sexuality. Recall that researchers asked a sample of 1784 people to choose a label to define their sexuality and found considerable variation (Table 8.2). They also found that women and men are on average simultaneously attracted to same-sex and other-sex partners. This is true even for people who identify themselves as heterosexual. Thus, on a 5-point scale, men who defined themselves as heterosexual scored on average 1.15 on same-sex attraction, where a high score indicates high attraction. The comparable score for heterosexual women was 1.49 (Vrangalova and Savin-Williams, 2012: 91). The fact that neither self-identified heterosexual women nor self-identified heterosexual men scored 1 means that, on average, members of both categories experienced some sexual attraction to people of the same sex.

Here it must be emphasized that the sexual orientations listed in Table 8.2 are fluid (Green, 2007; Sullivan, 2003). According to a relatively new stream of sociological thought known as **queer theory**, when we apply labels like heterosexual, bisexual, gay, and lesbian to ourselves or others, we are adopting official or at least socially accepted labels that fail to capture the degree to which people move between sexual identities and performances. That is, people are increasingly inclined to adopt different sexual orientations at different points in their life or even as they move back and forth between different social settings (Better, 2014). From this point of view, sexual orientation labels like those in Table 8.2 impose social conventions on people, acting as forms of control and domination and deflecting attention from the uniqueness of each individual.

The sexual fluidity highlighted by queer theory is a consequence of the fact that marriage, reproduction, and romantic love are becoming progressively decoupled, giving people more opportunity to redefine their sexuality however they wish; because it is

> **heterosexuals** People who prefer members of the opposite sex as sexual partners.
>
> **homosexuals** People who prefer sexual partners of the same sex. People usually call homosexual men *gays* and homosexual women *lesbians*.
>
> **bisexuals** People who enjoy sexual partners of either sex.
>
> **sexual orientation** A person's preference(s) with respect to sexual partners.
>
> **queer theory** Examines empirical mismatches among sex, gender, and sexual desire to debunk the notion that sex, gender, and sexuality are highly correlated; emphasizes how changing social contexts influence sexual identities and the performance of sexual acts.

### FIGURE 8.3 Homosexuality Indicators, North American University Students (percentage)

| | Men | Women |
|---|---|---|
| Homosexual identity | 3.4 | 2.4 |
| Had homosexual sex or desire | 12 | 13.4 |

Source: L. Ellis, B. Robb, and D. Burke. 2005. "Sexual Orientation in United States and Canadian College Students." *Archives of Sexual Behavior* 34: 569–81.

### TABLE 8.2  Self-Reported Sexual Orientation by Sex (percentage)

|  | Men | | Women | |
|---|---|---|---|---|
|  | Self-Identification (percentage) | Same-Sex Attraction Score (out of 5) | Self-Identification (percentage) | Same-Sex Attraction Score (out of 5) |
| Heterosexual | 81 | 1.15 | 71 | 1.49 |
| Mostly heterosexual | 9 | 2.03 | 20 | 2.79 |
| Bisexual | 3 | 3.56 | 6 | 4.08 |
| Mostly gay/lesbian | 2 | 4.87 | 1 | 4.70 |
| Gay/lesbian | 5 | 4.93 | 2 | 4.94 |
| Total | 100 | | 100 | |

Source: Zhana Vrangalova and Ritch C. Savin-Williams. 2012. "Mostly Heterosexual and Mostly Gay/Lesbian: Evidence for New Sexual Orientation Identities." *Archives of Sexual Behavior* 41: 85–101.

increasingly socially permissible to have sex without pregnancy, pregnancy without sex, sex and romance without marriage, and marriage without sex or romance, myriad new forms of intimate relationships are possible and experimentation with them is increasingly common (Giddens, 1992). Thus, researchers studied 188 young adults between the ages of 18 and 26 with same-gender sexual orientations. They found that 63 percent of females and 50 percent of males reported change over time in their sexual attractions, while 48 percent of females and 34 percent of males reported change over time in their sexual orientation (Katz-Wise and Hyde, 2015).

In sum, wide variation exists in attitudes toward sex, sexual identity, sexual orientation, and sexual conduct over time and place. For any one person, sexuality is not "fixed." Nor are men and women, or heterosexuals and homosexuals, sexual "opposites."

## THE EMERGENCE OF HOMOSEXUALITY

Homosexuals were not identified as a distinct category of people until the 1860s, when the term *homosexuality* was coined. The term *lesbian* is of even more recent vintage. Nevertheless, homosexual behaviour has existed in every society. Some societies, such as ancient Greece, have encouraged it. More frequently, homosexual acts have been forbidden.

We do not yet understand well why some individuals develop homosexual orientations. Some scientists believe that the cause of homosexuality is mainly genetic, others think it is chiefly hormonal, while still others point to life experiences during early childhood as the most important factor. According to the American Psychological Association (1998), it "emerges for most people in early adolescence without any prior sexual experience.... [It] is not changeable."

In any case, sociologists are less interested in the origins of homosexuality than in the way it is socially constructed, that is, in the wide variety of ways it is expressed and repressed (Foucault, 1990 [1978]; Plummer, 1995).

Homosexuality has become less of a stigma over the past century. Two factors are chiefly responsible for this, one scientific, the other political. In the twentieth century, sexologists—psychologists and physicians who study sexual practices scientifically—first recognized and stressed the wide diversity of existing sexual practices.

On April 1, 2001, the Netherlands became the first country to recognize full and equal marriage rights for homosexual couples. Within hours, Dutch citizens were taking advantage of the new law. The Dutch law is part of a worldwide trend to legally recognize long-term same-sex unions. On July 20, 2005, Canada became the fourth country to legalize homosexual marriage. As of July 2016, same-sex marriage was legal in 21 countries and some jurisdictions within countries.

Alfred Kinsey was among the pioneers in this field. He and his colleagues interviewed thousands of men and women. In the 1940s, they concluded that homosexual practices were sufficiently widespread that homosexuality could hardly be considered an illness affecting a tiny minority (Kinsey, Pomeroy, and Martin, 1948; Kinsey, Pomeroy, Martin, and Gebhard, 1953).

If sexologists provided a scientific rationale for belief in the normality of sexual diversity, sexual minorities themselves provided the social and political energy needed to legitimize sexual diversity among a large section of the public. Especially since the middle of the twentieth century, gays and lesbians have built large communities and subcultures, particularly in major urban areas (Greenhill, 2001; Ingram, 2001). They have gone public with their lifestyles (Owen, 2001). They have organized demonstrations, parades, and political-pressure groups to express their self-confidence and demand equal rights with the heterosexual majority (Goldie, 2001). These actions have done much to legitimize homosexuality and sexual diversity in general.

## Opposition to Homosexuality

Nonetheless, opposition to people who don't conform to conventional gender roles remains strong at all stages of the life cycle. When you were a child, did you ever poke fun at a sturdily built girl who was good at sports by calling her a "dyke"? As an adolescent or young adult, have you ever attempted to insult a man by calling him a "fag"? If so, your behaviour was not unusual. Many children and young adults continue to express the belief that heterosexuality is superior to homosexuality (Bibby, 2001). "That's gay!" is a common expression of disapproval among teenagers.

Among adults, opposition to people who don't conform to conventional gender roles is also strong. Do you happen to think that relations between adults of the same sex are always, or almost always, wrong? If so, you are not that unusual. In Canada, about 4 out of 10 adults hold that opinion. Rejection of homosexuality is correlated with age, gender, and region. Older adults, men, and residents of provinces other than Quebec and British Columbia are most inclined to reject homosexuality (Bibby, 2006: 21–22).

Antipathy to homosexuals is so strong among some people that they are prepared to back up their beliefs with force. A study of about 500 young adults in the San Francisco Bay area (one of the most sexually tolerant areas in North America) found that 1 in 10 admitted physically attacking or threatening people they believed were homosexuals. Twenty-four percent reported engaging in anti-gay name-calling. Among male respondents, 18 percent reported acting in a violent or threatening way and 32 percent reported name-calling. In addition, a third of those who had *not* engaged in anti-gay aggression said they would do so if a homosexual flirted with or propositioned them (Franklin, 2000). Clearly, **homophobia**, or fear of homosexuality, is widespread.

Research suggests that some anti-gay crimes may result from repressed homosexual urges on the part

**homophobia** Fear of homosexuality

of the aggressor (Adams, Wright, and Lohr, 1998). From this point of view, aggressors are homophobic because they cannot cope with their own, possibly subconscious, homosexual impulses. Their aggression is a way of acting out a denial of these impulses. Although this psychological explanation may account for some anti-gay violence, it seems inadequate when set alongside the finding that fully half of all young male adults admitted to some form of anti-gay aggression in the San Francisco study cited above. An analysis of the motivations of these San Franciscans showed that some of them did commit assaults to prove their toughness and heterosexuality. Others committed assaults just to alleviate boredom and have fun. Still others believed they were defending themselves from aggressive sexual propositions. A fourth group acted violently because they wanted to punish homosexuals for what they perceived as moral transgressions. It seems clear, then, that anti-gay violence is not just a question of abnormal psychology but a broad cultural problem with several sources. Still, opposition to anti-gay violence is also growing and public opinion polls report increasing acceptance of homosexuality.

## Opposition to Sexual Minorities in General

Opposition to homosexuals is part of a larger phenomenon. Like the Calgary bus driver who said he would quit his job if he was assigned to drive a bus wrapped in a rainbow flag during the city's 2015 Pride Week, some people oppose sexual minorities in general ("Calgary Transit," 2015).

Consider how most people react to babies who are born with an unusually large clitoris or small penis. Most parents and physicians believe that, in such cases, early surgery is required because children with these characteristics will have great difficulty adjusting to a society that, for the most part, finds it difficult to accept people with "ambiguous genitalia." They justify their belief with the research finding that, while babies first develop a vague sense of being a boy or a girl at about the age of one, they develop a full-blown sense of gender identity only between the ages of two and three. Accordingly, they hold that a child's sex and gender can be successfully reassigned before the age of 18 months by means of reconstructive surgery, socialization by family members, the instruction and influence of medical professionals and, beginning at puberty, hormone therapy (Creighton and Mihto, 2001; Lightfoot-Klein et al., 2000).

Others hold that sex and gender reassignment is coercive and inhumane if conducted at an early age. They hold that young children should not be forced to undergo sex reassignment surgery. Instead, they should be allowed to choose their sex and gender identity at puberty and, if they wish, undergo sex reassignment at that time. The problem, they contend, is not that children with ambiguous genitalia will have great difficulty adjusting to a society that can't tolerate them but that society is intolerant of sexual minorities. From this point of view, babies should not be mutilated because of widespread intolerance. Rather, rejection of sexual minorities should give way to greater tolerance so that people with ambiguous genitalia can choose their own sexual destiny once they are old enough to make responsible decisions.

In sum, **heteronormativity**—the expression of a preference for heterosexuality—is a durable norm in our society. Strong social and cultural forces lead us to distinguish men from women and heterosexuals from homosexuals. We learn these distinctions throughout the socialization process, and we continuously construct them anew in our daily interactions. Most people use positive and negative sanctions to ensure that others conform to conventional heterosexual gender roles. Some people resort to violence to enforce conformity and punish deviance.

Our discussion also suggests that the social construction of conventional gender roles helps create and maintain social inequality between women and men. In the remainder of this chapter, I examine some of the present-day consequences of gender inequality.

## LO5 GENDER INEQUALITY

### THE EARNINGS GAP

The earnings gap between men and women is one of the most important expressions of gender inequality today. When Canadian data on female and male earnings were first collected in 1967, the ratio of female-to-male earnings for full-year, full-time workers stood at about 58 percent. This means that women were earning 58 cents for every dollar men earned. By 1980, the ratio was 64 percent and it rose fairly steadily to about 73 percent in 1993 (Statistics Canada, 2003c). Since then, however, the ratio has fluctuated between about 68 percent and 74 percent. In 2011, women earned 72.0 cents for every dollar men earned (see Figure 8.4). At the 1967–2011 rate of improvement, women will achieve earnings equality with men in 2089! Even that projection may be optimistic because in 2014, the ratio was still 74 percent (Moyser, 2017).

Table 8.3 shows the gender wage gap in the average earnings of people in the 10 broad occupational categories used

**heteronormativity** A norm that expresses preference for heterosexuality.

**FIGURE 8.4** Ratio of Female-to-Male Earnings, Canada

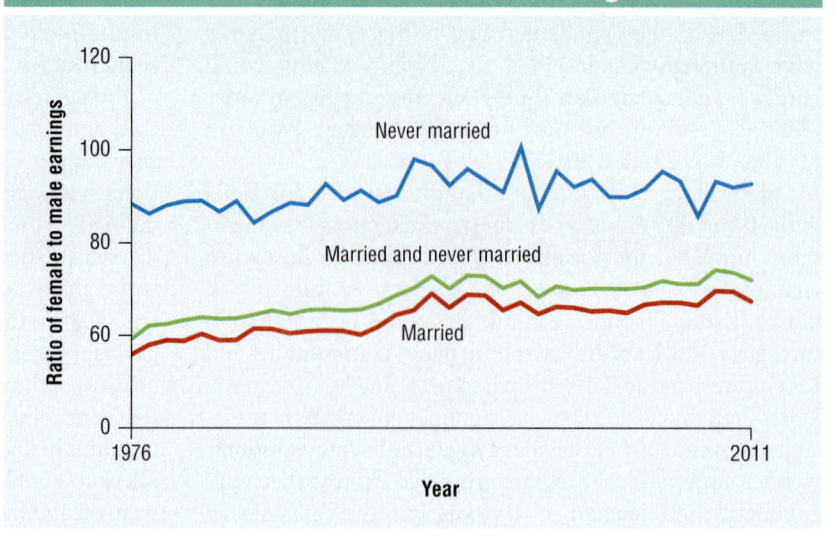

Source: Adapted from Statistics Canada, 2015i. "Female-to-Male Earnings Ratios, by Selected Characteristics, 2011 Constant Dollars, Annually (percentage)." CANSIM database, Table 2020104.

**TABLE 8.3** Female–Male Earnings Ratio in Broad Occupational Categories, Canada

| Occupational Category | Female–Male Earnings Ratio |
|---|---|
| Management | 0.72 |
| Business, finance, and administration | 0.67 |
| Natural and applied science | 0.84 |
| Health | 0.47 |
| Social science, education, government, and religion | 0.69 |
| Art, culture, recreation, and sport | 0.76 |
| Sales and service | 0.55 |
| Trades, transport, and equipment operation | 0.55 |
| Primary industry | 0.42 |
| Processing, manufacturing, and utilities | 0.64 |

Note: The data in this table are for 2015.
Source: Adapted from Statistics Canada, 2015f. "Earnings of Individuals, by Selected Characteristics and National Occupational Classification (NOC-S), 2011 Constant Dollars, Annually." CANSIM database, Table 2020106.

178 CHAPTER 8 Sexualities and Genders

by Statistics Canada. If the wage gap were due to universal gender differences, it would not vary across occupational categories. However, it does vary considerably, from 0.42 in primary industries (farming, fishing, and the like) to 0.84 in occupations in natural and applied science. This variation suggests that social conditions specific to given occupations account in part for the magnitude of the gender wage gap. In particular, the gender gap tends to be lower in occupations requiring more years of education (Moyser, 2017).

Four main factors contribute to the gender gap in earnings (Bianchi and Spain, 1996; England, 1992):

1. *Gender discrimination*. In February 1985, when Microsoft already employed about 1000 people, it hired its first two female executives. According to a well-placed source involved in the hiring, both women got their jobs because Microsoft was trying to win a U.S. Air Force contract. Under government's guidelines, Microsoft didn't have enough women in top management positions to qualify. The source quotes then 29-year-old Bill Gates, president of Microsoft, as saying, "Well, let's hire two women because we can pay them half as much as we will have to pay a man, and we can give them all this other 'crap' work to do because they are women" (quoted in Wallace and Erickson, 1992: 291).

   This incident is a clear illustration of gender discrimination, rewarding women and men differently for the same job. Discrimination on the basis of sex is against the law in Canada. Yet progress is slow; as noted earlier, the female-to-male earnings ratio has barely budged since 1993.

2. *Women tend to be concentrated in low-wage occupations and industries*. The second factor leading to lower earnings for women is that the programs they select in high school and afterward tend to limit them to jobs in low-wage occupations and industries. The concentration of women in certain occupations and men in others is referred to as **occupational sex segregation**. Although women have made big strides since the 1970s in several fields, including management, business and financial professions, medicine, and law, they are still concentrated in lower-paying clerical and service occupations, nursing, teaching, and social work, and underrepresented in higher-paying occupations (see Table 8.4). As intersectionality theory would predict, this pattern is particularly strong for women of colour, Aboriginal women, and women with disabilities (Chard, 2000: 229).

3. *Heavy domestic responsibilities reduce women's earnings*. In 2011, women who had never been married earned 92.8 cents for every dollar earned by men. The comparable figure for all women was 72.0 cents (refer back to Figure 8.4). Most of this 20.8-cent gap represents the economic cost to women of getting married and assuming disproportionately heavy domestic responsibilities. Of course, raising children can be one of the most emotionally satisfying experiences. That should not, however, blind us to the fact it is also work that decreases the time available for education, training, and paid work. Because women are disproportionately involved in child-rearing, they suffer the brunt of this economic reality. They devote fewer hours to paid work than men do, experience more labour-force interruptions, and are more likely than men are to take part-time jobs, which pay less per hour and offer fewer benefits than full-time work does. Women also do considerably more housework and elder care than men do. Even when they work full-time in the paid labour force, women continue to shoulder a disproportionate share of domestic responsibilities (Chapter 9, Families).

4. *Paid work done by women is commonly considered less valuable than work done by men, because it is viewed as involving fewer skills*. Women tend to earn less than men do because the skills involved in their work are often undervalued. For example, kindergarten teachers (nearly all of whom are women) earn less than office machine repair

**gender discrimination** Rewarding men and women differently for the same work.

**occupational sex segregation** The concentration of women in certain occupations and men in others.

### TABLE 8.4 Percentage of Women by Occupational Category, Canada, 1987 and 2015

| | 1987 | 2015 | Change (percentage) |
|---|---|---|---|
| Management | 30.4 | 35.1 | 4.8 |
| Business, finance, administration | 70.6 | 68.3 | −2.3 |
| Natural and applied sciences | 19.8 | 23.9 | 4.1 |
| Health | 78.1 | 79.9 | 1.7 |
| Social science, education, government services, religion | 56.3 | 70.8 | 14.6 |
| Art, culture, recreation, sport | 47.8 | 55.5 | 7.7 |
| Sales & service | 54.1 | 57.1 | 2.9 |

Source: Statistics Canada (2015j). "Labour force survey estimates (LFS), by National Occupational Classification for Statistics (NOC-S) and sex, annually." CANSIM database, Table 2820010.

**acquaintance rape** Sexual assault involving intercourse committed by a non-relative whom the victim knows.

technicians (nearly all of whom are men). It is, however, questionable whether it takes less training and skill to teach a young child the basics of counting and cooperation than it takes to get a photocopier to collate paper properly. As this example suggests, we apply somewhat arbitrary standards to reward different occupational roles. In our society, these standards systematically undervalue the kinds of skills needed for jobs in which women are concentrated.

We thus see that the gender gap in earnings is based on several social circumstances rather than on any inherent difference between women and men. This means that we can reduce the gender gap if we want to. Later in the chapter, I discuss social policies that could create greater equality between women and men. But first, to stress the urgency of such policies, I explain how the persistence of gender inequality encourages sexual harassment and rape.

## LO6 MALE AGGRESSION AGAINST WOMEN

Serious acts of aggression between men and women are common. In the overwhelming majority of such acts, men are the perpetrators and women are the victims. In 2014, Canadian women reported nearly 1.3 million violent victimization incidents to the police—85 for every 1000 women over the age of 14. Nearly 51 percent of those incidents were physical assaults, nearly 44 percent were sexual assaults, and nearly 6 percent were robberies (Mahony, Jacob, and Hobson, 2017).

## SEXUAL ASSAULT

The rate of sexual assault is higher among young, single women than among all women in the population. More than 44 percent of sexual assaults against women are committed by an acquaintance, nearly 35 percent by a current or former spouse, intimate partner, or family member, and 21 percent by a stranger (Mahony, Jacob, and Hobson, 2017).

**Acquaintance rape** is sexual assault involving intercourse committed by a non-relative whom the victim knows. A Canadian study conducted in the early 1990s found that more than a fifth of female postsecondary students said they had given in to unwanted sexual intercourse because they had been overwhelmed by a man's continued arguments and pressure. Nearly 7 percent reported they had unwanted sexual intercourse because a man threatened or used some degree of physical force, and almost 14 percent claimed that a man had attempted unwanted sexual intercourse while they were either intoxicated or under the influence of drugs (DeKeseredy and Kelly, 1993).

No subsequent Canadian research that would allow us to identify trends across time on this subject has been conducted (Sawa and Ward, 2015). However, research in the United States may be instructive. One study interviewed 483 university students at several time points. By the start of their second year, 48 percent of the women had experienced attempted or completed rape (Carey et al., 2015; see Figure 8.5).

Canadian law requires that people take "reasonable steps to ascertain consent" before engaging another person in any sexual act. However, interpretations of "reasonable steps" vary, partly because the courts have failed to define the term. Therefore, the largest category of cases in which men accused of sexual assault successfully argue "reasonable steps" and win acquittals are cases in which women have been deliberately drugged or are unconscious because of excessive alcohol use at the time of the assault (Sheehy, 2003: 579).

## EXPLANATIONS FOR MALE AGGRESSION AGAINST WOMEN

Why do men commit more frequent (and more harmful) acts of aggression against women than women commit against men? It is not because men on average are physically more powerful

*Lipstick and Blood* by Cuban artist José Gómez Fresquet (Frémez), circa 1970

**FIGURE 8.5** Percentage of University Students Who Severely Assaulted a Dating Partner in the Past Year, by Country (n = 6700)

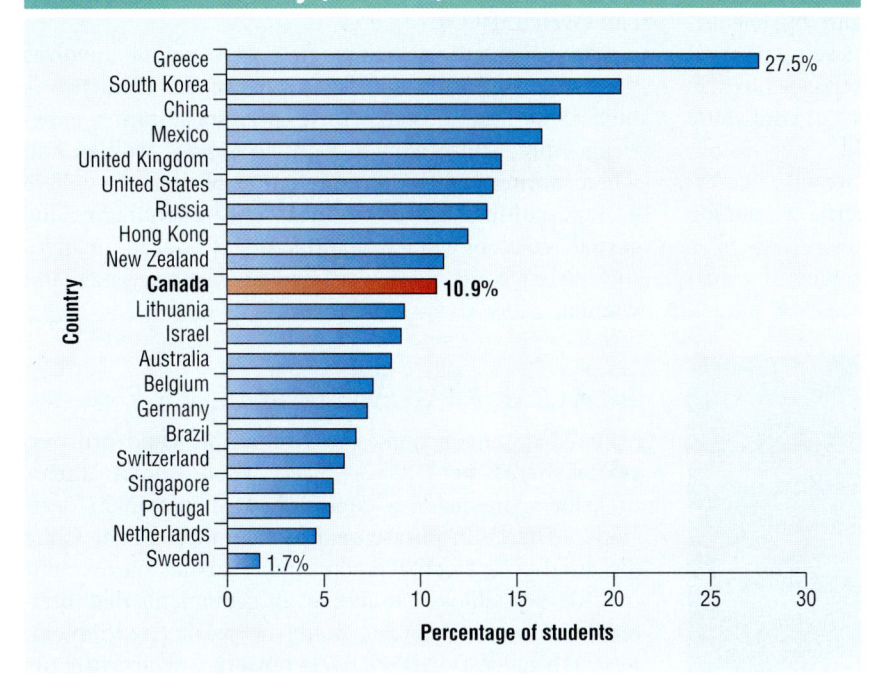

| Country | Percentage |
|---|---|
| Greece | 27.5% |
| South Korea | |
| China | |
| Mexico | |
| United Kingdom | |
| United States | |
| Russia | |
| Hong Kong | |
| New Zealand | |
| Canada | 10.9% |
| Lithuania | |
| Israel | |
| Australia | |
| Belgium | |
| Germany | |
| Brazil | |
| Switzerland | |
| Singapore | |
| Portugal | |
| Netherlands | |
| Sweden | 1.7% |

Note: Some of the U.S. data were collected in 1998. Data from other countries were collected between 2001 and 2005. "Severely assaulted" was defined as students who, in the year preceding the survey, used a knife or a gun on a partner, punched or hit a partner with something that could hurt, choked a partner, slammed a partner against a wall, beat up a partner, burned or scalded a partner, or kicked a partner.

Source: *International Dating Violence Study*. Tabulation courtesy of Murray A. Straus based on Emily M. Douglas and Murray A. Straus (2006), "Assault and injury of dating partners by university students in 19 nations and its relation to corporal punishment experienced as a child," *European Journal of Criminology* 3:293–318. Reprinted with permission by the authors.

than women are. Greater physical power is more likely to be used to commit acts of aggression only when norms justify male domination and men have much more *social* power than women have. When women and men are more equal socially, and norms justify gender equality, the rate of male aggression against women is lower. This fact is evident if we consider sexual assault and sexual harassment (see also the discussion of wife abuse in Chapter 9, Families).

Some people think rapists are men who suffer a psychological disorder that compels them to achieve immediate sexual gratification even if violence is required. Others think rape occurs because of flawed communication. They believe some victims give mixed signals to their assailants by, for example, wearing revealing clothes or flirting.

Such explanations are not completely invalid. Interviews with victims and perpetrators show that some offenders do suffer from psychological disorders. Others misinterpret signals in what they regard as sexually ambiguous situations (Hannon et al., 1995). But such cases account for only a small proportion of the total. Men who commit sexual assault rarely have a mental illness, and it is abundantly clear to most assailants that they are doing something their victims strongly oppose.

What then accounts for sexual assault being as common as it is? A sociological answer is suggested by the fact that sexual assault is sometimes not about sexual gratification at all. Some offenders cannot ejaculate or even achieve an erection. Significantly, however, all forms of sexual assault involve domination and humiliation as principal motives. It is not surprising, therefore, that some offenders were physically or sexually abused in their youth. They develop a deep need to feel powerful as psychological compensation for their early powerlessness. Others are men who, as children, saw their mothers as potentially hostile figures who needed to be controlled or as mere objects available for male gratification. They saw their fathers as emotionally cold and distant. Raised in such an atmosphere, rapists learn not to empathize with women. Instead, they learn to want to dominate them (Lisak, 1992).

Social-psychological factors aside, certain social situations also increase the rate of sexual aggression. One such situation is war. In war, conquering male soldiers often feel justified humiliating the vanquished, who are powerless to stop them. Rape is often used for this purpose.

The relationship between male dominance and sexual aggression is also evident in research on fraternities, especially in the United States. Many fraternities tend to emphasize male dominance and aggression as a central part of their culture. Sociologists who have interviewed fraternity members have shown that most fraternities try to recruit members who can reinforce a macho image and avoid any suggestion of effeminacy and homosexuality. Research also shows that fraternity houses that are especially prone to sexual assault tend to sponsor parties that treat women in a particularly degrading way. By emphasizing a narrow and aggressive form of masculinity, some fraternities tend to facilitate sexual assault on campuses (Boswell and Spade, 1996).

Another social circumstance that increases the likelihood of sexual assault is participation in athletics. Of course, the overwhelming majority of athletes are not rapists. However, there are proportionately more rapists among men who participate in athletics than among non-athletes (Welch, 1997). That is because many sports embody a particular vision of masculinity in North

**quid pro quo sexual harassment** Takes place when sexual threats or bribery are made a condition of employment decisions.

**hostile environment sexual harassment** Involves sexual jokes, touching, and comments that interfere with work or create an unfriendly work environment.

American culture: competitive, aggressive, and domineering. By recruiting men who display these characteristics and by encouraging the development of these characteristics in athletes, sports can contribute to off-field aggression, including sexual aggression. Furthermore, among male athletes, there is a distinct hierarchy of sexual aggression. Male athletes who engage in contact sports are more prone to be rapists than other athletes. There are proportionately even more rapists among athletes involved in collision and combative sports, notably football (Welch, 1997).

Sexual assault against women, we conclude, involves the use of sex to establish dominance. Its incidence is highest in situations in which early socialization experiences predispose men to want to control women and where norms justify the domination of women—where a "rape culture" exists. A third factor encouraging the sexual assault of women, about to be introduced, involves the existence of a big power imbalance between men and women.

## SEXUAL HARASSMENT

Sexual harassment comes in two forms. **Quid pro quo sexual harassment** takes place when sexual threats or bribery are made a condition of employment decisions. (The Latin phrase *quid pro quo* means "one thing for another.") **Hostile environment sexual harassment** involves sexual jokes, touching, and comments that interfere with work or create a hostile work environment. Research suggests that relatively powerless women are the most likely to be sexually harassed. Specifically, women who are young, unmarried, and employed in nonprofessional jobs are most likely to become objects of sexual harassment, particularly if they are temporary workers, if the ratio of women to men in the workplace is low, and if the organizational culture of the workplace tolerates sexual harassment (Welsh, 1999).

Ultimately then, male aggression against women, including sexual harassment and sexual assault, is encouraged by a lesson most of us still learn at home, in school, at work, through much of organized religion, and in the mass media: it is natural and right for men to dominate women. To be sure, recent decades have witnessed important changes in the way women's and men's roles are defined. Nevertheless, in the world of paid work, in the household, in government, and in all other spheres of life, men still tend to command substantially more power and authority than women. Daily patterns of gender domination, viewed as legitimate by most people, are built into our courtship, sexual, family, and work norms. From this point of view, male aggression against women is simply an expression of male authority by other means.

These facts do not mean that all men endorse the principle of male dominance, much less that all men are inclined to engage in sexual assault or other acts of aggression against women. Indeed, scholars increasingly speak of *masculinities* in the plural, rather than the singular, to acknowledge differences among men and to emphasize that "masculinity" is neither innate nor a fixed entity, with many men favouring gender equality and most men never abusing a woman (Messerschmidt, 1993). Yet the

In the 1990s, the Canadian Federation of Students introduced the slogan, "No means no" when it comes to sex. The problem is that some versions of "no," such as "not now" or "maybe later" are sufficiently ambiguous that they may be taken as consent. Therefore, in 2014, the State of California passed a law that sexual partners must consent by saying "yes" to sex. At Dalhousie, McGill, Concordia, and other Canadian universities, campaigns were soon initiated to publicize the higher level of consent now expected of sexual partners (Anderssen, 2014).

fact remains that many aspects of our culture legitimize male dominance, making it seem valid or proper.

For example, mainstream pornography, jokes about "dumb blondes," and leering might seem to be examples of harmless play. At a subtler, sociological level, however, they are assertions of the appropriateness of male domination. Such frequent and routine reinforcements of male authority increase the likelihood that some men will consider it their right to assault women physically or sexually if the opportunity to do so exists or can be created. During 2013 frosh week at St. Mary's University in Halifax and the University of British Columbia in Vancouver, students chanted a cheer celebrating non-consensual sex with a minor. Some participants said the cheer was harmless fun, failing to recognize that "just kidding" has a cost. Research has established that university men who enjoy sexist jokes are more likely than others are to report engaging in acts of sexual aggression against women (Romero-Sánchez et al., 2017; Ryan and Kanjorski, 1998).

We thus see that male aggression against women and gender inequality are not separate issues. Gender inequality is the foundation of aggression against women.

## GENDER RISK ACROSS 137 COUNTRIES

Women face dangers everywhere but the level of risk varies around the world. Combining data on rates of female homicide, rape, and domestic violence, we find that women are physically safest in southwestern Europe and parts of Scandinavia and at greatest risk in northern and eastern Africa, the Middle East, and much of south Asia. How can we explain this variation?

Research shows that three main factors contribute to female gender risk (Brym, 2018c). One important factor is average national income. The richer the country, the less the female gender risk. Why? As economic development occurs, factories and offices grow, while farming shrinks in importance. Demand for women's paid work increases, so women are drawn out of the home and into the system of formal education and the paid labour force. There, men are paid more than women are for doing similar work. Domestic work, child care, and care of the elderly remain disproportionately the responsibility of women even after they start working full-time in the paid labour force. Women enter new social settings in which they may be exposed to violence. These and other issues encourage many women to demand the vote, run for office, and champion government policies that promise to correct the many problems they face. In short, economic development increases women's independence and power, leading many women to achieve movement toward greater gender equality and safety.

However, exceptions abound; even in some rich countries, female gender risk is relatively high. The biggest exceptions are Qatar, Kuwait, and the United Arab Emirates, all in the Persian Gulf region. All three of these countries are rich but in all three of them male authority predominates inside and outside the home. They illustrate a general pattern: in general, where patriarchy is most deeply entrenched, women are most likely to be killed, raped, and subjected to domestic violence.

Even when we take wealth and patriarchy into account, we still find exceptions. Consider Tunisia, a Middle Eastern nation with a long history of patriarchy. The United Nations classifies it as an upper-middle-income country in the same league economically as Argentina and Hungary (United Nations Development Programme, 2014: 148). Women face less risk in Tunisia than one would expect, based on its historical level of patriarchy and its level of economic well-being. That is because Tunisian governments have been pushing to improve women's rights since the 1950s. Equality of women and men is affirmed in many Tunisian laws, and young women are as well educated as young men are. Tunisia is not Norway when it comes to female gender risk, but it does illustrate a pattern that exists around the world: the more governments pass laws promoting equality between women and men, the lower the level of female homicide, rape, and domestic abuse (Brym and Andersen, 2016).

## LO7 TOWARD 2089

The twentieth century witnessed growing equality between women and men in many countries. In Canada, the decline of the family farm made children less economically useful and more costly to raise. As a result, women started having fewer children. The industrialization of Canada, and then the growth of the economy's service sector, increased demand for women in the paid labour force. In 1950, just 21.6 percent of women between the ages of 25 and 54 were in the paid labour force, compared to 97.1 of men in that age range. In 2010, the comparable figures were 82.0 percent for women and 90.9 percent for men (Moyser, 2017). Labour force demand gave women substantially more economic power and also encouraged them to have fewer children. The legalization and availability of contraception made it possible for women to exercise unprecedented control over their bodies. The women's movement fought for, and won, increased rights for women on a number of economic, political, and legal fronts. All of these forces brought about a massive cultural shift, a fundamental reorientation of thinking on the part of many Canadians about what women could and should do in society.

One indicator of the progress of women is the Gender Inequality Index, computed annually by the United Nations (United Nations Development Programme, 2016). It takes into account inequality between men and women in terms of health, participation in the paid labour force, and political

**FIGURE 8.6** Gender Inequality Index, Top 10 and Bottom 10 Countries plus Canada, 2015

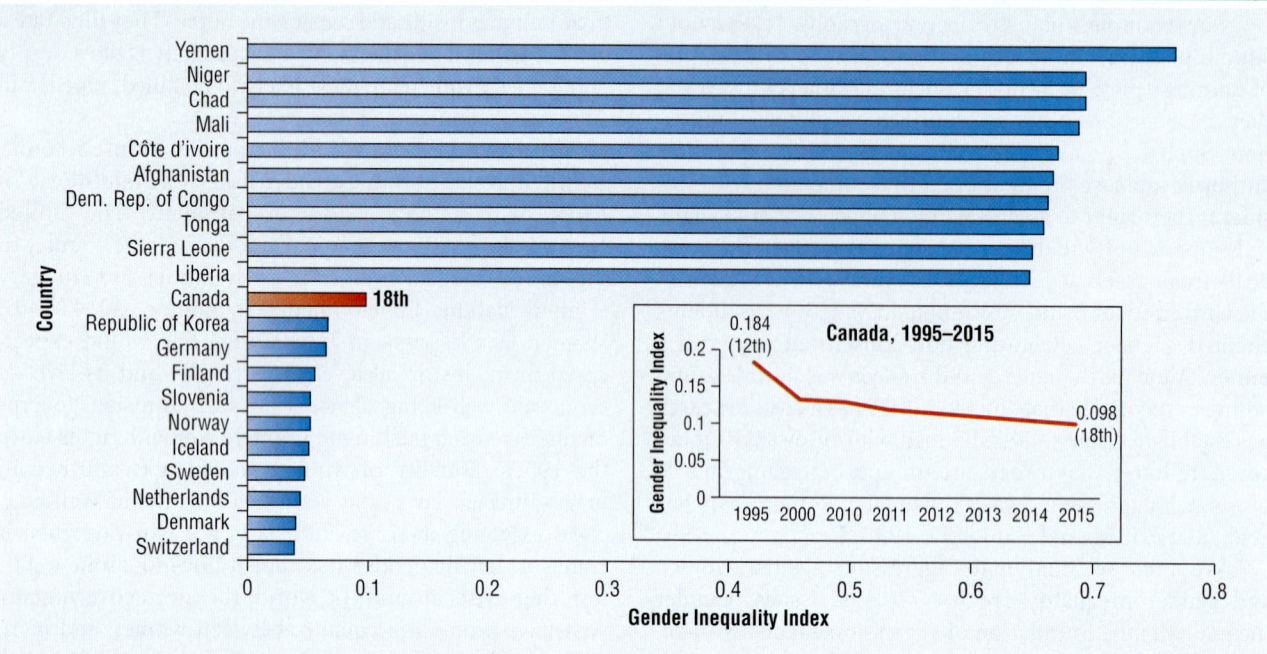

Source: United Nations Development Programme. 2016. "Gender Inequality Index (GII)." *Human Development Report 2016.* http://hdr.undp.org/en/data# (retrieved 4 February 2018). http://hdr.undp.org/en/content/copyright-and-terms-use

influence. A score of zero indicates equality with men on these three dimensions, while a score of 1 indicates maximum inequality. Data for 2015 are available for 160 countries. As Figure 8.6 shows, eight of the ten most gender-egalitarian countries, including all five Scandinavian countries, are in northern Europe. Women in these countries are closest to equality with men. The line graph inserted into Figure 8.6 shows that Canada's level of gender inequality has been falling for the last two decades. On the other hand, Canada's rank fell from 12th to 18th between 1995 and 2015.

In general, more gender equality exists in rich than in poor countries. The top-ranked countries are all rich, suggesting that gender equality is a function of economic development. However, my analysis data suggest that political factors are important too. For example, in some of the former communist countries of Eastern Europe, gender equality is higher than one would expect, given their level of economic development. Meanwhile, in some Muslim-majority countries, gender inequality is lower than one would expect, given their level of economic development. These anomalies exist because the former communist countries tend to make gender equality a matter of public policy, while many Muslim-majority countries discriminate against women in the public sphere.

The Gender Inequality Index figures suggest that Canadian women still have a considerable way to go before they achieve equality with men. We have also seen that the gender gap in earnings is shrinking but will not disappear until 2089—and then only if it continues to diminish at the same rate as it did from 1967 to 2011. That is a big "if," because progress is never automatic.

Socializing children at home and in school to understand that women and men are equally adept at all jobs is important in motivating them to excel in non-traditional fields. Hiring more women to compensate for past discrimination in hiring, firing, promotion, and training is also important. However, without in any way minimizing the need for such initiatives, we should recognize that their impact will be muted if women continue to undertake disproportionate domestic responsibilities and if occupations with a high concentration of women continue to be undervalued in monetary terms.

Two main policy initiatives will probably be required to lower gender inequality in Canada. One is the development of a better child-care system. The other is the development of better pay equity policy. As you learn about these issues in the remainder of this chapter, remember that gender inequality is not just a matter of money and power. It is also a matter of women's safety.

## CHILD CARE

High-quality, government-subsidized, affordable child care is widely available in most western European countries. Sixty percent of children in the United Kingdom are in regulated child care, as are 69 percent of children in France and 78 percent in Denmark. The comparable figure for Canada is less than 21 percent (Ferns and Friendly, 2014: 7).

As a result, many Canadian women with small children are either unable to work outside the home or able to work outside the home only on a part-time basis. This circumstance facilitates the persistence of a higher level of gender inequality than in most western European countries.

A universal system of daycare was proposed in Canada as early as 1970 but little progress has been made in this regard. Quebec is an exception. In 1997, Quebec introduced a comprehensive family policy that attempts to integrate family benefits, paid parental leave, child care, and kindergarten. Its child-care component heralded universally available, affordable child care. A rapid expansion in the number of spaces occurred, although waiting lists grew as well and issues concerning quality of care remain (Cleveland, 2016). Still, about 62 percent of the regulated daycare spaces available in Canada are in Quebec (Ferns and Friendly, 2014: 9).

Parents' average monthly cost of daycare for infants and toddlers ranges from about $170 in Montreal and Quebec City to about $1400 in Toronto and Vancouver (Macdonald and Friendly, 2017: 12, 15). The Quebec system has increased women's participation in the paid labour force and median family income, so the government spends less on social assistance and earns more from income tax. Consequently, Quebec's daycare system more than pays for itself (Fortin, 2017).

Outside of Quebec, the most important development in child care took place in 2017. The federal government announced it was setting aside $7 billion in new spending over ten years for early learning and child-care programs on top of the $500 million for one year it pledged in 2016 (Alini, 2017). This may seem like a lot of money, but it is not nearly enough to meet demand for affordable, high-quality daycare spaces. The International Monetary Fund calculates that Canada can spend more than 10 times that amount and the daycare program would still pay for itself, as it does in Quebec (Petersson, Mariscal, and Ishi, 2017).

## EQUAL PAY FOR WORK OF EQUAL VALUE

The second major stumbling block to increasing gender equality in Canada concerns the fact that women tend not to receive equal pay for work of the same value done by men. On paper, Canadian women have had the right to equal pay for the same jobs done by men since the 1950s. Unfortunately, although early laws proclaimed lofty goals, they failed to result in fair wages.

In the 1980s, researchers found that women earned less than men did, partly because jobs in which women were concentrated were valued less than jobs in which men were concentrated. They therefore tried to establish gender-neutral standards by which they could judge the dollar value of work. These standards included such factors as the education and experience required to do a particular job and the level of responsibility, amount of stress, and working conditions associated with it. Researchers felt that, by using these criteria to compare jobs in which women and men are concentrated, they could identify pay inequities. The underpaid could then be compensated accordingly. In other words, women and men would receive equal pay for work of equal value, even if they did different jobs.

**pay equity** Equal pay for work of equal value, or the equal dollar value of different jobs. It is established in gender-neutral terms by comparing jobs in terms of the education and experience needed to do them and the stress, responsibility, and working conditions associated with them.

During the mid-1980s, some governments amended the law to state that women should be paid equally for work of equal value. This amendment required employers to compare the rates of pay for women and men in dissimilar jobs that nevertheless involved the same level of skill, effort, and responsibility, and the same working conditions. In 1985, Manitoba became the first Canadian province to demand that its public sector implement plans for equal pay for work of equal value—or **pay equity**, as it came to be called. Today, pay equity laws cover public and private employees in the federal jurisdiction, Ontario, and Quebec, and provincial government employees in Manitoba, New Brunswick, Nova Scotia, and Prince Edward Island. Policy frameworks for negotiating pay equity with certain public-sector employees exist in Saskatchewan, Newfoundland and Labrador, and British Columbia. Only Alberta has adopted no laws or policy frameworks for pay equity, either in the public or the private sector (Hay Group, 2018).

Legal and regulatory provisions vary widely. Enforcement mechanisms are meagre. Employers have found various ways to argue that unequal wages do not signify discrimination based on sex. Thus, although pay equity is undoubtedly a significant step toward achieving gender equality, inequity remains, as evidenced by the persistent wage gap between working men and women.

# THE WOMEN'S MOVEMENT

Improved daycare and pay equity would do much to bridge the gender gap in earnings between women and men. However, improvements in the social standing of women do not depend on just the sympathy of government and business leaders. Progress on this front has always depended in part on the strength of the organized women's movement. That is likely to be true in the future, too. In concluding this chapter, it is therefore fitting to consider the state of the women's movement and its prospects.

The "first wave" of the women's movement emerged during the late nineteenth century and lasted into the 1920s. The most important public achievements of this movement in Canada were the right to vote and the right to be considered persons under Canadian law. That's right: until 1929, Canadian women were not legally recognized as having the rights of persons (Persons Case, 2018.) In 1916, women in Alberta, Manitoba, and Saskatchewan won the right to vote in provincial elections. Other provinces and territories followed: British Columbia (1917), Ontario (1917), Nova Scotia (1918), New Brunswick (1919), Yukon (1919), Prince Edward Island (1922), Newfoundland and Labrador (1925), Quebec (1940), and, finally, the Northwest Territories (1951). These rights were first granted to white women. Women from certain ethnic and racial groups did not receive the franchise until later. All legal impediments to voting were removed for First Nations women only in 1985 ("Aboriginal Peoples," 2018; Nelson and Robinson, 2002).

In the mid-1960s, the "second wave" of the women's movement emerged. Second-wave feminists were inspired in part by the successes of the civil rights movement in the United States. They felt that women's concerns were largely ignored despite persistent and pervasive gender inequality. Like their counterparts more than a century earlier, they held demonstrations, lobbied politicians, and formed women's organizations to further their cause. They demanded equal rights with men in education and employment, the elimination of sexual violence, and women's control over reproduction.

Today, diversity exists in the feminist movement concerning ultimate goals. Four main streams may be distinguished:

The "first wave" of the women's movement achieved its main goal—the right of women to vote—as a result of much demonstrating, lobbying, organizing, and persistent educational work.

The "second wave" of the women's movement started to grow in the mid-1960s. Members of the movement advocated equal rights with men in education and employment, the elimination of sexual violence, and women's control over reproduction.

1. *Liberal feminism* is the most popular current. Its advocates believe that the main sources of women's subordination are learned gender roles and the denial of opportunities to women. Liberal feminists advocate non-sexist methods of socialization and education, more sharing of domestic tasks between women and men, and extending to women all of the educational, employment, and political rights and privileges that men enjoy.

2. *Socialist feminists* regard women's relationship to the economy as the main source of women's disadvantages. They believe that the traditional nuclear family emerged along with inequalities of wealth. In their opinion, once men possessed wealth, they wanted to ensure that their property would be transmitted to their children, particularly their sons. They accomplished this in two ways. First, men exercised complete economic control over their property, thus ensuring it would not be squandered and would remain theirs and theirs alone. Second, they enforced female monogamy, thus ensuring that their property would be transmitted only to *their* offspring. Thus, according to socialist feminists, the economic and sexual oppression of women has its roots in capitalism.

Socialist feminists assert that the reforms proposed by liberal feminists are inadequate because they can do little to help working-class women, who are too poor to take advantage of equal educational and work opportunities. Socialist feminists conclude that only the elimination of private property and the creation of economic equality can bring about an end to the oppression of all women.

3. *Radical feminists* find the reforms proposed by liberals and the revolution proposed by socialists inadequate. Patriarchy—male domination and norms justifying that domination—is more deeply rooted than capitalism, say the radical feminists. After all, patriarchy predates capitalism. Moreover, it is just as evident in self-proclaimed communist societies as it is in capitalist societies. Radical feminists conclude that the very idea of gender must be changed to bring an end to male domination. Some radical feminists argue that new reproductive technologies, such as in vitro fertilization, are bound to be helpful in this regard because they break the link between women's bodies and child-bearing (see Chapter 9, Families). However, the revolution envisaged by radical feminists goes beyond the realm of reproduction to include all aspects of male sexual dominance. From their point of view, mainstream pornography, sexual harassment, restrictive contraception, sexual assault, incest, sterilization, and physical assault must be eliminated so that women can reconstruct their sexuality on their own terms.

4. *A "third wave"* of feminism emerged in the mid-1980s, characterized by anti-racist and postmodernist feminists criticizing liberal, socialist, and radical feminists for generalizing from the experience of white women and for failing to understand how women's lives are rooted in particular historical and racial experiences (hooks, 1984). The origins of intersectionality theory, discussed in Chapter 5, Deviance and Crime, and again in Chapter 12, Health and Medicine, may be traced to third-wave feminism. These new currents have done much to extend the relevance of feminism to previously marginalized groups.

Partly because of the political and intellectual vigour of the women's movement, feminist ideas have gained widespread acceptance in Canadian society. Nonetheless, as this chapter documents, gender equality remains a remote goal.

## READY TO STUDY?

### IN THE BOOK YOU CAN:

- Refer to the Chapter in Review section at the back of the book to have a summary of the chapter and key terms handy.
- Test your knowledge of chapter contents by answering the multiple-choice questions in the Chapter in Review section. Answers are in the appendix at the end of the book.

### ONLINE YOU CAN:

- Stay organized and efficient with MindTap—a single destination with all the course material and study aids you need to succeed.
- Flashcards are pre-populated to provide you with a jump start for review—or you can create your own.
- You can highlight text and make notes in your MindTap Reader.
- Prepare for tests with quizzes.

**GO TO NELSON.COM/STUDENT TO PURCHASE THESE DIGITAL RESOURCES.**

# 9 Families

## LEARNING OBJECTIVES:

In this chapter, you will learn to

**LO1** Appreciate that the traditional nuclear family has been weakening since the 1800s, although it strengthened temporarily in the years immediately following World War II.

**LO2** List the factors contributing to variation in patterns of mate selection, marital satisfaction, divorce, reproductive choice, housework and child care, and spousal violence.

**LO3** Describe the characteristics of diverse family forms.

**LO4** Apply major sociological theories to the analysis of families.

**LO5** Explain how public policy can prevent the emergence of certain social problems that might otherwise result from the decline of the traditional nuclear family.

## INTRODUCTION

On January 12, 2018, in Brampton, near Toronto, Baljit Thandi and her mother were fatally stabbed by Dalwinder Singh, Baljit's husband. The couple's young child was in the home at the time. According to the local newspaper, a close friend of the family said the murders were "completely unfathomable." Farther afield, the *Times of India* reported that, according to Baljit's brother, "theirs was a happy family" (Rosella, 2018; Singh, 2018).

For better or for worse, our most intense emotional experiences are bound up with our families. We love, hate, protect, hurt, express generosity toward, and envy nobody as much as our parents, siblings, children, and mates. Some families are islands of domestic bliss. Many families harbour mixed emotions. A few, like the family described in the news story above, are sites of the most violent acts imaginable; in Canada, about 35 percent of homicides occur within family or intimate relationships (Mahony, Jacob, and Hobson, 2017). Given the intensity of our emotional involvement with our families, should we be surprised that most people are passionately concerned with the rights and wrongs, the dos and don'ts, of family life? Should we be surprised that family issues lie close to the centre of political debate in this country?

## LO1 IS "THE FAMILY" IN DECLINE?

Because families are emotional minefields, few subjects of sociological inquiry generate as much controversy. Much of the debate centres on a single question: Is the family in decline and, if so, what should be done about it? These questions are hardly new. John Laing, a Protestant minister in Ontario, wrote in 1878, "We may expect to see further disintegration until the family shall disappear.... In all things civil and sacred the tendency of the age is towards individualism...its plausible aphorisms and popular usages silently undermining the divine institution of the family" (quoted in Sager, 2000: vii). This alarm, or one much like it, is sounded whenever the family undergoes rapid change, and particularly when the divorce rate increases.

> **nuclear family** Consists of a cohabiting man and woman who maintain a socially approved sexual relationship and have at least one child.
>
> **traditional nuclear family** A nuclear family in which the husband works outside the home for money and the wife works without pay in the home.

Today, when some people speak about the decline of the family, they are referring to the **nuclear family**. The nuclear family comprises a cohabiting man and woman who maintain a socially approved sexual relationship and have at least one child. Others are referring more narrowly to what we call the **traditional nuclear family**. The traditional nuclear family is a nuclear family in which the wife works in the home without pay while the husband works outside the home for money. This makes him the primary provider and ultimate authority.

In the 1940s and 1950s, many sociologists and much of the Canadian public considered the traditional nuclear family to be the most widespread and ideal family form. However, for reasons we will examine below, just 39 percent of Canadian families in 2016 were nuclear families, compared with almost 57 percent in 1981 (Figure 9.1) and 69 percent in 1901. Moreover, because about 80 percent of mothers with school-aged children are in the paid labour force, only a small minority of Canadian adults live in traditional nuclear families today. New family forms, including single-parent families, common-law families, and gay and lesbian families, have become increasingly prevalent in recent decades (Table 9.1).

Some sociologists, many of them functionalists, view the decreasing prevalence of the married-couple family and the rise of the "working mother" as an unmitigated disaster (Popenoe, 1996, 1998). In their view, rising rates of crime, illegal drug use, poverty, and welfare dependency (among other social ills) can be traced to the fact that so many children are not living in two-parent households with stay-at-home mothers. They call for various legal and cultural reforms to shore up the traditional nuclear family. For instance, they want to make it harder to get a divorce, and they want people to place less emphasis on individual happiness at the expense of family responsibility.

Other sociologists, influenced by conflict and feminist theories, disagree with the functionalist assessment (Coontz, 1992; Stacey, 1996). In the first place, they argue that it is inaccurate to talk about *the* family, as if this important social institution assumes or should assume only a single form. They emphasize that families have been structured in many ways and that the diversity of family forms is increasing as people accommodate to new social pressures.

Second, they argue that changing family forms do not necessarily represent deterioration in the quality of people's lives. In fact, such changes often represent improvement in the way people live. These sociologists believe that the decreasing prevalence of the traditional nuclear family and the proliferation of diverse family forms have benefited many men, women, and children and have not harmed other children as much as the functionalists think. They also believe that various economic and political reforms, such as the creation of an affordable nation-wide daycare system, could eliminate most of the negative effects of single-parent households.

I first outline the functional theory of the family because the issues raised by functionalism are still a focus of sociological controversy. Borrowing from the work of conflict theorists and feminists, I next show that the nuclear family has been in decline since the nineteenth century and is less prevalent than is often assumed. I then explain how change in the distribution of power between husbands and wives has affected mate selection, marital satisfaction, divorce, reproductive choice, domestic labour, and wife abuse.

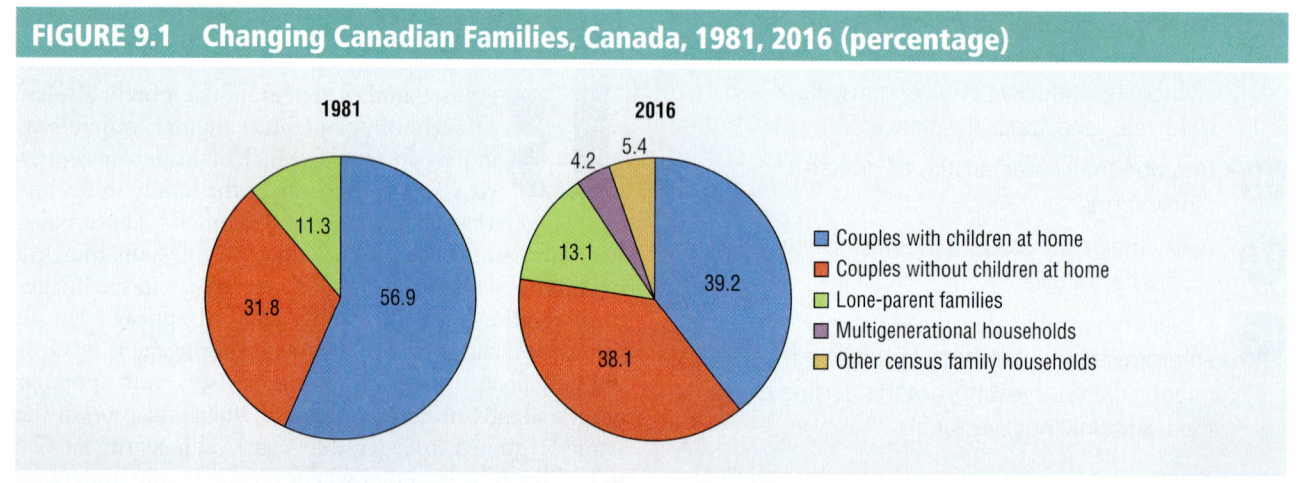

**FIGURE 9.1  Changing Canadian Families, Canada, 1981, 2016 (percentage)**

1981:
- Couples with children at home: 56.9
- Couples without children at home: 31.8
- Lone-parent families: 11.3

2016:
- Couples with children at home: 39.2
- Couples without children at home: 38.1
- Lone-parent families: 13.1
- Multigenerational households: 4.2
- Other census family households: 5.4

Sources: Statistics Canada, n.d., "Census Families Time Series, 1931–2001"; 2017p, "Private households by household type, 2016 counts, Canada, provinces and territories, 2016 Census – 100% Data." http://www12.statcan.gc.ca/census-recensement/2016/dp-pd/hlt-fst/fam/Table.cfm?Lang=E&T=21&Geo=00&SP=1&view=1 (retrieved 7 February 2018).

## TABLE 9.1 The Traditional Nuclear Family and New Alternatives

| Traditional Nuclear Family | New Alternatives |
| --- | --- |
| Legally married | Never-married singlehood, non-marital cohabitation |
| With children | Voluntary childlessness |
| Two-parent | Single-parent (never married or previously married) |
| Permanent | Divorce, remarriage (including binuclear family involving joint custody, stepfamily, or "blended" family) |
| Male primary provider, ultimate authority | Egalitarian marriage (including dual-career and commuter marriage) |
| Sexually exclusive | Extramarital relationships (including sexually open marriage, swinging, and intimate friendships) |
| Heterosexual | Same-sex intimate relationships or households |
| Two-adult household | Multi-adult households (including multiple spouses, communal living, affiliated families, and multigenerational families) |

Source: Adapted from Eleanor D. Macklin, 1980. "Nontraditional Family Forms: A Decade of Research." *Journal of Marriage and the Family* 42: 906.

The discussion then turns to alternative family forms—how they are structured and how their frequency varies by class and sexual orientation. Finally, you will learn that although postindustrial families solve some problems, they are hardly an unqualified blessing. The chapter's concluding section considers the kinds of policies that might help alleviate some of the most serious concerns facing families today.

# FUNCTIONALISM AND THE NUCLEAR IDEAL
## FUNCTIONAL THEORY

For any society to survive, its members must cooperate economically. They must have babies. And they must raise offspring in an emotionally supportive environment so the offspring can learn the ways of the group and eventually operate as productive adults. Since the 1940s, functionalists have argued that the nuclear family is ideally suited to meet these challenges. In their view, the nuclear family provides a basis for five main functions: regulated sexual activity, economic cooperation, reproduction, socialization, and emotional support (Murdock, 1949: 1–22; Parsons, 1955).

Functionalists cite the pervasiveness of the nuclear family as evidence of its ability to perform these functions. To be sure, other family forms exist. **Polygamy** expands the nuclear unit "horizontally" by adding one or more spouses (almost always wives) to the household. Polygamy is still legally permitted in many less industrialized countries in Africa and Asia. However, the overwhelming majority of families are monogamous because they cannot afford to support several wives and many children. The **extended family** expands the nuclear family "vertically" by adding another generation—one or more of the spouses' parents—to the household. Extended families used to be common throughout the world. They still are in some places. In Canada, about 4 percent of families are multigenerational. However, according

**polygamy** Expands the nuclear family "horizontally" by adding one or more spouses (usually women) to the household.

**extended family** Expands the nuclear family "vertically" by adding another generation—one or more of the spouses' parents—to the household.

The idealized North American family of the 1950s

**marriage** Traditionally defined, is a socially approved, presumably long-term sexual and economic union between a man and a woman. It involves reciprocal rights and obligations between spouses and between parents and children.

to the functionalists, the basic building block of the extended family is the nuclear unit.

George Murdock was a functionalist who conducted a famous study of 250 mainly preliterate societies in the 1940s. Murdock wrote, "Either as the sole prevailing form of the family or as the basic unit from which more complex familial forms are compounded, [the nuclear family] exists as a distinct and strongly functional group in every known society" (Murdock, 1949: 2). Moreover, the nuclear family, Murdock continued, is everywhere based on **marriage**. He defined marriage as a socially approved, presumably long-term, sexual and economic union between a man and a woman. It involves rights and obligations between spouses and between spouses and their children.

## FUNCTIONS OF THE NUCLEAR FAMILY

Let's consider the five main functions of marriage and the nuclear family in more detail:

1. *Sexual regulation*. The nuclear family defines the boundaries within which legitimate sexual activity is permitted, thus making an orderly social life possible. Of course, sex is readily available outside marriage. Murdock found that only 22 percent of 250 mainly preliterate societies forbade or disapproved of premarital sex between non-relatives, and in more than half the societies, a married man could legitimately have an extramarital affair with one or more female relatives (Murdock, 1949: 5–6). It is hardly news that premarital and extramarital sex are common in postindustrial societies. So sex is not the primary motivation for marrying.

2. *Economic cooperation*. People marry also because "a man and a woman make an exceptionally efficient cooperating unit" (Murdock, 1949: 7). Historically, pregnancy and nursing have restricted women in their activities, whereas men possess superior strength. Therefore, women have traditionally performed lighter tasks close to home while men have specialized in lumbering, mining, quarrying, land clearing, house building, hunting, fishing, herding, and trade (Murdock, 1937). Thus, "marriage exists only when the economic and the sexual are united into one relationship, and this combination occurs only in marriage" (Murdock, 1949: 8).

3. *Reproduction*. Before the invention of modern contraception, sex often resulted in the birth of a baby. In pre-modern societies, children are an investment in the future. By the age of six or seven, children in such societies do some chores. Their economic value to the family increases as they mature. When children become adults, they often help support aging parents. Consequently, there is a big economic incentive to having children.

4. *Socialization*. The investment in children can be realized only if adults rear the young to maturity. This involves not only caring for them physically but also teaching them language, values, beliefs, skills, religion, and much else. Some functionalists regard socialization as the "basic and irreducible" function of the family (Parsons, 1955: 16).

5. *Emotional support*. Functionalists note that the nuclear family universally gives its members love, affection, and companionship. In the nuclear family, it is mainly the mother who is responsible for ensuring the family's emotional well-being. It falls on the father to take on the role of earning a living outside the family (Parsons, 1955: 23). The fact that he is the "primary provider" makes him the ultimate authority.

Does this functionalist account provide an accurate picture of family relations across history? To assess the adequacy of the theory, let's discuss the families in which the early functionalists themselves lived: families in urban and suburban middle-class North America in the 1950s.

## THE CANADIAN MIDDLE-CLASS FAMILY IN THE 1950s

As a description of family patterns in the 15 years after World War II, functionalism has its merits. During the Great Depression (1929–39) and World War II (1939–45), many Canadians were forced to postpone marriage because of widespread poverty, government-imposed austerity, and physical separation. After this ordeal, many Canadians wanted to settle down, have children, and enjoy the peace, pleasure, and security that family life seemed to offer. Conditions could not have been better for doing just that. The immediate postwar era was one of unparalleled optimism and prosperity. Real per capita income rose, as did the percentage of Canadians who owned their own homes. Laws passed out of necessity during World War II to encourage women to join the paid labour force were cancelled. Things were now supposed to return to "normal," meaning that women were supposed to go back to being housewives and men to being breadwinners.

As a result of these conditions, Canadians experienced a marriage boom (see Figure 9.2). Increasingly, Canadians lived in married-couple families. The proportion of "never married" Canadians decreased and the average age at first marriage dropped for both women and men (McVey and Kalbach, 1995: 225; see Figure 9.3). As we might expect, the marriage boom soon gave way to a baby boom. The average Canadian family had four children; nearly all married women stayed home to raise their children (Nikiforuk, 1999). In 1951, 90 percent of married men but only 11.2 percent of married women worked in the paid labour force. Most women engaged in what has been called an "orgy of domesticity" in the postwar years, devoting increasing attention to child-rearing and housework. They also became increasingly concerned with the emotional quality of family life as love and companionship became firmly established as the main motivations for marriage (Coontz, 1992: 23–41; Skolnick, 1991: 49–74).

### The 1950s: An Historical Anomaly

What many functionalists fail to appreciate is that the immediate postwar period was in many respects an historical anomaly. Trends in divorce, marriage, and child-bearing show a gradual *weakening* of the nuclear family from the second half of the nineteenth century until the mid-1940s, and continued weakening after the 1950s. Specifically, throughout the nineteenth century, the crude divorce rate rose slowly. The **crude divorce rate** is the number of divorces that occur in a year for every 1000 people in the population. Meanwhile, the crude marriage rate fell. The **crude marriage rate** is the number of marriages that occur in a year for every 1000 people in the population. (Remarkably, data on these indicators have not been published by Statistics Canada for years after 2008.) The total fertility rate also fell (see Figure 9.4). The **total fertility rate** is the average number of children that would be born to a woman over her lifetime if she had the same number of children as do women in each age cohort in a given year.

Canada's marriage rate started falling after 1946. The divorce rate started rising in the 1960s, when the law was changed to make it easier to divorce. The total fertility rate started falling after 1961. Thus, by the early 1960s, the earlier trends had reasserted themselves. Only the peculiar historical circumstances of the postwar years, noted above, temporarily reversed them. The big picture from the nineteenth century until the present is that of a gradually weakening nuclear family. The early functionalists, it seems, generalized too hastily from the families they knew best— their own (see Theories in Dispute, Is the Heterosexual, Monogamous Family Ideally Functional After All?).

**crude divorce rate** The number of divorces that occur in a year for every 1000 people in the population.

**crude marriage rate** The number of marriages that occur in a year for every 1000 people in the population.

**total fertility rate** The average number of children that would be born to a woman over her lifetime if she had the same number of children as do women in each age cohort in a given year.

**FIGURE 9.2  Crude Marriage Rate, Canada, 1921–2008**

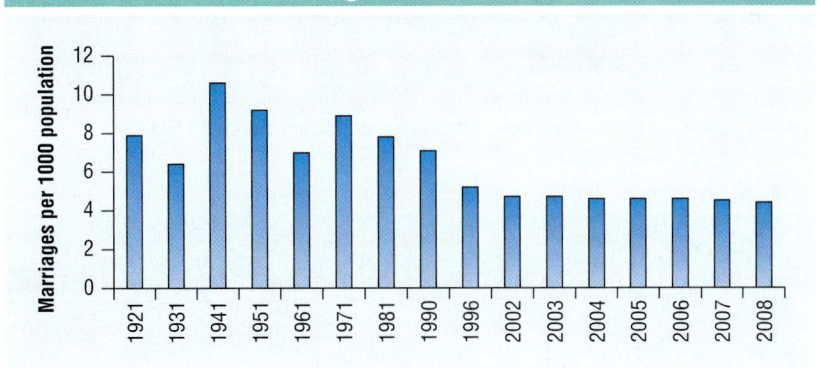

Sources: Adapted from the Statistics Canada products: 1992a. "Selected Marriage Statistics, 1921–1990," Catalogue No. 82-552, and *The Daily*, Catalogue No. 11-001; 2007, "Table 101-1002: Mean Age and Median Age of Males and Females, by Type of Marriage and Marital Status, Canada, Provinces and Territories, Annual"; 2013c, "Chart 6: Crude Marriage Rate and Crude Divorce Rate, Canada, 1926 to 2008."

**FIGURE 9.3  Average Age at First Marriage, Canada, 1921, 1970, and 2008**

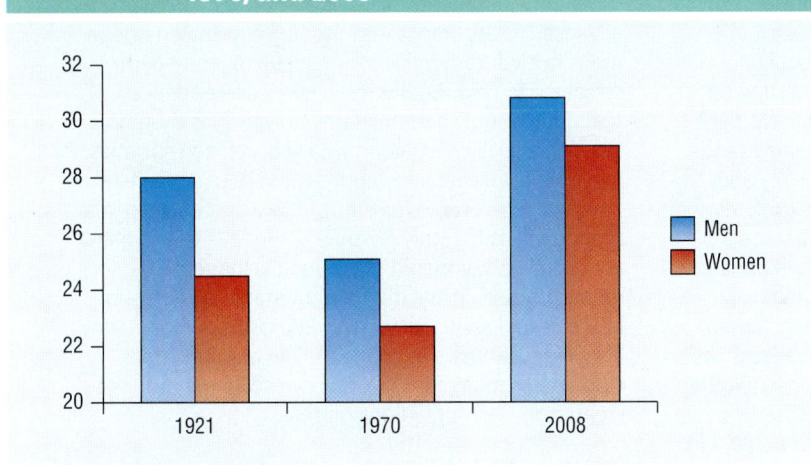

Sources: Statistics Canada. 2007, "Table 101-1002: Mean Age and Median Age of Males and Females, by Type of Marriage and Marital Status, Canada, Provinces and Territories, Annual"; Statistics Canada publications, 1992b, "Marriage and Conjugal Life in Canada, 1991"; 2003d, *The Daily*, Monday, June 2; and 2013c, "Mean Age and Median Age of Males and Females, by Marital Status, Canada, Provinces and Territories, 2005 to 2008." Special tabulation prepared by the Health Statistics Department.

## FIGURE 9.4  Total Fertility Rate, Canada, 1950–2017

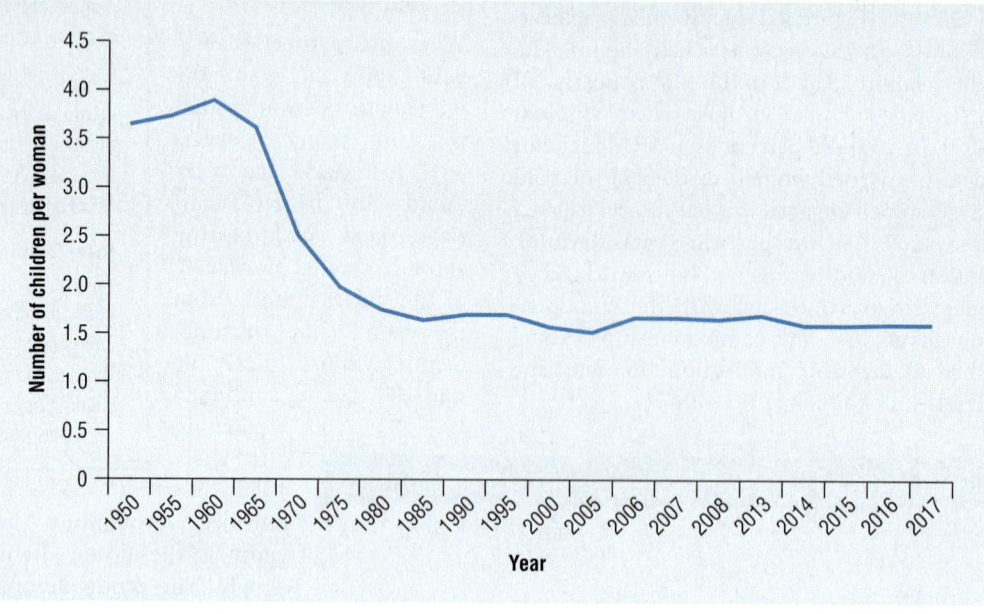

Source: *CIA World Factbook*. Various years. "Canada." https://www.cia.gov/library/publications/the-world-factbook/geos/ca.html (retrieved 7 February 2018).

# THEORIES IN DISPUTE

## Is the Heterosexual, Monogamous Family Ideally Functional After All?

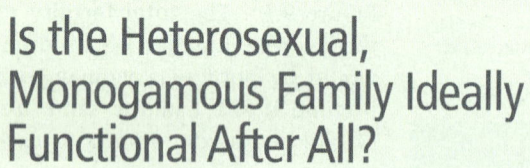

In 2012, an intriguing twist was added to the ongoing debate about whether the heterosexual, monogamous nuclear family is the ideal family form in modern societies. A team of researchers showed that about 85 percent of human societies have permitted polygamy, but heterosexual monogamy tends to take root as societies develop economically and socially because it solves some big social problems (Henrich, Boyd, and Richerson, 2012). In particular, societies in which polygamy is widespread experience intense competition for women because relatively few wealthy men marry a disproportionately large number of women. This circumstance leaves relatively few women for the non-wealthy men. Consequently, the rate of rape tends to be high in such societies. Moreover, because non-wealthy men must engage in intense competition for resources that enable them to attract women, rates of homicide, assault, robbery, and fraud are high too. Finally, societies that practise widespread polygamy are characterized by relatively high levels of gender inequality and woman abuse. In contrast, when heterosexual monogamy becomes a strong norm, gender inequality falls, as do crime rates and incidents of violent household conflict. In that sense it is highly functional.

In my judgment, this argument does nothing to advance the argument that the heterosexual, monogamous nuclear family is ideally functional in modern societies. To be sure, the researchers cite evidence that convincingly demonstrates polygamy is dysfunctional in socially and economically developed societies because it removes women from the pool of eligible partners. However, it does not follow that heterosexual monogamy is the only possible alternative to polygamy. For example, compared to polygamy, the replacement of heterosexual marriage by stable *common-law* heterosexual relationships and *homosexual* monogamy also increases the size of the female marriage pool. Apparently, many family forms can solve the problem created by widespread polygamy.

### Critical Thinking Questions
- What family forms other than those mentioned earlier could solve the polygamy problem?

Kody Brown has four wives and 18 children, all members of a pro-polygamy group of fundamentalist Mormons. They have allowed their lives to be documented in *Sister Wives* since 2010 because they want to legitimize polygamy as a reasonable lifestyle choice. Polygamy may indeed be a reasonable lifestyle choice for Kody Brown and his four wives. However, when entire societies allow polygamy, it can cause serious social problems that many alternative family forms can solve.

## Conflict and Feminist Theories

The nuclear family has become less prevalent since the nineteenth century because many of the traditional functions of the nuclear family have been eroded or partly taken over by other institutions. For example, the traditional division of labour, based on the physical capabilities and limitations of husband and wife, has weakened. That is because contraception and child-care services are now available, while demand for women to enter the paid labour force and pursue a higher education has increased. Because women are no longer tied to the home in the way they once were, part of the task of socialization has been taken over by schools, peer groups, and the mass media. Meanwhile, reproduction outside the nuclear family is possible because of the introduction of in vitro fertilization and other reproductive technologies. Thus, the traditional nuclear family has been in decline for more than a century because other institutions perform many of the economic, reproductive, and socialization functions that were formerly reserved for the nuclear family.

Conflict and feminist theorists argue that all of the institutional displacements just listed are responses to changes in power relations between women and men. The idea that power relations between women and men explain the prevalence of different family forms was first suggested by Engels, whose ideas on the subject were outlined in Chapter 8, Sexualities and Genders.

To recap: Engels argued that the traditional nuclear family emerged along with private property and inequalities of wealth (Engels, 1970 [1884]). Little inequality existed in pre-agricultural societies. Nomads, hunters and gatherers, cattle owners, and people who merely used small hand tools for planting and harvesting considered land common property. A family might graze their cattle or work on a particular plot of land for some time, even generations, but if the plot fell into disuse, another family had the right to use it. Substantial inequalities in wealth emerged only when people attached large animals, such as oxen, to plows and it became possible to farm large tracts of land. That was when private property began to be legally recognized. That was when some families began to amass wealth. And that was when men came to enjoy legal control of property and the wealth it generated.

Once legal control of property was concentrated in the hands of a man, wrote Engels, he became concerned about how to transmit it to his children, particularly his sons. How could a man safely pass on an inheritance, asked Engels? Only by controlling his wife sexually and economically. Economic control ensured that the man's property would not be squandered and would remain his and his alone. Sexual control, in the form of enforced female monogamy, ensured that his property would be transmitted only to *his* offspring. Engels concluded that only the elimination of private property and the creation of economic equality could bring an end to gender inequality and the traditional nuclear family. Inequality deriving from men's control of private property was the basis of the nuclear family in Engels's view, and the elimination of private property (communism) would spell its end.

Engels was right to note the long history of male economic and sexual domination in the traditional nuclear family. In 1900, any money a wife earned typically belonged to her husband. Until 1929, Canadian women did not enjoy the legal rights of a person. As recently as the 1950s, a Canadian wife could not rent a car, take a loan, or sign a contract without her husband's permission. It was only in the 1980s that it became illegal in Canada for a husband to rape his wife.

However, Engels was wrong to think that communism would eliminate gender inequality in the family. Gender inequality has been as common in societies that call themselves communist as in those that call themselves capitalist. For example, the Soviet Union left "intact the fundamental family structures, authority relations, and socialization patterns crucial to personality formation and sex-role differentiation. Only a genuine sexual revolution [or, as I prefer to call it, a *gender revolution*] could have shattered these patterns and made possible the real emancipation of women" (Lapidus, 1978: 7).

Because gender inequality exists in noncapitalist societies, most feminists believe something other than, or in addition to, capitalism accounts for gender inequality and the persistence of the traditional nuclear family. In their view, *patriarchy*—male dominance and norms justifying that dominance—is more deeply rooted in the economic, military, and cultural history of humankind than the classical Marxist account allows. For them, only a genuine gender revolution can alter this state of affairs.

Just such a revolution in family structures, authority relations, and socialization patterns picked up steam in Canada and other rich industrialized countries in the 1960s, although its roots extend back to the eighteenth century. As you will now learn, the revolution is evident in the rise of romantic love and happiness as bases for marriage, the rising divorce rate, and women's increasing control over reproduction through their use of contraceptives, among other factors. Let's first consider the sociology of mate selection.

# LO² POWER AND FAMILIES

## LOVE AND MATE SELECTION

Most Canadians take for granted that marriage ought to be based on love. Our assumption is evident, for example, in the way most popular songs celebrate love as the sole basis of long-term intimacy and marriage. Most of us view marriage devoid of love as tragic.

Yet in most societies throughout human history, love had little to do with marriage. Marriages were typically arranged by third parties, not by brides and grooms. The selection of marriage partners was based mainly on calculations intended to increase their families' prestige, economic benefits, and political advantages.

The idea that love should be important in the choice of a marriage partner first gained currency in eighteenth-century England with the rise of liberalism and individualism, philosophies that stressed the freedom of the individual over community welfare (Stone, 1977). The intimate linkage between love and marriage that we know today emerged only in the early twentieth century, when Hollywood and the advertising industry began to promote self-gratification on a grand scale. For these new spinners of fantasy and desire, an important aspect of self-gratification was heterosexual romance leading to marriage (Rapp and Ross, 1986).

Today, wherever individualism is highly prized, love has come to be defined as the essential basis for marriage.

Hollywood glamorized heterosexual romantic love and solidified the intimate linkage between love and marriage that we know today. Clark Gable and Vivien Leigh in *Gone with the Wind* (1939).

A survey of college undergraduates in 11 countries asked, "If a man (woman) had all the qualities you desired, would you marry this person if you were not in love with him (her)?" In the five developing countries, an average of 27.8 percent of students said they would marry someone they were not in love with if that person possessed all the qualities they were looking for in a partner. The comparable average for the five rich countries plus Brazil was 3.6 percent (Levine et al., 1995; see Figure 9.5).

You learned in Chapter 4, From Social Interaction to Social Organizations, that certain social factors influence who people fall in love with and marry. The resources people bring to the marriage market, demographic factors such as the ratio of men to women in one's community, and the constraints imposed by third parties continue to affect mate selection. However, mate selection is less constrained than it used to be. We can see clear evidence of this fact in the growing percentage of Canadians who consider themselves to be multi-ethnic (Figure 9.6). We also find a hint of this fact in the process of dating and mate selection on the Web (see Sociology and the Media, Race and Date Selection on the Web).

## MARITAL SATISFACTION

Just as mate selection came to depend more on romantic love over the years, so marital stability came to depend more on having a happy rather than merely a useful marriage. This change occurred because women in Canada and many other societies have become more autonomous, especially over the past half century. One aspect of the gender revolution that women are experiencing is that they are freer than ever to leave marriages in which they are unhappy.

One factor that contributed to women's autonomy was the legalization of birth control measures in Canada in 1969. The birth control

**FIGURE 9.5** Responses to the Question: "If a Man (Woman) Had All of the Other Qualities You Desired, Would You Marry This Person If You Were Not in Love with Him (Her)?"

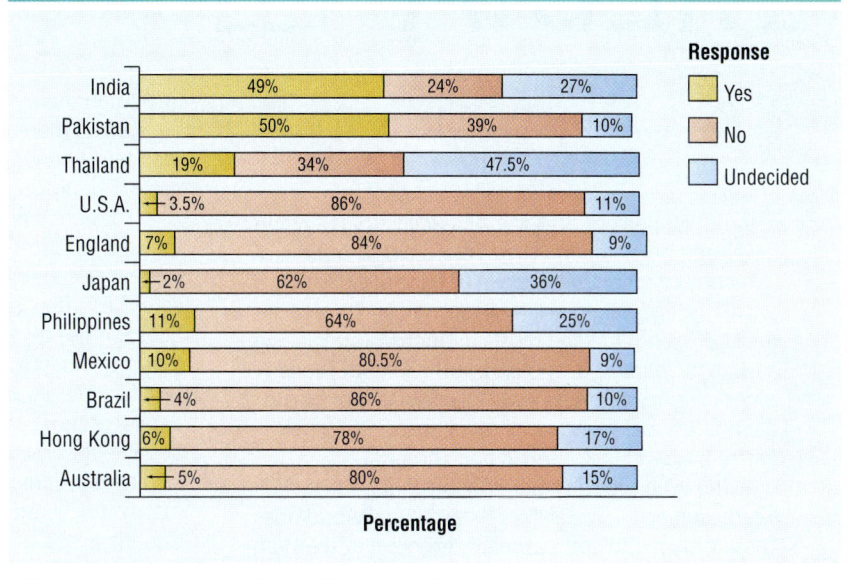

| Country | Yes | No | Undecided |
|---|---|---|---|
| India | 49% | 24% | 27% |
| Pakistan | 50% | 39% | 10% |
| Thailand | 19% | 34% | 47.5% |
| U.S.A. | 3.5% | 86% | 11% |
| England | 7% | 84% | 9% |
| Japan | 2% | 62% | 36% |
| Philippines | 11% | 64% | 25% |
| Mexico | 10% | 80.5% | 9% |
| Brazil | 4% | 86% | 10% |
| Hong Kong | 6% | 78% | 17% |
| Australia | 5% | 80% | 15% |

Note: Percentages may not add up to 100 because of rounding.

Source: Republished with permission of SAGE Publications, Inc., from R. Levine, S. Sato, T. Hashimoto, and J. Verma. (1995). "Love and Marriage in Eleven Cultures." *Journal of Cross-Cultural Psychology* Vol. 26 (5) pp. 554–71; permission conveyed through Copyright Clearance Center, Inc.

**FIGURE 9.6** Multi-Ethnic Canadians, Selected Groups, by Generation (percentage)

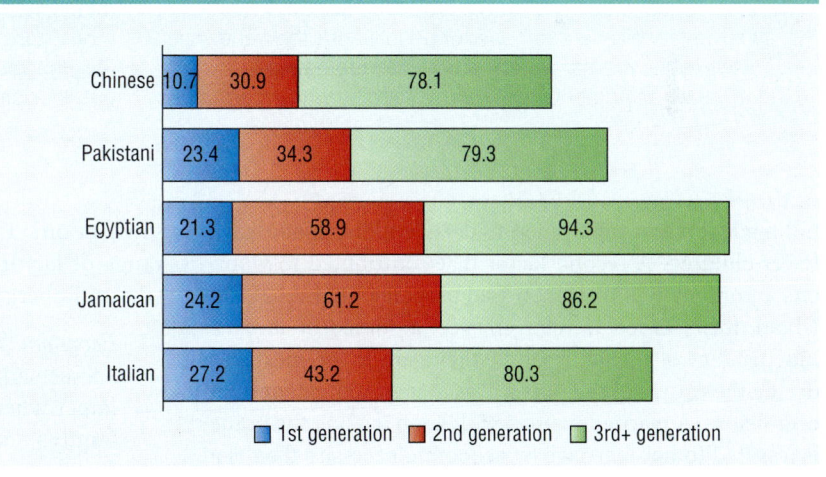

| Group | 1st generation | 2nd generation | 3rd+ generation |
|---|---|---|---|
| Chinese | 10.7 | 30.9 | 78.1 |
| Pakistani | 23.4 | 34.3 | 79.3 |
| Egyptian | 21.3 | 58.9 | 94.3 |
| Jamaican | 24.2 | 61.2 | 86.2 |
| Italian | 27.2 | 43.2 | 80.3 |

Note: The census asks each Canadian to specify one or more ethnic identities. One's ethnic identity is strongly influenced by the ethnic identity of one's parents. This graph shows the percentage of people in each generation of selected groups who indicated multiple ethnic identities. For example, 21.3 of first-Generation Egyptian Canadians had multiple ethnic identities, compared to 94.3 percent of 3rd+ generation Egyptian-Canadians. In all groups, the overwhelming majority of people think of themselves as multi-ethnic by the 3rd+ generation. This finding indicates a loosening of the ethnic constraint on mate selection over time.

Source: Statistics Canada. 2018i. "Ethnic Origin (279), Single and Multiple Ethnic Origin Responses (3), Generation Status (4), Age (12) and Sex (3) for the Population in Private Households of Canada, Provinces and Territories, Census Metropolitan Areas and Census Agglomerations, 2016 Census - 25% Sample Data." http://www12.statcan.gc.ca/census-recensement/2016/dp-pd/dt-td/Rp-eng.cfm?TABID=2&LANG=E&APATH=3&DETAIL=0&DIM=0&FL=A&FREE=0&GC=0&GK=0&GRP=1&PID=110528&PRID=10&PTYPE=109445&S=0&SHOWALL=0&SUB=0&Temporal=2017&THEME=120&VID=0&VNAMEE=&VNAMEF= (retrieved 8 February 2018).

# SOCIOLOGY AND THE MEDIA

## Race and Date Selection on the Web

Close to 40 percent of North American adults say they have used online dating sites. About a fifth of heterosexuals now meet their spouse or romantic partner online. Online dating still ranks second to "meeting through friends" as the most common way of finding a romantic partner or spouse but the help of friends is declining in importance as the popularity of online dating increases (Ansari with Klinenberg, 2015: 81; Baym, 2015: 115; Rosenfeld and Thomas, 2012).

The Web provides more opportunities for friendly interaction across racial lines than the real world does. Therefore, one might reasonably expect that the Web increases the likelihood that people will date and select mates across racial lines. This argument is consistent with the contact hypothesis, discussed in the Chapter 7 boxed feature, Theories in Dispute, From the Contact Hypothesis to Critical Race Theory.

Almost all of the research on the subject of online interracial dating comes from the United States. It finds that the Web actually tends to *reinforce* real-world racial divides, with a strong tendency to prefer dating and mating within one's racial group (Buggs, 2017). Only a few biracial categories of people buck the trend: Asian/white biracial women are viewed more favourably than any other category of women by white men and Asian men. Asian/white and Hispanic/white men are viewed more favourably than any other category of men by Asian women and Hispanic women, respectively (Curington, Lin, and Lundquist, 2015).

These findings may be valid only for countries like the United States that are deeply divided along racial lines. A rare study of interracial dating in nine European countries offers an intriguing finding that leads one to question the generalizability of the American studies (Potârcă and Mills, 2015). It turns out that the more racially heterogeneous a country is, the greater online daters' preference for interracial partners; it seems possible that racial heterogeneity in the real world increases the frequency of interracial online dating.

As you learned in Chapter 7, Race and Ethnicity, Canada is one of the world's most racially heterogeneous countries, and the level of heterogeneity is rising due to our high level of immigration. A hypothesis worthy of future research is that Canada provides an environment in which online daters are especially inclined to seek out partners from other races.

### Critical Thinking Questions

- How would you design a research project to determine whether online dating loosens racial and ethnic constraints on mate selection in Canada? Assume you have all the resources needed to carry out your project.

---

pill made it easier for women to delay childbirth and have fewer children. A second factor that contributed to women's autonomy was their increased participation in the paid labour force. Once women enjoyed a source of income independent of their husbands, they gained the means to decide the course of their own lives to a greater extent than ever before. A married woman with a job outside the home is less tied to her marriage by economic necessity than is a woman who works only at home. If a woman who works outside the home is deeply dissatisfied with her marriage, she can more easily leave. In addition, in 1968 and again in 1985, Canadian laws governing divorce were changed to make divorce easier.

## The Social Roots of Marital Satisfaction

If marital stability now depends largely on marital satisfaction, what are the main factors underlying marital satisfaction? The sociological literature provides a wide range of factors, four of which may be singled out here (Brym, Roberts, and Strohschein, 2018: 397-98):

1. *Economic forces.* Money issues are the most frequent subjects of family quarrels, and money issues loom larger when there isn't enough money to satisfy a family's needs and desires. Accordingly, marital satisfaction tends to fall and the divorce rate tends to rise as one moves down the socioeconomic hierarchy. The lower the social class and the lower the educational level of the spouses, the more likely it is that financial pressures will make them unhappy and the marriage unstable.

2. *Divorce laws.* Many surveys show that, on average, married people are happier than unmarried people are. Moreover, when people are free to end unhappy marriages and remarry, the average level of happiness

increases among married people. Thus, the level of marital happiness has increased in Canada over the past few decades, especially for wives. That is partly because it has become easier to get a divorce and more acceptable to remarry and create a **blended family**, which includes the children of one or both spouses from a previous marriage. In countries where getting a divorce is more difficult (e.g., Italy and Spain), husbands and wives tend to be less happy than in countries where getting a divorce is easier.

3. *The family life cycle.* Divorce is most common in the first five years of marriage. For marriages that last, marital satisfaction generally starts high, falls (especially for wives) when children are born, reaches a low point when children are in their teenage years, and rises again when children reach adulthood. Couples without children and parents whose children have left home (so-called *empty nesters*) enjoy the highest level of marital satisfaction. Parents who are just starting families or who have adult children living at home enjoy intermediate levels of marital satisfaction. Marital satisfaction is lowest during the "establishment" years, when children are attending school. Although most people get married at least partly to have children, it turns out that children, and especially teenagers, usually put big emotional and financial strains on families. These strains typically lower marital satisfaction.

4. *Housework and child care.* Marital happiness is higher among couples who have an equitable distribution of housework and child care. The farther couples are from an equitable sharing of domestic responsibilities, the more tension there is among all family members. Research finds that equitable sharing of household responsibilities tends to increase with spouses' level of education.

# DIVORCE

Before 1968, adultery was the only grounds for divorce in Canada, except in Nova Scotia, where cruelty was sufficient grounds even before Confederation (Morrison, 1987). The Divorce Act of 1968, the first federal divorce statute, expanded the grounds under which a divorce could be granted. The amendment of Canada's Divorce Act in 1985 allowed only one ground for divorce—marital breakdown, defined in three ways: (1) the spouses have lived apart for one year, (2) one of the spouses has committed an act of adultery, (3) one spouse has treated the other with mental or physical cruelty. Today, a spouse seeking divorce no longer has to prove grounds. Instead, a marriage is legally "dissolved" because the relationship is "irretrievably broken." Following these amendments, the divorce rate reached a historic high in 1987 but has since declined. Some 41 percent of Canadian marriages now end in divorce.

## Economic Effects

Women's income usually falls after divorce, while men's income generally stays about the same (Le Bourdais et al., 2016). That is because husbands tend to earn more than wives do, children typically live with their mothers after divorce, and child-support payments are often inadequate.

> **blended family** Includes the children of one or both spouses from a previous marriage.
>
> **child support** Money paid by the noncustodial parent to the custodial parent for the purpose of supporting the children of a separated marital, cohabiting, or sexual relationship.

In the past, Canadian laws regarding the division of marital assets on divorce and the awarding of alimony contributed to women's declining living standards after divorce. For example, in the early 1970s, Irene Murdoch, a farm wife, claimed that her labour over 15 years had earned her a share in the family farm. However, the Supreme Court of Canada ruled that her work was simply that of an "ordinary farm wife" and did not entitle her to share in the property that she and her husband had accumulated during their marriage (Steel, 1987: 159).

Although all Canadian provinces and territories now have laws requiring spouses to share assets in the event of marital breakdown, the precise definition of what constitutes a family asset varies and creates inconsistencies across jurisdictions (Dranoff, 2001: 257). In addition, although the monetary value of tangible family assets such as money in the bank or a house can be calculated and shared, the valuable "new property" today is the earning power of a professional degree, highly paid employment, work experience, a skilled trade, or other human capital. On divorce, the wife may receive an equal share of tangible property, but that does not usually result in her beginning post-divorce life on an equal footing with her former husband, especially if she retains physical custody of the couple's children and if she sacrificed her education and career so that he could earn a college or university degree.

**Child support** is money paid by the non-custodial parent to the custodial parent to support the children of a separated marital, cohabiting, or sexual relationship. Under the Divorce Act, either parent can be ordered to pay child support. However, because mothers retain custody in the great majority of cases—and because women are more likely to be economically disadvantaged in employment—those ordered to pay child support are usually fathers.

Every jurisdiction in Canada requires parents to support their children following separation or divorce. However, court orders do not guarantee that child support will be paid. In practice, orders for child and spousal support have often been difficult to enforce, and default rates have been high. All Canadian provinces and territories now have their own programs to protect against nonpayment of child support. Nonetheless, the problem of "deadbeat parents" (especially fathers) remains serious.

### Emotional Effects

Although divorce enables spouses to leave unhappy marriages, questions have been raised about the emotional consequences of divorce for children. Some scholars claim that divorcing parents are simply trading the well-being of their children for their own happiness. What does research say about this issue?

Three factors account for much of the distress among children of divorce:

1. *A high level of parental conflict.* A high level of parental conflict creates long-term distress among children and is the most important factor with negative consequences for the emotional health of children. Divorce without parental conflict does children much less harm. In fact, children in divorced families have a higher level of well-being on average than do children in high-conflict intact families. The effect of parental conflict on the long-term well-being of children is substantially greater than the effect of any other factor.

2. *A decline in living standards.* By itself, the economic disadvantage experienced by most children in divorced families influences their emotional well-being. Children of divorce who do not experience a decline in living standards suffer less harm.

3. *The absence of a parent.* Children of divorce often lose a parent as a role model and a source of emotional support, practical help, and supervision. By itself, this factor affects children's emotional well-being. Some non-custodial parents have contact with their children after divorce, but such contact helps the children emotionally only if the parents have a cooperative relationship. If conflict persists between the parents, time spent with the non-custodial parent doesn't help the child (Sobolewski and King, 2005).

In sum, claiming that divorcing parents selfishly trade the well-being of their children for their own happiness is an exaggeration. A high level of parental conflict is the biggest danger to the emotional well-being of children. It can have negative consequences for them even in adulthood. In high-conflict marriages, divorce can benefit children as long as the conflict does not persist post-divorce. Contact with the non-custodial parent and the maintenance of pre-divorce living standards also have positive effects on a child's emotional well-being, although these benefits can be wiped out if a high level of parental conflict persists.

## REPRODUCTIVE CHOICE

You have seen that the power women gained from working in the paid labour force put them in a position to leave a marriage if it made them deeply unhappy. Another aspect of the gender revolution women are experiencing is that they are increasingly able to decide what happens in the marriage if they stay. For example, women now have more say over whether they will have children and, if so, when they will have them and how many they will have.

Children are increasingly expensive to raise. They no longer give the family economic benefits, as they did on the family farm. Most women want to work in the paid labour force, many of them to pursue a career. As a result, most women decide to have fewer children, to have them farther apart, and to have them at an older age. Some decide to have none at all.

Women's reproductive decisions are carried out by means of contraception and abortion. Abortion was declared a criminal offence in Canada in 1892. In the 1960s, an abortion reform movement spearheaded by Dr. Henry Morgentaler urged the repeal of abortion laws that, in his words, "compelled the unwilling to bear the unwanted" (quoted in Dranoff, 2001: 16). In 1969, the law was changed to permit "therapeutic abortion" if performed by a physician in an accredited hospital and if a three-member committee certified that the continuation of the pregnancy would likely endanger the health of the mother.

In 1988, the Supreme Court of Canada struck down the law on abortion on the grounds that it contravened a woman's right to control her own reproductive life and, as such, contravened her constitutionally protected guarantees to security of her person. In 1989, the Supreme Court also unanimously determined that the civil law in Quebec, the Quebec Charter, and the common law do not protect fetal life or interests. In 1993, the Supreme Court of Canada struck down legislation that banned abortion clinics. Today, abortion clinics outside hospitals operate in most provinces and abortions are available in hospitals in all provinces and territories except Prince Edward Island.

A minority of Canadians continue to express opposition to abortion.

In 2015, 100 104 Canadian women obtained abortions (Abortion Rights Coalition of Canada, 2017). On a global scale, data on the abortion rate is available for 61 countries. Canada ranks 26th at 15.2 abortions per 1000 women between the ages of 15 and 44. Russia tops the list at 43.7 (United Nations, 2008).

In 1998, 36 percent of Canadians agreed that abortion should be permitted whenever a woman decides she wants one, but by 2016 that figure had increased to 57 percent. Another 21 percent of Canadians agreed abortion should be permitted only under certain circumstances, such as rape. Eight percent believed abortion should be permitted only when the mother's life is in danger and 3 percent said it should not be permitted under any circumstance (Russell, 2016). Attitudes toward abortion vary by age, with younger Canadians more likely than older Canadians to approve of the availability of legal abortion for any reason.

Right-to-life versus pro-choice activists have been clashing since the 1970s. Right-to-life activists object to the decriminalization of abortion; pro-choice activists want the current situation preserved. Both groups have tried to influence public opinion and lawmakers to achieve their aims. A few extreme right-to-life activists (almost all men) have resorted to violence.

## HOUSEWORK AND CHILD CARE

As we have seen, women's increased participation in the paid labour force, their rising participation in the system of higher education, and their greater control over reproduction transformed several areas of family life. Despite this far-ranging gender revolution, however, one domain remains more resistant to change: housework, child care, and senior care.

Men take a more active role in the day-to-day running of the household than they used to. Still, according to the most recent census data, Canadian women are two-and-a-half times more likely than men to devote 30 hours or more to unpaid household work every week. Men were nearly twice as likely as women to devote no time to such work (Table 9.2). Many women still work a "double shift"—one in the paid labour force and one at home (Hochschild with Machung, 1989).

Even these figures do not reveal the whole picture, however. Men tend to do low-stress chores that can often wait a day or a week. These jobs include mowing the lawn, repairing the car, and painting the fence. Although fathers of young children under the age of five are often happy to play with their children, they spend less time than mothers do providing more time-intensive forms of child care, such as feeding, washing, dressing, and medical care. In general, women tend to do the repetitive, higher stress chores that cannot wait. In short, the picture falls short of a revolution (Harvey, Marshall, and Frederick, 1991).

Two main factors shrink the gender gap in housework, child care, and senior care. First, the smaller the difference between the husband's and the wife's earnings, the more equal the division of household labour. Women who earn relatively high incomes use some of their money to pay outsiders to do domestic work. In addition, such women are able to translate earning power into domestic influence. Their increased financial status enables them to get their husbands to do more around the house.

Attitude is the second factor that shrinks the gender gap in domestic labour. The more the husband and wife agree that there *should* be equality in the household division of labour, the more equality there is. Seeing eye to eye on this issue is often linked to both spouses having a postsecondary education (Greenstein, 1996). Thus, if greater equality is going to exist between men and women in doing household chores, two things have to happen: There must be greater equality between men and women in the paid labour force, and broader cultural acceptance of the need for gender equality.

**TABLE 9.2  Unpaid Housework in Canada for Women and Men over the Age of 14 (percentage)**

|  | Women | Men |
|---|---|---|
| No hours | 7 | 12 |
| Fewer than 5 hours | 18 | 30 |
| 5 to 14 hours | 31 | 34 |
| 15 to 29 hours | 24 | 16 |
| 30 or more hours | 20 | 8 |
| Total | 100 | 100 |

Note: These data are for 2006. Statistics Canada has not collected data on domestic labour since then.

Source: Statistics Canada. 2010f. "Unpaid Work (20), Age Groups (9) and Sex (3) for the Population 15 Years and Over of Canada, Provinces, Territories, Census Divisions and Census Sub-divisions, 2006 Census—20% Sample Data."

"Yes, this is a two career household. Unfortunately I have both careers."

## SPOUSAL VIOLENCE

About 12 percent of police-reported violent crime in Canada involves spousal violence, and 83 percent of victims of spousal violence are women. Women are three times as likely as men are to suffer an injury, five times as likely to require medical attention, and five times as likely to report that the violence they experienced caused them to fear for their lives. Compared with men, women are more likely to report being beaten, choked, or threatened with a gun or knife, or having these weapons used against them. Compared with women, men are more likely to report being slapped, having something thrown at them, or being kicked, bitten, or hit (Bunge, 2000; Statistics Canada, 2009b).

Three main types of spousal violence exist (Johnson and Ferraro, 2000):

1. *Common couple violence* occurs when partners have an argument and one partner lashes out physically at the other. For a couple that engages in this type of violence, violent acts are unlikely to occur often, escalate over time, or be severe. Both partners are about equally likely to engage in common couple violence, regardless of their gender.
2. *Intimate terrorism* is part of a general desire of one partner to control the other. Where one partner engages in intimate terrorism, violent acts are likely to occur often, escalate over time, and be severe. Among heterosexual couples, the aggressor is usually the man.
3. *Violent resistance* is the third main type of domestic violence. Among heterosexual couples, it typically involves a woman violently defending herself against a man who has engaged in intimate terrorism.

### Gender Inequality and Spousal Violence

For heterosexual couples, spousal violence is associated with the level of gender equality in the family and in the larger society. The higher the level of gender inequality, the greater the frequency of spousal violence. Severe wife assault is therefore more common in lower-class, less highly educated families in which gender inequality tends to be high and men are likely to believe that male domination is justified. Severe wife abuse is also more common among couples who witnessed their mothers being abused and who were themselves abused when they were children, although research suggests that these socialization factors are considerably less influential than was once believed (Gelles, 1997). Still, male domination in both childhood socialization and current family organization increases the likelihood of severe wife assault.

Wife assault is also associated with gender inequality in the larger society (Brym, 2018c; Straus, 1994). As women and men become more equal in the larger society, wife assault declines. I conclude that for heterosexual couples, the incidence of domestic violence is highest where a big power imbalance between men and women exists, where norms justify the male domination of women, and, to a lesser extent, where early socialization experiences predispose men to behave aggressively toward women.

Summing up, conflict theorists and feminists have performed a valuable sociological service by emphasizing the importance of power relations in structuring family life. A substantial body of research shows that the gender revolution that started half a century ago has influenced the way we select mates, our reasons for being satisfied or dissatisfied with marriage, our propensity to divorce, the reproductive choices women make, the distribution of housework and child care, variations in the rate of spousal violence—in short, all aspects of family life. As you will now learn, the gender revolution has also created a much greater diversity of family forms.

## LO³ FAMILY DIVERSITY

### HETEROSEXUAL COHABITATION

About 90 percent of Canadians marry at least once, but marriage is becoming less important for many Canadians. Even in 1995, when asked, "In order for you to be happy in life, is it very important, important, not very important, or not at all important to be married?" just two-thirds of Canadian women rated marriage as important or very important. Younger Canadians were less likely than older Canadians to consider marriage important or very important. Those living in Quebec were markedly less likely to do so: 53 percent of women and 59 percent of men in Quebec considered marriage important or very important (Wu, 2000: 65–66). And although living in a common-law relationship may be a prelude to marriage for some people, for others it has become an alternative to marriage.

Since the Canadian census first started collecting information on cohabitation in 1981, the number of cohabiting people 15 years of age and older has increased dramatically. The proportion of common-law families in Canada nearly quadrupled between 1981 and 2016—from 5.6 percent to 21.3 percent of all families. In Quebec, the 2016 figure was 39.8 percent (Statistics Canada, 2017m). A majority of women outside Quebec and three-quarters of women in Quebec believe it is acceptable for couples to live together when they have no intention of making a long-term commitment and are simply sexually attracted to each other. Younger women and women in Quebec are particularly likely to voice such approval (Wu, 2000: 59).

### SAME-SEX UNIONS

In 2001, the Netherlands became the first country to legalize same-sex marriage. By the end of 2017, 31 countries (nationwide or in some parts) had followed suit. Canada did so in 2005. In 2016, there were 72 880 same-sex families in Canada, 0.9 percent of the families in the country. In one-third of

## FIGURE 9.7 Same-Sex Unions in Canada, 2001–16

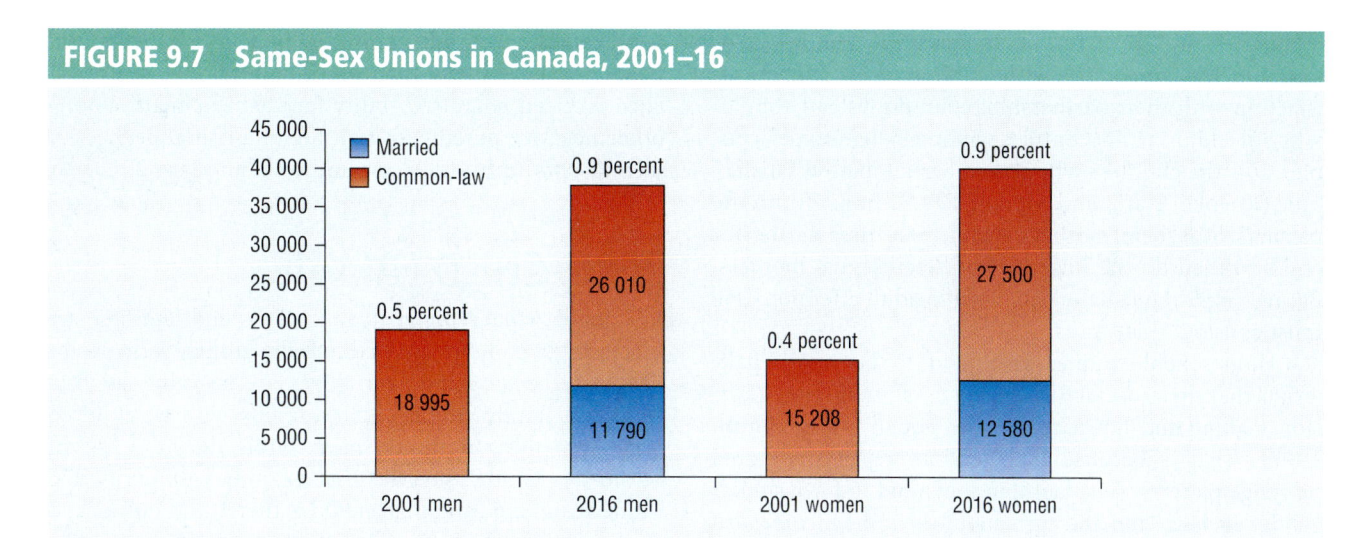

| Category | 2001 men | 2016 men | 2001 women | 2016 women |
|---|---|---|---|---|
| Married | — | 11 790 | — | 12 580 |
| Common-law | 18 995 | 26 010 | 15 208 | 27 500 |
| Percent of families | 0.5 percent | 0.9 percent | 0.4 percent | 0.9 percent |

Note: The figures at the top of each bar indicate the percentage of families in the category. For example, the second bar from the left says that in 2016, same-sex families involving men represented 0.9 percent of all families involving men. There were no same-sex marriages in 2001 because Canada recognized same-sex marriage only in 2005.

Source: Statistics Canada. 2017m. "Marital status and opposite- and same-sex status by sex for persons aged 15 and over living in private households for both sexes, total, presence and age of children, 2001 counts, Canada, provinces and territories, 2001 Census – 100% Data." http://www12.statcan.gc.ca/census-recensement/2016/dp-pd/hlt-fst/fam/Table.cfm?Lang=E&T=11&Geo=00&SP=1&view=4&sex=1&presence=1 (retrieved 8 February 2018).

same-sex families, the spouses were married. In the remainder, they were living common-law (see Figure 9.7).

Despite continuing opposition to same-sex marriage, the ultimate direction of change in many parts of the world is clear. Often amid controversy, the legal and social definition of "family" is being broadened to include cohabiting same-sex partners in long-term relationships. This change reflects the fact that most homosexuals, like most heterosexuals, want a long-term, intimate relationship with another adult (Chauncey, 2005).

### Raising Children in Homosexual Families

Some same-sex couples raise children who are (1) the offspring of previous heterosexual marriages, (2) adopted, or (3) result from artificial insemination.

Some people believe that children brought up in homosexual families develop a confused sexual identity, exhibit a tendency to become homosexuals themselves, and suffer discrimination from children and adults in the "straight" community. A growing body of literature, mostly on lesbian families, suggests the contrary.

Research suggests that children who grow up in homosexual families are much like children who grow up in heterosexual families (Orgibet, Le Heuzey, and Mouren, 2008). For example, a 14-year American study assessed 25 young adults who were the offspring of lesbian families and 21 young adults who were the offspring of heterosexual families (Tasker and Golombok, 1997). The researchers found that the two groups were equally well adjusted and displayed little difference in sexual orientation.

A review of French research on the subject found no difference between children of lesbian mothers and those of heterosexual parents in child development, sexual orientation, gender identity, gender role behavior, emotional/behavioral development, social relationships, and cognitive functioning. In French studies of gay fathers, no differences in sexual orientation, socialization, or psychological outcomes were found between children of gay fathers and children of heterosexual fathers (Fond, Franc, and Purper-Ouakil, 2012).

Homosexual and heterosexual families do differ in some respects, and those differences seem to favour

In 2002, in a precedent-setting move hailed by gay rights activists as the first of its kind in the world, full parental rights were extended to same-sex couples in Quebec. In addition, same-sex couples were granted the same status and obligations as heterosexual married couples when they entered into a civil union. Here, lesbians react as the Quebec legislature passes the law.

children who grow up in homosexual families. For example, lesbian couples with children record higher satisfaction with their partnerships than do lesbian couples without children. In contrast, among heterosexual couples, it is the childless who record higher marital satisfaction (Koepke, Hare, and Moran, 1992). In addition, the partners of lesbian mothers spend more time caring for children than do the husbands of heterosexual mothers. Because children usually benefit from adult attention, one must consider this a plus.

Homosexual couples also tend to be more egalitarian than heterosexual couples are, sharing most decision making and household duties equally (Rosenbluth, 1997). That is because they tend to reject traditional marriage patterns. The fact that they tend to have similar gender socialization and earn about the same income also encourages equality (Kurdek, 1996; Reimann, 1997). In sum, available research suggests being raised in a lesbian family has few if any negative consequences for the children and some benefits over and above being raised in a heterosexual family (Balkissoon, 2011; Foster, 2006; Wolpert, 2012).

## LONE-PARENT FAMILIES

During the first half of the twentieth century, lone-parent families were generally the result of the death of one parent. Today, solo parenting is usually the product of separation or divorce, after which child custody is typically granted to mothers. In 2016, more than 13 percent of Canadian families were headed by a lone parent and more than 80 percent of those families were headed by women.

Poverty is far more prevalent among female-headed single-parent families than among any other type of family. The poverty rate in female-headed single-parent families is more than double the rate in male-headed single-parent families. Children who grow up in low-income households are more likely than other children are to experience reduced cognitive ability and achievement, among other negative outcomes, with lifelong consequences for income and health (de Boer, Rothwell, and Lee, 2013).

## ZERO-CHILD FAMILIES

In Canada, what I prefer to call "zero-child families" are increasingly common. My admittedly clumsy term seems necessary because the alternatives are so value-laden: a "childless family" implies that a family without children lacks something it should have, while the more recent "child-free family" suggests that a family without a child is unencumbered and that a child is therefore a burden. To maintain neutrality, I resort to clumsiness.

Roughly a fifth of women between the ages of 40 and 44 have never given birth (Lamanna and Riedmann, 2003: 369). To explain this fact, we must first recognize that not having a child may be the result of circumstances beyond a couple's control. For example, one or both partners may be infertile, and some evidence suggests that infertility is a growing issue, perhaps because of chemical pollutants in the air and water. It seems that not having a child is more often a matter of choice, however, and the main reasons for the increasing prevalence of zero-child families are the rising cost of raising a child and the growth of attractive alternatives.

Just how expensive are children? In 2015, the best estimate of the average cost of raising a Canadian child up to the day before his or her nineteenth birthday was $253 954 (Brown, 2015). Add the cost of college or university and that is a lot of money that could be spent on investments, the couple's own education, and other desirable things. Mothers bear most of the cost of lost economic opportunities. Usually, they are the ones whose careers are disrupted when they decide to stay home to raise children and who lose income, benefits, and pension payments in the process.

Couples also incur non-economic costs when they have a child, the most important of which is stress. The birth of a child requires that couples do more work in the home, give up free time and time alone together, develop an efficient daily routine, and divide responsibilities. All of this adds sources of disagreement and tension to daily life, so it is little wonder that marital satisfaction declines with a child in the house, as noted earlier.

Alternative attractions decrease the desire of some couples to have a child. People with high income, high education, and professional and managerial occupations are most likely to have zero-child families. Such people tend to place an especially high value on mobility, careers, and leisure-time pursuits. Usually, they are neither frustrated nor unhappy that they do not have a child. Despite their tendency to feel negatively stereotyped as "selfish," they tend to be more satisfied with their marriage than are couples with a child (Lamanna and Riedmann, 2003: 380).

More than 80 percent of Canadian lone parent families are headed by women.

## MIXED-RACE FAMILIES: A SYMBOLIC INTERACTIONIST APPROACH

In 1633, Samuel de Champlain, the founder of New France (later Quebec), said this to his Indigenous allies: "Our young men will marry your daughters, and we shall become one people" (quoted in Bascaramurty, 2018). Nearly four centuries later, we remain far from Champlain's vision. Although the number of mixed-race families in Canada is growing, I estimate that in 2018 they comprised about 6 percent of all Canadian families—more than 10 percent in Vancouver and Toronto (based on Statistics Canada, 2016c). As symbolic interactionism would lead us to expect, members of these families face unique issues negotiating their identity and raising their children because the meaning they attach to their racial status differs from the meaning that others commonly attach to it.

Children of mixed-race families often think of themselves as Canadian but many others don't see them that way. "You walk into a room full of strangers," said a young mixed-race Edmonton woman who participated in one study, "and all they see is a brown person. And then they...want to know all about your race and stuff. But then it's almost anti-climactic when you're saying 'well, I'm Canadian.'" (quoted in Paragg, 2015: 22). Faced with the frequent demand to, in effect, justify their Canadianness, many children of mixed-race couples face contradictory pressures: they may feel that their brown-ness is perfectly Canadian while others repeatedly send the message that "Canadian" should be associated with "white." Consequently, by the time they are adults and have to answer census questions on ethnic identity, few mixed-race people select "Canadian." The great majority of people who say they are of Canadian ethnicity in the census have French or English as a mother tongue, and their parents were born in Canada. This may change, however, because young Canadians with mixed-race parents seem to be increasingly inclined to insist that they are Canadian when asked the "What are you?" question. By doing so, they are challenging the prevailing notion that "Canadian" must be associated with "white" (Paragg, 2015).

Mixed-race couples commonly experience tension when in public—people routinely stare at them as if they are a curiosity—and their children are still frequent victims of racial slurs in the schoolyard, at least in schoolyards with relatively few such children (Walji, 2017). As a Winnipeg study showed, parents in such families may be called upon to help their children cope with everything from discrimination in public settings to grandparents who do not value relationships with them. In families where one parent is white and the other is non-white, young children sometimes internalize the dominant societal view that white is inherently superior (Kouritzin, 2016; Walji, 2017).

## LO4 APPLICATION OF MAJOR SOCIOLOGICAL THEORIES

See Theories at a Glance, Families.

## THEORIES AT A GLANCE

### Families

| Theory | Main Question | Application |
|---|---|---|
| Functionalism | How do social structures and the values underlying them contribute to social stability? | For any society to survive, its members must cooperate economically. They must have babies. And they must raise offspring in an emotionally supportive environment so the offspring can learn the ways of the group and eventually operate as productive adults. Since the 1940s, functionalists have argued that the nuclear family—a cohabiting man and woman who maintain a socially approved sexual relationship and have at least one child—is ideally suited to meet these challenges. In their view, the nuclear family provides a basis for five main social functions: regulated sexual activity, economic cooperation, reproduction, socialization, and emotional support. Functionalists cite the supposed pervasiveness of the nuclear family as evidence of its ability to perform these functions. |

*(Continued)*

| | | |
|---|---|---|
| Conflict theory | How does the structure of inequality between privileged groups seeking to maintain their advantages and subordinate groups seeking to increase theirs lead to conflict and often to social change? | According to conflict theorists, rising demand for women to pursue a higher education and enter the paid labour force, together with the availability of contraception, child-care services, and reproduction outside the nuclear family have altered the traditional division of labour between husband and wife and, more generally, power relations between women and men. |
| Symbolic interactionism | How do people communicate to make their social settings meaningful, thus helping to create their social circumstances? | Mixed-race families face unique issues negotiating their identity and raising their children because the meaning they attach to their racial status typically differs from the meaning that others commonly attach to it. For example, children with mixed-race parents commonly think of themselves as Canadian but others tend to equate "Canadian" with "white." Consequently, such children are often asked where they come from, making them feel as if they do not belong. This feeling is reinforced by racial discrimination, sometimes from members of the extended family; in mixed-race families with a white parent, it can even lead to young children developing the view that whites are superior to non-whites. |
| Feminism | How do social conventions maintain male dominance and female subordination, and how do these conventions get overturned? | Like conflict theorists, feminist theorists highlight change in power relations between women and men as the driving force behind change in family structures. However, unlike Marxist-inspired conflict theorists, most feminist theorists think these changes have less to do with class relations than with the gender revolution in patriarchy that has been taking place since the 1960s. |

## LO5 FAMILY POLICY

Having discussed several aspects of the decline of the traditional nuclear family and the proliferation of diverse family forms, I can now return to the big question posed at the beginning of this chapter: Is the decline of the nuclear family a bad thing for society? Said differently, do two-parent families—particularly those with stay-at-home moms—provide the kind of discipline, role models, help, and middle-class lifestyle that children need to stay out of trouble with the law and grow up to become well-adjusted, productive members of society? Conversely, are family forms other than the traditional nuclear family the main source of teenage crime, poverty, welfare dependency, and other social ills?

The answer suggested by research is clear: yes and no (Brown, 2010; McLanahan, Tach, and Schneider, 2013). Yes, the decline of the traditional nuclear family can be a source of many social problems. No, it doesn't have to be that way.

The United States is a good example of how social problems can emerge from nuclear family decline. Sweden is a good example of how such problems can be averted. As Table 9.3 shows, Sweden leads the United States in 4 out of 5 measures of nuclear family decline. Swedes tend to get married at a much older age than Americans do. In Sweden, the out-of-marriage birth rate is about 16 percent higher than in the United States. The number of one-parent households with children under the age of 18 is around 9 percent higher. And the number of women with children under the age of 3 who are in the paid labour force is approximately 18 percent higher.

Significantly, however, on 4 out of 5 measures of children's well-being, Sweden leads the United States. Because the Swedish state spends about two-and-a-half times more on family support than the American state does, the poverty rate for children and the infant mortality rate are less than half the comparable American rates. Overall, then, the decline of the traditional nuclear family has gone farther in Sweden than in the United States, but children are much better off on average. How is this possible?

One explanation is that Sweden has something the United States lacks: a substantial family support policy. When a child is born in Sweden, a parent is entitled to a year of parental leave at 80 percent of his or her salary and an additional 90 days at a flat rate. Fathers can take 10 days of leave with pay when the baby is born. Parents are entitled to free consultations at "well-baby clinics." Like all citizens of Sweden, they receive free health care from the state-run system. Temporary parental benefits

### TABLE 9.3 The "Decline" of the Nuclear Family and the Well-Being of Children: The United States and Sweden Compared

| Indicators of Nuclear Family "Decline" | United States | Sweden | #1 "Decline" |
|---|---|---|---|
| **Median Age at First Marriage** | | | |
| Men | 29.7 | 35.8 | Sweden |
| Women | 27.8 | 33.3 | Sweden |
| Non-marital birth rate | 38.5 | 54.6 | Sweden |
| One-parent households with children aged < 18 as % of all households with children aged <18 | 27.4 | 18.2 | U.S. |
| Percentage of mothers with children aged < 3 in labour force | 54.2 | 71.9 | Sweden |
| **Indicators of Child Well-Being** | **United States** | **Sweden** | **#1 "Well-Being"** |
| Mean reading performance score at age 15 | 498 | 483 | U.S. |
| Percentage of children in poverty | 20.0 | 9.1 | Sweden |
| Public spending on families as a percentage of GDP | 1.2 | 3.1 | Sweden |
| Infant mortality rate | 5.8 | 2.5 | Sweden |
| Suicide rate for children aged 15–24 (per 100 000) | 12.5 | 9.5 | Sweden |

Source: From BRYM/ROBERTS/STROHSCHEIN/LIE. Sociology: Your Compass for a New World, 6E. © 2019 Nelson Education Ltd. Reproduced by permission. www.cengage.com/permissions.

are available for parents with a sick child under the age of 12. One parent can take up to 60 days off per sick child per year at 80 percent of salary. All parents can send their children to heavily government-subsidized, high-quality daycare facilities. Finally, Sweden offers its citizens generous direct cash payments based on the number of children in each family.*

Among industrialized countries, the United States stands at the other extreme. Since 1993, a parent has been entitled to 12 weeks of *unpaid* parental leave. Nearly 15 percent of Americans have no health care insurance, and under the Trump government's reforms, that percentage will increase significantly in the coming years. Health care is at a low standard for many millions more. There is no system of state daycare and no direct cash payments to families based on the number of children they have. The value of the dependant deduction on income tax has fallen nearly 50 percent in current dollars since the 1940s. Thus, when an unwed Swedish woman has a baby, she knows she can rely on state institutions to maintain her standard of living and help give her child an enriching social and educational environment. When an unwed American woman has a baby, she is pretty much on her own. She stands a good chance of

Painting class in a state-subsidized daycare facility in Stockholm, Sweden

* I am grateful to Gregg Olsen, Department of Sociology, University of Manitoba, for some of this information.

sinking into poverty, with all of the negative consequences that has for her and her child.

In a study of 33 countries, Canada tied for fifth place in the number of weeks it allows new parents to take time off work, but stood in fifteenth place in terms of the generosity of its maternity leave payments (Smyth, 2003). There are enough regulated daycare spaces for only a fifth of Canadian children up to age 12, and on average, governments allocate less than $500 a year per child for child care. These averages are far below comparable figures for western European countries. Moreover, they are boosted by Quebec, where regulated daycare spaces are twice as plentiful as in the rest of the country, and government support for regulated daycare is more than three times as generous. Overall, Canada stands between the United States and Sweden. Much of the debate surrounding family policy in Canada concerns whether we should move in the direction of the American or the Swedish model.

In Canada, three criticisms are commonly raised against generous family support policies. First, some people say these policies encourage long-term dependence on welfare, illegitimate births, and the breakup of two-parent families. However, research conducted two decades ago established that the divorce rate and the rate of births to unmarried mothers are not higher when welfare payments are more generous (Albelda and Tilly, 1997). Moreover, not all people who prefer to work are able to find full-time, secure employment, and part-time jobs offer little in the way of job security, decent wages, or benefits.

A second criticism of generous family support policies focuses on child care. Some critics say that non-family child care is bad for children under the age of three. In their view, only parents can provide the love, interaction, and intellectual stimulation that infants and toddlers need for proper social, cognitive, and moral development. However, when studies compare family care with daycare involving a strong curriculum, a stimulating environment, plenty of caregiver warmth, low turnover of well-trained staff, and a low ratio of caregivers to children, they find that daycare has no negative consequences and many positive consequences for children over the age of one or two (Cleveland, 2016).

Research also shows that daycare has some benefits, notably enhancing a child's ability to make friends and improve cognitive performance. The benefits of high-quality daycare are especially evident in low-income families, which often cannot provide the kind of stimulating environment offered by high-quality daycare.

The third criticism lodged against generous family support policies is that they are expensive and have to be paid for by high taxes. That is true. Swedes are one of the most highly taxed people in the world. They have made the political decision to pay high taxes, partly to avoid the social problems and associated costs that sometimes emerge when the traditional nuclear family is replaced with other family forms and no institutions are available to help family members in need. The Swedish experience teaches us, then, that there is a clear trade-off between expensive family support policies and low taxes. It is impossible to have both, and the degree to which any country favours one or the other is a political choice.

## READY TO STUDY?

### IN THE BOOK YOU CAN:

- Refer to the Chapter in Review section at the back of the book to have a summary of the chapter and key terms handy.
- Test your knowledge of chapter contents by answering the multiple-choice questions in the Chapter in Review section. Answers are in the appendix at the end of the book.

### ONLINE YOU CAN:

- Stay organized and efficient with MindTap—a single destination with all the course material and study aids you need to succeed.
- Flashcards are pre-populated to provide you with a jump start for review—or you can create your own.
- You can highlight text and make notes in your MindTap Reader.
- Prepare for tests with quizzes.

**GO TO NELSON.COM/STUDENT TO PURCHASE THESE DIGITAL RESOURCES.**

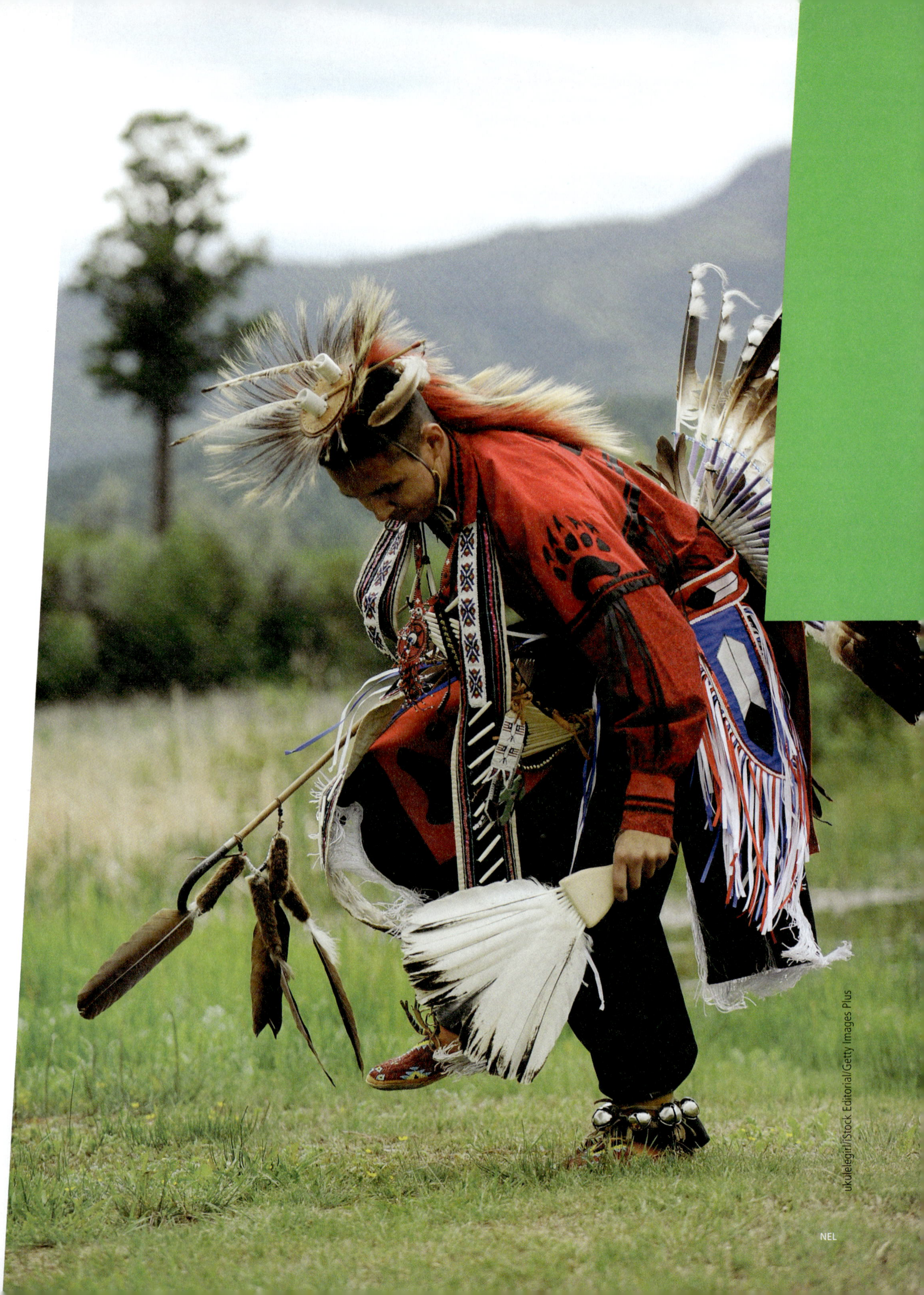

ukulelegirl/iStock Editorial/Getty Images Plus

# 10 Religion

## LEARNING OBJECTIVES:

In this chapter, you will learn to

- **LO¹** Explain how, under some circumstances, religion creates social cohesion and how, under other circumstances, religion reinforces social inequality and promotes social conflict, both non-violent and violent.
- **LO²** Describe the social forces causing secularization.
- **LO³** Analyze the social forces encouraging religious revivals.
- **LO⁴** Outline change in the distribution of religious membership in Canada.
- **LO⁵** List the main sociological factors associated with religious involvement.

## RELIGION

In 1902, psychologist William James observed that religion is the common human response to the fact that we all stand at the edge of an abyss. It helps people cope with the terrifying fact that we must die. It offers believers immortality, the promise of better times to come, and the security of benevolent spirits who watch over them. It provides meaning and purpose in a world that might otherwise seem cruel and senseless (James, 1976 [1902]: 116).

The motivation for religion may be psychological, as James argued. However, the content and intensity of religious beliefs, and the form and frequency of religious practices, are influenced by the structure of society and a person's place in it. Why does one religion predominate here, another there? Why is religious belief stronger at one time than at another? Under what circumstances does religion act as a source of social stability, and under what circumstances does it act as a force for social change? Are people becoming more or less religious? These are all questions that have occupied sociologists of religion, and I will touch on all of them here. Note that I have nothing to say about the truth of religion or of any religious belief. That is a question of faith, not science. It lies outside the province of sociology. As the New Testament says, "Faith is the substance of things hoped for, the evidence of things not seen" (Hebrews 11:1).

The cover of *Time* magazine once asked, "Is God dead?" As a sociological observation, the idea that God is dead is preposterous. Seventy-three percent of Canadians say they believe in God or a universal spirit (Bibby, 2017:66). By this measure (and by other measures I will examine below), God is still very much alive in Canada. In fact, among some categories of Canada's population, evidence of a religious revival exists. Overall, however, the scope of religious authority has declined in Canada and in other parts of the world. That is, religion governs fewer aspects of life than it used to. Some Canadians still look to religion to deal with all of life's problems, but an increasing proportion of Canadians expect that religion can help them deal with only a restricted range of spiritual issues. Other institutions—medicine, psychiatry, criminal justice, education, and so on—have grown in importance as the scope of religious authority has declined. Moreover, an increasing proportion of Canadians are irreligious.

# LO¹ CLASSICAL APPROACHES IN THE SOCIOLOGY OF RELIGION

## DURKHEIM'S FUNCTIONALIST THEORY

More than one person has said that hockey is Canada's "national religion." Before you decide whether that opinion is sensible or silly, consider that 80 percent of Canadians tuned in to at least part of the gold medal men's hockey game between Canada and the United States at the 2010 Vancouver Winter Olympics, making them the largest TV audience in Canadian history ("Gold Medal," 2010). And when Canada's men's hockey team came from behind to defeat the Soviets in 1972, the nation virtually came to a standstill.

Few events attract the attention and enthusiasm of Canadians as much as the annual Stanley Cup finals. Apart from drawing a huge audience, the Stanley Cup playoffs generate a sense of what Durkheim would have called "collective effervescence." That is, the Stanley Cup finals excite us by making us feel part of something larger than us: the Montreal Canadiens, the Edmonton Oilers, the Toronto Maple Leafs, the Vancouver Canucks, the Calgary Flames, the Ottawa Senators, the institution of Canadian hockey, the spirit of Canada itself. As celebrated Canadian writer Roch Carrier (1979: 77) wrote in his famous short story "The Hockey Sweater," "School was...a quiet place where we could prepare for the next hockey game, lay out our next strategies. As for church...there we forgot school and dreamed about the next hockey game. Through our daydreams it might happen that we would recite a prayer: We would ask God to help us play as well as Maurice Richard."

For many hours each year, hockey enthusiasts transcend their everyday lives and experience intense enjoyment by sharing the sentiments and values of a larger collectivity. In their fervour, they banish thoughts of their own mortality. They gain a glimpse of eternity as they immerse themselves in institutions that will outlast them and athletic feats that people will remember for generations to come.

So, do you think the Stanley Cup playoffs are a religious event? There is no god of the Stanley Cup, although the nickname of Canadian hockey legend Wayne Gretzky—The Great One—certainly suggests that he transcended the status of a mere mortal. Nonetheless, the Stanley Cup playoffs may meet Durkheim's definition of a religious experience.

Durkheim said that when people live together, they come to share common sentiments and values. These common sentiments and values form a **collective conscience** that is larger than any individual. On occasion, we experience the collective conscience directly. This causes us to distinguish the secular everyday world of the **profane** from the religious, transcendent world of the **sacred**. We designate certain objects as symbolizing the sacred. Durkheim called these objects **totems**. We invent set practices to connect us with the sacred. Durkheim referred to these practices as **rituals**.

The effect (or function) of rituals and of religion as a whole is to reinforce social solidarity, said Durkheim. The ritual heightens our experience of group belonging, increases our respect for the group's institutions, and strengthens our belief in the validity of the group's culture. So, in Durkheim's terms, the Stanley Cup playoffs share certain features with religious rituals. They cement society in the way Durkheim said all religious rituals do (Durkheim, 1976 [1915/1912]).

Durkheim would have found support for his theory in research showing that, in Quebec, the suicide rate among young men is higher when the Montreal Canadiens are not in the Stanley Cup playoffs than when they are (Trovato, 1998). Similarly, in the United States, the suicide rate dips during the two days preceding Super Bowl Sunday and on Super Bowl Sunday itself, just as it does for the last day of the World Series (Curtis, Loy, and Karnilowicz, 1986). These patterns are consistent with Durkheim's theory of suicide, which predicts a lower suicide rate when social solidarity increases (see the appendix to Chapter 1, A Brief History of Sociological Theory).

And what happens when favoured teams lose? Experimental research conducted at the University of

*Are the Stanley Cup playoffs a religious event?*

**collective conscience** The common sentiments and values that people share as a result of living together.

**profane** Refers to the secular, everyday world.

**sacred** Refers to the religious, transcendent world.

**totems** Objects that symbolize the sacred.

**rituals** Set practices designed to connect people to the sacred.

Religious rituals are set practices that help unite people into a moral community.

Alberta shows that threats to cherished beliefs promote thoughts of death (Schimel et al., 2007). It follows that a small number of people who strongly believe in the supremacy of their team and find their belief threatened by losses may become more suicidal. Core beliefs, it seems, are indeed prophylactic against thoughts of death.

## RELIGION, FEMINIST THEORY, AND CONFLICT THEORY

Durkheim's theory of religion is a functionalist account. It offers useful insights into the role of religion in society. Yet conflict and feminist theorists lodge two main criticisms against it. First, it overemphasizes religion's role in maintaining social cohesion. In reality, religion often incites social conflict. Second, it ignores the fact that when religion does increase social cohesion, it often reinforces social inequality.

### Religion and Social Inequality

Consider first the role of world religions in reinforcing social inequality. (Following convention, we regard the world religions as those that have the largest number of adherents and are widely dispersed geographically—Christianity, Islam, Hinduism, and Buddhism—plus Judaism, which has exerted disproportionate influence historically and globally; see Figure 10.1 and Table 10.1. Two large religious groupings do not meet these criteria.

Chinese traditional religion, with about 400 million adherents, has many local variants and is a blend of Buddhism, Confucianism, and Taoism. Sikhism has about 23 million adherents, roughly 80 percent of them living in the state of Punjab, India.)

Little historical evidence helps us understand the social conditions that gave rise to the first world religions, Judaism and Hinduism, 3800 to 4000 years ago. But we know enough about the rise of Buddhism, Christianity, and Islam between 2700 and 1500 years ago to say that the impulse to find a better world is often encouraged by adversity in this one. We also know that Moses, Jesus, Muhammad, and Buddha all promoted a message of equality and freedom. Finally, we know that over generations, the charismatic leadership of the world religions became "routinized." The **routinization of charisma** is Weber's term for the transformation of divine enlightenment into a permanent feature of everyday life. It involves turning religious inspiration into a stable social institution—a church—with defined roles, such as interpreters of the divine message, teachers, dues-paying laypeople, and so on. The routinization of charisma typically makes religion less responsive to the needs of ordinary people, and it often supports social inequalities and injustices, as you will now see.

### Religion and the Subordination of Women

Marx first stressed how religion often tranquilizes the underprivileged into accepting their lot in life. He called religion "the opium of the people" (Marx, 1970 [1843]: 131).

Evidence in support of Marx's interpretation can be drawn from many times, places, and institutions. For example, the major world religions have traditionally placed women in a subordinate position. Catholic priests, Muslim mullahs, and Jewish orthodox rabbis must be men. Women have been allowed to serve as Protestant ministers only since the mid-nineteenth century and as rabbis in the more liberal branches of Judaism since the 1970s. Many scriptures that emphasize the subordination of women

**routinization of charisma**
Weber's term for the transformation of divine enlightenment into a permanent feature of everyday life. It involves turning religious inspiration into a stable social institution with defined roles (interpreters of the divine message, teachers, dues-paying laypeople, and so on).

## FIGURE 10.1 The World's Predominant Religions

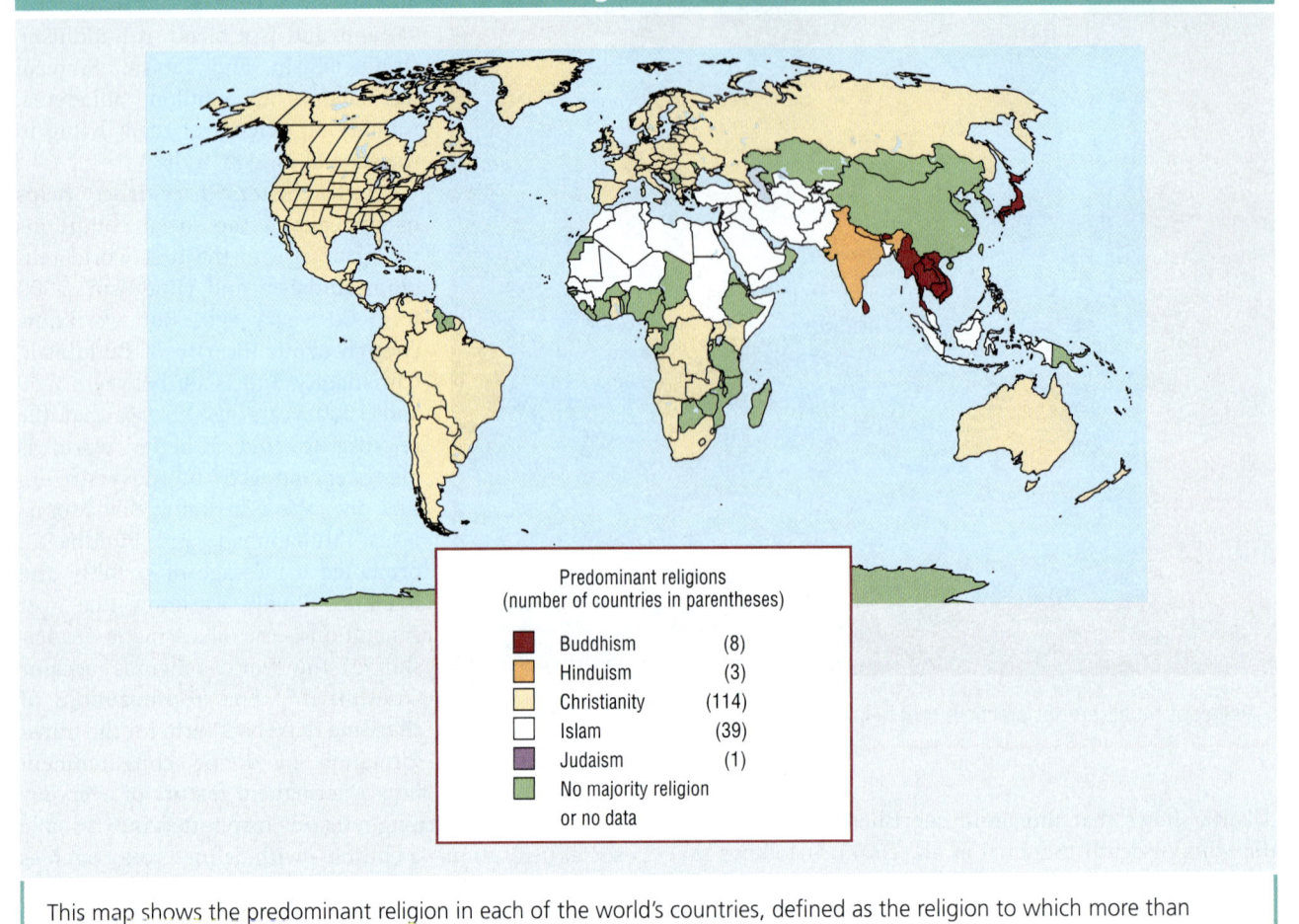

**Predominant religions (number of countries in parentheses)**
- Buddhism (8)
- Hinduism (3)
- Christianity (114)
- Islam (39)
- Judaism (1)
- No majority religion or no data

This map shows the predominant religion in each of the world's countries, defined as the religion to which more than 50 percent of a country's population adheres.

Source: Adherents.com (2001). *Religion Statistics: Predominant Religions*. Retrieved November 30, 2001 (http://www.adherents.com/adh_predom.html).

continue to inform that practice to a greater or lesser degree. For example:

1. Corinthians (14: 34–35) in the New Testament emphasizes that "women should remain silent in the churches. They are not allowed to speak, but must be in submission, as the law says. If they want to inquire about something, they should ask their own husbands at home."

2. The Sidur, the Jewish prayer book, includes this morning prayer, recited by Orthodox and ultra-Orthodox men: "Blessed are you, Lord our God, King of the Universe, who has not made me a woman."

3. The Koran, the holy book of Islam, contains a Book of Women in which it is written (4: 34) that "men are in charge of women by right of what Allah has given one over the other.... So righteous women are devoutly obedient.... But those from whom you fear arrogance, advise them; forsake them in bed; and strike them."

Religious feminists have challenged such ideas. For example, Muslim feminists have established that what many religious clerics present as divine Islamic law regarding women is actually based on interpretations that were authored by men over the centuries (Zakaria, 2014). Moreover, they contend that Islamic legal principles such as that of the "public interest" contradict and override principles that deny women equality with men. Meanwhile,

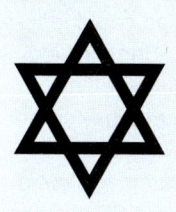

## TABLE 10.1 Five World Religions: Origins, Beliefs, and Divisions

| Religion | Origins | Beliefs | Divisions |
|---|---|---|---|
| Judaism | Judaism originated about 4000 years ago in what is now Iraq, when Abraham first asserted the existence of just one God. About 800 years later, Moses is said to have led the Jews out of Egyptian bondage. The emancipation of the Jews from slavery was a defining moment in the history of Judaism. | The central teachings rest on belief in one God (Yahweh) and on the idea that God sanctions freedom and equality. The 613 divine commandments (*mitzvot*) mentioned in the Five Books of Moses (the Torah) form the core of orthodox Jewish practice. The *mitzvot* include prescriptions for justice, righteousness, and observance: Rest and pray on the Sabbath, honour the old and the wise, do not wrong a stranger in buying or selling, do not seek revenge or hold a grudge, and so on. The Torah forms part of the Old Testament. | In seventeenth-century Eastern Europe, ecstatic Chasidic sects broke away from the bookish Judaism of the time. In nineteenth-century Germany, the Reform movement allowed prayer in German, the integration of women in worship, and other liberal reforms. Orthodox Judaism was a reaction against the liberalizing tendencies of Reform and involved a return to traditional observance. Conservative Judaism crystallized in Britain and the United States in the nineteenth century to reconcile what its practitioners regarded as the positive elements in Orthodoxy with the dynamism of Reform. Reconstructionism is a liberal twentieth-century movement known for its social activism and gender egalitarianism. |
| Christianity | Christianity originated about 35 CE* in what is now the disputed West Bank. Jesus, a poor Jew, criticized the Judaism of his time for its external conformity to tradition and ritual at the expense of developing a true relationship to God as demanded by the prophets.<br><br>* To avoid ethnocentrism, I designate dates as BCE (before the Christian era) and CE (Christian era) rather than BC (before Christ) and AD (anno domini—the year of our Lord). | Believe in God and love him; love your neighbour—these are the two main lessons of Jesus. These teachings were novel because they demanded that people match outward performance with inner conviction. It was not enough not to murder. One could not even hate. Nor was it enough not to commit adultery. One could not even lust after a neighbour's wife (Matthew 5: 21–30). These teachings made Jesus anti-authoritarian and even revolutionary. Admonishing people to love their neighbours impressed on them the need to emancipate slaves and women. Christians retained the Jewish Bible as the Old Testament, adding the gospels and letters of the apostles as the New Testament. | In 312 CE, the Roman Emperor converted to Christianity and turned Christianity into a state religion, after which the church became the dominant institution in Europe. In the sixteenth century, Martin Luther, a German priest, challenged the Christian establishment by seeking to establish a more personal relationship between the faithful and God. His ideas quickly captured the imagination of half of Europe and led to the split of Christianity into Catholicism and Protestantism. In the Middle Ages, Christianity had split into Western and Eastern halves, the former centred in Rome, the latter in Constantinople (now Istanbul, Turkey). Various Orthodox churches today derive from the Eastern tradition. Protestantism has been especially prone to splintering because it emphasizes the individual's relationship to God rather than a central authority. Today, there are hundreds of different Protestant churches. |

(*Continued*)

| TABLE 10.1 | Five World Religions: Origins, Beliefs, and Divisions *(Continued)* | | |
|---|---|---|---|
| **Religion** | **Origins** | **Beliefs** | **Divisions** |
| Islam | Islam originated about 600 CE in what is now Saudi Arabia. The powerful merchants of Mecca had become greedy and corrupt, impoverishing and enslaving many people. Also, fear grew that the Persian and Roman Empires might soon fall, bringing the end of the world. Into this crisis stepped Muhammad, who claimed to have visions from God. | People who profess Islam have five duties. At least once in their life they must recite the Muslim creed aloud, correctly, with full understanding, and with heartfelt belief. (The creed is "There is no god but Allah and Muhammad is his prophet.") Five times a day, they must worship in a religious service. They must fast from sunrise to sunset every day during the ninth month of the lunar calendar (Ramadan). They must give charity to the poor. And at least once in their life, they must make a pilgrimage to the holy city of Mecca. Muhammad's teachings were written down in the Koran. | A dispute broke out over how the followers of Muhammad could identify his successor. The Sunni argued that the successor should be an elected member of a certain Meccan tribe. The Shi'a claimed that the successor should be Muhammad's direct descendant. Today, about 85 percent of Muslims are Sunni. The Shi'a are concentrated in Iran, Bahrain, and southern Iraq. Islam spread rapidly in the Middle East, Africa, and parts of Europe. From the eighth century to the eleventh century it initiated a great cultural flowering and encouraged considerable religious tolerance. Wahabbism, a Sunni fundamentalist movement, originated in the eighteenth century and became the state religion of what is now Saudi Arabia. |
| Hinduism | Hinduism originated about 2000 BCE in India in unknown circumstances. It had no single founder. | Hinduism has many gods, all of them thought to be aspects of the one true God. The major texts are epic poems such as the Bhagavad Gita. Only the body dies in Hindu belief. The soul returns in a new form after death. The form in which it returns depends on how one lives one's life. Hindus believe that people who live in a way that is appropriate to their position in society will live better future lives. One may reach a state of spiritual perfection (*nirvana*) that allows the soul to escape the cycle of birth and rebirth, and reunite with God. But people who do not live in a way that is appropriate to their position in society supposedly live an inferior life when they are reincarnated. These ideas made upward social mobility nearly impossible because, according to Hindu belief, striving to move out of one's station in life ensures reincarnation in a lower life form. | Unlike the Western religions, Hinduism assimilates rather than excludes other religious beliefs and practices. Traditionally, Western religions rejected non-believers unless they converted. God tells Moses on Mount Sinai, "You shall have no other gods before me" (Exodus 20:2). In contrast, in the Bhagavad Gita (9: 23), Krishna says that "even those...who faithfully worship other gods also worship me." This attitude of acceptance helped Hinduism absorb many of the ancient religions of the peoples on the Indian subcontinent. It also explains why there are such wide regional and class variations in Hindu beliefs and practices. Hinduism as it is practised bears the stamp of many other religions. |

## TABLE 10.1 Five World Religions: Origins, Beliefs, and Divisions (*Continued*)

| Religion | Origins | Beliefs | Divisions |
|---|---|---|---|
| Buddhism | Sometime around 450 BCE in India, Siddhartha Gautama was deemed a "Buddha" or awakened one. The Buddha objected to the stale ritualism of Hinduism and sought to achieve a direct relationship with God. He rejected Hindu ideas of caste and reincarnation, and offered a new way for everyone to achieve spiritual enlightenment, promising salvation to everyone. | Buddha promoted the "Four Noble Truths": (1) Life is suffering. Moments of joy are overshadowed by sorrow. (2) All suffering derives from desire. We suffer when we fail to achieve what we want. (3) Suffering ceases by training ourselves to eliminate desire. (4) We can eliminate desire by behaving morally, focusing intently on our feelings and thoughts, meditating, and achieving wisdom. Buddhism does not presume the existence of one true God. Rather, it holds out the possibility of everyone becoming a god of sorts. Similarly, it does not have a central church or text such as the Bible. | Buddhism is notable for the diversity of its beliefs and practices. It spread rapidly across Asia after India's ruler, Ashoka, adopted it as his own religion in the third century BCE. He sent missionaries to convert people in Tibet, Cambodia (Kampuchea), Nepal, Sri Lanka (formerly Ceylon), Myanmar (formerly Burma), China, Korea, and Japan. The influence of Buddhism in the land of its birth started to die out after the fifth century CE and is negligible in India today. One of the reasons for the popularity of Buddhism in East and Southeast Asia is that Buddhism is able to coexist with local religious practices. Unlike Western religions, Buddhism does not insist on holding a monopoly on religious truth. |

Sources: Brown (1996); Flood (1996); Gombrich (1996); Gottwald (1979); Hodgson (1974); Lapidus (2002 [1988]); Lopez (2001); McManners (1990); Robinson and Johnson, 1997[1982]); Rodinson (1996); Roth (1961); Schwartz (2003).

Catholic and Orthodox Jewish feminists have been struggling for the ordination of women as priests and rabbis and the progressive reinterpretation of their own holy texts (Manson, 2014; Sigal, 2014).

### Religion and Inequality of Sexual Orientation and Class

Most established religions have also for the most part supported inequality of sexual orientation. Thus, while homosexuality is quite widely tolerated in Buddhism, it is unacceptable in Islam, Hinduism, and the more conservative denominations of Christianity and Judaism (Mackay, 2000: 73).

After becoming routinized, religions also typically support class inequality. They often emphasize charity, too—but not so much charity as to change the basic structure of inequality in society. Thus, in medieval and early modern Europe, Christianity, while collecting alms for the poor, promoted the view that the Almighty ordains class inequality, promising rewards to the lowly in the afterlife ("The meek shall inherit the earth"). As an Anglican hymn put it:

> All things bright and beautiful,
> The Lord God made them all.
> The rich man in his castle,
> The poor man at his gate,
> God made them high and lowly
> And ordered their estate.

(This verse was removed from the Anglican hymnal in 1920.)

Similarly, the Hindu scriptures say that the highest caste sprang from the lips of the supreme creator, the next highest caste from his shoulders, the next highest from his thighs, and the lowest, "polluted" caste from his feet. They warn that if people attempt to achieve upward mobility, they will be reincarnated as animals. And the Koran says that social inequality is due to the will of Allah (Ossowski, 1963: 19–20).

### Religion and Social Conflict

In the sociological sense of the term, a **church** is any bureaucratic religious organization that has accommodated itself to mainstream society and culture. As we have seen, church authorities often support various forms of inequality. However, religiously inspired protest against inequality often erupts from below.

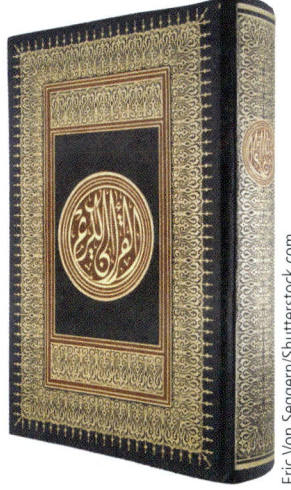

**church** A bureaucratic religious organization that has accommodated itself to mainstream society and culture.

For example, the radical Christianity of the early twentieth-century Social Gospel movement played an important role played in the creation of Canada's health care system and our social welfare network. The Social Gospel movement became a strong political force in the depths of the Great Depression (1929–39). It emphasized that Christians should be as concerned with improving the here and now as with life in the hereafter. Tommy Douglas, a Baptist minister, became the leader of the Co-operative Commonwealth Federation (precursor of the New Democratic Party). He spearheaded the creation of a socialized medical system, first in Saskatchewan and then in the country as a whole. His efforts exemplify the Social Gospel concern with social justice and, more generally, the way in which religion sometimes promoted conflict and change.

Another famous example of such protest involves the role of black parishioners' churches in spearheading the American civil rights movement during the 1950s and 1960s (Morris, 1984). Their impact was both organizational and inspirational. Organizationally, black people's churches supplied the ministers who formed the civil rights movement's leadership and the congregations whose members marched, boycotted, and engaged in other forms of protest. Additionally, Christian doctrine inspired the protesters. Perhaps their most powerful religious idea was that black people, like the Jews in Egypt, were slaves who would be freed. (It was, after all, Archangel Michael—regarded by Christians as the patron saint of the Jews—who rowed the boat ashore, leading the Jews back to the Promised Land.) Some white segregationists reacted strongly against efforts at integration, often meeting the peaceful protesters with deadly violence. However, the American South was never the same again. Religion had helped promote the conflict needed to make the South a more egalitarian and racially integrated place.

## Religious Violence

Religiously inspired conflict is by no means always progressive and non-violent. No religion is innocent of slaughter. Until Emperor Constantine declared Christianity the official religion of the Roman Empire in 313 CE, the Romans, who worshipped many gods and deified the Emperor, threw Christians to the lions for sport because the Christians recognized only their own God. In 2014, Sunni Islamic extremists belonging to ISIS shot, raped, crucified, and pillaged members of the Shia Muslim, Christian, and Yazidi minorities, as ISIS marched across much of Syria and Iraq. Extremist Hindus routinely attack Muslim temples in India, and on the West Bank, extremist Jews (whose settlements are illegal under international law), just as routinely attack their Muslim and Christian Palestinian neighbours.

Historically speaking, it seems that Christians have been the most violent of all religious groups. While the Romans killed a few thousand Christians in the first 300 years CE, Christians slaughtered millions—mainly other Christians but also Jews and Muslims—between the eleventh century and the nineteenth century, and particularly during Europe's religious wars in the sixteenth century and the seventeenth century. One historian reminds us of the following episode:

> On 23 August 1572, French Catholics who stressed the importance of good deeds attacked communities of French Protestants who highlighted God's love for humankind. In this attack, the St. Bartholomew Day's massacre, between 5000 and 10 000 Protestants were slaughtered in less than 24 hours. When the pope in Rome heard the news from France, he was so overcome by joy that he organized festive prayers to celebrate the occasion and commissioned Giorgio Vasari to decorate one of the Vatican's rooms with a fresco of the massacre (the room is currently off-limits to visitors) (Harari, 2014: 216).

## Violence against Nature: Useful Lessons from Indigenous Religions

The major world religions, and especially the Abrahamic religions (Judaism, Christianity, and Islam), tell people they have the right to rule Nature. It says so right in Exodus (1: 26), where God proclaims: "They shall rule over the fish of the sea, the birds of the sky, and over the animals, the whole earth, and every creeping thing that crawls upon the earth."

We have taken these words to heart (Harari, 2017: Chapters 2 and 3). However, in the process of achieving dominion over Nature, we drove to extinction other human species (*Homo Neanderthals* was the last to go) and half of all the large land mammals in existence. We domesticated other animals and modelled our industrialized system of animal food production on the concentration camp—separating the young from their parents, tightly confining them for most of their lives, and then killing them. In fact, as you will learn in Chapter 15, Technology, the Environment, and Social Movements, we have brought Nature to the point where more than 16 000 species of mammals, birds, reptiles, amphibians, fish, and insects—not to mention large swaths of humanity—are now endangered by human actions that are responsible for climate change and other catastrophes (International Union for Conservation of Nature, 2016).

Monotheistic religions like Judaism, Christianity, and Islam legitimize human domination over Nature by teaching that only humans have souls. Since pigs and cows and chickens lack souls—as does the air as well as rivers, lakes, and oceans—it follows that we can do whatever we want with them. In contrast, most traditional Indigenous religions are animistic. **Animism** also teaches that humans have souls, but in the animistic worldview, so do animals, plants, and natural phenomena such as rain. As such, animism accords the beings and things that populate Nature a level of respect that monotheistic religions lack. Traditional Indigenous religions implore people to live in harmony with Nature, not to dominate it.

For example, the Mi'kmaq of Atlantic Canada tell instructive stories like this one about Glooskap, the Creator: One day when Glooskap was a boy, the wind was blowing so hard Glooskap couldn't paddle his canoe into the bay to hunt ducks. So he found the source of the wind—the flapping wings of the Wind Eagle. He then tricked the Wind Eagle into getting stuck in a crevice, preventing him from flapping his wings. Now Glooskap could go hunting. However, the air soon grew so hot he found it difficult to breathe. The water became dirty, and began to smell bad, and there was so much foam on it he found it hard to paddle. When he complained to his grandmother, she explained that the wind was needed to cool the air, wash the earth, and move the waters to keep them clean. And so Glooskap freed the Wind Eagle. The winds returned, and Glooskap decided it was better to wait for good weather before going duck hunting rather than trying to force Nature's hand ("Gluscabi and the Wind Eagle," n.d.). Destroyers of the environment fail to learn from such stories at their peril—and ours.

### Summing Up

Based on the foregoing, it seems reasonable to conclude that Durkheim was right when he said that religion can maintain social order under some circumstances. However, Durkheim neglected to mention two facts that must qualify his observation. First, when religion maintains social order, it often reinforces social inequality. Second, under some circumstances, religion can promote social conflict, sometimes non-violent and progressive, at other times violent and, in the judgment of all but religious extremists, sickening. Religions that promote mastery over Nature rather than a balanced relationship with Nature can even contribute to damaging human society as a whole.

## WEBER AND THE PROBLEM OF SOCIAL CHANGE: A SYMBOLIC INTERACTIONIST INTERPRETATION

If Durkheim highlighted the way religion contributes to social order, Max Weber stressed the way religion can contribute to social change. Weber captured the core of his argument in a memorable image: if history is like a train, pushed along its tracks by economic and political interests, then religious ideas are like railroad switches, determining exactly which tracks the train will follow (Weber, 1946: 280).

Weber's most famous illustration of his thesis is his short book, *The Protestant Ethic and the Spirit of Capitalism*. Like Marx, Weber was interested in explaining the rise of modern capitalism. Again like Marx, he was prepared to recognize the "fundamental importance of the economic factor" in his explanation (Weber, 1958 [1904–05]: 26). But Weber was also bent on proving the one-sidedness of any exclusively economic interpretation. He did so by offering what we would today call a symbolic interactionist interpretation of religion. True, the term *symbolic interactionism* was not introduced into sociology until more than half a century after Weber wrote *The Protestant Ethic*. Yet Weber's focus on the worldly significance of the *meanings* people attach to religious ideas makes him a forerunner of the symbolic interactionist tradition.

For specifically religious reasons, wrote Weber, followers of the Protestant theologian John Calvin stressed the need to engage in intense worldly activity and to display industry, punctuality, and frugality in their everyday life. In the view of such men as John Wesley and Benjamin Franklin, people could reduce their religious doubts and ensure a state of grace by working diligently and living simply. Many Protestants took up this idea. Weber called it the Protestant ethic (Weber, 1958 [1904–05]: 183). According to Weber, the Protestant ethic had wholly unexpected economic consequences. Where it took root, and where economic conditions were favourable, early capitalist enterprise grew most robustly.

Subsequent research showed that the correlation between the Protestant ethic and the strength of capitalist development is weaker than Weber thought. In some places, Catholicism has coexisted with vigorous capitalist growth and Protestantism with relative economic stagnation (Samuelsson, 1961 [1957]). Nonetheless, Weber's treatment of the religious factor underlying social change is a useful corrective to Durkheim's emphasis on religion as a source of social stability. Along with Durkheim's work, Weber's contribution stands as one of the most important insights into the influence of religion on society. (See Theories at a Glance, Religion.)

> **animism** A type of religion that teaches that humans, animals, plants, and natural phenomena such as rain have souls. As such, animism accords the beings and things that populate Nature a level of respect that monotheistic religions lack, teaching people to live in harmony with Nature, not to dominate it.

# THEORIES AT A GLANCE

## Religion

| Theory | Main Question | Application |
|---|---|---|
| Functionalism | How do social structures and the values underlying them contribute to social stability? | Durkheim said that when people live together, they come to share common sentiments and values. These common sentiments and values form a collective conscience that is larger than any individual. On occasion, we experience the collective conscience directly. This causes us to distinguish the secular everyday world of the profane from the religious, transcendent world of the sacred. We designate certain objects as symbolizing the sacred. Durkheim called these objects *totems*.<br><br>We invent set practices to connect us with the sacred. Durkheim referred to these practices as *rituals*. The function of rituals and of religion as a whole is to reinforce social solidarity, said Durkheim. Religion heightens our experience of group belonging, increases our respect for the group's institutions, and strengthens our belief in the validity of the group's culture. |
| Conflict theory | How does the structure of inequality between privileged groups seeking to maintain their advantages and subordinate groups seeking to increase theirs lead to conflict and often to social change? | After becoming routinized, religions typically support class inequality. They often emphasize charity, too—but not so much charity as to change the basic structure of inequality in society. For example, in medieval and early modern Europe, Christianity, while collecting alms for the poor, promoted the view that the Almighty ordains class inequality, promising rewards to the lowly in the afterlife ("The meek shall inherit the earth"). However, religiously inspired protest against inequality often erupts from below, as the twentieth-century Social Gospel movement in Canada and the civil rights movement in the United States illustrate.<br><br>Religiously inspired conflict is by no means always progressive and non-violent; no religion is innocent of slaughter. Nor are the major world religions, and especially Judaism, Christianity, and Islam, innocent of violence against Nature. Proponents of these religions view God as having granted humans the right to dominate Nature; and in the process of exercising what they regard as their God-given right, humans have driven many species to extinction and caused great environmental damage. By imbuing all living and inanimate things with a soul, animistic Indigenous religions prescribe a more harmonious relationship between humans and Nature, which is especially instructive in an era of environmental danger caused by humans. |
| Symbolic interactionism | How do people communicate to make their social settings meaningful, thus helping to create their social circumstances? | Weber wrote that if history is like a train, pushed along its tracks by economic and political interests, then religious ideas are like railroad switches, determining exactly which tracks the train will follow. His most famous illustration of his thesis is *The Protestant Ethic and the Spirit of Capitalism*.<br><br>Like Marx, Weber recognized the fundamental importance of the economic factor in explaining the rise of capitalism. But Weber also sought to establish the one-sidedness of any exclusively economic interpretation. He did so by offering what we would today call a *symbolic interactionist interpretation*. For specifically religious reasons, wrote Weber, followers of the Protestant theologian John Calvin stressed the need to engage in intense worldly activity and to display industry, punctuality, and frugality in their everyday life. In the view of such men as John Wesley and Benjamin Franklin, people could reduce their religious doubts and ensure a state of grace by working diligently and living simply.<br><br>Many Protestants took up this idea. Weber called it the *Protestant ethic*. According to Weber, the Protestant ethic had wholly unexpected economic consequences. Where it took root, and where economic conditions were favourable, early capitalist enterprise grew most robustly. Weber's focus on the worldly significance of the meanings people attach to religious ideas makes him a forerunner of the symbolic interactionist tradition. |

| Feminism | How do social conventions maintain male dominance and female subordination, and how do these conventions get overturned? | The major world religions have traditionally placed women in a subordinate position. Catholic priests, Muslim mullahs, and Jewish Orthodox rabbis must be men. Women have been allowed to serve as Protestant ministers only since the mid-nineteenth century and as rabbis in the more liberal branches of Judaism since the 1970s. Many scriptures that emphasize the subordination of women continue to inform practice to a greater or lesser degree. Religious feminists have challenged such ideas. For example, Muslim feminists have established that what many religious clerics present as divine Islamic law regarding women is actually based on interpretations that were authored by men over the centuries. They also contend that Islamic legal principles such as that of the "public interest" contradict and override principles that deny women equality with men. |

# THE RISE, DECLINE, AND PARTIAL REVIVAL OF RELIGION

## LO² SECULARIZATION

In 1651, British political philosopher Thomas Hobbes described life as "poore, nasty, brutish, and short" (Hobbes, 1968 [1651]: 150). The standard of living in medieval and early modern Europe was abysmally low. On average, a person lived only about 35 years, mainly due to the high rate of infant mortality, but also due to famines, wars, and epidemics. The forces of nature and human affairs seemed entirely unpredictable. In this context, magic was popular. It offered easy answers to mysterious, painful, and capricious events.

As material conditions improved, popular belief in magic, astrology, and witchcraft gradually lost ground (Thomas, 1971). Christianity substantially replaced them. The better and more predictable times made Europeans more open to the teachings of organized religion. In addition, the church campaigned vigorously to stamp out opposing belief systems and practices. The persecution of witches in this era was partly an effort to eliminate competition and establish a Christian monopoly over spiritual life.

The church succeeded in its efforts. In medieval and early modern Europe, Christianity became a powerful presence in religious affairs, music, art, architecture, literature, and philosophy. Popes and saints were the rock stars and movie celebrities of their day. The church was the centre of life in both its spiritual and its worldly dimensions. The authority of the Catholic Church was supreme in marriage, education, morality, economic affairs, politics, and so on. European countries proclaimed Catholicism the official state religion and persecuted Protestants, Jews, and Muslims.

In contrast, a few hundred years later, Max Weber remarked on how the world had become thoroughly "disenchanted." By the turn of the twentieth century, he said, scientific and other forms of rationalism were replacing religious authority. His observations formed the basis of what came to be known as the **secularization thesis**, undoubtedly the most widely accepted argument in the sociology of religion until the 1990s. According to the secularization thesis, religious institutions, actions, and consciousness are unlikely to disappear, but they are certainly on the decline worldwide. That is because science and rational thinking in general fail to find any evidence for many religious beliefs (such as belief in the afterlife) and instead provide evidence-based alternative explanations (when our bodily functions cease, we are gone forever) (see the Sociology and the Media feature, From *South Park* to *The Book of Mormon*).

Figure 10.2 and Figure 10.3 provide two indicators of how far secularization has progressed in Canada. The percentage of Canadians who said they had no religion remained below 0.5 percent for each Canadian census from 1881 to 1951. In 1961 it nudged just above 0.5 percent. It then started to climb rapidly. The most recent census figures on religion come from 2011, at which time nearly a quarter of Canadians said they had no religion.

Figure 10.3 illustrates another aspect of secularization. The percentage of Canadians who attend religious services at least weekly fell rapidly from 1945 to 1975 and more slowly from 1975 to 2000, when it reached one-third of the 1945 figure. There was a modest uptick in 2005 but

**secularization thesis**
Theory that religious institutions, actions, and consciousness are on the decline worldwide.

# SOCIOLOGY AND THE MEDIA

## From *South Park* to *The Book of Mormon*

Viewers knew something was up in 1992 when the very first four-minute *South Park* short (available on YouTube) featured Frosty the Snowman killing Santa Claus. At last count, the South Park Archives on the Web listed nine Christmas specials (including 2003's "It's Christmas in Canada") and 23 other episodes about religion. They are all of course irreverent and, from the point of view of the believer, blasphemous. Such television programs would have been unthinkable as late as the 1980s; "secularization" hardly does justice to the way in which Trey Parker and Matt Stone's *South Park* ridicules every known religion and then some.

The pinnacle of Parker and Stone's antireligious diatribe came in 2011, when *The Book of Mormon* premiered in New York. In the play, young Mormon missionaries depart for Uganda to find poverty, filth, violence, and such profound disbelief that the locals sing "*Hasa eiga eebowai*," which they translate as "Fuck you, God." The missionaries fail to convert any of the natives, who find the Mormon belief system ridiculous and irrelevant. All seems lost until one of the missionaries accidentally initiates a new and (from the audience's viewpoint) equally ridiculous religious belief system that answers the natives' needs. Mass conversion follows.

When *The Book of Mormon* opened in Melbourne, Australia, in 2017, cries of "Jesus" were heard in the crowd—not in disgust but in amazement. That pretty well sums up audience reaction throughout the English-speaking world and now in Sweden, Norway, and Denmark. Audience members can't believe their eyes and ears as the norm-breaking musical comedy unfolds. They love it. The play has critics reaching for their thesauri. As the Australian reviewer wrote, "Parker and Stone have produced a work of comedic genius that exceeds critical hype and hyperbole: *The Book of Mormon* is an exceptional, visionary and all-round entertaining musical masterpiece" (Van Schilt, 2017). The play won nine Tony Awards, one for best musical. As of this writing, it has grossed more than half a billion U.S. dollars.

It would be easy to conclude that *The Book of Mormon* is a critique of religion in general and an anthem for secularization. But that would be hasty. After all, the new religion founded by the missionaries was embraced by the natives because it filled their need for hope and joy, otherwise unattainable. The stories on which religions base their message may indeed seem ridiculous from a rational or scientific point of view, but the message nonetheless speaks to many people in a meaningful way. Secularization may go only so far.

### Critical Thinking Question

- Skip ahead to Figure 10.3. Notice the 2005 uptick in the percentage of Canadians who attended religious services weekly. Is it a statistical fluke in the context of a long downward trend or might it signify something meaningful? If the latter, what might it signify?

---

**FIGURE 10.2    Canadians with "No Religion," 1881–2011 (percentage)**

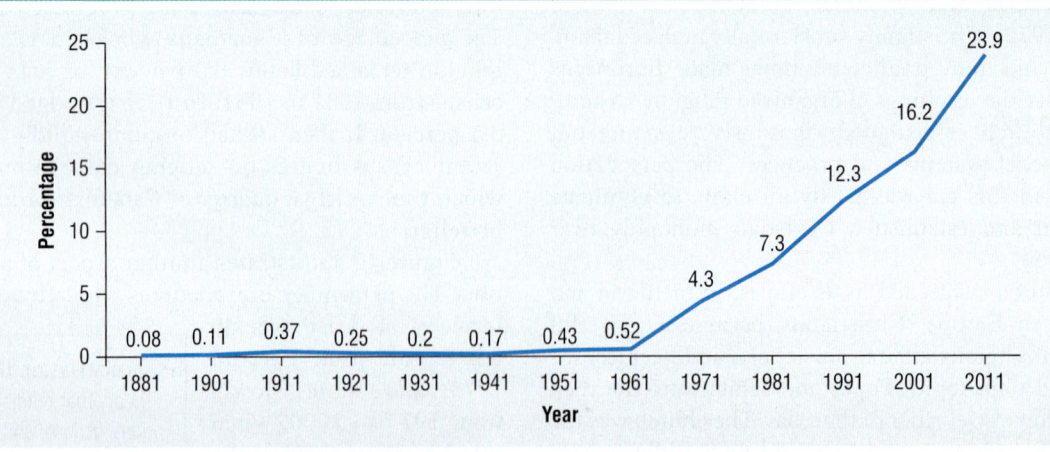

| Year | Percentage |
|---|---|
| 1881 | 0.08 |
| 1901 | 0.11 |
| 1911 | 0.37 |
| 1921 | 0.25 |
| 1931 | 0.2 |
| 1941 | 0.17 |
| 1951 | 0.43 |
| 1961 | 0.52 |
| 1971 | 4.3 |
| 1981 | 7.3 |
| 1991 | 12.3 |
| 2001 | 16.2 |
| 2011 | 23.9 |

Sources: Statistics Canada. 1994. "1991 Census Highlights"; 2005c. "Population by religion, by province and territory (2001 Census)"; 2014f. "Table A164-184. Principal religious denominations of the population, census dates, 1871 to 1971"; 2017u. "Religion (108), Immigrant Status and Period of Immigration (11), Age Groups (10) and Sex (3) for the Population in Private Households of Canada, Provinces, Territories, Census Metropolitan Areas and Census Agglomerations, 2011 *National Household Survey*."

## FIGURE 10.3 Weekly Attendance at Religious Services, Canada, 1945–2015, (percentage)

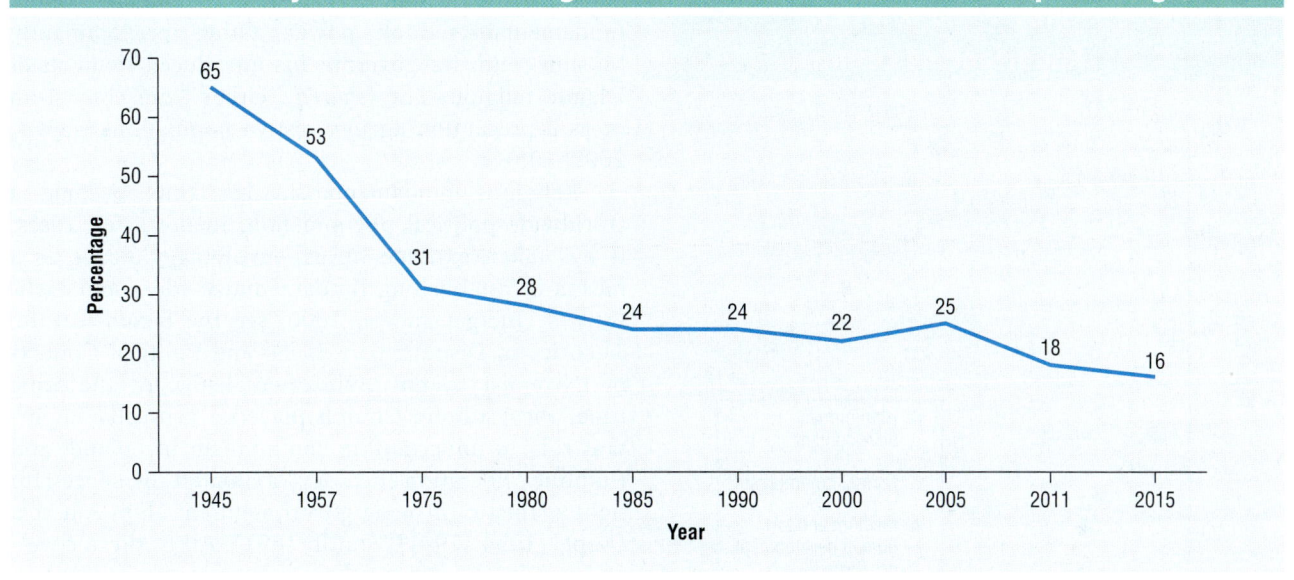

| Year | Percentage |
|------|------------|
| 1945 | 65 |
| 1957 | 53 |
| 1975 | 31 |
| 1980 | 28 |
| 1985 | 24 |
| 1990 | 24 |
| 2000 | 22 |
| 2005 | 25 |
| 2011 | 18 |
| 2015 | 16 |

Note: The 1945 figure is based on a poll of Canadians over the age of 20 who said they had attended a religious service in the three weeks following Easter Sunday. Some 95 percent of Canadians were Christian in 1945. The other figures are based on survey questions that determined how many Canadians over the age of 17 attended religious services at least weekly.

Sources: Bibby (2017: 12, 33, 41, 49, 66); Wilson-Laflamme, (2014).

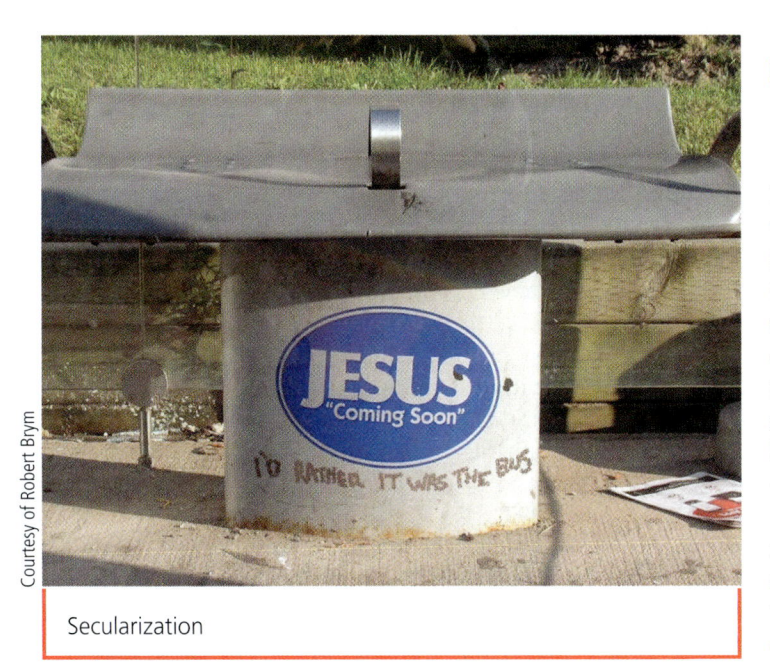

Secularization

## LO³ RELIGIOUS REVIVAL AND RELIGIOUS FUNDAMENTALISM

Despite the consensus about secularization that was evident in the 1980s, many sociologists modified their judgments in the 1990s. One reason for the change was that accumulated survey evidence showed that religion was not in an advanced state of decay in many places (see Figure 10.4). Even in a rich, secularized country like Canada, two-thirds of adults continue to say they have spiritual needs and believe in the existence of God or a higher power (Bibby, 2017: 74, 148).

The second reason many sociologists have modified their views about secularization is that an intensification of religious belief and practice has taken place among some people in recent decades. For example, since the 1960s, fundamentalist religious organizations have increased their membership in the Canada and the United States.

the overall downward trend resumed in 2011. By 2015, the rate of weekly religious service attendance was just one-quarter of the 1945 rate. The seven-decade drop in attendance has many religious leaders worried. If it weren't for some recent counter-trends—the increased vigour of fundamentalist Protestant denominations and the surge in immigration of Muslims and Chinese and Filipino Christians—the story would be even more dire (Xu, 2017). Figure 10.3 and Figure 10.2 thus add weight to the secularization argument.

**Fundamentalists** interpret their scriptures literally; seek to establish a direct, personal relationship with God; are relatively intolerant of nonfundamentalists; and often support conservative social and political issues. About 3 percent of Canada's 29 million adults are

**fundamentalists** People who interpret their scriptures literally; seek to establish a direct, personal relationship with God; are relatively intolerant of nonfundamentalists; and often support conservative social and political issues.

## FIGURE 10.4 Percentage of People Who Think Religion Is Very Important, 44 Countries

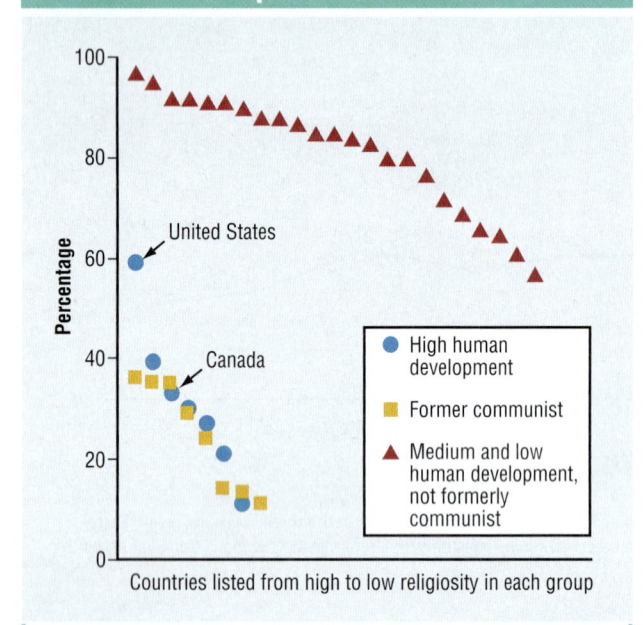

This figure is derived from a 2002 survey of 38 000 people in 44 countries. (Poland is a former communist country and the United Nations ranks it 37th in its list of 53 countries in the "high human development" group. It is classified here as a former communist country.)

Sources: Pew Research Center, 2002, *The Pew Global Attitudes Project: How Global Publics View Their Lives, Their Countries, the World, America*; United Nations, 2002, Human Development Report 2002, New York: Oxford University Press.

members of fundamentalist Protestant denominations (Bibby, 2017: 204). In the United States, where Protestant fundamentalists were a major force behind the election of Donald Trump as president in 2016, the comparable figure is about 25 percent (Pew Research Center, 2018).

Since the 1960s, religious movements have become dominant forces in many countries other than the United States. The Hindu nationalist Bharatiya Janata Party, in alliance with similar parties, formed the Indian government from 1998 to 2004 and from 2014 to the present. Jewish fundamentalists were always important players in Israeli political life, often holding the balance of power in Israeli governments, but they have become much more politically influential in recent years (Kimmerling, 2001: 173–207; Viorst, 2016: 185–284). A revival of Muslim fundamentalism began in Iran in the 1970s and then swept much of the Middle East, Africa, and parts of Asia. In Iran, Afghanistan, and Sudan, Muslim fundamentalists took power. Other predominantly Muslim countries' governments introduced elements of Islamic religious law (*shari'a*), either from conviction or as a precaution against restive populations (Lewis, 2002: 106).

Religious fundamentalism has thus become a worldwide political phenomenon. In not a few cases, it has taken extreme forms, involving violence as a means of establishing fundamentalist ideas and institutions (Juergensmeyer, 2000; see the boxed feature, Theories in Dispute, The Social and Political Context of Extremist Islamic Fundamentalism). At the same time, the Catholic Church played a critically important role in undermining communism in Poland, and Catholic "liberation theology" animated the successful fight against right-wing governments in Latin America (Kepel, 1994 [1991]; Smith, 1991). All of these developments amount to a religious revival that was unexpected in, say, 1970.

## THE REVISED SECULARIZATION THESIS

The spread of fundamentalist religion and the resilience of religion as a spiritual and political force in some countries led sociologists to revise the secularization thesis in the 1990s. The revisionists acknowledge that religion has become increasingly influential in the lives of some individuals and groups in recent decades. However, they insist that the scope of religious authority has continued to decline in most people's lives. That is, for most people, religion has less and less to say about education, family issues, politics, and economic affairs, even though it may continue to be an important source of spiritual belief and practice for some people. In this sense, secularization persists (Chaves, 1994; Yamane, 1997).

According to the **revised secularization thesis**, in most countries, worldly institutions have broken off (or "differentiated") from the institution of religion over time. One such worldly institution is the education system. Religious bodies used to run schools and institutions of higher learning that are now run almost exclusively by non-religious authorities. Like other specialized institutions that separated from the institution of religion, the education system is generally concerned with worldly affairs rather than spiritual matters.

The overall effect of the differentiation of secular institutions has been to make religion applicable only to the spiritual part of most people's lives, if that. Because the scope of religious authority has been restricted, people look to religion for moral guidance in everyday life less often than they used to. Most people have turned

**revised secularization thesis** Theory that worldly institutions break off from the institution of religion over time. As a result, religion governs an ever-smaller part of most people's lives and has become largely a matter of personal choice.

# THEORIES IN DISPUTE

## The Social and Political Context of Extremist Islamic Fundamentalism

In 1972, I was finishing my BA at the Hebrew University of Jerusalem. One May morning I switched on the radio to discover that a massacre had taken place at Lod (now Ben Gurion) International Airport, 42 km from the apartment I was sharing. Three Japanese men in business suits had arrived on Air France Flight 132 from Paris. They were members of the Japanese Red Army, a small, communist terrorist group with links to the nationalist Popular Front for the Liberation of Palestine–General Command. Both groups wanted to help wrest Israel from Jewish rule.

After they picked up their bags, the three men pulled out automatic rifles and started firing indiscriminately. Before pausing to slip in fresh clips, they lobbed hand grenades into the crowd at the ticket counters. One man ran onto the tarmac, shot some disembarking passengers, and then blew himself up. This was the first suicide attack in modern Middle East history. Security guards shot a second terrorist and arrested the third, Kozo Okamoto. When the firing stopped, 26 people lay dead. Half were non-Jews. In addition to the two terrorists, 11 Catholics were murdered. They were Puerto Rican tourists who had just arrived on a pilgrimage to the Holy Land.

Both the Japanese Red Army and the Popular Front for the Liberation of Palestine–General Command were strictly non-religious organizations. Yet something unexpected happened to Kozo Okamoto, the sole surviving terrorist of the Lod massacre. Israel sentenced him to life in prison but freed him in 1985 in a prisoner exchange. Okamoto wound up living in Lebanon's Beka'a Valley, the main base of the Iranian-backed Hezbollah fundamentalist organization. A revival of extremist Islamic fundamentalism was sweeping the Middle East. In 2000, Okamoto converted to Islam.

Kozo Okamoto's life tells us something important and not at all obvious about religious fundamentalism and politics in the Middle East and elsewhere. Okamoto was involved in extremist politics first and came to religion later. Extremist religious fundamentalism became a useful way for him to articulate and implement his political views when communism failed. That's not unusual. Religious fundamentalism often provides a convenient vehicle for framing political extremism, enhancing its appeal, legitimizing it, and providing a foundation for the solidarity of political groups.

Many people, including more than a few academic researchers, regard terrorism as the *effect* of extremist Islamic fundamentalism. In this view, some people happen to become religious fanatics, and then their fanaticism commands them to go out and kill others who don't share their beliefs. Typically, a few years ago, newspapers around the world screamed, "Religious extremism main cause of terrorism" (Arnett, 2014). The articles noted that fully two-thirds of all deaths due to terrorism in the preceding year were attributable to just four extremist Islamic fundamentalist groups. The statistic was based on a report from an Australian research institute that describes itself as one of the world's leading think tanks (Institute for Economics and Peace, 2018).

While the report's data seem sound, the interpretation of the data is highly suspect insofar as it ignores the social and political underpinning of most terrorist acts. Violent Islamic fundamentalism is typically an expression in religious form of opposition to colonialism, military occupation, and the highly unequal distribution of economic resources. Often, extreme religious forms of such opposition are adopted only after nationalist, communist, and other ideologies fail (Brym, 2008; Brym and Araj, 2011; 2012; Pape, 2003). Extremist organizations in the Middle East and elsewhere gain in strength to the degree that issues such as those just listed are not addressed in a meaningful way. What the headlines ignore is that violent fundamentalism, like all forms of religion, is powerfully influenced by the sociological context in which it emerges.

### Critical Thinking Question

- The newspaper headline quoted above really makes two claims—first, that an *association* exists between religious extremism and terrorism, and second, that religious extremism *causes* terrorism. Does the existence of an association always, sometimes, or never imply the existence of a cause-and-effect relationship?

religion into a personal and private matter rather than one imposed by an authoritative institution. Said differently, people feel increasingly free to combine beliefs and practices from various sources and traditions to suit their own tastes—like Leonard Cohen, the Canadian cultural icon who became a Buddhist monk in 1996 yet whose Jewish background and values featured prominently in his songs and poetry until his death in 2016 (Collins, 2009).

**religiosity** The degree to which religion is important to people.

## THE MARKET MODEL

Another way to understand how a religious revival can take place in the midst of an overall decline in religious participation is to think of religion as a market. In this view, religious organizations are suppliers of services such as counselling, pastoral care, youth activities, men's and women's groups, performance groups, lectures, and discussions. These services are demanded by people who desire religious activities. Religious denominations are similar to product brands offering different "flavours" of religious experience (Bibby, 2017: 42–46; Finke and Stark, 2005).

Some countries, such as the United States, permit vigorous competition among religions to satisfy the demands of the market for religious services. The market model predicts that in such countries, religiosity as measured by, say, frequency of attendance at religious services, will be relatively high. (**Religiosity** is the degree to which religion is important to people.) On the other hand, other countries allow less religious freedom. Some countries, like Saudi Arabia, even impose a national religion on its citizens. The market model predicts that religiosity will tend to be low in countries with restricted religious freedom because a single religion cannot adequately satisfy the religious needs of a diverse population.

Some evidence supports the market model. For instance, in 45 countries with an active Roman Catholic Church, the average Catholic's level of religious commitment is stronger where competition between the Catholic Church and other religions is stronger (Bibby and Stark, 2017). However, Figure 10.5 shows that the market model is not universally valid. Figure 10.5 compiles information on religious freedom (an indicator of religious competition) and weekly attendance at religious services in all 29 countries for which relevant data exist (Bibby, 2017: 184; Cato Institute, 2017). The trend in the data is for attendance to decline as religious freedom increases—just the opposite of what the market model predicts (see Figure 10.5).

The market model nonetheless raises the interesting question of what motivates people to participate in religion. Some sociologists highlight the role of otherworldly or supernatural rewards (Stark and Bainbridge, 1997). They argue that religion promises such rewards in exchange for particular types of behaviour. It follows that religion is particularly appealing to poor people because the wealthy enjoy material benefits and therefore have less need and desire for supernatural promises.

However, other sociologists question whether supernatural rewards interest only the poor, noting historical examples of people who gave up their wealth to live a simple, spiritual life. They also note that religions offer worldly benefits that attract the well-to-do (Collins, 1993). For instance, religious organizations regularly bestow public recognition on the wealthiest and most powerful people in society, as the name of Toronto's Timothy Eaton Memorial Church testifies. For such reasons, religion may appeal to the rich just as much as it appeals to the poor.

The market model does draw attention to the potential advantages of religious diversification. People often assume that an official or state religion, such as Christianity in the Roman Empire or Islam in contemporary Iran, is the best guarantee of religiosity. However, the market model emphasizes that religious diversity can also be a source

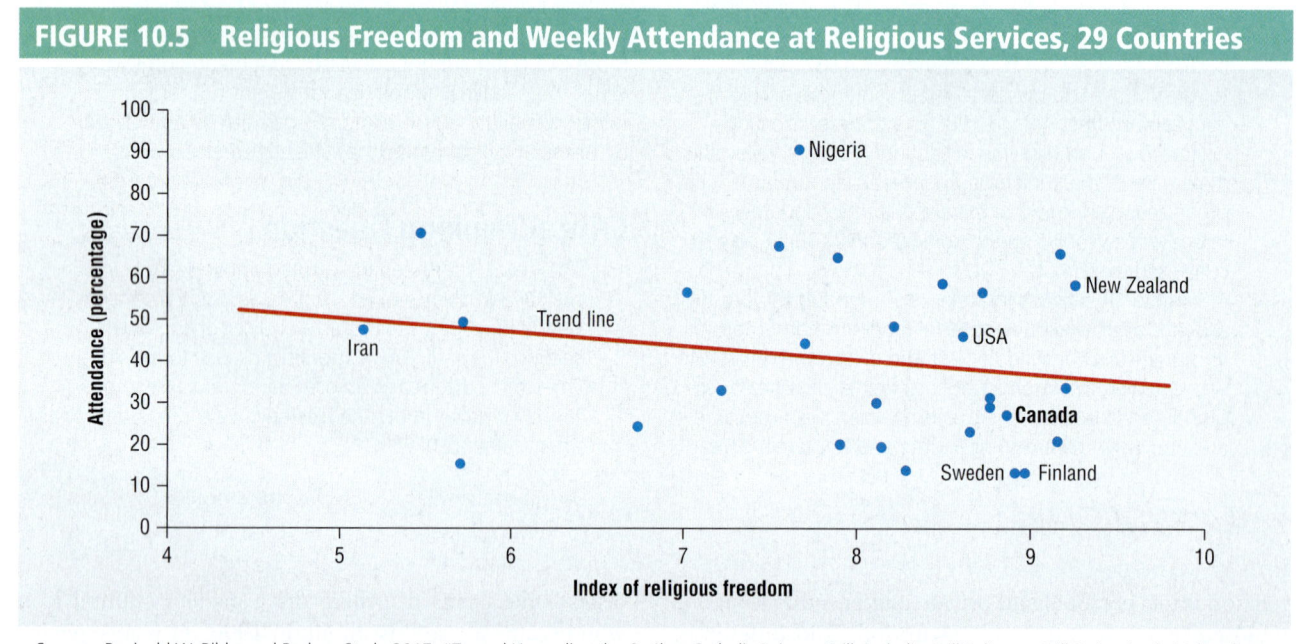

### FIGURE 10.5 Religious Freedom and Weekly Attendance at Religious Services, 29 Countries

Sources: Reginald W. Bibby and Rodney Stark. 2017. "Toward Unraveling the Québec Catholic Enigma: Still Catholic, Still Believers, Still Uninvolved: A View from Outside Québec"; Montreal: Étudier la religion au Québec: regards d'ici et d'ailleurs, symposium de la Société québécoise pour l'étude de la religion (SQÉR) en collaboration avec le Centre de recherche interdisciplinaire sur la diversité et la démocratie (CRIDAQ); Cato Institute. 2017. "Religious Freedom Index."

World meeting of religious leaders

of strength because it allows individuals to shop around for a religious organization that corresponds to their particular tastes. This may help explain why the United States, which constitutionally prohibits state involvement in religion, has a high rate of religious participation compared to most highly industrialized countries (refer back to Figure 10.4). In contrast, some regions in which state and religion remained entwined until quite recently, such as Quebec, have experienced some of the sharpest drop-offs in participation in religious organizations.

## LO⁴ RELIGION IN CANADA

### CHURCH, SECT, AND CULT

Sociologists generally divide religious groups into just three types: churches, sects, and cults (Troeltsch, 1931 [1923]; Stark and Bainbridge, 1979; see Table 10.2). As noted earlier, a *church* is a bureaucratic religious organization that has accommodated itself to mainstream society and culture. Because of this accommodation, it may endure for many hundreds, if not thousands, of years. The bureaucratic nature of a church is evident in the formal training of its leaders, its strict hierarchy of roles, and its clearly drawn rules and regulations. Its integration into mainstream society is evident in its teachings, which are generally abstract and do not challenge worldly authority. In addition, churches integrate themselves into the mainstream by recruiting members from all classes of society.

Churches take two main forms. First are **ecclesia**, or state-supported churches. For example, Christianity became the state religion in the Roman Empire in the fourth century, and Islam is the state religion in Iran and Sudan today. State religions impose advantages on members and disadvantages on non-members. Tolerance of other religions is low in societies with ecclesia.

Churches can also be pluralistic, allowing diversity within the church and expressing tolerance of non-members. Pluralism allows churches to increase their appeal by allowing various streams of belief and practice to coexist under their overarching authority. These subgroups are called **denominations**. For example, United Church, Anglican, Baptist, Lutheran, and Presbyterian are the major Protestant denominations in Canada today.

**Sects** typically form by breaking away from churches because of disagreement about church doctrine. Sometimes, sect members choose to separate themselves geographically, as the Hutterites do in their some 200 colonies, mostly in the western provinces. However, even in urban settings, strictly enforced rules concerning dress, diet, prayer, and intimate contact with outsiders can separate sect members from the larger society. Chasidic Jews in Toronto and Montreal prove the viability of this isolation strategy. Sects are less integrated into society and less bureaucratized than churches are. They are often led by **charismatic leaders**, men and women who claim to be inspired by supernatural powers and whose followers believe them to be so inspired. These leaders tend to be relatively intolerant of religious opinions other than their own. They tend to recruit like-minded members mainly from lower classes and marginal groups. Worship in sects tends to be highly emotional and based less on abstract

**ecclesia** State-supported churches.

**denominations** The various streams of belief and practice that some churches allow to coexist under their overarching authority.

**sects** Groups that usually form by breaking away from churches because of disagreement about church doctrine. Sects are less integrated into society and less bureaucratized than churches are. They are often led by charismatic leaders, who tend to be relatively intolerant of religious opinions other than their own.

**charismatic leaders** Religious leaders who claim to be inspired by supernatural powers and whose followers believe them to be so inspired.

### TABLE 10.2 Church, Sect, and Cult Compared

|  | Church | Sect | Cult |
| --- | --- | --- | --- |
| Integration into society | High | Medium | Low |
| Bureaucratization | High | Low | Low |
| Longevity | High | Low | Low |
| Leaders | Formally trained | Charismatic | Charismatic |
| Class base | Mixed | Low | Various but segregated |

Source: From BRYM/LIE. *Sociology*, 1E. © 2009 Nelson Education Ltd. Reproduced by permission. www.cengage.com/permissions.

**cults** Small groups of people deeply committed to a religious vision that rejects mainstream culture and society.

principles than immediate personal experience. Usually, sect-like groups appeal to the less affluent and churchlike groups to the more affluent. Many sects are short-lived, but those that do persist tend to bureaucratize and turn into churches. If religious organizations are to enjoy a long life, they require rules, regulations, and a clearly defined hierarchy of roles.

Although major Muslim subgroups are sometimes called denominations by non-Muslims, they are in some respects more appropriately seen as sects. That is because they sometimes do not recognize one another as Muslim and sometimes come into violent conflict with one another, like the Sunni and Shi'a in Iraq today.

**Cults** are small groups of people deeply committed to a religious vision that rejects mainstream culture and society. Cults are generally led by charismatic individuals. They tend to be class-segregated groups, recruiting members from only one segment of the stratification system: high, middle, or low. For example, many North American cults today recruit nearly all their members from among the university-educated. Some of these cults seek converts almost exclusively on university and college campuses (Kosmin, 1991).

Because they propose a radically new way of life, cults tend to recruit few members and soon disappear. There are, however, exceptions—and some extremely important ones at that. Jesus and Muhammad were both charismatic leaders of cults. They were so compelling that they and their teachings were able to inspire a large number of followers, including rulers of states. Their cults were thus transformed into churches.

Canada's immigration patterns have resulted in gains for some religious groups and declines in others over time.

Because worship in sects tends to be highly emotional and based less on abstract principles than immediate personal experience, ecstatic song and dance often takes on ritualistic importance. Here, members of the Habad Lubavich chasidic sect dance.

The number of Muslims more than doubled between 1991 and 2011, reaching an estimated 1.4 million or 3.2 percent of the population. More than two-thirds of Canada's population is Christian, but the proportion of Catholics declined from about 50 percent to 40 percent between 1871 and 2011, while the proportion of Protestants fell from around 45 percent to 27 percent over that 140-year period. The decline in the proportion of Christians is partly due to the growing number of Canadians specifying "no religion" since the 1961 census and partly due to the fact that about one-third of recent immigrants are not Christian. Hindus, Sikhs, Buddhists, and Jews each represent about 1 percent of the population (see Table 10.3 and Figure 10.6).

### TABLE 10.3  Religious Groups, Canada

| Group | Percentage |
| --- | --- |
| Catholic | 40.6 |
|     Roman | 38.7 |
|     Orthodox | 1.7 |
|     Other | 0.2 |
| Protestant | 26.6 |
|     United Church | 6.1 |
|     Anglican | 5.0 |
|     Baptist | 1.9 |
|     Lutheran | 1.5 |
|     Pentecostal | 1.5 |
|     Presbyterian | 1.4 |
|     Other | 9.2 |
| Muslim | 3.2 |
| Hindu | 1.5 |
| Sikh | 1.4 |
| Buddhist | 1.1 |
| Jewish | 1.0 |
| Other | 0.6 |
| No religion | 23.9 |
| **Total** | **99.9** |

Note: Total does not equal 100 percent because of rounding.

Source: Statistics Canada. 2013j. "Religion (108), Immigrant Status and Period of Immigration (11), Age Groups (10) and Sex (3) for the Population in Private Households of Canada, Provinces, Territories, Census Metropolitan Areas and Census Agglomerations," *2011 National Household Survey*.

### FIGURE 10.6  Religious Affiliations, Canada, 1871–2011

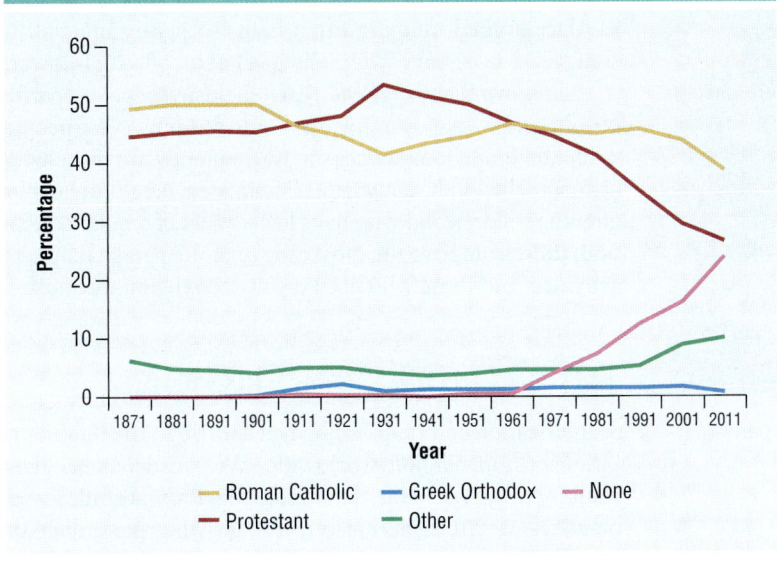

Sources: 1871–1971 from Statistics Canada, 1983, "Historical Statistics of Canada," Catalogue No. 11516XWE; 1981 from Ontario Consultants on Religious Tolerance, 2005, *Information about Religion in Canada*; 1991 and 2001 from Statistics Canada, 2003b, "Religions in Canada," Catalogue No. 96F0030XIE.

### FIGURE 10.7  Religious Involvement over the Life Cycle by Group

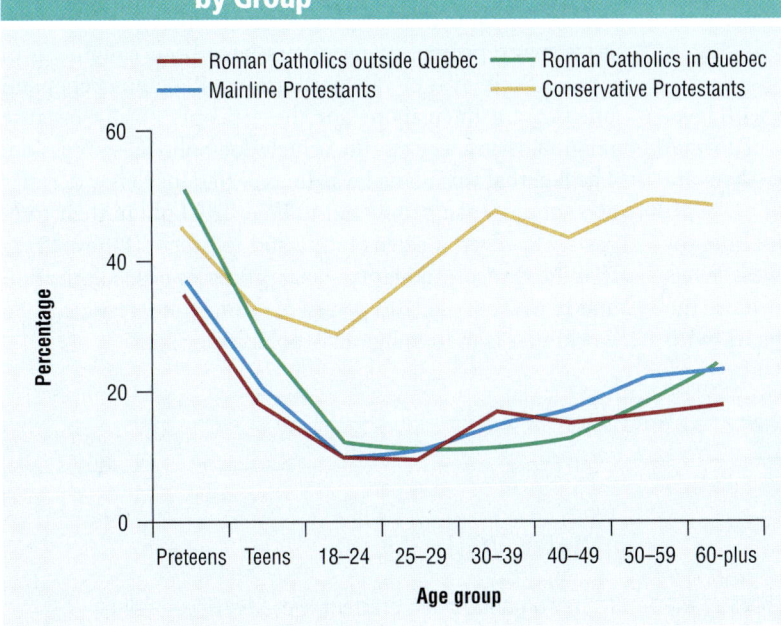

Source: Reginald W. Bibby, 2001. *Canada's Teens: Today, Yesterday, and Tomorrow*. Toronto: Stoddart. Reproduced by permission of the author.

## LO⁵ RELIGIOSITY

It is now time to consider some social factors that determine how important religion is to people, that is, their **religiosity**. It is possible to measure religiosity in various ways. Strength of belief, emotional attachment to a religion, knowledge about a religion, frequency of performing rituals, and frequency of applying religious principles in daily life all indicate how religious a person is. Ideally, one ought to examine many measures to get a fully rounded and reliable picture of the social distribution of religiosity. For simplicity, however, I focus on just one measure here. In a Canada-wide survey, respondents at various points in their lives were asked to indicate whether their level of involvement in religious activities was "high," "moderate," "low," or "none." Figure 10.7 summarizes the results.

Some fascinating patterns emerge from the data. First, the people most heavily involved in religious activities are preteens and seniors. As a result, involvement forms a U-shaped curve, falling among teenagers and young adults and then beginning to rise steadily after the age of about 24.

How can one explain this pattern? Preteens have little say over whether they attend Sunday school, confirmation classes, and the like. For many preteens, religious involvement is high because it is required of them, even if their parents do not always follow suit. At the other end of the lifespan, seniors sometimes have more time and need for religion. Because they are not usually in school, employed in the paid labour force, or busy raising a family, they have more opportunity than young people do to attend religious services. Moreover, because seniors are generally closer to illness and death than are young people, they are more likely to require the solace of religion. To a degree, then, involvement in religious activities is a life-cycle issue. Children are relatively involved in religious activities because they are required to be and seniors are relatively involved because they feel greater need for religious involvement and are in a position to act on that need.

Another issue is at stake here, too. Different age groups live through different times, and today's seniors reached maturity when religion was a more authoritative force in society. A person's current religious involvement depends partly on whether he or she grew up in more religious times. So, although young people are likely to become more religiously involved as they age, they are unlikely ever to become as involved as seniors are today.

A second factor influencing one's level of religious involvement is the region of

**religiosity** The degree to which religion is important to people.

CHAPTER 10 Religion  **229**

*Religiosity is partly a learned behaviour. Whether parents give a child a religious upbringing is likely to have a lasting impact on the child.*

the country in which one happens to live. Atlantic Canada, Saskatchewan, and Manitoba have the highest rates of religious involvement. Quebec and British Columbia have the lowest (Bibby, 2017: 71).

Third, respondents whose parents attended religious services frequently are more likely to do so themselves (Jones, 2000). Religiosity is partly a learned behaviour. Whether parents give a child a religious upbringing is likely to have a lasting impact on the child.

Fourth, religious involvement is associated with level of secular education. People with more years of formal schooling tend to be less religiously involved than are people with fewer years of formal schooling.

Fifth, research indicates that social inequality can promote religiosity, so rich countries with the lowest levels of social inequality, such as Denmark, tend to have the lowest levels of church attendance. Rich countries with high levels of social inequality, such as the United States, tend to have high levels of church attendance. Arguably, as Marx argued, religion often helps to justify inequality, so it is less necessary where the level of inequality is lower.

This overview suggests that religiosity depends partly on obligation, opportunity, need, and learning. The people who attend religious services most frequently are those who are compelled to be active; those who were taught to be religious as children and who have fewer years of secular education; those who have the most time to participate in religious activities; and those who need organized religion the most.

## THE FUTURE OF RELIGION

Secularization and religious revival are two of the dominant influences on religion worldwide. We can detect secularization in survey data that track religious attitudes and practices over time and also in the growing percentage of people who indicate in succeeding censuses that they have no religious affiliation. We also know that various secular institutions are taking over some of the functions formerly performed by religion, thus robbing it of its once pervasive authority over all aspects of life. It is an exaggeration to claim, as Max Weber did, that the whole world is gradually becoming "disenchanted." However, much of it certainly is.

At the same time, we know that even as secularization grips many people, many others have been caught up in a religious revival of vast proportions. Religious belief and practice are intensifying for these people, partly because religion serves as a useful vehicle for political expression. The fact that this revival was unexpected just a few decades ago should warn people not to be overly bold in their forecasts. However, it seems to me and to others (Bibby, 2017) that the two contradictory social processes of secularization and revival are likely to persist for some time, resulting in a world that is more religiously polarized.

## READY TO STUDY?

### IN THE BOOK YOU CAN:

- Refer to the Chapter in Review section at the back of the book to have a summary of the chapter and key terms handy.
- Test your knowledge of chapter contents by answering the multiple-choice questions in the Chapter in Review section. Answers are in the appendix at the end of the book.

### ONLINE YOU CAN:

- Stay organized and efficient with MindTap—a single destination with all the course material and study aids you need to succeed.
- Flashcards are pre-populated to provide you with a jump start for review—or you can create your own.
- You can highlight text and make notes in your MindTap Reader.
- Prepare for tests with quizzes.

GO TO NELSON.COM/STUDENT TO PURCHASE THESE DIGITAL RESOURCES.

# 11 Education

Chicago Tribune/Tribune News Service/Getty Images

## LEARNING OBJECTIVES:

In this chapter, you will learn to

**LO1** Describe how education was transformed from an elite phenomenon to a mass phenomenon.

**LO2** Apply major sociological theories to the analysis of how education promotes upward mobility, creates social cohesion, and reinforces class, racial, and gender inequalities.

**LO3** Analyze the corporatization of higher education.

**LO4** Assess attitudes toward the quality of schooling in Canada and compare the quality of Canadian schools to those in other countries.

# LO1 THE RISE OF MASS EDUCATION

You had spent nearly 15 000 hours in a classroom by the time you finished high school. This fact alone suggests that education dominates socialization outside the family in most rich countries. And of course, you are not alone. More than a fifth of Canadians are learning in educational institutions right now—over 5 million in school and over 2.5 million in college and university (Statistics Canada, 2017n).

Beyond its importance as an agent of socialization, education is a key determinant of opportunities for upward mobility. We care deeply about education, not just because it shapes us but also because it influences how well we do.

Because mass education is so intensive and extensive, we sometimes forget that it's a relatively recent phenomenon. In Europe 300 years ago, the nobility and the wealthy usually hired personal tutors to teach their children to read and write, learn basic history, geography, and foreign languages, and study how to dress properly, conduct themselves in public, greet status superiors, and so on. But few people went to college. Only a few professions, such as theologian and lawyer, required extensive schooling. The great majority of Europeans were illiterate. As late as the 1860s, more than 80 percent of Spaniards and more than 30 percent of the French could not read (Vincent, 2000). Even as recently as a century ago, most people in the world had never attended even a day of school. In 1950, only about 10 percent of the world's countries boasted systems of compulsory mass education (Meyer, Ramirez, and Soysal, 1992).

Today, the situation is vastly different. Compulsory mass education became a universal feature of European and North American life by the early twentieth century, and nearly universal literacy was achieved by the middle of the twentieth century (Curtis, 1988; Vincent, 2000). Every country in the world now has a system of mass schooling.

Still, universal literacy is a remote goal. Fourteen percent of the world's adults are illiterate. In sub-Saharan Africa, the figure is 65 percent. Sixty-three percent of the world's illiterate people are women. Twenty-one percent of primary school-aged children do not attend school. The country with the highest out-of-school rate for children of primary school age is Djibouti, at 48 percent (UNESCO, 2017, 2018). Canada leads the world in this respect at just 3 percent. Canada leads the world in a second respect, too: in 2016, 54 percent of Canadians between the ages of 25 and 64 had a certificate, diploma, or degree from a college or university (Statistics Canada, 2017i).

## UNIFORM SOCIALIZATION

Creating systems of education with enough resources to include all children was a social change of breathtaking scope. Training in families had been decentralized, unorganized, and uneven in quality. Religious training was never widely available and tended to set people apart from the surrounding community. Replacing these forms of instruction with a centralized and rationalized system created strong pressures toward uniformity and standardization. Diversity among families, regions, and religious traditions gradually gave way to homogenized indoctrination into a common culture.

Canada was in some ways exceptional because, in the nineteenth century, the provinces recognized separate school systems for Catholics and Protestants; doing so was necessary to convince Québec to join Confederation. However, the postsecondary institutions' lack of recognition of distinct religious tracks pressured secondary schools to cover the same topics in the same fashion in their efforts to prepare their students for more advanced training. As a result, students today can travel thousands of kilometres for higher education and experience no more discontinuity than do those who attend the nearest school.

Surrendering children to state control was not universally popular, especially at first. Some students preferred skipping class to sitting in school, and special police (truant officers) were charged with tracking down absentees, who were then punished. Effective mass education was achieved only through laws that made attendance compulsory. All Canadian provinces and territories now require parents to ensure their children are educated up to a certain age. Although variation exists, in most provinces about 95 percent of children are in public schools, about 4 percent are in independent schools, and less than 1 percent are home-schooled (Van Pelt et al., 2015). Some children resist schooling's forced drill toward cultural ideals that are at odds with their other experiences, but they are in a minority.

## JOBS AND EARNINGS

Higher educational attainment helps people get jobs and earn more. University graduates have employment rates about a third higher than those with just a high school diploma. The average annual income of university graduates is 82 percent higher than that of people with just a high school diploma (Council of Ontario Universities, 2015: 14). The relationship of education to income pattern is imperfect. People at every level of education are found at each level of earnings. However, the pattern is clear: more education and better earnings tend to go together.

## REASONS FOR THE RISE OF MASS EDUCATION

What accounts for the spread of mass schooling? Sociologists usually highlight four factors: the development of the printing press that led to inexpensive book production, the Protestant Reformation, the spread of democracy, and industrialism. Let us consider each of these factors in turn.

First, the printing press: In 1436, Johannes Gutenberg introduced the printing press with movable type in Europe. The effect was revolutionary. Books were expensive when scribes were the only source of new copies. The printing press led to a dramatic fall in book prices and an explosion of supply. Many of the new printed books were in the vernacular—languages used every day by common folk—and not in the Latin that only scholars understood. Literacy spread beyond elite circles, first in cities and eventually into rural areas, as inexpensive books fostered demand for schools to teach children the useful art of reading (Eisenstein, 1983).

Second, Protestantism: The Catholic Church relied on priests to convey dogma to believers. The education of priests was a primary motivation for the founding of European universities in the Middles Ages. However, in the early sixteenth century, Martin Luther began to criticize the Catholic Church. Protestantism grew out of his criticisms. The Protestants believed that the Bible alone, and not church doctrine, should guide Christians. They expected Christians to have more direct contact with the word of God than was allowed by the Catholic Church. Accordingly, Protestants needed to be able to read the scriptures for themselves. The rise of Protestantism was thus a spur to popular literacy.

Third, democracy: The rise of democracy led to the demand for free education for all children. Where local populations acquired the democratic means to tax themselves, tax-supported schools arose. The earliest school systems were established in Upper Canada and the northern United States about 1870. By 1900, Canada and the United States were the first countries in the world in which enrolment rates for all children aged 5 to 14 exceeded 90 percent. Another first: At least in elementary education, girls were enrolled at almost the same rate as boys were (Lindert, 2004).

The fourth and most important reason for the rise of mass schooling was industrialization. Mass education was widely recognized as an absolute necessity for creating an industrial economy. The Industrial Revolution began in England in the 1780s. Germany and the United States soon sought to catch up to England, and by the turn of the twentieth century, they had surpassed it. Germany and the United States had school systems that offered places to nearly all young people.

Literacy and numeracy were widespread, although what counted as literacy in those days would not impress us today. Historians assess the literacy of that period by counting the rate at which people signed marriage registers or similar documents with a name and not merely an X or another mark. However, as the number of people achieving such minimal performance rose, so did the number of people with much higher levels of literacy. Eventually, it was evident that a highly productive economy requires an education system large enough to create a mass labour force and rich enough to train and employ researchers able to work at the cutting edge of modern science. Democratic countries led the way, but communist countries, like the former Soviet Union, also invested heavily in education to foster economic development.

Today, investment in education is acknowledged as an important step in achieving great national wealth. But education is not only a source of wealth. It is also a product of wealth. After all, education is expensive. Raising education levels for entire populations requires overcoming a vicious cycle: A significant fraction of a country's population must invest a great deal of time and money to become educated before a sufficient number of teachers have been trained to instruct nearly everyone. This time and money must be saved from the time and income that are needed to supply necessities like food and shelter. What is true for individuals is also true for societies: Education enhances the ability to generate earnings and wealth, but educational accumulation is greatly facilitated by an earlier accumulation of wealth.

## LO² SOCIOLOGICAL THEORIES OF EDUCATION

### THE FUNCTIONS OF EDUCATION

Many Canadians believe that we enjoy equal access to basic schooling. They think schools identify and sort students based on merit and effort. They regard the education system as an avenue of upward mobility. From their standpoint, the brightest students are bound to succeed, whatever their economic, ethnic, racial, or religious background. In their view, **educational attainment** is largely an outcome of individual talent and hard work. Educational attainment refers to number of years of school completed. (In contrast, **educational achievement** refers to how much students actually learn.)

The view that the Canadian education system is responsible for sorting students based on talent and effort is a central component of the functional theory of education. The functional theory also stresses the training role of schools. That is, in schools, most people learn how to read, write, count, calculate, and perform other tasks essential to the workings of postmodern society. A third function of the education system involves the socialization of the young (Durkheim, 1956, 1961 [1925]). Schools teach the young to view Canada with pride, respect the law, think of democracy as the best form of government, and value capitalism. Finally, schools transmit culture from generation to generation, fostering a common identity and social cohesion in the process. Schools have played a particularly important role in assimilating the disadvantaged, minorities, and immigrants in Canadian society.

Durkheim emphasized the role of schools in socializing the young and promoting social integration. People, he said, are torn between egoistic needs and moral impulses. Like religion in an earlier era, educational institutions must ensure that the moral side predominates. By instilling a sense of authority, discipline, and morality in children, schools make society cohesive (Durkheim, 1956, 1961 [1925]).

Sorting, training, socializing, and transmitting culture are *manifest* functions, or positive goals that schools

**educational attainment**
The number of years of school that students complete.

**educational achievement**
How much students actually learn.

Apart from being rich and famous, what do Jon Bon Jovi, Bono, Snoop Dogg, Eminem, Mark Zuckerberg, Samuel L. Jackson, Ron Howard, and Jeff Daniels have in common? They all married women they first dated in high school or college or university, exemplifying how educational institutions act as marriage markets. LeBron James married his high school sweetheart, Savannah Brinson, in 2013 and they have three children together.

accomplish intentionally. However, schools also perform certain *latent*, or unintended, functions. For example, schools encourage the development of a separate youth culture that often conflicts with parents' values (Coleman, Campbell, and Hobson, 1966). Especially at the college and university levels, educational institutions bring potential mates together, thus serving as a "marriage market." Schools perform a useful custodial service by keeping children under surveillance for much of the day and freeing parents to work in the paid labour force. Finally, because they can encourage critical, independent thinking, educational institutions sometimes become "schools of dissent" that challenge authoritarian regimes and promote social change (Brower, 1975; Freire, 1972).

## THE EFFECT OF ECONOMIC INEQUALITY FROM THE CONFLICT PERSPECTIVE

From the conflict perspective, the chief problem with the functionalist view is that it exaggerates the degree to which schools sort students by ability and thereby ensure that the most talented students eventually get the most rewarding jobs. Conflict theorists argue that, in fact, schools distribute the benefits of education unequally,

**FIGURE 11.1** Educational Attainment by Income Group, Canada

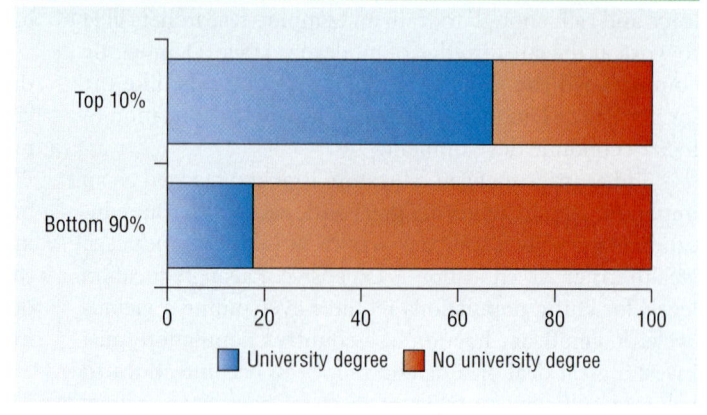

Source: Statistics Canada. 2013k. "Distribution of persons by income group and highest level of education attainment." https://www12.statcan.gc.ca/nhs-enm/2011/as-sa/99-014-x/2011003/c-g/desc/longdesc01_2-eng.cfm (retrieved 8 August 2015).

allocating most of the benefits to children from upper classes and higher-status racial and ethnic groups (see Theories in Dispute, Functionalist vs. Conflict Theories of the Community College). Amount and type of formal education are strongly correlated with earning power. As Figure 11.1 shows, two-thirds of the top 10 percent of income earners in Canada have a university degree compared to fewer than 18 percent of the remaining

## THEORIES IN DISPUTE

### Functionalist vs. Conflict Theories of the Community College

In 2016, more than 525 000 students were enrolled full-time in Canada's 179 colleges and another 202 000 were enrolled part-time. Functionalist and conflict theorists agree that increased demand for skilled workers in industry and services contributed heavily to the rise of the college system since the 1970s. However, the two camps part ways on the question of whether colleges promote upward mobility or simply help to reproduce the class structure.

Functionalists note that college tuition fees are generally lower than university fees and that most college students live with their parents, while many university students do not. Because college is relatively affordable, a disproportionately large number of students from lower socioeconomic strata and minority ethnic groups attend college. Once they are employed following graduation, their socioeconomic status tends to be higher than that of their parents. These facts support the functionalist view that the community college system not only creates new opportunities for disadvantaged youth who might otherwise have less rewarding jobs but also propels them up the socioeconomic hierarchy.

Nonetheless, conflict theorists deny that the college system increases upward mobility and equality. In the long run, they argue, it is the entire stratification system that is upwardly mobile. That is, the quality of nearly all jobs is improving but the *relative* position of college graduates versus university graduates remains the same (see Figure 11.2). Thus, conflict

**FIGURE 11.2** Functionalist vs. Conflict Views of Upward Mobility Due to College Education

**Functionalism:** College enables upward mobility.

**Conflict Theory:** College enables upward mobility only in that the whole stratification system is upwardly mobile.

---

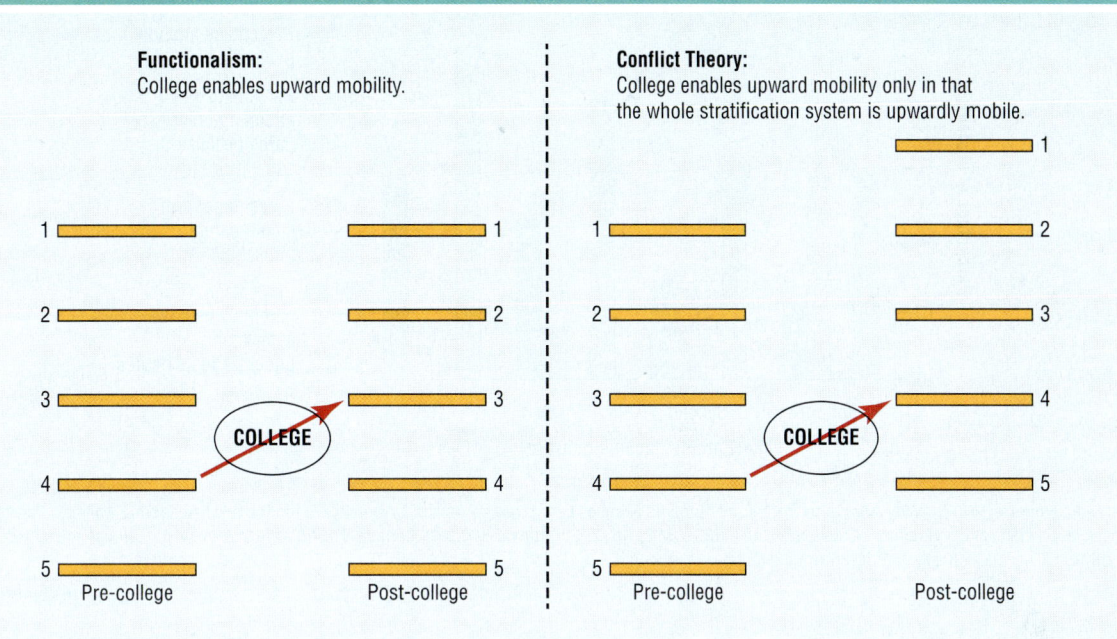

theorists argue that community colleges reinforce prevailing patterns of inequality by directing students from disadvantaged backgrounds away from universities and decreasing the probability that they will earn a four-year degree and a high-status position in society (Karabel, 1986: 18).

The evidence seems to support the conflict theorists' argument. The earnings gap and the employment gap between college and university graduates have not changed much if at all over time; on average, university graduates continue to have a significantly lower unemployment rate and significantly higher earnings than college graduates do. College graduates undoubtedly have better employment outcomes than they would if they did not attend college, but the relative positon of the two categories of graduates in the socioeconomic hierarchy seems to be holding steady (Walters, 2004).

## Critical Thinking Question

- In light of the discussion above, how would you describe the effect of attending college on intragenerational mobility and intergenerational mobility?

Canadians. Schools tend to reproduce the stratification system generation after generation.

Exactly how does the education system help to reproduce the class system? Sociologists have identified five social mechanisms at work.

First is *financial constraint*. Some people do not attend university or college because they feel they can't afford it, even if they work part-time and take advantage of student loans. More than twice as many 19-year-olds from low-income families feel this way, compared with 19-year-olds from high-income families (see the yellow columns in Figure 11.3).

Second is the increase in *one-parent households*. Low-income parents are more likely than are high-income parents to experience the kinds of financial problems that can make marriage difficult and contribute to divorce. In turn, children from one-parent households are often unable to rely on adults for tutoring, emotional support and encouragement, supervision, and role modelling to the same degree as children from two-parent households can. This puts children from one-parent households at a disadvantage. Significantly, the red columns in Figure 11.3 show that 19-year-olds from low-income families are six times as likely as 19-year-olds from high-income families to have been raised in a one-parent household.

The third mechanism linking class to educational outcomes involves *lack of cultural capital*. High-income

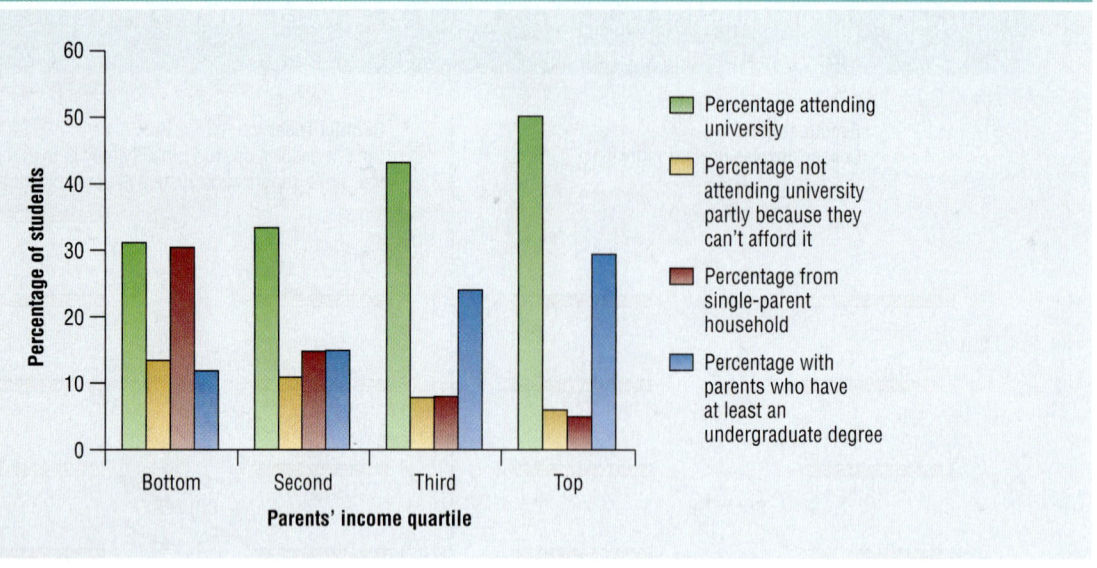

**FIGURE 11.3** The Effects of Parents' Social Class on the Education of 19-Year-Old Canadians

Source: Marc Frenette. 2007. "Why Are Youth from Lower-Income Families Less Likely to Attend University? Evidence from Academic Abilities, Parental Influences, and Financial Constraints." Catalogue No. 11F0019MIE, No. 295. Ottawa: Statistics Canada. Found at http://www.statcan.ca/english/research/11F0019MIE/11F0019MIE2007295.pdf (26 April 2007).

parents are two-and-a-half times as likely as low-income parents to have earned undergraduate degrees (see the blue columns in Figure 11.3). This fact is important because university education gives people cultural capital that they can transmit to their children, thus improving their chance of financial success. Cultural capital refers to "widely shared, high-status cultural signals (attitudes, preferences, formal knowledge, behaviours, goals, and credentials) used for social and cultural exclusion" (Lamont and Lareau, 1988: 156). If you possess a lot of cultural capital, you are more likely to have "highbrow" tastes in literature, music, art, and dance—and to behave according to established rules of etiquette. You are more likely to create a household environment that promotes refined taste and provides formal lessons to help instill such taste in your children, increasing their chance of success in school and, eventually, in the paid labour force (Bourdieu and Passeron, 1990; DiMaggio, 1982; Kingston, 2001).

Much evidence supports the conflict perspective. For instance, the green columns in Figure 11.3 show that Canadians from high-income families are 61 percent more likely than are those from low-income families to be enrolled in university at the age of 19. (Here, "high-income" families are those in the top 25 percent of family income and "low-income" families are those in the bottom 25 percent.) Research also shows that about 60 percent of 25- to 34-year-old Canadians whose fathers are professionals or managers attend university. The figure falls to 35 percent for those whose fathers are supervisory workers and to less than 30 percent for those whose fathers are skilled workers. Among those whose fathers are unskilled workers, fewer than 20 percent attend university, and for those whose fathers are farmers, the figure is around 10 percent (Guppy and Davies, 1998). Clearly, class strongly influences whether a person gets to university.

*Streaming* is the fourth mechanism that links class to educational outcomes. The more intelligent you are, the more likely you are to do well in school and to achieve economic success later in life. IQ and other standardized tests are employed to sort students by intelligence; test scores are used to channel them into high-ability ("enriched"), middle-ability, and low-ability ("basic" or "special education") classrooms. The trouble is that IQ and other standardized tests can measure only acquired proficiency in a given cultural system. The quantity and quality of a person's exposure to whatever is counted as proper or correct plays a large role here. Even the most able Anglo-Canadian children would perform abysmally if tested in Mongolian.

The results of IQ and other standardized tests therefore depend on two factors: (1) how effectively an individual absorbs what his or her environment offers, and (2) how closely his or her environment reflects what the test includes. Consequently, members of underprivileged groups tend to score low on IQ and other standardized tests—not because they are on average less intelligent than members of privileged groups are, but because they do not have the training and the cultural background needed to achieve higher scores (Fischer et al., 1996). Nonetheless, educators persist in using IQ and other standardized tests to sort students into different types of classes (Samuda et al., 1980). The result: Streaming reproduces class differences, determines who goes to university and who doesn't, and influences who enters which social class in the larger society.

Finally, the Internet helps to turn class inequality into inequality of educational attainment and achievement. The Internet is an increasingly important source of ideas and information, and people with high income are more likely to have easy access to the Internet than are people with low income. The access gap is shrinking over time, but recent Web-based developments are helping to ensure that class differences in educational attainment and achievement persist. Higher-education systems are turning to the Internet to offer MOOCs (Massive Open Online Courses), while some public schools are turning to largely unsupervised, computerized instructional systems (see Sociology and the Media, MOOCs and Virtual Classrooms: Who Benefits?)

## SOCIOLOGY AND THE MEDIA

### MOOCs and Virtual Classrooms: Who Benefits?

In the late 2000s, MOOCs were heralded as the most disruptive and democratizing innovation in higher education since the invention of the printed book. The year 2012 was proclaimed "the year of the MOOC," and Sebastian Thrun, sometimes called the godfather of free online education, predicted that in 50 years just 10 brick-and-mortar universities would remain in existence. According to Thrun, nearly everyone would be learning online for free.

Although the growth of MOOCs has not been as explosive as once imagined, enrolments have been impressive. In Canada (where the term "MOOC" was invented and one of the first MOOCs went online in 2008), 92 MOOCs were on offer in 2018, mainly by the University of Toronto, the University of British Columbia, the University of Alberta, and McGill University ("Canada MOOCs...," 2018). One of the leading proponents of MOOCs reported that, worldwide in 2017, more than 800 universities offered about 9400 MOOCs in which roughly 78 million students were enrolled (Shah, 2018).

Seventy-eight million is a huge number, but it turns out that the course completion rate is abysmal—according to one research finding, less than 7 percent of enrolments (Parr, 2013). Moreover, MOOCs are not the democratizing force they were anticipated to become. The modal MOOC student is an American or European male who enjoys a socioeconomic status well above average. He already has a university degree and is taking a course for purposes of professional development. Just a third of MOOC students and 15 percent of MOOC instructors are women, and a mere 4 percent of MOOC students are residents of Africa (Glass, Shiokawa-Baklan, and Saltarelli, 2015; Shah, 2017).

Meanwhile, at the K–12 level, we find educators taking advantage of another educational innovation that employs the Web and educational software: virtual classrooms. Virtual classrooms feature a bank of computers connected to the Internet but no teacher, just a poorly-paid, non-unionized "facilitator" to deal with technical issues and ensure that students make progress.

Virtual classrooms are concentrated in the United States. There, states pay for 43 percent of public school budgets and municipalities for 44 percent, so if you happen to live in a poor state and/or a poor municipality, there isn't a lot of money available to invest in public education (McCann, 2018). Virtual classrooms help; they save money since they don't require teachers.

In 2013–14, some 2.7 million American students were enrolled in virtual classrooms, up 80 percent since 2009–10 (Connections Academy, 2018). As for the quality of education, we may rely on the words of one high school sophomore taking advanced placement macroeconomics in a virtual classroom: "None of [us] want to be there" (quoted in Herrera, 2011).

Students attending public schools in richer states and/or municipalities—not to mention the nearly 10 percent of students attending private schools in North America—don't need to worry much about such technological "progress."

### Critical Thinking Question

- How has the Web influenced your education? Why has it exercised this influence?

**FIGURE 11.4** Ratio of Men to Women, Ages 25–64, with University Certificate, Diploma or Degree at Bachelor Level or Above, by Field, Canada, 2016

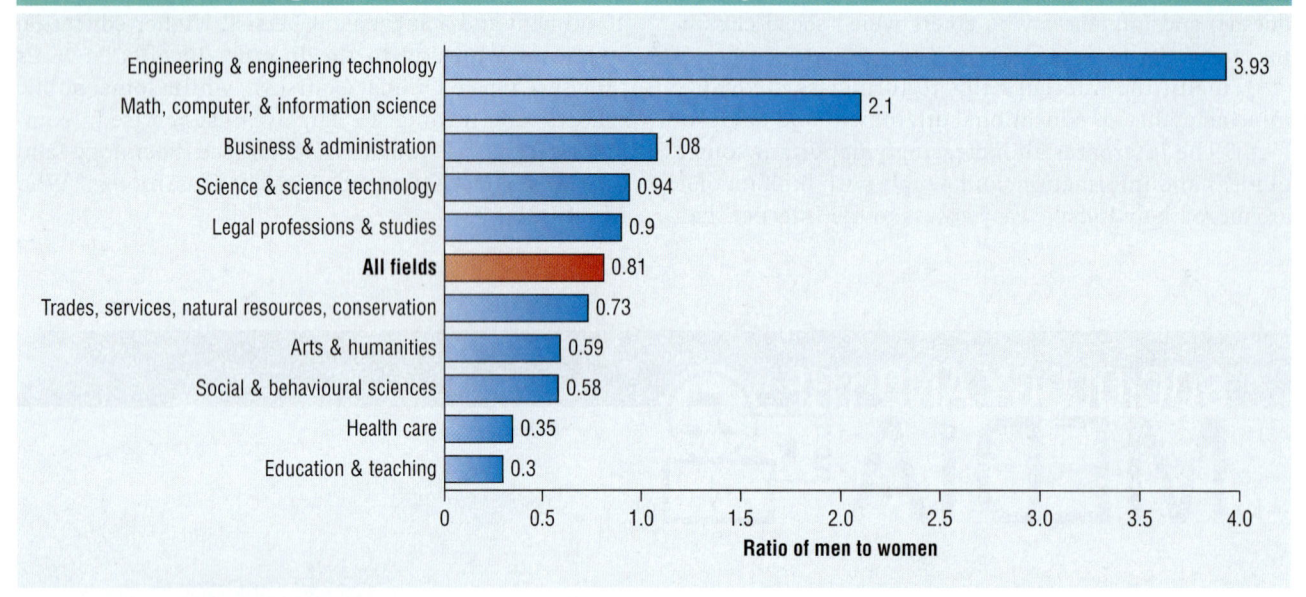

| Field | Ratio of men to women |
|---|---|
| Engineering & engineering technology | 3.93 |
| Math, computer, & information science | 2.1 |
| Business & administration | 1.08 |
| Science & science technology | 0.94 |
| Legal professions & studies | 0.9 |
| All fields | 0.81 |
| Trades, services, natural resources, conservation | 0.73 |
| Arts & humanities | 0.59 |
| Social & behavioural sciences | 0.58 |
| Health care | 0.35 |
| Education & teaching | 0.3 |

Source: Statistics Canada. 2017v. "Major field of study STEM and BHASE (non-STEM) groupings for selected age groups 25 to 64, both sexes, and selected highest levels of educational attainment (university certificate, diploma or degree at bachelor level or above), % distribution 2016, Canada, provinces and territories, 2016 Census – 25% Sample data." http://www12.statcan.gc.ca/census-recensement/2016/dp-pd/hlt-fst/edu-sco/Table.cfm?Lang=E&T=41&Geo=00&View=2&Age=2&Education=3 (retrieved 28 February 2018).

## GENDER AND EDUCATION: THE FEMINIST CONTRIBUTION

In some respects, women are doing better than men are in the Canadian education system. Women in colleges and universities have higher grade point averages than men do, and they complete their degrees faster. The number of women enrolled as college and university undergraduates has exceeded the number of men for decades, and more women than men are now enrolled in some graduate and professional programs, such as medicine and law. The enrolment gap between women and men is growing—not just in Canada but also in the United States, the United Kingdom, France, Germany, and Australia (Berliner, 2004). Men receive fewer than 40 percent of the quarter of a million degrees granted by Canadian colleges and universities annually.

The facts just listed represent considerable improvement over time in the position of women in the education system. Yet feminists who have looked closely at the situation have established that women are still at a disadvantage. Consider level of education and field of study. Although women receive more degrees than men do, the gap narrows considerably at the master's level and reverses at the PhD level, where men receive about 56 percent of degrees (Statistics Canada, 2013l). Moreover, a disproportionately large number of men earn degrees in engineering, computer science, dentistry, and specialized areas of medicine— all relatively high-paying fields, most requiring a strong math and science background. A disproportionately large number of women earn PhDs in education, English, foreign languages, and other relatively low-paying fields requiring little background in math and science (see Figure 11.4).

Parents and teachers are partly responsible for these choices because they tend to direct boys and girls toward what they regard as masculine and feminine fields of study. Gender segregation in the labour market also influences choice of field of study. University students know women are more likely to get jobs in certain fields than in others and they make career choices accordingly (Spade, 2001). Like class, gender structures the educational experience and its consequences.

## THE STEREOTYPE THREAT: A SYMBOLIC INTERACTIONIST VIEW

Macrosociological issues, such as the functions of education and the influence of class and gender on educational achievement, do not exhaust the interests of sociologists of education. They have also contributed much to our understanding of the face-to-face interaction processes that influence the educational process. Consider this finding from American research: When black and white children begin school, their achievement test scores are similar. Yet the longer they stay in school, the more black students fall behind. By Grade 6, blacks in many school districts are two full grades behind whites in achievement. Clearly, something happens in school to increase the gap between black and white students. Symbolic interactionists suggest that this something is the self-fulfilling prophecy, an expectation that helps to bring about what it predicts.

We encountered examples of self-fulfilling prophecies in educational settings in Chapter 4, From Social Interaction to Social Organizations. For instance, we discussed one famous experiment in which, at the beginning of a school year, researchers randomly identified students as high or low achievers to their teachers. At the end of the school year, they found that the students arbitrarily singled out as high achievers scored higher on an IQ test than those arbitrarily singled out as low achievers. The researchers concluded that teachers' expectations influenced students' performance (Rosenthal and Jacobson, 1968; Weinstein, 2002).

Many teachers expect members of lower classes and some visible-minority groups to do poorly in school. Rather than being treated as young people with good prospects, such students are often under suspicion of intellectual inferiority and often feel rejected by teachers, white middle-class classmates, and the curriculum. This expectation, sometimes called a **stereotype threat**, has a negative impact on the school performance of disadvantaged groups (Massey et al., 2003; Steele, 1997).

Minority-group students often cluster together because they feel alienated from dominant groups in their school or perhaps even from the institution itself. Too often, such alienation turns into resentment and defiance of authority. Many students from minority groups reject academic achievement as a goal because they see it as a value of the dominant culture. Discipline problems, ranging from apathy to disruptive and illegal behaviour, can result.

The corollary of identifying your race or ethnicity with poor academic performance is thinking of good academic performance as "selling out" to the dominant culture (Ogbu, 2003; Willis, 1984). Consistent with this argument, Indigenous and black students in Canada have higher-than-average school dropout rates. In 2011, the Toronto District School Board conducted research on students who were in Grade 9 five years earlier. The dropout rate was 14 percent overall. For black students, it was 23 percent, and for black students born in the Caribbean, it was 30 percent (Toronto District School Board, 2011). Among Indigenous peoples, the dropout rate in 2011 was 41 percent, four times the national average (Brown, 2014). In contrast, research shows that challenging lower-class and minority students, giving them emotional support and encouragement, giving greater recognition in the curriculum to the accomplishments of the groups from which they originate, creating an environment in which they can relax and achieve—all of these strategies explode the self-fulfilling prophecy and improve academic performance (Steele, 1992).

In sum, the stereotype threat at the microsociological level combines with the macrosociological processes described earlier to help reproduce the stratification system. These social mechanisms increase the chance that those who are socially marginal and already disadvantaged will earn low grades and wind up with jobs closer to the bottom than to the top of the occupational structure.

**stereotype threat** The impact of negative stereotypes on the school performance of disadvantaged groups.

**corporatization** The reshaping of universities on a business model. In practice, corporatization involves consumers of higher education paying a larger share of the cost of the services they enjoy and universities responding better to market demand for particular skills.

Although the composition of Canada's student population is becoming increasingly multicultural, this is less true of Canada's teachers. An ongoing debate in Canada is whether students at all levels would be better served by a faculty whose composition reflects the diversity of our population and who offer a more inclusive curriculum.

# LO 3 THE CORPORATIZATION OF THE UNIVERSITY

Observers have been documenting the corporatization of the Canadian university for three decades (Brownlee, 2015). By **corporatization**, they mean the reshaping of universities on a business model. In practice, corporatization involves consumers of higher education paying a larger share of the cost

# THEORIES AT A GLANCE

## Education

| Theory | Main Question | Application |
|---|---|---|
| Functionalism | How do social structures and the values underlying them contribute to social stability? | The view that the education system is responsible for sorting students based on talent and effort is a central component of the functional theory of education. The functional theory also stresses the training role of schools. That is, in schools, most people learn how to read, write, count, calculate, and perform other tasks essential to the workings of postmodern society.<br><br>A third function of the education system involves the socialization of the young. Schools teach the young to view their country with pride, respect the law, think of democracy as the best form of government, and value capitalism. Finally, schools transmit culture from generation to generation, fostering a common identity and social cohesion in the process.<br><br>Sorting, training, socializing, and transmitting culture are *manifest* functions, or positive goals that schools accomplish intentionally. Schools also perform certain *latent*, or unintended, functions. For example, schools encourage the development of a separate youth culture that often conflicts with parents' values. Especially at the college and university levels, educational institutions bring potential mates together, thus serving as a "marriage market." Schools perform a useful custodial service by keeping children under surveillance for much of the day and freeing parents to work in the paid labour force. Finally, because they can encourage critical, independent thinking, educational institutions sometimes become "schools of dissent" that challenge authoritarian regimes and promote social change. |
| Conflict theory | How does the structure of inequality between privileged groups seeking to maintain their advantages and subordinate groups seeking to increase theirs lead to conflict and often to social change? | From the conflict perspective, the chief problem with the functionalist view is that it exaggerates the degree to which schools sort students by ability and thereby ensure that the most talented students eventually get the most rewarding jobs. Conflict theorists argue that, in fact, schools distribute the benefits of education unequally, allocating most of the benefits to children from upper classes and higher-status racial and ethnic groups.<br><br>Five mechanisms allow the education system to help reproduce the class system. First, some people do not attend university or college because they feel they can't afford it, even if they work part-time and take advantage of student loans. Second, low-income parents are more likely than are high-income parents to experience the kinds of financial problems that can make marriage difficult and contribute to divorce. In turn, children from one-parent households are often unable to rely on adults for tutoring, emotional support and encouragement, supervision, and role modelling to the same degree as children from two-parent households can. This puts children from one-parent households at a disadvantage. The third mechanism linking class to educational outcomes involves lack of cultural capital. High-income parents are two-and-a-half times as likely as low-income parents to have earned undergraduate degrees. This fact is important because university education gives people cultural capital that they can transmit to their children, thus improving their chance of financial success. Fourth, IQ and other standardized tests are employed to sort students by intelligence; test scores are used to channel them into high-ability ("enriched"), middle-ability, and low-ability ("basic" or "special education") classrooms. The trouble is that IQ and other standardized tests can measure only acquired proficiency in a given cultural system. The quantity and quality of a person's exposure to whatever is counted as proper or correct plays a large role here. Fifth, the Internet helps to turn class inequality into inequality of educational attainment and achievement. The Internet is an increasingly important source of ideas and information, and people with high income are more likely to have easy access to the Internet than are people with low income. The access gap is shrinking over time, but recent Web-based developments (MOOCs and virtual classrooms) are helping to ensure that class differences in educational attainment and achievement persist. |

| | | |
|---|---|---|
| Symbolic interactionism | How do people communicate to make their social settings meaningful, thus helping to create their social circumstances? | Many teachers expect members of lower classes and some visible-minority groups to do poorly in school. Rather than being treated as young people with good prospects, such students are often under suspicion of intellectual inferiority and often feel rejected by teachers, white middle-class classmates, and the curriculum. This expectation, sometimes called a *stereotype threat*, has a negative impact on the school performance.<br><br>Minority-group students often cluster together because they feel alienated from dominant groups in their school or perhaps even from the institution itself. Too often, such alienation turns into resentment and defiance of authority. Many students from minority groups reject academic achievement as a goal because they see it as a value of the dominant culture. Discipline problems, ranging from apathy to disruptive and illegal behaviour, can result.<br><br>The corollary of identifying your race or ethnicity with poor academic performance is thinking of good academic performance as "selling out" to the dominant culture. Consistent with this argument, Indigenous and black students in Canada have higher-than-average school dropout rates.<br><br>In contrast, research shows that challenging lower-class and minority students, giving them emotional support and encouragement, giving greater recognition in the curriculum to the accomplishments of the groups from which they originate, creating an environment in which they can relax and achieve—all of these strategies explode the self-fulfilling prophecy and improve academic performance. |
| Feminism | How do social conventions maintain male dominance and female subordination, and how do these conventions get overturned? | Feminist theorists note that although women now constitute a majority of students in institutions of higher education, the gender gap narrows considerably at the master's level and reverses at the PhD level, where men receive most degrees. Moreover, a disproportionately large number of men earn degrees in engineering, computer science, dentistry, and specialized areas of medicine—all relatively high-paying fields, most requiring a strong math and science background. A disproportionately large number of women earn PhDs in education, English, foreign languages, and other relatively low-paying fields requiring little background in math and science. |

of the services they enjoy and universities responding to market demand for particular skills.

Corporatization is a change from the way universities were organized until the 1980s, when they were more heavily subsidized by government, academic personnel were freer to shape university priorities as they saw fit, and few instructors were cost-cutting part-timers. Average undergraduate university tuition fees for Canadian students are correlated with corporatization. Adjusted for inflation, fees fell from 1965 to 1981, remained steady from 1982 to 1989, and then started climbing sharply. By 2017–18, average fees were 2.6 times higher than in 1990–91, again adjusted for inflation. Ontario led the country in fee hikes, with 2017–18 fees standing 29 percent above the national average (Bank of Canada, 2018; Harris, 2017; Pelletier and Thomas, 1998; Strapagiel, 2013; Usher, 2017). Consumers—that is, students and their families—have paid dearly for corporatization.

True, government still contributes 41 percent of postsecondary revenue. Tuition contributes 28 percent, and private donations, mostly from big corporations and their owners, much of the remainder. However, of the 37 well-to-do countries in the Organisation for Economic Co-operation and Development, Canada ranks 32nd in the contribution of government to postsecondary education. In six northern European countries, governments pay more than 90 percent of postsecondary revenue (Organisation for Economic Co-operation and Development, 2018b; Statistics Canada, 2017g).

Another sign of corporatization is the growing tendency for Canadian university students to enrol in fields for which there is relatively high demand and therefore relatively high earnings. It is difficult to know how much of this shift is due to the changing priorities and enticements of the corporatized university and how much is due to student choice—or even if it is possible to disentangle these two sources of change.

In any case, the resulting pattern is laid out in Table 11.1. Rows shaded green indicate fields that grew in relative terms between 1992 and 2015. Fields that experienced no relative growth are shaded yellow. Rows shaded grey indicate fields in which enrolment shrunk relative to other fields. The big picture over the nearly quarter of a century summarized by Table 11.1 is a tendency for

## TABLE 11.1 University Enrolment by Field, Canada, 1992 and 2015

| | Enrolment 1992 | % of total 1992 | Enrolment 2015 | % of total 2015 | Relative change in % | |
|---|---|---|---|---|---|---|
| Health | 70 353 | 8 | 159 369 | 12 | +4 | Growing |
| Business | 136 845 | 15 | 237 354 | 18 | +3 | |
| Architecture, engineering | 64 341 | 7 | 131 253 | 10 | +3 | |
| Science | 73 275 | 8 | 126 990 | 10 | +2 | |
| Visual & performing arts | 25 167 | 3 | 45 822 | 4 | +1 | |
| Math & computer science | 31 938 | 4 | 48 687 | 4 | 0 | Stagnant |
| Agriculture & related | 13 470 | 2 | 22 359 | 2 | 0 | |
| Social science | 147 486 | 17 | 226 581 | 17 | 0 | |
| Education | 87 033 | 10 | 76 887 | 6 | −4 | Shrinking |
| Humanities | 148 362 | 17 | 162 246 | 12 | −5 | |
| Other | 87 375 | 10 | 69 726 | 5 | −5 | |

Source: Statistics Canada 2018c. "Postsecondary enrolments, by registration status, International Standard Classification of Education (ISCED), Classification of Instructional Programs, Primary Grouping (CIP_PG), sex and student status, annually (Number)." CANSIM Table 4770019.

Canadian students to look increasingly for greener pastures in health, business, engineering, and science.

It is likely significant that most of the criticism of corporatization comes from professors in the social sciences, education, and the humanities, all fields that are either stagnating or shrinking in terms of their relative share of the student body. Here, self-interest and idealism appear to coincide. Professors in fields that are growing relatively slowly, if at all, may be expressing both their sincere belief in the importance of humanistic, liberal arts education and a desire to protect their jobs. Adding to their discontent is that they are in fields that attract people with left-leaning political views in the first place and that reinforce such views (Brym and Nakhaie, 2009; Nakhaie and Brym, 1999; 2011).

It may also be significant in this regard that professors in the social sciences, education, and humanities are among the most likely to remain in their jobs past the age of 70. At 71, they earn their salary and are obliged by law to receive their university and government pensions—and to start withdrawing money from their private pension (RRSP) if they have one. People in this position are likely to enjoy an annual income of $234 700 or more, placing them in the top 1 percent of Canadian income earners (Younglai, 2017). I estimate that if a law were passed requiring professors over the age of 70 to earn either their salary *or* their pensions, then as many as 1000 young professors could be hired in the tenure stream in Ontario alone, something that students (not to mention unemployed and underemployed PhDs) would undoubtedly be happy to see (Brym, 2015c).

The corporatization of the university undoubtedly comes with risks, not the least of which is excessive corporate influence on university policy. Critics play a useful role in keeping a watchful eye on university governance, including at least one instance where critics exposed the case of a Canadian university president allegedly receiving payment for sitting on the board of a large corporation and sacrificing academic integrity by seeking to influence university policy in ways that would benefit that corporation (Srigley, 2018).

Paradoxically, however, it might make more sense for universities to broaden outside influence rather than seeking to eliminate it. In Denmark, umbrella organizations of universities, corporations, and unions consult frequently. They decide on funding priorities that result in educating university students so they can find interesting and well-paying jobs that the Danish economy needs. This arrangement helps to keep Denmark's per capita income higher than Canada's, its unemployment rate lower, and its people happier (Andersen, 2016; World Happiness Report 2017). Taxpayers are the ultimate constituents of the professoriate. It seems to me that if one favours a truly democratic system of higher education that is responsive to the wants and needs of the citizenry, one should want decision making to be as broadly based as possible. From this point of view, allowing excessive corporate *or* professorial influence does not serve the public interest.

# CANADIAN SCHOOLS: PUBLIC ATTITUDES AND INTERNATIONAL COMPARISON

Between 1979 and 2007, the percentage of adult Canadians giving public schools a grade of A or B declined from 59 percent to 48 percent (Canadian Education Association, 2007: 9). Ontario appears to be bucking the trend, with the percentage of adults expressing satisfaction with schools increasing from 51 percent to 60 percent between 1980 and 2015 (Hart and Kempf, 2015). Still, a large percentage of adults in Ontario and the rest of Canada are unhappy with the public school system. Many Canadians believe that the public school system has turned soft if not rotten. They argue that the youth of Japan and South Korea spend long hours concentrating on the basics of math, science, and language, while Canadian students spend fewer hours in school and study more non-basic subjects (art, music, drama, physical education) that are of little practical value. If students do not spend more school time on subjects that "really" matter, they warn, Canada will suffer declining economic competitiveness. Many Canadians—8 in 10 according to one poll—want province-wide standardized tests for students and teachers because they presumably allow school performance to be objectively assessed (Bricker and Greenspon, 2001: 165–6).

Partly because of the perceived decline in school standards, a growing number of Canadian children do not attend public schools. About 1 percent of Canadian children are home-schooled and about 7 percent attend private schools (Boyer, 2012). In relatively affluent cities, such as Toronto, the latter figure is roughly 10 percent.

Private schools offer specialized programs, small classes, contact with the "right" people, and facilities that students in public schools can only dream of. For the academic year 2018–19, the family of a Canadian boy entering Upper Canada College in Toronto in Grade 11 or Grade 12 and boarding at the school would have to pay $71 585 for the year (Upper Canada College, 2018). Among other amenities, the school has its own indoor regulation-sized hockey rink. A girl attending Bishop Strachan School in Toronto for a slightly lower fee is entitled to her own personal trainer.

Expensive private schools aside, international comparisons show that Canadians perform relatively well in standardized math, science, and literacy tests. In fact, according to the most comprehensive and widely respected international study of 15-year-old student performance, Canada's school system ranks sixth in the world (see Table 11.2). Moreover, Canada is among the top six countries in terms of providing a good education to students from all socioeconomic classes (the others are Finland, Iceland, Japan, South Korea, and Sweden; Sokoloff, 2001). This is not cause for complacency, though. We still need to do a lot to improve the quality of Canadian education, particularly for students from disadvantaged families. High dropout rates among black and Indigenous students are of particular concern. However, the public's fears about mediocre and declining educational standards are likely overdrawn.

Recent surveys suggest that Canadians have only a moderate level of confidence in the job being done by the public education sector.

### TABLE 11.2 The World's Top 10 School Systems

| Rank | Reading | Science | Math | Overall |
|---|---|---|---|---|
| 1 | Singapore | Singapore | Singapore | Singapore |
| 2 | **Canada** | Japan | Taiwan | Japan |
| 3 | Finland | Estonia | Japan | Estonia |
| 4 | Ireland | Taiwan | South Korea | Taiwan |
| 5 | Estonia | **Canada** | Switzerland | Finland |
| 6 | South Korea | Viet Nam | Estonia | **Canada** |
| 7 | Japan | South Korea | **Canada** | Viet Nam |
| 8 | Norway | New Zealand | Netherlands | South Korea |
| 9 | New Zealand | Slovenia | Finland | New Zealand |
| 10 | Germany | Australia | Denmark | Slovenia |

Source: Organisation for Economic Co-operation and Development. 2018. "PISA 2015 Results in Focus," https://www.oecd.org/pisa/pisa-2015-results-in-focus.pdf (retrieved 28 February 2018).

# 12
# Health and Medicine

## LEARNING OBJECTIVES:

In this chapter, you will learn to

**LO¹** Recognize that health risks are unevenly distributed by class, gender, race, and country of residence.

**LO²** Explain why low-income people and people who belong to groups that experience a high level of discrimination, such as Indigenous Canadians, have limited access to health services.

**LO³** Clarify the ways in which gender affects health outcomes.

**LO⁴** Identify the ways in which the social organization of health care systems influences people's health.

**LO⁵** Describe how the rise of medical science is linked to (1) successful treatments and (2) the way doctors excluded competitors and established control over their profession and their clients.

**LO⁶** Appreciate the benefits and dangers of alternative medical treatments.

## THE BLACK DEATH

In 1346, rumours reached Europe of a plague sweeping the East. Originating in Asia, the epidemic spread along trade routes to China and Russia. A year later, 12 galleys sailed from southern Russia to Italy. Diseased sailors were onboard. Their lymph nodes were swollen and eventually burst, causing painful death. Anyone who came in contact with the sailors was soon infected. As a result, the ships were driven out of several Italian and French ports. Yet the disease spread relentlessly, again moving along trade routes to Spain, Portugal, and England. Within two years, the Black Death, as it came to be known, killed a third of Europe's population. More than 650 years later, the plague still ranks as the most devastating catastrophe in human history (Herlihy, 1998; McNeill, 1976; Zinsser, 1935).

Today we know that the cause of the plague was a bacillus that spread from fleas to rats to people. It spread so efficiently because many people lived close together in unsanitary conditions. However, in the middle of the fourteenth century nobody knew anything about germs. Pope Clement VI sent a delegation to Europe's leading medical school in Paris to discover the cause of the plague. The learned professors studied the problem. They reported that a particularly unfortunate conjunction of Saturn, Jupiter, and Mars in the sign of Aquarius had occurred in 1345. The resulting hot, humid conditions caused the earth to emit poisonous vapours. To prevent the plague, they said, people should refrain from eating poultry, waterfowl, pork, beef, fish, and olive oil. They should not sleep during the daytime or engage in excessive exercise. Nothing should be cooked in rainwater. Bathing should be avoided at all costs.

We do not know whether the Pope followed the professors' advice. We do know he made a practice of sitting between two large fires to breathe pure air. Because the plague bacillus is destroyed by heat, this may have saved his life. Other people were less fortunate. Some rang church bells and fired cannons to drive away the plague. Others burned incense, wore charms, and cast spells. But other than the Pope, the only people to have much luck in avoiding the plague were the well-to-do (who could afford to flee the densely populated cities for remote areas in the countryside) and the Jews (whose religion required that they wash their hands before meals, bathe once a week, and conduct burials soon after death).

Some of the main themes of the sociology of health and medicine are embedded in the story of the Black Death, or at least implied by it. First, recall that some groups were more likely to die of the plague than others were. This is a common

**life expectancy** The average age at death of the members of a population.

pattern. Health risks are always unevenly distributed. Women and men, upper and lower classes, rich and poor countries, and privileged and disadvantaged members of racial and ethnic groups are exposed to health risks to varying degrees. This fact suggests that health is not just a medical issue but also a sociological one. In this chapter, I first examine the sociological factors that account for the uneven distribution of health in society.

Second, the story of the Black Death suggests that health problems change over time. Epidemics of various types still break out, but there can be no Black Death where sanitation, hygiene, and the quarantine of infected people prevent the spread of disease. Today we are also able to treat many infectious diseases, such as tuberculosis and pneumonia, with antibiotics. Twentieth-century medical science developed these drugs and many other life-saving therapies.

Medical successes allow people to live longer than they used to. **Life expectancy** is the average age at death of the members of a population. Life expectancy in Canada in 1831 was approximately 40 years for men and 42 years for women (Lavoie and Oderkirk, 2000: 3). In contrast, a Canadian girl born in 2015 can hope to live 84 years, a boy 80 years (World Bank, 2018). Yet, because of increased life expectancy, degenerative conditions, such as cancer and heart disease, have an opportunity to develop in a way that was not possible a century ago (see Table 12.1). Other factors, notably galloping weight gains, contribute to disease burden (see Figure 12.1).

The Black Death

The story of the Black Death raises a third issue, too. One cannot help being struck by the superstition and ignorance surrounding the treatment of the ill in medieval times. Remedies were often herbal but also included earthworms, urine, and animal excrement. People believed it was possible to maintain good health by keeping body

### TABLE 12.1 Ten Leading Causes of Death, Canada, 1901 and 2014

**Percentage of Deaths**

| | 1901 | % | | 2014 | % |
|---|---|---|---|---|---|
| 1. | Tuberculosis | 12.0 | 1. | Cancer | 29.8 |
| 2. | Bronchitis and pneumonia | 10.0 | 2. | Heart disease | 19.7 |
| 3. | Infections of the intestines | 9.1 | 3. | Stroke | 5.2 |
| 4. | Senile debility | 7.4 | 4. | Chronic lower respiratory diseases | 4.6 |
| 5. | Congenital debility | 7.0 | 5. | Accidents | 4.5 |
| 6. | Diseases of the heart | 5.6 | 6. | Diabetes | 2.7 |
| 7. | Apoplexy and paralysis | 4.4 | 7. | Alzheimer's disease | 2.5 |
| 8. | Diphtheria and croup | 3.9 | 8. | Influenza and pneumonia | 2.5 |
| 9. | Accidents | 3.4 | 9. | Suicide | 1.6 |
| 10. | Cancer | 2.8 | 10. | Kidney disease | 1.2 |
| | Other | 34.4 | | Other | 25.7 |
| | Total | 100.0 | | Total | 100.0 |

Source: S. E. Dawson. 1906; Statistics Canada. 2017k. "Leading causes of death, by sex (Both sexes)." http://www.statcan.gc.ca/tables-tableaux/sum-som/l01/cst01/hlth36a-eng.htm (retrieved 17 February 2018).

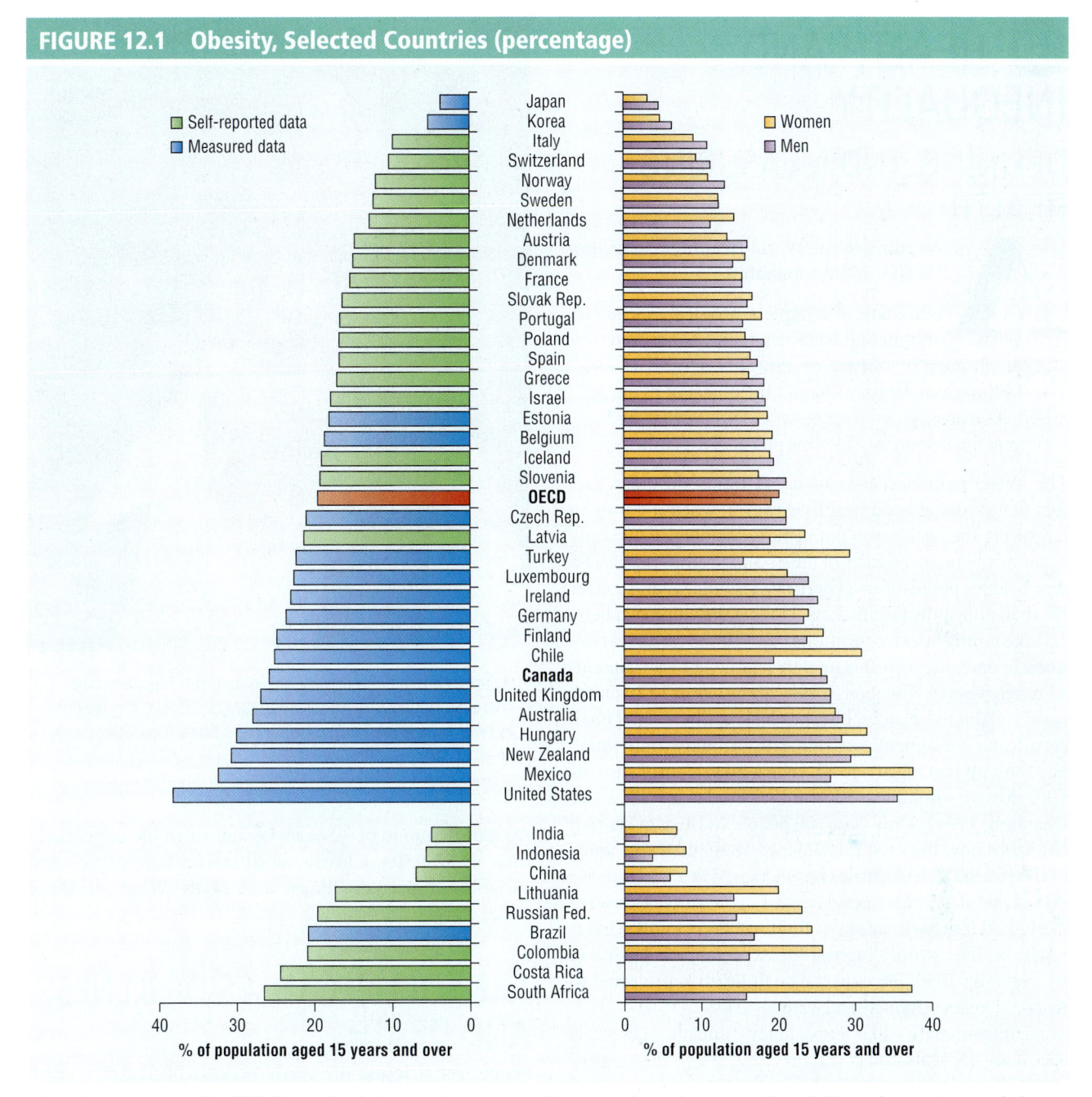

**FIGURE 12.1  Obesity, Selected Countries (percentage)**

Note: Member countries of the OECD (Organisation for Economic Co-operation and Development) are in the top pyramid. Non-OECD member countries are in the bottom pyramid. Data are for 2015. Body mass index (BMI) is equal to body mass in kilograms divided by the square of body height in metres. A BMI of 30 is considered obese.

Source: OECD (2017), Obesity Update 2017, https://www.oecd.org/els/health-systems/Obesity-Update-2017.pdf (retrieved 17 February 2018)

fluids in balance. Therefore, cures that released body fluids were common. These cures included hot baths, laxatives, and diuretics, which increase the flow of urine. If these treatments didn't work, bloodletting was often prescribed. No special qualifications were required to administer medical treatment. Barbers doubled as doctors.

However, the backwardness of medieval medical practice and the advantages of modern scientific medicine can be exaggerated. For example, medieval doctors stressed the importance of prevention, exercise, a balanced diet, and a congenial environment in maintaining good health. We now know this is sound advice. Conversely, one of the great shortcomings of modern medicine is its emphasis on high-tech cures rather than preventive and environmental measures. Therefore, in the final section of this chapter, I investigate how the medical professions gained substantial control over health issues and promoted their own approach to well-being, and how those professions have been challenged in recent years.

# LO¹ HEALTH AND INEQUALITY

## DEFINING AND MEASURING HEALTH

According to the World Health Organization (WHO, 2010b), **health** is

> …a state of complete physical, social and mental well-being, and not merely the absence of disease or infirmity. Health is a resource for everyday life, not the object of living. It is a positive concept emphasizing social and personal resources as well as physical capabilities.

The WHO definition lists in broad terms the main factors that promote good health. However, when it comes to *measuring* the health of a population, sociologists typically examine the negative: rates of illness and death. They reason that healthy populations experience less illness and longer life than unhealthy populations. I follow that approach here.

Assuming ideal conditions, how long can a person live? To date, the record is held by Jeanne Louise Calment, a French woman who died in 1997 at the age of 122. (Other people claim to be older, but they lack authenticated birth certificates.) Calment was an extraordinary individual. She took up fencing at age 85, rode a bicycle until she was 100, gave up smoking at 120, and released a rap CD at 121 (Matalon, 1997). Only 1 in 100 people in the world's rich countries now lives to be 100. Since 1840, life expectancy in the world's rich countries has increased at a fairly steady rate of about 2.5 years per decade. Further increases seem likely, and if there is an upper limit, we don't know what it might be. The world's highest life expectancy is Japan's at 84 years. By 2050, life expectancy in Japan is projected to reach 92 years (Oeppen and Vaupel, 2002).

Unfortunately, life expectancy outside Japan is less than 84 years today. Figure 12.2 shows life expectancy in selected countries. Life expectancy is two years shorter in Canada and in most other rich postindustrial countries than in Japan. In India, life expectancy is only 69 years. People in the Central African Republic, an impoverished African country south of the Sahara desert, have the world's shortest life expectancy at 52 years, just 17 years more than life expectancy in Europe in 1600.

If the maximum observed life expectancy in a population is now Japan's 84 years, then Canadians are being deprived of about two years of life because of avoidable social causes. Avoidable social causes deprive the citizens of the Central African Republic of 32 years of life, since life expectancy there is 52 years. Clearly, social causes have a big—and variable—impact on illness and death. What are those social causes?

> **health** According to the WHO, "A state of complete physical, social and mental well-being, and not merely the absence of disease or infirmity."

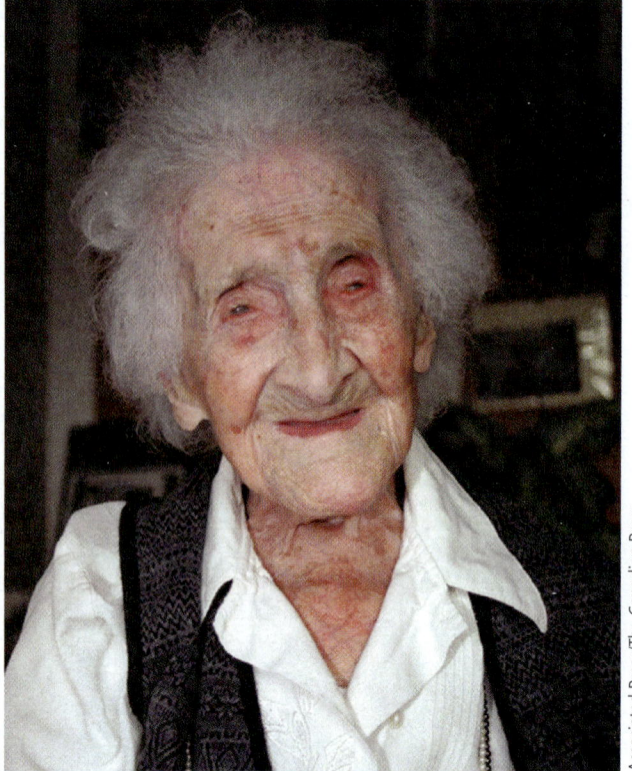

In the twenty-first century, the maximum lifespan may increase because of medical advances. So far, the record is held by Jeanne Louise Calment, a French woman who died in 1997 at the age of 122.

## THE SOCIAL CAUSES OF ILLNESS AND DEATH

People get sick and die partly because of natural causes. One person may have a genetic predisposition to cancer. Another may come in contact with the Ebola virus. However, other than such natural causes of illness and death, we can single out three types of *social* causes:

1. *Human-environmental factors.* Health risks arise from how human activity shapes the environments that people inhabit. Some environments foster good health, while others impose added risks for poor health. For example, in the 1980s, the pulp and paper industry's mercury poisoning of the English-Wabigoon river system in northwestern Ontario near the Manitoba border led to the virtual destruction of the Grassy Narrows First Nations way of life and means of livelihood. Mercury poisoning

## FIGURE 12.2  Life Expectancy, Selected Countries and Years

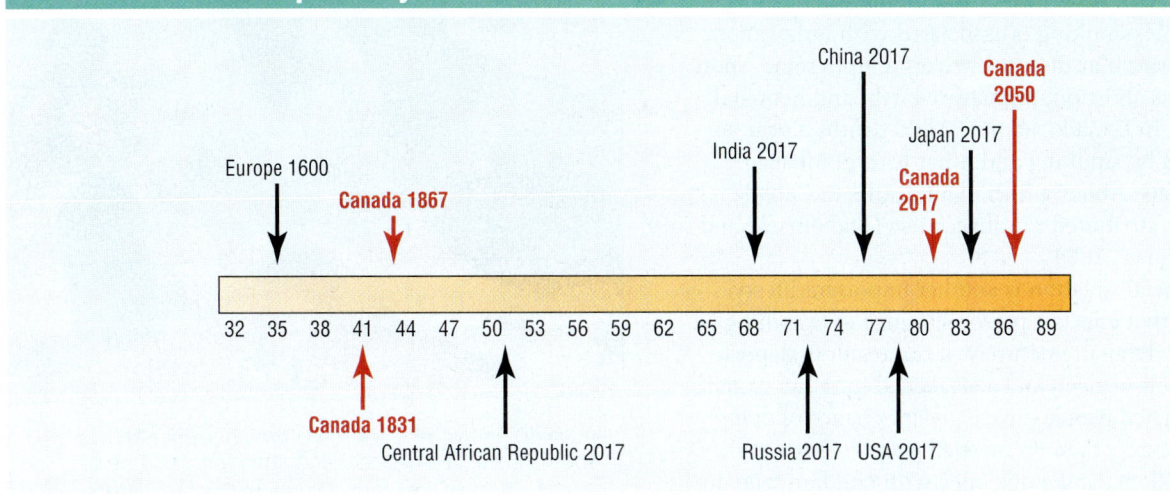

Europe 1600 — 35
Canada 1831 — 41
Canada 1867 — 44
Central African Republic 2017 — 53
India 2017 — 68
China 2017 — 71
Russia 2017 — 71
USA 2017 — 77
Canada 2017 — 80
Japan 2017 — 83
Canada 2050 — 86

Scale: 32 35 38 41 44 47 50 53 56 59 62 65 68 71 74 77 80 83 86 89

Sources: Yolande Lavoie and Jillian Oderkirk. (2000: 3), Population Reference Bureau. 2017. "2017 World Population Data Sheet," http://www.prb.org/Publications/Datasheets/2017/2017-world-population-data-sheet.aspx (retrieved 17 February 2017); Shripad Tuljapurkar, Nan Li, and Carl Boe. 2000. "A Universal Pattern of Mortality Decline in the G7 Countries." *Nature* 405: 789–92.

---

causes impaired peripheral vision, muscle weakness, impaired speech, hearing, and cognitive function, and numbness or stinging pain in the extremities and mouth (Shkilnyk, 1985). Mercury is still leaching into the river system today, even though the Ontario government discovered the problem in 1990 ("Ontario knew…," 2017). In 2016, the Ontario Superior Court decided that the American companies that owned the pulp and paper mills (Weyerhaeuser and Resolute) have no legal liability in the matter (Porter, 2016). Similarly, "patterns of atmospheric cycling have made the North a dumping ground for industrial chemicals that … [are] never used there. The chemicals bioaccumulate, delivering a higher level of toxic concentration to each level up the food chain. As a result, the breast milk of Inuit mothers is 10 times as contaminated as that of southern Canadian women" (Barlow and May, 2000: 184). In general, **environmental racism**, the tendency for hazardous waste sites and polluting industries to be located near Indigenous communities or areas populated by the poor, the politically marginalized, or certain visible-minority groups, also contributes to lower levels of health. This situation provides a striking illustration of how human-caused environmental conditions can cause illness and death (see Chapter 13, Technology, the Environment, and Social Movements).

2. *Factors related to the public health and health care systems.* The state of a nation's health depends partly on public and private efforts to improve people's well-being and treat their illnesses. The **public health system** comprises government-run programs that ensure access to clean drinking water, basic sewage and sanitation services, and inoculation against infectious diseases. The absence of a public health system is associated with high rates of disease and low life expectancy.

   The **health care system** comprises a nation's clinics, hospitals, and other facilities for ensuring health and treating illness. The absence of a system that ensures its citizens access to a minimum standard of health care is also associated with high rates of disease and shorter life expectancy. Thus, the 2014 Ebola outbreak killed 11 315 people. It originated in the West African country of Guinea and spread to nine other countries, four of them rich—Italy, Spain, the United Kingdom, and the United States. The total death toll from Ebola in the rich, Western countries: 1. The total death toll in the poor West African countries of Liberia, Sierra Leone, and Guinea, which lack what we would consider even rudimentary public health and health care systems: 11 300 ("Ebola", 2016).

3. *Lifestyle factors.* Smoking, excessive use of alcohol and drugs, poor diet, lack of exercise, and social

> **environmental racism** The tendency to heap environmental dangers on the disadvantaged.
>
> **public health system** Comprises government-run programs that ensure access to clean drinking water, basic sewage and sanitation services, and inoculation against infectious diseases.
>
> **health care system** Composed of a nation's clinics, hospitals, and other facilities for ensuring health and treating illness.

isolation are among the chief lifestyle factors associated with poor health and premature death. For example, smoking is associated with lung cancer, cardiovascular disease, strokes, emphysema, spontaneous abortion, premature birth, and neonatal death. In Canada, about 50 000 deaths a year are caused by smoking and other uses of tobacco products. About a fifth of all deaths in Canada can be attributed to tobacco use (Makomaski and Kaiserman, 2004).

Social isolation is another important lifestyle factor that affects a person's chance of becoming ill and dying prematurely; it can result in depression, self-neglect, and a weakened immune system. Unmarried people have a greater chance of dying prematurely than do married people. Single men living alone, and single men with children who do not live with them, have especially high mortality rates ("'Startlingly high mortality'," 2018). At any age, the death of a spouse increases a person's chance of dying, while remarrying decreases the chance of dying (Helsing, Szklo, and Comstock, 1981). Social isolation is a particularly big problem among older people who retire, lose a spouse and friends, and cannot rely on family members or state institutions for social and emotional support.

People often think of lifestyle factors like smoking as matters of individual choice. However, like human environmental factors and factors related to the public health and health care systems, they are associated with deeper social background factors, including country of residence, class, race, and gender. For example, smoking is one way of coping with stress, and stress is associated with occupying a lower class position and facing racial discrimination; like alcoholism and other lifestyle factors, smoking often has deeper social causes. Let's now consider the impact of social background factors, beginning with country of residence.

A health worker at Nazareth House in Cape Town, South Africa, lavishes care and attention on some of the 41 HIV/AIDS infected children in her care. Nearly 18 percent of South Africa's adult population is infected with HIV/AIDS.

with HIV/AIDS. Yet spending on research and treatment is concentrated overwhelmingly in the rich countries of North America and western Europe. As the case of HIV/AIDS illustrates, global inequality influences the exposure of people to different health risks.

You might think that prosperity increases health through biomedical advances, such as new medicines and diagnostic tools. If so, you are only partly correct. Biomedical advances do increase life expectancy. For

## Country of Residence

HIV/AIDS is the leading cause of death in the poverty-stricken part of Africa south of the Sahara desert. Figure 12.3 shows that by the end of 2015, 25.5 million sub-Saharan Africans were living with HIV/AIDS. Among adults, the prevalence of HIV/AIDS was 4.7 percent. In contrast, 0.5 percent of North American, western European, and central European adults were living

**FIGURE 12.3** People with HIV/AIDS (prevalence for adults in parentheses)

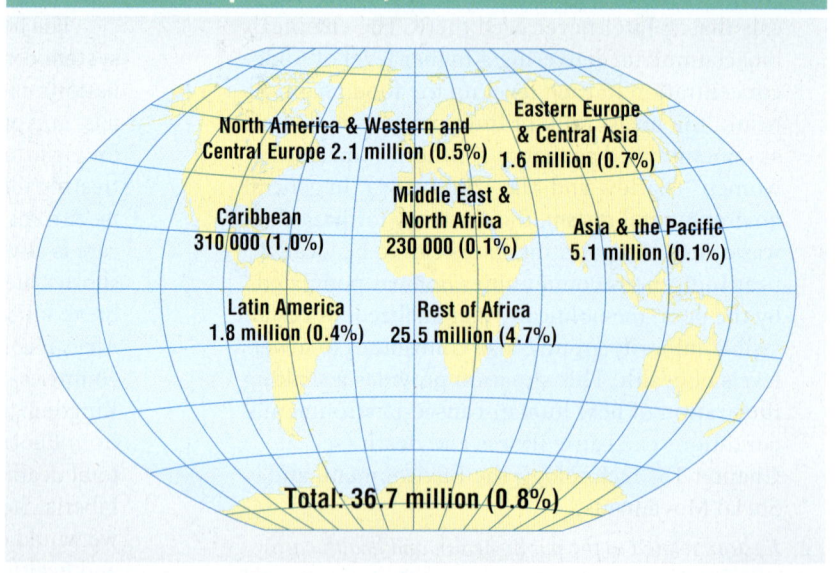

- North America & Western and Central Europe 2.1 million (0.5%)
- Eastern Europe & Central Asia 1.6 million (0.7%)
- Caribbean 310 000 (1.0%)
- Middle East & North Africa 230 000 (0.1%)
- Asia & the Pacific 5.1 million (0.1%)
- Latin America 1.8 million (0.4%)
- Rest of Africa 25.5 million (4.7%)

Total: 36.7 million (0.8%)

Note: Number of cases is for 2016. Prevalence data (percentage of cases in the adult population) are for 2015.
Source: "UNAIDS Data 2017," http://www.unaids.org/en/resources/documents/2017/2017_data_book (retrieved 17 February 2017).

example, vaccines against infectious diseases have done much to improve health and ensure longer life. However, the creation of a sound public health system is even more important in this regard. If a country can provide its citizens with clean water and a functional sewage system, epidemics decline in frequency and severity. Life expectancy soars.

The industrialized countries started developing public health systems in the mid-nineteenth century. Social reformers, concerned citizens, scientists, and doctors joined industrialists and politicians in urging governments to develop health policies that would help create a healthier labour force and citizenry (Bricker and Greenspon, 2001: 178–83; Goubert, 1989 [1986]; McNeill, 1976). But what was possible in North America and western Europe 150 years ago is not possible in many developing countries today. Most of us take clean water for granted, but more than a sixth of the world's people do not have access to a sanitary water supply (de Villiers, 1999).

Table 12.2 displays other indicators of health inequality for selected countries. We see that, in general, there is a positive association between national wealth and good health. Canada, the United States, and Japan are rich countries. They spend thousands of dollars per person on health care every year. More than two physicians serve every 1000 members of the population. **Infant mortality** (the annual number of deaths before the age of one for every 1000 live births) is low. India, which is poorer than Canada, the United States, and Japan, spends US$75 per person per year on health care. Accordingly, its population is less healthy in many respects. The Central African Republic is one of the poorest countries in the world. It spends little on health care, has few medical personnel, and suffers from a high rate of infant mortality. Nearly a third of its people lack safe drinking water.

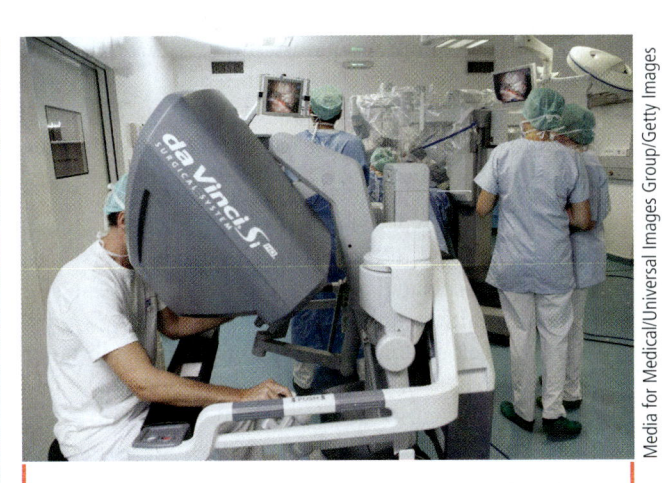

Biomedical advances increase life expectancy, but the creation of a sound public health system has even more dramatic benefits.

## LO² CLASS INEQUALITY AND HEALTH CARE

Despite Canada's system of universal health care, socioeconomic status is related to numerous aspects of health and illness (Raphael, 2004). On average, people with low income die at a younger age than do people with high income. Canadians enjoy a lower rate of illness and longer life expectancy at each step up the income ladder. Poverty is associated with high rates of tobacco

**infant mortality** The number of deaths before the age of one for every 1000 live births in a population in one year.

### TABLE 12.2 Health Indicators, Selected Countries

| Country | Per capita total expenditure on health* | Physicians per 1000 population* | Infant mortality per 1000 live births | Percentage of population with access to improved drinking water** |
|---|---|---|---|---|
| Canada | 5292 | 2.47 | 4 | 100 |
| Central African Republic | 16 | 0.05 | 89 | 69 |
| United States | 9403 | 2.55 | 6 | 99 |
| India | 75 | 0.73 | 35 | 94 |
| Japan | 3703 | 2.3 | 2 | 100 |

*Purchasing power in U.S. dollars.

**Piped water into dwelling, plot, or yard; public tap/stand pipe; tube well/borehole; protected dug well; protected spring; rainwater collection.

Note: Data are the most recent available as of February 2018.

Sources: World Bank. 2018b. "Improved water source (% of population with access)." https://data.worldbank.org/indicator/SH.H2O.SAFE.ZS (retrieved 17 February 2018); World Bank. 2018c. "Mortality rate, infant (per 1,000 live births)." https://data.worldbank.org/indicator/SP.DYN.IMRT.IN (retrieved 17 February 2018); World Bank. 2018d. "Physicians (per 1,000 people)." https://data.worldbank.org/indicator/SH.MED.PHYS.ZS (retrieved 17 February 2018).

and alcohol consumption, obesity, physical inactivity, and violence.

Why does health deteriorate as we move down the class hierarchy? Sociologists propose several explanations:

- *High stress and the inability to cope with it.* People in lower classes experience relatively high stress levels because of their difficult living conditions. Persistent stress is associated with a variety of physical and mental health problems, including high blood pressure, cancer, chronic fatigue, violence, and substance abuse. Stress is higher among people who have less autonomy at work. Moreover, people higher up in the class structure are often able to turn stress off. For instance, they can more easily take a few days off work or go on vacation.

   Many problems are more burdensome when such resources as money and influence are not available to address them. Upper-class people can pay others to fix their cars or their offspring's legal mishaps. Lower-class families may have to go into debt or simply accept some bad outcomes as unavoidable (Wilkinson and Marmot, 2003). Mishaps aside, lower-class families must endure greater crowding; poorer dwelling quality; working conditions that are more noxious, dangerous, and unpleasant; and longer hours of work to make ends meet (Brym, 2018d).
- *Differences in the earliest stages of development that have lifelong consequences.* Inequalities at the start of life have strong health consequences for a lifetime (Forrest and Riley, 2004). Poor nutrition during pregnancy, maternal smoking and misuse of drugs and alcohol, insufficient exercise, and inadequate prenatal care typically lead to suboptimal fetal development. Mothers with low income are more likely to provide such unfavourable starts to life.
- *Lack of knowledge.* People who are less educated and who have less exposure to educated advisers tend to have less knowledge about healthy lifestyles. For example, they are less likely to know what constitutes a nutritious diet. This, too, contributes to their propensity to illness. Illness, in turn, makes it more difficult for poor people to escape poverty.
- *Unequal access to health resources.* A disproportionately large number of poor Canadians live in areas that have inferior medical services. For example, there are fewer hospitals, physicians, and nurses per capita in rural areas than in urban areas. The problem is especially acute on First Nations reserves. As well, the quality of preventive, diagnostic, and treatment facilities is generally superior in urban areas. Moreover, many low- and middle-income Canadians have limited access to eye care, dentistry, mental health counselling, and prescription drugs (Boychuk, 2002).
- *Environmental exposure.* As you learned earlier, poor people are more likely than rich people are to be exposed to environmental risks that have a negative impact on their health. There is a striking lack of incinerators, pulp and paper mills, oil refineries, dumpsites, factories, and mines in the Bridle Path (Toronto) Shaughnessy Heights (Vancouver), Westmount (Montreal), Britannia (Calgary), South Tuxedo (Winnipeg), and other wealthy Canadian neighbourhoods (see Chapter 14, Social Change: Technology, the Environment, and Social Movements).

## INTERSECTIONALITY AND RACIAL INEQUALITIES IN HEALTH CARE

The life expectancy of Indigenous Canadians is about six years less than that of other Canadians. To put that number in perspective, it's about the same as the difference in life expectancy between Canadians and North Koreans, half of whom subsist on corn and kimchi (spicy pickled cabbage) and have little access to fuel for cooking and heating, let alone adequate health care (Newman, 2013; Population Reference Bureau, 2017; Statistics Canada 2017d).

Part of the Indigenous/non-Indigenous difference in life expectancy is a consequence of the fact that the median income of Indigenous Canadians is only about 60 percent of the median for all Canadians. Poor health is strongly associated with low income. But that is only half the story. In addition, researchers emphasize how Indigenous Canadians suffer negative health outcomes because of the cumulative effects of social exclusion based on race (Galabuzi, 2004). Here again we confront the issue of intersectionality, introduced in the Sociology and the Media boxed feature, *Highway of Tears* and the Problem of Intersectionality, in Chapter 5, Deviance and Crime.

Social exclusion based on race *compounds* the effect of low socioeconomic status on health (Veenstra, 2013; Williams and Sternthal, 2010). Specifically, even when Indigenous Canadians earn median Canadian income, they are more likely than other Canadians to live in unsafe and unhealthy areas. Many Indigenous Canadians live on remote reserves where medical services are meagre and drinking water is unsafe. Many of those who live in urban areas suffer systematic racial discrimination in housing. Their neighbourhoods typically suffer from poor access to medical services and healthy food options, and only overcrowded, unhealthy dwellings are available.

In addition to taking such institutional forms, racism operates at the individual level. To cope with the stress caused by everyday racism, some people smoke, take drugs, and drink alcohol excessively. Everyday racism can even kill people directly. Take the apparently common practice in Thunder Bay, Ontario, of flinging objects and racial slurs at Indigenous peoples from passing cars. In February 2017, Brayden Bushby threw a metal trailer hitch at Barbara Kentner, a First Nations woman, gleefully shouting "Oh, I got one." Five months later, Kentner died from her injuries (Porter, 2017).

Another form of everyday racism involves Indigenous peoples encountering racially based misunderstanding or even hostility when they seek medical services, like 45-year-old Brian Sinclair did when he visited the emergency ward of a Winnipeg hospital. Sinclair had a bladder infection that could have been cleared up with antibiotics. He was referred to emergency by a clinic because he hadn't urinated in 24 hours.

Presumably, he explained the problem to the triage nurse who interviewed him when he arrived. Sinclair then waited and dozed in the emergency room, vomiting several times because his body was going into shock. A security guard assumed he was intoxicated and just sleeping it off, so he summoned housekeeping staff to clean up the mess. Several other security guards raised concerns with triage staff but no medical staff saw Sinclair. He died in the emergency room 34 hours after arriving, the victim of the intersectional effects of class and race on health (Puxley, 2013).

The intersectional effects of class and race on Indigenous health are considerable. The rate of heart disease is 1.5 times higher among First Nations than among the Canadian population as a whole, type 2 diabetes is 3 to 5 times higher, tuberculosis infection is 8 to 10 times higher, and the percentage of those reporting poor or fair health is more than twice as high (Canadian Institute for Health Information, 2004: 81; Health Canada, 2014b).

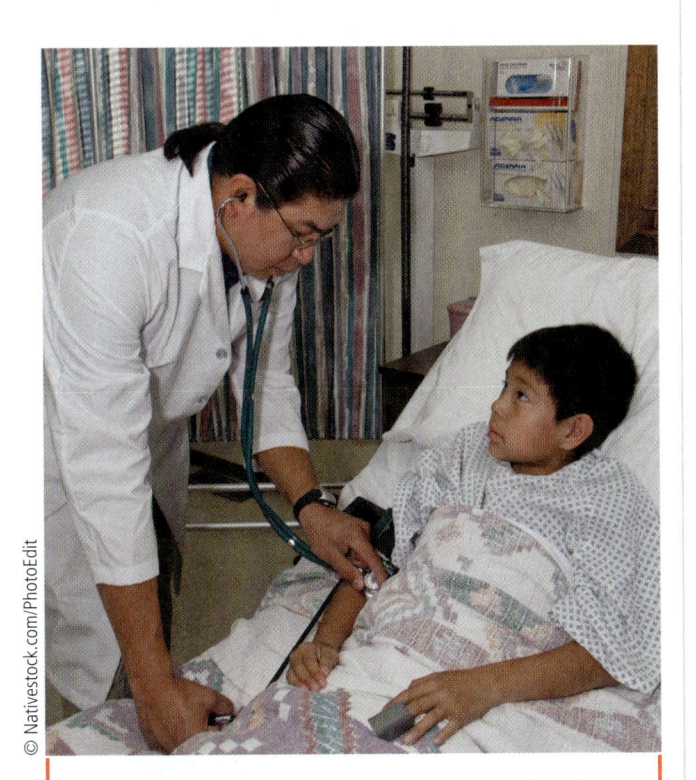

The average health status of Indigenous Canadians is relatively low, partly for economic reasons and partly due to racism.

# LO³ GENDER INEQUALITIES IN HEALTH CARE: THE FEMINIST CONTRIBUTION

Feminist scholars have brought another important basis of inequality in health to the attention of the sociological community: gender.

The gap between women's and men's health care is particularly evident in the Middle East, sub-Saharan Africa, and South Asia (Brym, 2018c). It's easy to see this by examining the **sex ratio**, that is, the number of males per 100 females in a population. *At birth*, the sex ratio for the entire world is 103, meaning that 103 boys are born for every 100 girls. But in India the sex ratio is an unusually high 112, while in China it is 115 (Central Intelligence Agency, 2018). Why? Because sex-selective abortion is widespread in India and China. A strong preference for boys leads many parents to pay for ultrasound tests that determine the sex of the fetus. A good number of those parents decide to abort the fetus if it's female. Sex-selective abortion apparently continues when women emigrate. Medical researchers studied 31 978 single-child live births to women born in India and living in Ontario between 2002 and 2007. They found that the sex ratio for first children was 111, increasing to 136 for second children (Henry, Ray, and Urquia 2012).

The United Arab Emirates and Qatar stand out if one examines the sex ratio for people *older than 64*. While the world's sex ratio for people older than 64 is 102, it stands at 169 for Qataris and 171 for Emiratis. Some observers say that the high sex ratio in these Persian Gulf countries is due to the large number of male migrant workers in the region. However, the work permits of nearly all migrant workers expire when the workers turn 60, at which time they must return home, mainly to India, Pakistan, Sri Lanka, the Philippines, and Bangladesh (Al Jandaly, 2009). It therefore seems that the high sex ratio for those over 64 may be due to women dying at a higher rate than men because, over their lifetime, they experience more violence and/or inferior nutrition and/or inferior health care compared to men.

In countries like Canada, where women and men have the same rights to health care and where the level of violence against women is more moderate, 60 percent of women and 60 percent of men say they are in excellent or very good health (Statistics Canada, 2016b). Nonetheless, gender bias in health is evident (Haas, 1998). For example, the health system has been slower to address and more likely to neglect women's health issues than men's health issues. So, until recent decades, more research focused on "men's diseases," such as cardiac arrest, than on "women's

**sex ratio** The number of males per 100 females in a population.

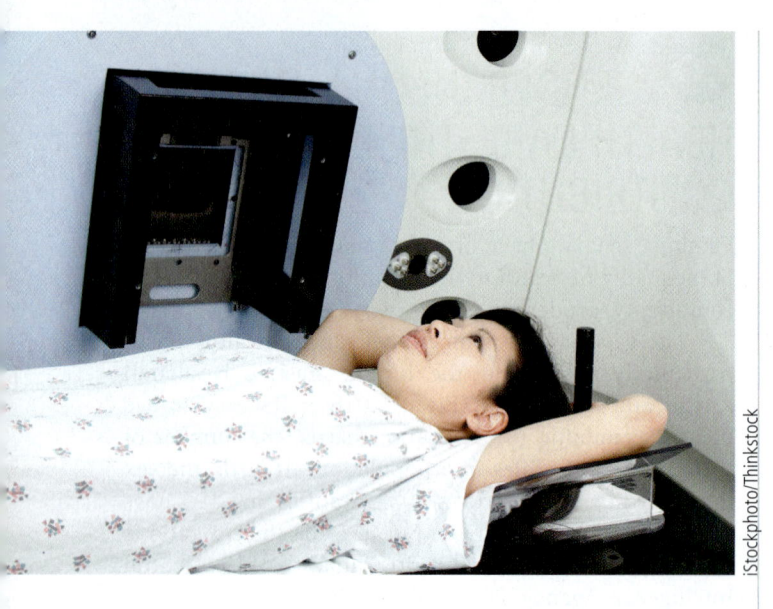

diseases," such as breast cancer. Similarly, women have until recently been excluded from participating in many major health research studies, which is significant because women may present with different symptoms than men who have the same illness and may require different treatment regimes.

In sum, although on average women live longer than men do, gender inequalities have a negative impact on women's health. Women's health is negatively affected by differences between women and men in access to gender-appropriate medical research and treatment, as well as the economic resources needed to secure adequate health care.

## LO4 COMPARATIVE HEALTH CARE FROM A CONFLICT PERSPECTIVE

### Health Care in the United States

I noted earlier that because rich countries spend more on health care than poor countries do, their populations enjoy longer life expectancy. This does not mean that money always buys good health. The United States spends 78 percent more per person on health care than Canada does, and 154 percent more than Japan does. It also has 3 percent more doctors per 1000 people than Canada does and 11 percent more than Japan does (refer back to Table 12.2). Yet the rate of infant mortality is 50 percent higher in the United States than in Canada and 200 percent higher than in Japan. Life expectancy is 2.9 years less than in Canada and 4.4 years less than in Japan. Clearly, spending more money on health care does not always improve the health of a nation.

What accounts for the American anomaly? Why do Americans spend more on health care than any other country, yet wind up with a population that, on average, is less healthy than the population of other rich countries?

One reason for the anomaly is that the gap between rich and poor is greater in the United States than in Canada, Japan, and other rich countries. In general, the higher the level of inequality in a country, the less healthy its population is (Wilkinson, 1996). Because the United States contains a higher percentage of poor people than other rich countries do, its average level of health is lower. Moreover, because income inequality has widened in the United States since the early 1970s, health disparities among income groups have grown.

A second reason for the American anomaly is that physicians, hospitals, pharmaceutical companies, and other providers of health care are able to charge substantially higher prices in the United States than elsewhere (Anderson et al., 2003: 89). To understand why, it is necessary to examine the American health care system from a comparative conflict perspective.

Recall that conflict theory is concerned mainly with the question of how privileged groups seek to maintain their advantages and subordinate groups seek to increase theirs. As such, conflict theory is an illuminating approach to analyzing the American health care system. We can usefully see health care in the United States as a system of privilege for some and disadvantage for others. It thus contributes to the poor health of less well-to-do Americans.

The United States, unlike all other rich countries, lacks a universal health care system. This means that it does not guarantee access to health care as a right of citizenship. Only elderly people, some of the poor, armed forces personnel, and some veterans receive medical benefits from the government under the Medicare, Medicaid, and military health care programs.

All told, the American government pays 53 percent of all medical costs out of taxes. In the United Kingdom, Sweden, and Denmark, the comparable figure is between 81 and 85 percent; in Japan and Germany, it is between 77 and 83 percent; and in France, Canada, and Italy, it is between 71 and 78 percent. Coverage in Germany, Italy, Belgium, Denmark, Finland, Greece, Iceland, Luxembourg, Norway, and Spain includes drugs, eyeglasses, dental care, and prostheses (Anderson et al., 2003; "Health Care Systems," 2001; Rogers, 2012; Schoen et al., 2004; Starr, 1994).

In 2010, the United States became the last of the world's rich countries to ensure that its population (or at least 95 percent of it) would at least be covered by health insurance, although they had to pay a lot for it. But even the gains of the Obama years were reversed soon after Donald Trump took office. During Trump's first year in office, the number of Americans without health insurance increased by 3.2 million, rising to 12.2 percent of adults. It is estimated that another 13 million American adults will lose coverage by 2028 (Mangan, 2018). And of course the distinctive feature of the American health care system—substantial private provision—remains in place. It is an expensive mechanism that leaves many people poorly served. The relatively privileged obtain health services at high prices, while the less well-off are effectively priced out of the market for health care (see Theories in Dispute, Free Market or State Regulation? The Case of Prescription Drugs).

# THEORIES IN DISPUTE

## Free Market or State Regulation? The Case of Prescription Drugs

Free markets are often said to encourage competition. Presumably, competition encourages innovation and keeps prices low, allowing successful businesses to increase market share and become more profitable. That's the theory. In practice, things are often not that simple, as the prescription drug industry illustrates.

In 2010, Valeant Pharmaceuticals started buying up other drug manufacturers, saving money by virtually shutting down their research and development departments, and making money by raising prices on their life-saving medicines. In 2015 alone Valeant raised the price on its brand name drugs by 66 percent. One of those drugs was syprine, used to treat people who can't metabolize copper and can't tolerate alternative drugs. Without syprine, they suffer liver and brain damage and eventually die. Valeant raised the cost of an average yearly supply of syprine from US$10 950.00 to US$233 081.70, far above what most people could pay (see the Netflix documentary, "Drug Short," 2018, an episode in the series *Dirty Money*).

Valeant is admittedly an extreme case. In general, however, Americans pay more for prescription drugs than anyone else in the world does—in 2016, over three times more than Canadians did (Patented Medicine Prices Review Board, 2016: 32). In recent decades, the price of prescription drugs in the United States has increased at more than twice the rate of inflation and more than any other item in the nation's health care budget. In contrast, the rise in the cost of prescription drugs in Canada has been below the rate of inflation since 1988 (Patented Medicine Prices Review Board, 2016: 31).

Rich countries other than the United States keep prescription drug prices down through government regulation. Since 1987, Canadian drug companies have not been allowed to increase prices of brand-name prescription drugs above the inflation rate. New brand-name prescription drugs cannot exceed the highest Canadian price of comparable drugs used to treat the same disease. For new brand-name prescription drugs that are unique and have no competitors, the price must be no higher than the median price for that drug in the United Kingdom, France, Italy, Germany, Sweden, Switzerland, and the United States. If a company breaks the rules, the government requires a price adjustment. If the government deems that a company has deliberately flouted the law, it imposes a fine. Not surprisingly, millions of Americans now buy prescription drugs from Canadian pharmacies.

American drug manufacturers justify their high prices by claiming they need the money for research and development (R&D). The American public benefits from R&D, they say, while lower prescription drug prices impair R&D in other countries. In fact, in the eight countries whose prescription drug prices and policies are monitored by the Canadian government, the correlation between drug prices and investment in R&D is precisely zero (calculated from data in Patented Medicine Prices Review Board, 2011: 25, 36). High prescription drug prices do not result in more R&D, and low prescription drug prices do not impair R&D.

What can be said with confidence is that (1) the pharmaceutical industry is by far the most profitable industry in the United States; (2) drug companies spend about half as much on advertising and promotions as they do on R&D, driving up prescription drug prices; and (3) they spend more on lobbying and political campaign contributions than any other United States industry does. Most of the lobbying effort is aimed at influencing members of Congress to maintain a "free market" in prescription drug prices (Barry, 2002a, 2002b, 2002c).

### Critical Thinking Questions

- Is the prescription drug market in the United States really free?
- Are manufacturers of prescription drugs suffering from government regulation?

## The Canadian Health Care System

> **socialized medicine** In countries with socialized medicine, the government (1) directly controls the financing and organization of health services, (2) directly pays providers, (3) guarantees equal access to health care, and (4) allows some private care for individuals who are willing to pay for their medical expenses.

Regulation of prescription drug prices is not the only feature of Canadian health care that differs from health care in the United States. In contrast to the United States, Canada also has a national health insurance system that is sometimes loosely described as **socialized medicine**. Despite differences in how socialized medicine works in different countries, common to all such systems is the fact that the government directly controls the financing and organization of health services, directly pays providers, guarantees equal access to health care, and allows some private care for individuals who are willing to pay for it (Cockerham, 1998). Canada does not have a true system of socialized medicine, however, because the government does not employ Canadian doctors. Most of Canada's doctors are independent practitioners who are paid on a fee-for-service basis and submit claims directly to the provincial or territorial health insurance plan for payment.

Tommy Douglas is widely credited with being Canada's "father of medicare." He led the Co-operative Commonwealth Federation (CCF) to political victory in Saskatchewan in 1944, making it the first socialist party to win a North American election. (Later, Douglas helped turn the CCF into the New Democratic Party.) He served as premier of Saskatchewan from 1944 to 1961, introducing many social reforms including universal medical care. His government's actions stirred up sharp opposition, including a province-wide physicians' strike, but Saskatchewan's medicare ultimately succeeded. In 1968 it became a model for the whole country.

Most Canadians think highly of their public health care system and often say it is Canada's core institution. Typically, one survey found that 94 percent of Canadians regard our public health care system as a source of collective pride, ranking it #1 in a long list of Canadian symbols, achievements, and attributes (Canadian Press, 2012). More than 86 percent of Canadians favour strengthening public health care rather than expanding for-profit medical services (Canadian Health Coalition, 2018).

Canadians also have issues with public health care. A particular source of concern is waiting times. Although our health care system is based on the premise that "all citizens will have access to the care they need within a reasonable time period" (Health Canada, 1999a), most people agree that some waits are too long, especially for elective surgery. Newfoundland and Labrador, Ontario, and especially Saskatchewan are making substantial progress in this regard, while Nova Scotia is a laggard.

Tommy Douglas (1904–86), leader of the Co-operative Commonwealth Federation (the precursor of the NDP) and the father of socialized medicine in Canada.

Still, about two-thirds of Canadians view their health care system positively. In contrast, only about one-third of Americans see their health care system in a positive light (Angus Reid Global Monitor, 2009). Most of the Canadians who hold negative opinions prefer a more American, two-tiered system that would allow people who can afford superior care to buy it. Most Americans who hold negative opinions prefer a Canadian-type system with greater government regulation. In both countries, therefore, health care remains a subject of political debate.

## LO5 THE PROFESSIONALIZATION OF MEDICINE

Earlier, we noted that from the conflict perspective, the health system can be viewed as a system of privilege and disadvantage. We now extend that argument by showing how physicians became such a privileged part of the health care system.

In the early nineteenth century, the practice of medicine was in a chaotic state. Herbalists, faith healers, midwives, druggists, and medical doctors vied to meet the health needs of the public. A century later, the dust had

## THEORIES AT A GLANCE

### Health

| Theory | Main Question | Application |
|---|---|---|
| Conflict theory | How does the structure of inequality between privileged groups seeking to maintain their advantages and subordinate groups seeking to increase theirs lead to conflict and often to social change? | Economic inequality is greater in the United States than in other rich countries, so American health care is more of a system of privilege for some and a disadvantage for others than it is in Canada and western Europe. The high level of inequality contributes to the poor health of less well-to-do Americans. All told, the American government pays 53 percent of all medical costs out of taxes. In the United Kingdom, Sweden, and Denmark, the comparable figure is between 81 and 85 percent; in Japan and Germany, it is between 77 and 83 percent; and in France, Canada, and Italy, it is between 71 and 78 percent. Moreover, in Germany, Italy, Belgium, Denmark, Finland, Greece, Iceland, Luxembourg, Norway, and Spain prescription drugs, eyeglasses, dental care, and prostheses are covered.<br><br>Even the cost of prescription drugs is unregulated in the United States, again in contrast to other rich countries, and many low-income people cannot afford the medication they need. In a successful political struggle, Canada's health care system was initiated by the CCF (the forerunner of the NDP) in Saskatchewan in 1968 and soon became a model for the whole country. |
| Feminism | How do social conventions maintain male dominance and female subordination, and how do these conventions get overturned? | Feminists have identified numerous gaps between women's and men's health. Globally, the gap is particularly evident in the Middle East, sub-Saharan Africa, and South Asia. Sex-selective abortion, violence against women, and gender discrimination with respect to nutrition and medical care are widespread in many countries in these regions. In wealthy Western countries like Canada, women and men have the same rights to health care and the level of violence against women is more moderate.<br><br>However, the health system has been slow to address and more likely to neglect women's health issues than men's health issues. Until recently, more research focused on "men's diseases," such as cardiac arrest, than on "women's diseases," such as breast cancer. Similarly, women have until recently been excluded from participating in many major health research studies, which is significant because women may present with different symptoms than men who have the same illness and may require different treatment regimes. |

settled. Medical science was victorious. Its first series of breakthroughs involved identifying the bacteria and viruses responsible for various diseases and then developing effective procedures and vaccines to combat them. These and subsequent triumphs in diagnosis and treatment convinced most people of the superiority of medical science over other approaches to health. Medical science worked, or at least it seemed to work more effectively and more often than did other therapies.

It would be wrong, however, to think that scientific medicine came to dominate health care only because it produced results. A second, sociological reason for the rise to dominance of scientific medicine is that doctors were able to professionalize. A **profession** is an occupation that requires extensive formal education. Professionals regulate their own training and practice. They restrict competition within the profession, mainly by limiting the recruitment of practitioners. They minimize competition with other professions, partly by laying exclusive claim to a field of expertise. Professionals are usually self-employed. They exercise considerable authority over their clients. And they profess to be motivated mainly by the desire to serve their community even though they earn a lot of money in the

> **profession** An occupation that requires extensive formal education and whose practitioners regulate their own training and practice, restrict competition, and exercise considerable authority over their clients.

CHAPTER 12 Health and Medicine  259

process. **Professionalization**, then, is the process by which people gain control and authority over their occupation and their clients. It results in professionals enjoying high occupational prestige and income, and considerable social and political power (Freidson, 1986; Johnson, 1972; Starr, 1982).

The professional organization of Canadian doctors is the Canadian Medical Association (CMA), founded in 1867 by 167 doctors in Quebec City. It quickly set about broadcasting the successes of medical science and criticizing alternative approaches to health as quackery and charlatanism. The CMA was able to have laws passed to restrict medical licences to graduates of approved schools and to ensure that only graduates of those schools could train the next generation of doctors. By restricting entry into the profession and by specifying what "paramedical" practitioners could and could not do, members of the medical establishment ensured their own status, prestige, and high incomes. For example, midwifery was originally included in the work of the Victorian Order of Nurses, founded in 1897 by the National Council of Women to assist rural women who otherwise lacked access to health care. However, "the opposition of the medical establishment in Canada was so great to what it saw as an infringement of its prerogatives that the idea was allowed to die" (Mitchinson, 1993: 396). When medicine became a profession, it also became a monopoly.

The modern hospital is the institutional manifestation of the medical doctor's professional dominance. Until the twentieth century, most doctors operated small clinics and visited patients in their homes. However, the rise of the modern hospital was guaranteed by medicine's scientific turn in the mid-nineteenth century. Expensive equipment for diagnosis and treatment had to be shared by many physicians. This required the centralization of medical facilities in large, bureaucratically run institutions that strongly resist deviations from professional conduct. Practically nonexistent in 1850, hospitals are now widespread. Yet despite their undoubted benefits, economic as well as health-related, hospitals and the medicine practised in them are not an unqualified blessing, as you are about to learn.

## LO6 THE SOCIAL LIMITS OF MODERN MEDICINE

In early February 2003, a 64-year-old professor of medicine from Guangzhou, the capital of Guangdong province in southern China, came down with an unidentified respiratory ailment. It did not bother him enough to cancel a planned trip to Hong Kong, so on February 12, he checked into that city's Metropole Hotel. Ironically, as it turned out, the desk clerk assigned him Room 911. Other ninth-floor guests included an older couple from Toronto and three young women from Singapore. All of these people, along with a local resident who visited the hotel during this period, fell ill between February 15 and 27 with the same medical problem as the professor. The professor died on March 4. The Canadian couple returned to Toronto on February 23 and the woman died at her home on March 5. The eventual diagnosis: severe acute respiratory syndrome, or SARS, a new (and in 9 percent of cases, deadly) pneumonia-like illness for which there is no vaccine and no cure.

By June 12, 8445 cases of SARS had been identified in 29 countries, and 790 people had died of the disease. Quickly and efficiently, global travel had spread HIV/AIDS, West Nile virus, and now SARS from remote and isolated locales to the world's capitals. As one of the world's most multicultural cities, Toronto has a large Chinese population. It is therefore not surprising that, outside of China, Hong Kong, and Taiwan, Toronto became the world's number one SARS hot spot (Abraham, 2003; World Health Organization, 2003).

Once identified as a potential SARS case, a person was quarantined at home for 10 days. However, if people exhibited symptoms of the disease, they were directed to a hospital, an institution where the air is maintained at a constant warm temperature that is ideal for the multiplication of germs. Furthermore, hospitals are places where there are many young and elderly people with weakened immune systems. A steady stream of germs pour in around the clock. Staff members often failed to follow elementary principles of good hygiene. Most of the 238 people in Toronto who had SARS caught it while in hospital before stringent isolation and disinfection procedures were imposed.

My characterization of hospitals as ideal environments for the spread of germs may seem harsh. It is not. Hospitals have become dangerous places. In Canada, about 80 percent of hospitals fall seriously short in preventing patients from getting hospital infections. Some 250 000 patients experience hospital infections every

Hong Kong during the 2003 SARS outbreak

year. According to one medical researcher, if the government classified hospital infections as a cause of death, it would be the fourth-leading cause of death in the country (Zoutman et al., 2003).

The situation has deteriorated largely because we invest disproportionately in expensive, high-tech, cutting-edge diagnostic equipment and treatment while we skimp on simple, labour-intensive, time-consuming hygiene. Cleaning staffs are too small and insufficiently trained. Nurses are too few. According to research by the Harvard School of Public Health, these are the kinds of factors correlated with hospital-acquired infections. As one registered nurse said, "When you have less time to save lives, do you take 30 seconds to wash your hands? When you're speeding up you have to cut corners. We don't always wash our hands. I'm not saying it's right, but you've got to deal with reality" (quoted in Berens, 2002).

It was not always the reality. Until the 1940s, North American hospital workers were obsessed with cleanliness. They had to be. In the era before the widespread use of antibiotics, infection often meant death. In the 1950s, however, the prevention of infections in hospitals became less of a priority because antibiotics became widely available. It was less expensive to wait until a patient got sick and then respond to symptoms by prescribing drugs than to prevent the sickness in the first place. Based on this logic, doctors and nurses grew lax about hygiene. One report cites a dozen health care studies showing that about half of doctors and nurses do not disinfect their hands between patients (Berens, 2002). One hospital north of Montreal cut serious infections by 80 percent simply by improving hygiene (CBC, 2004).

Using penicillin and antibiotics indiscriminately has other costs too. When living organisms encounter a deadly threat, only the few mutations that are strong enough to resist the threat survive and go on to reproduce. Accordingly, if you use a lot of antibiotics, "super germs" that are resistant to these drugs multiply. This is just what has happened. (It hasn't helped that antibiotics are routinely added to cattle feed to prevent disease and thereby lower beef production costs. This practice builds up resistance to antibiotics in humans.)

Penicillin could kill nearly all staphylococcus germs in the 1940s, but by 1982 it was effective in fewer than 10 percent of cases. In the 1970s, doctors turned to the more powerful methicillin, which in 1974 could kill 98 percent of staphylococcus germs. By the mid-1990s, it could kill only about 50 percent of them. Various strains of drug-resistant germs now cause pneumonia, blood poisoning, tuberculosis, and other infectious diseases. Drug-resistant germs that could formerly survive only in the friendly hospital environment have now adapted to the harsher environment outside the hospital walls. Some pharmaceutical companies are developing new antibiotics to fight drug-resistant bugs. However, their efforts lack energy because antibiotics are prescribed for only short periods and are therefore not big money makers (Groopman, 2008).

The epidemic of infectious diseases caused by slack hospital hygiene and the overuse of antibiotics suggest that market forces constrain the success of modern medicine. It is difficult to see how we can solve these problems without imposing stricter rules regarding hospital disinfection and getting governments to provide the incentive necessary to spur pharmaceutical companies to invest more in developing new antibiotics.

Meanwhile, many people are growing skeptical of the claims of modern medicine. They are beginning to challenge traditional medicine and explore alternatives that rely less on high technology and drugs and are more sensitive to the need for maintaining balance between humans and their environment in the pursuit of good health. In concluding this chapter, I explore some of these challenges and alternatives.

## CHALLENGES TO TRADITIONAL MEDICAL SCIENCE

### Patient Activism

By the mid-twentieth century, the dominance of medical science in Canada was virtually complete. Any departure from the dictates of scientific medicine was considered deviant. So when sociologist Talcott Parsons defined the **sick role** in 1951, he pointed out that illness suspends routine responsibilities and is not deliberate. He stressed that people playing the sick role must want to be well and must seek competent help, cooperating with health care practitioners at all times (Parsons, 1951: 428 ff.). Must they? According to Parsons's definition, a competent person suffering from a terminal illness cannot reasonably demand that doctors refrain from using heroic measures to prolong his or her life. And by his definition, a patient cannot reasonably question doctors' orders, no matter how well-educated the patient and how debatable the effect of the prescribed treatment. Although Parsons's definition of the sick role may sound plausible to many people born before the middle of the twentieth century, it probably sounds authoritarian and foreign to most other people today.

Ours is an era of patient activism, spurred on partly by a much more highly educated public than existed 60 or 70 years ago. Many people now have the knowledge, vocabulary, self-confidence, and political organization to participate in their own health care rather than passively accepting whatever the first expert tells them. Only about a third of Canadians say they

> **sick role** Playing the sick role, according to Talcott Parsons, involves the non-deliberate suspension of routine responsibilities, wanting to be well, seeking competent help, and cooperating with health care practitioners at all times.

follow a doctor's advice uncritically. Around 90 percent of Canadians prefer that their doctor offer several treatment options rather than a single course of action, 86 percent say they usually ask their doctor many questions about procedures, 76 percent say they are more likely to question their doctor now than they were in the past, and 70 percent claim to always ask their doctor about medicines that are prescribed (Bricker and Greenspon, 2001: 119–21).

Increasingly, patients are also taught to perform simple, routine medical procedures themselves. Many people now use WebMD and other websites to find information about various illnesses and treatments (although some find it difficult to distinguish reliable from unreliable information; see the boxed feature, Sociology and the Media, Gwyneth Paltrow and Celebrity Medical Advice). Doctors now routinely seek patients' informed consent for some procedures rather than deciding what to do on their own. Clearly, patients now play a more active role in their own care than was once the case.

## SOCIOLOGY AND THE MEDIA

### Gwyneth Paltrow and Celebrity Medical Advice

Gwyneth Paltrow is a successful and influential actress. In 2008, she introduced Goop.com, her lifestyle website and online store. Here is a sampling of some of the website's advice to women:

- Don't wear underwire and form-fitting bras. They constrain the lymph nodes around the breasts and underarms, causing a build-up of toxins that could cause cancer.
- Routinely steam-clean your vagina. Doing so increases your energy level.
- To promote fertility in yourself and your partner, drink a cup of milk or water into which you have stirred a teaspoon of "sex dust," described as "a lusty edible formula alchemized to ignite and excite sexy energy in and out of the bedroom" ("Sex Dust," 2018). The main ingredient of "sex dust," which costs nearly $50 for a 1.5 oz. (52.5 gram) jar, is cacao, the seed from which chocolate is made.
- Repeatedly flush your colon using warm water. Doing so clears out dangerous toxins.
- Cleanse your entire body by drinking large quantities of concentrated fruit juice.
- Remove heavy metals from your system by consuming Hawaiian algae, barley grass juice extract, cilantro, wild blueberries, and New Brunswick dulse, an edible seaweed.

The trouble with Paltrow's advice is that little of it is supported by scientific evidence (Caulfield, 2015; CBC News, 2018; Saul, 2015). Some of her recommendations, like using "sex dust," are ridiculous. Some are harmful. Vaginal steam-cleaning is associated with increased risk of yeast infection. Drinking lots of concentrated fruit juice can lead to weight again and diabetes. Colon cleanses can cause infection, tears in the intestine, and other complications.

Health professionals were horrified a few years ago when Paltrow misinformed people that vaccines cause autism. After all, measles can cause deafness and death, and mumps can cause inflammation of the brain and fertility problems. Yet some people heeded Paltrow, refusing to let their children receive vaccinations against these and other infectious diseases. As for the evidence supposedly underlying Paltrow's claim about the association between vaccines and autism, it turns out that the British doctor who said he conducted research demonstrating the connection was paid to falsify his data by a law firm that intended to sue vaccine manufacturers. He was stripped of his medical license in 2010.

Some celebrities mobilize their influence for good; Michael J. Fox and Elton John have each helped raise more than US$300 million for research on Parkinson's disease and HIV/AIDS, respectively. Other celebrities offer medical advice on the Web, TV, and in magazines with little or no knowledge of, or respect for, the methods and findings of medical science. I suppose they genuinely believe what they say. However, they must also appreciate that the many people who admire and trust them form a large market for celebrity ideas and branded products. They know that in an era when celebrity has become a cult, many people are willing to place their trust in the medical advice of famous people, apparently hoping that doing so will allow them to take on some of the desirable traits of the celebrities they admire (Hoffman and Tan, 2013).

### Critical Thinking Question

- Scientific theories are fallible. They are routinely disproved. Does this mean that people should trust celebrity medical advice over medical science? Why or why not?

Some challenges to the authority of medical science are organized and political. For example, in the early 1980s, AIDS activists started challenging the stereotype of AIDS as a "gay disease." They demanded more research funding to help find a cure and helped to change research and treatment priorities in a way that could never have happened earlier (Epstein, 1996). Even before that, feminists had started supporting the reintroduction of midwifery and argued against medical intervention in routine child births, thereby challenging the wisdom of established medical practice.

The previously male-dominated profession of medicine considered the male body the norm and paid relatively little attention to "women's diseases," such as breast cancer, and "women's issues," such as reproduction. This, too, is now changing thanks to feminist interventions. And although doctors and the larger society traditionally treated people with disabilities as incompetent children, various movements now seek to empower them.

## Alternative Medicine

Other challenges to the authority of medical science are less organized and political than those just mentioned. Consider, for example, the growing use of complementary and alternative therapies such as massage, chiropractic, acupuncture, and yoga. In 2016, 79 percent of Canadian adults said they had used at least one complementary or alternative therapy at least once in their lives (see Figure 12.4). Use of such therapies is most widespread in British Columbia and least common in Quebec. The most widely used health alternative is massage, followed closely by chiropractic services. Those with chronic disorders, including back problems and multiple chemical sensitivities, are more likely to consult an alternative health service provider. Use of alternative medicine increases with income and education, and decreases for those above the age of 44 (Esmail, 2017).

Despite its growing popularity, many medical doctors were hostile to alternative medicine until the late 1990s, lumping all alternative therapies together and dismissing them as unscientific (Campion, 1993). Today, a more tolerant attitude is evident. For some kinds of ailments, physicians began to recognize the benefits of at least the most popular forms of alternative medicine. For example, a 1998 editorial in the respected *New England Journal of Medicine* admitted that the beneficial effect of chiropractic on low back pain is "no longer in dispute" (Shekelle, 1998). This change in attitude was due in part to scientific evidence from Canada showing that spinal manipulation is a relatively effective and inexpensive treatment for low back pain (Manga, Angus, and Swan, 1993).

At the same time, however, alternative forms of medicine should not be assumed to be entirely risk-free. For example, to date, the majority of Canadian lawsuits against chiropractors have involved claims of muscular skeletal dysfunction, strains and sprains, and rib fractures. In other cases, however, more serious injury has occurred, including ruptured vertebral arteries and death.

The medical profession's grudging acceptance of chiropractic in the treatment of low back pain indicates what

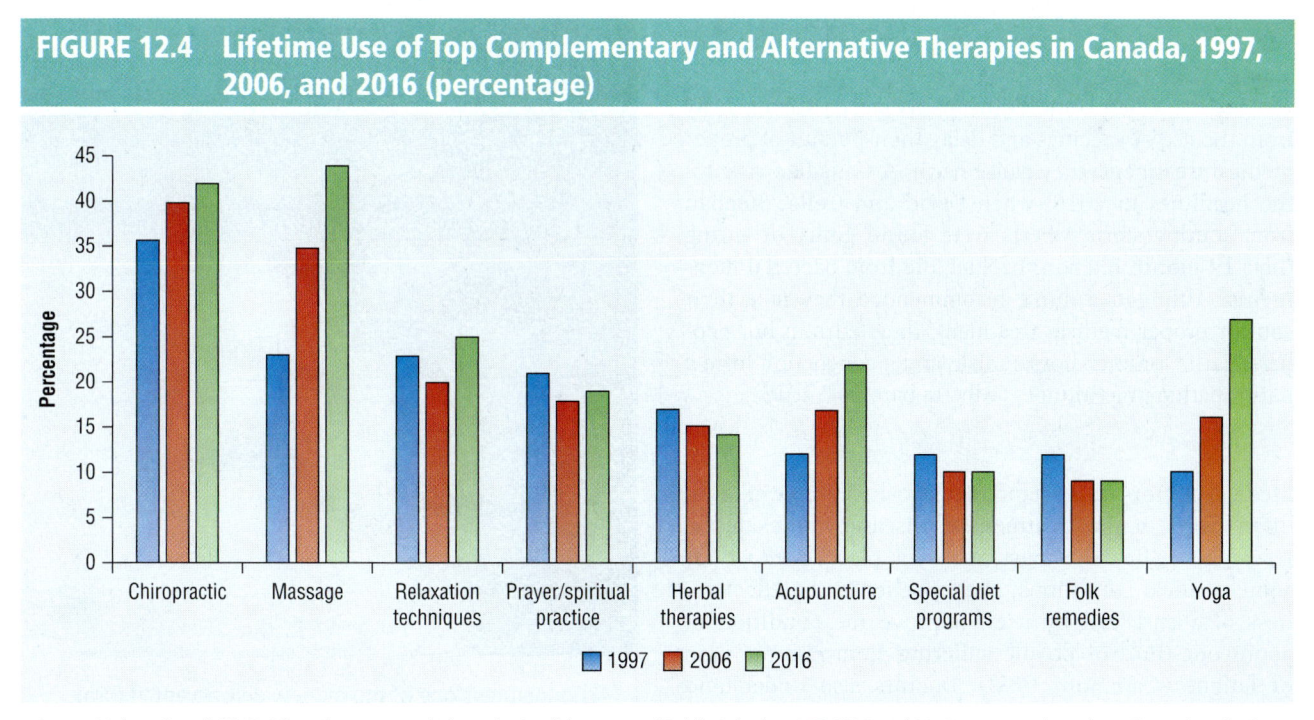

**FIGURE 12.4 Lifetime Use of Top Complementary and Alternative Therapies in Canada, 1997, 2006, and 2016 (percentage)**

Source: Nadeem Esmail. 2017. "Complementary and Alternative Medicine: Use and Public Attitudes 1997, 2006, and 2016," Fraser Institute, https://www.fraserinstitute.org/studies/complementary-and-alternative-medicine-use-and-public-attitudes-1997-2006-and-2016 (retrieved 17 February 2018).

**placebo effect** The positive influence on healing of a strong belief in the effectiveness of a cure.

**holistic medicine** Medical practice that emphasizes disease prevention. Holistic practitioners treat disease by taking into account the relationship between mind and body and between the individual and his or her social and physical environment.

we can expect in the uneasy relationship between scientific and alternative medicine in coming decades. Doctors will for the most part remain skeptical about alternative therapies unless properly conducted experiments demonstrate their beneficial effects. Most people agree with this cautious approach—but not all.

For example, Usain Bolt, David Beckham, Whoopi Goldberg, Queen Elizabeth II, Prince Charles, and Tony Blair have all used homeopathic medicine, as have many other less famous people (Ernst and Pittler, 2006). To prepare a homeopathic remedy, a substance such as salt, arsenic, duck liver, or human mucous is diluted with alcohol or distilled water. The dilution may be as strong as one part per 100 and as weak as one part per trillion or more, but usually it is so weak that no molecules of the original substance can be detected in it. Consumption of the preparation is alleged to alleviate ailments ranging from flu to cancer.

According to the American Medical Association, the National Health Service of the United Kingdom, and the National Health and Medical Research Council of Australia, hundreds of scientific studies find no scientific evidence to support the claim that homeopathic treatments have benefits other than the occasional placebo effect (National Health and Medical Research Council, 2015: 6). A **placebo effect** is the positive influence on healing of a strong belief in the effectiveness of a cure.

In fact, when some homeopaths steer patients away from the use of vaccines and delay their pursuit of proper medical treatment, they cause harm. A Canadian case hit the headlines in 2016, when David and Collet Stephan from southwestern Alberta were found guilty of letting their 19-month-old son, Ezekiel, die from bacterial meningitis. Although a nurse recommended they take their son for proper medical treatment, they fed him hot peppers, garlic, onions, horseradish, and a concoction from a naturopathic practitioner ("Alberta parents," 2016).

## Holistic Medicine

Medical doctors understand that a positive frame of mind often helps in the treatment of disease. For example, research verifies the existence of a placebo effect for some medical conditions; strong belief in the effectiveness of a cure can by itself improve the condition of about one-third of people suffering from chronic pain or fatigue (Campion, 1993). Doctors also understand that conditions in the human environment affect people's health. However, despite their appreciation of the effect of mind and environment on the human body, traditional scientific medicine tends to respond to illness by treating disease symptoms as a largely physical and individual problem. Moreover, scientific medicine continues to subdivide into more specialized areas of practice that rely more and more heavily on drugs and high-tech machinery. Most doctors are less concerned with maintaining and improving health by understanding the larger mental and social context within which people become ill.

Traditional Indian and Chinese medicine takes a different approach. India's Ayurvedic medical tradition views individuals in terms of the flow of vital fluids and their health in the context of their environment. In this view, maintaining good health requires not only balancing fluids in individuals but also balancing the relationship between individuals and the world around them (Zimmermann, 1987 [1982]).

Despite significant differences, the fundamental outlook is similar in traditional Chinese medicine. Chinese medicine and its remedies, ranging from acupuncture to herbs, seek to restore individuals' internal balance, as well as their relationship to the outside world (Unschuld, 1985).

Contemporary **holistic medicine**, the third and final challenge to traditional scientific medicine I will consider, takes an approach similar to these "ethnomedical" traditions. Practitioners of holistic medicine argue that good health requires maintaining a balance between mind and body, and between the individual and the environment.

Acupuncture is one of the more widely accepted forms of alternative medicine.

Most holistic practitioners do not reject scientific medicine. However, they emphasize disease *prevention*. Holistic practitioners seek to establish close ties with their patients and treat them in their homes or other relaxed settings. Rather than expecting patients to react to illness by passively allowing a doctor to treat them, they expect patients to take an active role in maintaining their good health. And some holistic practitioners, recognizing that industrial pollution, work-related stress, poverty, racial and gender inequality, and other social factors contribute heavily to disease, become political activists (Hastings, Fadiman, and Gordon, 1980).

In sum, patient activism, alternative medicine, and holistic medicine represent the three biggest challenges to traditional scientific medicine today. Few people think of these challenges as potential replacements for scientific medicine. However, many people believe that, together with traditional scientific approaches, these challenges will help improve the health status of people in Canada and throughout the world in the twenty-first century.

## READY TO STUDY?

### IN THE BOOK YOU CAN:

- Refer to the Chapter in Review section at the back of the book to have a summary of the chapter and key terms handy.
- Test your knowledge of chapter contents by answering the multiple-choice questions in the Chapter in Review section. Answers are in the appendix at the end of the book.

### ONLINE YOU CAN:

- Stay organized and efficient with MindTap—a single destination with all the course material and study aids you need to succeed.
- Flashcards are pre-populated to provide you with a jump start for review—or you can create your own.
- You can highlight text and make notes in your MindTap Reader.
- Prepare for tests with quizzes.

**GO TO NELSON.COM/STUDENT TO PURCHASE THESE DIGITAL RESOURCES.**

# 13
# Mass Media and Mass Communication

Columbia Pictures/Kobal/REX/Shutterstock

# THE SIGNIFICANCE OF THE MASS MEDIA
## ILLUSION BECOMES REALITY

In the 1982 science fiction classic *Blade Runner*, four "replicants" (artificial humans) escape the "off-world." They travel to Earth, trying to find their inventor, Eldon Tyrell. Their aim: to force him to extend their programmed lifespan. Rick Deckard (Harrison Ford) is a blade runner. His job is to hunt down and kill the escaped replicants. He does just that, but in the process he falls in love with Tyrell's assistant. She happens to be a replicant too.

Fast forward to 2017 and the release of the movie's sequel, *Blade Runner 2049*, directed by Denis Villeneuve and starring Ryan Gosling (both Canadians). This time, the blade runner's name is K. He discovers that a successful experiment conducted a couple of decades earlier allowed a replicant to give birth. K's boss realizes that war between humans and replicants might break out if the ability of replicants to reproduce became public knowledge; humans might fear that they would be replaced. To avoid that outcome, she orders K to hunt down and kill the offspring. However, K is a replicant himself, and a clue triggers a memory suggesting that he may be the offspring in question. Is his memory real or programmed? The movie's plot centres on K's attempt to answer that question.

If *Blade Runner* blurs the line between human and artificial human, *Blade Runner 2049* blurs the line between reality and artificial reality. As such, *Blade Runner 2049* may be an allegory for the fantasy worlds that the mass media create for us.

At the very least, the illusions created by the mass media today are every bit as pervasive and influential as religion was 500 or 600 years ago. If you think this is an exaggeration, recall what you learned in Chapter 2, Culture, and Chapter 3, Socialization: We spend more time absorbing and interacting with the mass media than we spend sleeping, working, or going to school. We have become so accustomed to interacting with the mass media that we find it increasingly difficult to be alone with our thoughts; recall the experiment that found that two-thirds of men and about a quarter of women chose electric shocks over their own company.

You might want to keep a tally of your activities for a day or two to see how you fit into this pattern of activity. Ask yourself, too, what you get out of your interactions with the mass media. Where do you get your ideas about how to dress, how to style your hair, and what music to listen to? Where do

## LEARNING OBJECTIVES:

In this chapter, you will learn to

**LO¹** Appreciate that, although the most popular mass media are products of the twentieth century, their growth is rooted in the rise of Protestantism, democracy, and capitalism.

**LO²** Explain how major sociological theories have been applied to the analysis of mass media and mass communication.

**LO³** Identify the ways in which centralized control and resistance to such control interact on the Internet.

**mass media** Print, radio, television, and other communication technologies that reach many people.

your hopes, aspirations, and dreams come from? If you're like most people, much of your reality is media-generated. Canadian media guru Marshall McLuhan, who coined the term *global village* in the early 1960s, said the media are extensions of the human body and mind (McLuhan, 1964). Six decades later, it is perhaps equally valid to claim that the human body and mind are extensions of the mass media (Baudrillard, 1983, 1988; Bourdieu, 1998).

## WHAT ARE THE MASS MEDIA?

The term **mass media** refers to print, radio, television, Internet, and other communication technologies that reach many people. Often, *mass media* and *mass communication* are used interchangeably to refer to the transmission of information from one person or group to another person or group. The word *mass* implies that the media reach many people. The word *media* signifies that communication does not take place directly through face-to-face interaction. Instead, technology intervenes or mediates in transmitting messages from senders to receivers.

Furthermore, communication via the mass media is often one-way, or at least one-sided. There are few senders (or producers) and many receivers (or audience members). Most newspapers print a few readers' letters in each edition, but journalists and advertisers write

Canadian media guru Marshall McLuhan said the media are extensions of the human body and mind.

The new media frontier blurs the distinction between producer and consumer and has the potential to make the mass media somewhat more democratic for those who can afford access.

virtually everything else. Ordinary people may appear on the *Dr. Phil* show or even delight in a slice of fame on *Survivor*, but producers choose the guests and create the program content. Similarly, a handful of people may visit your Facebook page, but Facebook chooses the ads you see based on what is known about your attributes (sex, age, and so on), and your likes and dislikes.

Usually, then, members of the audience cannot exert much influence on the mass media. They can choose only to tune in or tune out. And even tuning out is difficult because it excludes us from the styles, news, gossip, and entertainment most people depend on to grease the wheels of social interaction. Few people want to be cultural misfits. However, this doesn't mean that people are always passive consumers of the mass media. As discussed later, people tend to filter, interpret, and resist what they see and hear if it contradicts their experiences and beliefs. Even so, in the interaction between audiences and media sources, the media sources usually dominate.

To appreciate fully the impact of the mass media on life today, it's necessary to trace their historical development. That is the first task I set myself in the following discussion. I then critically review theories of the mass media's effects on social life. As you will see, each of these theories contributes to our appreciation of media effects. Finally, I assess developments on the media frontier formed by the Internet, television, and other mass media. I show that, to a degree, the new media frontier blurs the distinction between producer and consumer, and has the potential to make the mass media more democratic.

## THE RISE OF THE MASS MEDIA

It may be difficult for you to imagine a world without the mass media. Yet, as Table 13.1 shows, most of the mass media are recent inventions. The first developed

## TABLE 13.1 The Development of the Mass Media

| Year | Media Development |
|---|---|
| 1450 | Movable metal type used in Germany, leading to the Gutenberg Bible |
| 1702 | First daily newspaper, London's *Daily Courant* |
| 1833 | First mass-circulation newspaper, *The New York Sun* |
| 1837 | Louis Daguerre invented a practical method of photography in France |
| 1844 | Samuel Morse sent the first telegraph message between Washington and Baltimore |
| 1875 | Alexander Graham Bell sent the first telephone message |
| 1877 | Thomas Edison developed the first phonograph |
| 1895 | Motion pictures were invented |
| 1901 | Italian inventor Guglielmo Marconi transmitted the first transatlantic wireless message from England to St. John's, Newfoundland |
| 1906 | First radio voice transmission |
| 1920 | First regularly scheduled radio broadcast, Pittsburgh |
| 1928 | First commercial TV broadcast in United States; Canada followed in 1931 |
| 1949 | Network TV began in the United States |
| 1952 | VCR invented |
| 1961 | First cable television, San Diego |
| 1969 | First four nodes of the United States Department of Defense's ARPANET (precursor of the Internet) set up at Stanford University; University of California, Los Angeles; University of California, Santa Barbara; and the University of Utah |
| 1975 | First microcomputer marketed |
| 1976 | First satellite TV broadcast |
| 1983 | Cellphone invented |
| 1989 | World Wide Web conceived by Tim Berners-Lee at the European Laboratory for Particle Physics in Switzerland |
| 1990 | Windows 3.0 released (first mass-marketed graphical operating system) |
| 1991 | The World Wide Web became publicly accessible |
| 1999 | Wi-Fi (wireless Internet) became publicly available |
| 2001 | First iPod released<br>Digital satellite radio introduced |
| 2003 | Camera phone invented<br>First BlackBerry smartphone released in Waterloo, Ontario |
| 2005 | Facebook.com became public<br>YouTube founded |
| 2007 | First iPhone released |
| 2010 | FaceTime released; E Ink (Pearl display) invented, making e-readers like Kindle widely available |
| 2016 | Amazon Echo and Google Home released, followed by Apple HomePod a year later. |

Sources: Tim Berners-Lee, 1999, *Tim Berners-Lee: Biography*, www.w3.org/People/Berners-Lee/Overview.html (retrieved May 2, 2000); David Croteau and William Hoynes, 1997: 9–10, *Media/Society: Industries, Images, and Audiences*. Thousand Oaks, CA: Pine Forge Press; "Silent Boom," Peter Brimelow, *Forbes*, July 7, 1997: 170–71.

systems of writing appeared only about 5500 years ago in Mesopotamia (now southern Iraq). The print media became truly a mass phenomenon only in the nineteenth century. The inexpensive daily newspaper, costing a penny, first appeared in the United States in the 1830s. At that time, long-distance communication required physical transportation. To spread the news, you needed a horse, a railroad, or a ship. The slow speed of communication was costly. For instance, the last military engagement between Britain and the United States in the War of 1812–14 was the Battle of New Orleans. It took place 15 days after a peace treaty was signed. The good news did not reach the troops near the mouth of the Mississippi until they had suffered 2100 casualties, including 320 dead.

The newspaper was the dominant mass medium even as late as 1950 (Schudson, 1991; Smith, 1980). However, change was already in the air in 1844, when Samuel Morse sent the first telegraphic signal (Pred, 1973). From then on, long-distance communication no longer required physical transportation. The transformative power of the new medium was soon evident. For example, until 1883, hundreds of local time zones existed in North America. The correct time was determined by local solar time and was typically maintained by a clock in a church steeple or a respected jeweller's shop window. Virtually instant communication by telegraph made it possible to coordinate time and establish just six time zones in Canada. Railroad companies spearheaded the move to standardize time.

One of the most famous photographs in Canadian history is the driving of the last spike of the Canadian Pacific Railway (CPR) on November 7, 1885, at Craigellachie, British Columbia. The man holding the hammer is Donald Smith, who financed much of the construction of the CPR. The taller man standing behind him in the stovepipe hat is Sir Sandford Fleming, the mastermind behind standard time. The railroads spearheaded the introduction of standard time, which could be coordinated thanks to the introduction of the telegraph.

A Canadian civil and railway engineer, Sir Sandford Fleming, was the driving force behind the worldwide adoption of standard time (Blaise, 2001).

Most of the electronic media are creatures of the twentieth century. The first commercial television broadcasts date from the 1920s. The U.S. Department of Defense established ARPANET in 1969. It was designed as a system of communication between computers that would automatically find alternative transmission routes if one or more nodes in the network broke down because of, say, nuclear attack. ARPANET begat the Internet, which in turn begat the hyperlinked system of texts, images, and sounds known as the World Wide Web in 1991. By December 2017, nearly 4.2 billion people out of a world population of just over 7.63 billion used the Web (Internet World Stats, 2018). It was a quick trip—a mere 151 years separate the Pony Express from FaceTime.

## LO1 CAUSES OF MEDIA GROWTH

The rise of the mass media can be explained by three main factors—one religious, one political, and one economic:

1. *The Protestant Reformation.* At the beginning of the sixteenth century, Catholics relied on priests to tell them what was in the Bible. In 1517, however, Martin Luther protested certain practices of the church. Among other things, he wanted people to develop a more personal relationship with the Bible. Within 40 years, Luther's new form of Christianity, known as Protestantism, was established in half of Europe. Suddenly, millions of people were being encouraged to read. The Bible became the first mass media product in the West and is still today the best-selling book.

   Technological improvements in papermaking and printing made the diffusion of the Bible and other books possible (Febvre and Martin, 1976 [1958]). The most significant landmark was Johann Gutenberg's invention of the printing press. In the 50 years after Gutenberg produced his monumental Bible in 1455, more books were produced than in the previous 1000 years. The printed book enabled the widespread diffusion and exchange of ideas. It contributed to the Renaissance (a scholarly and artistic revival that began in Italy around 1300 and spread to all of Europe by 1600) and to the rise of modern science (Johns, 1998).

   A remarkable feature of the book is its durability. Many electronic storage media became obsolete just a few years after being introduced. Eight-track tapes are icons of the 1970s and 5.25-inch floppy disks are icons of the early 1980s. They are barely remembered today. In contrast, books are still

*In the 50 years after Johann Gutenberg invented the printing press, more books were produced than in the previous 1000 years.*

being published today, more than 560 years after Gutenberg published his Bible. Book publishing in Canada is a billion dollar a year industry, with tens of thousands of new titles published every year and 50 million books sold (Sparkes, 2017).

2. *Democratic movements.* A second force that promoted the growth of the mass media was political democracy. From the eighteenth century on, the citizens of France, the United States, and other countries demanded and achieved representation in government. At the same time, they wanted to become literate and gain access to previously restricted centres of learning. Democratic governments, in turn, depended on an informed citizenry and therefore encouraged popular literacy and the growth of a free press (Habermas, 1989).

Today, the mass media mould our entire outlook on politics. TV's influence first became evident in the 1960 U.S. presidential election. Soon, Canadian politicians were hiring "image consultants" too. Often, the media consultants' advice influenced the results. This included much maligned "negative advertising" techniques. While voters claim they do not approve of negative advertising, it is effective, although less often in Canada than in the United States sometimes (Kinsella, 2007). For example, in 2011, the Conservative Party branded Liberal Party leader Michael Ignatieff disloyal and power-hungry. The campaign was widely held to be partly responsible for undermining Liberal support in that year's federal election. On the other hand, four years later, the Conservatives framed Liberal Party leader Justin Trudeau as "just not ready" to lead the country. The campaign backfired and the Liberals won the election handily.

It is commonly claimed that television and other mass media have oversimplified politics. Some analysts say that politics has been reduced to a series of more or less well-managed images, catchy slogans, and ever-shorter uninterrupted comments or "sound bites." From this point of view, candidates are marketed for high office like breakfast cereal, and a politician's stage presence is more important than his or her policies in determining success at the polls. Political messaging on the Web has added a whole new dimension to the problem (see the Sociology and the Media boxed feature, Does the Web Endanger Democracy?)

3. *Capitalist industrialization.* The third major force stimulating the growth of the mass media was capitalist industrialization. Modern industries required a literate and numerate workforce. They also needed rapid means of communication to do business efficiently. Moreover, the mass media turned out to be a major source of profit in their own right.

Clearly, the sources of the mass media are deeply embedded in the religious, political, and economic needs of our society. Moreover, the mass media are among the most important institutions in our society today. How, then, do sociologists explain the effects of the mass media on society? To answer this question, I'll now summarize the relevant sociological theories.

# LO² THEORIES OF MEDIA EFFECTS

## FUNCTIONALISM

As societies develop, they become larger and more complex. The number of institutions and roles proliferate. Because of the sheer scale of society, face-to-face interaction becomes less viable as a means of communication. As a result, the need increases for new means of coordinating the operation of the various parts of society. For example, people in Nova Scotia must have at least a general sense of what is happening in Alberta, and they need to share certain basic values with Albertans if they are going to feel that they are citizens of the same country. The mass media do an important job in this regard. The nineteenth-century

# SOCIOLOGY AND THE MEDIA

## Does the Web Endanger Democracy?

For the first dozen or fifteen years of its existence, the Internet was regarded as democracy's best hope. Some observers saw it as a new "public square" that would encourage the free, open, and widespread exchange of ideas. Others thought home computers connected to the Internet would become electronic voting booths through which a growing proportion of citizens would be able to elect candidates and express support for, or opposition to, proposed legislative change. Still others regarded the Internet as a platform that would allow the voices of previously marginalized groups to be heard. Even as late as 2010–12, when the Arab Spring, the Occupy movement, the Idle No More movement, and other forces for change took to the streets demanding more democracy and tolerance, and less economic inequality, some sociologists optimistically believed that world was on the threshold of a better future (Castells, 2015 [2012]).

Although researchers had been looking into it for years (Deibert and Pauly, 2018), only in 2016 did many members of the public became aware of a less democratic, tolerant, and egalitarian side of politics on the Web. The occasion of their awakening to a grimmer reality was the election of Donald Trump to the U.S. presidency (Brym et al., 2018).

In 2012, social scientists published an article outlining how they had administered a questionnaire to 58 000 volunteers, who also provided detailed demographic profiles and access to their Facebook "likes" (Kosinski, Stillwell, and Graepel, 2012). The researchers showed they could accurately predict people's personality characteristics and personal attributes from their data. The researchers said that with 300 likes per person, they could know more about a respondent than the respondent's intimate partner knows. With still more likes, they claimed that their knowledge could exceed what people think they know about themselves. Data analysts in the Trump campaign latched onto the political potential of this technology.

One of the campaign's leading data scientists combined data from Facebook, the Republican National Committee, donor lists, email addresses gathered at campaign rallies, and other sources to identify several million persuadable voters living in a short hit list of states where the race was tight and Trump had the best chance of winning. He peppered those people with made-to-measure ads designed to appeal to their deepest hopes and anxieties, delivered for the most part digitally through Facebook, Twitter, and email. Off-the-shelf Facebook advertising tools were especially important in matching virtual profiles to real people, classifying individuals by race, income, residence, likes, dislikes, interests, and other characteristics, and maximizing the effectiveness of ads by first testing variants of them on hundreds of thousands of potential voters.

Two population categories were critically susceptible to these targeted, digital appeals: (1) alienated, older, white, small-town and rural voters, many of whom were reluctant to admit their pro-Trump sympathies to pollsters and many of whom had declined to vote in earlier elections; and (2) African-Americans who only tepidly supported Hillary Clinton and could be persuaded by anti-Clinton appeals not to vote at all. The strategy of mobilizing some voters and suppressing the vote of others worked better than expected. Trump won all of the states on the campaign's hit list, three of them by a total of just 0.09 percent of the ballots cast, barely enough to fill the University of Michigan's football stadium. If Clinton had won those three states, she would have been elected president.

### Critical Thinking Question
- Could something like the Trump victory occur in Canada?

---

German philosopher Georg Hegel once said that the daily ritual of reading the newspaper unites the secular world, just as the ritual of daily prayer once united the Christian world. Stated more generally, his point is valid. The nationwide distribution of newspapers, magazines, movies, television, and the Internet cements the large, socially diverse, and geographically far-flung population of Canada. In a fundamental sense, the nation is an imagined community, and the mass media make it possible for us to imagine it (Anderson, 1991).

The mass media perform an important function by coordinating the operation of industrial and postindustrial societies. However, according to functionalist theorists, their significance does not stop there (Wright, 1975). In addition, the mass media are also important agents of socialization. Families have relinquished their former nearly exclusive right to transmit norms, values, and culture. The mass media have stepped into the breach, reinforcing shared ideals of democracy, competition, justice, and so on (see Chapter 3, Socialization).

A third function of the mass media involves social control; the mass media help to ensure conformity. For example, news broadcasts, TV dramas, and reality TV programs pay much attention to crime, and they regularly sing the praises of heroes who apprehend and convict criminals. By exposing deviants and showcasing law enforcement officials and model citizens, the mass media reinforce ideas about what kinds of people deserve punishment and what kinds of people deserve rewards. In this way, they reproduce the moral order. Some people think *The Jerry Springer Show* is outlandish, and in a way it is. From a sociological point of view, however, it is also a deeply conservative program, for when television audiences become upset about marital infidelities and other outrages, they are reinforcing some of the most traditional norms and thus serving as agents of social control. As Nobel Prize-winning author Saul Bellow wrote, "a scandal [is] after all a sort of service to the community" (Bellow, 1964: 18).

The mass media's fourth and final function is to provide entertainment. Television, movies, magazines, and so on give us pleasure, relaxation, and momentary escape from the tension and tedium of everyday life. How often have you come home after a long and frustrating day at school or work, picked up the remote control, channel-surfed, concluded that there's nothing really worth watching, but settled for a sitcom or some other form of easily digestible entertainment? How about checking out the latest YouTube postings? It is precisely because some products of the mass media require little effort on the part of the audience that they are important. They relieve stress. Moreover, they do so in a way that doesn't threaten the social order. Without such escapes, who knows how our daily tensions and frustrations might express themselves?

From a sociological point of view, *The Jerry Springer Show* is a deeply conservative program that reinforces some of the most traditional norms and therefore serves as an agent of social control.

# CONFLICT THEORY

Clearly, functionalism offers valuable insights into the operation of the mass media. However, conflict theorists have criticized the functional approach for paying insufficient attention to the social inequality fostered by the mass media. Specifically, conflict theorists say functionalism exaggerates the degree to which the mass media serve the interests of the entire society. They contend that some people benefit from the mass media more than others do. In particular, the mass media favour the interests of dominant classes and political groups (Gitlin, 1983; Herman and Chomsky, 1988; Horkheimer and Adorno, 1986 [1944]; Iyengar, 1991).

Conflict theorists maintain that there are two ways in which dominant classes and political groups benefit disproportionately from the mass media. First, the mass media broadcast beliefs, values, and ideas that create widespread acceptance of the basic structure of society, including its injustices and inequalities. Second, ownership of the mass media is highly concentrated in the hands of a small number of people and is highly profitable for them. Thus, the mass media are a source of economic inequality. Let us consider these issues in more detail.

## Media Ownership

For decades, most of the Canadian mass media have been owned by fewer than a dozen families: the Siftons, the Thomsons, the Bassetts, the Southams, the Irvings, the Honderiches, the Blacks, and, more recently, the Shaws, the Rogerses, and the Péladeaus. Today, there are just five multimedia giants in the country with combined annual revenue of more than $45 billion. They include BCE, Rogers, Shaw, Québecor, and, by far the smallest of the five, with only 4 percent of total media revenue, *CBC/Radio-Canada*. The first four enterprises are privately owned while the fifth is government-owned.

In the 1930s, it was not at all obvious that 96 percent of the Canadian mass media would be privately owned and controlled. Here is what Prime Minister R. B. Bennett had to say on the subject in 1932:

> The use of the air...that lies over the...land of Canada is a natural resource over which we have complete jurisdiction....I cannot think that any government would be warranted in leaving the air to private exploitation and not reserving it for...the use of the people. Without [complete government control of broadcasting from Canadian sources, radio] can never become the agency by which national consciousness may be fostered and national unity...strengthened.
>
> —Quoted in Competition Bureau (2002)

What was self-evident to Prime Minister Bennett is a matter of controversy today. A minority of Canadians, like Bennett, still argue for strict government control of the mass media. Like Bennett, they believe that the mass media should be used to strengthen Canadian culture. Others want a more or less free market in which the great bulk of programming is American in origin or, failing that, American in style.

The Canadian Radio-television and Telecommunications Commission (CRTC) was established by an act of Parliament in 1968 as an independent agency responsible for regulating Canada's broadcasting and telecommunications systems. Its self-described mandate is to promote Canadian culture and economic competitiveness ("CRTC's Mandate," 2002). In practice, promoting Canadian culture means ensuring that 35 percent of the popular music played on English-language commercial radio stations between 6 a.m. and 6 p.m., Monday through Friday, is Canadian. Regulations for "ethnic" and French-language stations are somewhat different. Privately owned television stations must achieve a yearly Canadian content level of 60 percent between 6 a.m. and midnight and 50 percent between 6 p.m. and midnight. Canadian content rules for the CBC are slightly more demanding. "Canadian" means that the producer of the program is Canadian, key creative personnel are Canadian, and 75 percent of service costs and postproduction lab costs are paid to Canadians.

As a result of these regulations, about half of TV broadcasts in English Canada and 65 percent of popular music broadcasts are American. Moreover, many American TV and radio stations are widely available in Canada via cable, satellite, or the airwaves. (More than three-quarters of Canadian households subscribe to cable, satellite, or Internet protocol services: CRTC, 2017). It seems reasonable to conclude that at least three-quarters of the TV and popular music to which Canadians have access is American.

Over time, concentration of the privately owned media has increased. That is, fewer and fewer people control Canada's mass media with every passing decade. Moreover, it is not just the degree of media concentration that has changed. The form of media concentration began to shift in the 1990s, too. Until the 1990s, media concentration involved mainly "horizontal integration." A small number of firms tried to control as much production as possible in their particular fields (newspapers, radio, television, and so on). In the 1990s, however, "vertical integration" increased. Media firms sought to control production and distribution in many fields. They became media "conglomerates."

Today, a media conglomerate may own any combination of television networks, stations, and production facilities; magazines, newspapers, and book publishers; cable channels and cable systems; sports teams; Web portals; and software companies. A media conglomerate can create content and deliver it in a variety of forms. For instance, Rogers Communications Inc. owns the Toronto Blue Jays, creates sports entertainment, broadcasts it on its television stations, carries the signal to viewers' homes via its cable system, and spins off Blue Jays merchandise that it can sell in its stores.

## Media Bias

Does the concentration of the mass media in fewer and fewer hands deprive the public of independent sources of information, limit the diversity of opinion, and encourage the public to accept their society as it is? Conflict theorists think so. They argue that when a few conglomerates dominate the production of news in particular, they shut out alternative points of view.

Occasionally, corporate attempts to control the news are blatant, as in 2011, when Québecor Media launched a 24-hour television news network (*Sun News*) with an unapologetically right-wing, conservative slant. However, according to Edward Herman and Noam Chomsky (1988), more subtle mechanisms help to bias the news in a way that supports powerful corporate interests and political groups. These biasing mechanisms include advertising, sourcing, and flak:

- *Advertising.* Most of the revenue earned by television stations, radio stations, newspapers, and magazines comes from advertising by large corporations. According to Herman and Chomsky, these corporations routinely seek to influence the news so it will reflect well on them. In one American survey, 93 percent of newspaper editors said advertisers have tried to influence their news reports. Thirty-seven percent of newspaper editors admitted to being influenced by advertisers (Bagdikian, 1997). In addition, big advertisers may influence the news even without overtly trying to influence news carriers. For fear of losing business, news carriers may soften stories that big advertisers might find offensive.
- *Sourcing.* Studies of news-gathering show that most news agencies rely heavily for information on press releases, news conferences, and interviews organized by large corporations and government agencies. These sources routinely slant information to reflect favourably on their policies and preferences. Unofficial news sources are consulted less often. Moreover, unofficial sources tend to be used only to provide reactions and minority viewpoints that are secondary to the official story.
- *Flak.* Governments and big corporations routinely attack journalists who depart from official and corporate points of view.

On the whole, the conflict theorists' arguments are compelling. However, I don't find them completely convincing (Gans, 1979). *Sun News* was unpopular and stopped broadcasting in 2015. And if it is true that 37 percent of newspaper editors have been influenced by advertisers, 63 percent have not. News agencies may rely heavily on government and corporate sources, but this does not stop them from routinely biting the hand that offers to feed them and evading flak shot their way. The daily newspaper is full of examples of mainstream journalistic opposition to government and corporate viewpoints. Even mainstream news sources, although owned by media conglomerates, do not always act like the lap dogs of the powerful (Hall, 1980).

Still, conflict theorists make a valid point if they restrict their argument to how the mass media support core societal values. In their defence of core values, the mass media are virtually unanimous: they enthusiastically support democracy and capitalism. No Canadian news outlet has ever advocated a fascist government or a socialist economy.

Similarly, the mass media virtually unanimously endorse consumerism as a way of life. As discussed in Chapter 2, Culture, consumerism is the tendency to define ourselves in terms of the goods and services we purchase. Endorsement of consumerism is evident in the fact that advertising fills the mass media and is its lifeblood. Estimated expenditures for Canadian Internet, TV, radio, newspaper, magazine, and billboard advertising are more than $11 billion a year, nearly as much as the federal government spends on children's benefits and more than half the amount it spends on national defence (Department of Finance Canada, 2014; Houpt, 2014). We are exposed to a staggering number of ads each day. Companies pay filmmakers to use their brand-name products conspicuously in their movies. In some magazines, ads figure so prominently that readers have to search for the articles.

It is only when the mass media deal with news stories that touch on less central values that we can witness a diversity of media opinion. Specific government and corporate policies are often the subject of heated debate in the mass media. So, despite the indisputable concentration of media ownership, the mass media are diverse and often contentious on specific issues that do not touch on core values.

## INTERPRETIVE APPROACHES

The view that the mass media powerfully influence a passive public is common among both functionalists and conflict theorists. Many people believe that violence on TV causes violence in real life, pornography on the magazine stands or online leads to immoral sexual behaviour, and adolescents are more likely to start smoking cigarettes when they see popular movie stars lighting up.

Functionalists and conflict theorists share this top-down, deterministic view; members of both schools of thought stress how the mass media bridge social differences and reinforce society's core values. True, the two schools of thought differ in that functionalists regard core values as serving everyone's interests, while conflict theorists regard them as favouring the interests of the rich and powerful. By focusing so tightly on core values, however, both approaches understate the degree to which audience members interpret media messages in different ways.

The signal contribution of symbolic interactionist and related approaches, such as **cultural studies**, is that they highlight the importance of such interpretive acts.

Just how much influence do the mass media actually exert over audiences? The question is mired in controversy, but it seems that the top-down, deterministic view is one-sided (see Theories in Dispute, Does Violence on TV Cause Real-World Violence?). A persuasive argument that leads us to question the effects of mass media comes from interpretive sociologists, such as symbolic interactionists and interdisciplinary cultural studies experts. They use in-depth interviewing and participant observation to study how people interpret media messages.

British sociologist Stuart Hall (1980), one of the foremost proponents of cultural studies, emphasizes that people are not empty vessels into which the mass media pour a defined assortment of beliefs, values, and ideas. Rather, audience members take an active role in consuming the products of the mass media. They filter and interpret mass media messages in the context of their own interests, experiences, and values. Therefore, in Hall's view, any adequate analysis of the mass media needs to take into account both the production and the consumption of media products. First, he says, we need to study the meanings intended by the producers. Then we need to study how audiences consume or evaluate media products. Intended and received meanings may diverge; audience members may interpret media messages in ways other than those intended by the producers (Seiter, 1999).

Even children's television viewing turns out to be complex when viewed through an interpretive lens. Research shows that young children easily distinguish "make-believe" media violence from real-life violence (Woolley

> **cultural studies** Focus not just on the cultural meanings that producers try to transmit but also on the way audiences filter and interpret mass media messages in the context of their own interests, experiences, and values.

CHAPTER 13 Mass Media and Mass Communication

# THEORIES IN DISPUTE

## Does Violence on TV Cause Real-World Violence?

Social scientists are divided on whether violence on TV causes violence in the real world, even though they have been studying the issue since the 1960s, when the first generation of North American children raised on TV reached their teenage years (Brym, 2018e).

Some of the research is based on experiments. In a typical experiment, a group of children is randomly divided into experimental and control groups. The experimental group is shown a violent TV program. The level of aggressiveness of both groups at play is measured before and after the showing. If, after the showing, members of the experimental group play significantly more aggressively than they did before the showing, and significantly more aggressively than members of the control group, the researchers conclude that TV violence affects real-world behaviour.

Many such experiments show that exposure to media violence increases violent behaviour in young children, especially boys, over the short term. Results are mixed when it comes to assessing longer-term effects, especially on older children and teenagers.

Sociologists have also used surveys to measure the effect of media violence on behaviour. The results of most surveys show a significant relationship between exposure to violent mass media and violent behaviour—but a weaker relationship than experiments show.

Field research that systematically observes people in their natural social settings has also been employed to help us understand how media violence may influence behaviour. For example, sociologists have spent time in schools where shooting rampages have taken place. They have developed a deep appreciation of the context of school shootings by living in the neighbourhoods where they occur, interviewing students, teachers, neighbourhood residents, and shooters' family members, and studying police and psychological reports, the shooters' own writings, and other relevant materials. They have tentatively concluded that only a small number of young people—those who are weakly connected to family, school, community, and peers—are susceptible to translating media violence into violent behaviour.

Lack of social support allows the personal problems of such young people to become greatly magnified, and if guns are readily available, they are prone to using violent media messages as models for their own behaviour. In contrast, for the overwhelming majority of young people, violence in the mass media is just a source of entertainment and a fantasy outlet for emotional issues, not a template for action.

Finally, sociologists have analyzed official statistics to place the effect of media violence on real-world behaviour into broader perspective. For example, police statistics show that the homicide rate has historically been about three to four times higher in the United States than in Canada. Yet TV programming (as well as movies and video games) are nearly identical in the two countries, so exposure to media violence can't account for the difference. Most researchers attribute the difference to the higher level of economic and social inequality and the wider availability of handguns in the United States.

Apparently, then, the strength of the relationship between TV violence and real-world violence depends heavily on the methodology employed to examine it, with experiments showing the strongest relationship and analyses of official statistics showing the weakest relationship.

### Critical Thinking Question

- How is the argument presented here related to the problem of validity discussed in Chapter 1, Introducing Sociology?

and Ghossainy, 2013). That is one reason why watching *South Park* has not produced a nation of *South Park* clones. Similarly, research shows differences in the way working-class and middle-class women relate to TV. Working-class women tend to evaluate TV programs in terms of how realistic they are more than middle-class women do. This critical attitude reduces their ability to identify strongly with many characters, personalities, and storylines. For instance, working-class women know from their own experience that families often don't work the way they are shown on TV. They view the idealized, middle-class nuclear family depicted in many television shows with a mixture of nostalgia and skepticism (Press, 1991).

Age also affects how people relate to television. Senior viewers tend to be selective and focused in their television viewing. People who grew up with cable TV and a remote control often engage in channel-surfing, conversation, eating, and housework, zoning in and out of programs in anything but an absorbed fashion (Press, 1991). The idea that such viewers are sponges, passively soaking up the values embedded in TV programs and then mechanically acting on them, is mistaken.

## FEMINIST APPROACHES

Finally, let's consider feminist approaches to the study of mass media effects. In the 1970s, feminist researchers focused on the representation—more accurately, the misrepresentation—of women in the mass media. They found that in TV dramas, women tended to be cast as homemakers, as secretaries, and in other subordinate roles, while men tended to be cast as professionals and authority figures. Women usually appeared in domestic settings, men in public settings. Advertising targeted only women as purchasers of household products and appliances. Furthermore, researchers discovered that the news rarely mentioned issues of importance for many women, such as wage discrimination in the paid labour force, sexual harassment and abuse, childcare problems, and so on. News reports sometimes trivialized or denounced the women's movement. Newsworthy issues (the economy, party politics, international affairs, and crime) were associated with men, and men were more likely than women were to be used as news sources and to deliver the news (Watkins and Emerson, 2000: 152–53).

Most of this early feminist research assumed that audiences are passive. Analysts argued that the mass media portray women in stereotypical fashion, audience members recognize and accept the stereotypes as normal and even natural, and the mass media thereby reinforce existing gender inequalities. However, in the 1980s and 1990s, feminist researchers started criticizing this simple formula. Influenced by cultural studies, they realized that audience members selectively interpret media messages and sometimes even contest them.

A good example of this subtler and less deterministic approach is a study by Andrea Press and Elizabeth Cole (1999) of audience reaction to abortion as portrayed on TV shows. Over a four-year period, Press and Cole conducted 34 discussion groups involving 108 women. The women watched three TV programs focusing on abortion and then discussed their own attitudes and their reactions to the shows. The programs were pro-choice and dealt with women who chose abortion to avoid poverty.

Press and Cole found complex, ambivalent, and sometimes contradictory attitudes toward abortion among audience members. However, four distinct categories of opinion emerged:

1. *Pro-life women from all social classes* form the most homogeneous group. They think abortion is never justified. On principle, they reject the mass media's justifications for abortion.
2. *Pro-choice working-class women who think of themselves as members of the working class* adopt a pro-choice stand as a survival strategy, not on principle. They do not condone abortion, but they fear that laws restricting abortion would be applied prejudicially against women of their class. Therefore, they oppose any such restrictions. At the same time, they reject the TV message that financial hardship justifies abortion.
3. *Pro-choice working-class women who aspire to middle-class status* distance themselves from the "reckless" members of their own class who sought abortions on the TV shows. They tolerate abortion for such people but they reject it for themselves and for other "responsible" women.
4. *Pro-choice middle-class women* believe that only an individual woman's feelings can determine whether abortion is right or wrong in her own case. Many pro-choice middle-class women have deep reservations about abortion, and many of them reject it as an option for themselves. However, they staunchly defend the right of all women, especially the kind of women portrayed in the TV shows they watched, to choose abortion.

One of the most striking aspects of Press and Cole's findings is that, for different reasons, three of the four categories of audience members (categories 1, 2, and 3) are highly skeptical of TV portrayals of the abortion issue. Their class position and attitudes act as filters influencing how they react to TV shows and how they view the abortion issue. Moreover, three of the four categories of audience members (categories 2, 3, and 4) reject the simple pro-choice versus pro-life dichotomy often portrayed by the mass media. Many pro-choice women express ambivalence about abortion and even reject it as an option for themselves. We must

Missy Elliott

conclude that real women are typically more complicated than the stereotypes promoted in the mass media, and that women in the audience typically know that.

In recent years, some feminists have focused on the capacity of the mass media to reproduce and change the system of racial inequality in North American society. In the work of these scholars, the twin issues of female misrepresentation and active audience interpretation reappear, this time with a racial twist. On the one hand, they find that certain stereotypical images of women of colour recur in the mass media. Black women, for example, often appear in the role of the welfare mother, a highly sexualized Jezebel.

On the other hand, they recognize that some mass media, especially independent filmmaking and popular music, have enabled women of colour to challenge these stereotypes. The music and videos of Erykah Badu, Missy Elliott, Lauryn Hill, Beyoncé Knowles, and Alicia Keys are especially noteworthy in this regard. These artists write and produce their own music. They often direct their own videos. Their work is a running critical commentary on real-world issues confronting young black women. Thus, in terms of both production and content, their work breaks down the established roles and images of black women in North America (Watkins and Emerson, 2000: 159–56).

Still, stereotypes persist. Consider the results of a study of (1) 129 top-grossing family films released between September 2006 and September 2011; (2) 275 prime-time TV programs on 10 North American broadcast and cable channels in the spring of 2012; and (3) 36 children's TV shows across three networks in 2011 (Smith et al., 2012). Across all three categories, just 32.7 percent of characters were women. Women were grossly underrepresented in prestigious, high-paying occupational roles. For example, there were more than five times more male than female scientists in family films. Finally, women were hypersexualized (judged to be thin, attractive, wearing sexy clothes, and partly nude) 3.4 times more often than men were (see Figure 13.1 and Figure 13.2).

### FIGURE 13.1 Representation of Women in the Mass Media

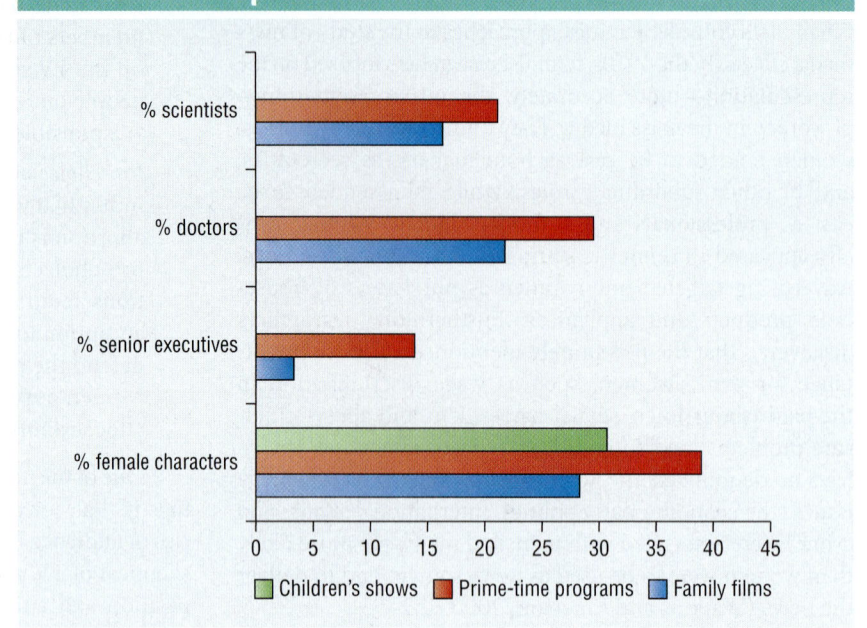

Source: Stacy L. Smith et al. 2012. "Gender Roles and Occupations: A Look at Character Attributes and Job-Related Aspirations in Film and Television." Emmitsburg, MD: Mount St. Mary's University, https://seejane.org/wp-content/uploads/full-study-gender-roles-and-occupations-v2.pdf (retrieved November 12, 2016).

### FIGURE 13.2 Hypersexuality in the Mass Media

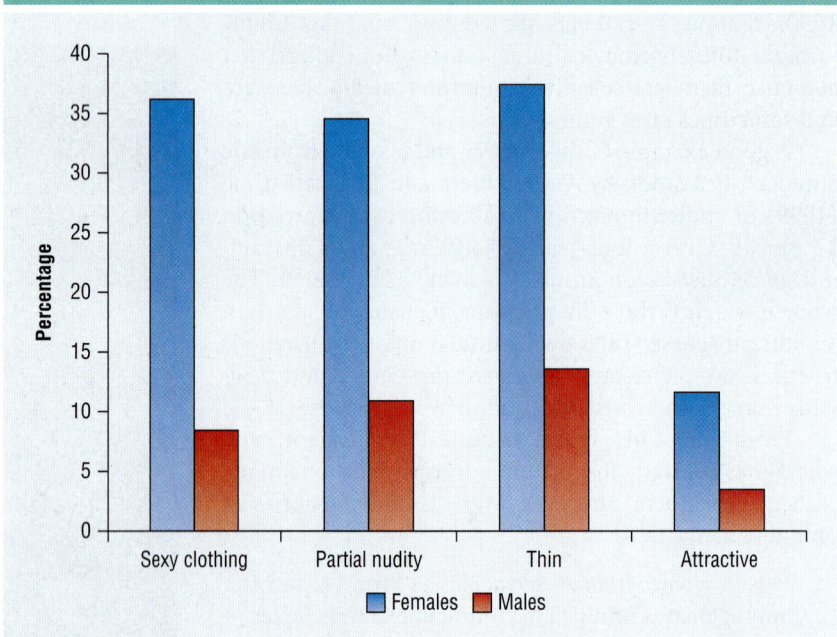

Source: Stacy L. Smith et al. 2012. "Gender Roles & Occupations: A Look at Character Attributes and Job-Related Aspirations in Film and Television." Emmitsburg, MD: Mount St. Mary's University (accessed November 12, 2016). Adapted by permission of the Geena Davis Institute on Gender in Media.

The way in which the mass media treat women and members of various minority groups has for the most part improved over time. We have come a long way since the 1950s, when virtually the only blacks on TV were men who played butlers and buffoons. Research suggests that the mass media still have a long way to go before they cease reinforcing traditional stereotypes in North America; *Wonder Woman* notwithstanding, just 24 percent of leading roles in the 100 top-grossing films of 2017 belonged to women, down from 29 percent in 2016 (Nathoo, 2018). But research also suggests that audiences and artists are hardly passive vehicles of these stereotypes, instead struggling to diversify the way the mass media characterize them.

## THEORIES AT A GLANCE

### Mass Media and Mass Communication

| Theory | Main Question | Application |
| --- | --- | --- |
| Functionalism | How do social structures and the values underlying them contribute to social stability? | The mass media perform an important function by coordinating the operation of industrial and postindustrial societies. In addition, the mass media are important agents of socialization. A third function of the mass media involves social control; the mass media help to ensure conformity. The mass media's fourth and final function is to provide entertainment, that is, pleasure, relaxation, and momentary escape from the tension and tedium of everyday life. Without such escapes, daily tensions and frustrations might express themselves more openly and disruptively. |
| Conflict theory | How does the structure of inequality between privileged groups seeking to maintain their advantages and subordinate groups seeking to increase theirs lead to conflict and often to social change? | Conflict theorists criticize functionalism for paying insufficient attention to the social inequality fostered by the mass media. Specifically, conflict theorists say functionalism exaggerates the degree to which the mass media serve the interests of the entire society. They contend that some people benefit from the mass media more than others do. In particular, the mass media favour the interests of dominant classes and political groups.<br><br>Conflict theorists maintain that there are two ways in which dominant classes and political groups benefit disproportionately from the mass media. First, the mass media broadcast beliefs, values, and ideas that create widespread acceptance of the basic structure of society, including its injustices and inequalities. Second, ownership of the mass media is highly concentrated in the hands of a small number of people and is highly profitable for them. In this way, the mass media are a source of economic inequality. |
| Symbolic interactionism | How do people communicate to make their social settings meaningful, thus helping to create their social circumstances? | Both functionalism and conflict theory stress how the mass media bridge social differences and reinforce society's core values. By focusing on core values, both approaches understate the degree to which audience members interpret media messages in different ways. Symbolic interactionist and related approaches highlight the importance of such interpretive acts. |
| Feminism | How do social conventions maintain male dominance and female subordination, and how do these conventions get overturned? | Early feminist research focused on the misrepresentation of women in the mass media. It found that in TV dramas, women tended to be cast in subordinate roles and men as authority figures. Women usually appeared in domestic settings, men in public settings. Advertising targeted only women as purchasers of household products and appliances. The news rarely mentioned issues of importance for many women and sometimes trivialized or denounced the women's movement. Newsworthy issues were associated with men, and men were more likely than women were to be used as news sources and to deliver the news.<br><br>In the 1980s and 1990s, feminist researchers, influenced by cultural studies, began demonstrating that audience members selectively interpret media messages and sometimes contest them. And in recent years, some feminist scholars have broadened their focus to analyze the capacity of the mass media to reproduce and change the system of racial inequality in North America. On the one hand, they find that certain stereotypical images of women of colour recur in the mass media. On the other hand, they recognize that some mass media, especially independent filmmaking and popular music, have enabled women of colour to challenge these stereotypes. |

# LO³ CENTRALIZED CONTROL AND RESISTANCE ON THE INTERNET

I've emphasized that the interaction between audiences and the traditional mass media (television, radio, and newspapers) is generally weighted in favour of the media. Audience members do not mindlessly absorb messages from these sources. However, they exercise little control over content.

In contrast, the Internet, especially its social media applications, offers better prospects for audience influence than do the traditional mass media. True, the Internet provides fresh opportunities for media conglomerates to restrict access to paying customers and accumulate vast wealth. Simultaneously, however, the Internet gives consumers new creative capabilities, partially blurring the distinction between producer and consumer. In short, the Internet can and sometimes does make the mass media more democratic.

To develop this idea, let's first consider the forces that restrict Internet access and augment the power of media conglomerates, and then discuss counter-trends.

## ACCESS

The Internet requires an expensive infrastructure of personal computers, servers, and routers; an elaborate network of fibre-optic, copper-twist, and coaxial cables; and many other components. This infrastructure has to be paid for, primarily by individual users. Access is growing, as are other indicators of usage (see Figure 13.3), but it is still restricted. In Canada, for example, households that are richer, better educated, urban, and younger are most likely to enjoy Internet access (Statistics Canada, 2010e).

Nor is Internet access evenly distributed globally. In Iceland and Denmark, close to 100 percent of the population is connected. In Sweden, the United Kingdom, Japan, and Sweden, the figure is about 95 percent. Canada boasts a penetration rate of around 90 percent, and the United States comes in at a few percentage points below that. In contrast, Africa has a 35 percent penetration rate; 13 African countries have rates in the single digits.

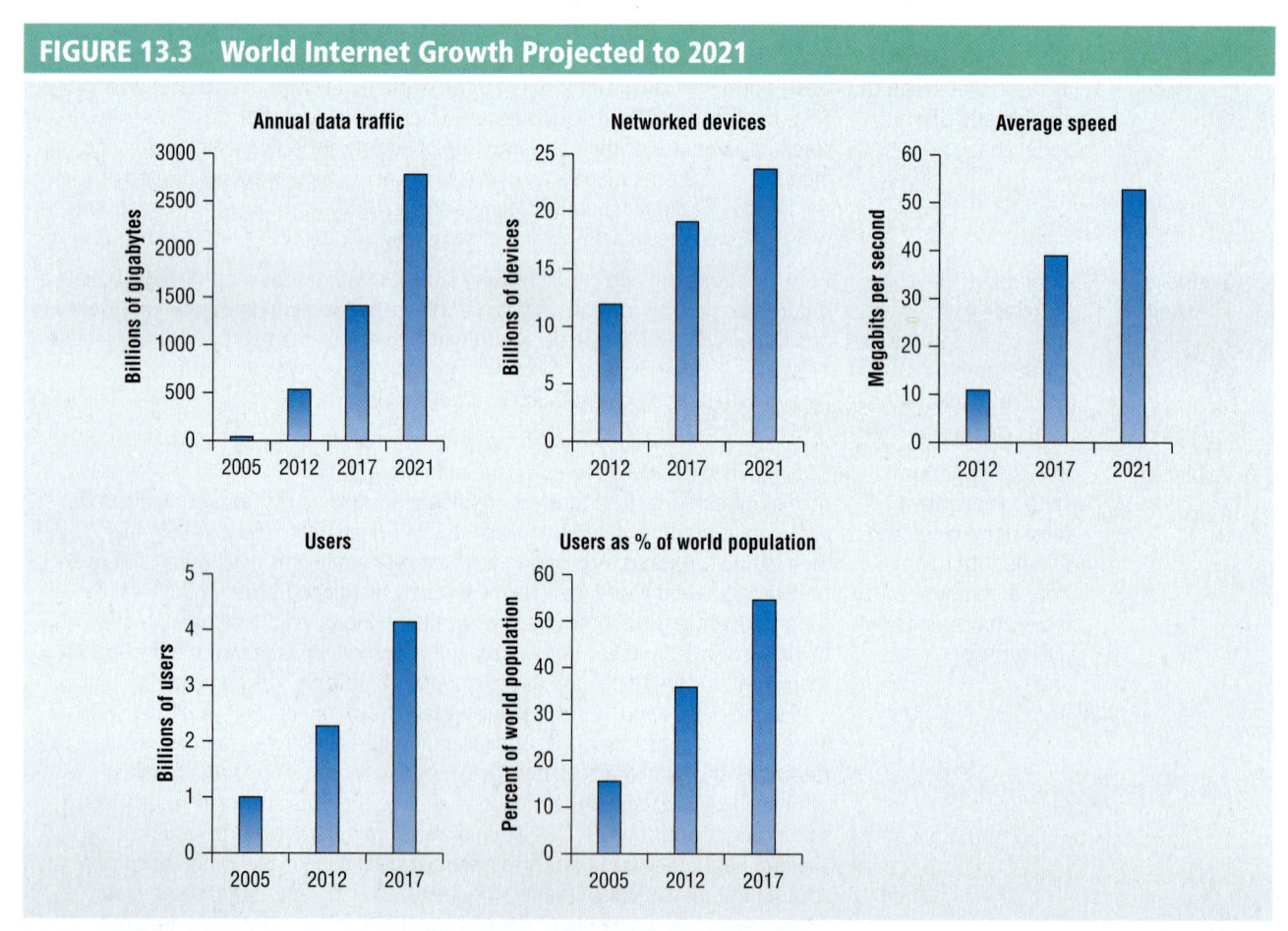

**FIGURE 13.3  World Internet Growth Projected to 2021**

Source: Cisco. 2017. "Cisco Visual Networking Index: Forecast and Methodology, 2016–2021." https://www.cisco.com/c/en/us/solutions/collateral/service-provider/visual-networking-index-vni/complete-white-paper-c11-481360.pdf.

Clearly, the rate of Internet connectivity is much higher in rich countries than in poor countries (Internet World Stats, 2018).

## CONTENT

According to some analysts, American domination is another striking feature of Internet content, as evidenced by the fact that 7 of the 10 world's most popular websites are American-owned and 9 of the 10 most followed people on Twitter are Americans (Bruner, 2018; World Economic Forum, 2018). Some analysts say that American domination of the Web is an example of **media imperialism**, the control of a mass medium by a single national culture and the undermining of other national cultures.

### Internet Advertising

Advertising is the major source of revenue for most big Internet companies. To cite just one example, Google earned US$89.5 billion in 2016, two-thirds of which came from advertising (Rosenberg, 2016).

Advertising seeks to influence (some would say "manipulate") consumers to buy products and services. Companies invest a lot in advertising because it works—and the Internet provides advertisers with ways to influence consumers more effectively than newspaper, magazine, radio, and TV ads do. For instance, targeted ads are widely used on the Internet. Google Search, YouTube (which is owned by Google), and other Internet services routinely collect information on which websites you visit, what you buy online, your locale, and your demographic characteristics. Advertisers buy this information so they can target specific market segments. It is no accident that when Indigo or Amazon suggests books for you to consider purchasing, they recommend titles that actually interest you. Nor should you be surprised to see a pop-up announcing that your favourite rock star is holding a concert in your city next month. Such ads are tailored to suit your interests and are therefore more cost-effective than, say, a roadside billboard for a refrigerator you don't need.

> **media imperialism**
> Domination of a mass medium by a single national culture and the undermining of other national cultures.

### Biased Algorithms

In 2016, investigators discovered that, in some cases, the autocomplete function in Google's search engine promoted information that was false and/or slanted with extreme right-wing bias. Investigators typed "climate change is" into the search engine and the first autocomplete result was "a hoax." When they typed "are women," the autocomplete function responded with "evil." Typing "are Muslims" produced "bad." Investigators also discovered that on job sites, men are more likely than women are to see ads for high-paying executive jobs popping up on their screen. When Flickr introduced image recognition tools, black people were sometimes tagged as "apes" or "animals" (Carpenter, 2015; Hern, 2015; Solon and Levin, 2016).

People write algorithms—rules that computers follow to solve problems—to drive the Internet and social media. As suggested by the examples just cited, the biases they have incorporated into their algorithms to date tend to favour privileged and/or right-wing groups. This circumstance has led some mathematicians and computer scientists to identify algorithms on the Internet and in social media that increase inequality and threaten democracy. One expert in the field labelled such biased algorithms "weapons of math destruction" (O'Neil, 2016).

## ONLINE PIRACY VS. NET NEUTRALITY

Some researchers argue that the Internet not only restricts access, promotes American content, manipulates audiences, and biases information but also increases the power of media conglomerates.

Media conglomerates like Bell, Rogers, and Shaw compete against each other to offer the most appealing content at the fastest speeds but they are united on industry-wide tactics to maximize profit. For instance, both companies strongly favour user-based billing (the more you use, the more you pay). Opponents of this policy argue that technology has lowered costs so much that user-based billing is just a money grab by some of the most profitable businesses in Canada—an unfair practice

Modern means of mass communication reach every corner of the earth.

**Online piracy** The term used by Internet service providers and online distributors of movies, music, and books to describe the downloading of copyright material without paying for it.

**Net neutrality** The principle that Internet service providers should not restrict access to any online content.

that restricts the poorest Canadians' access to the Internet and cellphones.

A related area of contention concerns the debate about **online piracy** versus **net neutrality**. Online piracy is the term used by Internet service providers and online distributors of movies, music, and books to describe the downloading of copyright material without paying for it. Net neutrality is the principle that Internet service providers should not restrict access to any online content.

Advocates of net neutrality claim that unrestricted access maximizes freedom of expression, innovation, and user choice. They also say that net neutrality provides access to online materials that offer education, information, and entertainment to people who would otherwise not be able to afford these benefits.

In contrast, those who decry online piracy note that musicians, actors, and authors expend enormous creative effort producing their works, while companies invest huge sums to advertise and distribute them. From this point of view, creators and distributors own the products of their labour and investment. They are therefore legally entitled to be compensated for their efforts. Distributing their work without paying for it is theft and should be dealt with accordingly.

While the debate between opponents of online piracy and supporters of net neutrality rages, one thing is clear: media conglomerates can never fully dominate the Internet because it is the first mass medium that makes it relatively easy for consumers to become producers.

## THE RISE OF SOCIAL MEDIA

Every minute, people upload 400 hours of digital video to YouTube (DMR, 2018). Nearly all laptops sport webcams and nearly all university and college students own laptops, so video chats through Skype and other services are commonplace. In February 2018, Facebook boasted 2.13 billion monthly active users (Zephoria Digital Marketing, 2018). There were 330 million monthly active Twitter users in December 2017 (Statista, 2018a). Add to this the many millions of personal websites, public-access cameras, alternate reality and multiple-user gaming sites, and discussion groups devoted to every imaginable topic, and one must temper the image of the Internet as a medium that is subject to increasing domination by large conglomerates.

In many respects, the trend is the contrary: individual users are making independent, creative contributions to Internet growth. And they react negatively if they lack access to computer-mediated communication. A recent experiment found that inability to answer a cellphone while completing word search puzzles caused anxiety, blood pressure and heart rate to increase, and cognitive performance to drop (Clayton, Leshner, and Almond, 2015).

Using social media affects identity (how people see themselves), social relationships (the connections people form with others), and social activism (the ways in which people seek to cause social change) (Bookman, 2014). Let's briefly consider each of these issues in turn:

- *Identity.* Social media offer people opportunities to manipulate the way they present themselves to others and explore aspects of their selves that they may suppress in embodied social interaction. Of course, people do not shift shapes, as it were, just because they can. The difference between self-presentation offline and online is typically modest. Nonetheless, differences exist, and they can change self-conceptions in ways that are usually minor but sometimes major.

  Some users find that social media have taken over such a large slice of life that their online identity performances start to feel like their real selves (Turkle, 2011: 12). Some learn to become more assertive online than they are offline, and it is possible that once they learn to be bolder, they carry the lesson into real life to a degree. In some cases, people "in the closet" with respect to their sexual preferences use social media as a gateway to "coming out." In these and other ways, social media serve as "identity workshops" (Turkle, 1995).

  On the other hand, some social media users are well aware that the selves they present on Facebook and Instagram are problematic. Increasingly, people are concerned they might reveal something that would stand in the way of their getting a job they want and/or they recognize that they construct their online selves to place themselves in the best possible light, thereby losing the opportunity to express themselves authentically. Because of these concerns, some Instagram users have started creating "finsta" and "rinsta" accounts (Pringle, 2017). A rinsta is a real Instagram account. It's the one a stranger would find by looking you up, so it presents you as you would like to be seen by, say, a potential employer. A finsta is a fake Instagram account. It uses a screen name based on an inside joke or identifying characteristic that only your close friends would know. On a finsta account, you can be your authentic self.

- *Social relations.* In the 1990s, some analysts expected the Internet to isolate people, creating private worlds that would lead to the decline of family and community life. Others held the opposite opinion—that the Internet would create opportunities for people to form new communities based on common interests rather than geographical proximity or blood ties. Both scenarios contain an element of truth but both are problematic as assessments of the overall impact of the Internet in general, and social media in particular, on social relations. A few people do retire to the basement, keep the curtains on their windows tightly drawn, avoid face-to-face interaction, and spend their days in virtual worlds. Some people do form close and even intimate friendships online in communities of common interest, dropping nearly all real-world social relations. For most people, however, social media have not replaced real life—social media have become an integral part of their life (Wellman, 2014).

Thus, research shows that people tend to use social media to augment telephone and face-to-face communication, not to replace them. Most of the people we e-mail, message, and text are people we already know, and when we use social media to contact people we don't know, it is often to see whether we want to proceed to a phone call or a face-to-face meeting.

For most people, then, social media increase interaction and build community—but not community in the traditional sense. Traditional communities are fixed locations. To interact in them, you have to reside in them physically. You don't get to select community members. Everybody knows your business. In contrast, social media allow for the crystallization of communities that are multiplex (you can belong to many of them), variegated (you can decide how intimately you want to interact with different members of different communities), personalized (you can decide who to allow in and who to exclude), portable (you can take them with you), and ubiquitous (you can take them anywhere you please). Social media thus breed what sociologist Barry Wellman calls "networked individualism" (Wellman, 2014).

Nonetheless, some people spend so much time managing online profiles and relationships, and instantly responding to e-mails, tweets, and Facebook messages, that social media may be causing a decline in the depth and quality of face-to-face social interaction. Going on holiday with the family, having dinner with friends, and other traditional ways of enjoying the presence of others are now punctuated with social media interruptions and distractions that can have consequences for our well-being. In fact, a recent survey showed that the sense of well-being of people between the ages of 18 and 34 declined the more frequently they communicated with acquaintances and co-workers (as opposed to relatives and close friends) using a variety of platforms (mobile and landline phones; desktop and laptop computers). In other words, frequent electronic communication with many acquaintances and co-workers on multiple platforms seems to burden younger people and make them less happy (Chan, 2014). Research also shows that the more often people use Facebook and the larger the size of their Facebook network, they more likely they are to be victimized by scam artists (Vishwanath, 2015). We thus see that an excess of networked individualism can have more than one downside.

- *Social activism.* Finally, social media open up new ways of engaging in social change. People advocate and spread awareness of a wide variety of environmental, human rights, and other causes using blogs, Twitter, Facebook, and activist websites containing reports, news, videos, announcements, and Web links. People also use social media to mobilize others for demonstrations, petitions, meetings, support concerts, and fundraising. The most celebrated use of social media for these purposes occurred during the heyday of the Occupy movement and the Arab Spring in 2010–11 and the Idle No More movement in Canada in 2012. Many analysts expect that the role of social media in advocating and mobilizing for social and political change will grow in the coming years.

Other researchers are not so sure. They identify two counter-trends. First, they observe that in Syria, Egypt, Russia, China, and other non-democratic countries, authorities systematically monitor and analyze social media messages. Doing so allows them to identify, harass, and arrest anti-regime activists, including those who support democratization. Some observers worry about online surveillance in democratic countries, too, fearing that by monitoring social media, authorities in Canada and elsewhere will inhibit legitimate radical discourse.

A second counter-trend involves social media acting as a replacement for high-risk activism. By, say, allowing people to sign an online petition or contribute a dollar to a cause instead of engaging in an illegal strike or demonstration, social media may encourage "slacktivism" rather than activism (Brym et al., 2014; Gunitsky, 2015). Thus, in addition to facilitating advocacy and mobilization for social and political change, social media can have the opposite effect.

In sum, the Internet is a mass medium unlike any other in the sense that it provides unique opportunities for user autonomy and creativity. To be sure, it also increases opportunities for corporations and authorities to engage in the homogenization, surveillance, and possible control of users, but at least on this mass medium, users enjoy many means of resistance (Lyon, 2007).

Even so-called American "media imperialism" seems to be less threatening than some analysts assume because of the decentralized nature of the Internet. Non-American influence is growing rapidly on the Web, while websites based in the United States adopt content liberally from Latin America, Asia, and elsewhere. Just as international influences are evident in today's hairstyles, clothing fashions, foods, and popular music, so we can see the Internet less as a site of American media imperialism than a site of globalization (Widyastuti, 2010). In 2018, the world's 25 most frequently visited websites included 13 from outside the United States (Alexa, 2018).

Of course, nobody knows exactly how the social forces we have outlined will play themselves out. In 1999, Napster emerged, enabling millions of people to share recorded music freely on the Web using a central server. Some analysts pointed to Napster as evidence of Internet democratization. Then the media conglomerates took Napster to court, forcing it to stop the giveaway on the grounds it was effectively stealing royalties from musicians and profits from music companies. Some analysts saw the court case as evidence of growing corporate control on the Web. However, a few years later, BitTorrent emerged, allowing people to share recorded music and videos without a central server, making it virtually impossible to shut it down.

Despite repeated legal actions to try to curb organizations like the Pirate Bay (a large torrent hub in Sweden), the dispersed locations of management, servers, developers, and users make litigation and enforcement extremely problematic. And so the tug-of-war between central control and democratization continues, with no end in sight. One thing is clear, however: The speed of technological innovation and the many possibilities for individual creativity on the Internet make this an exciting era to be involved in the mass media and to study it sociologically.

Some people say that social media are causing a decline in the depth and quality of social interaction.

## READY TO STUDY?

### IN THE BOOK YOU CAN:

❏ Refer to the Chapter in Review section at the back of the book to have a summary of the chapter and key terms handy.

❏ Test your knowledge of chapter contents by answering the multiple-choice questions in the Chapter in Review section. Answers are in the appendix at the end of the book.

### ONLINE YOU CAN:

❏ Stay organized and efficient with MindTap—a single destination with all the course material and study aids you need to succeed.

❏ Flashcards are pre-populated to provide you with a jump start for review—or you can create your own.

❏ You can highlight text and make notes in your MindTap Reader.

❏ Prepare for tests with quizzes.

GO TO NELSON.COM/STUDENT TO PURCHASE THESE DIGITAL RESOURCES.

# 14
# Social Change: Technology, the Environment, and Social Movements

# WHAT IS SOCIAL CHANGE?

**Social change** refers to the alteration of social structures and cultures. Sociological theorists have characterized large-scale social change in three main ways—as technology-driven progress; as a series of responses to environmental challenges; and as the product of large-scale conflict (Form and Wilterdink, 2018). In this chapter, I find merit in each of these characterizations but I also find weaknesses.

First, I show that while technological innovation is an important cause of social change, it becomes so only when it is driven by deep social need. Moreover, social change caused by technological innovation does not always represent unqualified progress: some new technologies put all of humanity, and especially disadvantaged groups, at great environmental risk.

Second, I recognize the benefit of viewing social change as a series of responses to environmental challenges. However, I also argue that responses involving ruthless competition (survival of the fittest) now seem riskier than do responses based on cooperation.

Third, I acknowledge that responses to environmental risk are likely to involve considerable conflict between groups with different ideas about how we should move forward. Much hinges on the outcome of these conflicts. Perhaps everything does, for the outcome will decide how successfully we, as a species, are able to adapt to the environmental challenges we face, or whether we are able to adapt at all.

I begin developing these ideas by first considering the role of technology in social change.

# TECHNOLOGY: SAVIOUR OR FRANKENSTEIN?

On August 6, 1945, the United States Air Force dropped an atomic bomb on Hiroshima. The bomb killed about 200 000 Japanese, almost all of them civilians. It hastened the end of World War II, making it unnecessary for American troops to suffer heavy losses in a land invasion of Japan.

Scholars interested in the relationship between technology and society recognize that Hiroshima

**social change** The alteration of social structures, cultural symbols, rules of behaviour, and/or value systems.

# LEARNING OBJECTIVES:

In this chapter, you will learn to

- **LO¹** Analyze the circumstances in which environmental issues are transformed into social problems.
- **LO²** Assess the unequal social distribution of environmental risks.
- **LO³** Summarize the role of market/technological and cooperative solutions to environmental problems.
- **LO⁴** Identify the social conditions that encourage people to rebel against the status quo.
- **LO⁵** List the characteristics of new social movements.

**technology** The practical application of scientific principles.

**normal accident** An accident that occurs inevitably although unpredictably because of the complexity of modern technologies.

divided the twentieth century into two periods. I call the period before Hiroshima the era of naive optimism. During that time, technology could do no wrong, or so it seemed to nearly all observers. **Technology** was widely defined as the application of scientific principles to the *improvement* of human life. It seemed to be driving humanity down a one-way street named progress, picking up speed with every passing year thanks to successively more powerful engines: steam, turbine, internal combustion, electric, jet, rocket, and nuclear.

Technology produced tangible benefits. Its detailed workings rested on scientific principles that were mysterious to all but those with advanced science degrees. Therefore, most people regarded scientists and technologists with reverence and awe. They were viewed as a sort of priesthood whose objectivity allowed them to stand outside the everyday world and perform near-magical acts.

With Hiroshima, the blush was off the rose. Growing pessimism was, in fact, evident three weeks earlier, when the world's first nuclear bomb exploded at the Alamogordo Bombing Range in New Mexico. Dr. J. Robert Oppenheimer had been appointed scientific director of the top-secret Manhattan Project just 28 months earlier. After recruiting what General Leslie Groves called "the greatest collection of eggheads ever," including three past and seven future Nobel Prize winners, Oppenheimer organized the largest and most sophisticated technological project in human history up to that time. As an undergraduate at Harvard, Oppenheimer had studied Indian philosophy, among other subjects. On the morning of July 16, 1945, as the flash of intense white light faded and the purplish fireball rose, sucking desert sand and debris into a mushroom cloud more than 12 kilometres high, Oppenheimer quoted from Hindu scripture: "I am become Death, the shatterer of worlds" (quoted in Parshall, 1998).

Most people value science and technology highly. Still, in the postwar years, a growing number of people came to share Oppenheimer's doubts about the bomb. Indeed, they extended those doubts not just to the peaceful use of nuclear energy but also to technology in general. Increasingly, people are beginning to think of technology as a monster run amok, a Frankenstein rather than a saviour.

In the 1970s and 1980s, a series of horrific disasters alerted many people (including sociologists) to the fact that technological advance is not always beneficial, not even always benign. A gas leak at a poorly maintained Union Carbide pesticide plant in Bhopal, India, killed about 4000 people in 1984 and injured 30 000, a third of whom died excruciating deaths in the following years. In 1986, the No. 4 reactor at Chernobyl, Ukraine, exploded,

Dr. J. Robert Oppenheimer, the "father" of the atomic bomb

releasing 30 to 40 times as much radioactivity as the blast at Hiroshima. It resulted in mass evacuations, more than 10 000 deaths, countless human and animal mutations, and hundreds of square kilometres of unusable cropland. In 1989, the *Exxon Valdez* ran aground in Prince William Sound, Alaska, spilling 42 million litres of crude oil, producing a dangerous slick more than 1600 kilometres long, causing billions of dollars of damage, and killing hundreds of thousands of animals.

By the mid-1980s, sociologist Charles Perrow was referring to such events as "normal accidents." The term **normal accident** recognizes that the very complexity of modern technologies ensures they will *inevitably* fail, although in unpredictable ways (Perrow, 1984). For example, a large computer program contains many thousands of conditional statements. They take the form "if $x = y$, do $z$; if $a = b$, do $c$." When in use, the program activates many billions of *combinations* of conditional statements. As a result, complex programs cannot be tested for all possible eventualities, so when rare combinations of conditions occur, they may have unforeseen consequences that are usually minor, occasionally amusing, sometimes expensive, and too often dangerous. You experience a minor normal accident when your computer crashes or hangs.

The public is now well aware of global warming and climate change. Their dangers are embedded in movies, TV shows, and even video games. Here we see a screen shot from *FUEL*, a video game in which race cars compete in extreme weather conditions caused by global warming.

and animal diversity, and normal weather patterns.

These considerations raise two tough questions. First, is technology *the* great driving force of social change? This is the opinion of both cheerleaders and naysayers, those who view technology as our saviour and those who fear it is a Frankenstein. In contrast, I show that technology is able to transform society only when it is coupled with a powerful social need. People control technology as much as technology transforms people. Second, if some people control technology, then exactly who are they? I argue against the view that scientific and engineering wizards are in control. The military and big corporations now decide the direction of most technological research and its application.

> **risk society** A society in which technology distributes environmental dangers among all categories of the population, although to varying degrees.
>
> **technological determinism** The belief that technology is the main factor shaping human history.

German sociologist Ulrich Beck also coined a term that stuck when he said we live in a risk society. A **risk society** is a society in which technology distributes danger among all categories of the population. Some categories, however, are more exposed to technological danger than others are. Moreover, in a risk society, danger does not result from technological accidents alone: increased risk is due to mounting *environmental* threats that are more widespread, chronic, and ambiguous than technological accidents—and therefore more stressful (Beck, 1992 [1986]; Freudenburg, 1997). New and frightening terms—climate change, global warming, acid rain, ozone depletion, endangered species—have entered our vocabulary. To many people, technology seems to be spinning out of control. From their point of view, it enables the production of ever more goods and services, but at the cost of breathable air, drinkable water, safe sunlight, plant

## TECHNOLOGY AND *PEOPLE* CAUSE SOCIAL CHANGE

Russian economist Nikolai Kondratiev was the first social scientist to notice that technologies are invented in clusters. As Table 14.1 shows, a new group of major inventions has cropped up every 40 to 60 years since the Industrial Revolution. Kondratiev argued that these flurries of creativity cause major economic growth spurts, beginning 10 to 20 years later and lasting 25 to 35 years each. Thus, Kondratiev subscribed to a form of **technological determinism**, the belief that technology is the major force shaping the development of human society (see also Ellul, 1964 [1954]).

Is it true that technology helps shape society? Of course it is. James Watt invented the steam engine in Britain in 1781. It was the main driving force in the mines, mills, factories, and railways of the Industrial Revolution. Gottlieb Daimler invented the internal combustion engine

**TABLE 14.1** "Kondratiev Waves" of Modern Technological Innovation and Economic Growth

| Wave | Invention Dates | New Technologies | Centre(s) | Economic Growth Spurt |
|---|---|---|---|---|
| 1 | 1760s–70s | Steam engine, textile manufacturing, chemistry, civil engineering | Britain | 1780–1815 |
| 2 | 1820s | Railways, mechanical engineering | Britain, Continental western Europe | 1840–70 |
| 3 | 1870s–80s | Chemistry, electricity, internal combustion engine | Germany, United States | 1890–1914 |
| 4 | 1930s–40s | Electronics, aerospace, chemistry | United States | 1945–70 |
| 5 | 1970s | Microelectronics, biotechnology | United States, Japan | 1985–? |

Source: Adapted from Arnold Pacey. 1983:32. *The Culture of Technology*. Cambridge, MA: MIT Press.

in Germany in 1883. It was the foundation stone of two of the world's biggest industries: automobiles and petroleum. John Atanasoff invented the first digital computer in 1939 at Iowa State College (now Iowa State University). It utterly transformed the way we work, study, and entertain ourselves. It also put the spurs to one of the most sustained economic booms ever. It would be easy to cite other examples of how technology transforms society.

However, probing a little deeper into almost any technology, one notices a pattern: technologies do not become engines of economic growth until *social* conditions allow them to do so. The original steam engine, for instance, was invented by Hero of Alexandria in the first century CE. He used it as an amusing way of opening a door. People then promptly forgot the steam engine. Some 1700 years later, when the Industrial Revolution began, factories were first set up near rivers and streams, where water power was available. That was several years before Watt patented his steam engine. Watt's invention was all the rage once its potential became evident, but the Industrial Revolution began before the steam engine was invented and the steam engine was adopted on a wide scale only after the social need for it emerged (Pool, 1997: 126–7).

Similarly, Atanasoff stopped work on the computer soon after the outbreak of World War II. However, once the military potential of the computer became evident, development rapidly resumed. The British computer, Colossus, helped decipher secret German codes in the last two years of the war and played an important role in the Allied victory. The University of Illinois delivered one of the earliest computers, ORDVAC, to the Ballistic Research Laboratory at the Aberdeen Proving Ground of the U.S. Army. Again, a new technology became a major force in society and history only after it was coupled with an urgent social need. I conclude that technology and society influence each other. Scientific discoveries, once adopted on a wide scale, often transform societies. But scientific discoveries are turned into useful technologies only when social need demands it.

## HOW HIGH TECH BECAME BIG TECH

Enjoying a technological advantage usually translates into big profits for businesses and military superiority for countries. In the nineteenth century, gaining technological advantage was still inexpensive. It took only modest capital investment, a little knowledge about the best way to organize work, and a handful of highly trained workers to build a shop to manufacture stirrups or even steam engines. In contrast, mass-producing cars, sending people to outer space, and unlocking the mysteries of the genome require enormous capital investment, detailed attention to the way work is organized, and legions of scientific and technical experts. Add to this the intensely competitive business and geopolitical environment of the twentieth and twenty-first centuries, and you can readily understand why ever larger sums have been invested in research and development over the past hundred years.

It was in fact already clear in the last quarter of the nineteenth century that turning scientific principles into technological innovations was going to require not just genius, but also substantial resources, especially money and organization. For this reason, Thomas Edison established the first "invention factory" at Menlo Park, New Jersey, in the late 1870s. Historian of science Robert Pool (1997: 22) notes that

> the most important factor in Edison's success—outside of his genius for invention—was the organization he had set up to assist him. By 1878, Edison had assembled at Menlo Park a staff of thirty scientists, metalworkers, glassblowers, draftsmen, and others working under his close direction and supervision. With such support, Edison boasted that he could turn out "a minor invention every ten days and a big thing every six months or so."

The phonograph and the electric light bulb were two such "big things." Edison inspired both. Both, however, were also expensive team efforts, motivated by vast commercial possibilities. Edison founded General Electric, still one of the largest companies in the world—in 9th place with 333 000 employees in 2017, after 139 years in operation, (World Economic Forum, 2017).

At the beginning of the twentieth century, the scientific or engineering genius operating in isolation was only rarely able to contribute much to technological

ORDVAC, an early computer developed at the University of Illinois, was delivered to the Ballistic Research Laboratory at the Aberdeen Proving Ground of the United States Army. Technology typically advances when it is coupled with an urgent social need.

U.S. Army Photos

innovation. Steve Wozniak inventing the first Apple computer in his garage in the 1970s was such an exception. By mid-century, most technological innovation was organized along industrial lines. Entire armies of experts and vast sums of capital were required to run the new invention factories. The prototype of today's invention factory was the Manhattan Project, which built the atomic bomb in the last years of World War II. By the time of Hiroshima, the manufacturing complex of the U.S. nuclear industry was about the same size as that of the U.S. automobile industry. The era of big science and big technology had arrived. Only governments and, increasingly, giant multinational corporations could afford to sustain the research effort of the second half of the twentieth century.

As the twentieth century ended, there seemed to be no limit to the amount that could be spent on research and development. During the twentieth century, the number of research scientists in North America increased a hundredfold. In the last 40 years of the century, research and development spending tripled, taking inflation into account. Between 1953 and 2015, industry's share of spending on research and development rose to 72 percent of the total (Hobsbawm, 1994: 523; National Science Foundation, 2017). Innovation accelerated (Figure 14.1).

As a result of these developments, it should come as no surprise that military and profit-making considerations now govern the direction of most research and development. Sometime in the 1930s, a reporter is supposed to have asked bank robber Willie Sutton why he robbed banks. Sutton answered, "Because that's where the money is." Of course, money is hardly the only motivation prompting scientists and engineers to research particular topics. Personal interests, individual creativity, and the state of a field's intellectual development still influence the direction of inquiry. This is especially true for theoretical work done in universities, as opposed to applied research funded by governments and private industry. However, it would be naive to think that practicality doesn't also enter the scientist's calculation of what he or she ought to study. Many researchers—even many of those who do theoretically driven research in universities—are pulled in particular directions by large research grants, well-paying jobs, access to expensive state-of-the-art equipment, and the possibility of winning patents and achieving commercial success.

Economic lures, increasingly provided by the military and big corporations, have generated moral and political qualms among some researchers. Some scientists and engineers wonder whether work on particular topics achieves optimum benefits for humanity. Certain researchers are troubled by the possibility that some scientific inquiries may be harmful to humankind. However, a growing number of scientists and engineers recognize that to do cutting-edge research, they must put their misgivings aside, hop on the bandwagon, and adhere to military and industrial priorities. That, after all, is where the money is.

**global warming** The gradual worldwide increase in average surface temperature.

## GLOBAL WARMING

The side effect of technology that has given people the most serious cause for concern is environmental degradation and, in particular, global warming resulting in climate change. Since the Industrial Revolution, humans have been burning increasing quantities of fossil fuels (coal, oil, gasoline, natural gas, and so on) to drive their cars, furnaces, and factories. Burning these fuels releases carbon dioxide into the atmosphere. The accumulation of carbon dioxide allows more solar radiation to enter the atmosphere and less heat to escape. This process contributes to **global warming**, a gradual increase in the world's average surface temperature. Figure 14.2 graphs the world's annual average surface air temperature and the concentration of carbon dioxide in the atmosphere from 1880 to 2016. It shows a warming trend that mirrors the increased concentration of carbon dioxide in the atmosphere. It also shows that the concentration of carbon dioxide and global warming started intensifying sharply in the 1950s.

### FIGURE 14.1 Speed of Market Penetration for Selected Technologies

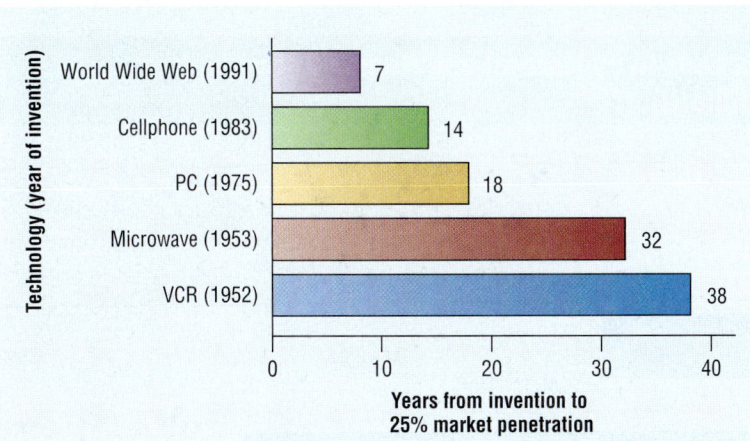

| Technology (year of invention) | Years from invention to 25% market penetration |
|---|---|
| World Wide Web (1991) | 7 |
| Cellphone (1983) | 14 |
| PC (1975) | 18 |
| Microwave (1953) | 32 |
| VCR (1952) | 38 |

Because large multinational corporations now routinely invest astronomical sums in research and development to increase their chance of being the first to bring innovations to market, the time lag between new scientific discoveries and their technological application is continually shrinking.

Source: Based on data from "The Silent Boom," *Forbes*, July 7, 1997. Adapted by permission of ESR Research.

## FIGURE 14.2 Average Annual Surface Air Temperature and Atmospheric Carbon Dioxide, 1880–2016

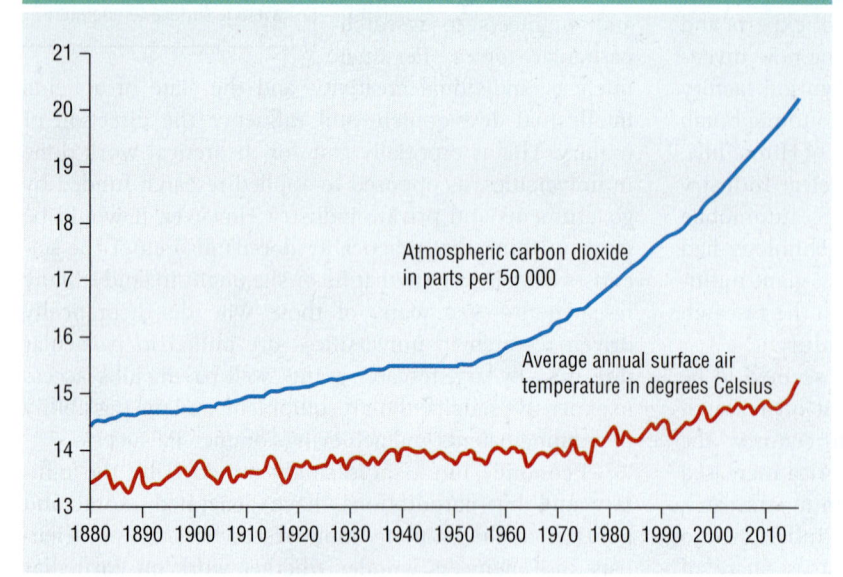

Sources: D. M. Etheridge et al. 1998. "Historical CO2 Record from the Law Dome DE08, DE08-2, and DSS Ice Cores," http://cdiac.ornl.gov/ftp/trends/co2/lawdome .combined.dat (retrieved 2 August 2015); Goddard Institute for Space Studies. 2017. "Global-mean monthly, seasonal, and annual means, 1880—present, updated through most recent month," http://data.giss.nasa.gov/gistemp (retrieved 16 November 2017); National Oceanic and Atmospheric Administration. 2017. "Mauna Loa CO2 annual mean data"; National Oceanic and Atmospheric Administration. 2017. "Mauna Loa CO2 annual mean data," ftp://aftp.cmdl.noaa.gov/products/trends/co2/co2_annmean_mlo.txt (retrieved 16 November 2017).

From 1974 to 2016, surface air temperature rose at a rate of 3.09 degrees Celsius per century. This figure may not seem like much until you realize that the warming trend is much stronger in the northern hemisphere than in the southern hemisphere and that, at a certain temperature, even slight warming turns ice to water. In recent years, many communities in Nunavut, including Arviat, Igloolik, Saniqiluaq, Repulse Bay, and Cape Dorset (the latter just 240 kilometres south of the Arctic Circle) have had to install refrigeration systems to keep the ice frozen in their hockey arenas (Klein, 2013).

As temperatures rise, more water evaporates. More evaporation causes more rainfall and bigger storms, which lead to more soil erosion, which in turn destroys cultivable land. Warming melts ice, causing the sea level to rise and increasing the chance of flooding in heavily populated coastal regions in Egypt, Bangladesh, the United States, and elsewhere. In the Far North, melting ice reveals tundra, areas of land above the tree line that are covered by grass, moss, and shrubs. Newly uncovered tundra contains rotting vegetation and animal remains, so it releases methane into the atmosphere—and methane is 21 times more effective in trapping heat than carbon dioxide is. The new water from melted ice reflects less heat than the ice did because it is darker than ice, thus speeding up global warming. Higher levels of carbon dioxide in the air interact with bodies of water to produce carbonic acid, destroying plant and animal life in oceans and lakes.

In short, global warming causes widespread climate change, resulting in much suffering and death among all living things. One indication of this fact is provided by Figure 14.3, which graphs the worldwide dollar cost

## FIGURE 14.3 Worldwide Insured losses Caused by Natural and Human Catastrophes, 1970–2016 (in 2005 $US billions)

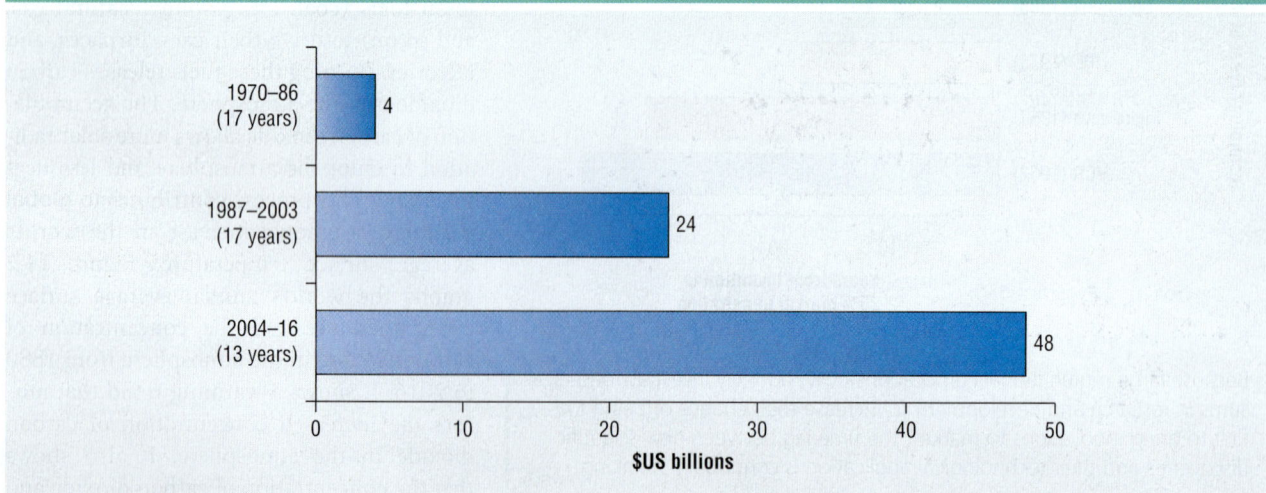

| Period | $US billions |
|---|---|
| 1970–86 (17 years) | 4 |
| 1987–2003 (17 years) | 24 |
| 2004–16 (13 years) | 48 |

Sources: Swiss Re. 2017. "Natural catastrophes and man-made disasters in 2016: a year of widespread damages," http://institute.swissre.com/research/overview/sigma/2_2017.html (retrieved 26 February 2018); U.S. Department of Labor. 2018. "CPI Inflation Calculator," https://data.bls.gov/cgi-bin/cpicalc.pl (retrieved 26 February 2018).

# LO¹ THE SOCIAL CONSTRUCTION OF ENVIRONMENTAL PROBLEMS

Environmental problems do not become social issues spontaneously. Before they can enter the public consciousness, policy-oriented scientists, the environmental movement, the mass media, and respected organizations must discover and promote them. People have to connect real-life events to the information learned from these groups. Because some scientists, industrial interests, and politicians dispute the existence of environmental threats, the public can begin to question whether environmental issues are, in fact, social problems that require human intervention. For this reason, environmental issues are not inevitably perceived as problematic. Rather, they are socially contested phenomena. They can be socially constructed by proponents, and they can be socially demolished by opponents (Hannigan, 1995).

The controversy over global warming is a good example of how people create and contest definitions of environmental problems (Ungar, 1992, 1999). The theory of global warming was first proposed about a century ago, but an elite group of scientists began serious research on the subject only in the late 1950s. They attracted no public attention until the 1970s, when the environmental movement emerged and gave new legitimacy and momentum to the scientific research and helped secure public funds for it. Respected and influential scientists now began to promote the issue of global warming. The mass media, always thirsting for sensational stories, were receptive to these efforts. Newspaper and television reports about the problem began to appear in the late 1970s and proliferated in the mid-to late 1980s.

The summer of 1988 brought the worst drought in half a century to North America. Respected organizations outside the scientific community, the mass media, and the environmental movement began expressing concern about the effects of global warming. By the early 1990s, public opinion polls showed that most North Americans with an opinion on the subject thought that using coal, oil, and gas contributes to global warming.

However, some industrialists, politicians, and scientists began to question whether global warming was, in fact, taking place. This group included Western coal and oil companies, the member states of the Organization of the Petroleum Exporting Countries (OPEC), other coal- and oil-exporting nations, and right-wing think-tanks, such as Canada's Fraser Institute in Vancouver, which is subsidized in part by major oil companies operating in

Because of global warming, glaciers are melting, the sea level is rising, and extreme weather events are becoming more frequent.

of insured damage due to "natural" and human disasters from 1970 to 2014. (I wrap "natural" in quotation marks because, as you've have just seen, an increasingly large number of meteorological events are rendered extreme by human action.) Clearly, the damage caused by extreme meteorological events is on the upswing—and if the dollar value of non-insured damage were included, the upswing would be even more dramatic (Swiss Re, 2017: 5). Worldwide, the number of events that the insurance industry classifies as "natural catastrophes" increased steadily from 40 to 191 between 1970 and 2016 (Swiss Re, 2013: 1). (Some of these incidents are earthquakes, which do not have human causes, but the number of earthquakes shows no trend.)

Global warming threatens everyone. However, as you will now see, the degree to which it is perceived as threatening depends on certain social conditions being met. Moreover, the threat is not evenly distributed in society.

**environmental racism** The tendency to heap environmental dangers on the disadvantaged, and especially on disadvantaged racial minorities.

Canada. "Bad scientific reporting, bad economics and bad judgement" is how the Fraser Institute summarized the analyses of those who regarded global warming as a serious issue requiring immediate action (Jones, 1997). Largely as a result of this onslaught, public concern about global warming began to falter.

Yet the evidence that global warming was substantial, dangerous, and caused by human activity continued to accumulate. In Canada, for example, ordinary people experienced ongoing drought on the Prairies, falling water levels in the Great Lakes, and the melting of glaciers in the north. In 2007, a large blue-ribbon panel of international climate experts, the Intergovernmental Panel on Climate Change (IPCC) issued a definitive report showing that global warming was real, dangerous, but stoppable through human intervention (Intergovernmental Panel on Climate Change, 2007). The public mood again shifted, and all of Canada's political parties adopted "green" platforms that promised swift and effective action. In 2009, the IPCC report was shown to contain a couple of errors, while scientists responsible for one of its data sets stupidly kept the data from public scrutiny. Again a furor erupted, although it was soon shown that the report's conclusions were accurate ("U.K. Panel," 2010). The ongoing debate clearly demonstrates that environmental issues become social problems only when social, political, and scientific circumstances allow them to be defined as such.

As you will now see, in addition to being socially defined, environmental problems are socially distributed. That is, environmental risks are greater for some groups than for others.

## LO² THE SOCIAL DISTRIBUTION OF RISK

You may have noticed that after a minor tornado touches down on some unlucky community, TV reporters often rush to interview the surviving residents of trailer parks. The survivors stand amid the rubble that was their lives. They heroically remark on the generosity of their neighbours, their good fortune in still having their family intact, and our inability to fight nature's destructive forces. Why trailer parks? Small twisters aren't particularly attracted to them, but reporters are. That is because trailers are flimsy in the face of even a small tornado. They often suffer a lot of damage from twisters and therefore make a more sensational story than the minor damage typically inflicted on upper-middle-class homes with firmly shingled roofs and solid foundations. This is a general pattern. Whenever disaster strikes, economically and politically disadvantaged people almost always suffer most. That is because their circumstances render them most vulnerable. In fact, the advantaged often consciously put the disadvantaged in harm's way to avoid risk themselves. This is what is known as **environmental racism**, the tendency to heap environmental dangers on the disadvantaged and especially on disadvantaged racial minorities.

### The Canadian Case

Environmental racism is evident in Canada. For example, the uranium used to construct the atom bombs that were dropped on Hiroshima and Nagasaki came from Port Radium in the Northwest Territories, the world's first uranium mine. More than 30 Dene hunters and trappers were recruited from the nearby village of Deline to haul and barge 45-kilogram burlap sacks of the raw ore along a 2100-kilometre route to Fort McMurray, Alberta, for $3 a day.

The American and Canadian governments had known about the dangers of exposure to uranium at least since 1931 (McClelland, 1931), yet they withheld this information from the workers, who were completely unprotected from the ore's deadly radiation. In the surrounding community, the Dene ate fish from contaminated dredging ponds and hunted and camped in contaminated areas. Dene children played with ore dust at docks and landings. Dene women sewed tents from used uranium sacks. Until recent decades, cancer was unknown in the community. Elders often lived into their 90s. By 1998, however, nearly

Ordinary people experienced first-hand the ongoing drought in Manitoba's Red River Valley.

The first shipment of uranium being transported on Great Bear Lake in 1931. The American and Canadian governments knew about the dangers of uranium exposure, yet paid more than 30 Dene hunters $3 per day to haul uranium in burlap sacks along a 2100-kilometre route to Fort McMurray.

half of the uranium workers had died of cancer while still in their 60s and 70s.

Cancer and lung disease are alarmingly widespread in the community. Deline is known locally as "The Village of the Widows." Neither the workers nor their families have received any compensation from the government, not even an apology (Nikiforuk, 1998). Broadly similar stories of environmental racism are legion, which is why in Nova Scotia, for instance, a strong correlation exists between (1) the location of black and Indigenous communities and (2) the placement of toxic waste sites (Waldron, 2018).

Class also structures exposure to environmental risk. Let's continue with the example of Nova Scotia, which has the second-lowest median income of any Canadian province. Cape Breton County is among the poorest counties in the province. Historically, Cape Breton County has been the only county in Nova Scotia where the incidence of cancer is significantly higher than the provincial average. Digging deeper, one finds that the county's main city, Sydney, has a cancer rate 45 percent higher than the Nova Scotia average (Waldron, 2018: 9; Figure 14.4). And the people who used to live on Frederick Street, the poorest part of Sydney, had the highest neighbourhood cancer rate in town. (The street has now been evacuated.) Skin ailments, birth defects, respiratory problems, diseases of the nervous system, and other medical conditions were also unusually common around Frederick Street.

The main reason? Sydney was home to a large steel mill that operated with no pollution controls between 1901 and 1988. Waste from the mill poured into the so-called tar ponds, a 50-hectare site polluted to a depth of 24 metres with cancer-causing chemicals. Frederick Street borders the tar ponds. Sludge oozed into people's basements, seeped into their vegetable gardens, and ran in open streams where children played (Barlow and May, 2000: 144). Many millions of federal and provincial tax dollars were spent subsidizing the steel mill that was the source of the problem. Yet a serious cleanup effort began only in 2010, nine long years after the Sydney Steel Corporation was shut down and a full three decades after elevated levels of toxins were first detected in Sydney Harbour and in local lobsters.

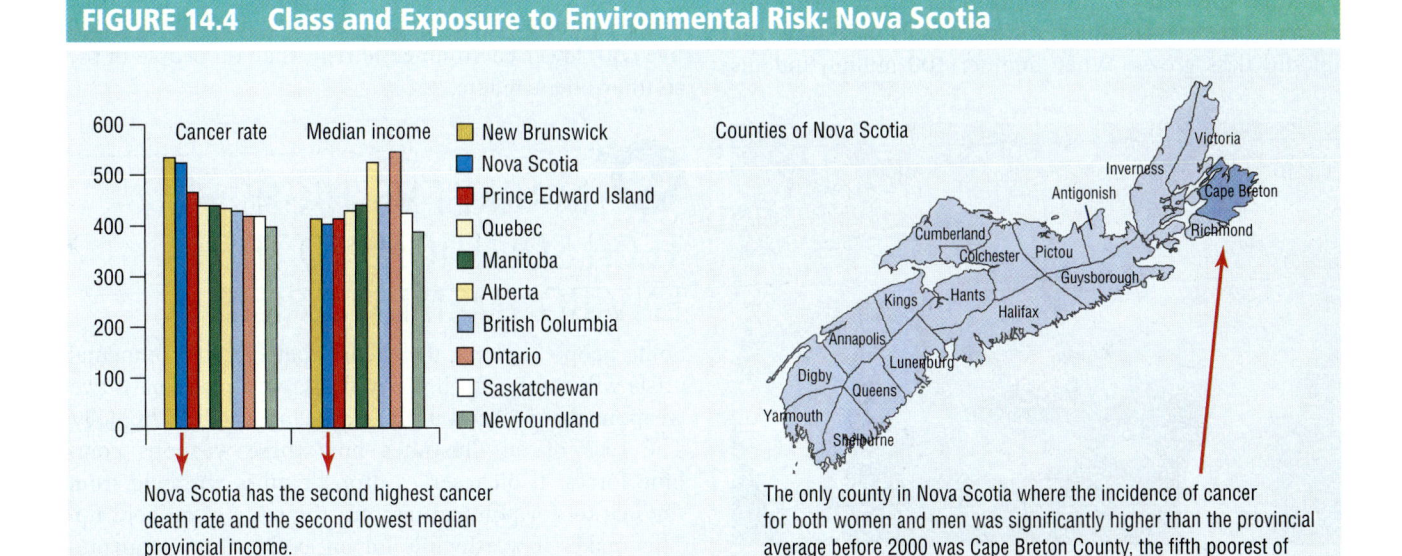

## FIGURE 14.4  Class and Exposure to Environmental Risk: Nova Scotia

Nova Scotia has the second highest cancer death rate and the second lowest median provincial income.

The only county in Nova Scotia where the incidence of cancer for both women and men was significantly higher than the provincial average before 2000 was Cape Breton County, the fifth poorest of 18 counties in Nova Scotia and the site of the Sydney Tar Ponds.

Sources: Cancer Care Nova Scotia, 2004, "Cancer Statistics in Nova Scotia"; Health Canada, 2003, "Canadian Cancer Statistics, 2003"; Province of Nova Scotia, 2010, "Counties of Nova Scotia"; Rural Communities Impact Policy Project, 2003, "Painting the Landscape of Rural Nova Scotia."

## The Less Developed Countries

What is true for disadvantaged classes and racial groups in Canada is also true for the less developed countries—the underprivileged face more environmental dangers than do the privileged. Mexico, Brazil, China, India, and other southern countries are industrializing rapidly, putting tremendous strain on their natural resources. Rising demand for water, electricity, fossil fuels, and consumer products is creating more polluted rivers, dead lakes, and industrial waste sites. At a quickening pace, rainforests, grazing land, cropland, and wetlands are giving way to factories, roads, airports, and housing complexes. Smog-blanketed megacities continue to sprawl. Of the world's 21 largest cities, 18 are in less developed countries, and 16 of the world's 20 most polluted cities are in China. In Beijing, official measurements of fine airborne particulates, which pose the greatest risk, are sometimes more than 40 times higher than WHO guidelines (*Bloomberg News*, 2013). When I wrote this sentence on July 14, 2018, the air quality index in Canada ranged from 8 in Calgary to 46 in Fort Smith, Northwest Territories (both in the "good" range). In Wuhai, China, the index stood at 999 ("hazardous") (World Air Quality Index, 2018).

Given the picture sketched above, it should be unsurprising that, on average, people in less developed countries are more concerned about the environment than people in rich countries are (Brechin and Kempton, 1994). However, the developing countries cannot afford much in the way of pollution control, so anti-pollution regulations are lax by North American, western European, and Japanese standards. This state of affairs is an incentive for some multinational corporations to place some of their foulest operations in the southern hemisphere. It is also the reason that the industrialization of the less developed countries is proving so punishing to the environment. For example, car ownership is growing rapidly in India as the middle class grows. When another 100 million Indians upgrade from bicycles to Tata Nanos, the result will not be pretty.

Ratan Tata, chairman of the Tata Group of India, stands beside the Tata Nano, which was unveiled in January 2008. Ticket price of the base model Tata Nano GenX in Delhi in 2018: $4460.70 (Tata Motors, 2018). The Nano is not sold in the West because it does not meet safety and pollution standards.

Taking a family selfie in Tiananmen Square, Beijing, January 21, 2013

For the time being, however, the rich countries do most of the world's environmental damage. That is because their inhabitants earn and consume much more than the inhabitants of less developed countries consume. For instance, the United States has only 4.5 percent of the world's population but uses about 25 percent of Earth's resources and produces more than 20 percent of global emissions of carbon dioxide, the pollutant responsible for about half of global warming. In general, the inhabitants of the northern hemisphere cause a disproportionately large share of the world's environmental problems, enjoy a disproportionate share of the benefits of technology, and live with fewer environmental risks than do people in the southern hemisphere.

## LO³ MARKET VS. HIGH-TECH SOLUTIONS TO THE ENVIRONMENTAL CRISIS

Some people endorse the theory that the environmental crisis will resolve itself. They think we already have two weapons that will end it: the market and high technology. The case of oil illustrates how these weapons combine forces. If oil reserves drop or oil is withheld from the market for political reasons, the price of oil goes up. This makes it worthwhile for oil exploration companies to develop new technologies to recover more oil. When they discover more oil and bring it to market, prices fall back to where they were. Generalizing this principle and projecting it into the future, optimists believe global warming and other forms of environmental degradation will be dealt with similarly. In their view, human inventiveness and the profit motive will combine to create the new technologies we need to survive and prosper.

Some evidence supports this optimistic scenario. For example, natural gas produces 50 to 60 percent less carbon dioxide than coal does. When new technology was developed in the late 1990s to capture natural gas from shale formations, it boosted natural gas production in North America and led to the replacement of coal by natural gas as the fuel powering many heating plants. Other new technologies that have been introduced to combat some of the worst excesses of environmental degradation include unleaded gas, refrigerants that don't destroy atmospheric ozone, efficient windmills and solar panels, pollution-control devices on cars and in factories, hybrid and electric cars, and so on.

However, three factors suggest that market forces and technological fixes cannot solve environmental problems on their own:

1. *Imperfect price signals*. The prices of many commodities do not reflect their actual cost to society. In Winnipeg, gasoline costs about $1.02 a litre at the time of this writing—inexpensive by world standards because Canadians pay relatively low taxes on gas. However, the *social* cost of gas, including the cost of repairing the environmental damage caused by burning it, may be three times that amount. Because of such price distortions, the market often fails to send signals that might result in the speedy adoption of technological and policy fixes.

2. *The slow pace of change*. Efforts so far to deal with global warming are insufficient; global warming continues to accelerate. One widely respected group of climate scientists and statisticians calculated that if we continue to burn fossil fuels at current rates, then by 2024 it will be exceedingly difficult to avert disaster (Carbon Tracker Initiative, 2012).

3. *The importance of political pressure*. Political pressure exerted by environmental activists, community groups, and public opinion is often necessary to motivate corporate and government action on environmental issues. Without the efforts of such organizations, it is doubtful that many environmental issues would be defined as social problems.

The alternative to the market and high-tech theory is a theory that emphasizes the need for cooperation to greatly reduce overconsumption of just about everything. This strategy includes investing more heavily in energy-saving technologies, doing more to clean up the environment, and subsidizing environmentally friendly industrialization in the developing countries. It would also require renewed commitment to voluntary efforts, new laws and enforcement bodies to ensure compliance, increased environmental research and development by industry and government, more environmentally directed foreign aid, and new taxes to help pay for it all (Livernash and Rodenburg, 1998).

Is the solution realistic? Not in the short term. It would be political suicide for anyone in the rich countries to propose such drastic measures as those just listed. Not too many Canadian drivers would be happy paying $3 a litre for gas, for example. For the solution to be politically acceptable, the broad public in North America, western Europe, Japan, and South Korea must be aware of the gravity of the environmental problem and willing to make substantial economic sacrifices to get the job done.

Survey data suggest that most Canadians people know about the environmental crisis, say they want it dealt with, but are unwilling to be inconvenienced or pay much of the cost themselves (Statistics Canada, 2006b). They regard environmental problems as too remote and abstract to justify making big personal sacrifices. It follows that more and bigger environmental catastrophes may have to occur before more people are willing to take massive remedial action.

**collective action** Occurs when people act in unison to bring about or resist social, political, or economic change.

**social movement** A collective attempt to change all or part of a political or social order by means of rioting, petitioning, striking, demonstrating, and/or establishing pressure groups, unions, and political parties.

# SOCIAL MOVEMENTS

I noted above that governments and corporations are inclined to act on environmental issues only if the public pressures them to do so. This observation raises some interesting questions: Under what circumstances do many individuals engage in **collective action**, working in unison to bring about or resist social, political, and economic change by means of demonstrations, strikes, riots, and the like? And under what circumstances is collective action turned into a **social movement**, an enduring collective attempt to change or resist change to part or all of society by establishing organizations, lobbies, unions, and political parties?

Answers to these questions are unclear, as I found out in Grade 11. One day in chemistry class, I learned that water combined with sulphur dioxide produces sulphurous acid. The news shocked me. To understand why, you have to know that I lived in Saint John, New Brunswick, about 100 metres downwind of one of the largest pulp and paper mills in Canada. Waves of sulphur dioxide billowed from the mill's smokestacks day and night. The town's pervasive rotten-egg smell was a long-standing complaint

**relative deprivation** An intolerable gap between the social rewards people receive and the social rewards they expect to receive.

**breakdown theory** Suggests that social movements emerge when traditional norms and patterns of social organization are disrupted.

in the area. But, for me, disgust turned to upset when I realized the fumes were toxic. Suddenly, it was clear why many people I knew—especially people living near the mill—woke up in the morning with a kind of "smoker's cough." Through the simple act of breathing, we were causing the gas to mix with the moisture in our bodies and form an acid that our lungs tried to expunge, with only partial success.

Twenty years later, I read the results of a medical research report showing that area residents suffered from rates of lung disease, including emphysema and lung cancer, significantly above the North American average. But even in 1968, it was evident my hometown had a serious problem. I therefore hatched a plan. Our high school was about to hold its annual model parliament. The event was notoriously boring, partly because, year in, year out, virtually everyone voted for the same party, the Conservatives. But here was an issue, I thought, that could turn things around. A local man, K. C. Irving, owned the pulp and paper mill. *Forbes* magazine ranked him as one of the richest men in the world. I figured that when I told the other students what I had discovered, they would quickly demand the closure of the mill until Irving guaranteed a clean operation.

Was *I* naive. As head of the tiny Liberal Party, I had to address the entire student body during assembly on election day to outline the party platform and rally votes. When I got to the part of my speech that explained why Irving was our enemy, the murmuring in the audience, which had been growing like the sound of a hungry animal about to pounce on its prey, erupted into loud boos. A couple of students rushed the stage. The principal suddenly appeared from the wings and commanded the student body to settle down. He then took me by the arm and informed me that, for my own safety, my speech was finished. So, I discovered on election day, was our high school's Liberal Party. And so, it emerged, was my high school political career.

This incident troubled me for years, partly because of the embarrassment it caused, partly because of the puzzles it presented. Why didn't the other students rebel in the way I thought they would? Why did they continue to support an arrangement that was enriching one man at the cost of a community's health? Couldn't they see the injustice? I didn't know it at the time, but to answer such questions, it is necessary to turn to the sociological literature on social movements.

## LO4 BREAKDOWN THEORY: A FUNCTIONALIST ACCOUNT

Until about 1970, most sociologists believed that two conditions must be met for social movements to form:

1. *Social marginality.* The early leaders of social movements and their first recruits must be poorly integrated in society. Without such socially marginal people, social movements supposedly cannot form.

2. *Strain.* People's norms must be strained or disrupted. For example, one of the most popular variants of breakdown theory is **relative deprivation** theory. *Relative deprivation* refers to the growth of an intolerable gap between the social rewards people expect to receive and those they actually receive. (Social rewards are widely valued goods, such as money, education, security, prestige, and so forth.) Supposedly, people are most likely to form social movements when the gap between rising expectations (brought on by, say, rapid economic growth and migration) and the receipt of social rewards (sometimes lowered by economic recession or war) becomes intolerable (Davies, 1969; Gurr, 1970; see Figure 14.5).

Following sociologist Charles Tilly and his associates, we can group these two conditions together as the **breakdown theory** of collective action. That is because both conditions assume that social movements result from the disruption or breakdown of previously integrative social structures and norms (Tilly, Tilly, and Tilly, 1975: 4–6). At a more abstract level, breakdown theory

Protesting the effects of the Alberta tar sands

**FIGURE 14.5  Relative Deprivation Theory**

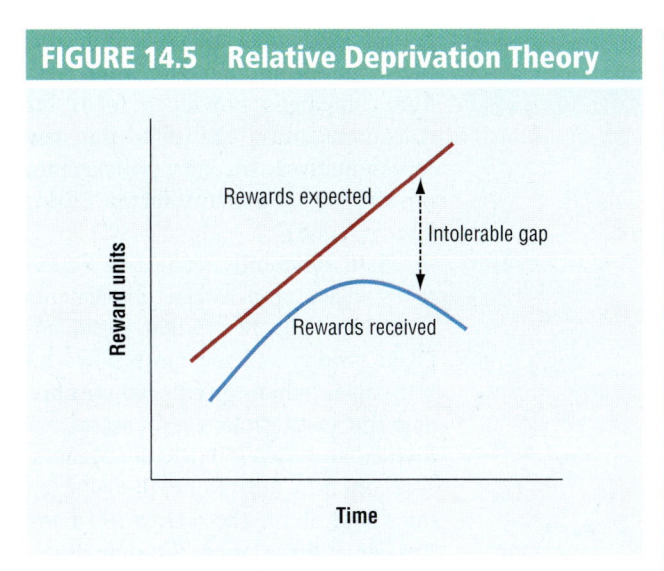

Source: From BRYM/LIE. *Sociology*, 1e. © 2009 Nelson Education Ltd. Reproduced by permission, www.cengage.com/permissions.

can be seen as a variant of functionalism because it regards collective action as a form of social imbalance that results from the improper functioning of social institutions.

Can breakdown theory adequately account for the crystallization of social movements? The short answer is no. Since 1970, sociologists have uncovered two main flaws in the theory. First, research shows that in most cases, leaders and early joiners of social movements are well-integrated members of their community, not socially marginal outsiders (Brym, 1980; Lipset, 1971). Second, researchers have found that high levels of relative deprivation are generally not associated with the crystallization of social movements. That is because certain social conditions can prevent people from translating their discontent into an enduring social movement with a more or less stable membership, hired office personnel, a publicity bureau, a regularly published newsletter, and the like (McPhail, 1994; Tilly, Tilly, and Tilly, 1975; Torrance, 1986: 115–45). We now consider those social conditions.

## SOLIDARITY THEORY: A CONFLICT APPROACH

**Solidarity theory** is a type of conflict theory that focuses on the social conditions that allow people to turn their discontent into a unified (or "solidary") political force. It identifies three such social conditions: adequate resource mobilization, sufficient political opportunities, and weak or inconsistent social control.

### Resource Mobilization

Most collective action is part of a power struggle. The struggle usually intensifies as groups whose members feel disadvantaged become more powerful relative to other groups. How do disadvantaged groups become more powerful? By gaining new members, becoming better organized, and increasing their access to scarce resources, such as money, jobs, and means of communication (Bierstedt, 1974). **Resource mobilization** is the process by which groups engage in more collective action as their power increases because of their growing size and increasing organizational, material, and other resources (Jenkins, 1983; Zald and McCarthy, 1979).

**solidarity theory** Holds that social movements are social organizations that emerge when potential members can mobilize resources, take advantage of new political opportunities, and avoid high levels of social control by authorities.

**resource mobilization** The process by which social movements crystallize because of the increasing organizational, material, and other resources of movement members.

Consider the effect of resource mobilization on the frequency of strikes in Canada. Research shows that in Canada between the mid-1940s and the mid-1970s, strike frequency was high when (1) unemployment was low, (2) union membership was high, and (3) governments were generous in their provision of social welfare benefits. *Low unemployment* indicates a strong economy. Workers are inclined to strike when business activity is robust because in such conditions they accumulate healthy strike funds, enjoy many alternative job opportunities, and know that employers and governments can afford to make concessions (employers make bigger profits and governments collect more taxes during economic booms). *A high level of unionization* is conducive to more strike activity because unions provide workers with leadership, strike funds, and coordination. Finally, *generous government benefits* give workers an economic buffer and thus increase their readiness to strike. So, as resource mobilization theory suggests, strong social ties among workers (as indicated by a high level of unionization) and access to jobs and money (as indicated by a booming economy and generous government benefits) increase challenges to authority (as indicated by strikes).

Figure 14.6 shows the pattern of strike activity in Canada between 1946 and 2017. It adds substance to the resource mobilization approach. Until 1974, the trend in strike activity was upward. This was a period of growing prosperity, low unemployment, expanding state benefits, and increasing unionization. With access to increasing organizational and material resources, workers challenged authority increasingly more often in the three decades after World War II. In 1973, however, economic crisis struck. As a result of war and revolution in the Middle East, oil prices tripled, and then tripled again at the end of the decade. Inflation increased and unemployment rose. Soon, the government was strapped for funds and had to borrow heavily to maintain social welfare programs. Eventually, the debt burden was so heavy, the government felt obliged to cut various social welfare programs. At the same time, federal and provincial governments introduced laws and regulations

## FIGURE 14.6 Weighted Frequency of Strikes, Canada, 1946–2017

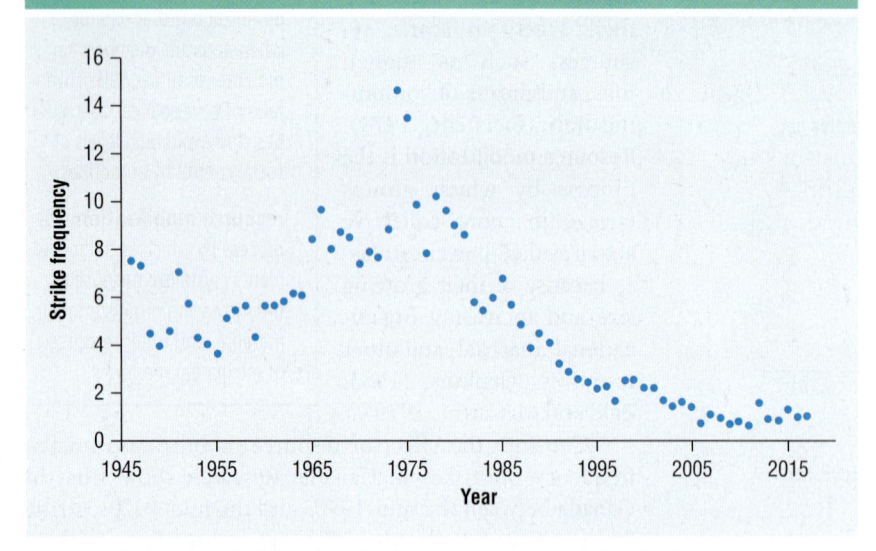

Note: "Strike frequency" is the number of strikes per 100 000 non-agricultural workers.

Sources: Republished with permission of Blackwell Publishing, from Robert Brym, Louise Birdsell-Bauer, and Mitch McIvor, "Is Industrial Unrest Reviving in Canada? Strike Duration in the Early 21st Century," *Canadian Review of Sociology* 50(2): pp. 227–38; © 2013 Canadian Sociological Association/La Société canadienne de sociologie; permission conveyed through Copyright Clearance Center, Inc.; Statistics Canada. 2018d. "Table 282-0088: Labour Force Survey estimates (LFS), employment by North American Industry Classification System (NAICS), seasonally adjusted and unadjusted monthly (persons × 1000)." http://www5.statcan.gc.ca/cansim/a26?id=2820088 (retrieved 27 February 2018).

---

**political opportunities**

Chances for collective action and social movement growth that occur during election campaigns, when influential allies offer support to insurgents, when ruling political alignments become unstable, and when elite groups become divided and conflict with one another.

---

limiting the right of some workers to strike and putting a cap on the wage gains that workers could demand.

The percentage of Canadian workers who belonged to unions began to decline. Strike action was made even more difficult when Canada signed free trade deals with the United States in 1988 and Mexico in 1994. It was now possible for employers to threaten to relocate in the United States or Mexico in the face of protracted strikes. So, in the post-1973 climate, the organizational and material resources of workers fell. As a result, strike activity plummeted. In 2017, the frequency of strikes per 100 000 Canadian non-agricultural workers was less than 7 percent that of 1974 (Brym, 2003; Brym, Birdsell-Bauer, and McIvor, 2013).

### Political Opportunities

A second social condition that allows mass discontent to be translated into social movement formation involves the emergence of new **political opportunities** (McAdam, 1982; Piven and Cloward, 1977; Tarrow, 2011). Specifically, chances for protest and social movement formation emerge when influential allies offer support, when ruling political alignments become unstable, when elite groups are divided and come into conflict with one another, and when election campaigns provide a focus for discontent and a chance to put new representatives with new policies into positions of authority (Tarrow, 2011; Useem, 1998).

Said differently, collective action takes place and social movements crystallize not just when disadvantaged groups become more powerful but also when privileged groups and the institutions they control are divided and therefore become weaker. As economist John Kenneth Galbraith once said about the weakness of the Russian ruling class at the time of the 1917 revolution, if someone manages to kick in a rotting door, some credit has to be given to the door.

### Social Control

The third main lesson of solidarity theory is that government reactions to protests influence subsequent protests. Specifically, governments can try to lower the frequency and intensity of protest by taking various *social control* measures (Oberschall, 1973: 242–83). These measures include making concessions to protesters, co-opting the most troublesome leaders (for example, by appointing them as advisers), and violently repressing collective action.

Note, however, that social control measures do not always have the desired effect. If grievances are very deeply felt, and yielding to protesters' demands greatly increases their hopes, resources, and political opportunities, government concessions may encourage protesters to press their claims further. And although the firm and decisive use of force usually stops protest, using force moderately or inconsistently often backfires. That is because unrest typically intensifies when protesters are led to believe that the government is weak or indecisive (Piven and Cloward, 1977: 27–36; Tilly, Tilly, and Tilly, 1975: 244).

## FRAMING THEORY: THE CONTRIBUTION OF SYMBOLIC INTERACTIONISM

As we have seen, solidarity theory helps to overcome the flaws in breakdown theory. Still, the rise of a social movement sometimes takes strict solidarity theorists by surprise, as does the failure of an aggrieved group to press its claims by means of collective action. It seems, therefore, that something lies between (1) the capacity of disadvantaged people to mobilize resources for collective action, and (2) the recruitment of a substantial number of movement members. That "something" is **frame alignment** (Benford, 1997; Goffman, 1974; Snow et al., 1986). Frame alignment is the process by which social movement leaders make their activities, ideas, and goals congruent with the interests, beliefs, and values of potential new recruits to their movement—or fail to do so. Thanks to the efforts of scholars operating mainly in the symbolic interactionist tradition, frame alignment has become the subject of sustained sociological investigation.

## Types of Frame Alignment

Frame alignment can be encouraged in several ways:

- Social movement leaders can reach out to other organizations that, they believe, include people who may be sympathetic to their movement's cause. For example, leaders of an anti-nuclear movement may use the mass media, telephone campaigns, Facebook, and direct mail to appeal to feminist, anti-racist, and environmental organizations. In doing so, they assume that these organizations are likely to have members who would agree, at least in general terms, with the anti-nuclear platform.
- Movement activists can stress popular values that have so far not featured prominently in the thinking of potential recruits. They can also elevate the importance of positive beliefs about the movement and what it stands for. For instance, in trying to win new recruits, movement members might emphasize the seriousness of the social movement's purpose. They might analyze the causes of the problem the movement is trying to solve in a clear and convincing way. Or they might stress the likelihood of the movement's success. By doing so, they can increase the movement's appeal to potential recruits and perhaps win them over to the cause.
- Social movements can stretch their objectives and activities to win recruits who are not initially sympathetic to the movement's original aims. This may involve a watering down of the movement's ideals. Alternatively, movement leaders may decide to take action calculated to appeal to non-sympathizers on grounds that have little or nothing to do with the movement's purpose. When rock, punk, hip hop, or reggae bands play at nuclear disarmament rallies or gay liberation festivals, it is not necessarily because the music is relevant to the movement's goals, nor do bands play just because movement members want to be entertained. The purpose is also to attract non-members. Once attracted by the music, non-members may make friends and acquaintances in the movement and then be encouraged to attend a more serious-minded meeting.

As we see, then, there are many ways in which social movements can make their ideas more appealing to a larger number of people. However, movements must also confront the fact that their opponents routinely seek to do just the opposite. That is, while movements seek to align their goals, ideas, and activities with the way potential recruits frame issues, their adversaries seek to *disalign* the way issues are framed by movements and potential recruits.

**frame alignment** The process by which individual interests, beliefs, and values become congruent and complementary with the activities, goals, and ideology of a social movement.

The B.C. Forest Alliance provides a good illustration of this process (Doyle, Elliott, and Tindall, 1997). Launched in British Columbia in 1991, the B.C. Forest Alliance was created and bankrolled by a group of senior forest industry executives and guided by the world's largest public relations firm. Its goal was to counter the province's environmental movement. It did so in two main ways. First, in its TV and print ads, the alliance claimed it represented the "middle ground" in the debate between forest companies and environmentalists. In practice, the alliance rarely criticized forest companies, while it routinely characterized environmentalists as dope-smoking hippies with untenable ideas, such as shutting down the entire forest industry. Actually, very few environmentalists hold such extreme opinions, and research shows that the middle class in British Columbia broadly supports environmental groups.

The second way the alliance sought to counter the environmental movement was by arguing that more environmentalism means fewer jobs. This was a huge oversimplification. Job losses in the forest industry were also caused by the introduction of new technologies in some areas, aging equipment in others, First Nations land claims, and resource depletion because of overharvesting and inadequate reforestation. Muddying the waters in this way is typical of social movement opponents. Frame alignment should therefore be viewed as a conflict-ridden process in which social movement partisans and their opponents use all the resources at their disposal to compete for the way in which potential recruits and sympathizers view movement issues.

## An Application of Frame Alignment Theory: Back to 1968

Frame alignment theory stresses the strategies employed by movement members to recruit non-members who are like-minded, apathetic, or even initially opposed to the movement's goals. Solidarity theory focuses on the broad social-structural conditions that facilitate the emergence of social movements. One theory usefully supplements the other.

The two theories certainly help clarify the 1968 high school incident described earlier in this chapter. In light of the foregoing discussion, it seems evident that two main factors prevented me from influencing my classmates when I spoke to them about the dangers of industrial pollution from the local pulp and paper mill.

First, I lived in a poor and relatively unindustrialized region of Canada where people had few resources they could mobilize on their own behalf. Per capita income and the level of unionization were among the lowest of any province or state in North America. The unemployment rate was among the highest. In contrast, K. C. Irving, who owned the pulp and paper mill, was so powerful that most people in the region could not even conceive of the need to rebel against the conditions of life he created for them. He owned most of the industrial establishments in the province. Every daily newspaper, most of the weeklies, all of the TV stations, and most of the radio stations were his, too. Little wonder anyone rarely heard a critical word about his operations. Many people believed that Irving could make or break local governments single-handedly. Should one therefore be surprised that mere high school students refused to take him on? In their reluctance, the students were only mimicking their parents, who, on the whole, were as powerless as Irving was mighty (Brym, 1979).

Second, many of my classmates did not share my sense of injustice. Most of them regarded Irving as the great provider. They saw that his pulp and paper mill, as well as his myriad other industrial establishments, gave many people jobs. They regarded that fact as more important for their lives and the lives of their families than the pollution problem I raised. Frame alignment theory suggests I needed to figure out ways to build bridges between their understanding and mine. I didn't, and I therefore received an unsympathetic hearing.

## THEORIES AT A GLANCE

### Social Movements

| Theory | Main Question | Application |
|---|---|---|
| Functionalism | How do social structures and the values underlying them contribute to social stability? | Breakdown theory is a variant of functionalism insofar as it regards collective action as a form of social imbalance that results from the improper functioning of social institutions. According to this theory, evidence of a breakdown in functioning is evident in the social marginality of early movement leaders and early recruits (who tend to be poorly integrated in society) and in the strain that tends to precede the emergence of movements (that is, the disruption of people's norms). One type of strain is relative deprivation (the growth of an intolerable gap between the social rewards people expect to receive and those they actually receive). |
| Conflict theory | How does the structure of inequality between privileged groups seeking to maintain their advantages and subordinate groups seeking to increase theirs lead to conflict and often to social change? | Solidarity theory is a type of conflict theory that focuses on the social conditions that allow people to turn their discontent into a unified (or "solidary") political force. It identifies three such social conditions: adequate resource mobilization, sufficient political opportunities, and weak or inconsistent social control. Resource mobilization is the process by which groups engage in more collective action as their power increases because of their growing size and increasing organizational, material, and other resources. A second social condition that allows mass discontent to be translated into social movement formation involves the emergence of new political opportunities. Specifically, chances for protest and social movement formation emerge when influential allies offer support, when ruling political alignments become unstable, when elite groups are divided and come into conflict with one another, and when election campaigns provide a focus for discontent and a chance to put new representatives with new policies into positions of authority.<br><br>The third main lesson of solidarity theory is that governments can try to lower the frequency and intensity of protest by taking various social control measures. These measures include making concessions to protesters, co-opting the most troublesome leaders (for example, by appointing them as advisers), and violently repressing collective action. |
| Symbolic interactionism | How do people communicate to make their social settings meaningful, thus helping to create their social circumstances? | Symbolic interactionists have developed the idea that frame alignment lies between (1) the capacity of disadvantaged people to mobilize resources for collective action, and (2) the recruitment of a substantial number of movement members.<br><br>Frame alignment is the process by which social movement leaders make their activities, ideas, and goals congruent with the interests, beliefs, and values of potential new recruits to their movement—or fail to do so. |

# LO⁵ NEW SOCIAL MOVEMENTS

Let's now turn to this chapter's final goal: sketching the history and prospects of social movements in broad, rapid strokes.

Around 1700, the modern state crystallized in western Europe. Typically, each new state amalgamated several regions distinguished from one another by ethnicity, language, or religion into a single entity with a central government, a national language, a unified army, a flag, and an anthem. For the next 250 years, social movements responded to the new political structure they faced by extending their focus from local to national issues. They became larger and generally less violent. Often, they struggled to expand the rights of citizens, fighting at first for the right to free speech, freedom of religion, and justice before the law; next for the right to vote and run for office; and then, in the twentieth century, for the right to a certain minimum level of economic security and full participation in social life (Marshall, 1965; Tilly, 1979a, 1979b).

In the 1960s, political structures started to undergo massive changes once again under the forces of globalization. "New social movements" responded by setting even broader goals, attracting new kinds of participants, and becoming global in scope (Melucci, 1980, 1995). Let's consider each of these developments in turn.

## Goals

Some new social movements promote the rights not of specific groups but of humanity as a whole to peace, security, and a clean environment. Such movements include the peace movement, the environmental movement, and the human rights movement. Other new social movements, such as the women's movement, the gay rights movement, the Black Lives Matter movement, the Idle No More movement, and the Me Too movement, seek to advance the rights of particular groups that have been excluded from full social participation due to various forms of discrimination:

- Since the 1960s, the women's movement has succeeded in getting admission practices altered in professional schools, placing women on an equal footing with men. It has also won more freedom of reproductive choice for women and opened up opportunities for women in the political, religious, military, educational, medical, legal, and business systems. To a degree, the women's movement has also helped alter the division of domestic labour, with many men now taking on a larger share of household work, including child care, than was the case in the past.
- Also originating in the 1960s, the gay rights movement (later broadened to include bisexual and transgender members as the LGBT movement) has achieved significant law reform involving the repeal of discriminatory legislation, such as anti-sodomy laws and laws that negatively affected parental custody of children. It has also fought, and, in two dozen countries, including Canada, succeeded in achieving equality under the law with respect to marriage rights.
- Disproportionate police violence is routinely visited on the black community throughout North America. For example, in Toronto, blacks are 3.2 times more likely than are whites to be stopped, questioned, and documented by the police. Often there is little or no apparent justification for the practice (*Toronto Star*, 2015). Between 2000 and 2017, the rate at which Canadians were killed or died while being subdued by police doubled. In Toronto, where about 8 percent of the population was black over this period, 37 percent of the people who died at the hands of police were black. Seventy percent of the people killed suffered from mental health problems, suggesting that a response other than violence would have been more appropriate in dealing with these cases (Marcoux and Nicholson, 2018). The Black Lives Matter movement emerged in 2013 to publicize and express outrage over such facts in the hope of achieving less discriminatory police practice.
- The Idle No More movement burst onto the scene in 2012. Founded by three Indigenous Canadian women and a non-Indigenous supporter in Saskatoon, and largely coordinated by social media, its members have blockaded railways, organized public round dances, and held demonstrations to promote land claims, environmental protection, and other issues of particular concern to Canada's Indigenous peoples.
- Originating in 2017 as a hashtag on social media, the Me Too movement seeks to publicize the magnitude of the problem of sexual harassment, publicly shame individuals who sexually harass others, and kindle a cultural change in norms surrounding the problem. With the vocal support of such movie stars as Alyssa Milano, Gwyneth Paltrow, Ashley Judd, Jennifer Lawrence, and Uma Thurman, the movement first centred on the film industry but has spread into the fields of sports, business, government, the military, and academia. It now has supporters in nearly a hundred countries.

Although diverse in terms of specific aims and membership characteristics, the movements just listed have in common the fact that they strive for the extension of equal citizenship rights to all adult members of society and to society as a whole (Roche, 1995; Turner, 1986: 85–105).

## Membership

New social movements are also novel in that they attract a disproportionately large number of highly educated, relatively well-to-do people from the social, educational, and cultural fields. Such people include teachers, professors, journalists, social workers, artists, actors, writers, and student apprentices. For several reasons, people in these occupations are more likely to participate in new social movements than are people in other occupations. Their higher education exposes them to radical ideas and makes those ideas appealing. They tend to hold jobs outside the business community, which often opposes their values. And they often become personally involved in the problems of their clients and audiences, sometimes even becoming their advocates (Brint, 1984; Rootes, 1995).

Not coincidentally, the explosion of native activism that Canada has recently witnessed with the emergence of the Idle No More movement is largely the doing of university-educated Indigenous Canadians. There were just a few hundred Indigenous students in Canada's colleges and universities in the 1970s, but now there are more than 30 000. Two-thirds of them are women. They have high expectations about their careers, they are eager to achieve equality with the rest of the country, and they have lent a loud, articulate voice to the aspirations of their community (Friesen, 2013).

## Globalization Potential

Finally, new social movements increase the scope of protest beyond the national level. For example, members of the peace movement view federal laws banning nuclear weapons as necessary. Environmentalists feel the same way about federal laws protecting the environment. However, environmentalists also recognize that the condition of the Brazilian rainforest affects climatic conditions worldwide. Similarly, peace activists understand that the spread of weapons of mass destruction could destroy all of humanity. Therefore, members of the peace and environmental movements press for *international* agreements binding all countries to protect the environment and stop the spread of nuclear weapons. Social movements have gone global.

Inexpensive international travel and communication facilitate the globalization of social movements. New technologies make it easier for people in various national movements to work with like-minded activists in other countries. In the age of CNN, inexpensive jet travel, instant messaging, Facebook, Skype, and email, it is possible not only to see the connection between apparently

The Idle No More movement is led mainly by university-educated First Nations women.

local problems and their global sources, but also to act both locally and globally.

Consider the Occupy movement, which spread quickly across the world in 2011, after Vancouver's anti-consumerist magazine, *Adbusters*, urged people to occupy Wall Street in protest against growing economic inequalities and the ravages of the Great Recession of 2008–09. Soon, scores of thousands of people in nearly a hundred cities in 82 countries took over parks and other public areas, holding demonstrations and setting up tent communities. They were mainly "millennials," people born after the early 1980s, who shared a deep sense of the injustice of growing economic inequality and argued that only mass movements like theirs could bring about enduring, progressive social change at a global level (see Sociology and the Media, *Mr. Robot*).

The remarkable spread of the Occupy Movement was facilitated by television stations with global reach, such as CNN, the BBC, and al Jazeera. Facebook, Twitter, Skype, and other Internet applications were widely used to coordinate protest activities. These media demonstrated the potential of new social movements to mobilize large numbers of people quickly and effectively in the era of instant, globalized communication.

Still, one must be careful not to exaggerate the role of the Internet in fostering the emergence and spread of global social movements. For example, some analysts have referred to the democracy movement that swept the Middle East and North Africa in 2010–11 as a "Twitter Revolution" or a "Facebook Revolution" because these Internet applications were used as organizing tools during the uprising in Tunisia, Egypt, and elsewhere in the region. However, survey research conducted in Egypt during this period paints a more subtle picture. While using new electronic communications media was associated with being a demonstrator, other factors were more important in distinguishing demonstrators from mere sympathetic onlookers. Protesters tended to be people with strong grievances related to unemployment, poverty, and corruption. They were more available for protest activities than others were because they tended to be unmarried men living in cities. And they tended to have strong, pre-existing ties to various charitable, political, and other civic associations. The use of new electronic communications media was less important than were strong grievances, high availability, and dense social connections in distinguishing demonstrators from sympathetic onlookers (Brym et al., 2014).

# SOCIOLOGY AND THE MEDIA

## Mr. Robot

Elliot Alderson suffers from some kind of mental disorder. He snorts morphine to cope. And he hates the way the top 1 percent of the top 1 percent controls the planet and grows ever richer by conning people, stealing from them, and manipulating their "needs." In an early episode of *Mr. Robot*, someone says, "Give a man a gun and he'll rob a bank. Give a man a bank and he'll rob the world." It's an attitude that pervades the TV series and, presumably, mirrors the views of its large fan base.

Elliot works for a cybersecurity firm by day and hacks the computers of people he doesn't like by night. However, given his precarious mental state, we have to wonder whether his unfolding drama is real or imagined. Is the head of a hacker group trying to recruit Elliot to delete records of most of the world's personal debt from E Corp computers, thus massively and almost instantly redistributing global wealth? Is E Corp trying to recruit Elliot to prevent hackers from wiping their servers clean? Could Elliot be working both sides at once?

Sam Esmail, the creator of *Mr. Robot*, has concocted a powerful formula for capturing his audience's attention. He draws a clear and rigid line between good and evil while injecting enough uncertainty into the boundary between reality and fantasy to keep us guessing. It helps that he cast the understated but intense Rami Malek as the hoodie-wearing Elliot, whose bulging eyes simultaneously suggest barely repressed rage over the world's injustices and the capacity to penetrate deeply into the working of people's minds, their computers, and their society.

At the same time, *Mr. Robot* challenges the view that only mass movements can bring about enduring, progressive social change at a global level.

### Critical Thinking Question

- If hackers can create social change, what kind of social change are they likely to create?

Elliott Anderson meets Mr. Robot.

The connection between computerized communication and the Egyptian uprising of 2011 is evident from this protester's demand for the overthrow of dictator Hosni Mubarak.

The globalization of social movements can be further illustrated by coming full circle and returning to my earlier anecdote. In the early 1990s, I visited my hometown. I hadn't been back in years. As I entered the city, I sensed something was different. I couldn't identify the change until I reached the pulp and paper mill. Then it became obvious. The rotten-egg smell was now faint. I discovered that in the 1970s, a local woman whose son developed a serious case of asthma took legal action against the mill and eventually won. The mill owner was forced by law to install a "scrubber" in the main smokestack to remove most of the sulphur dioxide emissions. Soon, the federal government was putting pressure on the mill owner to purify the polluted water that poured out of the plant and into the local river system.

Apparently, local citizens and the environmental movement had caused a deep change in the climate of opinion. The change influenced the government to force the mill owner to spend millions of dollars to clean up his operation. It took decades, but what was political heresy in 1968 became established practice by the early 1990s.

That is because environmental concerns had been amplified by the voice of a movement that had grown to global proportions. In general, as this case illustrates, globalization helps new social movements transcend local and national boundaries and promote universalistic goals.

## CONCLUSION

For many thousands of years, humans have done well on this planet. That is because we have created cultural practices including technologies that have allowed us to adapt to and thrive in our environment. Nonetheless, there have been failures along the way. Many tribes and civilizations are extinct. And our success to date as a species is no guarantee for the future. If we persist in using technologies that create an inhospitable environment, nature will deal with us in the same way it always deals with species that cannot adapt.

Broadly speaking, we have two survival strategies to cope with the challenges that lie ahead: competition and cooperation. Charles Darwin wrote famously about competition in *On the Origin of Species* (1859). He observed that members of each species struggle against one another and against other species in their struggle to survive. Most of the quickest, the strongest, the best camouflaged, and the smartest live long enough to bear offspring. Most of the rest are killed off. The traits passed on to offspring are those most valuable for survival. Ruthless competition, it turns out, is a key survival strategy of all species, including humans.

In *The Descent of Man*, Darwin mentioned our second important survival strategy: cooperation. In some species, mutual assistance is common. The species members that flourish are those that best learn to help one another: "When two tribes…came into competition, if the one tribe included (other circumstances being equal) a greater number of…members, who were always ready to…aid and defend each other, this tribe would without doubt succeed best" (Darwin, 1871: 162). The Russian geographer and naturalist Petr Kropotkin (1908 [1902]) elaborated on this idea. After spending five years studying animal life in Siberia, he concluded that "mutual aid" is at least as important a survival strategy as competition. Competition takes place when members of the same species compete for limited resources, said Kropotkin. Cooperation occurs when species members struggle against adverse environmental circumstances. According to Kropotkin, survival in the face of environmental threat is best assured if species members help one another. Kropotkin also showed that the most advanced species in any group—ants among insects, mammals among vertebrates, humans among mammals—are the most cooperative. Many evolutionary biologists now accept Kropotkin's ideas (Gould, 1988; Nowak, May, and Sigmund, 1995).

As you have seen, a strictly competitive approach to dealing with the environmental crisis—relying on the market and technological innovation to solve our problems—now seems inadequate. It appears that dominating nature may in some respects be more dangerous than cooperating with it, as Indigenous peoples have long appreciated (refer back to the Preface and the section on Violence against Nature in Chapter 10, Religion).

Practically speaking, a cooperative strategy involves substantially reducing consumption, paying higher taxes for environmental cleanup and energy-efficient industrial processes, subsidizing the developing countries to industrialize sustainably, placing pressure on governments and corporations to act in more environmentally responsible ways, and so on. Earlier, I outlined some grave consequences of relying too little on a cooperative survival strategy at this historical juncture, but which strategy you emphasize in your own life is, of course, your choice.

Similarly, throughout this book—when I discussed families, inequality, crime, race, and other topics—I raised social issues lying at the intersection of history, social structure, and biography. I set out alternative courses of action and outlined their consequences. I thus followed sociology's disciplinary mandate: helping people make informed choices based on sound sociological knowledge. In the context of the present chapter, however, I can make an even bolder claim for the discipline: Conceived at its broadest, sociology promises to help in the rational and equitable evolution of humankind.

Sociology promises to help in the rational and equitable evolution of humankind.

# READY TO STUDY?

## IN THE BOOK YOU CAN:

- Refer to the Chapter in Review section at the back of the book to have a summary of the chapter and key terms handy.
- Test your knowledge of chapter contents by answering the multiple-choice questions in the Chapter in Review section. Answers are in the appendix at the end of the book.

## ONLINE YOU CAN:

- Stay organized and efficient with MindTap—a single destination with all the course material and study aids you need to succeed.
- Flashcards are pre-populated to provide you with a jump start for review—or you can create your own.
- You can highlight text and make notes in your MindTap Reader.
- Prepare for tests with quizzes.

GO TO NELSON.COM/STUDENT TO PURCHASE THESE DIGITAL RESOURCES.

# REFERENCES

"19 years ago, Pamela George's killers were convicted of manslaughter." *Regina Leader-Post* 21 December. http://leaderpost.com/storyline/19-years-ago-pamela-georges-killers-were-charged-with-manslaughter (retrieved 26 January 2018).

23 and Me. 2018. "See sample report." https://www.23andme.com/en-ca/dna-reports-list (retrieved 1 February 2018).

"Aboriginal Peoples and the Fight for the Franchise." *The Canadian Encyclopedia* https://www.thecanadianencyclopedia.ca/en/article/aboriginal-peoples-and-the-fight-for-the-franchise (retrieved 6 February 2018).

Abortion Rights Coalition of Canada. 2017. *Statistics—Abortions in Canada.* https://www.google.ca/url?sa=t&rct=j&q=&esrc=s&source=web&cd=3&ved=0ahUKEwilkovSl5fZAhUhwYMKHQLrDsUQFggzMAI&url=http%3A%2F%2Fwww.arcc-cdac.ca%2Fbackrounders%2Fstatistics-abortion-in-canada.pdf&usg=AOvVaw34PtWUJZzLpO8at-JEyIrQ (retrieved 8 February 2018).

Abraham, Carolyn. 2003. "Hong Kong Hotel Is Focus of Pneumonia Investigation." *Globe and Mail*, March 20. Retrieved June 16, 2003 (http://globeandmail.workopolis.com/servlet/Content/fasttrack/20030320/UBUGGN?section=Healthcare).

Adams, Henry E., Lester W. Wright, Jr., and Bethany A. Lohr. 1998. "Is Homophobia Associated with Homosexual Arousal?" *Journal of Abnormal Psychology* 105: 440–45.

Adams, Michael. 1997. *Sex in the Snow: Canadian Social Values at the End of the Millennium.* Toronto: Penguin.

———. 2017. *Could It Happen Here? Canada in the Age of Trump and Brexit* (Toronto: Simon and Schuster).

Adler, Patricia A., and Peter Adler. 1998. *Peer Power: Preadolescent Culture and Identity.* New Brunswick, NJ: Rutgers University Press.

Akinsanya, Segun. 2016. "A History of Violence." *Toronto Life* 21 January. https://torontolife.com/city/life/my-life-in-street-gangs (retrieved 21 January 2018.

Akwagyiram, Alexis. 2009. "Hip-Hop Comes of Age." *BBC News.* Retrieved October 12 (http://news.bbc.co.uk/2/hi/uk_news/magazine/8303041.stm).

Alba, Richard. 2017. "Immigration and Mainstream Expansion in Canada and the United States." Pp. 11–27 in Robert Brym, ed. *Immigration and the Future of Canadian Society: Proceedings of the Second S. D. Clark Symposium on the Future of Canadian Society.* Oakville, ON: Rock's Mills Press.

Albas, Daniel, and Cheryl Albas. 1989. "Modern Magic: The Case of Examinations." *The Sociological Quarterly* 30: 603–13.

Albelda, Randy, and Chris Tilly. 1997. *Glass Ceilings and Bottomless Pits: Women's Work, Women's Poverty.* Boston: South End Press.

"Alberta parents convicted in toddler's meningitis death." *CBC News.* http://www.cbc.ca/news/canada/calgary/meningitis-trial-verdict-1.3552941 (retrieved 20 February 2018).

Alexa. 2018. "The top 500 sites on the web." https://www.alexa.com/topsites (retrieved 25 February 2018).

Alini, Erica. 2017. "Federal Budget 2017: Liberals extend parental leave to 18 months, boost childcare funding." *Global News.* https://globalnews.ca/news/3328107/federal-budget-2017-liberals-extend-parental-leave-to-18-months-boost-childcare-funding (retrieved 6 February 2018).

Al Jandaly, Bassma. 2009. "Working after Retirement in the UAE." Gulfnews.com, May 2. http://gulfnews.com/uaessentials/residents-guide/working/working-after-retirement-in-the-uae-1.440878 (retrieved 9 May 2013).

American Psychological Association. 1998. "Answers to Your Questions about Sexual Orientation and Homosexuality." Retrieved June 14, 2000 (http://www.apa.org/pubinfo/orient.html).

American Society of Plastic Surgeons. 2017. "Plastic Surgery Statistics Report 2016." https://www.plasticsurgery.org/news/plastic-surgery-statistics (retrieved 17 January 2018).

American Sociological Association. 1999. *Code of Ethics and Policies and Procedures of the ASA Committee on Professional Ethics.* Washington, DC: Author.

Andersen, Robert. 2016. "What Can Canada Learn from Europe? Policies to Promote Low Income Inequality and High Prosperity." Pp. 10–30 in Robert Brym, ed. *Inequality and the Future of Canadian Society.* Oakville ON: Rock's Mills Press.

Anderson, Benedict O. 1991. *The Imagined Community*, rev. ed. London, UK: Verso.

Anderson, Craig, and Brad J. Bushman. 2002. "The Effects of Media Violence on Society." *Science* 295, 5564: 2377–79.

Anderson, Gerald F., Uwe E. Reinhardt, Peter S. Hussey, and Varduhi Petrosyan. 2003. "It's the Prices, Stupid: Why the United States Is So Different from Other Countries." *Health Affairs* 22, 3: 89–105.

Anderson, Michael. 2003. "Reading Violence in Boys' Writing." *Language Arts* 80, 3: 223–31.

Anderssen, Erin. 2014. "Sex on campus: How no means no became yes means yes." *Globe and Mail* 14 November. Retrieved August 29, 2015 (http://www.theglobeandmail.com/life/relationships/sex-on-campus-how-no-means-no-became-yes-means-yes/article21598708/?page=all).

Andrew-Gee, Eric. 2018. "Your smartphone is making you stupid, antisocial and unhealthy. So why can't you put it down?" *Globe and Mail* 6 January. https://www.theglobeandmail.com/technology/your-smartphone-is-making-you-stupid/article37511900 (retrieved 11 January 2018).

Anesi, Charles. 1997. *The Titanic Casualty Figures.* Based on *British Parliamentary Papers*, "Shipping Casualties (Loss of the Steamship 'Titanic')," 1912, cmd. 6352, "Report of a Formal Investigation into the circumstances attending the foundering on the 15th April, 1912, of the British Steamship 'Titanic,' of Liverpool, after striking ice in or near Latitude 41°46′ N., Longitude 50°14′ W., North Atlantic Ocean, whereby loss of life ensued." London, UK: His Majesty's Stationery

Office, 1912. Retrieved March 11, 2010 (http://www.anesi.com/titanic.htm).

*Angus Reid Global Monitor.* 2009. "Views on Health Care Differ in Canada, U.S." Retrieved April 2, 2010 (http://www.angus-reid.com/polls/view/33946).

Ansari, Aziz, with Eric Klinenberg. 2015. *Modern Romance.* New York: Penguin.

Ariès, Phillipe. 1962 [1960]. *Centuries of Childhood: A Social History of Family Life*, Robert Baldick, trans. New York: Knopf.

Arnett, George. 2014. "Religious extremism main cause of terrorism, according to report." *The Guardian*, international ed. 18 November. https://www.theguardian.com/news/datablog/2014/nov/18/religious-extremism-main-cause-of-terrorism-according-to-report (retrieved 13 February 2018).

Asch, Solomon. 1955. "Opinion and Social Pressure." *Scientific American* July: 31–35.

Ayalon, Hanna, and Idit Livneh. 2013. "Educational Standardization and Gender Differences in Mathematics Achievement: A Comparative Study." *Social Science Research* 42(2): 432–55.

Babbie, Earl, and Lance Roberts. 2018 [2006]. *Fundamentals of Social Research*, 4th Canadian edition. Toronto: Nelson.

Bagdikian, Ben H. 1997. *The Media Monopoly*, 5th ed. Boston: Beacon.

Baghurst, T., D. B. Hollander, B. Nardella, and G. G. Haff. 2006. "Change in sociocultural ideal male physique: An examination of past and present action figures." *Body Image* 3(1): 87–91.

Balkissoon, Denise. 2011. "The Seven Habits of Highly Effective Lesbian Families." *Globe and Mail* 4 November. Retrieved February 2, 2013 (http://www.theglobeandmail.com).

Bank of Canada. 2018. "Inflation calculator." https://www.bankofcanada.ca/rates/related/inflation-calculator (retrieved 2 March 2018).

Baran, Paul A. 1957. *The Political Economy of Growth.* New York: Monthly Review Press.

Barlow, Maude, and Elizabeth May. 2000. *Frederick Street: Life and Death on Canada's Love Canal.* Toronto: HarperCollins.

Bar-On, Dan. 1999. *The Indescribable and the Undiscussable: Reconstructing Human Discourse after Trauma.* Ithaca, NY: Cornell University Press.

Barrera, Jorge. 2018. "The horrors of St. Anne's." *CBC News.* 29 March. https://newsinteractives.cbc.ca/longform/st-anne-residential-school-opp-documents (accessed 29 March 2018).

Barry, Patricia. 2002a. "Ads, Promotions Drive Up Drug Costs." AARP.

———. 2002b. "Drug Industry Spends Huge Sums Guarding Prices." AARP.

———. 2002c. "Drug Profits vs. Research." AARP.

Barth, Fredrik, ed. 1969. *Ethnic Groups and Boundaries: The Social Organization of Cultural Difference.* Boston: Little, Brown.

Bascaramurty, Dakshana. 2018. "As multi-ethnic population in Canada rises, complications arise for families." *Globe and Mail* 12 January. https://www.theglobeandmail.com/news/national/multi-ethnic-mixed-race-canada-census-2016/article37475308/ (retrieved 9 February 2018).

Baudrillard, Jean. 1983. *Simulations.* New York: Semiotext (e).

———. 1988 [1986]. *America.* Chris Turner, trans. London, UK: Verso.

Bauer, Nancy. 2010. "Lady Power." *New York Times*, 20 June. (Retrieved from http://opinionator.blogs.nytimes.com/2010/06/20/lady-power/?_r=0).

Bauman, Zygmunt. 1989. *Modernity and the Holocaust.* Ithaca, NY: Cornell University Press.

Baym, Nancy K. 2015. *Personal Connections in the Digital Age*, 2nd ed. Cambridge, UK: Polity Press.

Beck, Ulrich. 1992 [1986]. *Risk Society: Towards a New Modernity*, Mark Ritter, trans. London, UK: Sage.

Becker, Howard S. 1963. *Outsiders: Studies in the Sociology of Deviance.* New York: Free Press.

Bellow, Saul. 1964. *Herzog.* New York: Fawcett World Library.

Bellrichard, Chantelle. 2018. "Locked up at 12." *Globe and Mail* 28 March. https://newsinteractives.cbc.ca/longform/locked-up-at-12 (retrieved 31 March 2018).

Benford, Robert D. 1997. "An Insider's Critique of the Social Movement Framing Perspective." *Sociological Inquiry* 67: 409–39.

Berens, Michael J. 2002. "Infection Epidemic Carves Deadly Path." *Chicago Tribune*, 21 July. Retrieved June 16, 2003 (http://www.chicagotribune.com/news/specials/chi-0207210272jul21.story).

Berger, Peter L., and Thomas Luckmann. 1966. *The Social Construction of Reality: A Treatise in the Sociology of Knowledge.* Garden City, NY: Doubleday.

Berliner, Wendy. 2004. "Where Have All the Young Men Gone?" *Manchester Guardian* 18 May: 8.

Berners-Lee, Tim. 1999. *Tim Berners-Lee: Biography.* www.w3.org/People/Berners-Lee/Overview.html (retrieved May 2, 2000).

Better, Alison. 2014. "Redefining Queer: Women's Relationships and Identity in an Age of Sexual Fluidity." *Sexuality and Culture* 18(1): 16–38.

Bianchi, Suzanne M., and Daphne Spain. 1996. "Women, Work, and Family in America." *Population Bulletin* 51, 3: 2–48.

Bibby, Reginald W., 1985. *Project Canada National Survey Series.* Lethbridge, AB: University of Lethbridge.

———. 1987. *Fragmented Gods: The Poverty and Potential of Religion in Canada.* Toronto: Irwin.

———. 2001. *Canada's Teens: Today, Yesterday, and Tomorrow.* Toronto: Stoddart.

———. 2006. *The Boomer Factor: What Canada's Most Famous Generation Is Leaving Behind.* Toronto: Bastian.

———. 2017. *Resilient Gods.* Vancouver: University of British Columbia Press.

Bibby, Reginald, and Angus Reid, 2015. *Angus Reid Institute Religion Survey.*

Bibby, Reginald W., and Rodney Stark. 2017. "Toward Unraveling the Québec Catholic Enigma: Still Catholic, Still Believers, Still Uninvolved: A View from Outside Québec." Montreal: Étudier la religion au Québec: regards d'ici et d'ailleurs, symposium de la Société québécoise pour l'étude de la religion (SQÉR) en collaboration avec le Centre de recherche interdisciplinaire sur la diversité et la démocratie (CRIDAQ).

Bierstedt, Robert. 1963. *The Social Order: An Introduction to Sociology.* New York: McGraw-Hill.

———. 1974. "An Analysis of Social Power." Pp. 220–41 in *Power and Progress: Essays in Sociological Theory.* New York: McGraw-Hill.

Bissinger, Buzz. "Caitlyn Jenner: The Full Story." *Vanity Fair*, July 2015. Retrieved August 28, 2015 (http://www.vanityfair.com/hollywood/2015/06/caitlyn-jenner-bruce-cover-annie-leibovitz).

Blaise, Clark. 2001. *Time Lord: The Remarkable Canadian Who Missed His Train and Changed the World*. Toronto: Knopf Canada.

Blau, Peter M. 1964. *Exchange and Power in Social Life*. New York: Wiley.

Blauner, Robert. 1972. *Racial Oppression in America*. New York: Harper & Row.

Blazer, Dan G., Ronald C. Kessler, Katherine A. McGonagle, and Marvin S. Swartz. 1994. "The Prevalence and Distribution of Major Depression in a National Community Sample: The National Comorbidity Survey." *American Journal of Psychiatry* 151: 979–86.

*Bloomberg News*. 2013. "Eye-Stinging Beijing Air Risks Lifelong Harm to Babies." 6 February. Retrieved February 6, 2013 (http://www.bloomberg.com/news/2013-02-06/eye-stinging-beijing-air-risks-lifelong-harm-to-babies.html).

Blossfeld, Hans-Peter, and Yossi Shavit, eds. 1993. *Persistent Inequality: Changing Educational Attainment in Thirteen Countries*. Boulder, CO: Westview Press.

Blumberg, Paul. 1989. *The Predatory Society: Deception in the American Marketplace*. New York: Oxford University Press.

Blumer, Herbert. 1969. *Symbolic Interactionism: Perspective and Method*. Englewood Cliffs, NJ: Prentice-Hall.

Boal, Mark. 1998. "Spycam City." *The Village Voice*, 30 September–6 October. Retrieved March 26, 2001 (http://www.villagevoice.com/issues/9840/boal.shtml).

Bonacich, Edna. 1972. "A Theory of Ethnic Antagonism: The Split Labor Market." *American Sociological Review* 37: 547–59.

Bookman, Sonia. 2014. "Social Media: Implications for Social Life." Pp. 64–74 in Robert Brym, ed., *Society in Question*, 7th ed. Toronto: Nelson.

Boorstin, Daniel J. 1992. *The Image: A Guide to Pseudoevents in America*. New York: Vintage.

Boroditsky, Lera. 2010. "Lost in Translation." *Wall Street Journal*, 23 July. (Retrieved from http://online.wsj.com/article/SB10001424052748703467304575383131592767868.html).

Boswell, A. Ayres, and Joan Z. Spade. 1996. "Fraternities and Collegiate Rape Culture: Why Are Some Fraternities More Dangerous Places for Women?" *Gender and Society* 10: 133–47.

Bourdieu, Pierre. 1977 [1972]. *Outline of a Theory of Practice*, Richard Nice, trans. Cambridge, UK: Cambridge University Press.

_____. 1986. "The Forms of Capital." Pp. 241–58 in John Richardson, ed., *Handbook of Theory and Research for the Sociology of Education*. New York: Greenwood.

_____. 1998. *Acts of Resistance: Against the Tyranny of the Market*, Richard Nice, trans. New York: New Press.

Bourdieu, Pierre, and Jean-Claude Passeron. 1990. *Reproduction in Education, Society and Culture*, 2nd ed., Richard Nice, trans. London, UK: Sage.

Boychuk, Gerard W. 2002. "Federal Spending in Health: Why Here? Why Now?" Pp. 121–36 in G. Bruce Doern, ed., *How Ottawa Spends 2002–2003: The Security Aftermath and National Priorities*. Toronto: Oxford University Press.

_____. 2017. "Second Generation Educational and Occupational Attainment in Canada." Pp. 58–80 in Robert Brym, ed. *Immigration and the Future of Canadian Society*. Oakville ON: Rock's Mills Press.

Boyer, Dana. 2012. "Homeschooling 101." *Canadian Living*. Retrieved February 15, 2013 (http://www.canadianliving.com/moms/family_life/homeschooling_101.php).

Braithwaite, John. 1981. "The Myth of Social Class and Criminality Revisited." *American Sociological Review* 46: 36–57.

_____. 1989. *Crime, Shame and Reintegration*. New York: Cambridge University Press.

Brechin, Steven R., and Willett Kempton. 1994. "Global Environmentalism: A Challenge to the Postmaterialism Thesis." *Social Science Quarterly* 75: 245–69.

Brennan, Richard J. 2012. "Majority of Canadians support return of death penalty." *Toronto Star* 8 February 2012. Retrieved July 26, 2015 http://www.thestar.com/news/canada/2012/02/08/majority_of_canadians_support_return_of_death_penalty_poll_finds.html).

Bricker, Darrell, and Edward Greenspon. 2001. *Searching for Certainty: Inside the New Canadian Mindset*. Toronto: Doubleday Canada.

Briggs, Jean. 1970. *Never in Anger: Portrait of an Eskimo Family*. Cambridge MA: Harvard University Press.

Brint, Stephen. 1984. "New Class and Cumulative Trend Explanations of the Liberal Political Attitudes of Professionals." *American Journal of Sociology* 90: 30–71.

Brower, David. 1975. *Training the Nihilists: Education and Radicalism in Tsarist Russia*. Ithaca, NY: Cornell University Press.

Brown, Louise. 2014. "Number of aboriginal Canadians finishing high school is up, report says." *Toronto Star* 30 April. https://www.thestar.com/news/canada/2014/04/30/number_of_aboriginal_canadians_finishing_high_school_is_up_report_says.html (retrieved 1 March 2018).

Brown, Lyn Mikel, and Carol Gilligan. 1992. *Meeting at the Crossroads: Women's Psychology and Girls' Development*. Cambridge, MA: Harvard University Press.

Brown, Mark. 2015. "The real cost of raising kids." *MoneySense* 15 April. http://www.moneysense.ca/save/financial-planning/the-real-cost-of-raising-a-child/ (retrieved 8 February 2018).

Brown, Peter. 1996. *The Rise of Western Christendom: Triumph and Diversity, A.D. 200–1000*. Oxford: Blackwell.

Brown, Susan L. 2010. "Marriage and Child Well-Being: Research and Policy Perspectives." *Journal of Marriage and Family* 72(5): 1059–77.

Browning, Christopher R. 1992. *Ordinary Men: Reserve Police Battalion 101 and the Final Solution in Poland*. New York: HarperCollins.

Brownlee, Jamie. 2015. *Academia, Inc.: How Corporatization Is Transforming Canadian Universities*. Halifax: Fernwood.

Bruner, Raisa. 2018. "Katy Perry Reigns Supreme Still as Twitter's Most-Followed Celebrity." *Time*. 7 February. http://time.com/4591951/top-twitter-celebrities-2016/ (retrieved 25 February 2018).

Brym, Robert. 1979. "Political Conservatism in Atlantic Canada."

Pp. 59–79 in Robert J. Brym and R. James Sacouman, eds., *Underdevelopment and Social Movements in Atlantic Canada*. Toronto: New Hogtown Press.

_____. 1980. *Intellectuals and Politics*. London, UK: George Allen and Unwin.

_____. 2003. "Affluence, Strikes, and Power in Canada, 1973–2000." Pp. 243–53 in James Curtis, Edward Grabb, and Neil Guppy, eds., *Social Inequality in Canada: Patterns, Problems, Policies*, 4th ed. Scarborough, ON: Prentice-Hall.

_____. 2006. "How High School Drama Helped Me to Become a Sociologist: An Essay in the Sociology of Autobiography." *Canadian Journal of Sociology* 31: 245–57.

_____. 2008. "Religion, Politics, and Suicide Bombing: An Interpretative Essay." *Canadian Journal of Sociology* 33: 89–108.

_____. 2014. *2011 Census Update: A Critical Interpretation*. Toronto: Nelson.

_____. 2015c. "How Ontario dropped the ball on mandatory retirement." *iPolitics* 27 February. http://www.ipolitics.ca/2015/02/27/how-ontario-dropped-the-ball-on-mandatory-retirement/ (retrieved 2 March 2018).

_____. 2017. "More than half of Canada's Jews are missing." *Globe and Mail* 2 November. https://tgam.ca/2FQBpYf (retrieved 7 July 2018),

_____. 2018a. "Canadian Genocide." Pp. 125–46 in Robert Brym, *Sociology as a Life or Death Issue*, 4th Canadian ed. Toronto: Nelson 2018 [2009].

_____. 2018b. "Canadian Genocide." Pp. 133–46 in Robert Brym, *Sociology as a Life or Death Issue*, 4th Canadian ed. Toronto Nelson.

_____. 2018c. "Gender risk." Pp. 105–23 in Robert Brym, *Sociology as a Life or Death Issue*. Toronto: Nelson.

_____. 2018d. "The Social Bases of Cancer." Pp. 81–102 in Robert Brym, *Sociology as a Life or Death Issue*, 4th Canadian ed. Toronto: Nelson.

_____. 2018e. "Hip Hop from Caps to Bling." Pp. 13–31 in Robert Brym, *Sociology as a Life or Death Issue*, 4th Canadian ed. Toronto: Nelson.

Brym, Robert, and Robert Andersen. 2016. "Democracy, Women's Rights, and Public Opinion in Tunisia." *International Sociology* 31: 1–15.

Brym, Robert, and Bader Araj. 2011. "Intifada." Pp. 293–94 in *Sage Encyclopedia of Terrorism*, 2nd ed., C. Gus Martin, ed. Thousand Oaks CA: Sage.

_____. 2012. "Are suicide bombers suicidal?" *Studies in Conflict and Terrorism* 35: 432–43.

Brym, Robert, Louise Birdsell Bauer, and Mitch McIvor. 2013. "Is Industrial Unrest Reviving in Canada? Strike Duration in the Early 21st Century." *Canadian Review of Sociology* 50: 227–38.

Brym, Robert, Melissa Godbout, Andreas Hoffbauer, Gabe Menard, and Tony Huiquan Zhang. 2014. "Social Media in the 2011 Egyptian Uprising." *British Journal of Sociology* 65: 266–92

Brym, Robert, and Rhonda Lenton. 2001. *Love Online: A Report on Digital Dating in Canada*. Toronto: MSN Canada. Retrieved November 28, 2012 (http://projects.chass.utoronto.ca/brym/loveonline.pdf).

Brym, Robert, and John Lie. 2009. *Sociology: The Points of the Compass*. Toronto: Nelson.

Brym, Robert, and M. Reza Nakhaie. 2009. "Professional, critical, policy, and public academics in Canada." *Canadian Journal of Sociology* 34(3): 655–69.

Brym, Robert, Lance Roberts, and Lisa Strohschein. 2018. *Sociology: Compass for a New Social World*, 6th ed. Toronto: Nelson.

Brym, Robert, Anna Slavina, Mina Todosijevic, and David Cowan. 2018. "Social Movement Horizontality in the Internet Age? A Critique of Castells in Light of the Trump Victory." *Canadian Review of Sociology* 55(4).

Buggs, Shantel Gabrieal. 2017. "Does mixed race matter? The role of race in interracial sex, dating, and marriage." *Sociology Compass* 11(1). https://doi.org/10.1111/soc4.12531 (retrieved 8 February 2018).

Bunge, Valerie Pottie. 2000. "Spousal Violence." Pp. 11–21 in Statistics Canada, *Family Violence in Canada: A Statistical Profile 2000*. Catalogue No. 85-224-XIE. Ottawa: Minister of Industry.

Burger, Jerry. 2009. "Replicating Milgram: Would People Still Obey Today?" *American Psychologist* 64(1): 1–11.

Burnaby, Barbara, and Roderic Beaujot. 1987. *The Use of Aboriginal Languages in Canada: An Analysis of the 1981 Census*. Ottawa: Secretary of State of Canada;

Buss, David M. 2000. *Dangerous Passion: Why Jealousy Is As Necessary As Love and Sex*. New York: Free Press.

Butt, David. 2018. "How the justice system let race taint the Stanley verdict." *Globe and Mail* 10 February 2018. https://www.theglobeandmail.com/opinion/how-the-justice-system-let-race-taint-the-stanley-verdict/article37931748/ (retrieved 10 February 2018).

Cairns, James. 2017. *The Myth of the Age of Entitlement: Millennials, Austerity, and Hope*. Toronto: University of Toronto Press.

"Calgary Transit pride bus has driver threatening to quit." 2015. *CBC News* 28 August. Retrieved August 29, 2015 (http://www.cbc.ca/news/canada/calgary/calgary-transit-pride-bus-has-driver-threatening-to-quit-1.3207061).

Campbell, Donald, and Julian Stanley. 1963. *Experimental and Quasi-Experimental Designs for Research*. Chicago: Rand McNally.

Campbell, Frances A., and Craig T. Ramey. 1994. "Effects of Early Intervention on Intellectual and Academic Achievement: A Follow-up Study of Children from Low-Income Families." *Child Development* 65: 684–99.

Campion, Edward W. 1993. "Why Unconventional Medicine?" *New England Journal of Medicine* 328: 282.

"Canada MOOCs and Free Online Courses." https://www.mooc-list.com/countries/canada (retrieved 1 March 2018).

"Canada," Multicultural Policies in Contemporary Democracies, Queen's University. 2018. http://www.queensu.ca/mcp/immigrant-minorities/evidence/canada (retrieved 10 January 2018).

"Canada's Richest People." 2018. *Canadian Business* http://www.canadianbusiness.com/lists-and-rankings/richest-people/100-richest-canadians-complete-list/ (retrieved 27 January 2018).

Canadian Education Association. 2007. "Public Education in Canada: Facts, Trends, and Attitudes 2007." https://

www.edcan.ca/articles/public-education-in-canada-facts-trends-and-attitudes-2007 (retrieved 3 March 2018).

Canadian Health Coalition. 2018. "On eve of medical association's annual meeting: New poll shows overwhelming support for public health care; CMA president out of touch with most Canadians." https://www.newswire.ca/news-releases/on-eve-of-medical-associations-annual-meeting-new-poll-shows-overwhelming-support-for-public-health-care-cma-president-out-of-touch-with-most-canadians-538174651.html (retrieved 20 February 2018).

Canadian Institute for Health Information. 2004. *Improving the Health of Canadians*. Ottawa: Author.

Canadian Press. 2012. "Poll: Canadians are most proud of universal medicare." *CTV News*. 25 November. https://www.ctvnews.ca/canada/poll-canadians-are-most-proud-of-universal-medicare-1.1052929 (retrieved 20 February 2018).

Canadian Sociological Association and Department of Sociology, University of British Columbia. 2014. "Opportunities in Sociology." Montreal.

Cancer Care Nova Scotia. 2004. "Cancer Statistics in Nova Scotia." Retrieved February 27, 2008 (http://cancercare.ns.ca/media/documents/CancerinNS_Overview.pdf).

Carbon Tracker Initiative. 2012. "Unburnable Carbon—Are the World's Financial Markets Carrying a Carbon Bubble?" Retrieved March 31, 2013 (http://www.carbontracker.org/wp-content/uploads/downloads/2012/08/Unburnable-Carbon-Full1.pdf).

Cardoso, Fernando Henrique, and Enzo Faletto. 1979. *Dependency and Development in Latin America*, Marjory Mattingly Urquidi, trans. Berkeley, CA: University of California Press.

Carey, Kate B., Sarah E. Durney, Robyn L. Shepardson, and Michael P. Carey. 2015. "Incapacitated and Forcible Rape of College Women: Prevalence across the First Year." *Journal of Adolescent Health* 56(6): 678–80.

Carpenter, Julia. 2015. "Google's algorithm shows prestigious job ads to men, but not to women. Here's why that should worry you." *Washington Post* 6 July. https://www.washingtonpost.com/news/the-intersect/wp/2015/07/06/googles-algorithm-shows-prestigious-job-ads-to-men-but-not-to-women-heres-why-that-should-worry-you/?utm_term=.22994ff5bd55 (retrieved 25 February 2018).

Carreon, Justine. "Shop the best denim from every decade." *Elle* 30 January. http://www.elle.com/fashion/shopping/advice/g25646/denim-through-the-ages/ (retrieved 4 January 2018).

Carrier, Roch. 1979. *The Hockey Sweater and Other Stories*, Sheila Fischman, trans. Toronto: Anansi.

Caspi, Avshalom, Joseph McClay, Terrie E. Moffitt, Jonathan Mill, Judy Martin, Ian W. Craig, Alan Taylor, and Richie Poulton. 2002. "Role of Genotype in the Cycle of Violence in Maltreated Children." *Science* 297(5582) 851–54.

Castells, Manuel. 2015 [2012]. *Networks of Outrage and Hope: Social Movements in the Internet Age*, 2nd ed. (Cambridge UK: Polity).

Cato Institute. 2017. "Religious Freedom Index." https://www.cato.org/human-freedom-index (retrieved 14 February 2018).

Cavalli-Sforza, L. Luca, Paola Menozzi, and Alberto Piazza. 1994. *The History and Geography of Human Genes*. Princeton, NJ: Princeton University Press.

Caulfield, Timothy. 2015. *Is Gwyneth Paltrow Wrong about Everything?* New York: Random House.

*CBC News*. 2004. *Hospital Hygiene Cuts Severe Infections by 80 Per Cent*. Retrieved July 27, 2005 (http://www.cbc.ca/story/science/national/2004/01/15/hand_washque04015html?print).

———. 2018. "6 reasons doctors say to reconsider colon cleanses." 22 February. http://www.cbc.ca/news/health/colonics-colon-cleanses-doctor-warning-hydrotherapy-1.4543340 (retrieved 22 February 2018).

Central Intelligence Agency. 2018. *CIA World Factbook 2018*. https://www.cia.gov/library/publications/the-world-factbook/fields/2018.html (retrieved 21 February 2018).

Chagnon, Napoleon. 1992. *Yanomamö: The Last Days of Eden*. New York: Harcourt, Brace Yovanovich.

Chan, Michael. 2014. "Multimodal Connectedness and Quality of Life: Examining the Influences of Technology Adoption and Interpersonal Communication on Well-Being across the Life Span." *Journal of Computer-Mediated Communication* 20: 3–18.

Chard, Jennifer. 2000. "Women in a Visible Minority." Pp. 219–44 in *Women in Canada, 2000: A Gender-Based Statistical Report*. Ottawa: Statistics Canada.

Chauncey, George. 2005. *Why Marriage? The History Shaping Today's Debate over Gay Equality*. New York: Basic Books.

Chaves, Mark. 1994. "Secularization as Declining Religious Authority." *Social Forces* 72: 749–74.

Chrisman-Campbell, Kimberly. 2014. "The midi skirt, divider of nations." *The Atlantic*, 9 September. https://www.theatlantic.com/entertainment/archive/2014/09/the-return-of-the-midi-skirt/379543/ (retrieved 4 January 2018).

Cisco. 2017. "Cisco Visual Networking Index: Forecast and Methodology, 2016–2021." https://www.google.ca/url?sa=t&rct=j&q=&esrc=s&source=web&cd=2&ved=0ahUKEwi5gdfj2r_ZAhVBSK0KHXu2DdsQjBAIPDAB&url=https%3A%2F%2Fwww.cisco.com%2Fc%2Fen%2Fus%2Fsolutions%2Fcollateral%2Fservice-provider%2Fvisual-networking-index-vni%2Fcomplete-white-paper-c11-481360.pdf&usg=AOvVaw2jPqHwWAHY2eFHRnUSlNBQ (retrieved 24 February 2018).

City of Toronto. "Diversity." Retrieved July 22, 2015 (http://www1.toronto.ca/wps/portal/contentonly?vgnextoid=dbe867b42d853410VgnVCM10000071d60f89RCRD&vgnextchannel=57a12cc817453410VgnVCM10000071d60f89RCRD).

Clairmont, Donald H., and Dennis W. Magill. 1999. *Africville: The Life and Death of a Canadian Black Community*, 3rd ed. Toronto: Canadian Scholars' Press.

Clark, S. D. 1968. *The Developing Canadian Community*. Toronto: University of Toronto Press.

Clayton, Russell B., Glenn Leshner, and Anthony Almond. 2015. "The Extended Self: The Impact of iPhone Separation on Cognition, Emotion, and Physiology." *Journal of*

Clement, Wallace H. P. 1897. *The History of the Dominion of Canada*. Toronto: William Briggs.

Cleveland, Gordon. 2016. "What Is the Role of Early Childhood Education and Care in an Equality Agenda?" In Robert Brym, ed. *Inequality and the Future of Canadian Society*. Oakville, ON: Rock's Mills Press. Pp. 76–99.

Clinard, Marshall B., and Peter C. Yeager. 1980. *Corporate Crime*. New York: Free Press.

Cloward, Richard A., and Lloyd E. Ohlin. 1960. *Delinquency and Opportunity: A Theory of Delinquent Gangs*. New York: Free Press.

Cockerham, William C. 1998. *Medical Sociology*, 7th ed. Upper Saddle River, NJ: Prentice-Hall.

Cohen, Albert. 1955. *Delinquent Boys: The Subculture of a Gang*. New York: Free Press.

Cohen, Rachel, Toby Newton-John, and Amy Slater. 2017. "The relationship between Facebook and Instagram appearance-focused activities and body image concerns in young women." *Body Image*. https://doi.org/10.1016/j.bodyim.2017.10.002 (retrieved 4 February 2018).

Colapinto, John. 1997. "The True Story of John/Joan." *Rolling Stone* 11 December: 54–73, 92–97.

Cole, Michael. 1995. *Cultural Psychology*. Cambridge, MA: Harvard University Press.

Coleman, James S. 1961. *The Adolescent Society*. New York: Free Press.

_____. 1988. "Social Capital in the Creation of Human Capital." *American Journal of Sociology* 94: 95–120.

_____. 1990. *Foundations of Social Theory*. Cambridge, MA: Harvard University Press.

Coleman, James S., Ernest Q. Campbell, and Carol J. Hobson. 1966. *Equality of Educational Opportunity*. Washington, DC: United States Department of Health, Education, and Welfare, Office of Education.

Coll, Steve. 2017. "Donald Trump's 'fake news' tactics." *The New Yorker* 11 December. https://www.newyorker.com/magazine/2017/12/11/donald-trumps-fake-news-tactics (retrieved 1 January 2018).

Collins, Judy. 2009. "Interview about Leonard Cohen, 'Suzanne,'" YouTube. https://www.youtube.com/watch?v=Ijqp4s9JDOc (retrieved 14 February 2018).

Collins, Randall. 1979. *The Credential Society: An Historical Sociology of Education*. New York: Academic Press.

_____. 1982. *Sociological Insight: An Introduction to Nonobvious Sociology*. New York: Oxford University Press.

_____. 1993. "Review of a *Theory of Religion* by Rodney Stark and William S. Bainbridge." *Journal for the Scientific Study of Religion* 32, 4: 402–04, 406.

Connections Academy. 2018. "Infographic: Growth of K–12 Digital Learning." https://www.connectionsacademy.com/news/growth-of-k-12-online-education-infographic (retrieved 1 March 2018).

Conrad, Peter, and Joseph W. Schneider. 1992. *Deviance and Medicalization: From Badness to Sickness*, expanded ed. Philadelphia: Temple University Press.

Cooley, Charles Horton. 1902. *Human Nature and the Social Order*. New York: Scribner's.

Coontz, Stephanie. 1992. *The Way We Never Were: American Families and the Nostalgia Trap*. New York: Basic Books.

Costanzo, Mark. 1997. *Just Revenge: Costs and Consequences of the Death Penalty*. New York: St. Martin's Press.

Council of Ontario Universities. "2015 University Works: 2015 Employment Report." http://cou.on.ca/wp-content/uploads/2015/06/COU-University-Works-Report-2015.pdf (retrieved 14 November 2016).

Creighton, Sarah, and Catherine Mihto. 2001. "Managing Intersex." *BMJ: British Medical Journal* 323, 7324; December: 1264–65.

Crenshaw, Kimberlé. 2016. "The urgency of intersectionality." TEDWomen. https://www.ted.com/talks/kimberle_crenshaw_the_urgency_of_intersectionality/transcript (retrieved 27 February 2018).

Croteau, David, and William Hoynes. 1997. *Media/Society: Industries, Images, and Audiences*. Thousand Oaks, CA: Pine Forge Press.

Crozier, Michel. 1964. *The Bureaucratic Phenomenon*. Chicago: University of Chicago Press.

"CRTC's Mandate (The)." 2002. Canadian Radio-television and Telecommunications Commission. Retrieved May 15, 2003 (http://www.crtc.gc.ca/eng/BACKGRND/Brochures/B29903.htm).

_____. 2017. "Communications Monitoring Report 2017: Broadcasting sector overview." https://crtc.gc.ca/eng/publications/reports/policymonitoring/2017/cmr4.htm (retrieved 24 February 2018).

Culver, John H. 1992. "Capital Punishment, 1997–1998: Characteristics of the 143 Executed." *Sociology and Social Research* 76, 2 (January): 59–61.

Curington, Celeste Vaughan, Ken-Hou Lin, and Jennifer Hickes Lundquist. 2015. "Positioning Multiraciality in Cyberspace: Treatment of Multiracial Daters in an Online Dating Website." *American Sociological Review* 80(4): 764–88.

Curtis, Bruce. 1988. *Building the Educational State: Canada West, 1836–1871*. London, ON: Althouse Press.

Curtis, James, John Loy, and Wally Karnilowicz. 1986. "A Comparison of Suicide-Dip Effects of Major Sport Events and Civil Holidays." *Sociology of Sport Journal* 3: 1–14.

Damisch, L., B. Stoberock, and T. Mussweiler. 2010. "Keep Your Fingers Crossed! How Superstition Improves Performance." *Psychological Science* 21, 1014–20.

Darwin, Charles. 1859. *On the Origin of Species by Means of Natural Selection*. London, UK: John Murray.

_____. 1871. *The Descent of Man*. London, UK: John Murray.

Davies, James B. 1999. "Distribution of Wealth and Economic Inequality." Pp. 138–50 in James Curtis, Edward Grabb, and Neil Guppy, eds., *Social Inequality in Canada: Patterns, Problems, Policies*, 3rd ed. Scarborough, ON: Prentice Hall Allyn and Bacon Canada.

Davies, James C. 1969. "Toward a Theory of Revolution." Pp. 85–108 in Barry McLaughlin, ed. *Studies in Social Movements: A Social Psychological Perspective*. New York: Free Press.

Davis, Fred. 1992. *Fashion, Culture, and Identity*. Chicago: University of Chicago Press.

Davis, Kingsley, and Wilbert E. Moore. 1945. "Some Principles of Stratification." *American Sociological Review* 10: 242–49.

Davis, Mike. 1990. *City of Quartz: Excavating the Future in Los Angeles*. New York: Verso.

Dean, Jeremy. 2007. "Busting the myth 93% of communication is non-verbal." *Psyblog* 8 May. http://www.spring.org.uk/2007/05/busting-myth-93-of-communication-is.php (retrieved 20 January 2018).

de Boer, Kaila, David W. Rothwell, and Christopher Lee. 2013. "Child and family poverty in Canada: Implications for child welfare research." *Canadian Child Welfare Research Portal.* http://cwrp.ca/infosheets/child_poverty (retrieved 8 February 2018).

Deibert, Ronald J., and Louis W. Pauly. 2018. "Boundaries and Borders in Global Cyberspace." Pp. 27–48 in Robert Brym, ed. *The Future of Canada's Territorial Borders and Personal Boundaries* (Oakville ON: Rock's Mills Press).

DeKeseredy, Walter S., and Katherine Kelly. 1993. "The Incidence and Prevalence of Woman Abuse in Canadian University and College Dating Relationships." *Canadian Journal of Sociology* 18: 137–59.

DellaPergola, Sergio. 2018. "World Jewish Population, 2017." Pp. 297–377 in *American Jewish Yearbook 2017.* https://link.springer.com/chapter/10.1007/978-3-319-70663-4_7 (retrieved 7 July 2018).

Deloitte. 2018. *2017 Global Mobile Consumer Survey.* https://www2.deloitte.com/us/en/pages/technology-media-and-telecommunications/articles/global-mobile-consumer-survey-us-edition.html.

Denis, Jeffrey S. 2015. "Contact Theory in a Small-Town Settler-Colonial Context: The Reproduction of Laissez-Faire Racism in Indigenous–White Canadian Relations." *American Sociological Review* 80(1): 218–42.

_____. 2016. "Sociology of Indigenous Peoples in Canada," in Robert Brym, ed. *New Society*, 8th ed. Toronto: Nelson.

Department of Finance Canada. 2014. "Your Tax Dollar." Retrieved August 5, 2015 (http://www.fin.gc.ca/tax-impot/2014/2013-14-e.pdf).

Derber, Charles. 1979. *The Pursuit of Attention: Power and Individualism in Everyday Life.* New York: Oxford University Press.

Derrida, Jacques. 2004. *Positions*, Alan Bass, trans. London, UK: Continuum.

De Souza, Michael. 2016. "Here's what the science really says about Fort McMurray and climate change." *National Observer* 3 June. https://www.nationalobserver.com/2016/06/03/analysis/heres-what-science-really-says-about-fort-mcmurray-and-climate-change (retrieved 7 January 2018).

DeSteno, David, and Peter Salovey. 2001. "Evolutionary Origins of Sex Differences in Jealousy: Questioning the 'Fitness' of the Model." Pp. 150–56 in W. Gerrod Parrott, ed., *Emotions in Social Psychology: Essential Readings.* Philadelphia: Psychology Press.

Deutscher, Guy. 2010. "Does Your Language Shape How You Think?" *New York Times*, August 26. Retrieved June 7, 2011 (http://www.nytimes.com).

de Villiers, Marq. 1999. *Water.* Toronto: Stoddart Publishing.

DiMaggio, Paul. 1982. "Cultural Capital and School Success: The Impact of Status Culture Participation on the Grades of U.S. High School Students." *American Sociological Review* 47: 189–201.

_____. 2018. "160 Amazing YouTube Statistics and Facts (January 2018)." https://expandedramblings.com/index.php/youtube-statistics/ (retrieved 25 February 2018).

Donahue, John J., III, and Steven D. Levitt. 2001. "The Impact of Legalized Abortion on Crime." *Quarterly Journal of Economics* 116: 379–420.

Douglas, Emily M., and Murray A. Straus. 2006. "Assault and Injury of Dating Partners by University Students in 19 Nations and Its Relation to Corporal Punishment Experienced as a Child." *European Journal of Criminology* 3: 293–318.

Doyle, Aaron, Brian Elliott, and David Tindall. 1997. "Framing the Forests: Corporations, the B.C. Forest Alliance, and the Media." Pp. 240–68 in William Carroll, ed. *Organizing Dissent: Contemporary Social Movements in Theory and Practice*, 2nd ed. Toronto: Garamond Press.

"Do You Know Who Scored The First Basket in the NBA?" *The First Basket: A Jewish Basketball Documentary*, n.d.

Dranoff, Linda Silver. 2001. *Everyone's Guide to the Law.* Toronto: HarperCollins.

_____. 2014. "Poverty in Canada." Pp. 109–31 in Robert Brym, ed. *Society in Question.* Toronto: Nelson.

Dumont, Louis. 1980 [1966]. *Homo Hierarchicus: The Caste System and Its Implications*, translated by Mark Sainsbury, Louis Dumont, and Basi Gulati. Chicago: University of Chicago Press.

Durkheim, Émile. 1938 [1895]. *The Rules of Sociological Method*, G. E. G. Catlin, ed., S. A. Solovay and J. Mueller, trans. Chicago: University of Chicago Press.

_____. 1951 [1897]. *Suicide: A Study in Sociology*, G. Simpson, ed., J. Spaulding and G. Simpson, trans. New York: Free Press.

_____. 1956. *Education and Sociology*, Sherwood D. Fox, trans. New York: Free Press.

_____. 1961 [1925]. *Moral Education: A Study in the Theory and Application of the Sociology of Education*, Everett K. Wilson and Herman Schnurer, trans. New York: Free Press.

_____. 1973 [1899–1900]. "Two Laws of Penal Evolution." *Economy and Society* 2: 285–308.

_____. 1976 [1915/1912]. *The Elementary Forms of the Religious Life*, Joseph Ward Swain, trans. New York: Free Press.

_____. 1997 [1893]. *The Division of Labor in Society.* New York: Free Press.

Duster, Troy. 2015. "A post-genomic surprise: The molecular reinscription of race in science, law and medicine." *British Journal of Sociology* 66(1): 1–27.

"Ebola: Mapping the outbreak." *BBC News.* http://www.bbc.com/news/world-africa-28755033 (retrieved 18 February 2018).

Edmundson, Mark. 2003. "How Teachers Can Stop Cheaters." *New York Times*, 9 September. Retrieved September 9, 2003 (http://www.nytimes.com).

Ehlers, Cindy L. 2007. "Variations in ADH and ALDH in Southwest California Indians." *Alcohol Research Current Reviews* 30(1): 14–17.

Eichler, Margrit. 1987. *Nonsexist Research Methods.* Boston: Allen and Unwin.

_____. 1988. *Families in Canada Today*, 2nd ed. Toronto: Gage.

Eisenstein, Elizabeth L. 1983. *The Printing Revolution in Early Modern Europe.* Cambridge UK: Cambridge University Press.

Ekman, Paul. 1978. *Facial Action Coding System*. New York: Consulting Psychologists Press.

Elections Canada. 2012. "Voter Turnout at Federal Elections and Referendums." Retrieved from http://www.elections.ca.

_____. 2016. "Retrospective Report on the 42nd General Election of October 19, 2015." Retrieved January 10, 2016 (http://www.elections.ca/content.aspx?section=res&dir=rec/eval/pes2015/ege&document=p1&lang=e#a4).

Ellul, Jacques. 1964 [1954]. *The Technological Society*, John Wilkinson, trans. New York: Vintage.

Engels, Frederick. 1970 [1884]. *The Origins of the Family, Private Property and the State*, Eleanor Burke Leacock, ed., Alec West, trans. New York: International Publishers.

England, Paula. 1992. *Comparable Worth: Theories and Evidence*. Hawthorne, NY: Aldine de Gruyter.

Entine, J. 2000. *Taboo: Why Black Athletes Dominate Sports and Why We Are Afraid to Talk about It*. New York: Public Affairs.

Epstein, Steven. 1996. *Impure Science: AIDS, Activism, and the Politics of Knowledge*. Berkeley, CA: University of California Press.

Ernst, Edzard, and Max H. Pittler. 2006. "Celebrity-Based Medicine." *Medical Journal of Australia* 185, 11/12: 680–81.

Esmail, Nadeem. 2007. "Complementary and Alternative Medicine in Canada: Trends in Use and Public Attitudes, 1997–2006." *Public Policy Sources* 87. Retrieved August 7, 2015 (http://www.fraserinstitute.org/uploadedFiles/fraser-ca/Content/research-news/research/publications/complementary-alternative-medicine-in-canada-2007.pdf).

_____. 2017, Complementary and Alternative Medicine: Use and Public Attitudes 1997, 2006, and 2016. https://www.fraserinstitute.org/studies/complementary-and-alternative-medicine-use-and-public-attitudes-1997-2006-and-2016 (retrieved 17 February 2018).

Estrich, Susan. 1987. *Real Rape*. Cambridge, MA: Harvard University Press.

Etheridge, D. M., et al. 1998. Historical $CO_2$ Record from the Law Dome DE08, DE08-2, and DSS Ice Cores. Retrieved August 2, 2015 (http://cdiac.ornl.gov/ftp/trends/co2/lawdome.combined.dat).

European Monitoring Centre for Drugs and Drug Addiction. 2011. "Portugal." http://www.emcdda.europa.eu/publications/drug-policy-profiles/portugal (retrieved 26 January 2018).

Everitt, Joanna, Lisa A. Best, and Derek Gaudet. 2016. "Candidate Gender, Behavioral Style, and Willingness to Vote: Support for Female Candidates Depends on Conformity to Gender Norms." *American Behavioral Scientist* 60(14): 1737–55.

Fagot, Beverly I., Carie S. Rodgers, and Mary D. Leinbach. 2000. "Theories of Gender Socialization." Pp. 65–89 in Thomas Eckes, ed., *The Developmental Social Psychology of Gender*. Mahwah, NJ: Lawrence Erlbaum Associates.

Fausto-Sterling, Anne. 2000. "The five sexes, revisited." *The Sciences* 40: 18–23.

Fazel, S., and A. Wolf. 2015. "A Systematic Review of Criminal Recidivism Rates Worldwide: Current Difficulties and Recommendations for Best Practice." *PLoS One* 10(6). https://doi.org/10.1371/journal.pone.0130390 (retrieved 25 January 2018).

Febvre, Lucien, and Henri-Jean Martin. 1976 [1958]. *The Coming of the Book: The Impact of Printing 1450–1800*, David Gerard, trans. London, UK: NLB.

Federal–Provincial–Territorial Working Group on Restorative Justice, Subcommittee on Public and Justice Sector Education. 2009. Correctional Service Canada 22 December. Retrieved July 26, 2015 (http://www.csc-scc.gc.ca/restorative-justice/003005-4005-eng.shtml).

Felson, Richard B. 1996. "Mass Media Effects on Violent Behavior." *Annual Review of Sociology* 22: 103–28.

Fernandez-Dols, Jose-Miguel, Flor Sanchez, Pilar Carrera, and Maria-Angeles Ruiz-Belda. 1997. "Are Spontaneous Expressions and Emotions Linked? An Experimental Test of Coherence." *Journal of Nonverbal Behavior* 21: 163–77.

Ferns, Carolyn, and Martha Friendly. 2012. "The state of early childhood education and care in Canada 2012." Retrieved August 29, 2015 (http://childcarecanada.org/sites/default/files/StateofECEC2012.pdf).

Finke, Roger, and Rodney Starke. 1992. *The Churching of America, 1776–1990: Winners and Losers in Our Religious Economy*. New Brunswick, NJ: Rutgers University Press.

_____. 2005. *The Churching of America, 1776–2005: Winners and Losers in Our Religious Economy*, 2nd ed. New Brunswick, NJ: Rutgers University Press.

First Nations Information Governance Centre. 2018. "The First Nations Principles of OCAP®." http://fnigc.ca/ocap.html (retrieved 5 April 2018).

Fischer, Claude S., Michael Hout, Martín Sánchez Jankowski, Samuel R. Lucas, Ann Swidler, and Kim Voss. 1996. *Inequality by Design: Cracking the Bell Curve Myth*. Princeton, NJ: Princeton University Press.

Fleras, Augie, and Jean Leonard Elliott. 2002. *Engaging Diversity: Multiculturalism in Canada*. Toronto: Nelson.

Flood, Gavin D. 1996. *An Introduction to Hinduism*. Cambridge: Cambridge University Press.

Flores, Jerry. 2017. "Why I left Donald Trump's America." *Toronto Star*. https://www.thestar.com/opinion/contributors/2017/12/22/why-i-left-donald-trumps-america.html (retrieved 22 February 2018)

Flowers, Paul, and Katie Buston. 2001. "'I Was Terrified of Being Different:' Exploring Gay Men's Accounts of Growing-Up in a Heterosexist Society." *Journal of Adolescence*. Special Issue: *Gay, Lesbian, and Bisexual Youth* 24: 51–65.

Fond, G., N. Franc, and D. Purper-Ouakil. 2012. "Homoparentalité et développement de l'enfant: Données actuelles." *L'Encéphale* 38(1): 10–15.

Fong, Francis. 2017. "Income Inequality in Canada: The Urban Gap." Chartered Professional Accountants Canada. https://www.cpacanada.ca/en/the-cpa-profession/about-cpa-canada/cpa-canadas-key-activities/public-policy-and-government-relations/cpa-canada-economic-policy-research/income-inequality-in-canada (retrieved 27 January 2015).

Forbes.com. 2010. "The World's Billionaires." Retrieved March 11, 2010 (http://www.forbes.com/

lists/2010/10/billionaires-2010_The-Worlds-Billionaires_Rank.html).

Form, William, and Nico Wilterdink. 2018. "Social change." *Encyclopaedia Britannica*. https://www.britannica.com/topic/social-change (retrieved 27 February 2018).

Forman, Murray. 2001. "It Ain't All about the Benjamins: Summit on Social Responsibility in the Hip-Hop Industry." *Journal of Popular Music Studies* 13: 117–23.

Forrest, C. B., and A. W. Riley. 2004. "Childhood Origins of Adult Health: A Basis for Life-Course Health Policy." *Health Affairs* 23, 5: 155–64.

Fortin, Pierre. 2017. "You must be kidding: Confronting key myths about Quebec's childcare system." *Behind the Numbers*. http://behindthenumbers.ca/2017/04/25/must-kidding-confronting-key-myths-quebecs-childcare-system/ (retrieved 6 February 2018).

Forum Research Inc. 2015. "Instagram tops in user satisfaction." Retrieved July 6, 2015 (http://poll.forumresearch.com/data/Federal%20Social%20Media%20News%20Release%20%282015%2001%2006%29%20Forum%20Research.pdf).

Foster, Deborah. 2006. "Why Do Children Do So Well in Lesbian Households?" *Canadian Woman Studies* 24, 2, 3: 51–56.

Foucault, Michel. 1973. *The Birth of the Clinic: An Archaeology of Medical Perception*, A. M. Sheridan, trans. London UK: Routledge.

———. 1977 [1975]. *Discipline and Punish: The Birth of the Prison*, Alan Sheridan, trans. New York: Vintage.

———. 1988. *Madness and Civilization: A History of Insanity in the Age of Reason*, Richard Howard, trans. New York: Random House.

———. 1990 [1978]. *The History of Sexuality: An Introduction*, Vol. 1. Robert Hurley, trans. New York: Vintage.

Frank, Thomas, and Matt Weiland, eds. 1997. *Commodify Your Dissent: Salvos from the Baffler*. New York: W. W. Norton.

Franklin, Karen. 2000. "Antigay Behaviors among Young Adults." *Journal of Interpersonal Violence* 15, 4: 339–62.

Freidson, Eliot. 1986. *Professional Powers: A Study of the Institutionalization of Formal Knowledge*. Chicago: University of Chicago Press.

Freire, Paolo. 1972. *The Pedagogy of the Oppressed*. New York: Herder and Herder.

Frenette, Marc. 2007. "Why Are Youth from Lower-Income Families Less Likely to Attend University? Evidence from Academic Abilities, Parental Influences, and Financial Constraints." Catalogue No. 11F0019MIE. Ottawa: Statistics Canada.

Freudenburg, William R. 1997. "Contamination, Corrosion and the Social Order: An Overview." *Current Sociology* 45, 3: 19–39.

Friedenberg, Edgar Z. 1959. *The Vanishing Adolescent*. Boston: Beacon Press.

Friesen, Joe. 2013. "The Future Belongs to the Young." *Globe and Mail*, January 19: A4.

"Full parole granted to man who killed Regina woman." *CBC News* 10 November. http://www.cbc.ca/news/canada/full-parole-granted-to-man-who-killed-regina-woman-1.251523 (retrieved 26 January 2018).

Galabuzi, G.-E. 2004. *Social Inclusion as a Determinant of Health*. Ottawa: Public Health Agency of Canada.

Galper, Joseph. 1998. "Schooling for Society." *American Demographics* 20, 3: 33–34.

Gamson, William A., Bruce Fireman, and Steven Rytina. 1982. *Encounters with Unjust Authority*. Homewood, IL: Dorsey Press.

Gans, Herbert. 1979. *Deciding What's News: A Study of CBS Evening News, NBC Nightly News, Newsweek and Time*. New York: Pantheon.

———. 1991. "Symbolic Ethnicity: The Future of Ethnic Groups and Cultures in America." Pp. 430–43 in Norman R. Yetman, ed., *Majority and Minority: The Dynamics of Race and Ethnicity in American Life*, 5th ed. Boston, MA: Allyn and Bacon.

Garland, David. 1990. *Punishment and Modern Society: A Study in Social Theory*. Chicago: University of Chicago Press.

Gates, Gary J. 2011. "How many people are lesbian, gay, bisexual, and transgender?" *The Williams Institute* April. Retrieved August 27, 2015 (http://williamsinstitute.law.ucla.edu/wp-content/uploads/Gates-How-Many-People-LGBT-Apr-2011.pdf).

Gauvain, Mary, Beverly I. Fagot, Craig Leve, and Kate Kavanagh. 2002. "Instruction by Mothers and Fathers during Problem Solving with Their Young Children." *Journal of Family Psychology* 6, 1; March: 81–90.

Gelles, Richard J. 1997. *Intimate Violence in Families*, 3rd ed. Thousand Oaks, CA: Sage.

Ghosh, Bobby. 2011. "Rage, Rap and Revolution: Inside the Arab Youth Quake." *Time.com*, 17 February. Retrieved February 17, 2011 (http://www.time.com/time/world/article/0,8599,2049808,00.html).

Giddens, Anthony. 1987. *Sociology: A Brief but Critical Introduction*, 2nd ed. New York: Harcourt Brace Jovanovich.

———. 1990. *The Consequences of Modernity*. Stanford, CA: Stanford University Press.

———. 1992. *The Transformation of Intimacy: Sexuality, Love and Eroticism in Modern Society*. Stanford CA: Stanford University Press.

Gies, Miep, with Alison Leslie Gold. 1987. *Anne Frank Remembered: The Story of the Woman Who Helped to Hide the Frank Family*. New York: Simon and Schuster.

Gilman, Sander L. 1991. *The Jew's Body*. New York: Routledge.

Gitlin, Todd. 1983. *Inside Prime Time*. New York: Pantheon.

Glass, Chris R., Mitsue S. Shiokawa-Baklan, and Andrew J. Saltarelli, "Who Takes MOOCs?" New Directions for Institutional Research (167): 41–55.

Gleick, James. 2000. *Faster: The Acceleration of Just About Everything*. New York: Vintage.

Globescan, 2012. "China and India share relaxed Anglo-Saxon attitudes towards wealth." https://globescan.com/tag/wealth-inequality/ (retrieved 29 January 2018).

"Gluscabi and the Wind Eagle." n.d. http://www.angelfire.com/ia2/stories3/wind.html (retrieved 14 February 2018).

Goddard Institute for Space Studies, National Aeronautics and Space Administration. 2017. "Global-mean monthly, seasonal, and annual means, 1880–present, updated through most recent month." http://data.giss.nasa.gov/gistemp (retrieved November 16, 2017).

Goffman, Erving. 1959. *The Presentation of Self in Everyday Life*, reprinted ed. Garden City, NY: Anchor.

———. 1974. *Frame Analysis*. Cambridge, MA: Harvard University Press.

Goldie, Terry, ed. 2001. *In a Queer Country: Gay & Lesbian Studies in the Canadian Context*. Vancouver: Arsenal Pulp Press.

Goldhagen, Daniel Jonah. 1996. *Hitler's Willing Executioners: Ordinary Germans and the Holocaust*. New York: Alfred A. Knopf.

Goldman Amy D., and Andrew M. Penner. 2016. "Exploring international gender differences in mathematics self-concept." *International Journal of Adolescence and Youth* 21(4), 403–18.

"Gold Medal Men's Hockey Game Gets Record Canadian TV Audience." 2010. *The Province*, 1 March. Retrieved March 28, 2010 (http://www.theprovince.com/entertainment/Gold+medal+hockey+game+gets+record+Canadian+audience/2628644/story.html).

Gombrich, Richard Francis. 1996. *How Buddhism Began: The Conditioned Genesis of the Early Teachings*. London, UK: Athlone.

Goode, Erich, and Nachman Ben-Yehuda. 1994. *Moral Panics: The Social Construction of Deviance*. Cambridge, MA: Blackwell.

Gottfredson, Michael, and Travis Hirschi. 1990. *A General Theory of Crime*. Stanford, CA: Stanford University Press.

Gottwald, Norman K. 1979. *The Tribes of Yahweh: A Sociology of the Religion of Liberated Israel, 1250–1050 B.C.E.* Maryknoll, NY: Orbis.

Goubert, Jean-Pierre. 1989 [1986]. *The Conquest of Water*, Andrew Wilson, trans. Princeton, NJ: Princeton University Press.

Gould, Stephen J. 1988. "Kropotkin Was No Crackpot." *Natural History* 97, 7: 12–18.

———. 1996. *The Mismeasure of Man*, rev. ed. New York: W. W. Norton.

Government of Canada. 2002. "Study Released on Firearms in Canada." Retrieved 29 December 2005 (http://www.cfc-ccaf.gc.ca/media/news_releases/2002/survey-08202002_e.asp).

Gramsci, Antonio. 1957. *The Modern Prince and Other Writings*. L Marks, trans. New York: International Publishers.

———. 1971. *Selections from the Prison Notebooks*, Q. Hoare and G. Smith, eds. London, UK: Lawrence & Wishart.

Granovetter, Mark. 1973. "The Strength of Weak Ties." *American Sociological Review* 78: 1360–80.

Grassegger, Hannes, and Mikael Krogerus. 2017. "The data that turned the world upside down." *Vice* 28 January. Retrieved from https://motherboard.vice.com/en_us/article/mg9vvn/how-our-likes-helped-trump-win (24 February 2018).

Green, Adam Isaiah. 2007. "Queer Theory and Sociology: Locating the Subject and the Self in Sexuality Studies." *Sociological Theory* 25: 26–45.

Greenhill, Pauline. 2001. "Can You See the Difference: Queerying the Nation, Ethnicity, Festival, and Culture in Winnipeg." Pp. 103–21 in Terry

Greenland, Jacob, and Sraha Alam. 2017. "Police resources in Canada, 2016." https://www.statcan.gc.ca/pub/85-002-x/2017001/article/14777-eng.htm (retrieved 21 January 2018).

Greenstein, Theodore. 1996. "Husbands' Participation in Domestic Labor: Interactive Effects of Wives' and Husbands' Gender Ideologies." *Journal of Marriage and the Family* 58: 585–95.

Gregory. C. Jane, and Brian M. Petrie. 1975. "Superstitions of Canadian Intercollegiate Athletes: An Inter-Sport Comparison." *International Review for the Sociology of Sport* 10(1): 59–68.

Griner, Allison. 2013. "Aboriginal lawyers stride in footsteps of legal pioneer." *Thunderbird.ca*, 25 March. Retrieved August 2, 2015 (http://thethunderbird.ca/2013/03/25/aboriginal-lawyers-stride-in-footsteps-of-legal-pioneer).

Groopman, Jerome. 2008. "Superbugs." *The New Yorker* 11 August 2008.

Guillén, Mauro F. 2001. "Is Globalization Civilizing, Destructive or Feeble? A Critique of Five Key Debates in the Social Science Literature." *Annual Review of Sociology* 27.

Gunitsky, Seva. 2015. "Corrupting the Cyber-Commons: Social Media as a Tool of Autocratic Stability." *Perspectives on Politics* 13: 42–54.

Guppy, Neil, Kerry Greer, Nicole Malette, and Kristyn Frank. 2017. "The Future Lives of Sociology Graduates." *Canadian Review of Sociology* 54(2).

Guppy, Neil, and Scott Davies. 1998. *Education in Canada: Recent Trends and Future Challenges*. Ottawa: Ministry of Industry.

Gurr, Ted Robert. 1970. *Why Men Rebel*. Princeton, NJ: Princeton University Press.

Haas, Jack, and William Shaffir. 1987. *Becoming Doctors: The Adoption of a Cloak of Competence*. Greenwich, CT: JAI Press.

Habermas, Jürgen. 1989. *The Structural Transformation of the Public Sphere*, Thomas Burger, trans. Cambridge, MA: MIT Press.

Hagan, John. 1989. *Structuralist Criminology*. New Brunswick, NJ: Rutgers University Press.

———. 1994. *Crime and Disrepute*. Thousand Oaks, CA: Pine Forge Press.

Hagan, John, John Simpson, and A. R. Gillis. 1987. "Class in the Household: A Power-Control Theory of Gender and Delinquency." *American Journal of Sociology* 92: 788–816.

Haines, Herbert H. 1996. *Against Capital Punishment: The Anti-Death Penalty Movement in America, 1972–1994*. New York: Oxford University Press.

Hall, Edward. 1959. *The Silent Language*. New York: Doubleday.

———. 1966. *The Hidden Dimension*. New York: Doubleday.

Hall, Stuart. 1980. "Encoding/Decoding." Pp. 128–38 in Stuart Hall, Dorothy Hobson, Andrew Lowe, and Paul Willis, eds., *Culture, Media, Language: Working Papers in Cultural Studies, 1972–79*. London, UK: Hutchinson.

Hallgrimsdottir, Helga Kristin, Rachel Phillips, and Cecilia Benoit. 2006. "Fallen Women and Rescued Girls: Social Stigma and Media Narratives of the Sex Industry in Victoria, B.C., from 1980 to 2005." *Canadian Review of Sociology and Anthropology* 43, 3: 265–80.

Haney, Craig, W. Curtis Banks, and Philip G. Zimbardo. 1973. "Interpersonal Dynamics in a Simulated Prison." *International Journal of Criminology and Penology* 1: 69–97.

Hannigan, John. 1995. "The Postmodern City: A New Urbanization?" *Current Sociology* 43, 1: 151–217.

Hannon, Roseann, David S. Hall, Todd Kuntz, Van Laar, and Jennifer Williams. 1995. "Dating Characteristics Leading to Unwanted vs. Wanted Sexual Behavior." *Sex Roles* 33: 767–83.

Harari, Yuval Noah. 2014. *Sapiens: A Brief History of Humankind*. Toronto: McClelland and Stewart.

_____. 2017. *Homo Deus: A Brief History of Tomorrow*. New York: Harper.

Harding, David J., Cybelle Fox, and Jal D. Mehta. 2002. "Studying Rare Events through Qualitative Case Studies: Lessons from a Study of Rampage School Shootings." *Sociological Methods and Research* 31, 2: 174–217.

Harlequin. 2018. *Rev Up the Romance*. https://www.harlequin.com/shop/pages/rev-up-the-romance.html (retrieved 16 January 2018).

Harris, Marvin. 1974. *Cows, Pigs, Wars and Witches: The Riddles of Culture*. New York: Random House.

Harris, Kathleen. 2017 "University tuition fees in Canada jump 3.1% on average, StatsCan reports." *CBC News*. 6 September. http://www.cbc.ca/news/politics/statscan-university-tuition-1.4276740 (retrieved 2 March 2018).

Hart, Doug, and Arlo Kempf. 2015. "Public Attitudes toward Education in Ontario 2015." Toronto: Ontario Institute for Studies in Education of the University of Toronto.

Hartnagel, Timothy F. 2000. "Correlates of Criminal Behaviour." Pp. 94–136 in Rick Linden, ed., *Criminology: A Canadian Perspective*, 4th ed. Toronto: Harcourt Canada.

Harvey, Andrew S., Katherine Marshall, and Judith A. Frederick. 1991. *Where Does the Time Go?* Ottawa: Statistics Canada.

Harvey, Edward B., and Richard Kalwa. 1983. "Occupational Status Attainment of University Graduates: Individual Attributes and Labour Market Effects Compared." *Canadian Review of Sociology and Anthropology* 20: 435–53.

Hastings, Arthur C., James Fadiman, and James C. Gordon, eds. 1980. *Health for the Whole Person: The Complete Guide to Holistic Medicine*. Boulder, CO: Westview Press.

Hawking, Stephen. 2018. "Does God play dice?" http://www.hawking.org.uk/does-god-play-dice.html (retrieved 2 January 2018).

Hay Group. 2018. "Canadian pay equity requirements." http://www.haygroup.com/ca/services/index.aspx?id=43781 (retrieved 6 February 2018).

Haythornwaite, Caroline, and Barry Wellman. 2002. "The Internet in Everyday Life: An Introduction." Pp. 3–41 in Caroline Haythornwaite and Barry Wellman, eds., *The Internet in Everyday Life*. Oxford: Blackwell.

Health Canada. 1999a. *Statistical Report on the Health of Canadians*. Retrieved December 25, 1999 (http://www.hc-sc.gc.ca/hppb/phdd/report/state/englover.html).

_____. 2003. "Canadian Cancer Statistics, 2003." Retrieved March 30, 2010 (http://www.cancer.ca/Canada-wide/About%20cancer/Cancer%20statistics/Canadian%20Cancer%20Statistics.aspx?sc_lang=en).

_____. 2014b. First Nations and Inuit Health: Diseases and Health Conditions." Retrieved August 7, 2015 (http://www.hc-sc.gc.ca/fniah-spnia/diseases-maladies/index-eng.php).

"Health Care Systems: An International Comparison." 2001. Ottawa: Strategic Policy and Research, Intergovernmental Affairs. Retrieved June 13, 2003 (http://www.pnrec.org/2001papers/DaigneaultL ajoie.pdf).

Hechter, Michael. 1974. *Internal Colonialism: The Celtic Fringe in British National Development, 1536–1966*. Berkeley, CA: University of California Press.

_____. 1987. *Principles of Group Solidarity*. Berkeley, CA: University of California Press.

Helliwell, J., R. Layard, and J. Sachs. 2017. "World Happiness Report 2017." New York: Sustainable Development Solutions Network. http://worldhappiness.report/ed/2017/ (retrieved 2 March 2018).

Helsing, Knud J., Moyses Szklo, and George W. Comstock. 1981. "Factors Associated with Mortality after Widowhood." *American Journal of Public Health* 71: 802–09.

Hendrick, Dianne, and Lee Farmer. 2002. "Adult Correctional Services in Canada, 2000/01." *Juristat* 22, 10; October. Catalogue No. 85-002-XPE. Ottawa: Canadian Centre for Justice Statistics and Statistics Canada.

Henrich, Joseph, Robert Boyd, and Peter J. Richerson. 2012. "The Puzzle of Monogamous Marriage." *Philosophical Transactions of the Royal Society: Biological Sciences* 367: 657–69.

Henry, David A., Joel G. Ray, and Marcelo L. Urquia. 2012. "Sex Ratios among Canadian Liveborn Infants of Mothers from Different Countries." *Canadian Medical Association Journal* 184: E492–96.

Henry, Frances, Carol Tator, Winston Mattis, and Tim Rees. 2001. "The Victimization of Racial Minorities in Canada." Pp. 145–60 in Robert Brym, ed., *Society in Question: Sociological Readings for the 21st Century*, 3rd ed. Toronto: Harcourt Canada.

Herdt, Gilbert. 2001. "Social Change, Sexual Diversity, and Tolerance for Bisexuality in the United States." Pp. 267–83 in Anthony R. D'Augelli and Charlotte J. Patterson, eds., *Lesbian, Gay, and Bisexual Identities and Youth: Psychological Perspectives*. New York: Oxford University Press.

Herlihy, David. 1998. *The Black Death and the Transformation of the West*. Cambridge, MA: Harvard University Press.

Herman, Edward S., and Noam Chomsky. 1988. *Manufacturing Consent: The Political Economy of the Mass Media*. New York: Pantheon.

Hern, Alex. 2015. "Flickr faces complaints over 'offensive' auto-tagging for photos." https://www.theguardian.com/technology/2015/may/20/flickr-complaints-offensive-auto-tagging-photos (retrieved 25 February 2018).

Herrera, Laura. 2011. "In Florida, Virtual Classrooms with No Teachers." *New York Times*, January 17. Retrieved May 24, 2011 (http://www.nytimes.com).

Hersch, Patricia. 1998. *A Tribe Apart: A Journey into the Heart of American Adolescence*. New York: Ballantine Books.

Hesse-Biber, Sharlene, and Gregg Lee Carter. 2000. *Working Women in America: Split Dreams*. New York: Oxford University Press.

Hird, Myra J. 2005. *Sex, Gender and Science*. London, UK: Palgrave Macmillan.

Hirschi, Travis. 1969. *Causes of Delinquency*. Berkeley, CA: University of California Press.

Hobbes, Thomas. 1968 [1651]. *Leviathan*. Middlesex, UK: Penguin.

Hobsbawm, Eric. 1994. *Age of Extremes: The Short Twentieth Century, 1914–1991*. London, UK: Abacus.

Hochschild, Arlie Russell. 1979. "Emotion Work, Feeling Rules, and Social Structure." *American Journal of Sociology* 85: 551–75.

———. 1983. *The Managed Heart: Commercialization of Human Feeling*. Berkeley, CA: University of California Press.

Hochschild, Arlie Russell, with Anne Machung. 1989. *The Second Shift: Working Parents and the Revolution at Home*. New York: Viking.

Hodgson, Marshall G. S. 1974. *The Venture of Islam: Conscience and History in a World Civilization*, 3 vols. Chicago: University of Chicago Press.

Hoek, H. W. 2007. "Incidence, prevalence and mortality of anorexia nervosa and other eating disorders." *Current Opinion in Psychiatry* 19(4): 389–94.

Hoffman, Steven J., and Charlie Tan. 2013. "Following celebrities' medical advice: meta-narrative analysis." *British Medical Journal* 347(14): 1751. http://www.bmj.com/content/347/bmj.f7151 (retrieved 20 February 2018).

Hogan, Bernie, and Brent Berry. 2011. "Racial and Ethnic Biases in Rental Housing: An Audit Study of Online Apartment Listings." Oxford University, Oxford Internet Institute. Retrieved August 2, 2015 (http://people.oii.ox.ac.uk/hogan/wp-content/uploads/2011/06/Hogan-Berry_City_and_Community_Craigslist.pdf).

Homans, George Caspar. 1961. *Social Behavior: Its Elementary Forms*. New York: Harcourt, Brace and World.

hooks, bell. 1984. *Feminist Theory: From Margin to Center*. Boston: South End Press.

Horkheimer, Max, and Theodor W. Adorno. 1986 [1944]. *Dialectic of Enlightenment*, John Cumming, trans. London, UK: Verso.

Horwitz, Suzanne R., and John F. Dovidio. 2017. "The rich—love them or hate them? Divergent implicit and explicit attitudes toward the wealthy." *Group Processes and Intergroup Relations* 20(1): 3–31.

Houpt, Simon. 2014. "Digital ad revenue tops other media categories for first time: report." *Globe and Mail* 17 September. Retrieved August 5, 2015 (http://www.theglobeandmail.com/report-on-business/industry-news/marketing/digital-ad-revenue-tops-other-media-categories-for-first-time-report/article20638694).

"How Rich Am I?" 2018. https://www.givingwhatwecan.org/get-involved/how-rich-am-i/?country=CAN&income=76000&adults=2&children=1 (retrieved 29 January 2018.

Huesmann, L. Rowell, Jessica Moise-Titus, Cheryl-Lynn Podolski, and Leonard D. Eron. 2003. "Longitudinal Relations between Children's Exposure to TV Violence and Their Aggressive and Violent Behavior in Young Adulthood: 1977–1992." *Developmental Psychology* 39, 2: 201–21.

IAB Canada. "CMUST 2016 Executive Summary," Rob Young, December 2016. https://iabcanada.com/research/cmust/ (retrieved 13 January 2018). Reproduced by permission.

Ignatieff, Michael. 2000. *The Rights Revolution*. Toronto: Anansi.

Ignatiev, Noel. 1995. *How the Irish Became White*. New York: Routledge.

Ingram, Gordon Brent. 2001. "Redesigning Wreck: Beach Meets Forest as Location of Male Homoerotic Culture in Placemaking in Pacific Canada." Pp. 188–208 in Terry Goldie, ed., *In a Queer Country: Gay & Lesbian Studies in the Canadian Context*. Vancouver: Arsenal Pulp Press.

Inkeles, Alex, and David H. Smith. 1976. *Becoming Modern: Individual Change in Six Developing Countries*. Cambridge, MA: Harvard University Press.

Institute for Economics and Peace. 2018, "About Us." http://economicsandpeace.org/about/ (retrieved 13 February 2018).

Intergovernmental Panel on Climate Change. 2007. Retrieved 2 May 2007 (http://www.ipcc.ch/).

———. 2017. "Highest to Lowest—Prison Population Rate." Retrieved January 22, 2018 (http://www.prisonstudies.org/highest-to-lowest/prison-population-total).

*International Dating Violence Study*. Tabulation courtesy of Murray A. Straus, based on Emily M. Douglas and Murray A. Straus, (2006), "Assault and Injury of Dating Partners by University Students in 19 Nations and Its Relation to Corporal Punishment Experienced as a Child." *European Journal of Criminology* 3:293–318. Reprinted with permission of the authors.

International Union for Conservation of Nature. 2016. "IUCN Red List of Threatened Species." https://www.iucn.org/resources/conservation-tools/iucn-red-list-threatened-species (retrieved 14 February 2018).

*Internet World Stats*. 2017. "Internet Usage Statistics." http://www.internetworldstats.com/stats.htm (retrieved 16 January 2017).

———. 2018. "Internet usage statistics." https://www.internetworldstats.com/stats.htm (retrieved 24 February 2018).

Ipsos. 2017. "Three in Four (77%) Canadian Graduates Under 40 Regret Taking on Student Debt." https://www.ipsos.com/en-ca/news-polls/BDO-student-debt-2017-09-18 (retrieved 18 January 2018).

Isajiw, Wsevolod W. 1978. "Olga in Wonderland: Ethnicity in a Technological Society." Pp. 29–39 in L. Driedger, ed., *The Canadian Ethnic Mosaic: A Quest for Identity*. Toronto: McClelland & Stewart.

Iyengar, Shanto. 1991. *Is Anyone Responsible? How Television Frames Political Issues*. Chicago: University of Chicago Press.

James, William. 1976 [1902]. *The Varieties of Religious Experience: A Study in Human Nature*. New York: Collier Books.

Janis, Irving. 1972. *Victims of Groupthink*. Boston: Houghton Mifflin.

Jellinek, Rebecca D., Taryn A. Myers, and Kathleen L. Keller. 2016. "The impact of doll style of dress and familiarity on body dissatisfaction in 6- to 8-year-old girls." *Body Image* 18(1): 78–85.

Jenkins, J. Craig. 1983. "Resource Mobilization Theory and the Study of Social Movements." *Annual Review of Sociology* 9: 527–53.

Johns, Adrian. 1998. *The Nature of the Book: Print and Knowledge in the Making*. Chicago: University of Chicago Press.

Johnson, Jeffrey G., Patricia Cohen, Elizabeth M. Smailes, Stephanie Kasen, and Judith S. Brook. 2002. "Television Viewing and Aggressive Behavior during Adolescence and Adulthood." *Science* 295, 5564: 2468–71.

Johnson, Michael P., and Kathleen J. Ferraro. 2000. "Research on Domestic Violence in the 1990s: Making Distinctions." *Journal of Marriage and the Family* 62: 948–63.

Johnson, Terence J. 1972. *Professions and Power*. London, UK: Macmillan.

Johnston, Richard. 2012. "The Structural Bases of Canadian Party Preference." Pp. 154–79 in Mebs Kanji, Antoine Bilodeau, and Thomas J. Scotto, eds. *The Canadian Election Studies: Assessing Four Decades of Influence.* Vancouver: University of British Columbia Press).

Jones, Frank. 2000. "Are Children Going to Religious Services?" Pp. 202–25 in *Canadian Social Trends* 54 (Fall): 3–13. Catalogue No. 11-008-XPE.

Jones, Jeffrey M. 2014. "Americans' support for death penalty stable." *Gallup* 23 October. Retrieved July 26, 2015 (http://www.gallup.com/poll/178790/americans-support-death-penalty-stable.aspx).

Jones, Laura. 1997. "Global Warming Is All the Rage These Days...Which Enrages Many Doubting Scientists." The Fraser Institute. Retrieved May 5, 2002 (http:// oldfraser.lexi.net/media/media _releases/1997/19971201a.html).

Joseph, Bob. 2016. "10 Quotes John A. Macdonald Made about First Nations." https://www.ictinc.ca/blog/10-quotes-john-a.-macdonald-made-about-first-nations (retrieved 18 January 2018).

Josephson Institute. 2012. "The Ethics of American Youth: 2012." Retrieved September 9, 2013 (http:// charactercounts.org/programs/reportcard/2012/index.html).

Juergensmeyer, Mark. 2000. *Terror in the Mind of God: The Global Rise of Religious Violence.* Berkeley, CA: University of California Press.

Kalmijn, Matthijs. 1998. "Intermarriage and Homogamy: Causes, Patterns, Trends." *Annual Review of Sociology* 24: 395–421.

Karabel, Jerome. 1986. "Community Colleges and Social Stratification in the 1980s." In L. S. Zwerling, ed., *The Community College and Its Critics.* San Francisco: Jossey-Bass.

Kariv, Dafna, Teresa V. Menzies, Gabrielle A. Brenner, and Louis Jacques Filion. 2009. "Transnational networking and business performance: Ethnic entrepreneurs in Canada." *Entrepreneurship and Regional Development* 21(3): 239–64).

Katz-Wise, Sabra, and Janet S. Hyde. 2015. "Sexual Fluidity and Related Attitudes and Beliefs among Young Adults with a Same-Gender Orientation." *Archives of Sexual Behavior* 44(5): 1459–70.

Kay, Fiona, and John Hagan. 1998. "Raising the Bar: The Gender Stratification of Law Firm Capitalization." *American Sociological Review* 63: 728–43.

Keighley, Kathryn. 2017. "Police-reported crime statistics in Canada, 2016." http://www.statcan.gc.ca/pub/85-002-x/2017001/article/54842-eng.htm (retrieved 21 January 2018).

Kennedy, Paul. 1993. *Preparing for the Twenty-First Century.* New York: HarperCollins.

Kepel, Gilles. 1994 [1991]. *The Revenge of God: The Resurgence of Islam, Christianity and Judaism in the Modern World,* Alan Braley, trans. University Park, PA: Pennsylvania State University Press.

Kimmerling, Baruch. 2001. *The Invention and Decline of Israeliness: State, Society, and the Military.* Berkeley, CA: University of California Press.

King, Martin Luther. 1967. *Conscience for Change.* Toronto: CBC Learning Systems. Reprinted by arrangement with The Heirs to the Estate of Martin Luther King Jr., c/o Writers House as agent for the proprietor New York, NY Copyright © 1967 Dr. Martin Luther King Jr; copyright renewed 1991 Coretta Scott King.

Kingston, Paul W. 2001. "The Unfulfilled Promise of Cultural Capital Theory." *Sociology of Education* Supplement: 88–91.

Kinsella, Warren. 2007. *The War Room: Political Strategies for Business, NGOs, and Anyone Who Wants to Win.* Toronto: Dundurn.

Kinsey, Alfred C., Wardell B. Pomeroy, and Clyde E. Martin. 1948. *Sexual Behavior in the Human Male.* Philadelphia: W. B. Saunders.

Kinsey, Alfred, Wardell Pomeroy, Clyde Martin, and Paul Gebhard. 1953. *Sexual Behavior in the Human Female.* Philadelphia: W. B. Saunders.

Klein, Jeff Z. 2013. "Rinks in Canada's Arctic Turn to Cooling Systems." *New York Times* 4 January. Retrieved January 4, 2013 (http://www.nytimes.com).

Kling, Kristen C., Janet Shibley Hyde, Carolin J. Showers, and Brenda N. Buswell. 1999. "Gender Differences in Self-Esteem: A Meta-Analysis." *Psychological Bulletin* 125, 4: 470–500.

Koepke, Leslie, Jan Hare, and Patricia B. Moran. 1992. "Relationship Quality in a Sample of Lesbian Couples with Children and Child-Free Lesbian Couples." *Family Relations* 41: 224–29.

Kohlberg, Lawrence. 1981. The *Psychology of Moral Development: The Nature and Validity of Moral Stages.* New York: Harper and Row.

Kornblum, William. 1997. *Sociology in a Changing World,* 4th ed. © 1997 South-Western, a part of Cengage Learning, Inc. Reproduced by permission. www.cengage.com/permissions.

Kosinski, M., D. Stillwell, and T. Graepel. 2012. "Private traits and attributes are predictable from digital records of human behaviour." *Proceedings of the National Academy of Sciences of the United States of America.* 110(15): 5802–05. http://www.pnas.org/content/110/15/5802.full (retrieved 24 February 2018).

Kosmin, Barry A. 1991. *Research Report of the National Survey of Religious Identification.* New York: CUNY Graduate Center.

Kouritzin, Sandra G. 2016. "Mothering across colour lines: Decisions and dilemmas of white birth mothers of mixed-race children." *Journal of Multilingual and Multicultural Development* 37(8): 735–47. https://doi.org/10.1080/01434632.2015.1122604 (retrieved 9 February 2018).

Kropotkin, Petr. 1908 [1902]. *Mutual Aid: A Factor of Evolution,* rev. ed. London, UK: W. Heinemann.

Krupnik, Igor, and Ludger Müller-Wille. 2010. "Franz Boas and Inuktitut Terminology for Ice and Snow: From the emergence of the field to the 'Great Eskimo Vocabulary Hoax.'" Pp. 377–400 in Krupnik, Igor, Claudio Aporta, Shari Gearheard, Gita J. Laidler, and Lene Kielsen Holm, eds. *SIKU: Knowing Our Ice: Documenting Inuit Sea Ice Knowledge and Use.* Dordrecht, Netherlands: Springer.

Kurdek, Lawrence A. 1996. "The Deterioration of Relationship Quality for Gay and Lesbian Cohabiting Couples: A Five-Year Prospective Longitudinal Study." *Personal Relationships* 3: 417–42.

Kuther, Tara L., and Erin McDonald. 2004. "Early Adolescents' Experiences with and Views of Barbie. *Adolescence* 39(1): 39–52.

LaFeber, Walter. 1993. *Inevitable Revolutions: The United States in Central America*, 2nd ed. New York: W. W. Norton.

Lamanna, Mary Ann, and Agnes Riedmann. 2003. *Marriages and Families: Making Choices in a Diverse Society*, 8th ed. Belmont, CA: Wadsworth.

Lamont, Michele, and Annette Lareau. 1988. "Cultural Capital: Allusions, Gaps, and Glissandos in Recent Theoretical Developments." *Sociological Theory* 6: 153–68.

Lapchick, Richard. 2017. "The Racial and Gender Report Card." http://www.tidesport.org/reports.html (retrieved 1 February 2018).

Lapidus, Gail Warshofsky. 1978. *Women in Soviet Society: Equality, Development, and Social Change*. Berkeley, CA: University of California Press.

Lapidus, Ira M. 2002. *A History of Islamic Societies*, 2nd ed. Cambridge: Cambridge University Press.

Larson, Doran. 2013. "Why Scandinavian Prisons are Superior." *The Atlantic* https://www.theatlantic.com/international/archive/2013/09/why-scandinavian-prisons-are-superior/279949 (retrieved 25 January 2018).

Latimer, Jeff, Craig Dowden, and Danielle Muise. 2007. "The Effectiveness of Restorative Justice Practices: A Meta-Analysis." Research and Statistics Division, Department of Justice Canada. Retrieved July 26, 2015 (http://www.justice.gc.ca/eng/rp-pr/csj-sjc/jsp-sjp/rp01_1-dr01_1/rp01_1.pdf).

Lautard, Hugh, and Neil Guppy. 2008. "Multiculturalism or Vertical Mosaic? Occupational Stratification among Canadian Ethnic Groups." Pp. 120–29 in Robert J. Brym, ed., *Society in Question*, 5th ed. Toronto: Nelson.

_____. 2014. "Multiculturalism or Vertical Mosaic: Occupational Stratification among Canadian Ethnic Groups." Pp. 137–51 in Robert Brym, ed. *Society in Question*, 7th ed. Toronto: Nelson.

Lavoie, Yolande, and Jillian Oderkirk. 2000. "Social Consequences of Demographic Change." Pp. 2–5 in *Canadian Social Trends*, Volume 3. Toronto: Thompson Educational Publishing.

Law Society of British Columbia (The). 2015. "Quick Facts: About the Profession." Retrieved August 2, 2015 (https://www.lawsociety.bc.ca/page.cfm?cid=2189&t=About-the-Profession).

Le Bourdais, Céline, Sung-Hee Jeon, Shelley Clark, and Evelyne Lapierre-Adamcyk. 2016. "Impact of conjugal separation on women's income in Canada: Does the type of union matter?" *Demographic Research* 35(50): 1489–522.

Lee, Esther. 2015. "Caitlyn Jenner Insists Kris Jenner Knew about Women's Clothing, Breast Growth, Hormone Use." *US Weekly*. 1 June. Retrieved August 26, 2015 (http://www.usmagazine.com/celebrity-news/news/caitlyn-jenner-insists-kris-knew-about-womens-clothes-hormone-use-201516).

Lenton, Rhonda L. 1989. "Homicide in Canada and the U.S.A." *Canadian Journal of Sociology* 14: 163–78.

Levine, R. A., and D. T. Campbell. 1972. *Ethnocentrism: Theories of Conflict, Ethnic Attitudes, and Group Behavior*. New York: Wiley.

Levine, Robert, Suguru Sato, Tsukasa Hashimoto, and Jyoti Verma. 1995. "Love and Marriage in Eleven Cultures." *Journal of Cross-Cultural Psychology* 26, 5: 554–71.

Lewis, Bernard. 2002. *What Went Wrong? Western Impact and Middle Eastern Response*. New York: Oxford University Press.

Li, Peter. 1995. "Racial Supremacism under Social Democracy." *Canadian Ethnic Studies* 27, 1: 1–17.

_____. 1998. *The Chinese in Canada*, 2nd ed. Toronto: Oxford University Press.

"Life in plastic." 2002. *The Economist* 19 December. Retrieved August 29, 2015 (http://www.economist.com/node/1487595).

Lightfoot-Klein, Hanny, Cheryl Chase, Tim Hammond, and Ronald Goldman. 2000. "Genital Surgery on Children below the Age of Consent." Pp. 440–79 in Lenore T. Szuchman and Frank Muscarella, eds., *Psychological Perspectives on Human Sexuality*. New York: Wiley.

Lindert, Peter H. 2004. *Growing Public: Social Spending and Economic Growth since the Eighteenth Century*. Cambridge UK: Cambridge University Press.

Lips, Hilary M. 2014. *Gender: The Basics*. London, UK: Routledge.

Lipset, Seymour Martin. 1963. "Value Differences, Absolute or Relative: The English-Speaking Democracies." Pp. 248–73 in *The First New Nation: The United States in Historical Perspective*. New York: Basic Books.

_____. 1971. *Agrarian Socialism: The Cooperative Commonwealth Federation in Saskatchewan*, rev. ed. Berkeley, CA: University of California Press.

Lisak, David. 1992. "Sexual Aggression, Masculinity, and Fathers." *Signs* 16: 238–62.

Livernash, Robert, and Eric Rodenburg. 1998. "Population Change, Resources, and the Environment." *Population Bulletin* 53, 1. Retrieved August 25, 2000 (http://www.prb.org/pubs/population_bulletin/bu53-1.htm).

Lofland, John, and Lyn H. Lofland. *Analyzing Social Settings: A Guide to Qualitative Observation and Analysis*. Belmont, CA: Wadsworth/Thomson Learning.

Lopez, Donald S. 2001. *The Story of Buddhism: A Concise Guide to Its History and Teachings*. San Francisco: Harper.

López, Francesca A. 2017. "Altering the Trajectory of the Self-Fulfilling Prophecy: Asset-Based Pedagogy and Classroom Dynamics." *Journal of Teacher Education* 68(2): 193–212.

Lyon, David. 2007. *Surveillance Studies: An Overview* (Oxford, UK: Polity Press).

Lyon, David, and Elia Zureik, eds., 1996. *Computers, Surveillance, and Privacy*. Minneapolis, MN: University of Minnesota Press.

Macdonald, David, and Martha Friendly. 2017. *A Growing Concern: 2016 Child Care Fees in Canada's Big Cities*. Toronto: Canadian Centre for Policy Alternatives. https://www.policyalternatives.ca/growing-concern (retrieved 6 February 2018).

Mackay, Judith. 2000. *The Penguin Atlas of Human Sexual Behaviour*. New York: Penguin.

MacKinnon, Catharine A. 1979. *Sexual Harassment of Working Women*. New Haven, CT: Yale University Press.

Macklin, Eleanor D. 1980. "Nontraditional Family Forms: A Decade of Research." *Journal of Marriage and the Family* 42: 905–22.

MacLennan, Hugh. 1945. *Two Solitudes*. Toronto: Collins.

Mahony, Tina Hotton. 2013. "Women and the criminal justice system." Retrieved July 23, 2015 (http://www.statcan.gc.ca/pub/89-503-x/2010001/article/11416-eng.htm)

Mahony, Tina Hotton, Joanna Jacob, and Heather Hobson. 2017. "Women and the Criminal Justice System." Statistics Canada. http://www.statcan.gc.ca/pub/89-503-x/2015001/article/14785-eng.htm (retrieved 5 February 2018).

Makomaski, Illing E. M., and M. J. Kaiserman. 2004. "Mortality Attributable to Tobacco Use in Canada and Its Regions, 1998." *Canadian Journal of Public Health* 95: 38–44.

Manga, Pran, Douglas E. Angus, and William R. Swan. 1993. "Effective Management of Low Back Pain: It's Time to Accept the Evidence." *Journal of the Canadian Chiropractic Association* 37: 221–29.

Mangan, Dan. 2018. "Number of Americans without health insurance jumped by more than 3 million under Trump." *CNBC*. 16 January. https://www.cnbc.com/2018/01/16/americans-without-health-insurance-up-more-than-3-million-under-trump.html (retrieved 20 February 2018).

Manson, Jamie L. 2014. "Feminism in Faith: Sister Elizabeth Johnson's Challenge to the Vatican." Retrieved August 11, 2015 (http://www.buzzfeed.com/jamielmanson/feminism-in-faith-catholicism#.uu4gPgXOa).

Marcoux, Jacques, and Katie Nicholson. 2018. "Deadly Force: Fatal Encounters with Police in Canada, 2000–2017," *CBC News* https://newsinteractives.cbc.ca/longform-custom/deadly-force (retrieved 12 April 2018).

Marshall, S. L. A. 1947. *Men Against Fire: The Problem of Battle Command in Future War*. New York: Morrow.

Marshall, Thomas H. 1965. "Citizenship and Social Class." Pp. 71–134 in Thomas H. Marshall, ed., *Class, Citizenship, and Social Development: Essays by T. H. Marshall*. Garden City, NY: Anchor.

Martineau, Harriet. 1985. *Harriet Martineau on Women*, Gayle Graham Yates, ed. New Brunswick, NJ: Rutgers University Press.

Marx, Karl. 1904 [1859]. *A Contribution to the Critique of Political Economy*, N. Stone, trans. Chicago: Charles H. Kerr.

_____. 1967 [1867–94]. *Capital*, 3 vols. New York: International Publishers.

_____. 1970 [1843]. *Critique of Hegel's "Philosophy of Right,"* Annette Jolin and Joseph O'Malley, trans. Cambridge, MA: Harvard University Press.

Marx, Karl, and Friedrich Engels. 1972 [1848]. "Manifesto of the Communist Party." Pp. 331–62 in R. Tucker, ed., *The Marx–Engels Reader*. New York: Norton.

Massey, Douglas S., Camille Z. Charles, Garvey F. Lundy, and Mary J. Fischer. 2003. *The Source of the River: The Social Origins of Freshmen at America's Selective Colleges and Universities*. Princeton, NJ: Princeton University Press.

Matalon, Jean-Marc. 1997. "Jeanne Calment, World's Oldest Person, Dead at 122." *The Shawnee News-Star*, August 5. Retrieved May 2, 2000 (http://www.news-star.com/stories/080597/life1.html).

Matsueda, Ross L. 1988. "The Current State of Differential Association Theory." *Crime and Delinquency* 34: 277–306.

_____. 1992. "Reflected Appraisals, Parental Labeling, and Delinquency: Specifying a Symbolic Interactionist Theory." *American Journal of Sociology* 97: 1577–1611.

McAdam, Doug. 1982. *Political Process and the Development of Black Insurgency, 1930–1970*. Chicago: University of Chicago Press.

McCann, Clare. 2018. "School Finance." EdCentral. http://www.edcentral.org/edcyclopedia/school-finance/ (retrieved 1 March 2018).

McClelland, W. R. 1931. "Precautions for Workers in the Treating of Radium Ores." *Investigations in Ore Dressing and Metallurgy*. Ottawa: Bureau of Mines. Retrieved October 8, 2000 (http://www.ccnr.org/radium_warning.html).

McLanahan, Sara, Laura Tach, and Daniel Schneider. 2013. "The Causal Effects of Father Absence." *Annual Review of Sociology* 39: 399–427.

McLaren, Angus. 1990. *Our Own Master Race: Eugenics in Canada, 1885–1945*. Toronto: McClelland & Stewart.

McLuhan, Marshall. 1964. *Understanding Media: The Extensions of Man*. New York: McGraw-Hill.

McManners, John, ed. 1990. *Oxford Illustrated History of Christianity*. Oxford: Oxford University Press.

McNeill, William H. 1976. *Plagues and Peoples*. Garden City, NY: Anchor Press.

McPhail, Clark. 1994. "The Dark Side of Purpose: Individual and Collective Violence in Riots." *Sociological Quarterly* 35: 1–32.

McRoberts, Kenneth. 1988. *Quebec: Social Change and Political Crisis*, 3rd ed. Toronto: McClelland & Stewart.

McVey, Wayne W., Jr., and Warren E. Kalbach. 1995. *Canadian Population*. Scarborough, ON: Nelson.

Mead, George H. 1934. *Mind, Self and Society*. Chicago: University of Chicago Press.

Mehrabian, A. 1972. *Nonverbal Communication*. Chicago: Aldine-Atherton.

Melucci, Alberto. 1980. "The New Social Movements: A Theoretical Approach." *Social Science Information* 19: 199–226.

_____. 1995. "The New Social Movements Revisited: Reflections on a Sociological Misunderstanding." Pp. 107–19 in Louis Maheu, ed. *Social Classes and Social Movements: The Future of Collective Action*. London, UK: Sage.

Mendelson, Michael. 2006. "Aboriginal Peoples and Postsecondary Education in Canada." Caledon Institute of Social Policy. Retrieved August 2, 2015 (http://www.caledoninst.org/Publications/PDF/595ENG.pdf).

Menzies, C. R. 1999. "First Nations, Inequality and the Legacy of Colonialism." Pp. 236–44 in J. Curtis, E. Grabb, and N. Guppy, eds., *Social Inequality in Canada*, 3rd ed. Scarborough, ON: Prentice Hall Allyn and Bacon Canada Inc.

Merton, Robert K. 1938. "Social Structure and Anomie." *American Sociological Review* 3: 672–82.

_____. 1968 [1949]. *Social Theory and Social Structure*, enlarged ed. New York: Free Press.

Messerschmidt, James W. 1993. *Masculinities and Crime: Critique and Reconceptualization of Theory*. Lanham, MD: Roman and Littlefield.

_____. 2000. "Barbie Girls versus Sea Monsters: Children Constructing

Gender." *Gender & Society*, Special Issue 14, 6; December: 765–84.

Meyer, John W., Francisco O. Ramirez, and Yasemin Nuhoglu Soysal. 1992. "World Expansion of Mass Education, 1870–1980." *Sociology of Education* 65: 128–49.

Michael, Robert T., John H. Gagnon, Edward O. Laumann, and Gina Kolata. 1994. *Sex in America: A Definitive Survey*. Boston: Little, Brown and Company.

Microsoft Canada. 2015. Attention Spans. https://www.scribd.com/document/265348695/Microsoft-Attention-Spans-Research-Report (retrieved 11 January 2018).

Milanovic, Branko. 2005. *Worlds Apart: Measuring International and Global Inequality*. Princeton, NJ: Princeton University Press.

———. 2018. "There are two sides to today's global income inequality." *Globe and Mail* 22 January. https://www.theglobeandmail.com/report-on-business/rob-commentary/the-two-sides-of-todays-global-income-inequality/article37676680 (retrieved 29 January 2018).

Milgram, Stanley. 1974. *Obedience to Authority: An Experimental View*. New York: Harper.

Miller, J. R. 2018 [1989]. *Skyscrapers Hide the Heavens: A History of Native-Newcomer Relations in Canada*, 4th ed. Toronto: University of Toronto Press.

Milloy, John S. 1999. *A National Crime: The Canadian Government and the Residential School System, 1879 to 1986*. Winnipeg: University of Manitoba Press.

Mills, C. Wright. 1959. *The Sociological Imagination*. New York: Oxford University Press. Pp. 3–4.

Mitchinson, Wendy. 1993. "The Medical Treatment of Women." Pp. 391–421 in Sandra Burt, Lorraine Code, and Lindsay Dorney, eds., *Changing Patterns: Women in Canada*, 2nd ed. Toronto: McClelland & Stewart.

Montgomery, Malcolm. 1965. "The Six Nations and the Macdonald Franchise." *Ontario History* 57: 13.

Mooney, Linda A., David Knox, Caroline Schacht, and Adie Nelson. 2001. *Understanding Social Problems*. Toronto: Nelson Thomson Learning.

Morris, Aldon D. 1984. *The Origins of the Civil Rights Movement: Black Communities Organizing for Change*. New York: Free Press.

Morris, Norval, and David J. Rothman, eds. 1995. *The Oxford History of the Prison: The Practice of Punishment in Western Society*. New York: Oxford University Press.

Morrison, Nancy. 1987. "Separation and Divorce." Pp. 125–43 in M. J. Dymond, ed., *The Canadian Woman's Legal Guide*. Toronto: Doubleday.

Mosby, Ian. 2013. "Administering Colonial Science: Nutrition Research and Human Biomedical Experimentation in Aboriginal Communities and Residential Schools." *Histoire Sociale/Social History* 46(91): 145–72.

Moyser, Melissa. 2017. "Women and Paid Work." Statistics Canada. http://www.statcan.gc.ca/pub/89-503-x/2015001/article/14694-eng.htm (retrieved 4 February 2018).

Muir, Nicole, and Yvonne Bohr. 2014. "Contemporary Practice of Traditional Aboriginal Child Rearing: A Review." *First People Child and Family Review* 9(1): 66–69. http://journals.sfu.ca/fpcfr/index.php/FPCFR/article/download/231/218 (retrieved 5 April 2018).

Mundell, Helen. 1993. "How the Color Mafia Chooses Your Clothes." *American Demographics*, November. Retrieved May 2, 2000 (http://www.demographics.com/publications/ad/93_ad/9311_ad/ad281.htm).

Murdock, George Peter. 1937. "Comparative Data on the Division of Labor by Sex." *Social Forces* 15: 551–53.

———. 1949. *Social Structure*. New York: Macmillan.

Nakhaie, M. Reza, and Robert Brym. 1999. "The political attitudes of Canadian professors." *Canadian Journal of Sociology* (24, 3) 329–53.

———. 2011. "The ideological orientations of Canadian university professors." *Canadian Journal of Higher Education* 41(1): 18–33.

Nathoo, Zulekha. 2018. "Don't let Wonder Woman fool you: Female-led top movies still rare." *CBC News*. http://www.cbc.ca/news/entertainment/female-leads-still-exception-research-1.4550612 (retrieved 26 February 2018).

National Council of Welfare. 2004. *Poverty Profile 2001*. Catalogue No. SD25-1/2001E. Ottawa: Minister of Public Works and Government Services Canada.

National Health and Medical Research Council. 2015. https://www.nhmrc.gov.au/_files_nhmrc/publications/attachments/cam02a_information_paper.pdf (retrieved 24 May 2018).

National Oceanic and Atmospheric Administration. 2017. "Mauna Loa $CO_2$ annual mean data." ftp://aftp.cmdl.noaa.gov/products/trends/co2/co2_annmean_mlo.txt (retrieved 16 November 2017).

National Rifle Association. 2005. *Guns, Gun Ownership, & RTC at All-Time Highs, Less 'Gun Control,' and Violent Crime at 30-Year Low*. Retrieved December 29, 2005 (http://www.nraila.org/Issues/FactSheets/Read.aspx?ID5126).

National Science Foundation. 2017. "National Patterns of R&D Resources: 2014–15 Data Update." https://www-nsf-gov.myaccess.library.utoronto.ca/statistics/2017/nsf17311/#chp2 (retrieved 5 April 2018).

Native Women's Association of Canada. 2015. "Fact Sheet: Missing and Murdered Aboriginal Women and Girls." https://www.nwac.ca/wp-content/uploads/2015/05/Fact_Sheet_Missing_and_Murdered_Aboriginal_Women_and_Girls.pdf (retrieved 25 January 2018).

Neal, Mark Anthony. 1999. *What the Music Said: Black Popular Music and Black Public Culture*. New York: Routledge.

Neil, Christopher. 2014. "Just how many words does Arabic have for 'camel'?" *Medium.com*. https://medium.com/@chrisneil/just-how-many-words-does-arabic-have-for-camel-da5b58022564 (retrieved 14 March 2018).

Nelson, Adie, and Barrie W. Robinson. 2002. *Gender in Canada*, 2nd ed. Toronto: Prentice Hall.

Newman, Rick. 2013. "Here's How Lousy Life Is in North Korea." *U.S. News and World Report*. 12 April. https://www.usnews.com/news/blogs/rick-newman/2013/04/12/heres-how-lousy-life-is-in-north-korea (retrieved 18 February 2018).

Nikiforuk, Andrew. 1998. "Echoes of the Atomic Age: Cancer Kills Fourteen Aboriginal Uranium Workers." *Calgary Herald*, 14 March: A1, A4. Retrieved October 8, 2000 (http://www.ccnr.org/deline_deaths.html).

_____. 1999. "A Question of Style." *Time* 31; May: 58–59.

Nisbett, Richard E. 2011. "The Achievement Gap: Past, Present and Future." *Daedalus* 140(2): 90–100.

Nisbett, Richard E., Kaiping Peng, Incheol Choi, and Ara Norenzayan. 2001. "Culture and Systems of Thought: Holistic versus Analytic Cognition." *Psychological Review* 108: 291–310.

Norton, Kevin I., Timothy S. Olds, Scott Olive, and Stephen Dank. 1996. "Ken and Barbie at Life Size." *Sex Roles* 34, 3–4; February: 287–94.

Nowak, Martin A., Robert M. May, and Karl Sigmund. 1995. "The Arithmetics of Mutual Help." *Scientific American* 272, 6: 76–81.

O'Neil, Cathy. 2016. *Weapons of Math Destruction: How Big Data Increases Inequality and Threatens Democracy*. New York: Crown.

Oberschall, Anthony. 1973. *Social Conflict and Social Movements*. Englewood Cliffs, NJ: Prentice-Hall.

Oderkirk, Jillian, and Clarence Lochhead. 1992. "Lone Parenthood: Gender Differences." *Canadian Social Trends* 27; Spring: 16–19. Catalogue No. 11-008-XPE.

Oeppen, Jim, and James W. Vaupel. 2002. "Demography: Broken Limits to Life Expectancy." *Science* 296: 1029–31.

Office of the Correctional Investigator. 2013. "Aboriginal offenders—A critical situation." Retrieved July 23, 2015 (http://www.oci-bec.gc.ca/cnt/rpt/oth-aut/oth-aut20121022info-eng.aspx)

Ogbu, John U. 2003. *Black American Students in an Affluent Suburb: A Study of Academic Disengagement*. Mahwah, NJ: Erlbaum.

Omi, Michael, and Howard Winant. 1986. *Racial Formation in the United States*. New York: Routledge.

Ontario Consultants on Religious Tolerance. 2005. *Information about Religion in Canada*. Retrieved November 14, 2005 (http://www.religioustolerance.org/can_rel.htm).

"Ontario knew about mercury contamination near Grassy Narrows in 1990: Report." 2017. *CBC News* 12 November. http://www.cbc.ca/news/canada/thunder-bay/mercury-report-grassy-narrows-1.4399441 (retrieved 18 February 2018).

Ore, Timothy, and Astrid Birgden. 2003. "Does Prison Work: A View from Criminology." *Policy* 19, 2. Retrieved March 8, 2010 (http://www.cis.org.au/policy/winter03/polwin03-9.pdf).

Oreopoulos, Philip, and Diane Dechief. 2011. "Why do some employers prefer to interview Matthew, but not Samir?" University of British Columbia, Metropolis British Columbia, Working Paper Series, No. 11–13. Retrieved August 2, 2015 (http://mbc.metropolis.net/assets/uploads/files/wp/2011/WP11-13.pdf).

Organisation for Economic Co-operation and Development (OECD). 2017. "Obesity Update 2017." https://www.oecd.org/els/health-systems/Obesity-Update-2017.pdf (retrieved 17 February 2018).

_____.2018. "PISA 2015 Results in Focus." https://www.google.ca/url?sa=t&rct=j&q=&esrc=s&source=web&cd=13&ved=0ahUKEwir88Om0cjZAhWCtlkKHZd_CVUQFghtMAw&url=https%3A%2F%2Fwww.oecd.org%2Fpisa%2Fpisa-2015-results-in-focus.pdf&usg=AOvVaw3chnWopdeY00Tmps_4su2B (retrieved 28 February 2018).

_____. 2018a. "Income inequality." https://data.oecd.org/inequality/income-inequality.htm (retrieved 27 January 2018).

_____. 2018b. "Spending on tertiary education." https://data.oecd.org/eduresource/spending-on-tertiary-education.htm (retrieved 2 March 2018).

Orgibet, A., M.-F. Le Heuzey, and M.-C. Mouren. 2008. "Psychopathologie des enfants élevés en milieu homoparental lesbien: Revue de la littérature." *Archives de pédiatrie* 15: 202–10.

Ossowski, Stanislaw. 1963. *Class Structure in the Social Consciousness*, S. Patterson, trans. London, UK: Routledge and Kegan Paul.

Oved, Marco Chown. 2016. "CRA investigating 85 Canadians for tax evasion tied to Panama Papers." *Toronto Star* 14 November. https://www.thestar.com/news/world/2016/11/14/cra-investigating-85-canadians-for-tax-evasion-tied-to-panama-papers.html (retrieved 29 January 2018).

Owen, Michelle K. 2001. "'Family' as a Site of Contestation: Queering the Normal or Normalizing the Queer?" Pp. 86–102 in Terry Goldie, ed., *In a Queer Country: Gay and Lesbian Studies in the Canadian Context*. Vancouver: Arsenal Pulp Press.

Pammett, Jon H. 1997. "Getting Ahead Around the World." Pp. 67–86 in Alan Frizzell and Jon H. Pammett, eds., *Social Inequality in Canada*. Ottawa: Carleton University Press.

Pape, Robert A. 2003. "The Strategic Logic of Suicide Terrorism." *American Political Science Review* 97: 343–61.

Paragg, Jillian. 2015. "'Canadian-First': Mixed Race Self-Identification and Canadian Belonging." *Canadian Ethnic Studies* 47(2): 21–44.

Parke, Ross D. 2001. "Paternal Involvement in Infancy: The Role of Maternal and Paternal Attitudes." *Journal of Family Psychology* 15, 4; December: 555–58.

_____. 2002. "Parenting in the New Millennium: Prospects, Promises and Pitfalls." Pp. 65–93 in James P. McHale and Wendy S. Grolnick, eds., *Retrospect and Prospect in the Psychological Study of Families*. Mahwah, NJ: Lawrence Erlbaum Associates, Inc.

Parr, Chris. 2013. "Not Staying the Course." *Inside Higher Education* 10 May. https://www.insidehighered.com/news/2013/05/10/new-study-low-mooc-completion-rates (retrieved 1 March 2018).

Parshall, Gerald. 1998. "Brotherhood of the Bomb." *US News and World Report* 125, 7; 17–24 August: 64–68.

Parsons, Talcott. 1942. "Age and Sex in the Social Structure of the United States." *American Sociological Review* 7: 604–16.

_____. 1951. *The Social System*. New York: Free Press.

_____. 1955. "The American Family: Its Relation to Personality and to the Social Structure." Pp. 3–33 in Talcott Parsons and Robert F. Bales, eds., *Family, Socialization and Interaction Process*. New York: Free Press.

Patented Medicine Prices Review Board. 2011. *Annual Report 2011*. Retrieved March 16, 2013 (http://www.pmprb-cepmb.gc.ca/CMFiles/Publications/Annual%20Reports/2011/2011-Annual-Report_EN_Final-for-Posting.pdf).

_____. 2016. "Annual Report 2016." http://www.pmprb-cepmb.gc.ca/view.asp?ccid=1334#a1 (retrieved 20 February 2018).

Pelletier, Rose, and Terrence J. Thomas. 1998. "Financing University Education in Canada." Statistics Canada. http://publications.gc.ca/Collection-R/LoPBdP/BP/bp460-e.htm (retrieved 2 March 2018).

Perreault, Samuel. 2015. "Criminal victimization in Canada, 2014." *Juristat* (Statistics Canada). Retrieved July 1, 2016 (http://www.statcan.gc.ca/pub/85-002-x/85-002-x2015001-eng.htm).

Perrow, Charles B. 1984. *Normal Accidents*. New York: Basic Books.

Perry, Gina. 2013. *Behind the Shock Machine: The Untold Story of the Notorious Milgram Psychology Experiments*. New York: New Press.

"Persons Case." *The Canadian Encyclopedia* (https://www.thecanadianencyclopedia.ca/en/article/persons-case (retrieved 6 February 2018).

Peters, John F. 1994. "Gender Socialization of Adolescents in the Home: Research and Discussion." *Adolescence* 29: 913–34.

Petersson, Bengt Rodrigo Mariscal, and Kotaro Ishi. 2017. "Women Are Key for Future Growth: Evidence from Canada." *International Money Fund Working Paper*. https://www.imf.org/en/Publications/WP/Issues/2017/07/19/Women-Are-Key-for-Future-Growth-Evidence-from-Canada-45047 (retrieved 6 February 2018).

Pettigrew, Thomas F., and Linda R. Tropp. 2006. "A Meta-Analytic Test of Intergroup Contact Theory." *Journal of Personality and Social Psychology* 90(5): 751–83.

Pew Research Center. 2002. *The Pew Global Attitudes Project: How Global Publics View Their Lives, Their Countries, the World, America*. Reprinted by permission of The Pew Global Attitudes Project. Retrieved April 12, 2003 (http://www.people-press.org).

_____. 2018. "Religious Landscape Study." http://www.pewforum.org/religious-landscape-study (retrieved 12 February 2018).

Piaget, Jean, and Bärbel Inhelder. 1969. *The Psychology of the Child*, Helen Weaver, trans. New York: Basic Books.

Pittis, Don. 2018. "After years hidden in the background, artificial intelligence is getting pushy: and experts say we'll get used to it." *CBC News*. 22 May. http://www.cbc.ca/news/business/artificial-intelligence-intrusive-1.4667165 (retrieved 24 May 2018).

Piven, Frances Fox, and Richard A. Cloward. 1977. *Poor People's Movements: Why They Succeed, How They Fail*. New York: Vintage.

_____ and Richard A. Cloward. 1993. *Regulating the Poor: The Functions of Public Welfare*, updated ed. New York: Vintage.

Plummer, Kenneth. 1995. *Telling Sexual Stories: Power, Change and Social Worlds*. London, UK: Routledge.

Pool, Robert. 1997. *Beyond Engineering: How Society Shapes Technology*. New York: Oxford University Press.

Popenoe, David. 1988. *Disturbing the Nest: Family Change and Decline in Modern Societies*. New York: Aldine de Gruyter.

_____. 1996. *Life without Father: Compelling New Evidence that Fatherhood and Marriage Are Indispensable for the Good of Children and Society*. New York: Martin Kessler Books.

_____. 1998. "The Decline of Marriage and Fatherhood." Pp. 312–19 in John J. Macionis and Nijole V. Benokraitis, eds., *Seeing Ourselves: Classic, Contemporary and Cross-Cultural Readings in Sociology*, 4th ed. Upper Saddle River, NJ: Prentice Hall.

Population Reference Bureau. 2017. "2017 World Population Data Sheet." http://www.prb.org/Publications/Datasheets/2017/2017-world-population-data-sheet.aspx (retrieved 17 February 2017).

Porter, Jody. 2016. "Industry off the hook for mercury monitoring at mill that poisoned Grassy Narrows First Nation." http://www.cbc.ca/news/canada/thunder-bay/mercury-monitoring-grassy-narrows-1.3712441 (retrieved 18 February 2018).

_____. 2017. "First Nations woman dies after being hit by trailer hitch thrown from passing car in Thunder Bay, Ont." *CBC News*. 4 July. http://www.cbc.ca/news/canada/thunder-bay/trailer-hitch-death-1.4189426 (retrieved 20 February 2018.

Porter, John. 1965. *The Vertical Mosaic: An Analysis of Social Class and Power in Canada*. Toronto: University of Toronto Press.

_____. 1979. *The Measure of Canadian Society: Education, Equality, and Opportunity*. Toronto: Gage.

Postman, Neil. 1982. *The Disappearance of Childhood*. New York: Delacorte.

Potârcă, Gina, and Melinda Mills. 2015. "Racial Preferences in Online Dating across European Countries." *European Sociological Review* 31(3): 326–41.

Powers, Ann. 2009. "Frank Talk with Lady Gaga." *Los Angeles Times* 13 December.

Pred, Allan R. 1973. *Urban Growth and the Circulation of Information*. Cambridge, MA: Harvard University Press.

Press, Andrea L. 1991. *Women Watching Television: Gender, Class and Generation in the American Television Experience*. Philadelphia: University of Pennsylvania Press.

Press, Andrea L., and Elizabeth R. Cole. 1999. *Speaking of Abortion: Television and Authority in the Lives of Women*. Chicago: University of Chicago Press.

Pressman, Laurie. 2016. "PANTONE Fashion Color Report Spring 2017." https://www.pantone.com/fashion-color-report-spring-2017 (retrieved 30 March 2018);

_____. 2017. "Multi-faceted palette broadens opportunity for self-expression with 12 call-out shades and 4 seasonal classics." https://www.pantone.com/fashion-color-trend-report-new-york-spring-2018 (retrieved 30 March 2018).

Pringle, Ramona. 2017. "Finstas: Using 'fake' social media accounts to reveal your authentic self." *CBC News*. 11 September. http://www.cbc.ca/news/technology/instagram-finsta-rinsta-ramona-pringle-1.4279550 (retrieved 25 February 2018).

PROOF: Food Insecurity Policy Research. 2018. "Household Food Insecurity in Canada." http://proof.utoronto.ca/food-insecurity/ (retrieved 2 February 2018).

Provine, Robert R. 2000. *Laughter: A Scientific Investigation*. New York: Penguin.

Public Safety Canada. 2012. *Youth Gangs in Canada: What Do We Know?* Retrieved December 19, 2012 (http://www.publicsafety.gc.ca/prg/cp/bldngevd/2007-yg-1-eng.aspx).

Puxley, Chinta. 2013. "Brian Sinclair, Winnipeg Aboriginal Who Died

After 34-Hour Hour Hospital Wait, Assumed 'Sleeping It Off.'" *Huffpost* 29 October. http://www.huffingtonpost.ca/2013/08/29/brian-sinclair-winnipeg_n_3837008.html (retrieved 20 February 2018).

Raphael, D. 2004. *Social Determinants of Health: Canadian Perspectives*. Toronto: Canadian Scholars' Press.

Rapp, Rayna, and Ellen Ross. 1986. "The 1920s: Feminism, Consumerism and Political Backlash in the United States." Pp. 52–62 in J. Friedlander, B. Cook, A. Kessler-Harris, and C. Smith-Rosenberg, eds. *Women in Culture and Politics*. Bloomington, IN: Indiana University Press.

Reading, Charlotte Loppie, and Fred Wien. 2009. *Health Inequalities and Social Determinants of Aboriginal Peoples' Health*. National Collaborating Centre for Aboriginal Health.

Reimann, Renate. 1997. "Does Biology Matter? Lesbian Couples' Transition to Parenthood and Their Division of Labor." *Qualitative Sociology* 20, 2: 153–85.

Reiter, Keramet, Lori Sexton and Jennifer Sumner. 2016. "Denmark doesn't treat its prisoners like prisoners—and it's good for everyone." *Washington Post* 2 February. https://www.washingtonpost.com/posteverything/wp/2016/02/02/denmark-doesnt-treat-its-prisoners-like-prisoners-and-its-good-for-everyone/?utm_term=.5b76e6fe22de (retrieved 25 January 2018).

Reitz, Jeffrey G. 2011. "Tapping Immigrants' Skills." Pp. 178–93 in. Robert Brym, ed., *Society in Question*, 6th ed. Toronto: Nelson.

Reputation Institute. 2018. "Country RepTrak®—Annual Ranking of Most Reputable Countries Worldwide." https://www.reputationinstitute.com/ (retrieved 2 February 2018).

Richler, Mordecai. 1959. *The Apprenticeship of Duddy Kravitz*. Don Mills, ON: A. Deutsch.

Riley, Tasha, and Charles Ungerleider. 2012. "Self-fulfilling prophecy: How teachers' attributions, expectations, and stereotypes influence the learning opportunities afforded aboriginal students. *Canadian Journal of Education* 35(2): 303–33.

Roberts, Julian, and Thomas Gabor. 1990. "Race and Crime: A Critique." *Canadian Journal of Criminology* 92, 2; April: 291–313.

Robinson, Richard H., and Willard L. Johnson. 1997. *The Buddhist Religion: A Historical Introduction*, 4th ed. Belmont, CA: Wadsworth.

Roche, Maurice. 1995. "Rethinking Citizenship and Social Movements: Themes in Contemporary Sociology and Neoconservative Ideology." Pp. 186–219 in Louis Maheu, ed., *Social Classes and Social Movements: The Future of Collective Action*. London, UK: Sage.

Rodinson, Maxime. 1996. *Muhammad*, 2nd ed. Anne Carter, trans. London, UK: Penguin.

Roediger, David R. 1991. *The Wages of Whiteness: Race and the Making of the American Working Class*. London, UK: Verso.

Rogers, Simon. 2012. "Healthcare spending around the world, country by country." *The Guardian* 30 June. Retrieved August 7, 2015 (http://www.theguardian.com/news/datablog/2012/jun/30/healthcare-spending-world-country).

Romaniuc, Anatole. 1984. "Fertility in Canada: From Baby-Boom to Baby-Bust." *Current Demographic Analysis*. Ottawa: Statistics Canada.

Romero-Sánchez, Mónica, H. Carretero-Dios, J. L.Megías, M. Moya, and T. E. Ford. 2017. "Sexist Humor and Rape Proclivity: The Moderating Role of Joke Teller Gender and Severity of Sexual Assault Authors." *Violence against Women* 23(8): 951–72).

Rootes, Chris. 1995. "A New Class? The Higher Educated and the New Politics." Pp. 220–35 in Louis Maheu, ed., *Social Classes and Social Movements: The Future of Collective Action*. London, UK: Sage.

Rosella, Louie. 2018. "'Completely unfathomable': Brampton mother and daughter murdered in their home." *Brampton Guardian* 15 January. https://www.bramptonguardian.com/news-story/8072870--completely-unfathomable-brampton-mother-and-daughter-murdered-in-their-home/ (retrieved 7 February 2018).

Rosenberg, Eric. 2016. "The Business of Google (GOOG)." https://www.investopedia.com/articles/investing/020515/business-google.asp (retrieved 25 February 2016).

Rosenbluth, Susan C. 1997. "Is Sexual Orientation a Matter of Choice?" *Psychology of Women Quarterly* 21: 595–610.

Rosenfeld, Michael J., and Reuben J. Thomas. 2012. "Searching for a Mate: The Rise of the Internet as a Social Intermediary." *American Sociological Review* 77: 523–47.

Rosenthal, Robert, and Lenore Jacobson. 1968. *Pygmalion in the Classroom: Teacher Expectation and Pupils' Intellectual Development*. New York: Holt, Rinehart, and Winston.

Rostow, Walt W. 1960. *The Stages of Economic Growth: A Non-Communist Manifesto*. New York: Cambridge University Press.

Roth, Cecil. 1961. *A History of the Jews*. New York: Schocken.

Rough, Lisa. 2017. "The History of Cannabis in Canada." *Leafly*. https://www.leafly.com/news/canada/history-cannabis-canada (retrieved 26 January 2018).

Royal Canadian Mounted Police. 2015. "Missing and Murdered Aboriginal Women: 2015 Update to the National Operational Overview." http://www.rcmp-grc.gc.ca/en/missing-and-murdered-aboriginal-women-2015-update-national-operational-overview#p4 (retrieved 24 January 2018).

Rupp, Leila J., and Verta Taylor. 2010. "Straight Girls Kissing." *Contexts* 9, 4: 28–32.

Rural Communities Impact Policy Project. 2003. "Painting the Landscape of Rural Nova Scotia." Retrieved March 30, 2010 (http://www.ruralnovascotia.ca/RCIP/PDF/RR_final_full.pdf).

Russell, Andrew. 2016. "6 in 10 Canadians support abortion under any circumstances: Ipsos poll." https://globalnews.ca/news/2535846/6-in-10-canadians-support-abortion-under-any-circumstances-ipsos-poll (retrieved 8 February 2018).

_____. 2017. "Most Canadians say they have trust in traditional news media: Ipsos poll." *Global News* 26 May 2017. https://globalnews.ca/news/3478928/most-canadians-say-they-have-some-trust-in-traditional-news-media-ipsos-poll (retrieved 1 January 2018).

Ryan, Kathryn M., and Jeanne Kanjorski. 1998. "The Enjoyment of Sexist Humor, Rape Attitudes, and Relationship Aggression in College Students." *Sex Roles* 38: 743–56.

Sager, Eric. 2000. "Canadian Families—A Historian's Perspective." Pp. vii–xi in *Profiling Canada's Families II*. Nepean, ON: Vanier Institute for the Family.

Sampson, Robert, and John H. Laub. 1993. *Crime in the Making: Pathways and Turning Points through Life*. Cambridge, MA: Harvard University Press.

Samuda, R. J., D. Crawford, C. Philip, and W. Tinglen. 1980. *Testing, Assessment, and Counselling of Minority Students: Current Methods in Ontario*. Toronto: Ontario Ministry of Education.

Samuelsson, Kurt. 1961 [1957]. *Religion and Economic Action*, E. French, trans. Stockholm: Scandinavian University Books.

Sarlo, Christopher. 2001. *Measuring Poverty in Canada*. Vancouver, BC: The Fraser Institute.

Saul, Heather. 2015. "Gywneth Paltrow: Unusual advice from lifestyle website Goop." *The Independent* 10 December. http://www.independent.co.uk/news/people/gywneth-paltrows-goop-worst-advice-from-the-eccentric-lifestyle-website-a6704126.html (retrieved 19 February 2018).

Savoie, Josée. 2002. "Crime Statistics in Canada, 2001." *Juristat* 22, 6. Catalogue No. 85-002-XPE. Ottawa: Canadian Centre for Justice Statistics and Statistics Canada.

Sawa, Timothy, and Lori Ward. 2015. "Sex assault reporting on Canadian campuses worryingly low, say experts." *CBC News*. 6 February. http://www.cbc.ca/news/canada/sex-assault-reporting-on-canadian-campuses-worryingly-low-say-experts-1.2948321 (retrieved 5 February 2018).

Sawyer, Diane. 2015. "Bruce Jenner—The Interview." *20/20* 24 April. Retrieved August 26, 2015 http://abc.go.com/shows/2020/listing/2015-04/24-bruce-jenner-the-interview).

Saxton, Lloyd. 1990. *The Individual, Marriage, and the Family*, 9th ed. Belmont, CA: Wadsworth.

Schimel, J., J. Hayes, T. Williams, and J. Jahrig. 2007. "Is Death Really the Worm at the Core? Converging Evidence that Worldview Threat Increases Death-Thought Accessibility." *Journal of Personality and Social Psychology* 92(5): 789–803.

Schoen, Cathy, Robin Osborn, Phuong Trang Huynh, Michelle Doty, Karen Davis, Kinga Zapert, and Jordan Peugh. 2004. "Primary Care and Health System Performance: Adults' Experiences in Five Countries." *Health Affairs* (Web Exclusive) 4.487. Retrieved September 4, 2008 (http://content.healthaffairs.org/cgi/content/abstract/hlthaff.w4.487v1).

Schudson, Michael. 1991. "National News Culture and the Rise of the Informational Citizen." Pp. 265–82 in Alan Wolfe, ed., *America at Century's End*. Berkeley, CA: University of California Press.

Schwartz, Stephen. 2003. *The Two Faces of Islam: The House of Sa'ud from Tradition to Terror*. New York: Doubleday.

Scott, Wilbur J. 1990. "PTSD in DSM-III: A Case in the Politics of Diagnosis and Disease." *Social Problems* 37: 294–310.

Scutti, Susan. 2013. "Organ Trafficking: An International Crime Infrequently Punished." *Medical Daily* 9 July. http://www.medicaldaily.com/organ-trafficking-international-crime-infrequently-punished-247493 (retrieved 17 January 2018).

Seiter, Ellen. 1999. *Television and New Media Audiences*. Oxford, UK: Clarendon Press.

"Sex Dust." 2018. https://shop.goop.com/shop/products/sex-dust (retrieved 19 February 2018).

Shah, Dhawal. 2017. "MOOCs Find Their Audience: Learners and Universities." *Class Central*. https://www.class-central.com/report/moocs-find-audience-professional-learners-universities/ (retrieved 1 March 2018).

———. 2018. "By the Numbers: MOOCS in 2017." https://www.class-central.com/report/mooc-stats-2017/ (retrieved 1 March 2018).

Shanahan, Michael J., Shaun Bauldry, and Jason Freeman. 2010. "Beyond Mendel's Ghost." *Contexts* 9(4): 34–39.

Shattuck, Roger. 1980. *The Forbidden Experiment: The Story of the Wild Boy of Aveyron*. New York: Farrar, Straus, and Giroux.

Shea, Sarah E., Kevin Gordon, Ann Hawkins, Janet Kawchuk, and Donna Smith. 2000. "Pathology in the Hundred-Acre Wood: A Neurodevelopmental Perspective on A. A. Milne." *Canadian Medical Association Journal* 163, 12: 1557–59.

Retrieved December 12, 2000 (http://www.cma.ca/cmaj/vol-163/issue-12/1557.htm).

Sheehy, Elizabeth. 2003. "From Women's Duty to Resist to Men's Duty to Ask: How Far Have We Come?" Pp. 576–81 in T. Brettel Dawson, ed., *Women, Law and Social Change: Core Readings and Current Issues*, 4th ed. Concord, ON: Captus Press.

Shekelle, Paul G. 1998. "What Role for Chiropractic in Health Care?" *New England Journal of Medicine* 339: 1074–75.

Sherif, Muzafer, L. J. Harvey, B. Jack White, William R. Hood, and Carolyn W. Sherif. 1988 [1961]. *The Robber's Cave Experiment: Intergroup Conflict and Cooperation*, reprinted ed. Middletown, CT: Wesleyan University Press.

Sherrill, Robert. 1997. "The Year ('97) in Corporate Crime." *The Nation* 7 April: 11–20.

Shkilnyk, Anastasia. 1985. *A Poison Stronger than Love: The Destruction of an Ojibway Community*. New Haven, CT: Yale University Press.

Shorter, Edward. 1997. *A History of Psychiatry: From the Era of the Asylum to the Age of Prozac*. New York: John Wiley and Sons.

Sigal, Samuel. 2014. "Feminism in Faith: Sara Hurwitz's Road to Becoming the First Ordained Orthodox Jewish Rabba." Retrieved August 11, 2015 (http://www.buzzfeed.com/sigalsamuel/feminism-in-faith-orthodox-judaism#.yb9jXNxnVz).

Silberman, Steve. 2000. "Talking to Strangers." *Wired* 8, 5: 225–33, 288–96.

Silcoff, Sean. 2018. "More brains: Microsoft leads hunt to bring global AI experts to Canada." *Globe and Mail* 24 January. https://www.theglobeandmail.com/report-on-business/more-brains-microsoft-leads-hunt-to-bring-global-ai-experts-to-canada/article37712144/ (retrieved 24 January 2018).

"Silent Boom (The)." 1997. Peter Brimelow. *Forbes* 7 July: 170–71.

Simons, Gary F., and Charles D. Fennig, eds. 2017. Ethnologue: Languages of the World, 20th ed. Dallas: SIL International. http://www.ethnologue.com (retrieved 9 January 2018).

Singh, Hira. 2014. *Recasting Caste: From the Scared to the Profane*. New Delhi: Sage.

Singh, I. P. 2018. "Punjabi man kills wife, mother-in-law in Canada." *Times of*

*India* 15 January. https://timesofindia.indiatimes.com/city/chandigarh/punjabi-man-kills-wife-mother-in-law-in-canada/articleshow/62501448.cms (retrieved 7 February 2018).

Sissing, T. W. 1996. "Some Missing Pages: The Black Community in the History of Québec and Canada." Retrieved June 14, 2002 (http://www.qesnrecit.qc.ca/mpages/title.htm).

Skolnick, Arlene. 1991. *Embattled Paradise: The American Family in an Age of Uncertainty*. New York: Basic Books.

Slater, Amy, and Marika Tiggemann. 2016. "Little girls in a grownup world: Exposure to sexualized media, internalization of sexualization messages, and body image in 6–9-year-old girls." *Body Image* 18(1): 19–22.

Small, J. S. M. Chan, E. Drance, J. Globerman, W. Hulko, D. O'Connor, J. Perry, L. Stern, L. Ho. 2015. "Verbal and nonverbal indicators of quality of communication between care staff and residents in ethno-culturally and linguistically diverse long-term care settings." *Journal of Cross-Cultural Gerontology* 30(3): 285–304.

Smiler, Andrew P. 2011. "Sexual Strategies Theory: Built for the Short Term or the Long Term?" *Sex Roles* 64: 603–12.

———. 2013. *Challenging Casanova: Beyond the Stereotype of the Promiscuous Young Male*. San Francisco, CA: Jossey-Bass.

Smith, Anthony. 1980. *Goodbye Gutenberg: The Newspaper Revolution of the 1980s*. New York: Oxford University Press.

Smith, Christian. 1991. *The Emergence of Liberation Theology: Radical Religion and Social Movement Theory*. Chicago: University of Chicago Press.

Smith, Elliot Blair. 2012. "American Dream Fades for Generation Y Professionals." *Bloomberg.com*, December 21. Retrieved December 30, 2012 (http://www.bloomberg.com/news/2012-12-21/american-dream-fades-for-generation-y-professionals.html).

Smith, Noah. 2018. "Social Media Looks Like the New Opiate of the Masses." *Bloomberg.com* 4 April. https://www.bloomberg.com/view/articles/2018-04-04/social-media-use-bears-similarities-to-drug-addiction (retrieved 6 April 2018).

Smith, Stacy L., Marc Choueiti, Ashley Prescott, and Katherine Pieper. 2012. "Gender Roles and Occupations: A Look at Character Attributes and Job-Related Aspirations in Film and Television." Emmitsburg, MD: Mount St. Mary's University. https://www.google.ca/url?sa=t&rct=j&q=&esrc=s&source=web&cd=1&cad=rja&uact=8&ved=0ahUKEwjtkdWG3r_ZAhUO0IMKHZ3tDV0QFggpMAA&url=https%3A%2F%2Fseejane.org%2Fwp-content%2Fuploads%2Ffull-study-gender-roles-and-occupations-v2.pdf&usg=AOvVaw2O5WEaxl960TJpIvH9N-DA (retrieved November 12, 2016).

Smyth, Julie. 2003. "Sweden Ranked as Best Place to Have a Baby: Canada Places Fifth on Maternity Leave, 15th for Benefits." *National Post*, January 17. Retrieved June 27, 2004 (http://www.childcarecanada.org/ccin/2003/ccin1_17_03.html).

Snider, Laureen. 1999. "White-Collar Crime." P. 2504 in James H. Marsh, ed., *The Canadian Encyclopedia,* Year 2000 edition. Toronto: McClelland & Stewart.

Snow, David A., E. Burke Rochford, Jr., Steven K. Worden, and Robert D. Benford. 1986. "Frame Alignment Processes, Micromobilization, and Movement Participation." *American Sociological Review* 51: 464–81.

Sobolewski, Juliana M., and Valarie King. 2005. "The Importance of the Coparental Relationship for Nonresident Fathers' Ties to Children." *Journal of Marriage and Family* 67(5): 1196–212.

Sofsky, Wolfgang. 1997 [1993]. *The Order of Terror: The Concentration Camp*, William Templer, trans. Princeton, NJ: Princeton University Press.

Sokoloff, Heather. 2001. "Wealth Affects Test Scores." *National Post* December 5: A17. Retrieved January 22, 2004 (http://www.sgc.ca/Efact/emyths.htm).

Solon, Olivia, and Sam Levin. 2016. "How Google's search algorithm spreads false information with a right wing bias." *The Guardian* 16 December. https://www.theguardian.com/technology/2016/dec/16/google-autocomplete-rightwing-bias-algorithm-political-propaganda (retrieved 25 February 2018).

Spade, Joan Z. 2001. "Gender and Education in the United States." Pp. 270–78 in Jeanne H. Ballantine and Joan Z. Spade, eds., *Schools and Society: A Sociological Approach to Education*. Belmont, CA: Wadsworth.

Sparkes, Ainsley. 2017. "Canadian Book Market 2016: Infographic." https://www.booknetcanada.ca/blog/2017/3/8/canadian-book-market-2016-infographic (retrieved 24 February 2018).

Spines, Christine. 2010. "Lady Gaga Wants You." *Cosmopolitan*, UK edition May: 50–54.

Spitz, René A. 1945. "Hospitalism: An Inquiry into the Genesis of Psychiatric Conditions in Early Childhood." Pp. 53–74 in *The Psychoanalytic Study of the Child*, Vol. 1. New York: International Universities Press.

———. 1962. "Autoerotism Re-Examined: The Role of Early Sexual Behavior Patterns in Personality Formation." Pp. 283–315 in *The Psychoanalytic Study of the Child*, Vol. 17. New York: International Universities Press.

Spitzer, Steven. 1980. "Toward a Marxian Theory of Deviance." Pp. 175–91 in Delos H. Kelly, ed. *Criminal Behavior: Readings in Criminology*. New York: St. Martin's Press.

Srigley, Ron. 2018. "Whose university is it anyway?" *Los Angeles Review of Books* 22 February. https://lareviewofbooks.org/article/whose-university-is-it-anyway/ (retrieved 3 March 2018).

Stacey, Judith. 1996. *Brave New Families: Stories of Domestic Upheaval in Late Twentieth Century America*. New York: Basic Books.

Stark, Rodney, and William Sims Bainbridge. 1979. "Of Churches, Sects, and Cults: Preliminary Concepts for a Theory of Religious Movements." *Journal for the Scientific Study of Religion* 18: 117–31.

———. 1997. *Religion, Deviance, and Social Control*. New York: Routledge.

Starr, Paul. 1982. *The Social Transformation of American Medicine*. New York: Basic Books.

———. 1994. *The Logic of Health Care Reform: Why and How the President's Plan Will Work*, rev. ed. New York: Penguin.

"'Startlingly high mortality' among single dads in Canada." 2018. *CBC News*. 15 February. http://www.cbc.ca/beta/news/health/single-fathers-mortality-1.4535816 (retrieved 18 February 2018).

Statista. 2018a. "Number of monthly active Twitter users worldwide from 1st quarter 2010 to 4th quarter 2017 (in millions)." https://www.statista.com/statistics/282087/number-of-monthly-active-twitter-users/ (retrieved 25 February 2018).

_____. 2018b. "Penetration of leading social networks in Canada as of 4th quarter 2016." https://www.statista.com/statistics/284426/canada-social-network-penetration/ (retrieved 16 January 2018).

_____. 2018c. "Poverty rates in OECD countries as of 2015." https://www.statista.com/statistics/233910/poverty-rates-in-oecd-countries/ (retrieved 28 January 2018).

Statistics Canada. 1983. "Historical Statistics of Canada," Catalogue No. 11516XWE.

_____. 1992a. "Selected Marriage Statistics, 1921–1990," Catalogue No. 82-552 http://publications.gc.ca/site/eng/9.812865/publication.html).

_____. 1992b. "Marriage and Conjugal Life in Canada, 1991," Catalogue 91-534.

_____. 1994. "1991 Census Highlights." http://publications.gc.ca/site/archivee-archived.html?url=http://publications.gc.ca/collections/collection_2013/statcan/rh-hc/CS96-304-1994-eng.pdf (retrieved 12 February 2018).

_____. 1999. "National Longitudinal Survey of Children and Youth: Transition into Adolescence 1996/97." *The Daily* July 6. Retrieved May 10, 2001 (http://www.statcan.ca/Daily/English/990706/d990706a.htm).

_____. 2003a. "Earnings of Canadians: Making a Living in the New Economy." Catalogue No. 96F0030XIE2001014. Retrieved 16 July 2018 (http://www.statcan.ca/census01/products/analytic/companion/earn/contents.cfm).

_____. 2003b. "Religions in Canada." Catalogue No. 96F0030XIE2001015. Ottawa: Minister of Industry. Retrieved January 24, 2004 (http://www12.statcan.ca/english/census01/Products/Analytic/companion/rel/canada.cfm).

_____. 2003c. "Non-Wage Job Benefits, 2000." *The Daily* May 21. Retrieved September 15, 2004 (http://www.statcan.ca/Daily/English/030521/d030521c.htm).

_____. 2003d. *The Daily*, Catalogue 11-001, Monday, June 2, 2003.

_____. 2005c. "Population by religion, by province and territory (2001 Census)." http://www.statcan.gc.ca/tables-tableaux/sum-som/l01/cst01/demo30a-eng.htm (retrieved 12 February 2018).

_____. 2006b. "Households and the Environment 2006." Retrieved September 22, 2007 (http://www.statcan.ca/english/freepub/11-526-XIE/11-526-XIE2007001.pdf).

_____. 2007. "Table 101-1002: Mean Age and Median Age of Males and Females, by Type of Marriage and Marital Status, Canada, Provinces and Territories, Annual" (http://www5.statcan.gc.ca/cansim/a26?lang=eng&id=1011002).

_____. 2009b. "Family Violence in Canada: A Statistical Profile." Retrieved March 25, 2010 (http://www.phac-aspc.gc.ca/ncfv-cnivf/pdfs/fv-85-224-XWE-eng.pdf).

_____. 2010a. "Persistence of Low Income, by Selected Characteristics, Every 3 Years." CANSIM Table 202087.

_____. 2010c. "Projections of the Diversity of the Canadian Population, 2006 to 2031." Catalogue No. 91-551-XIE 2010001, 2006 to 2031. Released March 9, 2010. Retrieved March 13, 2010 (http://www.statcan.gc.ca/pub/91-551-x/91-551-x2010001-eng.pdf).

_____. 2010e. "Canadian Internet Use Survey." Retrieved September 20, 2011 (http://www.statcan.gc.ca/daily-quotidien/110525/dq110525b-eng.htm).

_____. 2010f. "Unpaid Work (20), Age Groups (9) and Sex (3) for the Population 15 Years and Over of Canada, Provinces, Territories, Census Divisions and Census Sub-divisions, 2006 Census—20% Sample Data."

_____. 2011. "General Social Survey – 2010. Overview of the Time Use of Canadians." https://www.statcan.gc.ca/pub/89-647-x/89-647-x2011001-eng.htm (retrieved 10 January 2018).

_____. 2013a. "Aboriginal Identity (8), Age Groups (11B), Sex (3) and Area of Residence (7) for Population, for Canada, Provinces and Territories, 2001 Census - 20% Sample Data." http://www12.statcan.ca/English/census01/products/standard/themes/Rp-eng.cfm?TABID=2&LANG=E&APATH=3&DETAIL=0&DIM=0&FL=C&FREE=0&GC=0&GK=0&GRP=0&PID=62715&PRID=0&PTYPE=55430,53293,55440,55496,71090&S=0&SHOWALL=0&SUB=0&Temporal=2001&THEME=45&VID=0&VNAMEE=&VNAMEF= (retrieved 24 January 2018).

_____. 2013c. "Chart 6: Crude Marriage Rate and Crude Divorce Rate, Canada, 1926 to 2008." Retrieved January 28, 2013 (http://www.statcan.gc.ca/pub/89-503-x/2010001/article/11546/c-g/c-g006-eng.htm).

_____. 2013g. "Table 1. Proportion of Aboriginal people by selected levels of educational attainment, sex and age groups, Canada, 2011." Retrieved August 2, 2015 (http://www12.statcan.gc.ca/nhs-enm/2011/as-sa/99-012-x/2011003/tbl/tbl1-eng.cfm.

_____. 2013j. "Religion (108), Immigrant Status and Period of Immigration (11), Age Groups (10) and Sex (3) for the Population in Private Households of Canada, Provinces, Territories, Census Metropolitan Areas and Census Agglomerations, *2011 National Household Survey*." Retrieved September 19, 2013 http://www12.statcan.gc.ca/nhs-enm/2011/dp-pd/dt-td/Rp-eng.cfm?LANG=E&APATH=3&DETAIL=0&DIM=0&FL=A&FREE=0&GC=0&GID=0&GK=0&GRP=0&PID=105399&PRID=0&PTYPE=105277&S=0&SHOWALL=0&SUB=0&Temporal=2013&THEME=95&VID=0&VNAMEE=&VNAMEF=).

_____. 2013k. "Distribution of persons by income group and highest level of education attainment." https://www12.statcan.gc.ca/nhs-enm/2011/as-sa/99-014-x/2011003/c-g/desc/longdesc01_2-eng.cfm (retrieved 8 August 2015).

_____. 2013l. "University Degrees, Diplomas, and Certificates Granted, by Program Level, Classification of Instructional Programs, Primary Grouping (CIP_PG) and Sex, Annually (number)." CANSIM Table 4770014.

_____. 2015e. "Market, total and after-tax income, by economic family type and income quintiles, 2011 constant dollars, annually." CANSIM, Table 202-0701. Retrieved July 27, 2015 (http://dc2.chass.utoronto

.ca.myaccess.library.utoronto.ca/cgi-bin/cansimdim/c2_getArrayDim.pl).

———. 2015f. "Earnings of Individuals, by Selected Characteristics and National Occupational Classification (NOC-S), 2011 Constant Dollars, Annually." CANSIM Table 2020106. (dc2.chass.utoronto.ca.myaccess.library.utoronto.ca/cgi-bin/cansimdim/c2 _arrays.pl).

———. 2015h. *National Household Survey* (NHS) PUMF, 2011: Individual's file. Retrieved August 2, 2015 (http://sda.chass.utoronto.ca.myaccess.library.utoronto.ca/ cgi-bin/sdacensus/hsda?harcsda +nhs11).

———. 2015i. "Female-to-Male Earnings Ratios, by Selected Characteristics, 2011 Constant Dollars, Annually (percentage)." CANSIM database, Table 2020104.

———. 2015j. "Labour force survey estimates (LFS), by National Occupational Classification for Statistics (NOC-S) and sex, annually." CANSIM database, Table 2820010.

———. 2016c. "Mixed unions in Canada." http://www12.statcan.gc.ca/nhs-enm/2011/as-sa/99-010-x/99-010-x2011003_3-eng.cfm (retrieved 9 February 2018).

———. 2016d. "Table 1: Number and proportion of the population aged 25 to 64 by highest level of educational attainment, Canada, 2011." http://www12.statcan.gc.ca/nhs-enm/2011/as-sa/99-012-x/2011001/tbl/tbl01-eng.cfm (retrieved 16 January 2018).

———. 2016e. "Visible minority of person." http://www23.statcan.gc.ca/imdb/p3Var.pl?Function=DEC&Id=45152 (retrieved 3 February 2018).

———. 2017a. "Aboriginal identity population by both sexes, total-age, 2016 counts, Canada, provinces and territories, 2016 Census – 25% Sample data." http://www12.statcan.gc.ca/census-recensement/2016/dp-pd/hlt-fst/abo-aut/Table.cfm?Lang=Eng&T=101&S=99&O=A (retrieved 25 January 2018).

———. 2017b. Canadian health characteristics, two-year period estimates, by age group and sex, Canada, provinces, territories and health regions. http://www5.statcan.gc.ca/cansim/a47 (retrieved 17 January 2017).

———. 2017c. "Chart 1: Average full-time hourly wage by broad occupational group, 2016." CANSIM Table 285-0050. http://www.statcan.gc.ca/daily-quotidien/170615/cg-a001-eng.htm (retrieved 28 January 2018).

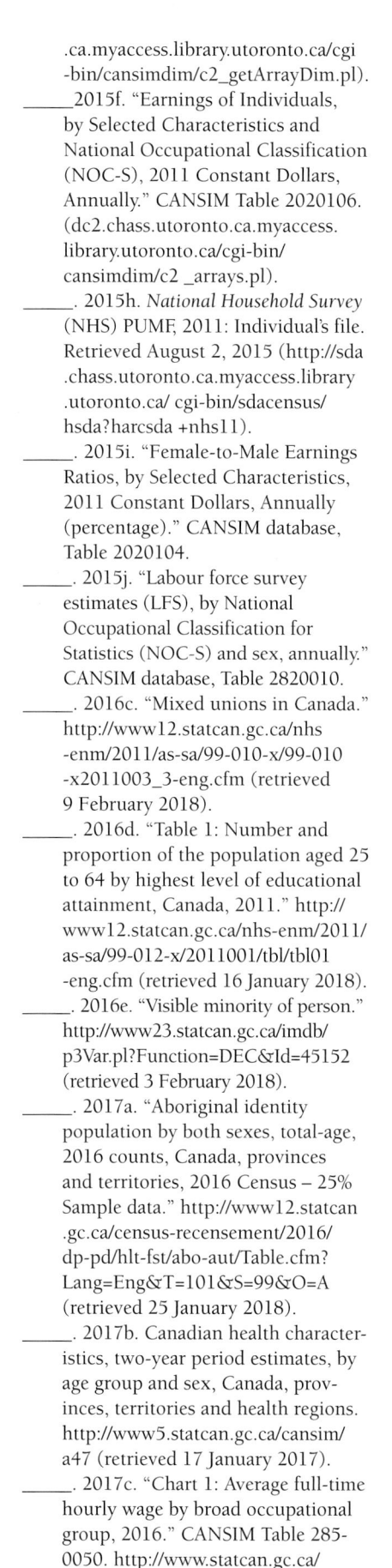

———. 2017d. "Chart 13. Projected life expectancy at birth by sex, by Aboriginal identity, 2017." http://www.statcan.gc.ca/pub/89-645-x/2010001/c-g/c-g013-eng.htm (retrieved 18 February 2018).

———. 2017f. "Ethnic Origin, both sexes, age (total), Canada, 2016 Census – 25% Sample data." http://www12.statcan.gc.ca/census-recensement/2016/dp-pd/hlt-fst/imm/Table.cfm?Lang=E&T=31&Geo=01&SO=4D (retrieved 31 January 2018).

———. 2017g. "Financial information of universities and degree-granting colleges, 2015/2016." www.statcan.gc.ca/daily-quotidien/170713/dq170713c-eng.pdf (retrieved 2 March 2018).

———. 2017h. "Household income in Canada: Key results from the 2016 Census." *The Daily* 13 September. http://www.statcan.gc.ca/daily-quotidien/170913/dq170913a-eng.htm (retrieved 29 January 2018).

———. 2017i. "Highest level of educational attainment (general) by selected age groups 25 to 64, both sexes, % distribution 2016, Canada, provinces and territories, 2016 Census – 25% Sample data." http://www12.statcan.gc.ca/census-recensement/2016/dp-pd/hlt-fst/edu-sco/Table.cfm?Lang=E&T=11&Geo=00&View=2&Age=2 (retrieved 21 February 2018).

———. 2017k. "Leading causes of death, by sex (both sexes)." http://www.statcan.gc.ca/tables-tableaux/sum-som/l01/cst01/hlth36a-eng.htm (retrieved 17 February 2018).

———. 2017l. "Low income statistics by age, sex and economic family type, Canada, provinces and selected census metropolitan areas (CMAs), annually." CAMSIM Table 2060041. http://dc2.chass.utoronto.ca.myaccess.library.utoronto.ca/cgi-bin/cansimdim/c2_getArrayDim.pl (retrieved 29 January 2018).

———. 2017m. "Marital status and opposite- and same-sex status by sex for persons aged 15 and over living in private households for both sexes, total, presence and age of children, 2001 counts, Canada, provinces and territories, 2001 Census – 100% Data." http://www12.statcan.gc.ca/census-recensement/2016/dp-pd/hlt-fst/fam/Table.cfm?Lang=E&T=11&Geo=00&SP=1&view=4&sex=1&presence=1 (retrieved 8 February 2018).

———. 2017n. "Postsecondary enrolments by institution type, registration status, province and sex (Both sexes)." http://www.statcan.gc.ca/tables-tableaux/sum-som/l01/cst01/educ71a-eng.htm (retrieved 28 February 2018).

———. 2017p. "Private households by household type, 2016 counts, Canada, provinces and territories, 2016 Census – 100% Data." http://www12.statcan.gc.ca/census-recensement/2016/dp-pd/hlt-fst/fam/Table.cfm?Lang=E&T=21&Geo=00&SP=1&view=1 (retrieved 7 February 2018).

———. 2017q. "Table 205-0004: Survey of Financial Security (SFS), assets and debts by net worth quintile, Canada, provinces and selected census metropolitan areas (CMAs)." http://www.statcan.gc.ca/daily-quotidien/140225/dq140225b-eng.htm (retrieved 27 January 2018).

———. 2017r. "Visible minority (visible minority), both sexes, age (total), Canada, provinces and territories, 2016 Census – 25% Sample data." http://www12.statcan.gc.ca/census-recensement/2016/dp-pd/hlt-fst/imm/Table.cfm?Lang=E&T=41&Geo=00&SP=1&vismin=2&age=1&sex=1 (retrieved 31 January 2018).

———. 2017s. "Young adults living with their parents in Canada in 2016." http://www12.statcan.gc.ca/census-recensement/2016/as-sa/98-200-x/2016008/98-200-x2016008-eng.cfm (retrieved 18 January 2018).

———. 2017t. "The Aboriginal languages of First Nations people, Métis and Inuit." http://www12.statcan.gc.ca/census-recensement/2016/as-sa/98-200-x/2016022/98-200-x2016022-eng.cfm (retrieved 9 January 2018).

———. 2017u. "Religion (108), Immigrant Status and Period of Immigration (11), Age Groups (10) and Sex (3) for the Population in Private Households of Canada, Provinces, Territories, Census Metropolitan Areas and Census Agglomerations, 2011 National Household Survey." http://www12.statcan.gc.ca/nhs-enm/2011/dp-pd/dt-td/Rp-eng.cfm?LANG=E&APATH=3&DETAIL=0&DIM=0&FL=A&FREE=0&GC=0&GID=0&GK=0&

GRP=0&PID=105399&PRID=0&PTYPE=105277&S=0&SHOWALL=0&SUB=0&Temporal=2013&THEME=95&VID=0 (retrieved 12 February 2018).

———. 2017v. "Major field of study STEM and BHASE (non-STEM) groupings for selected age groups 25 to 64, both sexes, and selected highest levels of educational attainment (university certificate, diploma or degree at bachelor level or above), % distribution 2016, Canada, provinces and territories, 2016 Census – 25% Sample data." http://www12.statcan.gc.ca/census-recensement/2016/dp-pd/hlt-fst/edu-sco/Table.cfm?Lang=E&T=41&Geo=00&View=2&Age=2&Education=3 (retrieved 28 February 2018).}

———. 2018a. "Adult correctional services, average counts of offenders in federal programs, annually." CANSIM, Table 2510006. http://dc2.chass.utoronto.ca.myaccess.library.utoronto.ca/cgi-bin/cansimdim/c2_getArrayDim.pl (retrieved 22 January 2018).

2018b. "Cannabis Stats Hub." http://www.statcan.gc.ca/pub/13-610-x/13-610-x2018001-eng.htm (retrieved 26 January 2018).

———. 2018c. "Postsecondary enrolments, by registration status, International Standard Classification of Education (ISCED), Classification of Instructional Programs, Primary Grouping (CIP_PG), sex and student status, annually (Number)." CANSIM Table 4770019. http://dc2.chass.utoronto.ca.myaccess.library.utoronto.ca/cgi-bin/cansimdim/c2_getArrayDim.pl (retrieved 3 March 2018).

———. 2018d. "Table 282-0088: Labour Force Survey estimates (LFS), employment by North American Industry Classification System (NAICS), seasonally adjusted and unadjusted monthly (persons x 1,000)." http://www5.statcan.gc.ca/cansim/a26?id=2820088 (retrieved 27 February 2018).

———. 2018e. "The Internet and digital technology." https://www.statcan.gc.ca/pub/11-627-m/index-eng.htm (retrieved 10 January 2018).

———. 2018f. "Youth Courts, guilty cases by type of sentence, annually (number)." CANSIM Table 2520067. Retrieved January 27, 2018) (http://dc2.chass.utoronto.ca.myaccess.library.utoronto.ca/cgi-bin/cansimdim/c2_getArrayDim.pl).

———. 2018g. Immigrant population in Canada. Retrieved January 10, 2018 (https://www.statcan.gc.ca/pub/11-627-m/index-eng.htm).

———. 2018h. Infographics. Retrieved January 27, 2018 (https://www.statcan.gc.ca/pub/11-627-m/index-eng.htm).

———. 2018i. "Ethnic Origin (279), Single and Multiple Ethnic Origin Responses (3), Generation Status (4), Age (12) and Sex (3) for the Population in Private Households of Canada, Provinces and Territories, Census Metropolitan Areas and Census Agglomerations, 2016 Census - 25% Sample Data." http://www12.statcan.gc.ca/census-recensement/2016/dp-pd/dt-td/Rp-eng.cfm?TABID=2&LANG=E&APATH=3&DETAIL=0&DIM=0&FL=A&FREE=0&GC=0&GK=0&GRP=1&PID=110528&PRID=10&PTYPE=109445&S=0&SHOWALL=0&SUB=0&Temporal=2017&THEME=120&VID=0&VNAMEE=&VNAMEF= (retrieved 8 February 2018).

Steel, Freda M. 1987. "Alimony and Maintenance Orders." Pp. 155–67 in Sheilah L. Martin and Kathleen E. Mahoney, eds., *Equality and Judicial Neutrality*. Toronto: Carswell.

———. 1997. "A Threat in the Air: How Stereotypes Shape the Intellectual Identities and Performance of Women and African-Americans." *American Psychologist* 52: 613–29.

Stein, Joel. 2013. "Millennials: The Me Me Me Generation." *Time* 20 May. http://time.com/247/millennials-the-me-me-me-generation/ (retrieved 18 January 2018).

Steiner-Adair, Catherine, with Teresa and H. Barker, eds. 2013. *The Big Disconnect: Protecting Childhood and Family in the Digital Age*. New York: Harper.

Sternberg, Robert J. 1998. *In Search of the Human Mind*, 2nd ed. Fort Worth, TX: Harcourt Brace.

Sternheimer, Karen. 2014. "Do Video Games Kill?" Pp. 87–95 in Robert Brym, ed., *Society in Question*, 7th ed. Toronto: Nelson.

Stone, Lawrence. 1977. *The Family, Sex and Marriage in England, 1500–1800*. New York: Harper and Row.

Stouffer, Samuel A., et al. 1949. *The American Soldier*, 4 vols. Princeton, NJ: Princeton University Press.

Strapagiel, Lauren. 2013. "University fees have tripled since 1990: Report." Canada.com. http://o.canada.com/business/university-fees-have-tripled-since-1990-report (retrieved 2 March 2018).

Straus, Murray A. 1994. *Beating the Devil Out of Them: Corporal Punishment in American Families*. New York: Lexington Books.

Strauss, Anselm L. 1993. *Continual Permutations of Action*. New York: Aldine de Gruyter.

Strother, Eric, Raymond Lemberg, Stevie Chariese Stanford, and Dayton Turberville. 2012. "Eating Disorders in Men: Underdiagnosed, Undertreated, and Misunderstood." *Eating Disorders* 20(5): 346–55. https://www.ncbi.nlm.nih.gov/pmc/articles/PMC3479631/ (retrieved 6 February 2018).

Sullivan, Mercer L. 2002. "Exploring Layers: Extended Case Method as a Tool for Multilevel Analysis of School Violence." *Sociological Methods and Research* 31, 2: 255–85.

Sullivan, Nikki. 2003. *A Critical Introduction to Queer Theory*. New York: New York University Press.

Sumner, William Graham. 1940 [1907]. *Folkways*. Boston: Ginn.

Sun, Lena H., and Juliet Eilperin. 2017. "CDC gets list of forbidden words: Fetus, transgender, diversity." *The Washington Post* 15 December. https://www.washingtonpost.com/national/health-science/cdc-gets-list-of-forbidden-words-fetus-transgender-diversity/2017/12/15/f503837a-e1cf-11e7-89e8-edec16379010_story.html?utm_term=.14edbe44dde6 (retrieved 1 January 2018).

Suomi, Stephen J., and Helen A. Leroy. 1982. In memoriam: Harry F. Harlow (1905–1981). *American Journal of Primatology* 2: 319–42. https://doi.org/10.1002/ajp.1350020402.

Sutherland, Edwin H. 1939. *Principles of Criminology*. Philadelphia: Lippincott.

———. 1949. *White Collar Crime*. New York: Dryden.

Swiss Re. 2013. "Natural Catastrophes and Man-Made Disasters in 2012." Retrieved March 31, 2013 (http://

media.swissre.com/documents/sigma2_2013_en.pdf).

Sykes, Gresham, and David Matza. 1957. "Techniques of Neutralization: A Theory of Delinquency." *American Sociological Review* 22: 664–70.

Szalavitz, Maia. 2015. "No, Native Americans aren't genetically more susceptible to alcoholism." *The Verge* 2 October. https://www.theverge.com/2015/10/2/9428659/firewater-racist myth-alcoholism-native-americans (retrieved 3 February 2018).

Tajfel, Henri. 1981. *Human Groups and Social Categories: Studies in Social Psychology*. Cambridge, UK: Cambridge University Press.

Tannen, Deborah. 1994a. *Talking from 9 to 5: How Women's and Men's Conversational Styles Affect Who Gets Heard, Who Gets Credit, and What Gets Done at Work*. New York: William Morrow.

———. 1994b. *Gender and Discourse*. New York: Oxford University Press.

Tarrow, Sidney. 2011. *Power in Movement*, 3rd ed. Cambridge UK: Cambridge University Press.

Tasker, Fiona L., and Susan Golombok. 1997. *Growing Up in a Lesbian Family: Effects on Child Development*. New York: The Guilford Press.

Tata Motors. 2018 "GenX Nano ex-showroom price list." http://nano.tatamotors.com/price-list.php (retrieved 26 February 2018).

Taylor, Laramie D., and Jhunehl Fortaleza. 2016. "Media Violence and Male Body Image." *Psychology of Men and Masculinity* 17(4): 380–84.

TD Economics. 2015. "Aboriginal women outperforming in labour markets." 6 July. Retrieved August 2, 2015 (https://www.td.com/document/PDF/economics/special/Aboriginal Women.pdf).

Tec, Nechama. 1986. *When Light Pierced the Darkness: Christian Rescue of Jews in Nazi-Occupied Poland*. New York: Oxford University Press.

Television Bureau of Canada. 2015. *Cross-Media Reach and Time Spent: Major Media Comparison*." Pp. 6, 13. Retrieved July 5, 2015 (http://www.tvb.ca/pages/RTS).

Thomas, Keith. 1971. *Religion and the Decline of Magic*. London, UK: Weidenfeld and Nicolson.

Thomas, Mikhail. 2002. "Adult Criminal Court Statistics, 2000/01." *Juristat* 22, 2 (March). Catalogue No. 85-002-XPE. Ottawa: Canadian Centre for Justice Statistics and Statistics Canada.

Thomas, William Isaac. 1966 [1931]. "The Relation of Research to the Social Process." Pp. 289–305 in Morris Janowitz, ed., *W. I. Thomas on Social Organization and Social Personality*. Chicago: University of Chicago Press.

Thompson, E. P. 1967. "Time, Work Discipline, and Industrial Capitalism." *Past and Present* 38: 59–67.

Thompson, Nicole. 2017. "2 richest businessmen hold same wealth as 11 million Canadians: Oxfam report." *Global News* 15 January. https://globalnews.ca/news/3183007/richest-canadians-wealth-income-inequality/ (retrieved 27 January 2018).

Thorne, Barrie. 1993. *Gender Play: Girls and Boys in School*. New Brunswick, NJ: Rutgers University Press.

Tilly, Charles. 1979a. "Collective Violence in European Perspective." Pp. 83–118 in H. Graham and T. Gurr, eds., *Violence in America: Historical and Comparative Perspective*, 2nd ed. Beverly Hills, CA: Sage.

———. 1979b. "Repertoires of Contention in America and Britain, 1750–1830." Pp. 126–55 in Mayer N. Zald and John D. McCarthy, eds. *The Dynamics of Social Movements: Resource Mobilization, Social Control, and Tactics*. Cambridge, MA: Winthrop Publishers.

Tilly, Charles, Louise Tilly, and Richard Tilly. 1975. *The Rebellious Century, 1830–1930*. Cambridge, MA: Harvard University Press.

Tjepkema, Michael. n.d. "Measured Obesity: Adult obesity in Canada: Measured height and weight." Statistics Canada. Retrieved January 14, 2013 (http://www.aboutmen.ca/application/www.aboutmen.ca/asset/upload/tiny_mce/page/link/Adult-Obesity-in-Canada.pdf).

Tkacik, Maureen. 2002. "The Return of Grunge." *Wall Street Journal*, December 11: B1, B10.

Tönnies, Ferdinand. 1988 [1887]. *Community and Society (Gemeinschaft und Gesellschaft)*. New Brunswick, NJ: Transaction.

"Top 100 Richest Rappers & Hip-Hop Artists." 2018. https://justrichest.com/top-100-richest-rappers-hip-hop-artists/ (retrieved 19 April 2018).

Toronto District School Board. 2011. "The TDSB Grade 9 Cohort 2006-2011: Trend Data, Fact Sheet No. 1." https://www.google.ca/url?sa=t&rct=j&q=&esrc=s&source=web&cd=8&ved=0ahUKEwjj2_eyp8vZAhXixYMKHS2OAM8QFgiEATAH&url=http%3A%2F%2Fwww.tdsb.on.ca%2FPortals%2F0%2FCommunity%2FCommunity%2520Advisory%2520committees%2FICAC%2Fresearch%2FSeptember%25202012%2520Cohort%2520dataAcrobat%2520Document.pdf&usg=AOvVaw36opgrQy92zriOFFvdIyKX (retrieved 1 March 2018).

*Toronto Star*. 2015. "Known to police." Retrieved July 22, 2015 (http://www.thestar.com/news/gta/knowntopolice.html).

Torrance, Judy M. 1986. *Public Violence in Canada*. Toronto: University of Toronto Press.

Troeltsch, Ernst. 1931 [1923]. *The Social Teaching of the Christian Churches*, Olive Wyon, trans. 2 vols. London, UK: George Allen and Unwin.

Trovato, Frank. 1998. "The Stanley Cup of Hockey and Suicide in Quebec, 1951–1992." *Social Forces* 77: 105–27.

Tufts, Jennifer. 2000. "Public Attitudes Toward the Criminal Justice System." *Juristat* 20, 12 (December). Catalogue No. 85-002-XPE. Ottawa: Canadian Centre for Justice Statistics and Statistics Canada.

Tuljapurkar, Shripad, Nan Li, and Carl Boe. 2000. "A Universal Pattern of Mortality Decline in the G7 Countries." *Nature* 405: 789–92.

Tumin, M. 1953. "Some Principles of Stratification: A Critical Analysis." *American Sociological Review* 18: 387–94.

Turcotte, Martin. 2007. "Time Spent with Family During a Typical Workday, 1986 to 2005." *Canadian Social Trends* 82: 2–11. Catalogue No. 11-008-XPE. Retrieved March 26, 2007 (http://www.statcan.ca/english/freepub/11-008-XIE/2006007/pdf/11-008-XIE20060079574.pdf).

Turkle, Sherry. 1995. *Life on the Screen: Identity in the Age of the Internet*. New York: Simon & Schuster.

———. 2011. *Alone Together: Why We Expect More from Technology and Less from Each Other*. New York: Basic Books.

Turner, Bryan S. 1986. *Citizenship and Capitalism: The Debate over Reformism*. London, UK: Allen and Unwin.

"U.K. Panel Calls Climate Data Valid." 2010. *New York Times*, March 30. Retrieved April 1, 2010 (http://www.nytimes.com).

UNAIDS. 2016. *Global Report: UNAIDS Report on the Global AIDS Epidemic 2013*. Pp. A3–A15. http://www.unaids.org/en/resources/documents/2017/2017_data_book (retrieved 17 August 2015).

UNESCO. 2017a. "Literacy Rates Continue to Rise from One Generation to the Next." http://uis.unesco.org/en/topic/literacy (retrieved 28 February 2018).

———. 2017b. "Data 2017." http://www.unaids.org/en/resources/documents/2017/2017_data_book (retrieved 17 February 2017).}

———. 2018. "Out-of-school; rate for children of primary school age." http://data.uis.unesco.org/Index.aspx?queryid=242 (28 February 2018).

Ungar, Sheldon. 1992. "The Rise and (Relative) Decline of Global Warming as a Social Problem." *Sociological Quarterly* 33: 483–501.

United Nations. 1998. Universal Declaration of Human Rights. www.un.org/Overview/rights .html.

———.2004. *Human Development Report 2004*. New York. http://hdr.undp.org/sites/default/files/reports/265/hdr_2004_complete.pdf (retrieved 6 July 2018).

———. 2008. "Abortion rate." http://data.un.org/Data.aspx?d=GenderStat&f=inID%3A12 (retrieved 8 February 2018).

United Nations Development Programme. 2014. "Country Classification." Retrieved April 2, 2016 (http://www.un.org/en/development/desa/policy/wesp/wesp_current/2014wesp_country_classification.pdf).

———. 2016. "Gender Inequality Index (GII)." *Human Development Report 2016*. http://hdr.undp.org/en/data# (retrieved 4 February 2018).

Unschuld, Paul. 1985. *Medicine in China*. Berkeley, CA: University of California Press.

U.S. Department of Labor. 2013. "CPI Inflation Calculator." Retrieved 31 March 2013 (http://www.bls.gov/data/inflation_calculator.htm).

Useem, Bert. 1998. "Breakdown Theories of Collective Action." *Annual Review of Sociology* 24: 215–38.

Usher, Alex. 2017. "Tuition Fees in Canada, 2017–18." Higher Education Strategy Associates. http://higheredstrategy.com/tuition-fees-in-canada-2017-18/ (retrieved 2 March 2018).

Vago, Stephen, and Adie Nelson. 2003. *Law and Society*. Don Mills, ON: Pearson Educational Publishing.

Van Pelt, Deani Neven, Jason Clemens, Brianna Brown, and Milagros Palacios. 2015. "Where Our Students Are Educated: Measuring Enrolment in Canada." The Fraser Institute. https://www.fraserinstitute.org/sites/default/files/where-our-students-are-educated-measuring-student-enrolment-in-canada.pdf (retrieved November 14, 2016).

Van Schilt, Stephanie. 2017. "*The Book of Mormon* review—a visionary musical masterpiece, genital jokes and all." *The Guardian*, international ed., 6 February. https://www.theguardian.com/stage/2017/feb/06/the-book-of-mormon-review-a-visionary-musical-masterpiece-genital-jokes-and-all (retrieved 13 February 2018).

Veenstra, Gary. 2013. "Race, gender, class, sexuality (RGCS) and hypertension." *Social Science and Medicine* 89: 16–24.

Vevo. 2017. "How Influential Are Music Videos on Beauty & Style?" https://www.google.ca/search?q=VEVO+How+InfluentialAre+Music+Videos on+Beauty+%26+Style%3F&ie=utf-8&oe=utf-8&client=firefox-b-ab&gfe_rd=cr&dcr=0&ei=9lC-Wp__C7HU8geBhIPYCQ# (retrieved 30 March 2018).

Vidal, John. 2017. "Camille Parmesan: 'Trump's extremism on climate change has brought people together'." *The Guardian* 17 December. https://www.theguardian.com/science/2017/dec/31/camille-parmesan-trump-extremism-climate-change-interview (retrieved 1 January 2018).

Vincent, David. 2000. *The Rise of Mass Literacy: Reading and Writing in Modern Europe*. Cambridge, England: Polity Press.

Viorst, Milton. 2016. *Zionism: The Birth and Transformation of an Ideal*. New York: Thomas Dunne.

Vishwanath, Arun. 2015. "Habitual Facebook Use and Its Impact on Getting Deceived on Social Media." *Journal of Computer-Mediated Communication* 20: 83–98.

Vrangalova, Zhana, and Ritch C. Savin-Williams. 2012. "Mostly Heterosexual and Mostly Gay/Lesbian: Evidence for New Sexual Orientation Identities." *Archives of Sexual Behavior* 41: 85–101.

Vygotsky, Lev S. 1987. *The Collected Works of L. S. Vygotsky*, Vol. 1, N. Minick, trans. New York: Plenum.

Wait Time Alliance. 2015. "Eliminating Code Gridlock in Canada's Health Care System: 2015 Wait Time Alliance Report Card." http://www.waittimealliance.ca/wta-reports/2015-wta-report-card/ (retrieved 20 February 2018).

Wald, Matthew L., and John Schwartz. 2003. "Alerts Were Lacking, NASA Shuttle Manager Says." *New York Times* July 23. Retrieved July 23, 2003 (http://www.nytimes.com).

Waldron, Ingrid. 2018. "Re-thinking waste: mapping racial geographies of violence on the colonial landscape." *Environmental Sociology* 4(1): 36–52. DOI: https://doi.org/10.1080/23251042.2018.1429178.

Walji, Nazima. 2017. "'We were just gawked at': Mixed-race families common in Canada but still face challenges." *CBC News*. 3 November. http://www.cbc.ca/news/canada/mixed-race-families-in-canada-1.4376379 (retrieved 9 February 2018).

Wallace, James, and Jim Erickson. 1992. *Hard Drive: Bill Gates and the Making of the Microsoft Empire*. New York: John Wiley.

Wallerstein, Immanuel. 1974–89. *The Modern World-System*, 3 vols. New York: Academic Press.

Walters, David. 2004. "A comparison of the labour market outcomes of post-secondary graduates of various levels and fields over a four-cohort period." *Canadian Journal of Sociology* 29(1): 1–27.

Wanner, R. 1999. "Expansion and Ascription: Trends in Educational Opportunity in Canada, 1920–1994." *Canadian Review of Sociology and Anthropology* 36; August: 409–42.

Wasserman, Stanley, and Katherine Faust. 1994. *Social Network Analysis: Methods and Applications.* Cambridge: Cambridge University Press.

Watkins, S. Craig, and Rana A. Emerson. 2000. "Feminist Media Criticism and Feminist Media Practices." *Annals of the American Academy of Political and Social Science* 571: 151–66.

Weber, Bruce. 2011. "J. Paul Getty III, 54, Dies; Had Ear Cut Off by Captors." *New York Times* 7 February. http://www.nytimes.com/2011/02/08/world/europe/08gettyobit.html (retrieved 30 January 2018).

Weber, Max. 1946. *From Max Weber: Essays in Sociology*, rev. ed., H. Gerth and C. W. Mills, eds. and trans. New York: Oxford University Press.

———. 1958 [1904–05]. *The Protestant Ethic and the Spirit of Capitalism.* New York: Scribner.

———. 1964 [1947]. *The Theory of Social and Economic Organization*, T. Parsons, ed., A. M. Henderson and T. Parsons, trans. New York: Free Press.

———. 1968 [1914]. *Economy and Society*, Guenther Roth and Claus Wittich, eds. Berkeley, CA: University of California Press.

Weeks, Jeffrey. 1986. *Sexuality.* London, UK: Routledge.

Weiner, Melissa F. 2012. "Towards a Critical Global Race Theory." *Sociology Compass* 6(4) 332–50.

Weinreich, Max. 1945. "Der YIVO un di problemen fun unzer tzayt." [Yiddish: "YIVO and the problems of our time"] *YIVO bleter: shrift fun yidishn visenshaftlikhn institut* [*YIVO Pages: Writing from the Yiddish Scientific Institute* 25, 1:3–18.

Weinstein, Rhona S. 2002. *Reaching Higher: The Power of Expectations in Schooling.* Cambridge, MA: Harvard University Press.

Weinstein, R. S., A. Gregory, and M. J. Strambler. 2004. "Intractable self-fulfilling prophecies fifty years after Brown vs. Board of Education." *American Psychologist* 59(6): 511–20.

Weis, Joseph G. 1987. "Class and Crime." Pp. 71–90 in Michael Gottfredson and Travis Hirschi, eds. *Positive Criminology.* Beverly Hills, CA: Sage.

Welch, Michael. 1997. "Violence Against Women by Professional Football Players: A Gender Analysis of Hyper-masculinity, Positional Status, Narcissism, and Entitlement." *Journal of Sport and Social Issues* 21: 392–411.

Wellman, Barry. 2014. "Connecting Communities On and Offline." Pp. 54–63 in Robert Brym, ed., *Society in Question*, 7th ed. Toronto: Nelson.

Wellman, Barry, and Stephen Berkowitz, eds. 1997. *Social Structures: A Network Approach*, updated ed. Greenwich, CT: JAI Press.

Wellman, Barry, Peter J. Carrington, and Alan Hall. 1997 [1988]. "Networks as Personal Communities." Pp. 130–84 in Barry Wellman and Stephen D. Berkowitz, eds., *Social Structures: A Network Approach*, updated ed. Greenwich, CT: JAI Press.

Welsh, Sandy. 1999. "Gender and Sexual Harassment." *Annual Review of Sociology* 25: 169–90.

West, Candace, and Don Zimmerman. 1987. "Doing Gender." *Gender and Society* 1: 125–51.

Whitaker, Reg. 1987. *Double Standard.* Toronto: Lester and Orpen Dennys.

Whorf, Benjamin Lee. 1956. *Language, Thought, and Reality*, John B. Carroll, ed. Cambridge, MA: MIT Press.

Widyastuti, Adeline. 2010. *The Globalization of New Media Exposure: The Dependency on the Internet.* Saarbrücken, Germany: Lambert.

Wikipedia. 2018. "List of Playboy Playmates of the Month." https://en.wikipedia.org/wiki/List_of_Playboy_Playmates_of_the_Month (retrieved 4 February 2018).

Wilensky, Harold L. 1967. *Organizational Intelligence: Knowledge and Policy in Government and Industry.* New York: Basic Books.

Wilkinson, Richard G. 1996. *Unhealthy Societies: The Afflictions of Inequality.* London, UK: Routledge.

Wilkinson, Richard, and Michael Marmot, eds. 2003. *Social Determinants of Health: The Solid Facts.* Copenhagen: World Health Organization Regional Office for Europe.

Williams, David R., and Michelle Sternthal. 2010. "Understanding racial–ethnic disparities in health: Sociological contributions." *Journal of Health and Social Behavior* 51 (supplement): S15–S27.

Willis, Paul. 1984. *Learning to Labour: How Working-Class Kids Get Working-Class Jobs*, reprinted ed. New York: Columbia University Press.

Wilson, T. D., D. Reinhard, E. C. Westgate, D. T. Gilbert, N. Ellerbeck, C. Hahn, C. L. Brown, & A. Shaked. 2014. "Just think: The challenges of the disengaged mind." *Science* 345(6192), 75–77. http://science.sciencemag.org/content/345/6192/75?sid=386a6acc-cf07-4e73-b2ad-7b57fde43d4c (retrieved 11 January 2018).

Wilson, William Julius. 1987. *The Truly Disadvantaged: The Inner City, the Underclass, and Public Policy.* Chicago: University of Chicago Press.

Wolf, Naomi. 1997. *Promiscuities: The Secret Struggle for Womanhood.* New York: Vintage.

Wolpert, Stuart. 2012. "Foster Kids Do Equally Well When Adopted by Gay, Lesbian or Heterosexual Parents." *UCLA Newsroom* 18 October. Retrieved February 2, 2013 (http://newsroom.ucla.edu/portal/ucla/foster-children-adopted-by-gay-239748.aspx).

"Woman Soldier in Abuse Spotlight." 2004. *BBC News World Edition* 7 May. Retrieved March 3, 2005 (http://news.bbc.co.uk/2/hi/americas/3691753.stm).

Wong, Lloyd, and Michele Ng. 1998. "Chinese Immigrant Entrepreneurs in Vancouver: A Case Study of Ethnic Business Development." *Canadian Ethnic Studies* 30: 64–85.

Woodbury, Anthony. (2003). "Endangered Languages." *Linguistic Society of America.* Woodrow Federal Reserve Bank of Minneapolis.

Woolley, Jacqueline D., and Maliki E. Ghossainy. 2013. "Revisiting the Fantasy–Reality Distinction: Children as Naïve Skeptics." *Child Development* 84(5): 1496-1510.

World Air Quality Index. 2018. http://aqicn.org/city/beijing/ (retrieved 5 April 2018).

World Bank. 2018a. "Life expectancy at birth, total (years)." https://data.worldbank.org/indicator/SP.DYN.LE00.IN (retrieved 18 February 2018).

———. 2018b. "Health expenditure per capita (current US$)." https://data.worldbank.org/indicator/SH.XPD.PCAP (retrieved 17 February 2018).

———. 2018c. "Improved water source (% of population with access)." https://data.worldbank.org/indicator/SH.H2O.SAFE.ZS (retrieved 17 February 2018).

———. 2018d. "Mortality rate, infant (per 1,000 live births)." https://data

.worldbank.org/indicator/SP.DYN .IMRT.IN (retrieved 17 February 2018).

———. 2018e. "Physicians (per 1,000 people)." https://data.worldbank .org/indicator/SH.MED.PHYS.ZS (retrieved 17 February 2018).

World Economic Forum. 2017. "These are the world's 10 biggest corporate giants." https://www.weforum.org/ agenda/2017/01/worlds-biggest -corporate-giants (retrieved July 13, 2018).

———. 2018. "These are the world's most popular websites." https://www .weforum.org/agenda/2017/04/most -popular-websites-google-youtube -baidu/ (retrieved 25 February 2018).

World Health Organization. 2003. *Cumulative Number of Reported Probable Cases [SARS]*. Retrieved June 16, 2003 (http://www.who.int/ csr/sars/country/2003_06_16/en).

———. 2010b. *WHO Statistical Information System (WHOSIS)*. Retrieved April 1, 2010 (http://www .who.int/whosis/en/index.html).

World Hunger Education Service. 2015. "2015 World Hunger and Poverty Facts and Statistics." Retrieved July 28, 2015 (http://www.worldhunger.org/ articles/Learn/world%20hunger%20 facts%202002 .htm).

World Prison Brief, Institute for Criminal Policy Research. 2017. "Highest to Lowest—Prison Population Rate." http://www.prisonstudies.org/ highest-to-lowest/prison-population -total (retrieved 22 January 2018).

Wortley, Scot, David Brownfield, and John Hagan. 1996. *The Usual Suspects: Race, Age and Gender Differences in Police Contact*. Paper presented at the 48th Annual Conference of the American Society of Criminology, Chicago: November.

Wortley, Scot, and Julian Tanner. 2008. "Money, Respect and Defiance: Explaining Ethnic Differences in Gang Activity among Canadian Youth." Pp. 181–210 in Frank van Gemert, Dana Peterson, and Inger-Lise Lien, eds., Youth Gangs, Migration and Ethnicity. London, U.K.: Willan Publishing.

Wright, Charles Robert. 1975. *Mass Communication: A Sociological Perspective*. New York: Random House.

Wu, Zheng. 2000. *Cohabitation: An Alternative Form of Family Living*. Don Mills, ON: Oxford University Press.

X, Malcolm. 1965. *The Autobiography of Malcolm X*. New York: Grove.

Xu, Xiao. 2017. "Immigrants providing a boost to declining church attendance in Canada." *Globe and Mail* 22 December. https://www .theglobeandmail.com/news/british -columbia/immigrants-providing -a-boost-to-declining-church -attendance-in-canada/article 37423409/ (retrieved 12 February 2018).

Yamane, David. 1997. "Secularization on Trial: In Defense of a Neosecularization Paradigm." *Journal for the Scientific Study of Religion* 36: 109–22.

Yancey, William L., Eugene P. Ericksen, and George H. Leon. 1979. "Emergent Ethnicity: A Review and Reformulation." *American Sociological Review* 41: 391–403.

Young, Rob. 2016. "Canadian Media Usage Trends Study 2016." Retrieved 13 January 2018 (https://iabcanada .com/research/cmust).

Younglai, Rachelle. 2017. "Canada's 1 per cent gets another big income boost." *Globe and Mail* 15 November. https:// www.theglobeandmail.com/report -on-business/economy/canadas-1-per -cent-gets-another-big-income-boost/ article36993871/ (retrieved 2 March 2018).

Zakaria, Rafia. 2014. "Feminism in Faith: Zainah Anwar's Quest to Reinterpret the Qur'an's Most Controversial Verse." Retrieved August 11, 2015 (http://www.buzzfeed.com/ rafiazakaria/feminism-in-faith -islam-1#.mao3MLngoX).

Zald, Meyer N., and John D. McCarthy. 1979. *The Dynamics of Social Movements*. Cambridge, MA: Winthrop.

Zephoria Digital Marketing. 2018. "The Top 20 Valuable Facebook Statistics – Updated February 2018." https:// zephoria.com/top-15-valuable -facebook-statistics/ (retrieved 25 February 2018).

Zimbardo, Philip G. 1972. "Pathology of Imprisonment." *Society* 9, 6: 4–8.

Zimmermann, Francis. 1987 [1982]. *The Jungle and the Aroma of Meats: An Ecological Theme in Hindu Medicine*, Janet Lloyd, trans. Berkeley, CA: University of California Press.

Zinsser, Hans. 1935. *Rats, Lice and History*. Boston: Little, Brown.

Zoutman, D. E., B. D. Ford, E. Bryce, M. Gourdeau, G. Hebert, E. Henderson, S. Paton, Canadian Hospital Epidemiology Committee, Canadian Nosocomial Infection Surveillance Program, Health Canada. 2003. "The State of Infection Surveillance and Control in Canadian Acute Care Hospitals." *American Journal of Infection Control* 31, 5: 266–73.

# INDEX

Aboriginal peoples. *See* Indigenous peoples
abortion, 201, 277
abstraction, 34
achievement-based stratification system, 134
acquaintance rape, 180
adolescence, 65–66, 72–75
adults
    increasing responsibilities, 73
    socialization, 70–71
    supervision and guidance, 73
advertising, 274, 281
age
    and crime, 102
    and television viewing, 276
agents of socialization, 63–70
Akinsanya, Segun, 103–104
*All the Money in the World,* 121
alternative medicine, 263–264
altruistic suicide, 10
American Revolution, 6, 45
analysis of existing documents and official statistics, 21–22
animism, 219
anomic suicide, 10
anticipatory socialization, 70
Asch, Solomon, 93–94
ascription-based stratification system, 134
Asian Canadians, 158–160
assimilation, 150, 151, 156, 159
association, 25–26
atomic bomb, 288, 294–295
authority structures, 87

bias
    algorithms and, 281
    media bias, 274–275
    racism, 145, 149–150
    self-fulfilling prophecy, 65
"big historical projects," 47–48
*The Big Sick,* 90–91
Bill C-10, 114–115
biology, 59
bisexuals, 175
black Canadians, 156–158
Black Death, 247
Black Lives Matter movement, 303
*Blade Runner* movies, 268
blended family, 199
body image, 171–173
body language, 82–83, 84
Bonacich, Edna, 158
*The Book of Mormon,* 222
bourgeoisie, 129
breakdown theory, 298–299
Buddhism, 213, 217

bureaucracy, 87–89, 95–97
bystander apathy, 94

Canada
    adolescents, 65–66
    alternative medicine, 263
    belief in God or a higher power, 47
    carding, 83–85
    death, leading causes of, 248
    earnings gap, 178
    education, 234, 240, 243–244, 245
    environmental racism, 294–295
    families, 190
    fertility, 194
    health care system, 258
    immigration, 43, 157–158, 228
    income and income inequality, 122–123
    largest ethnic groups, 161
    marriage, 193
    mass media, 67
    middle-class family in the 1950s, 192–193
    postmodernism in, 48–50
    race and ethnicity, 162, 163
    religion, 222, 223, 227–229
    strikes, 299–300
    suicide, by age and sex, 10
    voter turnout, 47
    women, and post-secondary education, 171
    women, by occupational category, 179
    youth offenders, 109
capitalist industrialization, 271
capital punishment, 115
caste, 39, 40–41
change, 17
charismatic leaders, 227–228
child care, 63, 184–185, 199, 201, 208
childhood socialization, 72–75
child support, 199–200
Chinese script, 50
Christianity, 213, 214, 215, 218
church, 217, 227
civilization differences, 62
civil rights movement, 218
Clark, S.D., 9
class, 129
    *see also* social class
class conflict, 11
class consciousness, 11
closed-ended question, 26
cohabitation, 202
collective action, 297, 300
collective conscience, 212
colonialism, 139, 150, 159
common couple violence, 202

community college, 236–237
competition, 80–81, 94–95
confidentiality, 23
conflict, 17
conflict theory, 11, 17–18, 20
    community college, 236–237
    crime and deviance, 107–108, 110
    critical evaluation of, 129–130
    culture, 44–45, 49
    dependency theory, 136–138
    education, 236–239, 242
    essentialism, 167
    families, 195–196, 206
    and fashion, 17–18
    gender, 167, 174
    health, 256–258, 259
    Karl Marx, 11
        see also Marx, Karl
    mass media, 273–275, 279
    race and ethnic relations, 150–159
    religion, 213, 217–218, 220
    school, 64
    sexualities, 174
    social interaction, 80–81, 86
    socialization, 63, 69
    social movements, 299–300, 302
    social organization, 86
    social stratification, 127–130, 132
    solidarity theory, 299–300
conformity, 86–87, 92–95
conquest, 153, 159
constraint
    financial, and education, 237
    freedom and, 40, 50–55
    organizational constraints, 97
consumerism, 53
contact hypothesis, 154
contraception, 197–198
control group, 25
control theory, 108
Cooley, Charles, Horton, 60
cooperation, 35, 192
core countries, 138–139
core values, 47–48
corporatization, 241–244
counterculture, 54–55
cow worship, 39, 40
crime, 99–100
    see also deviance; specific types of crime
    conflict theory, 107–108, 110
    control theory, 108
    criminal profiles, 102–103
    criminal subcultures, 107
    explanations of, 103–110
    feminism, 109–110
    functionalist theory, 106–107, 110
    get-tough policies, 113–115
    measuring crime, 101–102
    moral panic, 113
    prison, 112–113

    punishment, 100, 110–111, 115–117
    sanctions, 100
    and social class, 107
    social definition, 99
    symbolic interactionist theory, 104–106, 110
    vs. deviance, 99–100
criminal justice system, 103, 113
critical race theory, 154
crude divorce rate, 193
crude marriage rate, 193
cults, 228
cultural capital, 125, 237–238
cultural hegemony, 12
cultural relativism, 44
cultural studies, 275
cultural turn, 12
culture, 34
    blending cultures, 46
    components of, 34–36
    conflict analysis, 44–45
    as constraint, 40, 50–55
    and ethnicity, 146
    ethnocentrism, 39–40
    as freedom, 40–42
    functionalist analysis, 39–40
    multiculturalism, 42–44
    origins of, 34–36
    as problem solving, 33–34
    and social class, 35–36
    sociological theories, 49

Darwin, Charles, 307
date rape, 109
Davis, Kingsley, 130–131, 133
death, 248, 250–253
death penalty, 115
decriminalization, 116
democracy, 23, 271, 272
Democratic Revolution, 6–8
Denis, Jeff, 154
denominations, 227
dependent variable, 25
detached observation, 27–28
deterrence, 112
deviance, 99
    see also crime
    conflict theory, 107–108, 110
    explanations of, 103–110
    feminism, 109–110
    functionalist theory, 106–107, 110
    learning deviance, 104–105
    medicalization of deviance, 111–112
    social definition, 99
    symbolic interactionist theory, 104–106, 110
    vs. crime, 99–100
discrimination, 144, 159, 179
diversion, 116–117
diversity, 45–46, 202–205
division of labour, 179
divorce, 193, 198–200

dominant culture, 36
Douglas, Tommy, 258
dramaturgical analysis, 81–82
Dumont, Louis, 40–41
Durkheim, Émile, 25–26, 106, 212–213
    *see also* functionalist theory
dysfunctions, 11

earnings gap, 178–180
ecclesia, 227
economic capital, 124
economic cooperation, 192
economic inequality, 236–239
education
    conflict theory, 236–239, 242
    corporatization of the university, 241–244
    and employment, 234
    feminist theory, 240, 243
    functionalist theory, 235–236, 242
    hidden curriculum, 64
    international comparison, 245
    mass education, rise of, 233–235
    school conflicts, 64
    school functions, 64
    sociological theories, 235–241, 242–243
    symbolic interactionist theory, 240–241, 243
educational achievement, 235
educational attainment, 235
efficiency, 89
egoistic suicide, 10
Eichler, Margrit, 15
emotional labour, 79–80
emotional support, 192
emotion management, 79
emotions, 79–80
employment, and education, 234
Engels, Friedrich, 167, 195–196
environment
    environmental exposure, 254
    environmental racism, 251, 294–296
    global warming, 291–293
    market *vs.* high-tech solutions, 296–297
    risk, social distribution of, 294–296
    social construction of environmental problems, 293–294
environmental racism, 251, 294–296
erosion of authority, 46–47
essentialism, 166–168
ethics in sociological research, 23–24
ethnic group, 146
ethnic identity, 147–150
ethnicity, 146
    advantages of, 160–161
    choice *vs.* imposition, 149–150
    future of, 161–163
    social construction of, 147–150
    sociological theories, 147–159
ethnocentrism, 39–40
exchange, 80–81
existing documents, 28–29
experimental group, 25
experiments, 24–26, 29
expulsion, 150
extended family, 191
extracurricular activities, 73

facial expressions, 82–83
families
    as agents of socialization, 63
    conflict theory, 195–196, 206
    decline, 189–191
    family diversity, 202–205
    feminism, 206
    feminist theory, 195–196
    functional theory, 191–193, 205
    middle-class family in the 1950s, 192–193
    mixed-race families, 205
    nuclear family, 190, 191–192, 195–196, 207
    and power, 196–202
    sociological theories, 190, 205–206
    symbolic interactionist theory, 205, 206
family policy, 206–208
fashion, and sociological theories, 15–21
feminism and feminist theory, 14–15, 19–20
    crime and deviance, 109–110
    culture, 49
    education, 240, 243
    essentialism, 167
    families, 195–196, 206
    and fashion, 19–20
    feminization of poverty, 128–129
    gender, 167, 174
    Harriet Martineau, 15
    health, 255–256, 259
    liberal feminism, 186
    mass media, 68, 277–279, 279
    modern feminism, 15
    radical feminists, 187
    religion, 213–217, 221
    sexualities, 174
    social interaction, 77–79, 86
    socialist feminists, 186
    socialization, 63, 68, 69
    social organization, 86
field research, 27–28
First Nations, 148
    *see also* Indigenous peoples
folkway, 35
formal organizations, 95
formal punishment, 100
Foucault, Michel, 12–13
frame alignment, 301–302
freedom, 29–30
    culture as freedom, 40–42
    religious freedom, 226
    social collectivities, 97
French Revolution, 6, 45
functionalist theory, 8–11, 16–17, 20
    breakdown theory, 298–299
    community college, 236–237
    crime and deviance, 106–107, 110

functionalist theory (*continued*)
    critical evaluation of, 130–131
    culture, 39–40, 49
    education, 235–236, 242
    Émile Durkheim, 8–9
    essentialism, 167
    families, 191–193, 205
    family, 63
    and fashion, 16–17
    gender, 167, 174
    mass media, 271–272, 279
    modernization theory, 136
    religion, 212–213, 220
    school, 64
    sexualities, 174
    socialization, 63, 69
    social movements, 298–299, 302
    social stratification, 130–131, 133
    suicide, 9–10
functionalist theory of stratification, 130–131
fundamentalists, 223–224, 225

gangs, 107
gay rights movement, 303
gays, 175
gender, 166
    *see also* women
    and crime, 102
    essentialism, 166–168
    gender differences, 62
    gender risk, global, 183
    gender theories, 166
    male-female interaction, 173
    mass media, and body image, 171–173
    segregation and interaction, 170–171
    socialization, 169–171
    social learning of gender, 166–173
    sociological theories, 167–169, 174
gender discrimination, 179
gender identity, 166
gender ideologies, 171
gender inequality, 178–180, 202
Gender Inequality Index, 183–184
gender roles, 66, 68
generalized other, 62
gene-society interactions, 59
genetic testing companies, 142–143
genocide, 150, 159
geopolitical position, 139
gestures, 82–83
Gilligan, Carol, 62
global inequality, 135–139
globalization, 30, 31, 45–46, 304–307
global structures, 5
global village, 46, 268
global warming, 291–293
Goffman, Erving, 14, 68, 81–82, 83
Gramsci, Antonio, 12
group conformity, 92–95
groups. *See* social groups
groupthink, 94

Harlow, Harry and Margaret, 58
health
    *see also* medicine
    Canadian health care system, 258
    class inequality, and health care, 253–254
    comparative health care, 256–258
    conflict theory, 256–258, 259
    country of residence, 252–253
    feminism and feminist theory, 255–256, 259
    gender inequalities, 255–256
    health indicators, selected countries, 253
    human-environmental factors, 250–251
    and inequality, 250–253
    intersectionality and racial inequalities, 105–106, 254–255
    lifestyle factors, 251–252
    public health and health care systems, 251
    social causes of illness and death, 250–253
    sociological theories, 259
    WHO definition, 250
health care system, 251
heteronormativity, 178
heterosexuals, 175
hidden curriculum, 64
high culture, 36
*Highway of Tears,* 105–106
Hinduism, 39, 40, 213, 216
hip-hop, 54–55
Hirschi, Travis, 109
HIV/AIDS, 252–253, 263
Hochschild, Arlie Russell, 79–80
holistic medicine, 264–265
the Holocaust, 85–86
homelessness, 125
homophobia, 177
homosexuality, 173–178, 202–204, 303
homosexuals, 175
hostile environment sexual harassment, 182
hourly wage, 124
housework, 199, 201
human agency, 19
human capital, 124

"I," 60
identity
    gender identity, 166
    racial and ethnic identity, 147–150
    self-identity, 58, 70–72
    social media, 282
Idle No More movement, 153, 272, 303
illness, 250–253
impression management, 82
incarceration rates, 112–115
income, 122–123
income inequality, 123–125
independent variable, 25
India, 39, 40–41
Indigenous peoples
    and criminal justice system, 103
    health care, 255
    *Highway of Tears,* 105–106
    Idle No More movement, 153, 272, 303

labelling of, 148
languages, disappearance of, 37–38
religion, 218–219
and research, 23–24
residential schools, 38, 151–152
treatment of, by European settlers, 150–153
well-being, relative, 152
Industrial Revolution, 8, 11, 129
inequality, 17
infant mortality, 253
informal punishment, 100
informed consent, 23
initiation rite, 68
institutional racism, 149–150
intelligence, 141, 238–239
interaction. *See* social interaction
intergenerational mobility, 133
internal colonialism, 150
Internet
    access, 280–281
    advertising, 281
    biased algorithms, 281
    content, 281
    and culture, 51–53
    and democracy, 272
    and education, 239
    global social movements, 305
    health information, 262
    online piracy *vs.* net neutrality, 281–282
    race, and dating, 198
    reach of, 66–67
    self-identity, 71–72
    social media, 67, 282–284
    social networks, 72
    virtual communities, 71–72
interpersonal communication, 12
intersectionality, 105–106, 254–255
intersex, 166
intimate terrorism, 202
intragenerational mobility, 133
Inuit, 148
Islam, 213, 214, 216, 225, 228

Japanese Red Army, 225
Jenner, Caitlyn, 165, 166
job search, 89–92
Judaism, 213, 214, 215

Korea, 139

labelling theory, 105
labels, 147–148
language, 36–37
    decline and disappearance of languages, 37–38
    Sapir-Whorf hypothesis, 36–37
    social context of, 82
latent functions, 27, 236
law, 100
legalization, 116
lesbians, 175, 176, 203
less developed countries, 296

life expectancy, 248
lifestyle factors, 251–252
lone-parent families, 204, 237
looking-glass self, 59–60
love, 196–197

macrostructures, 5, 19
male aggression against women, 180–183, 202
manifest functions, 27, 235–236
marital satisfaction, 197–199
marriage, 192, 197–199
Martineau, Harriet, 15
Marx, Karl, 11, 13, 127–129
    *see also* conflict theory
mass communication, 279
    *see also* mass media
mass culture, 36
mass media, 268
    *see also* specific film and television titles
    body image, 171–173
    causes of media growth, 270–271
    celebrity medical advice, 262
    conflict theory, 273–275, 279
    feminist approaches, 277–279, 279
    functionalist theory, 271–272, 279
    gender roles, 68
    influence, increasing, 73
    Internet. *See* Internet
    interpretive approaches, 275–276
    makeover reality shows, 61
    media bias, 274–275
    media violence, effect of, 28
    and moral panic, 113
    ownership of media, 273–274
    racist TV ads, 142–143
    rise of, 268–270
    socialization, 66–68, 68
    social media, 51–53
    sociological theories, 271–279
    symbolic interactionism, 275–276, 279
    television, and violence, 26, 28, 276
material culture, 35
mate selection, 196–197
McLuhan, Marshall, 46, 268
"me," 60
Mead, George Herbert, 13–14, 60, 62, 81
    *see also* symbolic interactionist theory
media. *See* mass media
media imperialism, 281, 284
medicalization of deviance, 111–112
medicine
    *see also* health
    alternative medicine, 263–264
    holistic medicine, 264–265
    patient activism, 261–263
    prescription drugs, 257
    professionalization of medicine, 258–260
    social limits of modern medicine, 260–261
mental disorders, 111–112
Merton, Robert, 11, 106–107
mesostructures, 5

Métis, 148
Me Too movement, 303
microstructures, 5, 19
Milgram, Stanley, 87, 88
Millennials, 74–75
Mills, C. Wright, 4
modernization theory, 136
MOOCs (Massive Open Online Courses), 239
Moore, Wilbert, 130–131, 133
moral panic, 113
more, 35
*Mr. Robot*, 306
multiculturalism, 42–44
Muslim. *See* Islam

net neutrality, 281–282
network analysis, 89–92
network structure, 97
new social movements, 303–307
    globalization potential, 304–307
    goals, 303
    membership, 303–304
non-status Indians, 148
nonverbal communication, 82–85
normal accident, 288
norms, 35, 78–79
norms of solidarity, 86–87
Nova Scotia, 295
nuclear family, 190, 191–192, 195–196, 207
Nunavut, 155

obedience study, 87, 88
obesity, 249
occupational sex segregation, 179
Occupy movement, 305
official statistics, 28–29
Okamoto, Kozo, 225
online piracy, 281–282
open-ended question, 26–27
opportunities, 146–147

Paltrow, Gwyneth, 262
Parsons, Talcott, 9
participant observation, 28, 29
parties, 132
patient activism, 261–263
patriarchy, 5, 15, 19, 196
pay equity, 185
peer groups, 65–66, 73
peripheral countries, 138–139
Perry, Gina, 88
placebo effect, 264
*Playboy* "Playmate of the Month," 172
pluralism, 159, 162
political opportunities, 300
politics, and class inequality, 135
polygamy, 191, 194
popular culture, 36
population, 26
Porter, John, 14, 147
postindustrialism, 30

Postindustrial Revolution, 30
postmodernism, 46–50
poststructuralism, 12, 20–21
poverty, 125–127, 128–129, 137
power, 13, 19, 120, 196–202
prejudice, 143–144, 159
prescription drugs, 257
primary group, 95
primary socialization, 63
prison, 112–113
privacy, 23
production, 35
profane, 212
profession, 259
professionalization of medicine, 258–260
proletariat, 129
Protestant ethic, 13
Protestant Reformation, 45, 270–271
public health system, 251
punishment, 100, 110–111, 115–117

qualitative method, 27
quantitative methods, 27
Québécois, 153–156
queer theory, 175–176
questionnaires, 26
quid pro quo sexual harassment, 182

race
    choice vs. imposition, 149–150
    conflict theories, 150–159
    and crime, 102–103
    future of, 161–163
    and health care, 254–255
    and intelligence, 141
    online dating, 198
    racial mixing, 144–145
    social construction of, 147–150
    sociological definition, 145
    sociological theories, 147–159
    and sports, 141–144
    symbolic interactionist theory, 147–150
racism, 145, 149–150, 251, 254–255
randomization, 18
rape, 109
    *see also* sexual assault
rape culture, 37
rate, 25
rationalization, 50–51
reactivity, 20–21
recidivism rate, 116
reference groups, 95
rehabilitation, 112, 115–116
relative deprivation, 298–299
reliability, 18
religion, 34, 214, 215–217
    in Canada, 227–229
    class, 217
    conflict theory, 213, 217–218, 220
    feminist theory, 213–217, 221
    functionalist theory, 212–213, 220

fundamentalism, 223–224, 225
future of, 230
Indigenous religions, 218–219
market model, 226–227
and Nature, 218–219
religious freedom, 226
revised secularization thesis, 224–225
revival, 223–224, 226–227
secularization, 221–223
sexual orientation, 217
social conflict, 217–218
social inequality, 213
sociological theories, 212–221
symbolic interactionist theory, 219, 220
and violence, 218
women, subordination of, 213–217
religiosity, 224, 226, 229–230
reproduction, 192
reproductive choice, 200–201
research, 8
    ethics of, 23–24
    research cycle, 22–23
    research methods, 24–29
residential schools, 38, 151–152
resocialization, 68–70
resource mobilization, 299–300
resources, 146–147
restorative justice, 116–117
*Revenge Body*, 61
revised secularization thesis, 224–225
rights revolution, 44–45
risk, social distribution of, 294–296
risk society, 289
rites of passage, 45
rituals, 212
Robbers Cave Study, 95
Robinson Crusoe (Dafoe), 119, 131
role, 57, 78
role conflict, 78
role distancing, 81
role strain, 78
role-taking, 60–62
routinization of charisma, 213

sacred, 212
safety, 23
same-sex unions, 202–204
sample, 26
sanctions, 100
Sapir, Edward, 37
Sapir-Whorf hypothesis, 36–37
scapegoat, 145
schools. *See* education
Scientific Revolution, 6, 7, 45
secondary group, 95
secondary socialization, 64
sects, 227
secularization thesis, 221–223
self, 58, 59–60, 60–62
self-esteem, 94–95
self-fulfilling prophecy, 64–65

self-identity, 58, 70–72
self-report surveys, 101
semiperipheral countries, 138–139
sex, 165–166
sex ratio, 255
sexual assault, 37, 109, 180–182
sexual harassment, 182–183
sexuality, 20, 21–22
sexual minorities, 177–178
sexual orientation, 175–176, 217
sexual regulation, 192
shipwrecks, 119–120
sick role, 261
significant others, 60
Singh, Hira, 40–41
slavery, 156, 159
smartphones, 51–53
social activism, 283–284
social capital, 124–125
social category, 92
social change, 287
    environmental problems, 293–297
    social movements. *See* social movements
    technology, 287–293
social class, 11, 129
    and crime, 107
    culture and, 35–36
    and politics, 135
    religion, 217
social constructionism, 166, 169
social control, 108, 110, 300
social convention, 15, 19
social function, 16
social groups, 86–89, 92
    boundaries, 94–95
    group conformity, 92–95
    primary group, 95
    reference groups, 95
    secondary group, 95
social inequality patterns, 120–127
social interaction, 77
    conflict theories, 80–81
    and feminist theory, 77–79
    sociological theories, 86
    symbolic interactionist theory, 81–85
social isolation, 57–58, 252
socialization, 57, 192
    across the life course, 70–75
    adolescence, 72–75
    adult socialization, 70–71
    agents of socialization, 63–70
    anticipatory socialization, 70
    childhood, 72–75
    education and, 234
    gender socialization, 169–171
    primary socialization, 63
    resocialization, 68–70
    secondary socialization, 64
    and social isolation, 57–58
    sociological theories, 69
    symbolic interactionist theory, 59–62

socialized medicine, 258
social marginality, 298
social media, 51–53, 67, 282–284
social mobility, 133–135
social movements, 297
    breakdown theory, 298–299
    framing theory, 300–302
    new social movements, 303–307
    sociological theories, 298–302
    solidarity theory, 299–300
social networks, 72, 89–92
social organizations, 86–97
social relations, 282–283
social solidarity, 8
social stratification, 120
    conflict theory, 127–130, 132
    functionalist theory, 130–131, 133
    global inequality, 135–139
    income, 122–125
    Max Weber, 131–132, 133
    politics, and class inequality, 135
    poverty, 125–127
    shipwrecks and inequality, 119–120
    social inequality patterns, 120–127
    social mobility, 133–135
    wealth, 120–122
social structure, 4–6, 16, 17, 79–80, 139, 146
society, 34
sociological imagination, 4–8
sociological research. *See* research
sociological theories, 8–22
    *see also* specific sociological theories
    crime and deviance, 103–110
    culture, 49
    education, 235–241, 242–243
    families, 190, 205–206
    gender, 167–169, 174
    health, 259
    mass media, 271–279
    race and ethnicity, 147–159
    religion, 212–221
    sexualities, 174
    social interaction, 86
    socialization, 63–70, 69
    social organizations, 86
    social stratification, 127–133
sociology, 4, 8
solidarity theory, 299–300
*South Park*, 222, 276
split labour markets, 158–160, 159
sports, and race, 141–144
spousal violence, 202
Stanford prison experiment, 69–70
state policy, 139
Statistics Canada, 28, 126
status, 65, 78
status cues, 83–85
status groups, 131–132
Status Indians, 148
stereotypes, 83, 278
stereotype threat, 240–241

stigmatization, 100
strain, 106, 298
stratification. *See* social stratification
streaming, 238
street crimes, 103, 107
stress, 254
strikes, 299–300
subculture, 53–55, 107
subordinate culture, 36
suicide, 9, 10
surveys, 26–27, 29, 101
Sweden, and the nuclear family, 206–208
*Swept Away*, 119
symbol, 12, 34
symbolic ethnicity, 149
symbolic interactionist theory, 13–14, 18–19, 20
    childhood, foundations of, 59–62
    crime and deviance, 104–106, 110
    culture, 49
    education, 240–241, 243
    families, 205, 206
    and fashion, 18–19
    framing theory, 300–302
    gender, 169, 174
    George Herbert Mead, 13–14
    mass media, 275–276, 279
    racial and ethnic identity, 147–150, 159
    religion, 219, 220
    self-fulfilling prophecy, 64–65
    sexualities, 174
    social constructionism, 169
    social interaction, 81–85, 86
    socialization, 63, 69
    social movements, 300–302, 302
    social organization, 86
    Thomas theorem, 64

taboo, 35
Taiwan, 139
tax system, 127
technological determinism, 289
technology, 288
    environmental solutions, 296–297
    global warming, 291–293
    high tech, and big tech, 290–291
    Kondratiev waves, 289
    and social change, 289–290
television. *See* mass media
theory, 6
    *see also* sociological theories
Thomas theorem, 64
Tilly, Charles, 298
*Titanic*, 119–120
total fertility rate, 193
total institutions, 68–69
totems, 212
traditional nuclear family, 190, 191
transgender, 166
transnational communities, 161
Trump, Donald, 7

Uniform Crime Reporting Survey, 28
United Nations Universal Declaration of Human Rights, 44
United States
    health care, 256–257
    and the nuclear family, 206–208
uranium, 294–295
urban networks, 92

validity, 25
values, 8, 16, 35, 47–48
verbal communication, 82
vertical mosaic, 14, 147
victim-blaming, 154
victimization surveys, 101
victimless crimes, 101
violence
    male aggression against women, 180–183, 202
    religious violence, 218
    spousal violence, 202
    television and, 26, 276

violent resistance, 202
virtual communities, 71–72
visible minority, 147, 162

wage gap, 178–180
wealth, 120–122
Weber, Max, 11–12, 13, 50, 53, 87, 131–132, 133, 213, 219, 221
white-collar crimes, 103, 107
Whorf, Benjamin Lee, 37
"wild boy of Aveyron," 57
women
    *see also* gender
    child care, 184–185
    male aggression against women, 180–183, 202
    pay equity, 185
    and religion, 213–217
women's movement, 185–187, 303
world religions, 214, 215–217

zero-child families, 204

# CHAPTER 1 IN REVIEW

## INTRODUCING SOCIOLOGY

### LEARNING OBJECTIVES

### LO¹ DEFINE SOCIOLOGY

Most people take for granted that things happen in the world because physical and emotional forces cause them. They think that famine is caused by drought, economic success by hard work, marriage by love, and so on. But if drought causes famine, why have so many famines occurred in perfectly normal weather conditions or involved some groups hoarding or destroying food so others would starve? If hard work causes prosperity, why are so many hard workers poor? If love causes marriage, why does violence against women and children occur in so many families? The answer to these questions is that *social* forces influence all human behaviour. **Sociology** draws our attention to these forces; it is the systematic study of human behaviour in social context.

### LO² IDENTIFY THE SOCIAL RELATIONS THAT SURROUND YOU, PERMEATE YOU, AND INFLUENCE YOUR BEHAVIOUR

**Social structures** are stable patterns of social relations. Although you might not be aware of them, they affect your innermost thoughts and feelings, influence your actions, and help shape who you are. C. Wright Mills argued that the sociologist's job is to identify and explain the connection between people's personal troubles and the social structures in which they are embedded. He wrote that the **sociological imagination** allows us to see the connection between personal troubles and social structures (Mills, 1959). To broaden your sociological awareness, you need to recognize that four levels of social structure surround and permeate us:

1. **Microstructures** are patterns of intimate social relations formed during face-to-face interaction. Families and friendship cliques are examples of microstructures.
2. **Mesostructures** are patterns of social relations in organizations that involve people who are often not intimately acquainted and who often do not interact face to face. Social organizations such as colleges and government bureaucracies are examples of mesostructures.
3. **Macrostructures** are overarching patterns of social relations that lie above and beyond mesostructures. One such macrostructure is **patriarchy**, a system of power relations and customary practices that help to ensure male dominance in economic, political, and other spheres of life.
4. **Global structures** are social structures that span countries. Economic relations among countries and patterns of worldwide travel and communication are examples of global structures.

### LO³ DESCRIBE HOW THE SCIENTIFIC, DEMOCRATIC, AND INDUSTRIAL REVOLUTIONS GAVE RISE TO THE SOCIOLOGICAL IMAGINATION

The sociological imagination originated in three revolutions that caused people to think about society in an entirely new way:

1. The **Scientific Revolution** began in Europe about 1550. It promoted the view that conclusions about the workings of the world should be based on solid evidence, not just speculation.
2. The **Democratic Revolution** began about 1770, as citizens of France and the United States started demanding an increased say in the way they were governed. By eventually achieving popular control of government, they demonstrated that societies do not have to be ruled by kings and queens who claim their authority is ordained by God. Instead, society can be organized and run by ordinary people. This idea prepared the ground for the notion that a science of society aimed at improving human welfare is possible.
3. The **Industrial Revolution**, which involved rapid growth of mechanized industry, began in Britain in the 1780s. The application of science and technology to industrial processes, the creation of factories, massive migration from countryside to city, and the formation of an industrial working class transformed society and caused a host of social problems that attracted the attention of social thinkers.

### LO⁴ APPRECIATE THAT VALUES, THEORY, AND RESEARCH FORM THE BUILDING BLOCKS OF THE SOCIOLOGICAL ENTERPRISE

A **theory** is a conjecture about the way observable facts are related. When people formulate theories, their values inevitably influence them. **Values** are ideas about what is right and wrong, good and bad, desirable and undesirable, beautiful and ugly. **Research** is the systematic observation of facts for the purpose of showing that a theory is false. When research fails to show that a theory is false, investigators are obliged to conclude that the theory is valid—but only until further notice, that is, unless and until someone shows it is false. All people have values. Their values inevitably influence their theories. But research allows us to reject some theories as invalid.

## LO 5 SUMMARIZE THE FOUR MAIN SCHOOLS OF SOCIOLOGICAL THEORY

### THEORIES AT A GLANCE

**Sociology's Main Theories**

| Theory | Main Level(s) of Analysis | Main Foci | Main Question |
|---|---|---|---|
| Functionalism | Macro | Social structure; social function; values | How do social structures and the values underlying them contribute to social stability? |
| Conflict theory | Macro | Social structure; inequality; social conflict and change | How does the structure of inequality between privileged groups seeking to maintain their advantages and subordinate groups seeking to increase theirs lead to conflict and often to social change? |
| Symbolic interactionism | Micro | Meaning; interpersonal communication; human agency | How do people communicate to make their social settings meaningful, thus helping to create their social circumstances? |
| Feminism | Macro and micro | Patriarchy; power and social convention | How do social conventions maintain male dominance and female subordination, and how do these conventions get overturned? |

## LO 6 DISTINGUISH THE FOUR MAIN METHODS OF COLLECTING SOCIOLOGICAL DATA

**TABLE 1.3 Strengths and Weaknesses of the Four Main Sociological Research Methods**

| Method | Strengths | Weaknesses |
|---|---|---|
| Experiment | High reliability; excellent for establishing cause-and-effect relationships | Low validity for many sociological problems because of the unnaturalness of the experimental setting |
| Survey | Good reliability; useful for establishing cause-and-effect relationships | Validity problems exist unless researchers make strong efforts to deal with them |
| Participant observation | Allows researchers to develop a deep and sympathetic understanding of the way people see the world; especially useful in exploratory research | Low reliability and generalizability |
| Analysis of existing documents and official statistics | Often inexpensive and easy to obtain; provides good coverage; useful for historical analysis; nonreactive | Often contains biases reflecting the interests of the data creators rather than the interests of the researcher |

Source: From BRYM/LIE. *Sociology*, 1E. © 2009 Nelson Education Ltd. Reproduced by permission. www.cengage.com/permissions.

## LO 7 EXPLAIN HOW SOCIOLOGY CAN HELP US DEAL WITH MAJOR CHALLENGES THAT FACE SOCIETY TODAY

The greatest sociological puzzles of our time are (1) the **Postindustrial Revolution** (the technology-driven shift from employment in factories to employment in offices, and the consequences of that shift for nearly all human activity) and (2) **globalization** (the process by which formerly separated individuals, groups, institutions, economies, states, and cultures are becoming tied together and people are becoming increasingly aware of their growing interdependence). Both processes have allowed many people to become freer to choose their identity, their religion, their friends, and their intimate partners, and to enjoy more opportunities for education, political influence, entertainment, and good jobs. However, the Postindustrial Revolution and globalization have also restricted freedom and limited opportunities for many people. Whether the balance will tip toward more freedom and more opportunities for more people or in the opposite direction is unclear. However, the promise of sociology is that it makes tools available for figuring out how to achieve desirable social goals.

## Multiple-Choice Questions

Questions marked with an asterisk are higher-order questions on the Bloom taxonomy. Answers to these questions are available in the appendix on page CR-50.

*1. In 1960, women in South Korea had an average of about six babies each. Today, women in South Korea have fewer than two babies each. Which of the following statements offers the best *sociological* explanation of this change?
   a. Over the past six decades, most women in South Korea realized that the disadvantages of having large families outweighed the advantages and changed their child-bearing behaviour accordingly.
   b. As South Korea underwent rapid industrialization, increasing air and water pollution had a large, negative effect on women's fertility, so women started having fewer babies.
   c. South Korean industrialization turned many farmers into urban workers and housewives. Whereas it was valuable to have many children working on the farm, it was more costly and less useful to raise as many children in the city, so women started having fewer babies.
   d. When television came to South Korea, women learned that in the West there were only about two children per family.

*2. A sociologist observes that cow worship and malnourishment are common in rural India. He can't understand why rural Indians refuse to eat beef and engage in a variety of ritual practices involving cows when they need more food. He conducts research on the subject, leading him to theorize that rural Indians don't slaughter cows because cows provide things of great value. They give birth to oxen that can plough fields and yield abundant manure that can be used as a cooking fuel and a fertilizer. With which theoretical tradition is the sociologist's explanation for cow worship in rural India associated?
   a. symbolic interactionism
   b. functionalism
   c. conflict theory
   d. feminism

3. What is the purpose of research?
   a. To discover associations between observable facts
   b. To discover new theories
   c. To prove the validity of theories
   d. To disprove the validity of theories

4. Which of the following problems confront experiments that are designed to test sociological theories?
   a. low validity
   b. high reliability
   c. high reactivity
   d. low randomization

*5. A sociologist wants to research a problem about which little is known and concerning which theories are poorly developed. Which of the following research methods would be the most appropriate for her research?
   a. an experiment
   b. a survey
   c. participant observation
   d. analysis of existing documents and official data

# CHAPTER 2 IN REVIEW

## CULTURE

### LEARNING OBJECTIVES

#### LO1 DEFINE CULTURE AND ITS MAIN COMPONENTS

**Culture** consists of the socially transmitted ideas, practices, and material objects that people create to deal with real-life problems.

#### LO2 EXPLAIN HOW CULTURE HELPS HUMANS ADAPT AND THRIVE IN THEIR ENVIRONMENTS

Humans are able to create culture because of their capacity to engage in

- **abstraction** (using **symbols** or general ideas or ways of thinking that are not linked to particular instances)
- **cooperation** (building a complex social life by establishing **norms** or generally accepted ways of doing things, and values or ideas about what is right and wrong, good and bad, desirable and undesirable, beautiful and ugly)
- **production** (making and using tools and techniques that improve their ability to take what they want from nature).

#### LO3 RECOGNIZE THE CENTRALITY OF LANGUAGE IN ALL CULTURES

A **language** is a system of symbols strung together to communicate thought, and it is one of the most important parts of any culture. The **Sapir–Whorf hypothesis** holds that we experience important things in our environment and form concepts about those things. Then we develop language to express our concepts. Finally, language itself influences how we see the world.

For centuries, Great Britain, the United States, France, Portugal, and Spain gained economic, political, and cultural influence over much of the world by using military violence, supporting sympathetic local governments, helping to create new educational systems, fostering the spread of the mass media, and encouraging the use of their national languages. The usage of many languages has consequently decreased or disappeared entirely. Because Canadian governments have sought to assimilate Indigenous peoples, often by force, Indigenous languages in Canada are among the many endangered languages of the world.

#### LO4 APPRECIATE THAT ASSESSING OTHER CULTURES FROM THE STANDPOINT OF YOUR OWN CULTURE IMPAIRS SOCIOLOGICAL UNDERSTANDING

Judging another culture exclusively by the standards of our own is known as **ethnocentrism**. Ethnocentrism impairs sociological analysis insofar as it prevents you from understanding the meaning that members of other cultures attach to the people and things in their social environment.

#### LO5 DISTINGUISH WAYS IN WHICH CULTURE MAKES PEOPLE FREER AS IT BECOMES MORE DIVERSE, MULTICULTURAL, AND GLOBALIZED

Cultural diversification (an increase in the variety of cultures represented in a society), **multiculturalism** (a government policy that promotes and funds the maintenance of culturally diverse communities), and globalization (the process by which formerly separate individuals, groups, institutions, economies, states, and cultures are becoming tied together and people are becoming increasingly aware of their growing interdependence) increase freedom insofar as they provide people with more choices of food, fashion, friends, religion, intimate partners, and so on. One consequence of cultural diversification is the growth of **postmodernism**, which is characterized by an eclectic mix of cultural elements from different times and places, the erosion of authority, and the decline of consensus around core values. According to some analysts, Canada is the first truly postmodern society.

#### LO6 IDENTIFY WAYS IN WHICH CULTURE PLACES LIMITS ON PEOPLE'S FREEDOM

**Rationalization** (the application of the most efficient means to achieve given goals and the unintended, negative consequences of doing so) and **consumerism** (the tendency to define ourselves in terms of the goods and services we purchase) are powerful social forces that compel us to act in particular ways, thus restricting our freedom. For example, the drive to efficiency and high levels of consumption can lead to compulsive behaviour that impedes enriching face-to-face interaction.

# THEORIES AT A GLANCE

## Culture

| Theory | Main Question | Application |
|---|---|---|
| Functionalism | How do social structures and the values underlying them contribute to social stability? | Cow worship is a practice that seems bizarre to many Westerners but it makes sense if one considers its useful functions. As Harris noted, most Indian peasants can't afford tractors, so cows are needed to give birth to oxen, which are in high demand for plowing. Moreover, cows produce hundreds of millions of kilograms of recoverable manure, half of which is used as fertilizer and the other half as a cooking fuel—and all of which is useful in a society with oil, coal, wood, and chemical fertilizers too expensive for many peasants to afford. Cows in India don't cost much to maintain because they eat mostly food that is not fit for human consumption. And they represent an important source of protein as well as a livelihood for members of low-ranking castes, who have the right to eat beef and dispose of the bodies of dead cattle. These "untouchables" form the workforce of India's large leather craft industry. The protection of cows by means of cow worship is thus a functional practice.<br><br>Manifest functions are intended and easily observed, while latent functions are unintended and less obvious. Harris discovered that cow worship performs a range of latent functions, showing how a particular social practice has unintended consequences that make social order possible. |
| Symbolic interactionism | How do people communicate to make their social settings meaningful, thus helping to create their social circumstances? | Functionalists and conflict theorists view culture as an effect of patterns of social relations. Symbolic interactionists view culture as a result of human creativity and choice. From the latter viewpoint, freedom to choose one's culture has been enhanced over the past half-century by the ethnic and religious diversification of Canadian society, the development of Canada's policy of multiculturalism, the efforts of groups formerly excluded from full participation in Canadian economic and political life to assert their rights, and globalization. Some analysts regard the freedom to choose one's culture as having advanced to the point where it is necessary to characterize our culture as postmodern—a culture that blends elements from various times and places, erodes authority, and renders core values unstable. |
| Conflict theory | How does the structure of inequality between privileged groups seeking to maintain their advantages and subordinate groups seeking to increase theirs lead to conflict and often to social change? | Conflict theorists argue that if we probe beneath cultural diversification and multiculturalism, we find the rights revolution, the process by which socially excluded groups have struggled to win equal rights under the law and in practice. Today, indigenous rights, women's rights, minority rights, gay and lesbian rights, the rights of people with special needs, constitutional rights, and language rights are all part of our political discourse. Because of the rights revolution, democracy has been widened and deepened. Many categories of people are still discriminated against socially, politically, and economically. However, in much of the world, a widening circle of people participate more fully than ever before in the life of their societies because they have engaged in conflict with privileged groups. |
| Feminism | How do social conventions maintain male dominance and female subordination, and how can these conventions be overturned? | Income and power inequality between women and men encourage some men to use terms like fox, babe, bitch, ho, and doll to refer to women. The use of such words in itself influences men to think of women as sexual objects. Feminist theorists argue that thinking about women in this way sustains a rape culture in which sexual harassment, slut-shaming, the trivialization of rape, victim-blaming, and sexual assault are widespread and, for large sections of the population, these actions seem normal. As some feminists emphasize, if men are ever going to think of women as equals, actual gender inequality will have to be reduced—and male language conventions used to refer to women will also have to change. |

# Multiple-Choice Questions

Questions marked with an asterisk are higher-order questions on the Bloom taxonomy. Answers to these questions are available in the appendix on page CR-50.

1. The Sapir–Whorf hypothesis sets out the relationship among verbalization (language), conceptualization (thought), and experience. According to Sapir and Whorf, what is the causal order of these three elements?
    a. verbalization → conceptualization → experience → verbalization
    b. experience → conceptualization → verbalization → experience
    c. verbalization → experience → conceptualization → verbalization
    d. experience → verbalization → conceptualization → experience

2. According to the text, what is the main difference between class and caste?
    a. There is no difference; caste is simply the term for class in India.
    b. Castes existed in the distant past; classes exist now.
    c. Castes are justified mainly by religion; classes are not.
    d. There are four main classes in Canada; three are six main castes in India.

*3. Which of the following statements describes a latent function?
    a. A university is a "marriage market," that is, a competitive forum for the establishment of long-term, intimate relations between individuals.
    b. A university is an institution of advanced learning covering a wide range of subjects in the humanities, social sciences, and natural sciences that are important to the progress of society.
    c. A university is a waste of time.
    d. Even a small university costs more to run than most businesses.

4. In Canada, what have cultural diversification, multiculturalism, and globalization created?
    a. a rights revolution
    b. more social constraint
    c. heightened ethnocentrism and cultural relativism
    d. a postmodern society

*5. At a McDonald's restaurant, food ingredients, cooking times, portion sizes, and even the "specials" recited by people taking your order are precisely regulated, providing a uniform experience in McDonald's restaurants across the country. What does the McDonald's experience exemplify?
    a. postmodernism
    b. rationalization
    c. cultural freedom
    d. globalization

# CHAPTER 3 IN REVIEW

## SOCIALIZATION

### LEARNING OBJECTIVES

#### LO¹ RECOGNIZE THAT HUMAN ABILITIES REMAIN UNDEVELOPED UNLESS SOCIAL INTERACTION UNLEASHES THEM

The ability to learn culture and become fully human is only a potential. To be actualized, **socialization** must unleash this potential. Socialization is the process by which people learn their culture. They do so by (1) entering into and disengaging from a succession of roles and (2) becoming aware of themselves as they interact with others. (A **role** is the behaviour expected of a person occupying a particular position in society.) The formation of the self begins in infancy and continues throughout life.

#### LO² EXPLAIN HOW ONE'S SENSE OF SELF EMERGES AND CHANGES AS ONE INTERACTS WITH OTHERS

When infants cry out, driven by elemental needs, they are gratified by food, comfort, and affection. Because their needs are typically satisfied immediately, they do not at first seem able to distinguish themselves from their main caregivers, usually their mothers. However, they soon begin developing a self-image or sense of **self**—a set of ideas and attitudes about who they are as independent beings. Inherent biological and psychological traits set broad potentials and limits to what people can become. The broader society and culture define the general outlines of people's beliefs, symbols, values, and roles. However, as symbolic interactionists emphasize, people are continually socialized in face-to-face settings where they interact with others. In those settings they imaginatively interpret, accept, and sometimes reject the opportunities and demands of socialization in ways that suit them.

Charles Horton Cooley proposed that our sense of self develops largely as a result of the way we see ourselves evaluated by others; he referred to the **looking-glass self**. By this he meant that when we interact with others, they react to us with words and gestures. This allows us to imagine how we appear to them. We then judge how others evaluate us. Finally, from these judgments we develop a self-concept or a set of feelings and ideas about who we are.

George Herbert Mead took up and developed Cooley's ideas. Mead noted that a subjective and impulsive aspect of the self (the **I**) is present from birth. He also recognized that a storehouse of culturally approved standards (the **me**) emerges as part of the self during social interaction. He drew attention to the unique human capacity to "take the role of the other" as the source of the me. According to Mead, the self develops in four stages of role-taking:

1. First, children learn to use language and other symbols by imitating important people in their lives, such as their mother and father (their significant others).
2. Second, they use their imaginations to play the roles of others in games.
3. Third, children learn to play complex games that require them to take the role of several other people simultaneously.
4. Fourth, they learn to take the role of the generalized other. That is, years of experience teaches an individual that other people, employing the cultural standards of their society, usually regard him or her in particular ways. A person's image of these cultural standards and how they are applied to him or her is what Mead meant by the generalized other.

The structure of a person's society and his or her position in it also affects socialization because they influence the kinds of people with whom one is most likely to interact. For example, a person's gender and the civilization into which he or she is born have a bearing on the content of a person's socialization.

#### LO³ COMPARE CHANGE OVER THE PAST CENTURY IN THE SOCIALIZING INFLUENCE OF THE FAMILY, SCHOOLS, PEER GROUPS, AND THE MASS MEDIA

The family is the most important agent of **primary socialization**, the process of mastering the basic skills required to operate in society during childhood. The socialization function of the family was more pronounced a century ago, partly because adult family members were more readily available for child care and supervision than they are today. As industry grew across Canada, families left farming for city work in factories and offices. Many women had to work outside the home for a wage to maintain an adequate standard of living for their families. Child care—and therefore childhood socialization—became a big social problem that was partly alleviated by compulsory schooling.

Schools became increasingly responsible for **secondary socialization**, or socialization outside the family after childhood. Instructing students in academic and vocational subjects is the school's manifest function. One of its latent functions is to teach the **hidden curriculum**. The hidden curriculum instructs students in what will be expected of them in the larger society once they graduate—it teaches them to be conventionally "good citizens." Many students from working-class and racial-minority families struggle against the hidden curriculum because their experience and that of their friends, peers, and family members make them skeptical about the ability of school to open good job opportunities for them. As a result, they rebel against the authority of the school, do poorly academically, and eventually enter the work world near the bottom of the socioeconomic hierarchy. Some teachers expect that students from working-class and racial-minority families will do poorly in school, and this expectation itself helps to cause what it predicts, acting as a **self-fulfilling prophecy**.

Like schools, **peer groups** and the mass media have become increasingly important agents of socialization over the past century. Peer groups consist of individuals who are not necessarily friends but who are about the same age and of similar status. (**Status** refers to a recognized social position an individual can occupy.)

The mass media also constitute an important agent of socialization. TV reaches more Canadians than any other mass medium. However, Canadians spend more time using the Internet than any other mass medium. Although people are free to choose socialization influences from the mass media, they choose some influences more than others. Specifically, they tend to choose influences that are more pervasive, fit existing cultural standards, and are made especially appealing by those who control the mass media.

## LO 4 APPRECIATE THAT PEOPLE'S IDENTITIES CHANGE FASTER, MORE OFTEN, AND MORE COMPLETELY THAN THEY DID JUST A COUPLE OF DECADES AGO

Today, people's identities change faster, more often, and more completely than they did just a few decades ago. One important factor contributing to the growing flexibility of the self is globalization. A second factor increasing our freedom

## THEORIES AT A GLANCE

### Socialization

| Theory | Main Question | Application |
|---|---|---|
| Functionalism | How do social structures and the values underlying them contribute to social stability? | Families and schools contribute to social order because they are the main agents of primary and secondary socialization, respectively. |
| Conflict theory | How does the structure of inequality between privileged groups seeking to maintain their advantages and subordinate groups seeking to increase theirs lead to conflict and often to social change? | The experience of many minority-group and working-class students teaches them that even if they adhere to the hidden curriculum, it is unlikely they will become highly successful. Therefore, they often rebel against school authority—which helps to ensure they will not become highly successful. |
| Symbolic interactionism | How do people communicate to make their social settings meaningful, thus helping to create their social circumstances? | The expectations of students and teachers influence the learning opportunities and performance of students. The operation of self-fulfilling prophecies helps to ensure that, on average, working-class and minority-group students will have inferior learning opportunities and achieve lower grades than other students do. |
| Feminism | How do social conventions maintain male dominance and female subordination, and how do these conventions get overturned? | Media messages typically support conventional expectations about how males and females are supposed to behave. However, women's increasing power over the past 50 or 60 years has led them to assert their right to equality with men, and to a degree this change is reflected in the mass media. |

to design ourselves is our growing ability to fashion new bodies from old. The Internet also contributes to the flexibility of identity formation today.

## LO 5 LIST THE FACTORS TRANSFORMING THE CHARACTER OF CHILDHOOD, ADOLESCENCE, AND EARLY ADULTHOOD TODAY

In preindustrial societies, children were considered to be small adults. From a young age, they were expected to conform as much as possible to the norms of the adult world. Beginning around 1600 in Europe and North America, the idea of childhood as a distinct stage of life emerged, first for boys from well-to-do families, then for girls from well-to-do families. Most working-class children didn't enjoy much of a childhood until the twentieth century. Prolonged childhood was *necessary* in societies that required better-educated adults to do increasingly complex work, because childhood gave young people a chance to prepare for adult life. Prolonged childhood was *possible* in societies where improved hygiene and nutrition allowed most people to live more than 35 years, the average lifespan in Europe in the early seventeenth century.

## LO 6 IDENTIFY HOW THE SOCIALIZATION PATTERNS OF CANADIAN YOUTH HAVE CHANGED OVER THE PAST HALF-CENTURY DUE TO DECLINING ADULT SUPERVISION AND GUIDANCE, INCREASING MASS MEDIA AND PEER GROUP INFLUENCE, AND INCREASING ASSUMPTION OF SUBSTANTIAL ADULT RESPONSIBILITIES TO THE NEGLECT OF EXTRACURRICULAR ACTIVITIES

The socialization patterns of Canadian youth have changed considerably over the past half-century. The change is largely due to declining adult supervision and guidance (which provides more opportunities to engage in risky behaviour), increasing mass media and peer group influence (which often pulls young people in different directions from the school and the family, leaving them uncertain about what constitutes appropriate behaviour and making the job of growing up more stressful than it used to be), and increasing assumption of substantial adult responsibilities to the neglect of extracurricular activities (the latter of which provide important opportunities for students to develop concrete skills and thereby make sense of the world and their place in it).

Notwithstanding the changes just enumerated, many commentators characterize North Americans born between the early 1980s and the early 2000s—so-called "Millennials"—as lazy, entitled narcissists who still live with their parents. This characterization is inaccurate because (1) spoiled kids from well-to-do families are not a new phenomenon; (2) not all children from well-to-do families are spoiled; and (3) most Millennials are not from well-to-do families that can afford to spoil their children. In fact, a decline in the number of good jobs available to new entrants in the paid labour force, rising student debt, and the high cost of housing prevent many young adults from assuming the responsibilities of adulthood that their parents took on when they were in their twenties.

## Multiple-Choice Questions

Questions marked with an asterisk are higher-order questions on the Bloom taxonomy. Answers to these questions are available in the appendix on page CR-50.

1. Which of the following is NOT a stage of role-taking according to George Herbert Mead?
    a. imitating significant others
    b. pretending to be other people
    c. playing simple games
    d. playing complex games
    e. taking the role of the generalized other

2. Over the past century, which agent of socialization has declined in importance?
    a. the family
    b. the peer group
    c. the school
    d. the mass media

*3. When Sung Min's family was getting ready to move from South Korea to Canada, his mother started watching North American TV shows to learn about Canadian culture. However, she could only access "classic" shows like an old comedy series from the 1950s, *My Three Sons*. In that series, three brothers did all of the household chores. When Sung Min's family finally arrived in Canada, his mother insisted that Sung Min do all the chores while his sister didn't have to do any. When Sung Min objected, his mother said, "I'm sorry, but that's the way they do things in

Canada." What sociological concept does this anecdote (based on actual events) illustrate?

a. the looking-glass self
b. the "me"
c. the generalized other
d. anticipatory socialization

4. Why did the idea of childhood emerge beginning around 1600 in North America and Europe?

a. Life expectancy rose and the need for better-educated adults became apparent.
b. Humanitarian ideas spread, gradually causing people to put an end to child labour.
c. Early sociologists demonstrated that a sustained period of early life without adult responsibilities was healthy for the development of the self.
d. Early psychologists demonstrated that a sustained period of early life without adult responsibilities was healthy for the development of the self.

5. According to the text, about 35 percent of young adults in Canada live with their parents, and this percentage has been increasing since 2001. Why?

a. Poor child-rearing practices have produced a generation with a high proportion of slackers.
b. Lack of good jobs, high student debt, and expensive housing costs force many young adults to live with their parents.
c. Because the family has become a more important socializing agent over time, young adults are closer to their parents than they used to be and are therefore inclined to live with them as long as possible.
d. Housing conditions have improved over time, so many people now have finished basements where their young adult children can live.

# CHAPTER 4 IN REVIEW

## FROM SOCIAL INTERACTION TO SOCIAL ORGANIZATIONS

### LEARNING OBJECTIVES

#### LO1 DEFINE SOCIAL INTERACTION

**Social interaction** involves people communicating face to face, acting and reacting in relation to one another.

#### LO2 IDENTIFY HOW VARIOUS ASPECTS OF SOCIAL STRUCTURE INFLUENCE THE TEXTURE OF EMOTIONAL LIFE

Social interaction is structured by **social statuses** (recognized social positions), **roles** (sets of expected behaviours) and **norms** (generally accepted way of doing things). When a person holds two or more statuses with different role demands, the result is **role conflict**. When a person holds a single status with incompatible role demands, the result is **role strain**. Structural influences on social interaction are evident in **emotion management** (obeying "feeling rules" and responding appropriately to the situations in which people find themselves) and **emotional labour** (emotion management that many people do as part of their job and for which they are paid).

Social interaction is structured by competition for valued resources, including attention, approval, prestige, information, and money. Conflict never lies far below the surface of competitive social interactions marked by substantial inequality. However, norms often influence people to interact in ways that are noncompetitive.

#### LO3 RECOGNIZE THAT IN SOCIAL INTERACTION, NONVERBAL COMMUNICATION IS EXTREMELY IMPORTANT

To become competent communicators, people must be able to reduce ambiguity and make sense of words. They do so by learning the nuances of meaning in different cultural and social contexts over an extended time. Nonverbal cues assist them in that task.

The face is capable of more than 1000 distinct expressions, reflecting the whole range of human emotion. Arm movements, hand gestures, posture, and other aspects of body language send many more messages to a person's audience. Most researchers believe that the facial expressions of six emotions (happiness, sadness, anger, disgust, fear, and surprise) are similar across cultures although some analysts contend that facial expressions are not the readout of emotions but displays that serve social motives and are mostly determined by the presence of an audience.

#### LO4 SEE HOW EMOTIONAL AND MATERIAL RESOURCES FLOW THROUGH PATTERNS OF SOCIAL RELATIONS CALLED SOCIAL NETWORKS

A social network is a bounded set of units (individuals, organizations, countries, and so on) linked by the exchange of material or emotional resources. Network members exchange resources more frequently with each other than with nonmembers and they think of themselves as network members. Each network member is linked to people in other social networks. This linkage connects the member to others he or she has never met, creating a "small world" that extends far beyond the member's personal network.

#### LO5 EXPLAIN HOW SOCIAL GROUPS BIND PEOPLE TOGETHER, IMPOSE CONFORMITY ON THEM, AND SEPARATE THEM FROM NON–GROUP MEMBERS

**Social groups** consist of one or more social networks, the members of which identify with one another, routinely interact, and adhere to defined norms, roles, and statuses. In contrast, **social categories** consist of people who share similar status but do not routinely interact or identify with one another. Social groups typically compel people to conform, which has both advantages (armies and sports teams require a high level of conformity) and disadvantages (too much conformity can instill apathy, dampen creativity, and limit the visibility of danger).

People can act in ways that contradict their beliefs and values when norms of solidarity demand conformity, structures of authority demand obedience, and bureaucratic structures distance people from the negative effects of their actions.

# THEORIES AT A GLANCE

## Social Interaction and Social Organizations

| Theory | Main Question | Application |
|---|---|---|
| Conflict theory | How does the structure of inequality between privileged groups seeking to maintain their advantages and subordinate groups seeking to increase theirs lead to conflict and often to social change? | A large part of everyday conversation involves a subtle competition for attention. In fact, much social interaction is a competitive struggle in which people seek to gain the most—socially, emotionally, and economically—while paying the least. |
| Symbolic interactionism | How do people communicate to make their social settings meaningful, thus helping to create their social circumstances? | People frequently act in ways they consider fair or just, even if it does not maximize their personal gain. Some people even act altruistically. Thus, selfishness and conflict are not the only bases of social interaction.<br><br>When people behave fairly or altruistically, they are interacting with others based on norms they have learned. These norms say they should act justly and help people in need, even if it costs a lot to do so. |
| Feminism | How do social conventions maintain male dominance and female subordination, and how do these conventions get overturned? | Women laugh more than men do in everyday conversations. Men are more likely than women are to engage in long monologues and interrupt when others are talking. They are also less likely to ask for help or directions because doing so would imply a reduction in their authority. These research findings suggest that social interaction is structured by the relative power of women and men. |

## LO 6 APPRECIATE THAT BUREAUCRACIES CAN OFTEN BE MADE MORE EFFICIENT BY ADOPTING MORE DEMOCRATIC STRUCTURES WITH FEWER LEVELS OF AUTHORITY

Weber defined **bureaucracy** as a large, impersonal organization comprising many clearly defined positions arranged in a hierarchy. A bureaucracy has a permanent, salaried staff of qualified experts and written goals, rules, and procedures. Staff members typically try to find ways to run their organization more efficiently.

Usually, the more levels in a bureaucratic structure, the more difficult communication becomes because people have to communicate indirectly through department and division heads, rather than directly with one another. Information may be lost, blocked, reinterpreted, or distorted as it moves up the hierarchy, or an excess of information may cause top levels to become engulfed in a paperwork blizzard that prevents them from clearly seeing the needs of the organization and its clients. Bureaucratic heads may have only a vague and imprecise idea of what is happening on the ground.

Evidence suggests that bureaucracies with fewer levels of authority, decentralized decision making, and multiple lines of communication produce more satisfied workers, happier clients, and bigger profits. These efficiencies can be achieved by organizing bureaucracies along the lines of a network structure.

## Multiple-Choice Questions

Questions marked with an asterisk are higher-order questions on the Bloom taxonomy. Answers to these questions are available in the appendix on page CR-50.

*1. A man and a woman are having a conversation. The woman speaks. The man listens. Who tends to laughs more?

   a. the man
   b. the woman
   c. The amount of time they spent laughing is approximately equal.
   d. From the information given, it is impossible to say who laughs more.

2. What are people doing when they obey feeling rules and respond appropriately to the situations in which they find themselves?
   a. engaging in emotion management
   b. engaging in emotional labour
   c. experiencing role strain
   d. experiencing role conflict

*3. Azziza is a college student. She has a big test tomorrow and needs to study. However, her mother has the flu and can't take Mahmoud, Azziza's little brother, to hockey practice in the evening. Azziza feels an obligation to help out with Mahmoud and an obligation to study. What is Azziza experiencing?
   a. emotion management
   b. emotional labour
   c. role strain
   d. role conflict

4. On what grounds have the Milgram experiments been criticized?
   a. ethical breaches
   b. reliability problems
   c. validity problems
   d. all of the above

5. According to Mark Granovetter's research, what is the most efficient way to find a job?
   a. Respond to ads on employment websites with effective résumés.
   b. Respond to "Help Wanted" ads in newspapers with effective résumés.
   c. Solicit information about job opportunities from people to whom you are weakly tied.
   d. Solicit information about job opportunities from people to whom you are strongly tied.

# CHAPTER 5 IN REVIEW

## DEVIANCE AND CRIME

### LEARNING OBJECTIVES

**LO1 SEE HOW PEOPLE DEFINE DEVIANCE AND CRIME DIFFERENTLY IN DIFFERENT TIMES AND PLACES**

**Deviance** involves breaking a norm and evoking a negative reaction from others. Societies establish some norms as laws. **Crime** is deviance that breaks a law, which is a norm stipulated and enforced by government bodies. Because norms vary widely, deviance and crime are relative. What some people consider normal in some times and places, other people in other times and places consider deviant or criminal. No act is deviant or criminal in and of itself. People commit deviant or criminal acts only when they break a norm and cause others to react negatively. From a sociological point of view, *everyone* is a deviant in one social context or another.

Many otherwise deviant acts go unnoticed or are considered too trivial to warrant negative *sanctions*, or actions indicating disapproval. People who are observed committing more serious acts of deviance are typically punished, either informally or formally. **Formal punishment** results from people breaking laws. For example, criminals are usually formally punished by having to serve time in prison, pay a fine, or perform community service. **Informal punishment** is mild. It may involve raised eyebrows, a harsh stare, an ironic smile, gossip, ostracism, "shaming," or **stigmatization**. When people are stigmatized, they are negatively evaluated because of visible characteristics that distinguish them from others.

Types of deviance and crime vary in terms of the *severity of the social response*, which ranges from mild disapproval to capital punishment. They vary also in terms of the *perceived harmfulness* of the deviant or criminal act. Finally, deviance and crime vary in terms of the *degree of public agreement* about whether an act should be considered deviant.

**LO2 INTERPRET DIFFERENCES IN CRIME RATES OVER TIME AND BETWEEN DIFFERENT POPULATION CATEGORIES**

Information on crime collected by the police is the main source of crime statistics. These statistics have two main shortcomings. First, much crime is not reported to the police. This is particularly true of so-called **victimless crimes**, such as illegal gambling, which involves guilty parties not stepping forward and getting identified; common or "Level 1" assaults, often unreported because the assailant is a friend or relative of the victim; and sexual assaults, often unreported because victims are afraid they will be humiliated or not believed and stigmatized by making the crime public. The second main shortcoming of official crime statistics is that authorities and the wider public decide which criminal acts to report and which to ignore. Authorities may decide to crack down or be more lenient regarding certain crimes, and laws may be changed, creating new offences or amending existing offences. Such actions also influence the number of recorded offences.

Recognizing these difficulties, students of crime often supplement official crime statistics with other sources of information. In **self-report surveys**, respondents are asked to report their involvement in criminal activities, either as perpetrators or as victims. In **victimization surveys**, people are asked whether they have been victims of various crimes within a certain time period.

Official statistics show that the Canadian crime rate was 3.6 times higher in 1992 than in 1962, and 1.9 times higher in 1992 than in 2016. The crime rate has been falling since the early 1990s because more and better trained police are fighting crime; the proportion of young men (the most crime-prone category of the population) has fallen; the unemployment rate (which is generally associate with the crime rate) has declined; and possibly also because abortion was legalized a couple of decades before the decline started, so beginning in the early 1990s there were proportionately fewer unwanted and unsupervised young people in the population.

Crime rates are higher for certain racial groups, notably Indigenous peoples and black people, because people belonging to these groups tend to have below-average income; are younger than members of other groups on average; face a criminal justice system that may discriminate against them; and tend to commit street crimes rather than white-collar crimes (people are more often detected, apprehended, and prosecuted, and receive stiffer penalties for street crimes). In addition, contact with Western settlers and Western culture disrupted social life in indigenous communities, leading to a weakening of social control over community members.

# LO³ APPLY A VARIETY OF SOCIOLOGICAL THEORIES TO THE ANALYSIS OF VARIOUS ASPECTS OF DEVIANT AND CRIMINAL BEHAVIOUR

## THEORIES AT A GLANCE
### Deviance and Crime

| Theory | Main Question | Application |
|---|---|---|
| Symbolic interactionism | How do people communicate to make their social settings meaningful, thus helping to create their social circumstances? | Deviant and criminal roles must be learned in the course of social interaction if they are to become habitual activities. Moreover, deviance results not just from the actions of the deviant but also from the responses of others, who define some actions as deviant and other actions as normal. |
| Functionalism | How do social structures and the values underlying them contribute to social stability? | Deviance and crime have positive functions for society insofar as they provide opportunities to clarify societal values, define moral boundaries, increase social solidarity, and allow useful social change. They also have dysfunctions. In particular, if societies do not provide enough legitimate opportunities for everyone to succeed, strain results, one reaction to which is to find alternative and illegitimate means of achieving one's goals. |
| Conflict theory | How does the structure of inequality between privileged groups seeking to maintain their advantages and subordinate groups seeking to increase theirs lead to conflict and often to social change? | The rich and powerful are most likely to impose deviant and criminal labels on others, particularly those who challenge the existing social order. Meanwhile, the rich and powerful are often able to use their money and influence to escape punishment for their own misdeeds. Most people do not engage in deviance and crime because they are prevented from doing so by authorities. Deviants and criminals break norms and laws because social controls imposed by various authorities are too weak to ensure their conformity. |
| Feminist theory | How do social conventions maintain male dominance and female subordination, and how do these conventions get overturned? | Changes over time in the distribution of power between women and men influence the degree to which crimes against women are identified and prosecuted, and the degree to which women become criminals. |

## LO⁴ LEARN HOW FORMS OF PUNISHMENT HAVE CHANGED HISTORICALLY

Among the most important recent developments in social control are the "medicalization of deviance" and the widespread use of prisons.

The **medicalization of deviance** refers to the fact that medical definitions of deviant behaviour are becoming more prevalent in societies like ours. In an earlier era, much deviant behaviour was labelled as evil. Deviants tended to be chastised, punished, and otherwise socially controlled by members of the clergy, neighbours, family members, and the criminal justice system. However, what used to be regarded as willful deviance is now often regarded as involuntary deviance. Increasingly, what used to be defined as evil is defined as "sickness," and medical and psychiatric authorities and institutions increasingly seek to manage people with deviant "ailments."

In pre-industrial societies, criminals were publicly humiliated, tortured, or put to death, depending on the severity of their transgressions. In the industrial era, depriving criminals of their freedom by putting them in prison seemed more civilized. Today, some people think that prisons should perform a rehabilitative function, preparing prisoners for reintegration into society institutions. Others think that prisons should serve mainly to deter people from committing crime; as institutions of revenge; or simply as institutions that keep criminals out of society as long as possible.

## LO 5 EXPLAIN HOW FEAR OF CRIME IS SUBJECT TO MANIPULATION BY POLITICAL AND COMMERCIAL GROUPS THAT BENEFIT FROM IT

**Moral panic** is widespread fear that occurs when many people fervently believe that some form of deviance or crime poses a profound threat to society's well-being. Groups that may benefit from moral panic include the mass media, the crime prevention and punishment industry, the criminal justice system, and politicians. Canada experienced moral panic between 2004 and 2014. The crime rate was falling dramatically throughout this period but many Conservative politicians argued that the state should get tough on crime, imprisoning more people and imposing tougher sentences. Many people accepted their argument, which helped the Conservatives take power in 2006 and remain in power until 2015. The incarceration rate rose during this period despite the falling crime rate.

## LO 6 IDENTIFY WORKABLE ALTERNATIVES TO TOUGH PRISON REGIMES

**Rehabilitation** involves reducing the recidivism rate—the percentage of convicted offenders who commit another crime, usually within two years of release from prison—by means of education and job training, individual and group therapy, substance abuse counselling, behaviour modification, and simply treating prisoners with dignity. In the Scandinavian countries, rehabilitative prisons, based on the idea that the more closely a prison resembles the outside world, the easier it will be to train less violent prisoners to function well outside the prison, have produced recidivism rates significantly below those of Canada.

Decriminalization and legalization of certain actions have also been recommended as alternatives to tough prison regimes. (Decriminalization allows for fines or other non-prison penalties; legalization does not.) Canada legalized cannabis in 2018 and Portugal decriminalized all drugs in 2001, viewing drug use as an issue of harm reduction rather than a criminal problem. Portugal has developed a nationwide system of needle exchanges, detoxification/treatment/counselling centres, and training/employment/housing opportunities that have resulted in declining drug use among adolescents and adults, drug-related prosecutions, HIV infections among drug users, and drug-related deaths—all indicators that decriminalization has worked as planned.

The third reform to tough prison regimes that has been proposed in recent years involves reducing the number of incarcerated offenders by diverting them from the court and prison systems—so-called "diversion." Most cases referred for diversion involve a minor offence, such as theft under $5000. To be considered for diversion, offenders must first acknowledge that they are guilty of the act they have been accused of committing. Victims have the opportunity to explain to offenders the full impact of the criminal acts. Offenders must then seek reconciliation with the victims by, say, apologizing and agreeing to financial compensation. Offenders selected for the program generally complete the provisions of the agreements they make.

Similarly, the Supreme Court of Canada has urged judges to apply **restorative justice** principles when dealing with the sentencing of Indigenous peoples. Restorative justice addresses the harm caused by crime, holds the offender responsible, and gives the parties affected the chance to articulate their needs. It thus supports healing, reintegration, the prevention of future harm, and reparation. Research shows that participating in a restorative justice system generally results in higher victim satisfaction ratings, higher restitution compliance, and lower recidivism rates than participating in a nonrestorative justice program.

## MULTIPLE-CHOICE QUESTIONS

Questions marked with an asterisk are higher-order questions on the Bloom taxonomy. Answers to these questions are available in the appendix on page CR-50.

1. What is deviance?
    a. Committing an inherently evil act.
    b. Breaking a norm and being informally punished.
    c. Breaking a norm and evoking a negative reaction from others.
    d. Becoming stigmatized and being informally punished.

2. According to the textbook, which of the following is NOT a cause of the falling crime rate in Canada?
    a. the increased incarceration rate
    b. the declining number of young men in the population
    c. the falling unemployment rate
    d. the legalization of abortion

3. Which of the following factors insulates black Torontonians from police searches?
    a. age
    b. education
    c. lack of a criminal record
    d. none of the above

*4. Members of a political party promote the idea that the country is experiencing a crime wave and that to stop it, more people need to be thrown into jail and face stiffer sentences. Television stations, hungry for sensational stories that draw large audiences, adhere to the principle "if it bleeds, it leads," and place the most lurid crime stories as the number one item in their newscasts. What do sociologists call this situation?
   a. moral panic
   b. recidivism
   c. intersectionality
   d. none of the above

5. What are rehabilitation, decriminalization/legalization, and diversion?
   a. reforms to the prison regime that have NOT worked well in practice
   b. reforms to the prison regime that HAVE worked well in practice
   c. reforms to the prison regime that have NOT worked well when implemented in Canada but HAVE worked well in some European countries, such as Denmark and Portugal
   d. reforms to the prison regime that have NOT worked well when implemented in Denmark and Portugal but HAVE worked well in Canada.

# CHAPTER 6 IN REVIEW

## SOCIAL STRATIFICATION: CANADIAN AND GLOBAL PERSPECTIVES

### LEARNING OBJECTIVES

#### LO 1 DESCRIBE HOW WEALTH AND INCOME INEQUALITY IN CANADA HAVE CHANGED IN RECENT DECADES

**Social stratification** is the way society is organized in layers or strata according to wealth (assets minus debt), income (earnings per year), and **power** (the ability to achieve one's goals even against the resistance of others). In Canada, inequality in wealth has been increasing steadily since the 1980s. In 2016, the wealthiest fifth of Canadians owned more than two-thirds of national wealth, while the poorest fifth had more debt than assets. Income inequality rose from the late 1980s until the mid-2000s. In 2011, the top fifth of Canadian income earners earned more than 44 percent of all income while the bottom fifth earned less than 5 percent.

#### LO 2 LIST THE FACTORS UNDERLYING INCOME INEQUALITY

Natural talent, effort, and capital (economic, human, social, and cultural) all influence how much people earn. **Economic capital** is ownership of land, real estate, industrial plants and equipment, and stocks and bonds. **Human capital** is investment in education and training. **Social capital** refers to people's networks or connections. **Cultural capital** refers to the widely shared, high-status cultural signals (attitudes, preferences, formal knowledge, behaviours, goals, and credentials) used for social and cultural inclusion and exclusion.

#### LO 3 APPRECIATE THE SOCIAL ORIGINS OF POVERTY

Analysts disagree whether poverty should be defined in absolute or relative terms and whether it should be based on income or consumption. Canada does not have an official poverty line. However, Statistics Canada reports a low-income measure (half the median household income, adjusted for family size), below which people are considered to be in the low-income category. By this relative, income-based measure, 14.2 percent of Canadians in households (4.8 million people) were in the low-income category in 2015. Many low-income people want to work but can't because of poor health or a disability or because they must take care of their young children. Even people who work full-time for the minimum wage cannot earn enough to rise above the low-income line. While recent immigrants experience low-income rates significantly higher than the Canadian-born, they represent only a small fraction of all Canadian immigrants; once established, immigrants have lower poverty rates than do people born in Canada.

Considerable mobility out of low-income status takes place, with 80 percent of low-income people escaping low-income status within a year and another 12 percent escaping within two years. Many people explain poverty as a result of individual attributes such as low intelligence or disability. These factors account for only a small amount of poverty. Others explain poverty as a result of acquired attributes such as low self-esteem and low motivation to achieve. However, these factors are more the result of poverty than a cause of it. Social factors—the phase of the business cycle, minimum wage laws, tax and redistribution policies, and widely held negative images of certain groups—are the most important factors affecting the level of poverty.

#### LO 4 UNDERSTAND WHY DIFFERENT SOCIOLOGISTS ARGUE THAT HIGH LEVELS OF INEQUALITY ARE NECESSARY, WILL INEVITABLY DISAPPEAR, OR VARY UNDER IDENTIFIABLE CONDITIONS

## THEORIES AT A GLANCE

### Stratification

| Theory | Outline |
|---|---|
| Marx's conflict theory | In capitalist societies, the two main classes are the bourgeoisie (who own but do not work productive property) and the proletariat (who work but do not own productive property). During the Industrial Revolution, industrial owners were eager to become more productive so they could earn higher profits. Less efficient owners were driven out of business and forced to join the working class, where they were joined by former peasants pouring into the cities looking for factory jobs. The drive for profits motivated owners to concentrate workers in increasingly larger factories, keep wages as low as possible, and invest as little as possible in improving working conditions. Thus, as the bourgeoisie grew richer and smaller, the proletariat grew larger and more impoverished. Marx also believed that the impoverished proletariat would be unable to afford to buy all that industry could produce, creating economic crises, during which businesses would go bankrupt, unemployment would spread, and workers would become more aware of the severity of their exploitation. Their growing sense of "class consciousness" would encourage the growth of unions and workers' political parties that would eventually try to create a new, classless society in which there would be no private wealth. |
| Davis and Moore's functionalist theory | Davis and Moore observed that some jobs are more important than others, and important jobs require considerable education. Incentives are needed to motivate the most talented people to train for the most important jobs. The incentives, said Davis and Moore, are money and prestige. Thus, social stratification is necessary (or functional) because the prospect of high rewards motivates people to undergo the sacrifices needed to get a higher education. Without substantial inequality, Davis and Moore concluded, the most talented people would have no incentive to become judges, physicians, and so on. |
| Weber's compromise | Weber argued that the emergence of a classless society is highly unlikely but under some circumstances people can act to lower the level of inequality in society. He also held that a person's class position is determined by his or her possession of goods, opportunities for income, level of education, and level of technical skill. Four main classes based on these factors exist in capitalist societies: large property owners, small property owners, propertyless but relatively highly educated and well-paid employees, and propertyless manual workers.<br><br>Weber also recognized that two types of groups other than classes—status groups and parties—have a bearing on the way a society is stratified. Status groups differ from one another in the prestige or social honour they enjoy and in their lifestyle. Parties are organizations that seek to impose their will on others through the exercise of power. Just as a person can be rich and have low prestige, so control over parties does not depend just on wealth. Weber argued that to draw an accurate picture of a society's stratification system, we must analyze classes, status groups, and parties as somewhat independent bases of social inequality. |

## LO5 RECOGNIZE HOW PEOPLE MOVE UP AND DOWN THE STRUCTURE OF INEQUALITY

*Social mobility* refers to movement up and down the stratification system over time. Movement is measured using one of two benchmarks: your first full-time job and the position of your parents in the hierarchy. Comparing your first job with your current job is an examination of occupational or **intragenerational mobility**. Comparing the occupations of parents with their children's current occupation is an examination of the inheritance of social position or **intergenerational mobility**. Little evidence supports the view that greater equality of opportunity exists in societies with expanding education systems. In most countries, the openness of the system of inequality did not increase over the last half of the twentieth century.

## LO6 ANALYZE CHANGE IN THE MAGNITUDE OF INEQUALITY ON A WORLD SCALE

Since 1975, the annual income gap between the 20 or so richest countries and the rest of the world has grown enormously. The share of world income going to the top 10 percent of individuals increased, and the share of world income going to the bottom 20 percent of individuals fell. Since 1980, the world's richest 0.1 percent increased their wealth by the same amount as the poorest half of the world's population. The number of people in the world living on $1 a day or less peaked in 1950 and then started to decline gradually. Still, nearly half of the world's population lives on $2 a day or less.

## LO7 CONTRAST COMPETING EXPLANATIONS FOR THE PERSISTENCE OF GLOBAL INEQUALITY

According to **modernization theory**, a variant of functionalism, global inequality results from various dysfunctional characteristics of poor societies. Specifically, modernization theorists say the citizens of poor societies lack sufficient *capital* to invest in Western-style agriculture and industry. They lack rational Western-style *business techniques* of marketing, accounting, sales, and finance. As a result, their productivity and profitability remain low. They lack stable Western-style *governments* that could provide a secure framework for investment. Finally, they lack a Western *mentality*: values that stress the need for savings, investment, innovation, education, high achievement, and self-control in having children.

Proponents of **dependency theory** note that less global inequality existed in 1500 and even in 1750 than today. However, beginning around 1500, the armed forces of the world's most powerful countries subdued and then annexed or colonized most of the rest of the world. The Industrial Revolution began around 1780. It enabled the western European countries, Russia, Japan, and the United States to amass enormous wealth that they used to extend their global reach. They forced their colonies to become a source of raw materials, cheap labour, investment opportunities, and markets for the conquering nations. The colonizers thereby prevented industrialization and locked the colonies into poverty. Accordingly, dependency theorists hold that an adequate theory of global inequality should not focus on the internal characteristics of poor countries themselves but should follow the principles of conflict theory and focus on patterns of domination and submission—specifically, in this case, on the relationship between rich and poor countries.

The world does not consist just of **core countries** that are major sources of capital and technology (the United States, Japan, and Germany) and **peripheral countries** that are major sources of raw materials and cheap labour (the former colonies). In addition, a middle tier of **semiperipheral countries** consists of former colonies that are making considerable headway in their attempts to become prosperous. The semiperipheral countries tend to have been ruled by colonial powers that built up their infrastructure, to have received considerable economic assistance from the United States because of their favourable geopolitical position, to have adopted state policies that nourished the growth of domestic industry, and to be relatively socially cohesive.

## MULTIPLE-CHOICE QUESTIONS

Questions marked with an asterisk are higher-order questions on the Bloom taxonomy. Answers to these questions are available in the appendix on page CR-50.

1. Which of the following factors account for most of the variation in individual income?
   a. natural talent
   b. effort
   c. various forms of capital
   d. luck

2. What kind of measure is Statistics Canada's low-income measure (LIM-AT)?
   a. relative and income-based
   b. absolute and consumption-based
   c. relative and consumption-based
   d. absolute and income-based

3. In Canada, taxes other than income tax are regressive. Higher income earners are able to shelter part of their income and tend to earn income from sources that are taxed at a lower rate than are wages and salaries. The very rich can take advantage of overseas tax havens. Which of the following is a consequence of these circumstances?
   a. Canada is the world's top investment opportunity for foreign investors.
   b. Canada's tax system is approximately neutral.
   c. Canada is the world's top destination for immigrants.
   d. all of the above

*4. A new government is elected. It increases taxes on the wealthy to fund a countrywide system of free, high-quality daycare. Hundreds of thousands of single mothers with small children enter the paid labour force. Income inequality is substantially reduced. Which of the following theorists is/are most likely to regard these events as dysfunctional developments?

a. Marx
b. Weber
c. Davis and Moore
d. none of the above

5. According to dependency theorists, which of the following factors maintained dependency in the postcolonial era?

a. substantial foreign investment
b. support for authoritarian governments
c. mounting debt
d. all of the above

# CHAPTER 7 IN REVIEW

## RACE AND ETHNICITY

### LEARNING OBJECTIVES

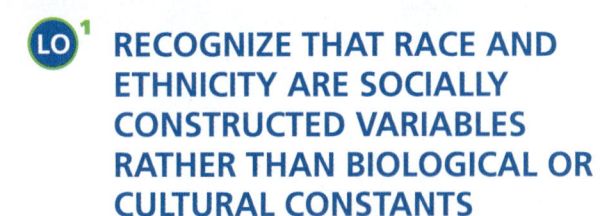

#### LO¹ RECOGNIZE THAT RACE AND ETHNICITY ARE SOCIALLY CONSTRUCTED VARIABLES RATHER THAN BIOLOGICAL OR CULTURAL CONSTANTS

**Race** is a social construct used to distinguish people in terms of one or more physical markers. Racial distinctions emerge and persist because they help to create and reinforce social, economic, and political inequalities. Thus, racial differences are not the inevitable outcome of physical or biological differences. An **ethnic group** comprises people whose perceived *cultural* markers (language, religion, customs, values, ancestors, and the like) are socially significant. However, just as physical distinctions do not cause differences in the behaviour of various races, so cultural distinctions are often not by themselves the major source of differences in the behaviour of various ethnic groups. Said differently, ethnic values and other elements of ethnic culture have less of an effect on the way people behave than we commonly believe. That is because social-structural differences (such as differences in access to material resources and differences in mobility opportunities) frequently underlie cultural differences. Thus, both race and ethnicity are socially constructed.

#### LO² ANALYZE WHY RACIAL AND ETHNIC LABELS AND IDENTITIES CHANGE OVER TIME AND PLACE

Racial and ethnic identity and the labels that people attach to different racial and ethnic groups are social constructs that emerge from, and are transformed by, social relations between previously separated peoples. Specifically, high levels of **pluralism** (the retention of racial and ethnic culture combined with equal access to basic social resources) and **assimilation** (the process by which a minority group blends into the majority population and eventually disappears as a distinct people in the larger society) are associated with low levels of **prejudice** (an attitude that judges a person on his or her group's real or imagined characteristics), **discrimination** (unfair treatment of people because of their group membership), and **institutionalized racism** (embeddedness of prejudice and discrimination in established ideologies and practices, not necessarily in the conscious actions of individuals).

#### LO³ APPRECIATE THAT CONQUEST AND DOMINATION ARE AMONG THE MOST IMPORTANT FORCES LEADING TO THE CRYSTALLIZATION OF DISTINCT ETHNIC AND RACIAL IDENTITIES

**Colonialism** involves people from one country invading another and engaging in conquest, the forcible capture of land, and the economic and political domination of its inhabitants. In the process of gaining control over the native population, the colonizers change or destroy the Indigenous culture, develop the belief that the natives are inherently inferior, and confine them to unskilled jobs. **Genocide** (the intentional extermination of an entire population defined as a race or a people) and **expulsion** (the forcible removal of a population from a territory claimed by another population) often accompany colonialism. Once entrenched, colonizers may engage in **internal colonialism**, preventing the assimilation of subordinate racial or ethnic groups by segregating them residentially, occupationally, and in social contacts ranging from friendship to marriage. **Slavery** (the ownership and control of people) has been a consequence of colonialism in certain times and places. Colonialism can also give rise to **split labour markets**, where low-wage workers of one race and high-wage workers of another race compete for the same jobs. In that situation, high-wage workers are likely to resent the presence of low-wage competitors. Conflict is bound to result and racist attitudes to develop or become reinforced.

#### LO⁴ DESCRIBE THE WAYS IN WHICH IDENTIFYING WITH A RACIAL OR ETHNIC GROUP CAN BE ECONOMICALLY, POLITICALLY, AND EMOTIONALLY ADVANTAGEOUS

The economic advantages of ethnicity are most apparent for immigrants, who often lack extensive social contacts and fluency in English or French. They commonly rely on

# THEORIES AT A GLANCE

## Race and Ethnicity

| Theory | Main Question | Application |
|---|---|---|
| Conflict theory | How does the structure of inequality between privileged groups seeking to maintain their advantages and subordinate groups seeking to increase theirs lead to conflict and often to social change? | Colonialism involves people from one country invading another and engaging in conquest, the forcible capture of land, and the economic and political domination of its inhabitants. In the process of gaining control over the native population, the colonizers change or destroy the Indigenous culture, develop the belief that the natives are inherently inferior, and confine them to unskilled jobs.<br><br>Genocide (the intentional extermination of an entire population defined as a race or a people) and expulsion (the forcible removal of a population from a territory claimed by another population) often accompany colonialism. Once entrenched, colonizers may engage in internal colonialism, preventing the assimilation of subordinate racial or ethnic groups by segregating them residentially, occupationally, and in social contacts ranging from friendship to marriage.<br><br>Slavery (the ownership and control of people) has also been a consequence of colonialism in certain times and places. Colonialism can also give rise to split labour markets, where low-wage workers of one race and high-wage workers of another race compete for the same jobs. In that situation, high-wage workers are likely to resent the presence of low-wage competitors. Conflict is bound to result and racist attitudes to develop or become reinforced. |
| Symbolic interactionism | How do people communicate to make their social settings meaningful, thus helping to create their social circumstances? | Racial and ethnic identity and the labels that people attach to different racial and ethnic groups are social constructs that emerge from, and are transformed by, social relations between previously separated peoples. Racial differences are not the inevitable outcome of physical or biological differences. Ethnic differences are based more on social-structural than cultural differences.<br><br>High levels of pluralism (the retention of racial and ethnic culture combined with equal access to basic social resources) and assimilation (the process by which a minority group blends into the majority population and eventually disappears as a distinct people in the larger society) are associated with low levels of prejudice (an attitude that judges a person on his or her group's real or imagined characteristics), discrimination (unfair treatment of people because of their group membership), and institutionalized racism (embeddedness of prejudice and discrimination in established ideologies and practices, not in the conscious actions of individuals). |

members of their ethnic group to help them find jobs and housing. In this way, immigrant communities become tightly knit. However, some economic advantages extend into the third generation and beyond. For example, community solidarity is an important resource for "ethnic entrepreneurs," businesspeople who operate largely within their ethnic community. They draw on their community for customers, suppliers, employees, and credit, and they may be linked economically to the homeland as importers and exporters. They often pass on their businesses to their children, who in turn can pass the businesses on to the next generation. In this way, strong economic incentives encourage some people to remain ethnic group members, even beyond the immigrant generation. Ethnic group membership can also be politically useful, enabling ethnic groups to obtain more resources from the government, for example. Finally, ethnic group membership can offer people emotional support, especially if they have suffered unusually high levels of prejudice and discrimination involving expulsion or genocide. Note also that retaining ethnic ties beyond the second generation has never been easier. Immigration used to involve cutting all or most ties to a country of origin because of the high cost of travel and long-distance telephone calls. Lack of communication encouraged assimilation in people's newly adopted countries. Today, however, ties to the ancestral communities are often maintained in ways that sustain ethnic culture—through visits abroad, bringing relatives to Canada for visits, the use of various types of electronic communication, and the establishment of economic relations with communities in the homeland. Thanks to these mechanisms, some ethnic groups have become **transnational communities**, the boundaries of which extend between or among countries.

## LO 5 UNDERSTAND THAT CANADA IS AMONG THE WORLD'S MOST TOLERANT COUNTRIES *AND* HOME TO PERSISTENT RACIAL INEQUALITY

In Canada, ethnic and racial tolerance has grown over the past two centuries. A country founded on principles that kept ethnic and racial groups socially segregated is now a place where ethnic and racial mixing is common in all spheres of life. Moreover, Canada is today one of the most ethnically and racially tolerant countries in the world. Nonetheless, inequalities persist and are especially evident with respect to Indigenous Canadians.

## Multiple-Choice Questions

Questions marked with an asterisk are higher-order questions on the Bloom taxonomy. Answers to these questions are available in the appendix on pages CR-50 and CR-51.

*1. Hutus and Tutsis lived harmoniously in Rwanda for centuries. The Hutus were mainly farmers and the Tutsis mainly cattle herders. The Tutsis were the ruling minority but they spoke the same language as the Hutus and shared the same religious beliefs. Members of the two groups lived side by side, and half the population of Rwanda was of mixed Hutu–Tutsi ancestry. The two groups never came into serious conflict.

   Then Belgium colonized Rwanda in 1916. Among other divisive policies, the Belgians passed a law saying that one had to be Tutsi to serve in any official capacity, and they started distinguishing Tutsis from Hutus by measuring the width of their noses. Animosity between Tutsis and Hutus grew until, in 1994, the Hutus massacred 800 000 Tutsis within just a few days. What does the history of Tutsi–Hutu relations illustrate? Choose *two* of the following.
   a. Race and ethnicity are socially constructed.
   b. The upward social mobility of ethnic and racial groups is typically a function of state policy.
   c. Blacks are generally less free to choose their racial identity than Whites are.
   d. Colonialism is often associated with an intensification of ethnic and racial differences.

*2. Among which of the following groups is symbolic ethnicity most widespread?
   a. Chinese Canadians
   b. black Canadians
   c. Irish Canadians
   d. Indigenous Canadians

*3. People convicted of a crime can sometimes avoid jail by paying a fine. Because Indigenous people are less likely than white people to be able to afford fines, they are more likely to go to jail. Which theory does this circumstance illustrate?
   a. critical race theory
   b. contact theory (or the contact hypothesis)
   c. split labour market theory
   d. symbolic interactionist theory

4. Which of the following circumstances led to the emergence of the separatist movement in Quebec?
   a. the potential demographic decline of the Québécois and the assimilation of immigrants into English culture
   b. persistent ethnic stratification and the continued use of English as the language of private industry
   c. both of the above
   d. none of the above

5. Among non-immigrants in Canada, which of the following groups has the highest percentage of low-income people?
   a. black
   b. Arab
   c. Chinese
   d. white

CR-24    Visit nelson.com/student for additional study tools!

# CHAPTER 8 IN REVIEW

## SEXUALITIES AND GENDERS

### LEARNING OBJECTIVES

#### LO1 DISTINGUISH BIOLOGICALLY DETERMINED SEX FROM SOCIALLY CONSTRUCTED GENDER

**Sex** depends fundamentally on one's genetic makeup. The overwhelming majority of people are born with 23 pairs of chromosomes, one pair of which determines their sex. If a person's sex chromosome is of the XX variety, she will be a woman. If a person's sex chromosome is of the XY variety, he will be a man. However, other sex chromosome types occur naturally. They often result in people who are **intersex,** that is, they do not fit the conventional male or female sex categories. Their genitals, reproductive system, and secondary sexual characteristics such as breasts and body hair may not be distinctly male or female in the conventional sense of the terms.

Being male or female involves not just biological characteristics but also certain "masculine" and "feminine" feelings, attitudes, and behaviours. Accordingly, sociologists distinguish biological sex from sociological **gender**. One's gender comprises the feelings, attitudes, and behaviours typically associated with being male or female. **Gender identity** is your identification with, or sense of belonging to, a particular sex—psychologically, socially, and usually biologically. People who are uncomfortable with the gender assigned to them at birth or who do not fit neatly into conventional male or female gender categories are considered **transgender**.

#### LO2 APPLY MAJOR SOCIOLOGICAL THEORIES TO THE ANALYSIS OF GENDER

## THEORIES AT A GLANCE

### Genders and Sexualities

| Theory | Main Question | Application |
|---|---|---|
| Functionalism | How do social structures and the values underlying them contribute to social stability? | Functionalists reinforce the essentialist viewpoint that gender roles are inherent when they claim that traditional gender roles help to integrate society. From this point of view, in the family, women traditionally specialize in raising children and managing the household. Men traditionally work in the paid labour force. Each generation learns to perform these complementary roles by means of gender role socialization in the family.<br><br>The larger society also promotes gender role conformity. It instills in men the fear that they won't be attractive to women if they are too feminine, and it instills in women the fear that they won't be attractive to men if they are too masculine. In the functionalist view, then, learning the essential features of femininity and masculinity integrates society and allows it to function properly. |
| Conflict theory | How does the structure of inequality between privileged groups seeking to maintain their advantages and subordinate groups seeking to increase theirs lead to conflict and often to social change? | Conflict theorists dating back to Friedrich Engels locate the root of male domination in class inequality. According to Engels, men gained substantial power over women when preliterate societies were first able to produce more than their members needed for their own subsistence. At that point, some men gained control over the economic surplus. They soon devised two means of ensuring that their offspring would inherit the surplus. First, they imposed the rule that only men could own property. Second, by means of socialization and force, they ensured that women remained sexually faithful to their husbands.<br><br>As industrial capitalism developed, Engels wrote, male domination increased because industrial capitalism made men still wealthier and more powerful, while it relegated women to subordinate domestic roles. |

*(Continued)*

| | | |
|---|---|---|
| Symbolic interactionism | How do people communicate to make their social settings meaningful, thus helping to create their social circumstances? | One of the things to which people attach meaning is what it means to be male or female. Boys and girls first learn masculine and feminine roles in their interactions in the family and at school, and these lessons are reinforced by the mass media. |
| Feminism | How do social conventions maintain male dominance and female subordination, and how do these conventions get overturned? | Feminist theorists doubt that male domination is closely linked to the development of industrial capitalism. They note that gender inequality is greater in agrarian than in industrial capitalist societies. Moreover, male domination is evident in societies that call themselves socialist or communist. These observations lead many feminists to conclude that male domination is rooted less in industrial capitalism than in the patriarchal authority relations, family structures, and patterns of socialization and culture that exist in most societies. Despite this disagreement, conflict and feminist theorists concur that behavioural differences between women and men result less from any essential differences between them than from men being in a position to advance their interests over the interests of women. |

## LO 3  APPRECIATE THAT GENDER IS SHAPED LARGELY BY THE WAY PARENTS RAISE CHILDREN, TEACHERS INTERACT WITH PUPILS, AND THE MASS MEDIA PORTRAY IDEAL BODY IMAGES

The major agents of socialization tend to encourage people to think of gender in binary terms—as men vs. women—and to adopt strict standards for identifying people as masculine vs. feminine. This tendency is evident from birth. Most parents treat boys and girls differently, for example by encouraging them to play with toys that help to teach them to conform to conventional gender expectations. Schools tend to reinforce the lesson, so that by the time adolescents are able to choose course options, most boys are strongly inclined to consider only their careers while most girls are inclined to consider both home responsibilities and careers. Consequently, boys tend to choose career-oriented courses, particularly in math and science, more often than girls do.

In college and university, the pattern is accentuated. Because they expect to devote a large part of their lives to child-rearing and housework, women's course choices typically lead to less demanding, lower-paying jobs. Outside school, children, adolescents, and adults find that the mass media reinforce conventional gender roles. This tendency is particularly evident in the way the mass media accentuate conventional feminine and masculine body images.

## LO 4  IDENTIFY THE SOCIAL FORCES PUSHING PEOPLE TOWARD HETEROSEXUALITY

**Heteronormativity** is a durable norm in our society. Strong social and cultural forces lead us to distinguish heterosexuals from homosexuals. We learn these distinctions throughout the socialization process, and we continuously construct them anew in our daily interactions. Most people use positive and negative sanctions to ensure that others conform to conventional heterosexual gender roles. Some people resort to violence to enforce conformity and punish deviance from those roles. However, as **queer theory** insists, and empirical research demonstrates, people's sexual preferences and performances are actually more heterogeneous and fluid than heteronormative standards allow.

## LO 5  RECOGNIZE THAT THE SOCIAL DISTINCTION BETWEEN MEN AND WOMEN SERVES AS AN IMPORTANT BASIS OF INEQUALITY IN THE WORKPLACE

The earnings gap between men and women is one of the most important expressions of gender inequality today. When Canadian data on female and male earnings were first collected in 1967, the ratio of female-to-male earnings for full-year, full-time workers stood at about 58 percent. By 1980, the ratio was 64 percent and it rose fairly steadily to about 73 percent in 1993. Since then, however, the ratio has fluctuated between about 68 percent and 74 percent. In 2011, women earned 72 cents for every dollar men earned. At the 1967–2011 rate of improvement, women will achieve earnings equality with men in 2089! Even that projection may be optimistic because in 2014, the ratio was still 74 percent. The earnings gap persists because of gender discrimination, the concentration of women in low-wage jobs and industries, the tendency of women to take on heavy domestic work responsibilities, and the fact that paid work done by women is commonly considered less valuable than work done by men insofar as it is commonly viewed as involving fewer skills.

## LO 6 EXPLAIN HOW MALE AGGRESSION AGAINST WOMEN IS ROOTED IN GENDER INEQUALITY

Serious acts of aggression between men and women are common. In the overwhelming majority of such acts, men are the perpetrators and women are the victims. Male aggression against women is highest in situations in which early socialization experiences predispose men to want to control women, where norms justify the domination of women, and where a big power imbalance exists between men and women.

## LO 7 OUTLINE SOCIAL POLICIES THAT COULD LOWER THE LEVEL OF INEQUALITY BETWEEN WOMEN AND MEN

Two major policy changes would help to eliminate gender inequality in income and wealth: the development of a high-quality, government-subsidized, affordable child-care system, and the regulation and enforcement of a wage and salary system that ensures women receive equal pay for work of the same value done by men. The development of a high-quality, government-subsidized, affordable child-care system would allow many women who do only unpaid domestic work or combine unpaid domestic work with part-time paid work to take full-time jobs in the paid labour force, thus boosting women's income and wealth. Mandating equal pay for work of equal value would eliminate the current tendency to devalue paid work that women tend to do, again boosting women's income and wealth.

## Multiple-Choice Questions

Questions marked with an asterisk are higher-order questions on the Bloom taxonomy. Answers to these questions are available in the appendix on page CR-51.

1. What label do sociologists conventionally assign to people who are uncomfortable with the gender assigned to them at birth or who do not fit neatly into conventional male or female gender categories?
   a. transsexual
   b. homosexual
   c. intersex
   d. transgender

2. One school of thought holds that male domination is rooted in rules of property ownership and enforced female monogamy. Which school of thought is that?
   a. radical feminism
   b. the Marxist variant of conflict theory
   c. symbolic interactionism
   d. essentialism

3. One school of thought emphasizes the fluidity of sexual preferences and performances. Which school of thought is that?
   a. symbolic interactionism
   b. liberal feminism
   c. queer theory
   d. social constructionism

*4. Some people believe that men tend to be more aggressive than women are because they have a higher level of the hormone testosterone in their system. Which school of thought is aligned most closely with this view?
   a. essentialism
   b. radical feminism
   c. "third wave" feminism
   d. the theory of hostile environment sexual harassment

*5. The level of gender risk for women is lower in country X than one would expect, based on its historical level of patriarchy and its level of economic well-being. What circumstance(s) likely account for this fact?
   a. Neighbouring countries have been pushing country X to lower the level of gender risk for decades.
   b. The country's women's movement has been especially well-organized and vocal.
   c. The country's government has been pushing to improve women's rights for decades.
   d. (b) and (c) only

CR-27

# CHAPTER 9 IN REVIEW

## FAMILIES

### LEARNING OBJECTIVES

**LO1 APPRECIATE THAT THE TRADITIONAL NUCLEAR FAMILY HAS BEEN WEAKENING SINCE THE 1800S, ALTHOUGH IT STRENGTHENED TEMPORARILY IN THE YEARS IMMEDIATELY FOLLOWING WORLD WAR II**

Trends in divorce, marriage, and child-bearing show a gradual weakening of the nuclear family from the second half of the nineteenth century until the mid-1940s, and continued weakening after the 1950s. Specifically, throughout the nineteenth century, the crude divorce rate rose slowly. The **crude divorce rate** is the number of divorces that occur in a year for every 1000 people in the population. Meanwhile, the marriage rate fell. The **crude marriage rate** is the number of marriages that occur in a year for every 1000 people in the population. The total fertility rate also fell. The **total fertility rate** is the average number of children that would be born to a woman over her lifetime if she had the same number of children as do women in each age cohort in a given year. Canada's marriage rate started falling after 1946. The divorce rate started rising in the 1960s when the law was changed to make it easier to divorce. The total fertility rate started falling after 1961. Thus, by the early 1960s, the earlier trends had reasserted themselves. Only the peculiar historical circumstances of the postwar years temporarily reversed them.

Specifically, during the Great Depression (1929–39) and World War II (1939–45), many Canadians were forced to postpone marriage because of widespread poverty, government-imposed austerity, and physical separation. After this ordeal, many Canadians wanted to settle down, have children, and enjoy the peace, pleasure, and security that family life seemed to offer. Conditions could not have been better for doing just that. The immediate postwar era was one of unparalleled optimism and prosperity. Real per capita income rose, as did the percentage of Canadians who owned their own homes. Laws passed out of necessity during World War II to encourage women to join the paid labour force were cancelled. Things were now supposed to return to "normal," meaning that women were supposed to go back to being housewives and men to being breadwinners.

**LO2 LIST THE FACTORS CONTRIBUTING TO VARIATION IN PATTERNS OF MATE SELECTION, MARITAL SATISFACTION, DIVORCE, REPRODUCTIVE CHOICE, HOUSEWORK AND CHILD CARE, AND SPOUSAL VIOLENCE**

In most societies throughout human history, marriages were typically arranged by third parties, not by brides and grooms. The selection of marriage partners was based mainly on calculations intended to increase their families' prestige, economic benefits, and political advantages. Especially since the early twentieth century, mate selection has come to depend more on romantic love. Yet social factors continue to affect mate selection. These factors include the resources people bring to the marriage market, demographic factors such as the ratio of men to women in one's community, and the constraints imposed by third parties. Nonetheless, mate selection is less constrained than it used to be, as evidenced by the growing percentage of Canadians (particularly young Canadians) who consider themselves to be multi-racial and multi-ethnic—a consequence of the increasing frequency of multi-racial and multi-ethnic marriages and common-law relationships.

Marital stability has come to depend more on having a happy rather than merely a useful marriage. This change occurred because women in Canada and many other societies have become more autonomous, especially over the past half-century. Factors contributing to women's growing autonomy were the legalization of birth control measures in Canada in 1969; the increased participation of women in the paid labour force; and changes in Canadian laws that made divorce easier. Marital satisfaction now depends on such factors as the economic security of the family (dissatisfaction grows as one moves down the socioeconomic hierarchy), the ease with which people can get a divorce (married people are more satisfied with their marriages in countries with liberal divorce laws), and the phase of the family life cycle (marital satisfaction reaches a low point when children are in their teenage years).

Women's income usually falls after divorce, while men's income generally stays about the same. That is because husbands tend to earn more than wives do, children typically live with their mothers after divorce, and child-support payments are often inadequate. On divorce, the wife may receive an equal share of tangible property, but that does not usually result in her beginning post-divorce life on an equal footing with her former husband, especially if she retains physical custody of the couple's children and if she sacrificed her education and career so that he could earn a college or university degree. The degree of emotional distress of children post-divorce is tied to three factors: the level of ongoing parental conflict, a decline in living standards, and the absence of one parent as a role model and a source of emotional support, practical help, and supervision.

Thanks to contraception and the availability of abortion, women now have more say than they used to over whether they will have children and, if so, when they will have them and how many they will have. Men take a more active role in the day-to-day running of the household than they used to. Still, Canadian women are two-and-a-half times more likely than men to devote 30 hours or more to unpaid household work every week while men are nearly twice as likely as women to devote no time to such work. In addition, men tend to do low-stress chores that can often wait a day or a week while women tend to do more stressful domestic work that requires their immediate attention. Domestic responsibilities tend to be shared more equally the smaller the difference between the husband's and the wife's earnings and the greater the agreement between spouses that equality in the household division of labour is desirable. Such agreement tends to be associated with the spouses' level of education.

For heterosexual couples, spousal violence is associated with the level of gender equality in the family and in the larger society. The higher the level of gender inequality, the greater the frequency of spousal violence. Severe wife assault is therefore more common in lower-class, less highly educated families in which gender inequality tends to be high and men are likely to believe that male domination is justified. Severe wife abuse is also more common among couples who witnessed their mothers being abused and who were themselves abused when they were children, although research suggests that these socialization factors are considerably less influential than was once believed.

## LO 3 DESCRIBE THE CHARACTERISTICS OF DIVERSE FAMILY FORMS

Several family forms are increasingly common in Canada: heterosexual cohabitation, same-sex unions, lone-parent families, zero-child families, and mixed-race families. Notable features of these family forms include the following: (1) The proportion of common-law families quadrupled between 1981 and 2016, reaching more than a fifth of Canadian families (nearly two-fifths in Quebec). (2) Same-sex marriage was first recognized in the Netherlands in 2001. Canada followed suit in 2005, and now 31 countries (nationwide or in some parts) recognize same-sex marriage. In 2016, nearly 1 percent of families in Canada were same-sex families. In about a third of them, the spouses were married and in the remainder, they were living common-law. Raising a child in a homosexual family has few if any negative effects on the child's development, sexual orientation, gender identity, gender role behavior, emotional/behavioral development, social relationships, and cognitive functioning, and it has some benefits in terms of child care and marital satisfaction. (3) Solo parenting is usually the product of separation or divorce, after which child custody is typically granted to mothers. The poverty rate in female-headed single-parent families is more than double the rate in male-headed single-parent families. Children who grow up in low-income households are more likely than other children are to experience reduced cognitive ability and achievement, among other negative outcomes, with lifelong consequences for income and health. (4) Roughly a fifth of women between the ages of 40 and 44 have never given birth. This may be due to infertility of one of the spouses or the decision not to have children because of the expense and stress associated with raising a child and the alternative attractions available to spouses. People with high income, high education, and professional and managerial occupations are most likely to have zero-child families. They tend to be neither frustrated nor unhappy that they do not have a child. Despite their tendency to feel negatively stereotyped as "selfish," they tend to be more satisfied with their marriage than are couples with a child. (5) Mixed-race families comprise about 6 percent of all Canadian families—more than 10 percent in Vancouver and Toronto. Children of mixed-race families often think of themselves as Canadian but many others don't see them that way. They may feel that they are perfectly Canadian but others repeatedly send the message that "Canadian" should be associated with "white." Consequently, by the time they are adults and have to answer census questions on ethnic identity, few mixed-race people select "Canadian." However, it seems that young Canadians with mixed-race parents seem to be increasingly inclined to insist that they are Canadian when asked the "What are you?" question, thus challenging the prevailing notion that "Canadian" must be associated with "white." Mixed-race couples commonly experience tension when in public—people routinely stare at them as if they are a curiosity—and their children are still frequent victims of racial slurs in the schoolyard, at least in schoolyards with relatively few such children.

# LO⁴ APPLY MAJOR SOCIOLOGICAL THEORIES TO THE ANALYSIS OF FAMILIES

## THEORIES AT A GLANCE

### Families

| Theory | Main Question | Application |
|---|---|---|
| Functionalism | How do social structures and the values underlying them contribute to social stability? | For any society to survive, its members must cooperate economically. They must have babies. And they must raise offspring in an emotionally supportive environment so the offspring can learn the ways of the group and eventually operate as productive adults. Since the 1940s, functionalists have argued that the nuclear family—a cohabiting man and woman who maintain a socially approved sexual relationship and have at least one child—is ideally suited to meet these challenges. In their view, the nuclear family provides a basis for five main social functions: regulated sexual activity, economic cooperation, reproduction, socialization, and emotional support. Functionalists cite the supposed pervasiveness of the nuclear family as evidence of its ability to perform these functions. |
| Conflict theory | How does the structure of inequality between privileged groups seeking to maintain their advantages and subordinate groups seeking to increase theirs lead to conflict and often to social change? | According to conflict theorists, rising demand for women to pursue a higher education and enter the paid labour force, together with the availability of contraception, child-care services, and reproduction outside the nuclear family have altered the traditional division of labour between husband and wife and, more generally, power relations between women and men. |
| Symbolic interactionism | How do people communicate to make their social settings meaningful, thus helping to create their social circumstances? | Mixed-race families face unique issues negotiating their identity and raising their children because the meaning they attach to their racial status typically differs from the meaning that others commonly attach to it. For example, children with mixed-race parents commonly think of themselves as Canadian but others tend to equate "Canadian" with "white." Consequently, such children are often asked where they come from, making them feel as if they do not belong. This feeling is reinforced by racial discrimination, sometimes from members of the extended family; in mixed-race families with a white parent, it can even lead to young children developing the view that whites are superior to non-whites. |
| Feminism | How do social conventions maintain male dominance and female subordination, and how do these conventions get overturned? | Like conflict theorists, feminist theorists highlight change in power relations between women and men as the driving force behind change in family structures. However, unlike Marxist-inspired conflict theorists, most feminist theorists think these changes have less to do with class relations than with the gender revolution in patriarchy that has been taking place for the past half-century. |

## LO 5 EXPLAIN HOW PUBLIC POLICY CAN PREVENT THE EMERGENCE OF CERTAIN SOCIAL PROBLEMS THAT MIGHT OTHERWISE RESULT FROM THE DECLINE OF THE TRADITIONAL NUCLEAR FAMILY

Many social problems develop in societies where the nuclear family is in decline and the state fails to provide much family support. These problems include high levels of child poverty, juvenile delinquency, suicide, and infant mortality. A comparison of Sweden and the United States shows that Sweden has experienced more of a decline in the nuclear family but has fewer social problems such as those just listed because, unlike the United States, it provides families with much more social support: substantial paid parental leave when a child is born or gets sick, free health care, heavily government-subsidized, high-quality daycare, and generous direct cash payments based on the number of children in each family. Swedes pay high taxes for these services, but they have decided to do so to avoid the social problems that crop up when the nuclear family is in decline and the state fails to provide much family support.

## Multiple-Choice Questions

Questions marked with an asterisk are higher-order questions on the Bloom taxonomy. Answers to these questions are available in the appendix on page CR-51.

1. In which historical period did North America witness an especially rapid increase in the number of nuclear families?
    a. during the nineteenth century
    b. during the Great Depression (1929–39)
    c. during World War II (1939–46)
    d. during the 1950s and early 1960s

2. In societies where polygamy is widespread, intense competition for women creates numerous social problems. Which of the following conclusions does the text reach about how these social problems can be minimized?
    a. The social problems caused by widespread polygamy can be minimized only if heterosexual monogamous families replace polygamous families.
    b. The social problems caused by widespread polygamy can be minimized if a wide variety of family forms, including common-law heterosexual families and homosexual monogamous families, replace polygamous families.
    c. The social problems caused by widespread polygamy can be minimized if the state intervenes to ban polygamy.
    d. The social problems caused by widespread polygamy can be minimized by economic development, which makes polygamy dysfunctional.

*3. Researchers conducted a survey of mate selection among online daters in Vancouver in January 2018. They discovered that 10 percent of the people surveyed developed long-term intimate partnerships with people whose race was different than their own. What could the researchers reasonably infer from this finding?
    a. The rate of interracial unions is significantly higher among Vancouver's online daters than it is among Vancouver's population in general.
    b. The rate at which Vancouver's daters form interracial unions has increased over time.
    c. both (a) and (b)
    d. none of the above

4. Why is marital satisfaction higher on average in countries with relatively liberal divorce laws?
    a. Liberal divorce laws encourage a high rate of divorce, and unmarried people are happier than married people.
    b. Liberal divorce laws allow people to leave unhappy marriages and find marriage partners with whom they are happy.
    c. In countries with less liberal divorces, more marriages are arranged, so couples are less frequently in love with one another.
    d. Countries with less liberal divorce laws tend to be poor countries, and since money issues often lead to unhappy marriages, married couples tend to be relatively unhappy in such countries.

5. In families that experience divorce, which of the following is the most important factor with negative consequences for the emotional health of children?
    a. persistent conflict between the spouses
    b. a decline in living standards
    c. absence of the non-custodial parent
    d. The three factors listed above are of approximately equal importance.

# CHAPTER 10 IN REVIEW

## RELIGION

### LEARNING OBJECTIVES

**LO 1** EXPLAIN HOW, UNDER SOME CIRCUMSTANCES, RELIGION CREATES SOCIAL COHESION AND HOW, UNDER OTHER CIRCUMSTANCES, RELIGION REINFORCES SOCIAL INEQUALITY AND PROMOTES SOCIAL CONFLICT, BOTH NON-VIOLENT AND VIOLENT

## THEORIES AT A GLANCE

### Religion

| Theory | Main Question | Application |
|---|---|---|
| Functionalism | How do social structures and the values underlying them contribute to social stability? | Durkheim said that when people live together, they come to share common sentiments and values. These common sentiments and values form a collective conscience that is larger than any individual. On occasion, we experience the collective conscience directly. This causes us to distinguish the secular everyday world of the profane from the religious, transcendent world of the sacred.<br><br>We designate certain objects as symbolizing the sacred. Durkheim called these objects *totems*. We invent set practices to connect us with the sacred. Durkheim referred to these practices as *rituals*. The function of rituals and of religion as a whole is to reinforce social solidarity, said Durkheim. Religion heightens our experience of group belonging, increases our respect for the group's institutions, and strengthens our belief in the validity of the group's culture. |
| Conflict theory | How does the structure of inequality between privileged groups seeking to maintain their advantages and subordinate groups seeking to increase theirs lead to conflict and often to social change? | After becoming routinized, religions typically support class inequality. They often emphasize charity, too—but not so much charity as to change the basic structure of inequality in society. For example, in medieval and early modern Europe, Christianity, while collecting alms for the poor, promoted the view that the Almighty ordains class inequality, promising rewards to the lowly in the afterlife ("The meek shall inherit the earth"). However, religiously inspired protest against inequality often erupts from below, as the twentieth-century Social Gospel movement in Canada and the civil rights movement in the United States illustrate.<br><br>Religiously inspired conflict is by no means always progressive and non-violent; no religion is innocent of slaughter. Nor are the major world religions, and especially Judaism, Christianity, and Islam, innocent of violence against Nature. Proponents of these religions view God as having granted humans the right to dominate Nature; and in the process of exercising what they regard as their God-given right, humans have driven many species to extinction and caused great environmental damage. By imbuing all living and inanimate things with a soul, animistic Indigenous religions prescribe a more harmonious relationship between humans and Nature, which is especially instructive in an era of environmental dangers caused by humans. |

*(Continued)*

| | | |
|---|---|---|
| Symbolic interactionism | How do people communicate to make their social settings meaningful, thus helping to create their social circumstances? | Weber wrote that if history is like a train, pushed along its tracks by economic and political interests, then religious ideas are like railroad switches, determining exactly which tracks the train will follow. His most famous illustration of his thesis is his *The Protestant Ethic and the Spirit of Capitalism*.<br><br>Like Marx, Weber recognized the fundamental importance of the economic factor in explaining the rise of capitalism. But Weber also sought to establish the one-sidedness of any exclusively economic interpretation. He did so by offering what we would today call a symbolic interactionist interpretation. For specifically religious reasons, wrote Weber, followers of the Protestant theologian John Calvin stressed the need to engage in intense worldly activity and to display industry, punctuality, and frugality in their everyday life. In the view of such men as John Wesley and Benjamin Franklin, people could reduce their religious doubts and ensure a state of grace by working diligently and living simply.<br><br>Many Protestants took up this idea. Weber called it the Protestant ethic. According to Weber, the Protestant ethic had wholly unexpected economic consequences. Where it took root, and where economic conditions were favourable, early capitalist enterprise grew most robustly. Weber's focus on the worldly significance of the meanings people attach to religious ideas makes him a forerunner of the symbolic interactionist tradition. |
| Feminism | How do social conventions maintain male dominance and female subordination, and how do these conventions get overturned? | The major world religions have traditionally placed women in a subordinate position. Catholic priests, Muslim mullahs, and Jewish orthodox rabbis must be men. Women have been allowed to serve as Protestant ministers only since the mid-nineteenth century and as rabbis in the more liberal branches of Judaism since the 1970s. Many scriptures that emphasize the subordination of women continue to inform practice to a greater or lesser degree.<br><br>Religious feminists have challenged such ideas. For example, Muslim feminists have established that what many religious clerics present as divine Islamic law regarding women is actually based on interpretations that were authored by men over the centuries. They also contend that Islamic legal principles such as that of the "public interest" contradict and override principles that deny women equality with men. |

## LO² DESCRIBE THE SOCIAL FORCES CAUSING SECULARIZATION

According to the **secularization thesis**, religious institutions, actions, and consciousness are unlikely to disappear, but they are certainly on the decline worldwide. That is because science and rational thinking in general fail to find any evidence for many religious beliefs (such as belief in the afterlife) and instead provide evidence-based alternative explanations (when our bodily functions cease, we are gone forever). Evidence supporting the secularization thesis includes census data on the percentage of Canadians claiming they have no religion (which climbed from about 0.5 percent in 1961 to nearly 24 percent in 2011) and survey data on the percentage of Canadians who attend religious services weekly (which fell from about 65 percent in 1945 to 16 percent in 2015).

## LO³ ANALYZE THE SOCIAL FORCES ENCOURAGING RELIGIOUS REVIVALS

Despite the consensus about secularization that was evident in the 1980s, many sociologists modified their judgments in the 1990s. One reason for the change was that accumulated survey evidence showed that religion was not in an advanced state of decay in many places. In addition, an intensification of religious belief and practice took place among some people in recent decades. For example, since the 1960s, fundamentalist religious organizations have increased their membership in Canada and the United States, and religious movements gained strength in much of Asia and Africa. These developments prompted some sociologists to propose the **revised secularization**

**thesis**, which acknowledges that religion has become increasingly influential in the lives of some individuals and groups in recent decades but also insists that the scope of religious authority has continued to decline in most people's lives. That is, for most people, religion has less and less to say about education, family issues, politics, and economic affairs, even though it may continue to be an important source of spiritual belief and practice for some people.

The introduction of a **market model** of religion was another important development in the field. According to the market model, religious organizations are suppliers of services such as counselling, pastoral care, youth activities, men's and women's groups, performance groups, lectures, and discussions. These services are demanded by people who desire religious activities. Religious denominations are similar to product brands offering different "flavours" of religious experience. Some countries, such as the United States, permit vigorous competition among religions to satisfy the demands of the market for religious services. The market model predicts that in such countries, religiosity as measured by, say, frequency of attendance at religious services, will be relatively high. (**Religiosity** is the degree to which religion is important to people.) On the other hand, other countries allow less religious freedom. Some countries, like Saudi Arabia, even impose a national religion on its citizens. The market model predicts that religiosity will tend to be low in countries with restricted religious freedom because a single religion cannot adequately satisfy the religious needs of a diverse population. Evidence supporting the market model is mixed.

## LO 4 OUTLINE CHANGE IN THE DISTRIBUTION OF RELIGIOUS MEMBERSHIP IN CANADA

Canada's immigration patterns have resulted in gains for some religious groups and declines in others over time. The number of Muslims more than doubled between 1991 and 2011, reaching an estimated 1.4 million or 3.2 percent of the population. More than two-thirds of Canada's population is Christian, but the proportion of Catholics declined from about 50 percent to 40 percent between 1871 and 2011, while the proportion of Protestants fell from around 45 percent to 27 percent over that 140-year period. The decline in the proportion of Christians is partly due to the growing number of Canadians specifying "no religion" since the 1961 census and partly due to the fact that about one-third of recent immigrants are not Christian. Hindus, Sikhs, Buddhists, and Jews each represent about 1 percent of the population.

## LO 5 LIST THE MAIN SOCIOLOGICAL FACTORS ASSOCIATED WITH RELIGIOUS INVOLVEMENT

Religiosity is highest near the beginning and near the end of the life cycle; in Atlantic Canada, Saskatchewan, and Manitoba; among people who had a religious upbringing; among those with fewer years of secular education; and among people who live in countries with a high level of inequality. These patterns suggest that religiosity depends partly on obligation, opportunity, need, and learning. The people who are most religiously active are those who are compelled to be active; those who were taught to be religious as children; those who have relatively little exposure to secular education; those who have the most time to participate in religious activities; and those who need organized religion the most.

## Multiple-Choice Questions

Questions marked with an asterisk are higher-order questions on the Bloom taxonomy. Answers to these questions are available in the appendix on page CR-51.

1. One sociological theory contends that religious institutions, actions, and consciousness are on the decline worldwide because science and rational thinking in general fail to find any evidence for many religious beliefs and instead provide evidence-based alternative explanations. Which theory makes this argument?
    a. the market model
    b. the secularization thesis
    c. the revised secularization thesis
    d. the Protestant ethic thesis

2. Which of the following has/have been proposed as an alternative/alternatives to the secularization thesis?
    a. the market model
    b. the functional theory
    c. the revised secularization thesis
    d. (a) and (c) only

3. Which of the following arguments most accurately summarizes what the text says about the relationship between extremist Islamic fundamentalism and terrorism?
    a. Colonialism, military occupation, and high inequality in the distribution of resources are associated with extremist Islamic fundamentalism, which is in turn associated with a relatively high level of terrorism.

b. Extremist Islamic fundamentalism is associated with a relatively high level of terrorism.
   c. Extremist Islamic fundamentalism is NOT associated with a relatively high level of terrorism.
   d. The text says nothing about the relationship between extremist Islamic fundamentalism and terrorism.

*4. A sociologist conducts research showing that (a) in countries where the Catholic Church is active, the average Catholic's level of religious commitment is stronger where competition between the Catholic Church and other religious is stronger; and (b) in all countries where relevant data are available, attendance at religious services tends to be low where religious freedom is high. What is the most appropriate conclusion to draw from these findings?
   a. The findings support the market model.
   b. The findings refute the market model.
   c. The findings are not relevant to the market model.
   d. The findings in support of the market model are mixed.

5. Which of the following factors is NOT associated with a high level of religious involvement?
   a. being in the middle of the life cycle
   b. living in a country with a low level of inequality
   c. being a Catholic
   d. (a) and (b) only

# CHAPTER 11 IN REVIEW

## EDUCATION

### LEARNING OBJECTIVES

**LO¹ DESCRIBE HOW EDUCATION WAS TRANSFORMED FROM AN ELITE PHENOMENON TO A MASS PHENOMENON**

Creating systems of education with enough resources to include all children was a social change of breathtaking scope. Training in families had been decentralized, unorganized, and uneven in quality. Religious training was never widely available and tended to set people apart from the surrounding community. Replacing these forms of instruction with a centralized and rationalized system created strong pressures toward uniformity and standardization. Diversity among families, regions, and religious traditions gradually gave way to homogenized indoctrination into a common culture.

The development of mass education was facilitated by the development of printing (which made relatively inexpensive books widely available), the spread of Protestantism (which expected Christians to read the scriptures for themselves), the rise of democracy (which led to the demand for free education for all children), and, most importantly, industrialization (which required a literate labour force with a good knowledge of basic math.)

**LO² APPLY MAJOR SOCIOLOGICAL THEORIES TO THE ANALYSIS OF HOW EDUCATION PROMOTES UPWARD MOBILITY, CREATES SOCIAL COHESION, AND REINFORCES CLASS, RACIAL, AND GENDER INEQUALITIES**

## THEORIES AT A GLANCE

### Education

| Theory | Main Question | Application |
|---|---|---|
| Functionalism | How do social structures and the values underlying them contribute to social stability? | The view that the education system is responsible for sorting students based on talent and effort is a central component of the functional theory of education. The functional theory also stresses the training role of schools. That is, in schools, most people learn how to read, write, count, calculate, and perform other tasks essential to the workings of postmodern society. A third function of the education system involves the socialization of the young. Schools teach the young to view their country with pride, respect the law, think of democracy as the best form of government, and value capitalism. Finally, schools transmit culture from generation to generation, fostering a common identity and social cohesion in the process.<br><br>Sorting, training, socializing, and transmitting culture are *manifest* functions, or positive goals that schools accomplish intentionally. Schools also perform certain *latent*, or unintended, functions. For example, schools encourage the development of a separate youth culture that often conflicts with parents' values. Especially at the college and university levels, educational institutions bring potential mates together, thus serving as a "marriage market." Schools perform a useful custodial service by keeping children under surveillance for much of the day and freeing parents to work in the paid labour force. Finally, because they can encourage critical, independent thinking, educational institutions sometimes become "schools of dissent" that challenge authoritarian regimes and promote social change. |

CR-36  Visit nelson.com/student for additional study tools!

| | | |
|---|---|---|
| Conflict theory | How does the structure of inequality between privileged groups seeking to maintain their advantages and subordinate groups seeking to increase theirs lead to conflict and often to social change? | From the conflict perspective, the chief problem with the functionalist view is that it exaggerates the degree to which schools sort students by ability and thereby ensure that the most talented students eventually get the most rewarding jobs. Conflict theorists argue that, in fact, schools distribute the benefits of education unequally, allocating most of the benefits to children from upper classes and higher-status racial and ethnic groups.<br><br>Five mechanisms allow the education system to help reproduce the class system. First, some people do not attend university or college because they feel they can't afford it, even if they work part-time and take advantage of student loans. Second, low-income parents are more likely than are high-income parents to experience the kinds of financial problems that can make marriage difficult and contribute to divorce. In turn, children from one-parent households are often unable to rely on adults for tutoring, emotional support and encouragement, supervision, and role modelling to the same degree as children from two-parent households can. This puts children from one-parent households at a disadvantage. The third mechanism linking class to educational outcomes involves lack of cultural capital. High-income parents are two-and-a-half times as likely as low-income parents to have earned undergraduate degrees. This fact is important because university education gives people cultural capital that they can transmit to their children, thus improving their chance of financial success. Fourth, IQ and other standardized tests are employed to sort students by intelligence; test scores are used to channel them into high-ability ("enriched"), middle-ability, and low-ability ("basic" or "special education") classrooms. The trouble is that IQ and other standardized tests can measure only acquired proficiency in a given cultural system. The quantity and quality of a person's exposure to whatever is counted as proper or correct plays a large role here. Fifth, the Internet helps to turn class inequality into inequality of educational attainment and achievement. The Internet is an increasingly important source of ideas and information, and people with high income are more likely to have easy access to the Internet than are people with low income. The access gap is shrinking over time, but recent Web-based developments (MOOCs and virtual classrooms) are helping to ensure that class differences in educational attainment and achievement persist. |
| Symbolic interactionism | How do people communicate to make their social settings meaningful, thus helping to create their social circumstances? | Many teachers expect members of lower classes and some visible-minority groups to do poorly in school. Rather than being treated as young people with good prospects, such students are often under suspicion of intellectual inferiority and often feel rejected by teachers, white middle-class classmates, and the curriculum. This expectation, sometimes called a stereotype threat, has a negative impact on the school performance.<br><br>Minority-group students often cluster together because they feel alienated from dominant groups in their school or perhaps even from the institution itself. Too often, such alienation turns into resentment and defiance of authority. Many students from minority groups reject academic achievement as a goal because they see it as a value of the dominant culture. Discipline problems, ranging from apathy to disruptive and illegal behaviour, can result.<br><br>The corollary of identifying your race or ethnicity with poor academic performance is thinking of good academic performance as "selling out" to the dominant culture. Consistent with this argument, Indigenous and black students in Canada have higher-than-average school dropout rates.<br><br>In contrast, research shows that challenging lower-class and minority students, giving them emotional support and encouragement, giving greater recognition in the curriculum to the accomplishments of the groups from which they originate, creating an environment in which they can relax and achieve—all of these strategies explode the self-fulfilling prophecy and improve academic performance. |

*(Continued)*

| Feminism | How do social conventions maintain male dominance and female subordination, and how do these conventions get overturned? | Feminist theorists note that although women now constitute a majority of students in institutions of higher education, the gender gap narrows considerably at the master's level and reverses at the PhD level, where men receive most degrees. Moreover, a disproportionately large number of men earn degrees in engineering, computer science, dentistry, and specialized areas of medicine—all relatively high-paying fields, most requiring a strong math and science background. A disproportionately large number of women earn PhDs in education, English, foreign languages, and other relatively low-paying fields requiring little background in math and science. |
|---|---|---|

## LO3 ANALYZE THE CORPORATIZATION OF HIGHER EDUCATION

The **corporatization** of the university means the reshaping of the university on a business model. In practice, corporatization involves consumers of higher education paying a larger share of the cost of the services they enjoy and universities responding to market demand for particular skills. Corporatization is a change from the way universities were organized up until the 1980s, when they were more heavily subsidized by government, academic personnel were freer to shape university priorities as they saw fit, and few instructors were cost-cutting part-timers. Evidence of corporatization includes the rapid rise in the cost of tuition since the 1990s, the decline of government funding, and the shift of enrolment to fields for which there is relatively high demand and therefore relatively high earnings.

It is likely significant that most of the criticism of corporatization comes from professors in the social sciences, education, and the humanities, all fields that are either stagnating or shrinking in terms of their relative share of the student body. Here, self-interest and idealism appear to coincide. Professors in fields that are growing relatively slowly, if at all, may be expressing both their sincere belief in the importance of humanistic, liberal arts education and a desire to protect their jobs.

The corporatization of the university undoubtedly comes with risks, not the least of which is excessive corporate influence on university policy. Critics play a useful role in keeping a watchful eye on university governance. Paradoxically, however, it might make more sense for universities to broaden outside influence rather than seeking to eliminate it. In Denmark, umbrella organizations of universities, corporations, and unions consult frequently. They decide on funding priorities that result in educating university students so they can find interesting and well-paying jobs that the Danish economy needs. This arrangement helps to keep Denmark's per capita income higher than Canada's, its unemployment rate lower, and its people happier.

## LO4 ASSESS ATTITUDES TOWARD THE QUALITY OF SCHOOLING IN CANADA AND COMPARE THE QUALITY OF CANADIAN SCHOOLS TO THOSE IN OTHER COUNTRIES

Adults Canadians are only moderately satisfied with their public schools, and dissatisfaction seems to be growing. A substantial number of Canadians think that educational standards are too low and require renewed emphasis on "the basics" of language, math, and science. They worry that the Canadian school system lags behind that of other countries, such as Japan and South Korea.

However, comparative analysis of the capabilities of 15-year-old students in reading, math, and science show that the quality of Canadian education compares favourably with the quality of education in 67 other countries. In standardized tests in these subjects in 2015, Japanese students ranked second, South Korean students ranked eighth, and Canadian students ranked sixth.

## Multiple-Choice Questions

Questions marked with an asterisk* are higher-order questions on the Bloom taxonomy. Answers to these questions are available in the appendix on page CR-51.

1. Which of the following is a latent function of schools?
   a. socializing students
   b. training students
   c. providing a custodial service for parents
   d. transmitting culture

*2. The following diagram illustrates a theory about the effect of colleges on social mobility. Which theory does it illustrate?
   a. functionalism
   b. conflict theory
   c. symbolic interactionism
   d. feminism

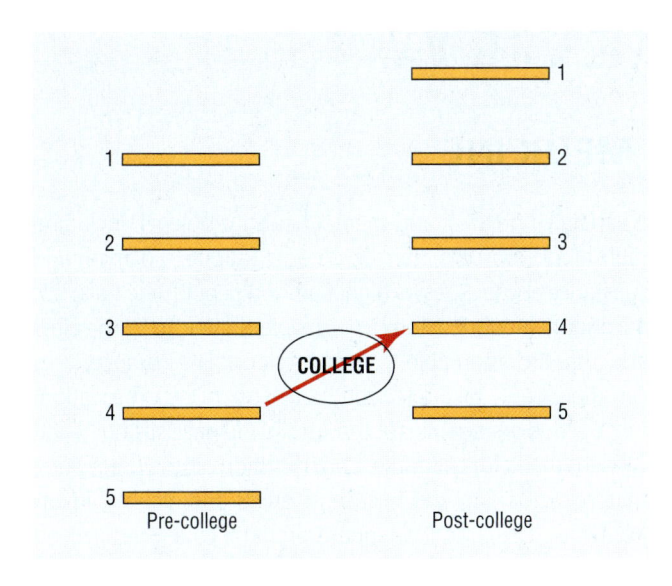

## EDUCATIONAL ATTAINMENT BY INCOME GROUP, CANADA

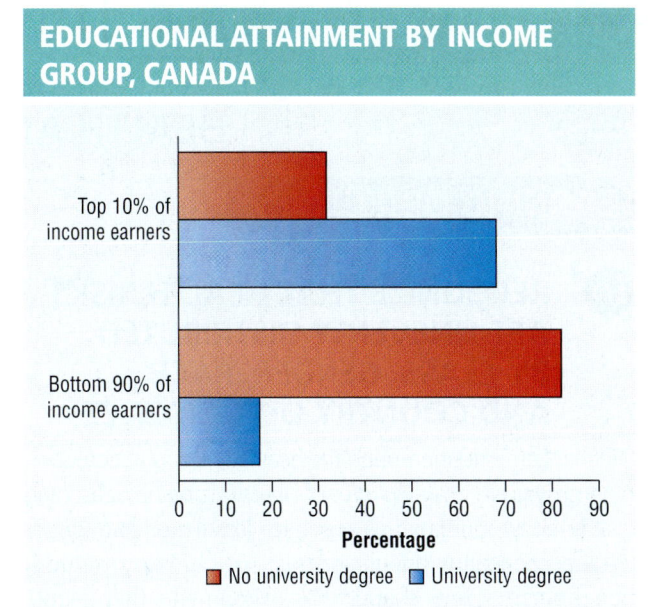

Source: Statistics Canada. 2013k. "Distribution of persons by income group and highest level of education attainment." https://www12.statcan.gc.ca/nhs-enm/2011/as-sa/99-014-x/2011003/c-g/desc/longdesc01_2-eng.cfm (retrieved 8 August 2015).

3. Which of the following statements is NOT accurate?
   a. Canada has the world's lowest out-of-school rate for children of primary school age.
   b. Canada has the highest percentage of residents between the ages of 25 and 64 with a certificate, diploma, or degree from a college or university.
   c. The earliest school systems were established in Upper Canada and the northern United States about 1870.
   d. Canada's public school system is ranked the best in the world.

*4. The following graph illustrates a theory about the relationship between education and income. Which theory, if any, does it illustrate?
   a. functionalism
   b. conflict theory
   c. symbolic interactionism
   d. none of the above

5. The text argues that certain groups may be influencing university policy in ways that do not best serve the public interest. What are these groups?
   a. professors
   b. corporations
   c. unions
   d. (a) and (b) only

# CHAPTER 12 IN REVIEW

## HEALTH AND MEDICINE

### LEARNING OBJECTIVES

**LO 1 RECOGNIZE THAT HEALTH RISKS ARE UNEVENLY DISTRIBUTED BY CLASS, GENDER, RACE, AND COUNTRY OF RESIDENCE**

When it comes to measuring the health of a population, sociologists typically examine rates of illness and death, reasoning that healthy populations experience less illness and longer life than unhealthy populations do. Health risks arise from how human activity shapes the environments that people inhabit. Some environments foster good health, while others impose added risks for poor health. Health risks also arise from the quality of a country's public health and health care systems. The **public health system** comprises government-run programs that ensure access to clean drinking water, basic sewage and sanitation services, and inoculation against infectious diseases. The **health care system** comprises a nation's clinics, hospitals, and other facilities for ensuring health and treating illness. Finally, lifestyle factors, including smoking, excessive use of alcohol and drugs, poor diet, lack of exercise, and social isolation are associated with poor health and premature death. People often think of lifestyle factors like smoking as matters of individual choice. However, like human environmental factors and factors related to the public health and health care systems, they are associated with deeper, social background factors, including country of residence, class, race, and gender.

**LO 2 EXPLAIN WHY LOW-INCOME PEOPLE AND PEOPLE WHO BELONG TO GROUPS THAT EXPERIENCE A HIGH LEVEL OF DISCRIMINATION, SUCH AS INDIGENOUS CANADIANS, HAVE LIMITED ACCESS TO HEALTH SERVICES**

There are several reasons why health care deteriorates as one moves down the class hierarchy. First, people in lower classes experience relatively high stress levels because of their difficult living conditions. Persistent stress is associated with a variety of physical and mental health problems, including high blood pressure, cancer, chronic fatigue, violence, and substance abuse. Stress is higher among people who have less autonomy at work. Moreover, people higher up in the class structure are often able to turn stress off. For instance, they can more easily take a few days off work or go on vacation.

Second, inequalities at the start of life have strong health consequences for a lifetime. Poor nutrition during pregnancy, maternal smoking and misuse of drugs and alcohol, insufficient exercise, and inadequate prenatal care typically lead to suboptimal fetal development. Mothers with low income are more likely to provide such unfavourable starts to life.

Third, People who are less educated and who have less exposure to educated advisers tend to have less knowledge about healthy lifestyles. For example, they are less likely to know what constitutes a nutritious diet. This, too, contributes to their propensity to illness. Illness, in turn, makes it more difficult for poor people to escape poverty.

Fourth, a disproportionately large number of poor Canadians live in areas that have inferior medical services. For example, there are fewer hospitals, physicians, and nurses per capita in rural areas than in urban areas. The problem is especially acute on Indigenous peoples' reserves. As well, the quality of preventive, diagnostic, and treatment facilities is generally superior in urban areas. Moreover, many low- and middle-income Canadians have limited or no access to eye care, dentistry, mental health counselling, and prescription drugs.

Fifth, poor people are more likely than rich people are to be exposed to environmental risks that have a negative impact on their health.

Negative health outcomes are also associated with being a member of a group that experiences a high level of discrimination, such as Indigenous Canadians. Part of the Indigenous/non-Indigenous difference in life expectancy is a consequence of the fact that the median income of Indigenous Canadians is only about 60 percent of the median for all Canadians. Poor health is strongly associated with low income. But that is only half the story. In addition, Indigenous Canadians suffer negative health outcomes because of the cumulative effects of social exclusion based on race. Specifically, even when Indigenous Canadians earn median Canadian income, they are more likely than other Canadians to live in unsafe and unhealthy areas and to experience discrimination that takes a toll on their health. Thus, it is the *intersection* of class and race that explains the health status of Indigenous Canadians.

## LO³ CLARIFY THE WAYS IN WHICH GENDER AFFECTS HEALTH OUTCOMES

A gap between women's and men's health care exists in many countries, especially in the Middle East, sub-Saharan Africa, and South Asia. It's easy to see this gap by examining the **sex ratio**, that is, the number of males per 100 females in a population. *At birth*, the sex ratio for the entire world is 103, meaning that 103 boys are born for every 100 girls. But in India, the sex ratio is an unusually high 112, while in China, it is 115, because sex-selective abortion is widespread in those two countries. A strong preference for boys leads many parents to pay for ultrasound tests that determine the sex of the fetus. A good number of those parents decide to abort the fetus if it's female.

The United Arab Emirates and Qatar stand out if one examines the sex ratio for *people older than 64*. While the world's sex ratio for people older than 64 is 102, it stands at 169 for Qataris and 171 for Emiratis. These unusually high sex ratios may be due to women dying at a higher rate than men because, over their lifetime, they experience more violence and/or inferior nutrition and/or inferior health care compared to men.

In countries like Canada, where women and men have the same rights to health care and where the level of violence against women is more moderate, there still exists a gender bias in health. The health system has been slower to address and more likely to neglect women's health issues than men's health issues. And women have until recently been excluded from participating in many major health research studies, which is significant because women may present with different symptoms than men who have the same illness and may require different treatment regimes.

## LO⁴ IDENTIFY THE WAYS IN WHICH THE SOCIAL ORGANIZATION OF HEALTH CARE SYSTEMS INFLUENCES PEOPLE'S HEALTH

The United States spends more per person on health care and has more physicians per 1000 people than Canada does, yet on average Americans live significantly shorter lives than Canadians do. One reason for this is that the gap between rich and poor is greater in the United States than in Canada. In general, the higher the level of inequality in a country, the less healthy its population is. A second factor is that physicians, hospitals, pharmaceutical companies, and other providers of health care are able to charge substantially higher prices in the United States than in Canada because the United States has a privatized system of health care in which extraordinarily powerful, organized interests (such as physicians and pharmaceutical companies) are able to set prices for their goods and services yet claim that they are protecting a free market. Canada's publicly funded health care system and government-regulated prescription drug regime prevent this outcome.

## THEORIES AT A GLANCE

### Health

| Theory | Main Question | Application |
|---|---|---|
| Conflict theory | How does the structure of inequality between privileged groups seeking to maintain their advantages and subordinate groups seeking to increase theirs lead to conflict and often to social change? | Economic inequality is greater in the United States than in other rich countries, so American health care is more of a system of privilege for some and a disadvantage for others than it is in Canada and western Europe. Inequality thus contributes to the poor health of less well-to-do Americans. All told, the American government pays 53 percent of all medical costs out of taxes. In the United Kingdom, Sweden, and Denmark, the comparable figure is between 81 and 85 percent; in Japan and Germany, it is between 77 and 83 percent; and in France, Canada, and Italy, it is between 71 and 78 percent. Moreover, in Germany, Italy, Belgium, Denmark, Finland, Greece, Iceland, Luxembourg, Norway, and Spain prescription drugs, eyeglasses, dental care, and prostheses are covered.<br><br>Even the cost of prescription drugs is unregulated in the United States, again in contrast to other rich countries, and many low-income people cannot afford the medication they need. In contrast, in a successful political struggle, Canada's "socialized" health care system was initiated by the CCF (the forerunner of the NDP) in Saskatchewan in 1968 and soon became a model for the whole country. |

*(Continued)*

| Feminism | How do social conventions maintain male dominance and female subordination, and how do these conventions get overturned? | Feminists have identified numerous gaps between women's and men's health. Globally, the gap is particularly evident in the Middle East, sub-Saharan Africa, and South Asia. Sex-selective abortion, violence against women, and gender discrimination with respect to nutrition and medical care are widespread in many countries in these regions. In wealthy Western countries like Canada, women and men have the same rights to health care and the level of violence against women is more moderate.
However, our health system has been slow to address and more likely to neglect women's health issues than men's health issues. Until recently, more research focused on "men's diseases," such as cardiac arrest, than on "women's diseases," such as breast cancer. Similarly, women have until recently been excluded from participating in many major health research studies, which is significant because women may present with different symptoms than men who have the same illness and may require different treatment regimes. |
|---|---|---|

Most Canadians think highly of their public health care system, often say it is Canada's core institution, and favour strengthening public health care rather than expanding for-profit medical services. Canadians also have issues with public health care, however. A particular source of concern is waiting times, especially for emergency care.

## LO 5 DESCRIBE HOW THE RISE OF MEDICAL SCIENCE IS LINKED TO (1) SUCCESSFUL TREATMENTS AND (2) THE WAY DOCTORS EXCLUDED COMPETITORS AND ESTABLISHED CONTROL OVER THEIR PROFESSION AND THEIR CLIENTS

In the early nineteenth century, the practice of medicine was in a chaotic state. Herbalists, faith healers, midwives, druggists, and medical doctors vied to meet the health needs of the public. A century later, the dust had settled. Medical science was victorious. Its first series of breakthroughs involved identifying the bacteria and viruses responsible for various diseases and then developing effective procedures and vaccines to combat them. These and subsequent triumphs in diagnosis and treatment convinced most people of the superiority of medical science over other approaches to health.

A second, sociological reason for the rise to dominance of scientific medicine is that doctors were able to professionalize. A **profession** is an occupation that requires extensive formal education. Professionals regulate their own training and practice. They restrict competition within the profession, mainly by limiting the recruitment of practitioners. They minimize competition with other professions, partly by laying exclusive claim to a field of expertise. Professionals are usually self-employed. They exercise considerable authority over their clients. And they profess to be motivated mainly by the desire to serve their community even though they earn a lot of money in the process. Professionalization, then, is the process by which people gain control and authority over their occupation and their clients. It results in professionals enjoying high occupational prestige and income, and considerable social and political power.

## LO 6 APPRECIATE THE BENEFITS AND DANGERS OF ALTERNATIVE MEDICAL TREATMENTS

Ours is an era of patient activism, spurred on partly by a much more highly educated public than existed 60 or 70 years ago. Patients are more likely now than in past decades to learn about their illnesses and treatment options, review treatment options with their doctors, ask their doctors many questions about procedures, and so on.

Some recent challenges to the authority of medical science are highly organized and political, such as the movement to increase funding for research on HIV/AIDS. Others, such as the increasing popularity of alternative medical treatments (chiropractic, acupuncture, massage, and so on) are less organized and political.

While in general patient activism is a positive development, it has a downside in that people are increasingly prone to being influenced by the medical advice of celebrities who lack scientific and medical training. Some of their advice is beneficial, some is benign but of little or no benefit, and some is harmful. Patient activism that includes paying careful attention to developments in medical science can help people evaluate celebrity advice.

## Multiple-Choice Questions

Questions marked with an asterisk are higher-order questions on the Bloom taxonomy. Answers to these questions are available in the appendix on page CR-51.

*1. Many factors underlie ill health. Which of the following factors is not based on a sociological understanding of the causes of ill health?
   a. smoking cigarettes
   b. living in an unhealthy environment
   c. living at or near the bottom of the class hierarchy
   d. living in a poor country

2. Which of the following factors is always associated with better health outcomes?
   a. per capita total expenditure on health
   b. physicians per 1000 population
   c. both (a) and (b)
   d. none of the above

*3. Juan is a senior manager in a company where Aiguo is a clerk. They had precisely identical upbringings and they have precisely equal access to excellent health services. Based only on this information, who, if either, is likely to be in better health?
   a. Aiguo
   b. Juan
   c. They are likely to be equally healthy.
   d. Note enough information has been provided to allow one to answer this question.

4. Which of the following statements is true?
   a. Poor health outcomes among Indigenous Canadians are solely a result of their relatively low class position.
   b. Poor health outcomes among Indigenous Canadians are solely a result of their experience of racial discrimination.
   c. Poor health outcomes among Indigenous Canadians are solely a result of their relatively low class position and their experience of racial discrimination.
   d. none of the above

*5. A country has an unusually high ratio of males to females for people over the age of 64. What does this fact suggest?
   a. Sex-selective abortion is widespread.
   b. Over their lifetime, women may experience more violence and/or inferior nutrition and/or inferior health care compared to men.
   c. both (a) and (b)
   d. none of the above

# CHAPTER 13 IN REVIEW

## MASS MEDIA AND MASS COMMUNICATION

### LEARNING OBJECTIVES

**LO¹ APPRECIATE THAT, ALTHOUGH THE MOST POPULAR MASS MEDIA ARE PRODUCTS OF THE TWENTIETH CENTURY, THEIR GROWTH IS ROOTED IN THE RISE OF PROTESTANTISM, DEMOCRACY, AND CAPITALISM**

At the beginning of the sixteenth century, Catholics relied on priests to tell them what was in the Bible. Then, in 1517, Martin Luther protested certain practices of the church. Among other things, he wanted people to develop a more personal relationship with the Bible. Within 40 years, Luther's new form of Christianity, known as Protestantism, was established in half of Europe. Suddenly, millions of people were being encouraged to read. The Bible became the first mass media product in the West, aided by technological improvements in papermaking and printing.

A second force that promoted the growth of the mass media was political democracy. From the eighteenth century on, the citizens of France, the United States, and other countries demanded and achieved representation in government. At the same time, they wanted to become literate and gain access to previously restricted centres of learning. Democratic governments, in turn, depended on an informed citizenry and therefore encouraged popular literacy and the growth of a free press.

The third major force stimulating the growth of the mass media was capitalist industrialization. Modern industries required a literate and numerate workforce. They also needed rapid means of communication to do business efficiently. Moreover, the mass media turned out to be a major source of profit in their own right.

**LO² EXPLAIN HOW MAJOR SOCIOLOGICAL THEORIES HAVE BEEN APPLIED TO THE ANALYSIS OF MASS MEDIA AND MASS COMMUNICATION**

## THEORIES AT A GLANCE

### Mass Media and Mass Communication

| Theory | Main Question | Application |
|---|---|---|
| Functionalism | How do social structures and the values underlying them contribute to social stability? | The mass media perform an important function by coordinating the operation of industrial and postindustrial societies. In addition, the mass media are also important agents of socialization. A third function of the mass media involves social control; the mass media help to ensure conformity. The mass media's fourth and final function is to provide entertainment, that is, pleasure, relaxation, and momentary escape from the tension and tedium of everyday life. Without such escapes, daily tensions and frustrations might express themselves more openly and disruptively. |
| Conflict theory | How does the structure of inequality between privileged groups seeking to maintain their advantages and subordinate groups seeking to increase theirs lead to conflict and often to social change? | Conflict theorists criticize functionalism for paying insufficient attention to the social inequality fostered by the mass media. Specifically, conflict theorists say functionalism exaggerates the degree to which the mass media serve the interests of the entire society. They contend that some people benefit from the mass media more than others do. In particular, the mass media favour the interests of dominant classes and political groups.<br><br>Conflict theorists maintain that there are two ways in which dominant classes and political groups benefit disproportionately from the mass media. First, the mass media broadcast beliefs, values, and ideas that create widespread acceptance of the basic structure of society, including its injustices and inequalities. Second, ownership of the mass media is highly concentrated in the hands of a small number of people and is highly profitable for them. In this way, the mass media are a source of economic inequality. |

| | | |
|---|---|---|
| Symbolic interactionism | How do people communicate to make their social settings meaningful, thus helping to create their social circumstances? | Both functionalism and conflict theory stress how the mass media bridge social differences and reinforce society's core values. By focusing on core values, both approaches understate the degree to which audience members interpret media messages in different ways. Symbolic interactionist and related approaches highlight the importance of such interpretive acts. |
| Feminism | How do social conventions maintain male dominance and female subordination, and how do these conventions get overturned? | Early feminist research focused on the misrepresentation of women in the mass media. They found that in TV dramas, women tended to be cast in subordinate roles and men as authority figures. Women usually appeared in domestic settings, men in public settings. Advertising targeted only women as purchasers of household products and appliances. The news rarely mentioned issues of importance for many women and sometimes trivialized or denounced the women's movement. Newsworthy issues were associated with men, and men were more likely than women were to be used as news sources and to deliver the news.<br><br>In the 1980s and 1990s, feminist researchers, influenced by cultural studies, began demonstrating that audience members selectively interpret media messages and sometimes contest them. And in recent years, some feminist scholars have broadened their focus to analyze the capacity of the mass media to reproduce and change the system of racial inequality in North America. On the one hand, they find that certain stereotypical images of women of colour recur in the mass media. On the other hand, they recognize that some mass media, especially independent filmmaking and popular music, have enabled women of colour to challenge these stereotypes. |

## LO3 IDENTIFY THE WAYS IN WHICH CENTRALIZED CONTROL AND RESISTANCE TO SUCH CONTROL INTERACT ON THE INTERNET

Interaction between audiences and the traditional mass media (television, radio, and newspapers) is generally weighted in favour of the media. Although audience members do not mindlessly absorb messages from these sources, they exercise little control over content. In contrast, the Internet, especially its social media applications, offers better prospects for audience influence than do the traditional mass media.

On the one hand, centralized control of the Internet is evident in the following circumstances: (1) Internet access requires payment, so usage is limited to people who can afford it (only about half the people in the world, and richer, better educated, urban, and younger people in rich countries like Canada). (2) American content dominates the Internet because most large Internet companies are American-owned and Americans are disproportionately heavy Internet users. (3) Advertising is the major source of revenue for most big Internet companies. Advertising seeks to influence (some would say "manipulate") consumers to buy products and services. The Internet is an especially effective means of advertising because it is able to influence consumers using ads that are targeted to their particular interests, likes, and dislikes. (4) Algorithms (rules that computers follow to solve problems) to drive the Internet and social media. To date, the biases they have incorporated into their algorithms tend to favour privileged and/or right-wing groups. This circumstance has led some mathematicians and computer scientists to identify many algorithms on the Internet and in social media that increase inequality and threaten democracy. (5) Owners of online content seek to prevent what they call "online piracy" by restricting access to paying customers and seeking legal redress for violations of ownership.

On the other hand, resistance to centralized control of the Internet is evident in the following circumstances: (1) Most Internet users favour net neutrality, demanding unrestricted access to online content so as to maximize freedom of expression, innovation, and user choice. (2) Users create an enormous amount of online content themselves, thus making independent, creative contributions to Internet growth. (3) The use of social media allows people to change how other people see them and how they see themselves (that is, their identity). Social media also give users the capacity to (4) augment the connections they form with others (that is, their social relationships), and (5) seek social change in new ways (that is, enhance their activism).

## Multiple-Choice Questions

Questions marked with an asterisk are higher-order questions on the Bloom taxonomy. Answers to these questions are available in the appendix on page pages CR-51 to CR-52.

1. According to the text, three factors account for the rise of the mass media. Which of the following is NOT one of those factors?
   a. the widespread use of the Bible after Christianity became the official religion of the Roman Empire in the fourth century
   b. the widespread use of the Bible after the Protestant Reformation in the sixteenth century
   c. the spread of democracy beginning in the eighteenth century
   d. capitalist industrialization

2. Which of the following is NOT a function of the mass media according to functionalist theory?
   a. coordinating the operation of industrial and postindustrial societies
   b. acting as important agents of socialization
   c. helping to ensure conformity
   d. providing many jobs that pay well

3. Which theory claims that the mass media are biased because of advertising, sourcing, and flak?
   a. feminist theory
   b. symbolic interactionist theory
   c. conflict theory
   d. functionalist theory

*4. Which of the following research methods provides the most valid assessment of the relationship between TV violence and real-world violence?
   a. laboratory experiments
   b. field research
   c. surveys
   d. natural experiments

5. What is net neutrality?
   a. The principle that Internet service providers should not restrict access to any online content.
   b. The principle that people should pay the same fee for Internet access regardless of how much data they use.
   c. The principle that political messaging on the Internet should avoid extremism.
   d. The principle that people should have equal access to the Internet and that the speed of their connection should also be equal.

# CHAPTER 14 IN REVIEW

## SOCIAL CHANGE: TECHNOLOGY, THE ENVIRONMENT, AND SOCIAL MOVEMENTS

### LEARNING OBJECTIVES

#### LO1 ANALYZE THE CIRCUMSTANCES IN WHICH ENVIRONMENTAL ISSUES ARE TRANSFORMED INTO SOCIAL PROBLEMS

Environmental problems do not become social issues spontaneously. Before they can enter the public consciousness, policy-oriented scientists, the environmental movement, the mass media, and respected organizations must discover and promote them. People have to connect real-life events to the information learned from these groups. Because some scientists, industrial interests, and politicians dispute the existence of environmental threats, the public can begin to question whether environmental issues are, in fact, social problems that require human intervention. Thus, environmental issues are not inevitably perceived as problematic. Rather, they are socially contested phenomena. They can be socially constructed by proponents, and they can be socially demolished by opponents.

#### LO2 ASSESS THE UNEQUAL SOCIAL DISTRIBUTION OF ENVIRONMENTAL RISKS

Whenever disaster strikes, economically and politically disadvantaged people almost always suffer most. That is because their circumstances render them most vulnerable. In fact, the advantaged often consciously put the disadvantaged in harm's way to avoid risk themselves. This phenomenon is known as **environmental racism**: the tendency to heap environmental dangers on the disadvantaged and especially on disadvantaged racial minorities. Class also structures exposure to environmental risk, as does citizenship in less economically developed or more economically developed countries. In general, the inhabitants of the northern hemisphere cause a disproportionately large share of the world's environmental problems, enjoy a disproportionate share of the benefits of technology, and live with fewer environmental risks than do people in the southern hemisphere.

#### LO3 SUMMARIZE THE ROLE OF MARKET/TECHNOLOGICAL AND COOPERATIVE SOLUTIONS TO ENVIRONMENTAL PROBLEMS

Some people endorse the theory that the environmental crisis will resolve itself. They think we already have two weapons that will end it: the market and high technology. The case of oil illustrates how these weapons combine forces. If oil reserves drop or oil is withheld from the market for political reasons, the price of oil goes up. This makes it worthwhile for oil exploration companies to develop new technologies to recover more oil. When they discover more oil and bring it to market, prices fall back to where they were. Generalizing this principle and projecting it into the future, optimists believe global warming and other forms of environmental degradation will be dealt with similarly. In their view, human inventiveness and the profit motive will combine to create the new technologies we need to survive and prosper.

While some evidence supports this optimistic scenario, three factors suggest that market forces and technological fixes cannot solve environmental problems on their own: (1) The price of some commodities does not reflect their actual cost to society. Because of such price distortions, the market often fails to send signals that might result in the speedy adoption of technological and policy fixes. (2) Despite some successes with market and technological fixes, efforts so far to deal with global warming are insufficient; global warming continues to accelerate. (3) Political pressure exerted by environmental activists, community groups, and public opinion is often necessary to motivate corporate and government action on environmental issues. Without the efforts of such organizations, it is doubtful that many environmental issues would be defined as social problems.

The alternative to the market and high-tech theory is a theory that emphasizes the need for cooperation to greatly reduce overconsumption of just about everything. This strategy includes investing more heavily in energy-saving technologies, doing more to clean up the environment, subsidizing environmentally friendly industrialization in the developing countries, renewing commitment to voluntary efforts, passing new laws and enforcement bodies to ensure compliance, increasing environmental research and development by industry and government, providing more environmentally directed foreign aid, and levying new taxes to help pay for it all.

However, the cooperative theory is not realistic in the short term. It would be political suicide for anyone in the rich countries to propose such drastic measures as those just listed. The plain fact is that most people are unwilling to be inconvenienced or pay much of the cost of such measures.

It follows that more and bigger environmental catastrophes may have to occur before more people are willing to take massive remedial action.

## LO⁴ IDENTIFY THE SOCIAL CONDITIONS THAT ENCOURAGE PEOPLE TO REBEL AGAINST THE STATUS QUO

## THEORIES AT A GLANCE

### Social Movements

| Theory | Main Question | Application |
|---|---|---|
| Functionalism | How do social structures and the values underlying them contribute to social stability? | Breakdown theory is a variant of functionalism insofar as it regards collective action as a form of social imbalance that results from the improper functioning of social institutions. According to this theory, evidence of a breakdown in functioning is evident in the social marginality of early movement leaders and early recruits (who tend to be poorly integrated in society) and in the strain that tends to precede the emergence of movements (that is, the disruption of people's norms). One type of strain is relative deprivation (the growth of an intolerable gap between the social rewards people expect to receive and those they actually receive). |
| Conflict theory | How does the structure of inequality between privileged groups seeking to maintain their advantages and subordinate groups seeking to increase theirs lead to conflict and often to social change? | Solidarity theory is a type of conflict theory that focuses on the social conditions that allow people to turn their discontent into a unified (or "solidary") political force. It identifies three such social conditions: adequate resource mobilization, sufficient political opportunities, and weak or inconsistent social control. Resource mobilization is the process by which groups engage in more collective action as their power increases because of their growing size and increasing organizational, material, and other resources.<br><br>A second social condition that allows mass discontent to be translated into social movement formation involves the emergence of new political opportunities. Specifically, chances for protest and social movement formation emerge when influential allies offer support, when ruling political alignments become unstable, when elite groups are divided and come into conflict with one another, and when election campaigns provide a focus for discontent and a chance to put new representatives with new policies into positions of authority.<br><br>The third main lesson of solidarity theory is that governments can try to lower the frequency and intensity of protest by taking various social control measures. These measures include making concessions to protesters, co-opting the most troublesome leaders (for example, by appointing them as advisers), and violently repressing collective action. |
| Symbolic interactionism | How do people communicate to make their social settings meaningful, thus helping to create their social circumstances? | Symbolic interactionists have developed the idea that frame alignment lies between (1) the capacity of disadvantaged people to mobilize resources for collective action, and (2) the recruitment of a substantial number of movement members.<br><br>Frame alignment is the process by which social movement leaders make their activities, ideas, and goals congruent with the interests, beliefs, and values of potential new recruits to their movement—or fail to do so. |

CR-48   Visit nelson.com/student for additional study tools!

## LO 5 LIST THE CHARACTERISTICS OF "NEW SOCIAL MOVEMENTS"

In the 1960s, political structures started to undergo massive changes under the forces of globalization. "New social movements" responded by setting broader goals, attracting new kinds of participants, and becoming global in scope.

## Multiple-Choice Questions

Questions marked with an asterisk are higher-order questions on the Bloom taxonomy. Answers to these questions are available in the appendix on page CR-52.

1. A new group of major inventions has cropped up every 40 to 60 years since the Industrial Revolution. These flurries of creativity cause major economic growth spurts, beginning 10 to 20 years later and lasting 25 to 35 years each. What term describes this phenomenon?
   a. Sutton's law
   b. Kondratiev waves
   c. social constructionism
   d. technological indeterminism

*2. More than two million used uranium fuel bundles are sitting at temporary storage sites in Canada. Their useful life fuelling nuclear reactors is over. Scientists and government officials know that they will be dangerously radioactive for at least another 10 000 years and that leakage could cause mass radioactive poisoning to nearby populations. Does this constitute a social problem?
   a. Yes. If the authorities know about the situation and many people are in harm's way, it is a big social problem.
   b. No. However, the situation could become a social problem if a social movement and the mass media publicize it and many people come to recognize that the situation could harm them.
   c. Maybe. The information provided is too vague to permit one to decide whether the situation constitutes a social problem or not.
   d. Probably. Governments can't keep secrets; there are always leaks.

*3. An intolerable gap develops between the social rewards people expect to receive and those they actually receive. What do they experience?
   a. strain
   b. social marginality
   c. resource mobilization
   d. relative deprivation

*4. Social movement leaders decide to water down their movement's ideals because they think that would enable them to recruit more members. What activity are they engaged in?
   a. frame alignment
   b. co-optation
   c. resource mobilization
   d. social control

5. What does survey research conducted in Egypt during the Arab Spring show?
   a. Using new electronic communications media was associated with being a protester.
   b. Protesters tended to be people with strong grievances related to unemployment, poverty, and corruption.
   c. Protesters were more available for protest activities than others were because they tended to be unmarried men living in cities and tended to have strong, pre-existing ties to various charitable, political, and other civic associations.
   d. all of the above

# APPENDIX

## ANSWERS TO MULTIPLE-CHOICE QUESTIONS

### Chapter 1 Introduction to Sociology

1. c. South Korean industrialization turned many farmers into urban workers and housewives. Whereas it was valuable to have many children working on the farm, it was more costly and less useful to raise as many children in the city, so women started having fewer babies

   **Explanation:** Option (a) locates the cause of the change exclusively in women's minds. Option (b) locates the cause of the change exclusively in the chemical properties of the environment. Option (d) fails to explain why South Korean women would want to mimic the behaviour of Western women. Only option (c) locates the cause of the change in the social world and identifies a plausible mechanism for why the cause would have the effect it did.

2. b. The sociologist's theory is that a set of *values* involving the worship of cows and a *social structure* that includes various worship practices exist in rural India because cow worship performs a useful *function*: it increases the ability of people to gain access to scarce, valuable resources.
3. d.
4. a.
5. c.

### Chapter 2 Culture

1. b. experience → conceptualization → verbalization → experience
2. c. Castes are justified mainly by religion; classes are not.
3. a. A university is a "marriage market," that is, a competitive forum for the establishment of long-term, intimate relations between individuals.
4. d. a postmodern society
5. b. rationalization

### Chapter 3 Socialization

1. c. playing simple games
2. a. the family
3. d. anticipatory socialization
4. a. Life expectancy rose and the need for better-educated adults became apparent.
5. b. Lack of good jobs, high student debt, and expensive housing costs force many young adults to live with their parents.

### Chapter 4 From Social Interaction to Social Organizations

1. b. the woman
2. a. engaging in emotion management
3. d. role conflict
4. d. all of the above
5. c. Solicit information about job opportunities from people to whom you are weakly tied.

### Chapter 5 Deviance and Crime

1. c. Breaking a norm and evoking a negative reaction from others.
2. a. the increased incarceration rate
3. b. education
4. d. none of the above

   **Explanation:** The situation described in the question stem is not necessarily a moral panic, because it provides no information about the actual crime rate. If the situation were accompanied by a falling or even a steady crime rate, it could be considered a moral panic. However, the situation could be considered a reasonable response if it were accompanied by a rapidly rising crime rate.

5. b. reforms to the prison regime that HAVE worked well in practice

### Chapter 6 Social Stratification: Canadian and Global Perspectives

1. c. various forms of capital
2. a. relative and income-based
3. b. Canada's tax system is approximately neutral.
4. c. Davis and Moore
5. d. all of the above

### Chapter 7 Race and Ethnicity

1. a and d
2. c. Irish Canadians

3. a. critical race theory
4. c. both of the above
5. b. Arab

## Chapter 8 Sexualities and Genders

1. d. transgender
2. b. the Marxist variant of conflict theory
3. c. queer theory
4. a. essentialism
5. d. (b) and (c) only

## Chapter 9 Families

1. d. during the 1950s and early 1960s
2. b. The social problems caused by widespread polygamy can be minimized if a wide variety of family forms, including common-law heterosexual families and homosexual monogamous families replace polygamous families.
3. d. none of the above

**Explanation:** According to the text, the rate of interracial unions among Vancouver's population in general is about 10 percent, so it seems there is no difference between the population and the sample estimate derived from the study. Moreover, the researchers did not themselves measure the rate of interracial union formation in Vancouver's general population, so they could not have checked to see if there was any difference between the general population and their sample of online daters. Therefore, (a) is false. The study did not measure the rate of interracial union formation at two or more time points. Therefore, (b) is false. Accordingly, (d) must be the right answer.]

4. b. Liberal divorce laws allow people to leave unhappy marriages and find marriage partners with whom they are happy.
5. a. persistent conflict between the spouses

## Chapter 10 Religion

1. b. the secularization thesis
2. d. (a) and (c) only
3. a. Colonialism, military occupation, and high inequality in the distribution of resources are associated with extremist Islamic fundamentalism, which is in turn associated with a relatively high level of terrorism.
4. d. The findings in support of the market model are mixed.
5. d. (a) and (b) only

## Chapter 11 Education

1. c. providing a custodial service for parents
2. b. conflict theory
3. d. Canada's public school system is ranked the best in the world.
4. d. None of the above

**Explanation:** The graph illustrates an association between income and education: people who earn high incomes are more likely than people without high incomes to have a university degree. It is possible that a high income allows people to earn a university degree (which would support conflict theory) or that having a university degree allows people to earn a high income (which is consistent with functionalism)—or both. By itself, however, the graph does not offer support for any one theory.

5. d. (a) and (b) only

## Chapter 12 Health and Medicine

1. a. smoking cigarettes

**Explanation:** Smoking is of course one of the most dangerous things a person can do. However, as noted in the text, smoking is one way of coping with stress, and stress is associated with occupying a lower class position and facing racial discrimination. Propensity to smoke is thus partly an effect of deeper social causes and is not a social cause in itself.

2. d. none of the above

**Explanation:** The United States spends more on health care per person and has more physicians per 1000 population than any other country but has worse health outcomes than all other rich countries.

3. b. Juan

**Explanation:** As a senior manager, Juan is likely to experience less stress than Aiguo does because he has more autonomy at work and can more easily turn stress off by, say, taking a few days off. Since persistent stress is associated with a variety of negative health outcomes, Juan is likely to be in better health.

4. c. Poor health outcomes among Indigenous Canadians are solely a result of their relatively low class position and their experience of racial discrimination.
5. b. Over their lifetime, women may experience more violence and/or inferior nutrition and/or inferior health care compared to men.

## Chapter 13 Mass Media and Mass Communications

1. a. the widespread use of the Bible after Christianity became the official religion of the Roman Empire in the fourth century
2. d. providing many jobs that pay well

3. c. conflict theory
4. b. field research
5. a. the principle that Internet service providers should not restrict access to any online content

## Chapter 14 Social Change: Technology, the Environment, and Social Movements

1. b. Kondratiev waves
2. b. No. However, the situation could become a social problem if a social movement and the mass media publicize it and many people come to recognize that the situation could harm them.
3. d. relative deprivation
4. a. frame alignment
5. d. all of the above